BAROQUE AND ROCOCO IN LATIN AMERICA

BAROQUE AND ROCOCO IN LATIN AMERICA

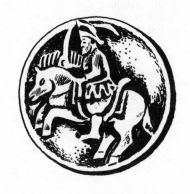

by Pál Kelemen

In Two Volumes:
VOLUME 1, TEXT

SECOND EDITION

DOVER PUBLICATIONS, INC., NEW YORK

This Dover edition, first published in 1967, is an unabridged and corrected republica-
tion of the work originally published in one volume by The Macmillan Company in
1951. New to this edition are a Preface by the author and a detailed List of Illustrations.

Parts of the text and some of the illustrations were used by the author in his book
Battlefield of the Gods; Aspects of Mexican History, Art, and Exploration (English
Copyright 1937), in articles for the *Bulletin of the Pan American Union, Boletín de la
Unión Panamericana* (Copyright 1941, 1942 by the Pan American Union, Washington,
D. C.), *Art in America* (Copyright 1944 by Art in America, Springfield, Massachusetts),
El Palacio (Copyright 1945 by the School of American Research, Santa Fe, New Mexico),
Gazette des Beaux-Arts (Copyright 1944 by Gazette des Beaux-Arts, New York, New
York), *Magazine of Art* (Copyright 1942 by the American Federation of Arts, Washing-
ton, D. C.), and the *Encyclopaedia Britannica* (in press).

The brief quotation from *The Selected Writings of John Marin*, edited by Dorothy
Norman, is reproduced by permission of the publisher, Pellegrini & Cudahy (Copyright
1944 by John Marin).

Standard Book Number: 486-21698-5
Library of Congress Catalog Card Number: 66-29056

Manufactured in the United States of America
Dover Publications, Inc., 180 Varick Street, New York, N. Y. 10014

To the millions of innocent and undefended children, women, and men, from the English Channel to the delta of the Danube, who were tortured and murdered by nations posing as cultured and Christian in the greatest massacre the world has ever known

PREFACE TO THE DOVER EDITION

$\cdots\bullet\!\!-\!\!\blacktriangleright\!\!\blacklozenge\!\!\blacktriangleright\!\!-\!\!\bullet\cdots$

Since the first appearance of this book, the appreciation of colonial art in Latin America has passed through various phases. Even the terms Baroque and Rococo—which caused raised eyebrows when the title was first made known and brought advice that it be changed to something less associated with the ridiculous and effeminate—are now common expressions.

Baroque and Rococo art in Latin America had for quite a while its enthusiasts, who delighted in those monuments standing in a picturesque, frequently dramatic ambiance. Artists, writers, photographers, museum men, and collectors were here also the avant garde. World War II and its aftermath increased the number of Americans who were reluctant to go to Europe and so "discovered" the other Americas. Airplane travel has enlarged the circle of *aficionados*, and a number of countries, with improved travel and lodging, are doing much to facilitate the enjoyment of their colonial glory.

On the campus, the growing interest in the anthropology, history, and sociology of our Southern neighbors has expanded also to investigation in the field of art. It should be pointed out, however, that some thirty years ago in the United States only five institutions, two of them women's colleges, listed regular classes in art history in their catalogues. Then, when the population explosion affected the campus, in many cases there was neither tradition nor experience in the teaching of art history. The shortage of teachers was alleviated partly by the influx of Central Europeans, whose education was based on the strict principles of the first years of our century. It is understandable, though regrettable, that in the effort to bring the elusive blend of styles of colonial Latin America into teachable form, Latin American art was forced into the ready-made pigeonholes of European art history. Attempt was made to tame this splendid bird, born in the freedom of lush tropical valleys or on the slopes of snow-capped volcanoes, to fit the display of styles of a sophisticated, self-centered, dank continent.

While World War II was still being fought on all fronts, at a meeting on Americanistic studies more than a half dozen scholars spoke on projects related to those presented in this book. Since that time, however, in spite of a great apparatus and benefits on hand, almost nothing has been produced. Obfuscation and atrophy took over. At the same time, a widely advertised encyclopedia, fired by the spirit of the Good Neighbor policy, solicited articles from leading scholars for their new edition, on the colonial art and architecture of a number of Latin American countries. The contributions were duly delivered, but even in the most recent edition of that publication, they were not included.

PREFACE TO THE DOVER EDITION

Meanwhile, a large public has been growing who recognize that the value of Latin American Baroque and Rococo lies in its unique character, which grew out of this hemisphere, out of the temperament, imagination, and craftsmanship of its native population, whether white, mixed, or Indian. It has its own beguiling charm and unsuspected power.

The libraries are looking for books and the museums for educated curators who can explain and evaluate this newly found and refreshing wealth of material. It is hoped that this corrected edition of *Baroque and Rococo in Latin America*, actuated by continued demand, will help bring this art into a clearer focus.

Norfolk, Connecticut   *PÁL KELEMEN*
September, 1966

PREFACE TO THE FIRST EDITION

Art—a something that exists completely within itself—gives of itself only to sensitive people—for they approach it rightly. . . . I would suggest (as an exercise) that sometime you take your two eyes along with you —and leave your *intellect* and your friends' *intellects* at home—you might without these handicaps begin to see things that would surprise you.
The Selected Writings of John Marin

Baroque and Rococo are almost strangers in the English language and sometimes carry a disparaging implication, though Chippendale, Chelsea, and Georgian, offshoots of these styles, enjoy widespread popularity. Michelangelo, Cervantes, and Bach expressed the Baroque age; Scarlatti, Molière, and Gainsborough, the spirit of the Rococo. And the list of distinguished names is long not in the arts alone. Many of the principles which govern the humanities and sciences of modern life were established in the seventeenth and eighteenth centuries, the epoch of the Baroque and Rococo.

Before the First World War these centuries still conditioned much of the social and artistic climate of Europe. To one, like myself, who grew up in the golden twilight of a Europe that vaunted her civilization, Baroque and Rococo provided a living background. Then the Austro-Hungarian Empire was full of palaces and churches built or refurbished in the Baroque age of Maria Theresa. Early travels in Europe—only Czarist Russia, Bourbon Spain, and the Sultan's Turkey required passports—acquainted me with the rarely graceful Rococo of the Asam churches in Bavaria and the playful pavilions around Versailles and brought me in touch with champions of the Baroque and Rococo. In Vienna, where I stayed often, Alois Riegl and his disciples had already analyzed the problems of these styles, and in Munich another pioneer in the field was then expounding his theories—Heinrich Wölfflin, whose classes it was my good fortune to attend.

The First World War greatly enlarged my horizon. In Transylvania the horses of my squadron were bedded down in the stables of Baroque manor houses, and I saw with anguished heart a Rococo mansion on the Polish plains—in which I had slept yesterday—going up in flames from Russian cannonading. When stationed in Turkish Novibazar, I was awakened each morning by the muezzin's call from a nearby Moslem minaret. In northern Italy the hills and plains of Friuli and Veneto were an open-air laboratory for the youthful art-historian. There in the castle of Pagnacco, before a group of officers, I gave one of my earliest lectures—on the art styles of Italy—using as illustrations art pieces gathered from the neighborhood.

In those agitated years I witnessed from inside the military cordon the last coronation of a Habsburg in Budapest and saw the embers of the Holy Roman Empire blaze up for the last time. Gilded Baroque coaches swinging on leather straps and drawn by milk-white horses rolled past, carrying the court ladies in the splendid costumes of their forebears. Behind the king rode the highest born of the land in the *banderium*, looking, in their velvets and damasks fringed with fur and their plumed shakos, as if they had stepped out of a gallery of ancestral portraits. Their mounted hussars in braided gala closed the ranks, each bearing the standard of a "shire." *Arcière* guards followed on foot, wearing their cream-colored capes lined with scarlet, tall patent-leather boots, and silver helmets with streaming white horsetails. The spirit may have been decadent in this final act of feudal Europe, but the art was magnificent and virile.

The last months of the war took me to parts of France and Belgium, where new impressions were added to those gained beyond the Alps. Bruges, with German howitzers parked beneath its plane trees, lay under a veil of mourning. Little did I dream as I walked along the streets of Ghent and army wagons rumbled across its bridges that, decades later, research on Charles V would bring me back to the birthplace of the first Habsburg emperor to mount the throne of Spain.

In the mid-1920's an ambition to study El Greco—then not yet a household word—to explore his Greek soul and persistent Byzantine leanings, took me to Spain. At that time Spain's monuments stood intact and her fragrant gardens were in full beauty. The last Bourbon king still sat on his shaky throne, though dominated by his dictator. Palaces and galleries, churches and monasteries, all were open to study. In Toledo I watched the full moon sharpen the contour of the Alcázar as Greco had painted it. And in a tower of the Alhambra, perched above Granada, I wrote a litany on the pale dust vibrating over the autumnal landscape and the elongating shadows of passers-by in the late September afternoon.

Indeed, shadows of apocalyptic portent were spreading over the world when I made my first trip to Spanish America in the spring of 1933. I did not feel a stranger there. I went to Mexico and Yucatán to study the remnants of their pre-Columbian past. But even while concentrating on the indigenous masterpieces of America, I was forced to pause before the stupendous art of the Spanish colonial period. Very soon the great and many differences between the art of the Spanish motherland and that of her former colonies made themselves felt. The farther I traveled, the more I became aware that the artistic production of the first century or so under Spanish administration—which resulted in a conglomeration of transplanted styles —is surpassed by more original manifestations on this continent. For the Indian and mestizo craftsmen and artists had yet to pour their imagination, their tremendous artistic talent, and their ancestral skills into the service of the new religion. Their efforts flowered in Latin America in a period which coincided with the spread of the Baroque and the appearance of the Rococo. Just as the tulip bulbs we bought from Holland produced within a few years a changed flower in our Florentine garden—as a result of different treatment, soil, and sun—so the many elements of the Baroque and Rococo which were brought over from Europe went through a fascinating transformation.

Within a month or two it will be forty years since my first essays on art appeared in print. The first two decades of this period were spent in Europe—and I have no wish to forget what this background means to me. But for the last two I have lived in the United States.

While nations that posed as cultured and Christian were torturing and murdering millions of innocent and undefended children, women, and men, from the English Channel to the delta of the Danube, in the greatest massacre the world has ever known, the Americas were offering me a new field of research full of inspiration.

Until recently the art of colonial Latin America either has been treated in a most perfunctory manner, merely as an appendix to that of the Iberian Peninsula, or ignored. As a rule, the more a building, statue, or canvas resembled a European prototype, the greater reverence it was accorded. With many writers a blind spot apparently blacked out the powerful non-European sources in this art, while others tried to cover them up or belittle them. However, in those very countries that have the most exciting colonial art—Mexico, Guatemala, Ecuador, Peru, and Bolivia—the majority of the people are not of the white race and even after more than four hundred years do not speak much Spanish. All too little has been done to understand the language (much less the psychology) of the Indian; there is today not a single scientifically reliable grammar of any South American Indian tongue; even for Quechua and Aymara, which are spoken by millions of people, most of the grammars and dictionaries available were written by seventeenth-century missionaries.

Further, certain misconceptions, which originated in Europe in the romantic epoch of discovery, are perpetuated in a number of misnomers. The Caribbean Islands are known as the West Indies, when they are thousands of miles away from India, and the redskin population of the American continent is called Indian, although it has long been established that this race is in no way related to the populace of India; Spanish writers still refer to these regions of the New World as "the Indies." Somewhat similarly the term Latin America is open to criticism, for it is used to denote a territory where even today European stock is in the minority.

In my survey of pre-Columbian art, I was faced with the presentation and evaluation of indigenous cultures, each of which had woven into its artistic fabric its own individuality. In the colonial art of Latin America, the warp is continuous throughout—from California to Chile; but through the weft runs the originality of local talent, making for considerable divergencies.

In this volume are gathered for the reader generally interested in art some of the aesthetic achievements of seventeenth- and eighteenth-century Latin America which demand attention for their beauty and originality, irrespective of dates and names. I have tried to present a humanistic subject in a humanistic way and have avoided "scientific" terminology whenever simple terms would suffice. For the reader's convenience the present-day names of cities and countries have been used, although care has been taken also to mention the colonial designations. Often the use of a modest magnifying glass will increase his enjoyment of the illustrations. To avoid overcrowding the text with cross references, the illustrations from each site have been grouped together in the Index.

Much of the research for this volume was done and a considerable part of the material was collected while I was working on my pre-Columbian survey, and by the summer of 1947 the first draft and the illustrations were more or less complete. It was then, upon rereading my statements and conclusions, that I realized that, after five trips to various parts of Latin America, a review of my impressions of Baroque and Rococo in Europe would be extremely beneficial. Thus the following spring I flew to Lisbon. The medieval sonority of Tomár was well balanced by the sunny Rococo of Braga. I found the radiant atmosphere of Seville unchanged, but Toledo, with half its profile blown off during the civil war, was a great shock, and I could not warm again to Granada, the city which had murdered its own poet. In Central Europe I saw with new eyes the regional variations of Baroque and Rococo, and a stay in Belgium confirmed my inferences concerning Flemish prints.

During the years in which this volume was in preparation, I had many stimulating and helpful discussions with scholars who knew little or nothing about the subject yet who recognized its freshness and originality. Bernard Berenson, on his terrace at Settignano overlooking the valley of the Arno, discussed with me the subtle apartness apparent in an art which drew from other sources than the Greco-Roman civilization. In the barren room of a professor at the war-ravaged University of Budapest, Tibor Gerevich pointed out folkloristic tendencies in the regional Baroque and Rococo of Europe similar to those in Latin America. Leo van Puyvelde, in his sunny modern villa in a suburb of Brussels, clarified some iconographical problems of Latin American colonial painting by linking it to lesser-known works of Flemish painters and engravers. In Lisbon, surrounded by masterpieces of Portuguese Gothic and Baroque, Reynaldo dos Santos brought into focus parallels between the Rococo in the Oporto and Braga region and that of Brazil.

Space does not permit individual mention of all the officials of the various governments, universities, museums, and libraries, the many ecclesiastics, archivists, photographers, and connoisseurs who facilitated my research. Therefore I request them to accept, in this collective acknowledgment, the expression of my sincere gratitude and the assurance that nothing can efface for me the color and flavor of those many delightful meetings.

Another group gave me assistance in such measure that public credit is due them:

From the Division of Cultural Relations in our State Department: Albert H. Gerberich, first in Bogotá, then in Washington; Howard Lee Nostrand, in Lima; James H. Webb, Jr., in Tegucigalpa; Jacob Canter, in Managua; Juana Vogt, in Mexico; and Hershel Brickell and Francis J. Colligan, in Washington.

Also from the United States: Elsie Brown, Lewis Hanke, Albert S. Fisher, Jean Richmond, in Washington; Mrs. Frank B. Freyer, Denver; Hans Tietze and Erika Tietze-Conrat, G. E. Kidder Smith, Elizabeth du Gué Trapier, Beatrice Proske, New York; Erwin Raisz, Cambridge, Massachusetts; Mrs. Dorothy W. Terrell, Norfolk, Connecticut; further, for special courtesies offered, the United Fruit Company, Pan American Airways, the Grace Line, and Panagra.

In Mexico: Manuel Toussaint, Jorge Enciso, Justino Fernández, Abelardo Carrillo y Gariel, Federico Hernández Serrano, Heinrich Berlin, Anita Brenner, H. H. Behrens, Dr. and Mrs. Joseph Lengyel, Mexico City; J. Germán Patiño D., Ignacio Herrera Tejeda, Querétaro; Manuel Leal, Guanajuato.

In Guatemala: the late Jorge Ubico, President of the Republic, J. Antonio Villacorta

C., Lilly de Jongh Osborne. In Honduras: Tiburcio Carias Andino, former President of the Republic, Federico Lunardi, Tegucigalpa; Dr. and Mrs. Wilson Popenoe, Zamorano; Gregorio F. Sanabria, Comayagua. In El Salvador: Emeriterio Oscar Salazar, San Salvador. In Nicaragua: Luis Cuadra Cea, Managua; E. R. McGuire, León. In Santo Domingo: Walter Erwin Palm, Ciudad Trujillo.

In Colombia: Antonio Rocha, Gregorio and Guillermo Hernández de Alba, Teresa Cuervo Borda, Miguel A. Rodríguez, Bogotá; Ramon C. Correa, Tunja; Manuel María Buenaventura, Cali; José María Arboleda Llorente, Jesús M. Otero, Popayán. In Venezuela: Carlos Manuel Möller, Caracas. In Ecuador: Nicolas Delgado, Carlos Manuel Larrea, J. Alberto Mena C., Juan Gorrell, Bodo Wuth, Quito; Mr. and Mrs. David Basile, Cuenca.

In Peru: Manuel Prado y Ugarteche, former President of the Republic, Rafael Marquina y Bueno, Albert A. Giesecke, Alberto Santibañez Salcedo, Pedro de Osma, Adolfo Cristóbal Winternitz, Lima; Rafael Larco Herrera and his sons, in Hacienda Chiclín; Victor M. Barriga, Arequipa; José Uriel García, David Chaparro, Luis A. Pardo, Cornejo Bouroncle, Cuzco; José M. Franco Hinojosa, Juli.

In Bolivia: the late Cecilio Guzmán de Rojas, Humberto Cuenca, F. Díez de Medina, Luis Herzog G., La Paz. In Argentina: Mario J. Buschiazzo, Buenos Aires. In Brazil: M. F. de Andrade, Rio de Janeiro.

In Spain: Diego Angulo Iñiguez, Madrid; Cristóbal Bermúdez Plata, Enrique Marco Dorta, Antonio Sancho Corbacho, Seville; José Gudiol Ricart, Martín Almagro, Antonio Rumeu de Armas, Barcelona. In Portugal: Mrs. Herbert Scoville, Azeitão; João Santos Simões, Tomár. In Hungary: Rudolph Bedö, Budapest. In Belgium: Mrs. F. C. Legrand, Brussels; Frank van den Wijngaert, Antwerp. In The Netherlands: M. A. Vente, Zwolle.

I was fortunate enough to have a scholar in each field consent to give my chapters a critical reading. I benefited greatly from their criticism and suggestions, but the responsibility for the text is mine alone.

Harold E. Wethey, of the University of Michigan, read Chapters 1, 5, 10, 11, 15, and parts of Chapter 3; he also generously put at my disposal the manuscript of his recently published book on colonial Peru as well as an exhaustive paper, now in press, on colonial Bolivia. Robert C. Smith, of the University of Pennsylvania, reviewed Chapter 14 and parts of Chapter 3; he also furnished me with many exquisite photographs on Brazil. For data on these three countries I have relied largely on the works of these two scholars. Alfred Neumeyer, of Mills College, a Wölfflin pupil like myself but of a later decade, read Chapters 2, 4, 7, 9, and 12. John McAndrew, of Wellesley College, read Chapter 6 and parts of Chapter 3; Verle L. Annis, of the University of Southern California, parts of Chapters 3 and 8; Carleton Sprague Smith, of the New York Public Library, Chapter 13, which was seen also by M. A. Vente of Zwolle, The Netherlands. Martin S. Soria, of Michigan State College, looked over Chapter 12 and checked on some data for me during his extended Latin American survey trip. Finally, my gratitude is due Elizabeth Wilder Weismann who was able to send me the proofs for the text of her book on sculpture in Mexico just before my manuscript went to the publisher.

My good luck held in obtaining the co-operation of two others, friends ever since they were associated with me in the preparation of my pre-Columbian survey. Edward C. Wolf left his *tusculanum* on the Virginia shore to lend his remarkable artistic sense and great technical knowledge to the arrangement of the photographs. Helen B. Hartman assisted me with unparalleled loyalty; with her fine feeling for the language and her editorial knowledge she made a definite contribution in the final draft of the manuscript. The styling of the bibliography and the compiling of the index are largely her accomplishment.

My wife Elisabeth accompanied me on all the trips; she was with me when we had to make comfortable a Maya hut in Yucatán or travel by muleback in the High Andes or hunt Flemish prints in the Royal Library at Brussels. She made a great number of photographs, frequently under trying circumstances—practically half of the illustrations in this volume were hers as well as hundreds of study pictures; the quality of her achievement speaks for itself. From the first typescript through page proof—a long and arduous way—she supported me with untiring spirit and intellectual alertness. She contributed many pertinent observations, and the musicological part of the chapter on organs is mainly hers. But she not only participated in the physically tiresome and mentally exhausting work—she shared with me in full measure the thrill of discovery and the experience of beauty.

Norfolk, Connecticut
April, 1951

PÁL KELEMEN

CONTENTS

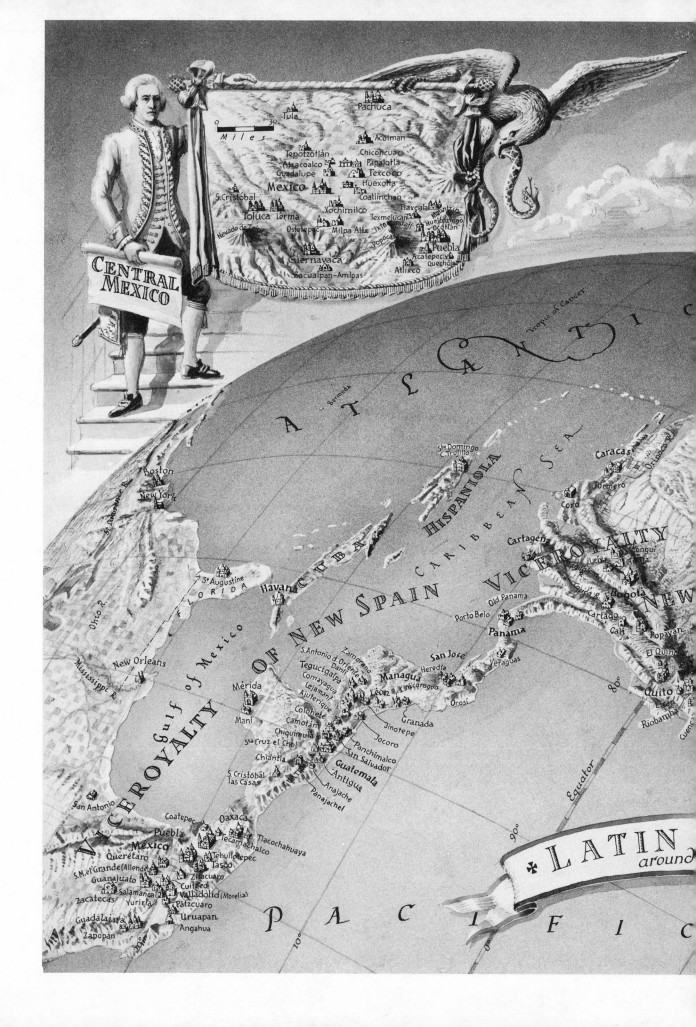

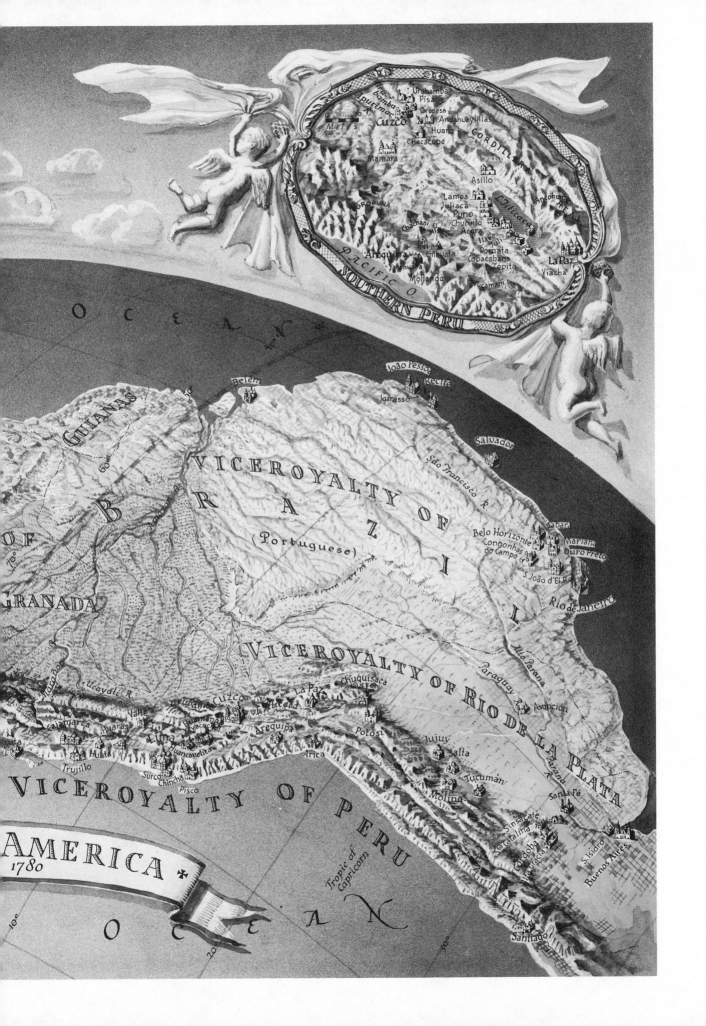

SOUTHERN PERU

Urubamba
bamba
Pisac
Apurimac R.
Oropesa
Cuzco
Andahuaylillas
Huaro
Checacupe
Mamara
Asillo
Lampa
Juliaca
Puno
Chucuito
Acora
Chachani
Ilave
Juli
Pomata
Copacabana
Zepita
Arequipa
Chiluata
Yahuma
Mollendo
Yucumani
La Paz
Yiacha
Titicaca
CORDILLERA
Ancohum
PACIFIC O.

João Pessoa
Belém
Recife
Igarassó
Salvador
São Francisco R.

GUIANAS
VICEROYALTY OF
BRAZIL
(Portuguese)
Belo Horizonte
Sabará
Congonhas
do Campo
Mariana
Ouro Preto
S. João d'El Rei
Rio de Janeiro
Alto Parana
Paraguay R.
Asuncíon

OF
GRANADA

70°

Maracaibo
Ucayali R.
Cajamarca
Huaras
Huanta
Cuzco
La Paz
Urubamba
Valle
Titicaca
Chuquisaca
Lima
Arequipa
Huancavelica
Potosí
VICEROYALTY OF RIO DE LA PLATA
Jujuy
Palta
Huata
Surco
Arica
Salta
Trujillo
Chincha
Pisco
Tucuman
Molinos

VICEROYALTY OF PERU

AMERICA
1780

OCEAN

Tropic of Capricorn

Santa Fé
Sinsacate
Sta Catalina
Córdoba
Villa Vieja
S. Isidro
Buenos Aires

Santiago

BAROQUE AND
ROCOCO
IN LATIN AMERICA

1

THE COLONIAL SCENE

SINCE the advent of Christianity, no single event in the history of mankind has produced such tremendous changes in the world as the conquest of the Americas. A territory many times as large as Europe was opened up to the material exploitation of, principally, Spain and Portugal, and in the process millions of natives in the Western Hemisphere became indoctrinated with the Roman Catholic culture of the Iberian Peninsula.

The Conquistadores, arriving on the American mainland during the early sixteenth century, found here a remarkably high civilization which, having developed in isolation, was very different from their own. So powerful were the tribal kingdoms and empires that it took years to bring about their final subjugation, even with the use of the horse, steel weapons, and gunpowder, all of which were unknown to the natives.

1

For the administration of the vast territory in the New World after the Conquest, the Spaniards established two viceroyalties, one north of the Isthmus and one south. This form of government had already proven itself useful to the crown of Castile in Aragon, Valencia, Sardinia, Sicily, and Naples; Venice had applied it in the Levant, and Portugal in the Orient. The first viceroyalty in the New World was created in 1535 to rule what is today Mexico and Central America, with Mexico City as its capital. It was known as Nueva España, or New Spain. The second, the Viceroyalty of Peru, established in 1544, governed all Spanish possessions in South America and had its seat at Lima. In 1717 this viceroyalty ceded territory to the new Viceroyalty of New Granada, comprising Colombia, Venezuela, and, later, Ecuador. In 1776 what is today Argentina, Bolivia, Paraguay, and Uruguay became the Viceroyalty of Rio de la Plata. Panama, closely tied up with the transshipment of treasure from the Andean Highlands to the motherland, was for a time under the administration of Peru and was later transferred to New Granada.

Portugal's holdings in the New World were consolidated into a single colony, later a viceroyalty, Brazil. Its history and artistic development differed from Spanish America's and will be discussed in Chapter 14.

The supreme authority in the Spanish colony was the viceroy, under whom a gigantic bureaucracy flourished; all civil and military matters came under his jurisdiction. Spiritual power was entrusted to the Roman Church, represented by its secular clergy and conventual orders. Through these two channels—the civil and the religious—the Spanish way of life was introduced into the New World.

The viceroy ruled in the king's name and his power was almost absolute. All officials were nominally answerable to him. He was responsible for the collection of the "royal fifth," the king's share of the bullion from the mines, aś well as for the other taxes. Since the Spanish crown claimed a share of all Indian treasures, the viceroy was obliged to maintain a diligent search for hidden wealth in the wrecked temples and undiscovered tombs of the pre-Columbian past. Tribute was paid by the Indians to both the crown and the church, just as it had been to the hierarchy in pre-Columbian times, in grains, dyes, herbs, and other produce of the land, as well as in blankets and manufactured goods; later they paid in money.

Early in the seventeenth century the manufacture of armaments and gunpowder, the latter needed also in great amounts for mining, became one of the few industries permitted in the colonies, and it too was under the supervision of the viceroy. Mints for hard currency, which were established near the great silver mines, were controlled by him. In some cases he even interfered with details of individual life. Remonstrating against the mode affected by the women in Lima, one viceroy forbade them to go about so closely veiled, and this same official also decreed better and more adequate garments for the Indians.[52]

The military also was under the control of the viceroy, and he was responsible for the fortification of important ports. In the early decades the army consisted largely of adventurers with commissions from the king; later it became a more professional organization. The officers as a rule were European veterans, not always Spaniards, and the ranks were made up mainly of creoles (Spaniards born in the colony) and of mestizos (native-born of half white and half Indian blood). Some men enlisted voluntarily, but most of the soldiers were drawn, as in contemporary Europe, through levies on town idlers, vagabonds, and deserters. Despite the rule of segregation, mestizos entered companies made up of whites and in less-favored border garrisons Negroes even became officers.

To facilitate military and civil administration, the immense territory within a single viceroyalty had to be subdivided. Military districts, called captaincies-general, were organized, and audiencias, or supreme-court districts, were established. This high court had legislative, judicial, and executive functions and powers, and against its decisions, in certain cases, appeal could be carried only to the crown. Because of the distances and the arduousness of travel, affairs often went unattended and crimes unpunished for years.

The arrival of a viceroy in the colony was a major event, and the towns along his route of travel arranged elaborate receptions. It must have been a long and tiring journey even for a Mexican viceroy, but for one whose duties called him to Lima it was little short of an ordeal. With good winds the journey across the Atlantic took from four to five weeks. The trip to the Canaries, where provisions were taken aboard, was made in about a week. Shortly thereafter the food was apt to deteriorate and the danger of meeting corsairs increased. The viceroy's quarters were an alcove in the poop, where the ship's motion was least felt; a curtain was hung across the front to afford him privacy. On arriving at Portobelo he, with other distinguished persons, traveled in a small boat up the Chagres River and then had a day's ride across the Isthmus on horseback or by mule litter to the city of Panama. From here he took another vessel, built on that side of the continent, to Paita, Peru, a journey of nearly six weeks. Finally, after another six weeks, with many stops at intermediate cities where he held audiences, he arrived at Callao, Lima's port. To accord all possible outward recognition to the authority of a viceroy, he was crowned upon ascending to his high office, the center of picturesque and luxurious—though often tedious—ceremonies.[42]

Some of the viceroys were intelligent, socially awake, and aware of their great responsibilities. But a goodly number of them were opportunists, educated for the military, seek-

[2]

ing their own advantages. And what advantages existed in this new land where favors were paid for in gold, silver, emeralds, and pearls and where a vast reservoir of Indian and Negro slave labor stood at the disposal of feudal landholders.

Government by viceroy continued in New Spain until 1821, with a roster of fifty-nine names; in Peru until 1817, with forty; and in New Granada and Rio de la Plata until 1810, with fourteen and eleven respectively. Of these 124 functionaries only four were American born; the others either were Spaniards or were drawn from European aristocracy and often were relatives of the reigning house. Three members of the Lemos family were viceroys in Italy in the seventeenth century and a fourth held a similar position in Peru.[186] In the beginning the length of a viceroy's tenure was not explicit; sometimes it lasted for life. Later it was limited to five years, but this rule was not always adhered to. Few viceroys remained in the colony after their term of office expired; more than a hundred of them returned to Spain laden with riches, where they added considerably to the glamour of the Spanish grandee.

By early seventeenth century in the colony, there were more than two hundred cities and many *villas*, or towns.[57] The system of communication between the main centers was called the *Camino Real*, or the Royal Highway, which often followed the network of roads laid down by the Indians in pre-Columbian times. Eyewitnesses of the Conquest report highways with sluices and causeways in the Aztec and Maya empires, as well as bridges anchored across mountain torrents and tunnels carved through living rock by the Incas to establish communication over the Andes. Between the two Inca capitals of Cuzco and Quito the road was said to be broad enough for six horsemen to ride abreast.[47] The state and quality of the Royal Highway differed according to the region it traversed; sometimes it was little more than a mule path and sometimes it was comparable to the average contemporary road in Europe. This disparity was due in part to the fact that the upkeep of the roads was entrusted to the civil authorities of the various districts; the work was done by Indian forced labor. In Guatemala until recently Indians who were unable to pay their taxes could work them off on the roads. The condition of the local roads leading to outlying towns, villages, and great estates depended largely on the needs of the region and on the enterprise and means of those whom they served. After mid-eighteenth century the standard of the Royal Highway was constantly improved, and its curving line lay across the green landscape like an endless ribbon. It was more than broad enough for two carts to pass. Generally it was paved with cobblestones set by hand; in some of the tropical countries the surface was of gravel. The pavement, as uncomfortable as it was for the traveler because of the constant shaking and rattling, proved a boon in the rainy season, for without it the roads would have been quagmires. Often in mountainous terrain the surface was sloped toward the center to guide off the water of torrential downpours.[191]

Side by side with the civil administration of the viceroy another system, nearly as powerful, was in operation—that of the Roman Catholic Church. With the Conquest came the various orders of friars—the Franciscans, Dominicans, Augustinians, Mercedarians, and, later, the Jesuits and Carmelites. Monasteries were constructed for the conversion and instruction of the Indians. The first buildings were modest and often temporary. Frequently mass baptisms were administered before improvised altars. But in an amazingly short time in both viceroyalties substantial edifices arose. By early seventeenth century the New World is said to have had seventy thousand churches and five hundred convents of the various orders. In most cases the earlier churches and monasteries, as well as the ecclesiastical and civil palaces, underwent repeated alterations and enlargements.

The Spanish church was, in a sense, a national church, a hotbed of royal protégés and bureaucrats. The King of Spain nominated the bishops and other ecclesiastics by papal concession. So absolute was his control in religious matters that not even papal bulls or briefs could be circulated in the New World without the sanction of the Council of the Indies, that arm of the Spanish crown which ruled upon American affairs from its Renaissance palace in Seville. All ecclesiastical positions in the colonies were licensed by the king, to whom all possible data on an aspirant had to be submitted. Once a priest was in the colonies, permission for him to sail back to Spain depended on prelate, diocese, and, in final instance, on the crown itself.[52]

Visitors to the colonial empire wrote in astonishment of the vast holdings of the church. In 1620 the convents in Lima, with their related properties, occupied more ground than all the rest of the city. Alexander von Humboldt reported after his visit to Mexico (1803–1804) that in some provinces as much as 80 per cent of the arable land was in the control of the church. The property of the individual cleric as well as that of the church was exempt from taxation. Secular priests were paid in tithes, 10 per cent of the income of the whites and 10 per cent of whatever produce of the Indian originally derived from Europe, such as wheat, cattle, silk. When serving on large estates, priests received salaries in addition to fees, gifts, and bequests.[122]

With the passage of time two classes of white religious personnel emerged: those born in Spain and those of Spanish antecedents born and educated in the colonies. The antagonism between these two important groups of society began to make itself felt in the second half of the sixteenth century—by which time the number of creole priests and friars had increased appreciably—and continued well beyond the colonial epoch; in some instances it is perceptible even today. Many of their quarrels were carried to the king, who had to rely for his final judgment on information furnished through his own channels. No Spanish king ever set foot on American soil, and the royal *camarilla* often had to check and double check because of the spying, the charges and countercharges that riddled colonial politics.

In 1551 Charles V authorized the establishment of two universities in the Americas "with the privileges, exemptions, and limitations of the University of Salamanca." In 1553 the Royal and Pontifical University of Mexico opened its gates and twenty-three years later the University of San Marcos in Lima. Some of the early professors in these institutions held the highest degree obtainable from Spanish universities. The subjects taught were theology, scripture, law, canons, decretals, rhetoric, and the arts—logic, metaphysics, and physics—all in Latin. In 1576 a chair for Indian languages was established, as these were recognized as vital to the propagation of the faith. Attendance seemingly was open to those mestizos and Indians who could qualify, chiefly descendants of highborn Indian families and relatives of ranking officials. But in places such as Lima, where Spanish social prejudice was ingrained, the right of students of pure Indian blood to attend the universities was disputed; a settlement in the Indians' favor was finally made there in 1697, but less than ten years later this privilege was revoked.[74]

The Roman Church of the Americas was a majestic machine but frequently managed by weak humans. Many of the prelates were earnest and sincere personalities. The secular clergy was of very mixed quality and often corrupt; immoralities of many kinds existed in the monastic orders, and embezzlement was not uncommon. This uneven quality of the priesthood was due in part to a lack of good seminaries. The Council of Trent—that longest of church conventions, lasting from 1545 to 1563—decreed that every diocese must have at least one seminary for the education of the oncoming priests. Yet throughout the colonial period there were many dioceses in the New World without seminaries. By royal decree every village was supposed to have a primary school; but it was left to civil authorities to erect and finance them and the order was never fully complied with. Special schools were established for the children of Indian caciques and others for mestizos, including the illegitimate children of priests and friars. The church had charge of all hospitals, which were always too few in number and in constant need of funds and supplies.[50]

Although Pope Alexander VI—Rodrigo Borgia, from the Spanish family of Borja—had early declared the Indian a human being possessed of a soul and thus capable of admission to the Roman Catholic faith, a later pope absolved him of heresy, ruling that he was not *gente de razón*—intelligent and rational enough to be held responsible for his acts. Bishop Bartolomé de las Casas (1474–1566), an enlightened churchman of the Spanish colonial empire, considered this latter judgment a great injustice to the native population.[56] However, this ruling had its advantage, for at least temporarily the Indian escaped the discipline of the Inquisition, though it was later applied in those districts where idolatry persisted.

The Holy Office of the Inquisition first functioned in Lima in 1569, in Mexico in 1571, and in Cartagena in 1610. By this last date it was solidly established throughout the New World, where it continued to operate until about 1820. Its investigations were concerned especially with freethinkers, Protestants, Freemasons, and converted Mohammedans and Jews who had reverted to their former faiths. Antonio de Mendoza (?–1552), viceroy first of Mexico and later of Peru, ordered the trial of several clerics and friars who instead of instructing the Indians had devoted themselves to the acquisition of wealth and, with certain bishops, had returned to Spain laden with silver. The Holy Office has been accused of misusing its power for political reasons. Those with disquieting popularity or suspicious riches sometimes were called up, their wealth confiscated, and the accused tortured or even put to death. In 1649 the auto-da-fé of Mexico

alone yielded three million pesos.[82] In Lima in 1743 Don Juan de Loyola y Haro, an elderly gentleman and relative of St. Ignatius, was arrested on a flimsy charge of a Negro slave that he was practicing Judaism. But even if the accused was finally acquitted, the summons and trial could ruin him, especially if he had to endure a trip from some remote spot to the tribunal of the Inquisition—a dangerous overland journey perhaps of hundreds of miles through wild territory on horseback—and, on arrival, a detention of unknown duration. A French writer described the activity of the church in the Spanish colonies with the phrase: "I plunder you, I crush you, I kill you, but I save you." [50]

The administration of church and state in the New World operated under many handicaps. The Spaniards were affected by the trying conditions of high altitudes and tropical climates here and by the unheard-of power and fabulous wealth suddenly placed in their trust. The tremendous distance from the motherland and the vastness of the colonial territory made a rigid control of the lazy and often unscrupulous bureaucracy impossible. Indeed the task was well-nigh unachievable: officials were supposed to foster a healthy commercial development in the colonies yet not compete with home industry; to maintain a steady flow of bullion; to exploit the wealth of the colonies to the full yet keep them economically and politically dependent on the motherland.[75] So long as the Habsburgs remained on the throne of Spain (1516–1700), the viceroys to the New World were grandees, who in general co-operated with ecclesiastic authorities but whose main purpose nevertheless was to bring in the vast revenues due the crown.

The accession of the Bourbons inaugurated an attempt toward a better administration, and viceroys eager for reform introduced a new spirit. This change produced clashes with the church which extended even to the pope; for in the interest of efficient co-ordination the church often had to give way to the state. In the front ranks of that struggle stood the Society of Jesus. The Jesuits, though they had started their work in the New World somewhat later than the other monastic orders, had risen rapidly to a most influential position. They excelled not only in the pacification and conversion of the Indians but also in their educational, agricultural, and industrial enterprises. An unyielding international organization, they came into conflict with the vigorous civil administration. Simultaneously with the action taken against them in Spain, came their expulsion from the Spanish colonies in 1767. They had been expelled from Brazil eight years earlier.

2

Everyone in Spanish America was conditioned by the two gigantic institutions of church and state and had to make his way in a society which was stratified into numerous layers, each set apart by its own distinctive garments. At the top stood the descendants of the Conquistadores and just below them were the first settlers and their descendants; these two groups made up the cream of creole society and often stood in opposition to the Spaniards recently arrived from Europe. On the one side the most ignorant Spaniard held himself superior to any creole, and on the other, in retaliation, the creoles made fun of the Europeans; in Mexico they nicknamed them *gachupines*, for their pointed city shoes, and in Peru, *chapetones*, from the gastric disturbances that generally befell a foreigner before he was acclimatized to the country. Below the white groups were the mestizos and the varying grades of mixed blood, the Negroes, and at the bottom the Indians, who greatly outnumbered the total of all the others. Their number at the time of the Conquest has been estimated at from twelve to sixteen million; more recent calculations would have this figure cover Mexico alone, and the total Indian population of Latin America number close to twice that amount.[124]

The white population was concentrated in the cities and towns; the Indians were segregated in special suburbs or in villages of their own.

The overwhelming disproportion of native population to white changed little during the centuries of colonial administration. Numerically and traditionally it was still an Indian world, and over it a layer of Spanish culture was superimposed. In the first decades few white women crossed the ocean, and even later, when conditions were more favorable, the number of white families was infinitesimally small against the millions of Indians and the number of mestizos. Though baptized in droves into the Roman Catholic faith, their ancient cultural traditions could not be exterminated. Though new plants were introduced by the Spaniards, the prehistoric ones—corn, beans, potatoes, and squash—remained the staple foods. Though new implements for household and agriculture were imported from Europe, the girdle-back loom and the planting stick were not discarded. The Indian's dress took on new elements in imitation of Spanish colonists but even today in districts where twentieth-century "overall-ization" has not entirely replaced his picturesque costume he still wears an untailored garment.

Arable lands, when not owned by the church, were often in the hands of the *encomenderos*, together with a right to the labor of certain of the Indians on the property. These feudal lords, usually knighted, numbered about four thousand at the end of the sixteenth century. Some estates were worked by Indians in the *mita* system of forced labor. As is usual under such circumstances, the treatment of the worker varied, depending on the landowner and his staff. The service most dreaded by the Indian was that in the *obrajes*, the cotton and woolen mills. This industry was among the few fostered in the colonies and was run on the principle of a prison. The workmen were forced to live under intolerable and inhuman conditions on the premises among criminals and the mentally and chronically ill. Only on Sundays and holy days might they be let free for a few hours and then only if their behavior had been impeccable; the overseer, too often cruel and brutal, was the judge.[60]

As a rule the family of the *encomendero* lived in town, sometimes quite a distance away, in order to enjoy the more civilized aspects of life, but the overlord and his Spanish or creole staff had to stay on his property for at least a portion of the year. Here they had their Indian mistresses—a custom common also in Brazil with Negresses—which explains in part the large percentage of mixed blood throughout Latin America.

Neither a white nor a Negro was permitted to live in the Indian towns; traveling merchants could remain there for only three days. In local matters the Indians governed themselves. The affairs of each village were directed by a group of elders, whose authority was based on birth or political astuteness and who lived at the expense of the rest. The governor of the region was empowered to purchase merchandise in the capital for resale among the Indians. The idea behind this scheme was to distribute the artifacts of civilization among the natives, weaning them away from their former habits and increasing their productivity. But in practice the system was subject to much abuse, and frequently an official foisted off useless articles on the Indians at exorbitant prices, exacting the same penalties for nonpayment as for failure to pay tribute.

By the end of the sixteenth century the Indian population was decreasing alarmingly, not only as a result of mass flight into the mountains because of cruel treatment but also because of ravages wrought by European diseases hitherto unknown in the Western Hemisphere. To carry out the various projects of the Spaniards, especially in tropical regions, Negro slaves began to be imported. Some two hundred thousand are said to have been brought into Mexico during the seventeenth century. Negroes, however, did not play as great a part in the economy of Mexico as they

did in that of the West Indies, tropical Central America, or Brazil. In Spanish South America, where they were employed mainly in the lower altitudes and along the coast, their number approached three-quarters of a million.[52] The viceregal Rococo splendor of Lima made the most picturesque use of the Negro, from the lavishly caparisoned lackeys who marched before the university rector on all festive occasions to the coquettishly arrayed washerwomen of private households.

Lima, as a colonial capital, offered a most brilliant scene. Hither came, by endless mule caravan, mineral wealth from the Andes, and here, in the nearby harbor of Callao, landed the commercial fleet—with its merchandise from the motherland to be exchanged for ingots—and those other vessels which carried on coastal trade. To Acapulco, the Pacific harbor for Mexico, went Peruvian gold and silver, and in return Lima received fine silks, velvets, metallic fringe, damask, and taffetas, which, coming from the Orient, were valued more highly than any others, even though Mexico was accused of keeping the better quality for herself. According to one traveler's tale, when the new viceroy, the Duke of Palata, entered the Peruvian capital in 1682, the street of La Merced for the length of two town-quarters was paved with silver ingots.[54] Both men and women in Lima dressed with reckless extravagance, the men in brocaded and embroidered waistcoats, with jeweled bands and buckles on their hats and shoes, and the ladies in imported silks and muslins, with ruffles of Brussels and Mechlin lace and stockings of thin white silk. Lima women were famed for their natural beauty, dainty feet, fine teeth, and flashing eyes. They displayed their graceful figures untrammeled by hoops and stays and wore their hair unpowdered, bedecked with colored ribbons and jewels. Even the slave had her ear-bobs and bangles, and so great was the love of perfume that nosegays were doused with it. The manner of life in Lima was suave and polished. The noble houses boasted paintings from

Rome, tapestries from Flanders, furniture from Seville and Lisbon, silver from Potosí, gold from Chile, and bric-a-brac from China.[186] There was plenty of opportunity for adventure and excesses; the afternoon siesta often was given over to affairs outside the household, and in the evening men and women went disguised for greater freedom. Social standing was adjudged, as in Europe, by the magnificence of one's equipages; early-eighteenth-century Lima boasted four thousand mule-drawn caleches.

Nevertheless the economic life of the colonies was hampered by the many restrictions imposed by Spain. The raising of sugar and cocoa was bound by strict regulation, sometimes favoring one region and sometimes another. To protect producers in Spain, olives could not be grown without a special permit, in spite of the fact that the colonists used olive oil in cooking, following the Spanish custom.[57] As late as the early nineteenth century, the wine growers of Cadiz, Spain, tried through a royal decree to stop the cultivation of grapes in the colonies in an effort to revive their diminishing export trade of sherry.

Merchandise from European countries other than Spain was subject to high duties, and local manufacture was limited to articles which would not compete with the industry of the mother country. In addition Spain forbade commerce between viceroyalties, whether by land or by sea, and even between different ports in the same viceroyalty—an embargo generally disregarded. Everything that was produced in the colonies had to be placed at the disposition of the motherland. Production was permitted in pottery, for which Puebla, Mexico, was justly famous, textiles, especially cotton cloth and blankets, and leather goods and furniture, which were often better made and always less expensive than in Spain. Ica, Peru, had a glass factory, and church bells were cast in Arequipa, to be distributed to the most remote Andean village on the shoulders of the Indian.

The mining of gold and silver was free from all restriction; the main reason for the encouragement of that industry was the royal fifth claimed by the crown. It was mining that made Potosí, 13,600 feet high in the Andes, without arable land and far above the timber line, a bustling city of 150,000 before Buenos Aires had outgrown the size of an outpost; Potosí produced three hundred fifty millions in silver in the first fifteen years of its existence. Its riches poured into Lima after a journey of nearly fifteen hundred miles, and there the precious metals were exchanged for Spanish, European, and the much-coveted contraband Oriental goods. Immense revenues were produced also in Mexico. Before the end of the colonial period the wooden machinery of Mexico's mint turned out some two billion dollars' worth of coin; and another two billion was exported in bars.[123]

To collect the royal fifth, the fleet sailed out from Spain every year, laden with goods for the colonial trade. In 1561 it was found expedient for the vessels to travel with an armed convoy, reinforced and protected by great high-pooped galleons. Generally the fleet divided in the Antilles, one section proceeding to Veracruz, the other to Cartagena in the Tierra Firme (now Colombia) and eventually to Portobelo, Panama. On the way single vessels were dispatched to lesser ports in Yucatán, Honduras, Venezuela, and elsewhere. For the return voyage the fleet reassembled at Havana to clear for Spain.

Cartagena, the gateway to New Granada and South America, was one of the richest and best fortified of the colonial cities. On arrival here the commander of the *flota* sent a messenger ahead to Portobelo with dispatches for the authorities in Panama and the viceroy at Lima, which were forwarded across the Isthmus and by boat down the Pacific coast. Other messengers started overland to Lima, Santa Fé de Bogotá, and such intermediate stations as Popayán, Antioquia, and Quito. To Cartagena, for shipment to Spain, came the gold and emeralds of the Colombian highlands and the pearls and tropical products of the lush Venezuelan shores.

Meantime in Callao the king's revenues had been accumulating from the great silver mines at Potosí, some three weeks' trip by muleback and ship. With this hoard Peru's Silver Fleet moved north, stopping on the way at Trujillo and Paita, and eventually was joined by a vessel with treasure from the Kingdom of Quito. In three weeks they lay off Panama and began transferring their cargoes to muleback for the hazardous crossing of the Isthmus. The Isthmian highway remained a rough mule path, varying in width and condition with the terrain and the season, until the eighteenth century, when a paved road was constructed. Indeed it was a large order to build and maintain forty miles of such a road over mountains and through tropical forest and swampland in the deadliest of climates.

On the occasion of the fleet's call, large fairs were held in every port. The one at Portobelo, as described by Thomas Gage in 1637, lasted for fifteen days. Eight galleons and ten merchant vessels put in at the port. The little town, stewing in tropical miasma, suddenly sprang to life; prices rose twentyfold, and lodging and food were at a premium as merchants and traders from distant places descended upon the port. Besides precious metals, a variety of colonial products from the various districts were awaiting shipment to Europe: indigo, cocoa, tobacco, and cinchona bark from Ecuador, cochineal and tortoise shell from Middle America, vicuña cloth from the Andes, dried meat, cordage, and leather from Chile, precious gums, and many kinds of rare woods as well as timber. Transactions were consummated not in coin but in silver bullion weighed out in bars, which lay piled in the marketplace without danger of theft. But many who had come to make their fortunes never returned home or they reached there only to die, for sickness overtook them and epidemics broke out. On its way back the *flota* was comprised of twenty-seven ships, having been joined by vessels from Honduras and the Caribbean islands.[55]

The gold-and-silver-laden flotilla was a much-coveted prize of English, Dutch, French, and other buccaneers. Its armed convoy, like the harbor fortifications in the colonies, rarely came up to requirements—a shortcoming often reported but seldom remedied. Thus much of the precious cargo either landed at a port other than that for which it was destined or sank to the bottom of the sea, where it still intrigues the imagination. The map of the Spanish Main is dotted with crosses marking sunken treasure ships, and undoubtedly millions in bullion and jewels lie scattered beneath the seaway between the New World and Europe. But in spite of harassment and losses, the convoys continued well into the eighteenth century (galleons sailed to Cartagena until 1748 and to Veracruz until 1778), when privileged trading companies took over the business. Between the fleet's visits, in the sixteenth and seventeenth centuries, dispatches were carried twice yearly on light, swift-sailing caravels of sixty to one hundred tons, two for Mexico and two for Peru; toward the end of the seventeenth century the schedule called for a trip every three months, calling at Cartagena (for all South America) and at Havana, where communications from Mexico, Central America, and the islands awaited them. Originally these ships were forbidden to carry either merchandise or passengers, but the rule was rarely observed.

In the early years commerce with foreigners was prohibited; later it was permitted under special licenses, which also ensured protection. England and certain other European nations were allowed to buy specified colonial products but only at a stated port, a scheme which gave all the intermediate profits of transport and handling to the colonials. Some foreign firms got round the regulations by establishing houses in Cadiz, Spain, which held the monopoly for overseas trade to the Spanish colonies during much of the eighteenth century. The English, who had a permit to send one ship a year to one Spanish American port, circumvented the authorities by replenishing this vessel constantly through reloading merchandise from other ships which lay in hiding nearby. All these restrictions resulted in such widespread smuggling that by the end of the eighteenth century half of the entire commerce of Spanish America was illicit.[75] Lima reveled in Chinese porcelains, brocades, and silks, in muslins from India and exotic spices, the importation of which was expressly prohibited. Sometimes a vessel was "blown off course" on its way from the Philippines to Acapulco, Mexico, and it then unloaded its cargo in a port much farther south, with considerable profit. Until mid-eighteenth century Buenos Aires was supposed to depend on wares brought across Panama, down the Pacific coast to Lima, and then over the trans-Andean mule trail to the Atlantic. But it was not long before Brazilian neighbors and a number of European traders realized the great profits to be had by landing in the small inlets of the Rio de la Plata, whence goods found their way more directly to and from the merchants of Buenos Aires.

Among such contraband, forbidden books and prints were smuggled in by devious and ingenious means. A ship captain and his officers would bring packages on board and neglect to list them in the official cargo; often the contents of bales and boxes would not correspond to official declarations. Untold quantities of material entered the Spanish colonies in wine casks and demijohns,[53] a method which the Spaniards might have learned from their earlier traffic with the Low Countries. Harbor officials were instructed to question the ship's master, pilot, sailors, and even some of its passengers whether it contained any images of saints, popes, or other revered figures which might evoke ridicule.[94]

Those crafts and industries which out of necessity had to be permitted in the New World were placed under the same rules as the Spanish guilds. Each guild had a judge to see that all ordinances were observed. An apprentice had to produce a "masterwork" and undergo a severe examination before he could graduate and open his own shop. Negroes and Indians at first were debarred from the guilds but later were admitted, though kept in the lower ranks; the rule was relaxed in the eighteenth century if not earlier, as some artistic examples presented in this book will demonstrate. Most of the guilds were located in the various capitals, where they were grouped according to craft, each within a special district if not on a single street. Silversmiths in Mexico had to have their shops on the street named San Francisco—now the Avenida Madero, the Fifth Avenue of the capital—so that they could be kept under the eye of the authorities who were responsible for the king's revenue.

The guilds formed lay brotherhoods, or *cofradías,* which through their industrial, economic, and often artistic prominence became important elements in the religious and social life of the cities. Their membership in gala habit, with their decorated standards and guild emblems, formed a substantial part of any procession or reception. The number of guilds in the viceroyalties of Mexico and Peru was about a hundred;[57] the best known were those of the bakers, barbers, silk growers and manufacturers, saddlemakers, weavers, hatters, potters, butchers, candlemakers, confectioners, tailors, silversmiths, carpenters, shoemakers, tanners, blacksmiths, and basketmakers. In Peru even a guild for miners existed at one time, abolished in 1779. Somewhat less in the foreground but similarly powerful were the lay sisterhoods, or *sodalidades,* which pulled many strings behind the scenes. The various strata of society—white, mestizo, mulatto, Negro, and Indian—each had its own fraternities and sodalities.

3

In all the capitals of Latin America immense power and wealth were concentrated. The viceroys, with their large and splendid retinues, vied with the archbishops, whose households were often equally lavish, in a pretentious imitation of life at the royal court in the mother country. The reception to a new viceroy was rivaled only by the obsequies accorded to him if he happened to die in office. The passing of the Marquis of Casa Fuerte, Juan de Acuña, was such an occasion. This nobleman was born in Lima in 1658, but after his thirteenth birthday he spent much time in Spain, where he was trained for a military career. A favorite of Philip V, he was appointed governor of Messina, viceroy and captain general in Aragon and Majorca, and in 1722 viceroy of Mexico, where as a creole he was enthusiastically received. He is best known for the beautification of the capital, especially the Alameda, with fountains and trees and for the reconstruction of the mint and customhouse. He was instrumental in acquiring from Macao, the Portuguese colony in China, material for the magnificent bronze grille which was cast in Mexico and set up in 1730 in Mexico City's cathedral.[88] Acuña was also watchful of morals in the parks and on the waterways of Xochimilco. He prohibited masks at carnival time and reformed the festivals to conform with Spanish custom. He patronized classic Spanish plays but also enjoyed an occasional comedy by a good Mexican playwright. In his time part of Belize was retaken from the English and colonized with settlers from the Canary Islands, groups of whom he sent also to Texas.[41]

When the people learned that the great viceroy lay dangerously ill, at the age of seventy-six, they began general prayers for him. At nightfall the last sacraments were administered by the archbishop and a bishop, and he expired shortly after midnight. Then the churches began to toll the hundred strokes of the passing bell and the artillery to fire its four hundred and seventy-seven salvos. Early the next morning the high court convened to verify the death. Later the royal provision for the succession was officially examined, and as customary the choice fell on the archbishop. Meantime the most skillful surgeons em-balmed the body with unguents, powders, and varnishes. Then, clad in the mantle of the Order of Santiago and adorned with many decorations, the remains lay in state upon a bed of carmine under a crimson canopy, a standard at the foot and lighted tapers about it. Respectful throngs filed past it while four hundred Masses were said in especially erected booths.

The burial took place the following Sunday. All along the route at each street corner palisades six feet high were erected to hold back the crowds. The funeral procession, almost a mile long, contained nearly all the officialdom of New Spain, the order of their precedence painstakingly observed. Eighty fraternities took part, with standards and insignia, each member bearing a scepter and a taper. Next came Indian delegations, their leaders bearing long staves of office. Then followed the colleges, in their dark robes with vivid bands and banners, and the many religious orders with crosses and candles. A miraculous crucifix was accompanied by the metropolitan clergy, dressed in crimson mantles, laces, and blue tippets. After them were the catafalque and the members of the viceroyal household, who were followed by two unshod horses bearing the dead grandee's heraldic symbols. Behind these came members of the lesser courts of New Spain, the staff of the university in full regalia, representatives of the royal treasury, and the archbishop in appropriate magnificence. The procession was closed by a guard of infantry and cavalry with reversed arms. At the end rolled the coaches of mourners draped in black, led by that of the dead marquis. It took over three hours for the funeral cortege to reach the cemetery.[73]

This description, as well as the details of life in Lima sketched earlier, gives an idea of the pomp and circumstance which attended important events in the colonies, and such fanfare was echoed throughout Latin America.

THE ARTISTIC CLIMATE

For an understanding of the Baroque and Rococo in Latin America, several factors and influences affecting the artistic climate there have to be taken into consideration. The development of the various art styles in the Old World and especially the conditions peculiar to the Iberian Peninsula must be reviewed, as well as the entirely strange cosmos of the New World onto which European art was grafted.

1

At the time when artistic activity in the Americas began to unfold (about mid-sixteenth century), art in Europe showed a complex picture. Italy was still leading all Europe. In regions separated by comparatively short distances, such as Tuscany and Venetia or Lombardy and Rome, people speaking practically the same language and confessing the same faith had already gone far along the road toward producing strongly regional styles.

In Venice—until the discovery of the New World the hub of international commerce—Titian, Tintoretto, Veronese, and the Bassano family were supplying oil paintings for Renaissance palaces and churches, built perhaps by Sansovino or the Lombardi brothers. Here also, a few blocks from the thousand-and-one-night's splendor of St. Mark's, lay the Borgo dei Greci, with its considerable Greek population—four thousand in 1550—among them not

merely seamen and merchants but mosaic workers, artists, and scholars.[22] In this quarter painters born in the Orthodox faith on the Greek Islands or in the Balkan hinterland still worked on panel or canvas in the Byzantine tradition. This Veneto-Byzantine school persisted well into the seventeenth century, as is testified by the surviving pictures in the church of San Giorgio dei Greci and its chapter house, both built by Lombardi. Through these piazzas and *rios* echoing with the Greek tongue, the young unknown Doménicos Theotocópoulos roamed before, by way of Rome, he reached Spain and fame. Venice, for all its fast tempo, commercial activity, and lavish manifestations in art, literature, music, and drama, could not entirely uproot the old Byzantine tradition.

The disciples of Byzantine art seldom signed even their masterpieces. They subordinated their individualities to orthodox expression, while the artist of Renaissance Italy was developing a self-expression so strong in its characteristics that many of his works—even without a monogram—betray the master. Earlier both the Romanesque and the Gothic had manifested such regional differences that the Romanesque of Spain can be distinguished from that of Central Europe and Portuguese Gothic from the English. But the Renaissance, as a powerful humanistic movement, burst the bounds of regionalism and implanted the spirit of individuality everywhere.

The Iberian Peninsula, off the main thoroughfare of artistic interchange, had a distinctive artistic past of its own. The foundations of some of its buildings had been laid when it was a Roman province. Later the Visigoths made their contributions. And still later the Moorish occupation, which in the southern portion of the peninsula lasted for seven centuries, left its indelible mark. Certain elements from the art of the Near East which reached other parts of Europe secondhand through the returning Crusaders [16] or were filtered in through Venice came to the Spaniards firsthand through the art and architecture of the Moors.

The Moorish tradition continued side by side with European artistic influences. When Granada fell (1492) the military grip of the Moors on Spain was broken, but the deep imprint they had stamped on Spanish life remained, whether in medicine, in arithmetic —with the exchange of the clumsy Roman numerals for the Arabic—in ceramics, or in architecture. The crescent-moon standards with their streamers of horses' tails may have departed across the narrows of Gibraltar, but the Moorish civilization had infiltrated into Spanish life and many Moors converted to Christianity stayed in Spain.

A converted Moor was called a "mudéjar" by the Spaniards, from the Arabic meaning "vassal." Later this term was applied to that art style which showed Moorish characteristics, for the most part in its treatment of brick, wood, and tile. The brick of the Spaniards frequently was thinner than that of contemporary Europe; wood was used and ornamented in the Moorish manner; and the ceramic work of Spain and Portugal—even of Italy—shows kinship to the famous majolica ware from the island of Majorca, long a Moorish colony.

At the close of the fifteenth century no country in Europe had an artistic soil more diversified, layer by layer, than that of the Iberian Peninsula. The distinctive florid Gothic style of both Spain and Portugal developed out of this diversity and in addition shows a certain time lag when compared with the rest of Europe, so that Seville was building its exquisite Gothic cathedral in 1506 when in Italy Bramante (1444?–1514) had already arrived at the expression of purest Renaissance.

The Renaissance in Spain, delayed by the long-drawn-out warfare against the Moors, did not take hold until after their final expulsion by Ferdinand and Isabella. Charles I of Spain, born in Ghent and brought up in a Flemish environment, succeeded his grandfather to the Spanish crown in 1516, the first Habsburg on the Spanish throne; three years later he was also made head of the Holy Roman Empire, as Charles V. At that time the Holy Roman Empire included nearly all of German-speaking Central Europe, the Low Countries, Luxembourg, Liechtenstein, Bohemia, some districts of eastern France, and much of northern Italy. To the Spanish crown belonged Sardinia, Naples, and Sicily, scattered provinces of North Africa, and the vast new colonies of the New World.

The administration of the huge Habsburg properties meant unremitting toil, but at the same time an unprecedented opportunity was offered for intellectual and artistic exchange among many different countries. Although the title of emperor passed from Charles to the Austrian branch of the family, the Habsburg dynasty remained on the Spanish throne until 1700 and at the head of the Holy Roman Empire more or less continuously until that empire was dissolved in 1806. In addition, through personal union and alliances by marriage, the Habsburgs ruled the kingdoms of Hungary and Poland, with their dependencies. Such extensive holdings—a veritable cauldron of European nationalities—under the control of one family functioned as a vast market for the exchange of ideas, from the Slavs on the east to the Gauls on the west and from the Scandinavian borders to the Mediterranean.

All over Europe the versatility of the individual artist during the Renaissance contributed much to the increasingly personal expression of that style. Architect, painter, and sculptor of note might be embodied in one person. Such versatility did much to break down the barriers between the various branches of the arts and to make the whole style integrated and pictorial. Certain artists attained a superlative command of their craft and expressed themselves with a virtuosity that would have seemed impossible in the preceding decades. The painter experimented successfully with extravagant forms and daring perspectives. The twisted column divided into three segments which were variously decorated can be found in Raphael's work, and Veronese made use of it in several of his murals; this form appears in three dimensions notably in Bernini's baldachin for the high altar at St. Peter's in Rome (about 1627–1633). Also the jeweler's art, which reached its height with Benvenuto Cellini—who was also famous as a sculptor—made use of the Renaissance vocabulary. Objects that combined gold and silver with pearls, other jewels, and intricate enamel work revealed the creator's talent in the handling of material, shape, and color.

About 1500 it became the mode for Spanish aristocrats and high ecclesiastics to order carved marble tombs from Genoa, and Italian sculptors often accompanied their works to Spain. Such carving may have been an early source in Spain of motifs from the Italian Renaissance—the *putti*, medallions, grotesques, the swags and garlands of flowers and fruit, and the candelabrum columns—which were adapted by Spanish builders with little sense of Italian architectural principles but with a remarkable feeling for their decorative value.[24]

Considerably later the name "Plateresque" was given to this early flowering of the Renaissance in Spain. The style is now believed to have been applied first in architecture when the artisans showed themselves *plateros en yeso* (silversmiths in stucco).[25] In the spread and persistence of its many motifs, however, the influence of the Renaissance jeweler should not be overlooked. The Spanish Plateresque

covers in general the first half of the sixteenth century, but its decorative ideals made themselves felt not only in the succeeding classicizing period but also even in the Baroque.

Spain found her way slowly out of the long domination of Flemish and Italian models to artistic self-assurance.[88] When Charles V—whose connoisseurship is documented by his continuous patronage of Titian—abdicated in 1556 in favor of his son Philip II, an interesting paradox existed there: Spain, one of the most powerful countries of Europe, was artistically behind not only the other Habsburg crown lands but also other sections of the Old World.

By the time Spain had made the Renaissance her own (mid-sixteenth century) a new style, the Baroque, was already incipient in Italy, the Germanic lands, and the Low Countries; in Rome it found its ideal climate and its most talented early artists. The word "Baroque" is said to derive from the Spanish *barrueco*, meaning "a pearl of irregular form"; some authorities [1] trace it back to the Visigothic and others to the Latin *verruca*, meaning "wart." It was first used by the scholastic writers—in a poem quoted by Antonio Abbondanti in 1627—later it appears in the works of Louis Saint-Simon (1675–1755), and still later it was taken over into art history.[3]

The Renaissance had been a self-conscious age and Baroque evolved, in part, out of the tendency to revolt against its rules, which had become pedantic, and a desire to try out new possibilities. It is impossible to confine an art style between two arbitrary dates, one for the beginning of its course and another for the termination. The roots of the Baroque can be traced beyond Michelangelo, who is often called its originator; before him the trend to break the classical forms was already in evidence.

The world then was inclining more and more to make of life a drama and of drama, life. It was a world of extreme contrasts, of arrogant magnificence and hopeless misery, of carnal indulgence and ecstatic asceticism. The coronation of an emperor or a viceroy, the birth of a royal child, the wedding of an archduke, the funeral of a high dignitary—all were occasions for elaborate architectural settings, with baldachins, tribunes, triumphal arches, and, when appropriate, catafalques. Such festivals of joy or mourning lasted for days. The preparations in the illusionistic field called for artists of renown and were equaled only by those of a sartorial or a culinary nature. There were theater performances requiring complicated machinery, waterfalls, fireworks, floats, parades, and all kinds of artful devices and tricks of perspective and illusion.

Thus Baroque was not merely an art style but a mode of living; it was the last grand spectacle of feudalism, and it also heralded the dawn of the epoch of the common man. It spread to the farthermost corners of Europe, disregarding religious boundaries. It manifested itself in the arts, literature, music, and drama and in many facets of everyday life, in Sweden as well as in Poland, in England and the Low Countries as well as in France.

The Council of Trent had remonstrated against the all-too-pagan representations of Renaissance painting and sculpture—the nudity, the carnal subjects, the unorthodox and overfamiliar treatment of religious figures—and prescribed in detail the religious iconography of the Counter Reformation. Since the service to religion was still a major function of art these directives were instrumental in bringing about in certain schools of painting and sculpture an emphasis on the ecstatic; and since the development of Baroque coincided with the immense expansion of the Jesuit order (founded by the Spanish-born Ignatius Loyola and recognized officially in 1540) it is often identified with that militant institution.

Spain also adopted the new style. Economically at that time the country was approaching its zenith; into it was pouring the immeasurable riches of a new world, and much of the gold and silver mined in faraway America by Indian and Negro slaves served to enlarge and embellish both civil and ecclesiastic estab-

lishments in the motherland. After generations of foreign artists and even artisans had been accepted, Spanish talent and ingenuity now took hold and created its own Baroque, with accents in its architecture on the heroic, the complex, and the ostentatious and in its sculpture and painting on the mystic, the ascetic, and the *larmoyant*.

Although the Baroque style developed out of the Renaissance it presents a marked contrast to it. The Renaissance manner is distinguished by a clarity of composition and a tranquillity of line; the Baroque, by a massivity of composition and a mobility of line. The careful subordination of the decorative elements in the Renaissance changes with the Baroque into a compact and vibrant complexity, in which the emphasis is not on the organization of the detail into the whole but on the impact of the total impression.

In addition to the ebullience and floridity of its effect, Baroque can be recognized by certain general characteristics. There was in this period considerable complication of the ground plan, a show of virtuosity in construction—in the use of octagonals and ovals both in plan and in certain members, such as cupolas—and an increased interest in interior lighting. Also, the exterior was less indicative of interior structure. Side walls were kept rather plain, and ornament was heaped on the façade. The stress on classic proportion was relaxed and a new pictorial emphasis took its place, characterized by vigor of rhythm and boldness of detail. Columns and pilasters often lost their function and became purely decorative. Columns were coupled into pairs, frequently twisted, and hung with wreaths and garlands. The classic triangular pediment was broken; sometimes its slanting segments were reversed to flare outward and sometimes they were replaced with scrolls. Sculpture was called upon to adorn window frames; consoles, capitals, balustrades, and finials were brought forward to embellish all suitable space.

Especial attention was given to the setting

and the grouping of buildings. The surrounding terrain was laid out for an impressive approach, with terraces, esplanades, and flights of steps. Monuments, fountains, and even cascades were arranged to climax harmonious vistas. The villas of royalty and aristocracy in Italy furnished principles and formulas which were used beyond the borders of that country. On the islands of Venice and on the mainland of Venetia, on Isola Bella in Lake Maggiore and on the shores of Lake Como, lavish formal gardens which drew the water's edge into the composition served as prototypes for Baroque landscaping.

It is important to note the continuance of an undercurrent, an academic, classicizing trend, which persisted throughout the seventeenth and eighteenth centuries until its ultimate resurgence into the neoclassic.

The evolution of the Rococo out of the Baroque is interestingly exemplified in France. When Louis XIV turned toward the indulgence of eye, ear, and palate, Italians were invited to France to refine and elevate the standards of court and country. The Sun King's mother was a Habsburg, and through her the Baroque gained new ground in the French court. With Louis' death in 1715 the five-year-old dauphin became king, but state matters were in the hands of a regency and the tradition of pomp continued. The mother of the youthful Louis XV, a princess of Savoy, doubtless introduced some of her taste preferences. A young artist from Turin, her home, arrived in Paris in 1723 and under the name of Juste Aurèle Meissonier rose to a leading position as architect, sculptor, and designer. The royal court and the aristocrats employed Italian painters, sculptors, and architects. And in addition from inexhaustible Italy came the actors of the Commedia dell' Arte (with their paraphernalia and their modes for the ladies to follow), singers, dancers, musicians (as immortalized by the Flemish-born Watteau), hairdressers, milliners, dressmakers, tailors, the makers of candles and fireworks, the gardeners, pastry cooks, and even the masters of the kitchens.

In the Rococo the interest of the decorative system—until then in general divided evenly between the horizontal and the vertical—made a distinct shift toward the vertical. There was a return to a clearer, definitely classical design, made visible through a regrouping of decorative elements. Surfaces were left plain and the contrasting ornament became thinner and more flowing. Blank panels were framed sometimes with only a slender pendent garland. The inner fields of panels were elongated and exchanged their gold for color; flowered patterns in various hues came into favor.

In painting and sculpture, too, the Rococo produced a liquidity of color, a lightness in the composition, and a delicacy and grace of line, frequently obtained by the use of tenuous elements and reduced dimensions. Even in Rococo gardens the change is noticeable, for the bulk of vegetation was lightened, clean-cut airy perspectives were opened, and graceful sculpture was applied for gaiety of effect.

The term "Rococo" is said to derive from a combination of the French words *rocaille* and *coquille* (rockwork and shell). But such a modern garbling of syllables would indeed be exceptional in an age famous for its literary precision and the purity of its language. Considering Italy's great contribution to this style, the word *roccioso* (rocky) would seem a somewhat less distant root. It is worth noting that while no French word ends in *-co*, the Italian has for art styles: *classico, gotico, barocco*. The implication is that from the Baroque garden with its contrived rockeries and grottoes—an Italian word from which grotesque is derived—were brought indoors its characteristic rocks, shells, marine figures, and ferns and moss as motifs for decoration. Allegedly the term occurs first in Stendhal's *Voyage d'Italie*.

In Spain in 1700 the Habsburg line was succeeded by the Bourbon when a grandson of Louis XIV was placed on the throne, and in the following era the Baroque gave way to the Rococo. The royal summer palace at Aranjuez, near Madrid, a showplace since the sixteenth century, displays the evolution of taste. As early as 1576 it was mentioned as one of the wonders of the world. The asparagus and strawberries grown there were famous; cotton, too, was cultivated, in one of the first botanical gardens of Europe, and the collection of animals there included specimens of exotic origin as well as European.[29] The entrance to the palace is Baroque, with its wide porte-cochere and its high curving pediment surmounted by statuary. Baroque too is the magnificent staircase inside, at the foot of which a coach and four could draw up with ease. Most of the furniture, woodwork, bronzes, tapestries, and porcelains of the interior were manufactured in Spain. The Rococo is exquisitely represented by a unique masterpiece, the Porcelain Salon, produced in the Buen Retiro factory in 1763. This entire room is faced with large panels of lustrous porcelain, a bower of polychromed flower and fruit patterns enlivened with birds and little animals, amid which human figures, about one-third life size, are grouped in picturesque Chinese garb.

Baroque flourished at a time when commerce with the Near East was quite regular and profited from the richness of form, color, and workmanship current in Mohammedan countries. Rococo reached full bloom when the Christian world was in frequent communication with China and her neighbors. The grace in the fine arts of the Far East, the hues and patterns of the silks, the colorfulness of the wallpapers, the perfection of the porcelain —all further enlivened the Rococo style.

2

The Spanish conquerors came to America from a world where Christianity was fifteen hundred years old, where a powerful hierarchy administered the firmly established religion. Its rites, its iconography, its philosophy, had evolved out of the mentality of the European and were attuned to his temperament. It was a religion that was stabilized not only in its ecclesiastical administration but also in its spiritual scope. Its dogma was supreme; and for the regulation of those who tried to leave the prescribed path, the Holy Office of the Inquisition was instituted.

The Indian, on his part, was not the "savage dog" that some chroniclers would have us believe. He also had built for himself a world which in many of its concepts was remarkably civilized; though he did not know the use of the wheel and had no iron tools, his stone temples stood more than a hundred feet high and were decorated with polychromed carvings of human, animal, and geometric forms. Even today the remnants of his ruined cities, ravaged by the jungle, climate, and man, awe us with their grandeur, maturity of planning, and artistic sensitivity. Although our understanding of pre-Columbian art is hampered by our Greco-Roman concept of beauty, nevertheless we feel its strange power. Much of the Indian's pottery compares favorably with ceramic products of contemporary Europe; one region achieved even a vitreous glaze. Woven materials, sometimes more than a thousand years old, have been taken from graves with colors still rich and vibrant and present a variety of weaving techniques that is yet to be matched. Whereas Europe had to wait until the sixteenth century and Benvenuto Cellini for the rediscovery of the lost wax process, the pre-Columbian Indian discovered this complex method of metal casting and produced by it ornaments in gold, platinum, and silver of rare artistic refinement.

But not merely in the arts can pre-Columbian America hold her own; in the intellectual field, also, the native American made outstanding achievements. The Maya's calendar was more accurate than that of sixteenth-century Europe. Not until the reform of Pope Gregory XIII in 1582 were the equinoxes brought into adjustment in the European system. Several pre-Columbian cultures had writing and made scrolls of vegetable fiber or animal skins on which the time count and matters of history were recorded. Some of them had literature, drama, and the dance—closer in imagination and poetry to works of the advanced nations of Asia than to those of the Christian world. Such surviving pieces of literature as the admonition of an Aztec mother to her young daughter and the dramatized Inca legend of ancestors elevated to godhood in *Ollantaytambo* make inspiring and revealing reading.[62]

The cities of pre-Columbian America—compared by the Conquistadores to Seville and Cordova—were spacious and clean, laid out according to plan, often with a fine feeling for topography; many of them had water channels and sewage systems. Roads and causeways connected one city with another, and commerce in the busy markets was supervised by special officials, who even checked the accuracy of weights and measures.

The Indian's knowledge of natural history was so well developed that it was made use of by the Spaniards, who found it not only accurate but also detailed. Such plants as cocaine, quinine, cocoa, tobacco, and curare were known and their stimulating and medicinal properties utilized.

These high pre-Columbian cultures came into clash with the European civilization of the Spanish conquerors. Not only were two absolutely different races involved but in addition all circumstances of their manner of living had developed after different patterns. The Indian was subjugated by weapons of iron and steel and by military tactics which confounded him, and he became a peon in his own land.

With the Conquistadores came the priests, imbued with missionary zeal and bearing their crucifixes, rosaries, censers, painted banners, and their books. On the one side was the paraphernalia of the new religion, on the other were the temples reaching toward the sky, the spiraling copal smoke, and the life-size statues of the gods of rain, maize, flowers, war, and death. First, all evidence of the pagan

religion had to be destroyed, the temples wrecked, the "sacerdotes of hellish practices" slaughtered or driven away, the idols broken and scattered or, if very large, buried out of sight. In many cases the expertly cut stones of a pre-Columbian building were reused in the construction of Christian churches.

The first churches were simple barnlike structures, but they were soon replaced by more pretentious edifices. Here in the New World the early colonial builder, whether priest or layman, was faced with a situation for which he had no precedent in the Old World. In Europe the architecture was composed into a landscape that had been shaped by the hand of man. In America the builder was confronted with a spectacular setting little touched by human hands; gone were the temples from their high platforms, sharply contoured against the tropical horizon, and the palaces with the ornaments on their roofs polychromed or glittering with gold. Here the Christian architecture had to be fitted into an untamed landscape.

The destruction of the social fabric brought about by the Conquest was so thorough that the new religion could not take subjective hold on the Indian for many years. Though he had been defeated in battle and had nominally accepted his conqueror's God, he could not immediately grasp the precepts of Christianity. For the European the Holy Land was a reality, as were the works of the Apostles and the lives of the saints. And the powerful philosophical and economic movements that had figured in the spread of Christianity were all part of his background and tradition. The Italian woodworker who carved a crucifix was following a long line of precursors who knew what it stood for. To the Indian the crucifix had no meaning; he looked uncomprehendingly at the images of the Virgin Mother, Santiago on horseback, and other holy figures painted on the banners which the Conquistadores bore. Even if he wished to embrace the new religion the whole mystic and symbolic content of Christianity was outside his ken. For him the entire development of Christianity prior to the sixteenth century was a sealed book. And above all else the Saviour was not an Indian but of the same white race as his subjugators and was not even a triumphant war chief. The Inca Atahuallpa taunted the Spaniards—even when their prisoner—that their God had been put to death by the very men he had created.[197]

Because the Indian was totally ignorant of the intellectual and spiritual past of the Christian European he had to be educated. The friar learned the native tongues and thus discovered what a different instrument was the soul of his charges. The catechism was transcribed into native picture writing to put the alien concepts at least into a familiar visual idiom. The children were taught Spanish, and pictures illustrating Biblical history were shown to them. The alphabet was adapted to the native languages, and quotations from Holy Scripture appeared on church walls placed below Latin and Spanish texts.

The Indian was accustomed to the rule of a hierarchy from pre-Columbian times and to obedience to a higher authority. He needed the ceremonial contact with those superior powers on whom depended his harvest and the health of his children. His ancestors had offered fowl, maize, and flowers to the priest of the sacrificial religion, and so he continued the custom, bringing offerings to the Christian church. In bygone centuries his ancestors had rejoiced to burn copal before their idols and carry flickering torches in processions, and it gave him pleasure to see his son, as an acolyte, swinging the censer during Mass, and perhaps it made him still happier to participate in the various processions of the Christian calendar. Bernal Díaz, that truly human chronicler of the conquest of Mexico and Central America, wrote with satisfaction in 1576:

Since the destruction of idolatry, by the Will of God, and by His holy aid . . . there have been baptised in this country all the natives whose souls formerly were sunk and lost in the infernal pit. It is a thing worthy to thank God on to

see the devotion which the natives exhibit when at Holy Mass. Men, women, and children are taught the holy orations in their mother-tongue. We, the conquerors, also taught them to keep wax candles lighted before the holy altars and crosses, for before our arrival they did not know the use of wax in making candles. We also taught them to behave with respect to the reverend fathers, and when they came to their towns, to go out and meet them and receive them with lighted wax candles, ringing the bells and giving them plentifully to eat. . . . They have also other holy and good customs, for on the day of Our Lady or of Corpus Christi and their solemn feasts they go in procession with crosses and lighted candles, bearing the image of the saint who is their patron or patroness, as richly dressed as they can afford; and they go singing litanies and other holy orations, and sound their flutes and trumpets.[100]

But behind this impressive façade of ritual, there were many traditional practices and subconscious reflexes that added up to a very different religion from that of the European. Furthermore, in time a considerable number of the ecclesiastic personnel were creoles, mestizos, and even Indians, and a change took place that had far-reaching religious and artistic implications. Increasingly the Indian became a fervent participant. Thus it became possible for him to perform Christian acts of mercy and to have Christian visions. After the shock from the collision of two civilizations had subsided he was able to express himself again also in art.

Since the success of the work of the Roman Church depended to a great extent on the participation of the Indian, the priest or missionary could or would not protest too strongly against the transformation brought about by Indian hands. He may have taken it as a sign of success; if the Christian iconography took on characteristics of the artistic and emotional idiom of the natives without serious divergence from dogma it could be interpreted as proof that the Indian had submerged himself in the new religion. Today in Chichicastenango, Guatemala, representatives of distant villages gather to burn copal and murmur prayers on the steps outside the church before entering in much the same way as the ancient Maya did on the stairways of their temple bases. Within this church the seed corn from the separate villages is laid out in rectangles on the floor and framed with flower petals and candles, forming a continuous pattern the length of the nave as it awaits the blessing of the priest. In Pisac, Peru, conch shells blare at the elevation of the Host.

The yielding to the new religion was aided by the *cofradías* and *sodalidades* of mestizo and Indian membership. Often an Indian region was without a resident priest and had only a visiting cleric who came on muleback from a distant valley. In the interim the leaders of the *cofradía* took over, performing many a duty which in Europe was entrusted only to the ordained clergy.

Climate provided another factor for change. Many church holidays in Europe had equivalents in pre-Christian religions, intimately connected in mood and spirit with the seasons. In Latin America such holidays cannot evoke the same feelings, for even the countries above the equator do not know our succession of four seasons and below the equator the seasons are reversed. Thus Christmas—par excellence a winter holiday, presaging the return of the sun—falls in South America in midsummer. And Easter, which in Europe on the threshold of spring is full of expectancy, in South America comes when the crops are harvested, when nature is at its drabbest and coldest, when rain and fog are due on the coast and the people are facing winter.

3

In forming an aesthetic evaluation of Latin American colonial art, we must not forget that a superb range of the Romanesque, Gothic, and Renaissance was part of the background of those who came to the New World: they had in their mind's eye those buildings of the homeland among which they had been brought up, the churches where they had worshiped,

the cities which had impressed them en route to the harbors whence they set sail for America. The intermingling of Romanesque, Gothic, and Renaissance elements which occurred in the first century or so of colonial life makes for a fascinating mixture. The compound character which resulted from this elastic application of styles prepared the way for the distinctive Baroque and Rococo of Latin America.

Amazingly small in proportion to the art production is the number of confirmed cases of renowned artists emigrating to the colonies —either from Spain or from other European countries—who through their outstanding personalities and originality might have set the direction. In the various memoirs, treatises, and contracts which remain from the colonial period, there is little mention of artists or art works going to America. The Flemish painter Simon Pereyns is one early exception; he came to Mexico in 1568, contributed to the decoration of the cathedral, and had many pupils. The paintings of Martin de Vos (1536–1693) are known to have been imported and to have influenced the manner of painting in Mexico. The Italian Mateo Pérez de Alesio was active in Lima toward the end of the sixteenth century, and his son carried on his school of painting. The sculptor Juan Martínez Montañés (1568–1649) contracted to execute an altar for Lima, Peru. Francisco de Zurbarán (1598–1669?) is reported to have sent some of his canvases out on commission with a ship captain.[27] In the early eighteenth century Jerónimo de Balbás came from Spain and built the Altar de los Reyes in the cathedral of Mexico City. About the same time and in the same place Lorenzo Rodríguez (1704?–1774), also an Andalusian, was active; his work on the Sagrario of the cathedral is especially noteworthy. Manuel Tolsa (1757–1816), a Spanish architect and sculptor who arrived in Mexico in 1791, was another to achieve distinction there. However, the number of European artists of rank working in the colony are too few (even though many more may be discovered through research) to have directed the entire artistic orientation of the vast territory comprising the New World. In spite of the many Italian and Flemish artists who worked in Spain no one would classify Spanish art as a mere subsidiary of the Italian or Flemish; and Latin American colonial art developed in a not too dissimilar manner its own individuality in the distant hemisphere.

Throughout the colonial period in whatever concerns the intellectual, artistic, and even sartorial fashions of Europe a time lag can be observed. Transportation was slow, and while a new mode might sweep a viceregal capital with the arrival of a new viceroy and his suite the rhythm of new ideas moved with increasing ritardando into the hinterland. By the seventeenth century the arts were flourishing on virile and articulate regional impulses; the importation of European ideas and art products continued throughout the colonial period, but everywhere it met strong competition from the growing artistic independence of the creole, the mestizo, and the Indian.

Nowhere else in the world was the religious iconography of one high civilization so successfully replaced with another. In the early years of the Conquest writers remarked on the astonishing ability of the Indian to copy any model placed before him. In fact, his representation of the European was much more accurate than the European's of him. But the chroniclers do not mention that the Indian was doing something else: he was also transforming his image of the model according to his own psychology.

It should be pointed out here that in those regions where advanced artistic cultures existed in pre-Columbian times, colonial art is its most striking and original; in Mexico, Guatemala, Colombia, Ecuador, Peru, and Bolivia especially, many of the Indian artifacts today have an ancient origin, many of them unchanged in design and technique until recently. Statistics published in 1945 give the population in these six countries as 10 per cent white, 30 per cent pure Indian, and 60 per cent mestizo. Two centuries earlier the proportion in favor of the Indian was considerably larger.[71] Millions of the Indians there even today speak languages that antedate Columbus; as many as fifty separate roots exist.

The imagination and the expressive gift of the native were not merely powerful but stubborn. The Spaniards brought over the same norms for art and architecture to all Latin America, and, in general, colonial buildings can be classified within the framework of European architectural forms. Yet frequently in the various areas a shift of emphasis occurs which results in distinguishable regional styles, especially in the decoration of the buildings. And often in sculpture and painting the psychology of the Christianized Indian and the double heritage of the mestizo come even more to the fore. No one who knows pre-Columbian pottery will confuse a Maya jar with an Inca; and an explanation of the great differences between Mexican and Peruvian colonial arts can be found partly in the different artistic abilities of the Indians—for instance, Zapotec and Aztec versus Mochica and Quechua.

Mexico City, Quito, and Cuzco were built on the foundations of pre-Columbian capitals and from the first had a vast reservoir of native craftsmen at hand to help erect the new cities. As the colonies grew in population and wealth new towns developed and the landscape was dotted with churches whose towers gazed alertly into the alien landscape. In principle the towns were laid out on the checkerboard plan of the Spanish colonial system, with one side of the central plaza reserved for the main church, another for the municipal building, a third for the military, and the fourth for the governor's house. Spanish building types served as models for the structures, large and small. The work was organized and directed mainly by Spaniards or other Europeans, but by far the greater portion, not only of the masonry but also of the decoration, was executed by natives. From the point of view of craftsmanship the Indian had little to learn; he had reached a high level with his own stone tools and the introduction of iron implements released his talent and gave it a new impulse. When the times were ready for real magnificence, the natives were proficient enough to produce it.

In 1556 the Dominican archbishop Alonso de Montúfar wrote to Philip II of monasteries in Mexico so grandiose that though only a handful of friars were to be accommodated in them they would be worthy of the Spanish city of Valladolid; of Indians called up in gangs of five hundred to a thousand to work on the construction, without wages or even food provided; of the Indian personnel for such establishments, including gardeners, doorkeepers, cleaners, cooks, sacristans, and messengers, some of them acting also as cantors, acolytes, and musicians and all serving without remuneration.[123] The participation of the Indians and mestizos in the construction of a church or convent was an act of faith, just as in the Middle Ages in Europe. In the colonies the haughty attitude of the Spaniards and creoles toward menial labor kept them from any occupation which might result in loss of face.

It was a custom at this time even in Europe for builders to solve many of their structural and decorative problems as a building progressed, with leeway left for extemporaneous detail; not every figure, columnette, garland, and rosette was worked out as a modern architect designs them for a blueprint, reduced to scale. The plans of many colonial buildings in Spanish America, still extant in the Archive of the Indies, gave only the general layout, with no specific designs for the decoration. Even recently this author observed stone carvers in San Miguel de Allende, Mexico, chiseling away in their traditional fashion on a design which the master builder had roughed out in pencil on a brick cornice. And at Cuenca, Ecuador, he saw expert masons, volunteer workers on a new cathedral—already more than fifty years in the making—using a late-nineteenth-century wooden model for inspiration but modifying the walls and arches, as they built them, to suit their own taste.

In Europe the rising artist could study with his own eyes the masterpieces of every branch of the arts. The mestizo and Indian, on the other hand, who produced the major portion of colonial art, seldom left their own districts and had only scanty plans and meager models to grasp at.

Colonial art in Spanish America is far from being a mere transplantation of Spanish forms into a new world; it grew out of the union of two civilizations which in many ways were the antithesis of each other. Non-European factors were at work also. Thus it incorporated the Indian's preferences, his characteristic sense of form and color, the power of his own heritage, all of which, as overtones, modulated the imported style. Furthermore, the different physical background contributed toward a new expression.

The Baroque style lent itself amazingly well to the fusion of these influences. A full-blooded Baroque spread to even the less accessible regions of Latin America and with its vast register of variations developed such regional expressions as the "Andean mestizo" and the "Mexican *poblano*" styles.

Throughout the colonial period two major art trends are noticeable. The first manifests itself in a painstaking copying and imitation of European models, primarily from Spain but also from Italy, the Low Countries, and other parts of Europe. Such work was often servile and uninspired, though it might be satisfactory from the standpoint of both iconography and craftsmanship. The second trend came into being after native talent had forged a new language, differing not only from the old but also from region to region. These two trends might be regarded as echoing two major motives of the mother country: the shaping of a colonial empire and the conversion of the Indian.

Structurally, Baroque architecture in Europe is complex, constantly concerned with the illusionistic principles of perspective; the effects of light and shade were calculated with virtuosity, and the traditional system of organization was kept in mind even in the most complex design. Colonial architecture, on the other hand, reveals a lack of knowledge of as well as respect for the traditional. The subtle balance of classical architecture which has repeatedly revitalized European styles was totally alien to the native of the New World. Usually the Spanish American Baroque building was simple in structure. The decoration rather than the design was elaborated. Because of the control of the Inquisition and the very different intellectual and physical climate, the sensualistic aspects of European Baroque never developed here. The art of colonial Latin America is characterized by the sincerity and power that marked the early Christian spirit; expressed in the current idiom—the flamboyant Baroque—it achieved a unique flavor.

Heretofore in discussions of Latin American colonial art a disproportionate emphasis has been placed upon architecture and little attention has been devoted to the decorative detail, where often the greatest originality is evident. Colonial sculpture presents not theater, as does frequently European Baroque, but drama experienced. Many colonial paintings have an unparalleled story-telling charm and a fairy-tale atmosphere. In colonial weaving, pre-Columbian taste and techniques continued long after the Conquest, producing a fascinating blend. Pictures fashioned of tiny brilliant feathers (a pre-Conquest technique) were applied with amazing skill to shields, miters, and stoles. The potter, combining indigenous and imported methods and decorative motifs, turned out ware which was pleasing in form and color. The great wealth of gold, silver, and other precious minerals stimulated the manufacture of countless attractive articles, from tableware to extravagant jewelry. Furniture and objects for interior decoration, sometimes more lavishly Baroque and Rococo than those in Europe, were made of the uniquely durable native woods, which showed up magnificently when processed. In the tooling of leather, a craft unknown in pre-Columbian America, many original ideas were developed.

Just as the artistic achievement of pre-Columbian civilization will always remain a torso—grand but incomplete—so also the splendor of the arts of colonial Latin America can never be fully recaptured. This is a hemisphere visited by volcanic eruptions, earthquakes, and tropical hurricanes, and the colonial builders were never able to outwit such violent phenomena of nature. Further, the colonies had no Vasari to chronicle for succeeding generations the story, the personalities, and the methods of local artists; in proportion to the immense output, few names can be identified through documentation.

Too often in the past Latin American colonial art has been evaluated by measuring it against the art of Europe, and the peculiar originality that is one of its chief values has been passed over as a less important "mestizo" feature. The art of the Byzantine and Romanesque epochs in Europe is being enjoyed whether or not it is documented with names and dates, and the folk art of many regions of the world serves as a great stimulus, despite anonymity. Just as the Greek Revival in the United States is not a soulless imitation of an Old World style but mirrors a North American spirit, so the Baroque and Rococo of Latin America reflect artistic impulses invigoratingly new and different from those of contemporary Europe.

3

CATHEDRALS

THE story of the cathedrals in Latin America reflects the rise and decline of the colonial empires there. The seat of the bishop was established in those towns to which the kings' officials attached considerable hope. Often the expectation was fulfilled, and today the cathedral dominates the main plaza of a bustling city. But it also happened that the reasons for choosing the location—geographical, military, or perhaps economic—lost pertinency with the passing of time, and the cathedral now stands on some sleepy square in a shrinking out-of-the-way town.

In sixteenth-century Europe the cathedral was a well-established institution, with both direction and continuity to its program. It had developed out of the Christian civilization of Western Europe and reflected the character of its age; the bishops and their functionaries were integrated into the pattern of the administrative, economic, and social life which made up the complex picture there. But for the bishop who was sent from Spain into the New World in those early decades the situation was without precedent. He came into the primitive beginnings of colonial city life, where he found little of the resplendent ceremony to which he was accustomed in the homeland. When he celebrated Mass, there were no rows of elegant gentlemen—and still fewer noble ladies—before him; splendid vestments were rare, priestly assistants were few, and the music and ecclesiastical vessels were far from later standards.

The community centered about the main plaza; beyond lay dusty plots with, for the most part, a few shacks scattered here and there. Horses and cattle grazed about, and in some places the howling of monkeys and the cry of tropical birds mingled with the ringing of the church bells. In most cases the early church in the New World was a barnlike structure of wood and reeds, with a peaked roof built of timber and thatched. Descriptions and sketches which remain from those days show little that is spectacular, either in magnitude or in design; the notable exceptions include the cathedral of Santo Domingo in the republic of the same name and the "fortress churches" in Mexico.

Yet before the Conquest was a century old, ambitious and spacious buildings had been erected. Sometimes only a handful of ecclesiastics carried through projects the grandeur of which amazes us even today. A bishop's church was an expression of his own eminence, an acclamation of his own renown, and its construction, enlargement, and embellishment were in his power; here he could exercise his authority in making his New World cathedral worthy of comparison with those in the motherland. Where a document connected with the construction of a church survives, the name of the prelate always is mentioned, that of the donor more rarely, and still less frequently—unless the paper be a contract—the names of the artists and craftsmen who actually carried out the work.

For the erection or re-edification of an important building in the Spanish colonies plans were sometimes sent from Spain at the instigation of high ecclesiastical authorities or as a part of the king's contribution; more often, however, they were drawn up in the colonies and were then, theoretically at least, submitted to Spain for approval. Of the nearly four hundred plans of buildings in the Americas and the Philippines which have been published from the material in the Archive of the Indies, in Seville, less than 6 per cent date before 1610. In some instances an architect or sculptor of renown in Spain designed a small-scale model of a church or an altar which could be sent over (Brazil even received dressed stone from Portugal for some of its coastal buildings). More rarely a famous architect or artist came over himself to supervise the erection of some important work. But even then, as was also the case in Europe, the original plan was usually modified considerably in the course of realization. Furthermore, even when a project was laid out by a Spaniard or other European in the colonies, the actual execution lay in the hands of the workmen of the New World. And almost incredible is the number—tens of thousands—of regional churches produced exclusively by local labor in Latin America.

The people of the countryside soon learned their crafts from the traveling carpenters, the *maestro canteros* (master masons), sculptors, painters, and the *ensambladores*, who might best be translated as the co-ordinators or foremen of the project and who might belong to any of the builders' guilds. Books, drawings, etchings, woodcuts, and other reproductions of European art and architecture as well as treatises on the techniques of construction and painting were a continuous source of information and inspiration. Printing, a new craft in Europe, was introduced into the New World

as early as 1539, and engravings were reproduced and widely circulated. The market was insatiable.

Labor and building material were available in abundance in the New World. Nearly always some type of stone suitable for the project was close at hand, and the natives in many districts were skilled in the manufacture of adobe bricks and blocks even before the Conquest. Some regions furnished a soft stone, easy to quarry and to carve, which hardened upon exposure to the air, and the magnificent virgin forests provided extremely durable lumber for beams, rafters, and columns. The problem of transporting the material was secondary, for the Indian was accustomed to carrying or, if necessary, rolling incredible weights over incredible distances.

The colonial cathedral is imposing and substantial, built of stone or, more rarely, of brick and nearly always employing masonry vaults. Often it was set on a stepped platform above the level of the plaza and boasted a broad atrium, or open court, before it. This provided a stage, a dramatic setting with the façade of the building as backdrop, for the various ceremonies and colorful processions that enlivened the religious life of the age. Decoration was lavished on this façade, with columns, pilasters, niches, and statues a part of the embellishment. Three entrances were usual and, in the early structures, one tower. In later centuries two towers became customary. These towers not only served as belfries but also buttressed the façade and helped anchor the side walls.

As a rule the interior of the colonial cathedral, like the European, was laid out in three aisles—corresponding to the three doorways in the façade—separated by the pillars or clustered columns which supported the vaulted ceilings. All three might be of the same height, as in the hall-type church, or the center one might be given greater importance by higher vaulting. In certain regions domes were favored, although they were not always placed over the main body of the structure, perhaps because of the ever-present danger from earthquakes. For side chapels, either bays or niche-like recesses were provided.

In the grander buildings, following the scheme common in Spanish cathedrals, the choir occupied part of the central area of the nave; it was enclosed on three sides and faced the main altar, with a relatively narrow space between. The choir stalls, the organs, retables, and pulpit all lent themselves to lavish ornamentation. The side chapels also were ornate, many of them being dedicated by individual families or brotherhoods, who vied with one another in this expression of their devotion.

By the first quarter of the seventeenth century ecclesiastical edifices were adorning the land, a justifiable source of pride to the inhabitants and, for posterity, documents of the artistic and technical ability of colonial craftsmanship. Only a few cathedrals exist today, however, which have not seen major renovations. Earthquakes, lightning, fires, and, later, revolutions took their toll of colonial beauty; finally, the execrable taste of mid-nineteenth century and later, which added little of artistic value, demolished numberless old buildings or "modernized" them in the atrocious French bourgeois style of Napoleon III and the Victorian fashion.

The cathedral of Santo Domingo, on account of its historical priority in the Conquest of the New World, must be given first place among the noteworthy façades there. Not two months after Columbus first set foot on the territory of the New World—the island which he named San Salvador—he discovered a neighboring island which in his correspondence he called Hispaniola, the Spanish Island. Its early capital, Santo Domingo, has seen much turbulence during the centuries.

This was the spot from which the conquest of the American mainland was directed. Here Hernán Cortés arrived at the age of twenty and, as a public scribe, learned the manners and customs of colonial life. From here Veláz-

quez sailed to become the governor of Cuba, intrigant and antagonist of Cortés in the conquest of Mexico. Figures both great and small in the most spectacular drama of the Americas passed through this port: Ojeda to the Tierra Firme of South America (1509), Ponce de León—later famous for his exploration of Florida—to Puerto Rico in the same year, Balboa to the Pacific (1513), and Pizarro to Peru (1522). For about a half-century Santo Domingo was the capital of "all the Indies" known at that time, but its importance waned after the conquest of Mexico, when Havana was made the port of reunion for the fleets, homeward bound with their valuable cargo.

In the first years of occupation the religious needs of the new colony grew so rapidly that Diego Colón, son of the great admiral and governor of the island, complained in a letter to the Spanish king that the very small straw-covered church then being used could not accommodate half the crowd. It was not long before plans for a new structure were taking form.

The cathedral as it stands today (*Pl. 1, fig. b*) was projected as early as 1514, but seemingly the first stone was not laid until 1521 or 1523. In 1541 the building was dedicated, and the tower was begun soon after. The main façade has been attributed to the Spanish architect Rodrigo Gil de Liendo and, more recently, to his successor, Luis de Moya.[154] This façade is clearly Plateresque in style. The double entrance, formed by two arches, is divided by a central column—a scheme that recalls the Gothic, as do also the gable and the round window above the cornice; but in the Gothic the dividing column is generally part of the recessed doorway whereas here it is on a plane with the outer wall. It is of the slim Corinthian type favored in the early Renaissance, and the form is repeated in the fluted columns which flank the two niches in the upper order. The two arches are splayed in a curious manner so that the recessed windows are brought close together, suggesting the eyes of an owl. Bands with typically Plateresque motifs outline the arches, and smaller patterns of the same type are ingeniously adapted to fit the curved soffits. The frieze, surmounted by a powerful cornice, and the medallions of allegorical figures applied to the face of the abutments, also in the spirit of the Plateresque, effectively frame the portal.

In the lower order, highly fanciful tempietti, each different, serve as baldachins for the niches (*fig. c*); the figures painted on the wall beneath them replace earlier statuary. In this façade can be observed two characteristics that are peculiar to colonial architecture: components of various styles are blended, and architectural elements which were originally functional are turned to purely decorative uses. The side walls are plain and the few windows comparatively small. Castellation along the roof is the only ornamentation. The vaults in the interior rest on round pillars and are of equal height, as in the medieval hall churches.

In this venerable edifice is said to be the tomb of Christopher Columbus. In 1586 the English corsair Francis Drake ransacked the colony and burned its archive; thus with the first building discussed here we encounter that ever-recurring shadow which beclouds colonial art history in Latin America—the lack of archival material.

In South America the region around Tunja, Colombia, likewise attained its greatest importance early in the period of occupation; in 1539 Jiménez de Quesada and his captains subdued this portion of the New World. Before the Conquest the site was the residence of Hunza, chief of the Chibcha people, whose many gold objects, cast in a characteristic wire technique, awakened Spanish greed; here an annual ceremony took place in which gold dust was blown over the glue-covered body of the chief—hence the name El Dorado (the gilded man). But the mineral wealth of gold and opals proved not so great as had been anticipated, and the region was later eclipsed by the richer gold and emerald mines to the west as well as by the fertile agricultural lands of the Cauca Valley further southwest, which had the additional advantage of direct connections with Ecuador and Peru. Tunja's colonial houses, with their adobe walls and stone corners and doorways, their balconies, their colonnaded patios, and their proud coats of arms, retain today the atmosphere of the sixteenth and seventeenth centuries.

The Tunja cathedral (*fig. a*), contracted for in 1569 and erected as the "principal church" of the town, was not raised to its present status until 1880. Fortunately, despite several alterations, it preserves the main features of the façade originally designed in 1598–1600 by the Castilian Bartolomé Carrión.[172] The building, constructed of a smooth, reddish stone, is set off from the plaza by a raised atrium. Great restraint was observed by the designer. The heavy entablature serves as a base for the central niche and its accompanying ornamentation. A classical pediment crowns the whole, resting on pilasters which frame the entire central section. Above the entrance is placed in Plateresque tradition a cherub head with spread wings. A great single tower, its square bulk built of a different stone, contrasts with the façade (its upper sections, as well as the balustrade and the central dome, are relatively late additions).

The house at the left, called the Atarazana, was a dependency of the church, and from its second-story balcony ecclesiastical pronouncements were read to the community.

The interior of Tunja cathedral is on the basilica plan, with a cruciform shape suggested by chapels at the sides. The nave is separated into three aisles by arcades and originally had a wooden ceiling of Mudéjar design. Many of Tunja's early buildings were Mudéjar-Gothic in atmosphere, as will be illustrated in Chapter 5.

This cathedral as it stands today, under Tunja's forbidding skies, between the early colonial mansion and the modern residence of the bishop, is a tangible expression of the frozen Renaissance which characterizes this part of Colombia.

The cathedral of Mexico dominates a vast square which, together with some of the adjoining blocks, was the site of the main Aztec temple and its annexes. After all the pagan edifices had been razed on the order of Cortés, the stones were used to fill in canals to form streets and as building material, usually in foundations and ground walls. The cathedral of Mexico, until recently the largest church building in the Western Hemisphere, is one of the most complex in the stylistic richness of its architecture and art.

But it, too, had its modest predecessor (*Pl. 2, inset*). This early building was started in 1525, and in 1584 it was thoroughly repaired. Usually this structure is referred to disparagingly as small and poor; however, a study of the subject by Manuel Toussaint, dean of Mexican art historians, gives a quite different picture.[129] Its portal is described as in classical style with fluted pilasters. The entrance had a central window and two round ones containing *encerados*, or paintings on waxed cloth, of the Virgin, St. Peter, and St. Paul. In the interior the grillework was gilded, and a beamed ceiling was executed in the Mudéjar manner. Among the artists and craftsmen who carved the plastic decoration, painted the canvases, and worked on the interior, such European names as the Flemish Simon Pereyns and Adrian Suster appear, as well as a number of Spaniards. Mention is repeatedly made also of Indian carpenters, painters, and gilders from Tlatelolco and Texcoco, to whom orders had to be given through interpreters. In the rich inventory of this cathedral, taken in 1588, chalices, ciboriums, monstrances, censers, and communion vessels of fine quality are listed, with vestments of exquisite workmanship and tapestries representing King Saul, Judith and Holofernes, and the history of Solomon among the other valuables. This early structure was in use until 1626, by which time all of its functions and many of its treasures had been transferred to the new building.

The present cathedral (*fig. a*) was begun close by in 1563. Originally a pretentious plan was proposed, one befitting an archbishop's seat in a capital of great promise. But a realistic view of the situation showed that first consideration must be given to the problem of laying firm foundations on the soft ground of a dry lake bed in an earthquake region. In 1558 a canal was constructed for transporting the materials and five years later the first stone was laid. By 1615 the walls were up only to about half their projected height and eight vaults had been completed. It is recorded that Alonso Pérez de Castañeda (1563–1615) proffered a design, taking into consideration the state of the building as it then was, and that the king had his own architect, Juan Gómez de Mora, look it over and contribute his advice. After considering these suggestions, the authorities in Mexico decided that the work should proceed according to the plans of Claudio de Arciniega and the model made by Juan Miguel de Agüero. Thus Arciniega is considered the "father" of the cathedral of Mexico.[44] In 1656, almost a century after the work was begun, the cathedral was dedicated to the Assumption of the Virgin Mary; the interior was completed in 1667. The towers, however, were not finished until 1791; their huge bell-shaped tops (1786–1793) are the work of José Damián Ortiz de Castro, a native of Coatepec, Veracruz.[120] To Manuel Tolsa are attributed some of the statues on the façade, as well as the design of the lanterned dome, which was completed in 1813.

Standing today at the very heart of a modern city, this cathedral presents a truly majestic appearance. It is a gigantic structure of basalt and gray sandstone, and in it diverse styles of several centuries are blended with a harmony that defies analysis and demonstrates the mellowing effect of time. Although certain details may suggest architectural masterpieces of Europe, in its total effect the building, consisting of divergent components, does not resemble any of them. Though numerous classical details decorate the façade, the protruding massive volutes across the front and the coupled twisted columns above the lesser doorways are unmistakably Baroque. The bases of the towers were made heavy to buttress the structure, and the upper sections were carefully pared to lighten the weight without sacrificing the imposing line; note the unusual arrangement for the accommodation of many bells of various sizes. It has been suggested with considerable authority that originally four such towers were planned for the edifice.[44]

Church bells, the resounding tones of which traveled far in the days when there was no appreciable city noise, figured significantly in colonial life. Not only were they rung to mark the passing hours and call the people to worship but they were also the announcers of disaster—such as fire, earthquakes, or the approach of an enemy—and pealed the joyful news of a fiesta, a victory, or some event in the life of the reigning family. They were of noble composition, often containing much silver and even gold, and their beautiful clear tones were a source of community pride. Names were given to them and usually they were dated. The largest bell of the cathedral of Mexico, called Nuestra Señora de Guadalupe, weighs 12,420 pounds; it was cast in Tacubaya by one Salvador de Vega, a Castilian, in 1782.

The interior of the cathedral has three aisles. The nave and transepts are roofed over with intersecting barrel vaults, pierced by lunettes; the side aisles are covered by means of groined vaults constructed to give the effect of shallow domes. Such domical vaults are common throughout Spanish America. A row of rectangular chapels line either side of the structure. As in Spanish cathedrals, a choir enclosed on three sides occupies the nave somewhat beyond the entrance and a sanctuary with the high altar faces it just beyond the transept (see Pl. 159).

This interior is an illuminating exposition of the various artistic styles and fashions which flourished during the colonial period. From chapel to chapel, from altar to altar, a splendid panorama unfolds: paintings attributed to Zurbarán and Murillo, statuary carved by Indians, and ecclesiastical paraphernalia from the fabulous East. There are chapels which admonish of the vanity of life in their somber simplicity and chapels where saintly figures with almost living gesture and color step out of their shining golden backgrounds to shed joy and benediction on the creatures of this earth.

At the right of the cathedral a second church, called the Sagrario Metropolitano, independent of it and intended to serve the surrounding parish, was inaugurated in 1768. This building, praised as one of the finest examples of Mexican Churrigueresque (see Chapter 6), is the work of Lorenzo Rodríguez, a Spanish-born architect, and Pedro Patiño Ixtolinque, its chief sculptor. Rodríguez (1704?–1774) was at first active in Mexico as a master carpenter, around 1731. The other, judging from his name, must have been of Indian parentage. A special characteristic of the Sagrario is its elaborate façades on the south and east, which are harmoniously joined at the corner in a daring solution. In effect the portals, which extend above the roof, are lavishly sculptured screens, loaded with garlands, medallions, and ornamental columns interspersed with statues. The white of the carved stone contrasts pleasingly with the deep rose color of the side walls. In plan, the church shows two intersecting barrel vaults with a central dome. Lower structures, built within each of the four angles of the intersection, are also domed, as can be seen in the illustration.

Some of the retables from the Jesuit church in the city were transferred here after the expulsion of that order in 1767; but in 1776 and again in 1796 the interior suffered from fires and many of the altars and much of the decoration that had been kept in a style congenial to the exterior perished.

Earthquakes have repeatedly damaged both the cathedral and the Sagrario. In the last decades, however, much has been done to solidify the structures, protect them from ground water, and anchor them more firmly by the use of modern materials and methods. Here and there on the gigantic building complex, great iron clamps grip together sections of the walls, cracked by earthquakes; inscribed in the plaster around the clamps are the year, month, and day of the shock. Side by side stand the massive cathedral, a monument of a heroic epoch, and the exuberant Sagrario, which expresses a more leisurely and artistically emancipated period of colonial Mexico.

Early writers of the Conquest reiterated that Yucatán was a peninsula, not an island as was originally believed. Its protruding northern end was first touched by the Spaniards in their voyages of exploration which covered the islands of the Caribbean Sea, and considering its distance from that section of the mainland with which they were familiar, it is small wonder that they first thought it a part of the archipelago. This peninsula was and still is distinct from the rest of Mexico, set apart not only geographically but also in its cultures; it has been the home of the Maya people since long before the Conquest, and even today their language is the official idiom. This Indian nation, the achievements of which rank highest in pre-Columbian art, is linked not so much to Mexico as to Guatemala, whence its people migrated to Yucatán through virgin forest and primeval jungle. Maps made early in the twentieth century still designated the southern half of Yucatán as uncharted territory populated by "independent Indians"; the discovery of Maya wall paintings in 1946 at Bonampak, Chiapas, once more threw into relief its continued isolation.

Yucatán was isolated also in the centuries of colonial expansion. Here there was no gold, the population was sparse and untamable, and the peninsula lay well to one side of any of the great land routes; it was a dead-end road. Its conquest took much longer than that of the high plateau of Mexico and the other more profitable regions; the seat of a Spanish viceroy had long been established upon the ruins of the Aztec capital when the struggle in Yucatán was still continuing. But eventually the Maya chiefs retreated to the south into

impenetrable jungle and the outer northern strip of the land was drawn into the network of colonization. Here Mérida was founded by Francisco de Montejo, the elder, in 1542, on the ruins of the Maya city Tihó, and, as in Mexico, the torn-down temples and palaces offered ready building material of high quality. The new city was laid out by the Spaniards in their usual checkerboard scheme, with one side of the main plaza allotted to the cathedral and another to the palace of the conqueror, the Casa de Montejo (*see Pl. 32*).

In Mérida also, a provisional building—which stood to the right of the present edifice—first served as the cathedral. For decades the squarish stones of Maya buildings were being gathered for the new structure (*fig. b*), and finally in 1579 its walls were up; it took a score of years, however, before the building was fully under roof—the façade is inscribed 1599. It is dedicated to San Ildefonso. The tower on the left was added in 1713. As has been observed, frequently the early cathedrals were planned with a single tower; the twin-tower scheme did not become general until toward mid-seventeenth century. Note that the two higher orders in the towers are placed on one side of the base.

That the Plateresque style in its ornate and ostentatious form was not unknown to the builders in Mérida is amply demonstrated by the Casa de Montejo, yet perhaps no cathedral in the New World, even that of Tunja, shows such austerity and simplicity in its façade as Mérida's. Here again the district did not keep pace economically with the mainland, and there was neither emotional nor economic stimulus for a reworking in the Baroque style.

The rectangular ground plan generally applied in the colonies is apparent here. The main portal of the cathedral shows on either side of the door twin pilasters and a niche between them, and above the three arched entrances are low unbroken pediments. Such a restrained decorative effect is almost lost against the vast plain surface of the wall. The most striking feature in the façade is the impressive central arch, which rests on two massive piers that frame the main portal and extends above the roof line to the level of the lower sections of the towers. The large heraldic medallion inside the arch bore the arms of Castile and León.

Within, all three aisles have dome-shaped vaulting of equal height, and the central cupola shows that ingenuity in dome construction which is so intriguing in the study of Mexican colonial architecture. Inside the dome is an inscription dated 1598, to the effect that the *maestro mayor* (chief architect) was Juan Miguel de Agüero, who was connected with the cathedral of Mexico and was also employed on the fortifications of Havana.[105]

Pizarro's conquest of the Inca Empire in South America laid open to Spanish colonization the region from the coastal strip of the Pacific up into the mountain valleys of the High Andes, then down again on the other side to the pampas. However, it soon became evident that Cuzco, the ancient seat of the Inca, was not a favorable site for a viceregal capital. This city, founded in 1534, was too far from the sea—main line of communication with Spain—and it was situated amid densely populated valleys in the heart of a most virile Indian nation; thus from an administrative as well as a military point of view the location had disadvantages. In 1535 the site for a new city was chosen, near a good harbor of the Pacific and on the left bank of the river Rimac (hence Lima, a corruption of the Indian name).

In the same year that the city was founded, Pizarro is said to have laid the ground stone and carried the first beam for the church with his own hands.[69] As building material, adobe was used, a sun-dried brick produced by the Indians and employed throughout the coastal region in pre-Columbian construction.

In 1543 Lima became the seat of a bishopric and work was begun on a cathedral, which was completed in 1551. Meanwhile the city was elevated to an archbishopric, and this factor, together with the requirements of a growing population, provided the impetus for alterations and an enlargement befitting the new rank. The history of the great cathedral is the tale of one unending struggle against earthquakes. Little headway seems to have been made with the grandiose project of Alonso Beltrán, begun between 1569 and 1575, and at the close of the century the famous Spanish architect Francisco Becerra was called from Cuzco to draw new plans, which are said to be incorporated in the ground layout of the present cathedral (*Pl. 3, fig. a*). They called for a nave and side aisles of equal height (the hall-type church), flanked by a row of side chapels and covered by means of groined vaults of stone. Within a few years after Becerra's death (1605), the vaults which had already been built were so badly damaged by earthquake shocks that it was decided to replace them with lower vaults of brick.[203] Destructive quakes in 1687 and 1746 made practically a complete reconstruction necessary, and both times the collapsed vaults were replaced with a wood, reed, and plaster construction; so they remain today. After the latter catastrophe the work was done under Juan Rher, a Jesuit friar born in Prague, and his mulatto assistant. Photographs made after shocks in the nineteenth and twentieth centuries show hanging ceilings, fallen sections of wall, and rubble all over the interior—torn paintings, broken sculpture, and splintered wood carvings—a heart-breaking ruin.

But despite alterations, repairs, and cement reinforcement, the general aspect of the building still suggests its powerful colonial past. Its façade—much restored after 1940—is drawn out into five parts and kept comparatively low. The lower half of the main portal follows the 1626 design of Juan Martínez de Arrona; the upper half, which according to the inscription was rebuilt in 1722, was made to harmonize with the whole. This central section, with its vertical arrangement of niches and its statuary, suggestive of a retable, has some Baroque touches, but the entire structure in general impression, with its classicizing columns and minimal decoration, belongs to that parallel stylistic movement—the cold and unindividual manner associated with Juan de Herrera, the architect of the Escorial. The heroic equestrian statue of Pizarro on the atrium and the flight of steps in the foreground give an idea of the size of the cathedral.

Inside is evidence of the many vicissitudes experienced by the structure, but some woodwork, extremely fine both in spirit and in execution, survives, which, together with the high altar of burnished silver, testifies to the grandeur that once distinguished this edifice. The chests in the sacristy, surmounted by reliefs of the Apostles, were carved by the same Martínez de Arrona who designed the early portal. The choir stalls (*fig. b*), noble in expression, are the work of the Catalan Pedro de Noguera, who won the hotly contested competition for the contract in 1623 and then engaged his rivals to assist him in carrying out the commission.[203] The imposing sequence of male and female saints, Evangelists, Church Fathers, and one Biblical group was disturbed late in the nineteenth century when the choir stalls were transferred to the sanctuary from their original position at the lower end of the nave.

In the first chapel on the right lies the body of Francisco Pizarro, who was murdered in 1541 at his palace on the great square in one of the first of those human upheavals which have since cursed the land.

Trujillo, on the northern coast of Peru, was named for Pizarro's home in Estremadura and was important from the beginning of the colony. Like Lima, it was a walled town. Situated within eight miles of the small harbor of Salaverry, it offered a **convenient resting** place for travelers coming from or going to Lima in the south. In mid-eighteenth century Juan Ulloa described the coastal road, which followed much the same route as the Pan American Highway today. It was marked by the bones of mules that had sunk beneath their burdens rather than by any track—which would soon have been obliterated by windblown sand—and was generally traversed by night because of the terrific heat in the daytime and the scarcity of water and forage for the animals.[61]

After Trujillo became the seat of the new bishopric covering all northern Peru (1616) a new cathedral was laid out; but the present structure (*fig. c*) dates from 1647. Diego Maroto, a Dominican architect who was for a time *maestro mayor* of Lima's cathedral, furnished the designs but probably was never in Trujillo to supervise their execution. The building, consecrated in 1666, withstood the earthquake of 1687 but that of 1759 caused considerable damage. It was restored under the direction of the famous architect Cristóbal de Vargas and reconsecrated in 1781; the towers were finished later.

This massive cathedral of brick, reinforced with stone at the corners and covered with stucco, stands on a stepped platform which extends around two sides. In plan it is a three-aisle church, vaulted in brick. Its fine dome on a square drum is placed over the raised sanctuary. The façade, striking in the simplicity of its linear composition, makes no use of figural decoration except for the single statue atop the rounded pediment. Classicizing columns support the open pediment above the main door, and the scheme of decoration is clear cut and well balanced. In the façade, the shape and position of the large central window and the line of the broken pediment are characteristics of many later churches to be seen in the same city and along the western coast. Note the treatment of the corners in the belfries. A comparison of the two cathedrals on this plate will bring out interesting contrasts: the one with its extremely broad façade and detailed decoration, the other with a compressed façade, bold in its solidity.

Cuzco, Peru, as the capital of the vast Inca Empire held a unique position in pre-Columbian times, and in a large measure it maintained its prominence during the entire colonial period. Its situation at the meeting of fertile valleys ensured its continued agricultural importance under Spanish rule, and, surrounded by mines, it soon became a gathering place for caravans en route with their mineral wealth from the Andes to the distant Pacific shores. From early times the Plaza de Armas has been a pulsing center of Cuzco; it is larger than most plazas in Spanish American towns and in general aspect preserved its picturesque and fascinating colonial character unmarred until the 1950 earthquake. Four churches look out upon it—unusual even in Latin America—and the rest of the space is occupied by arcaded and balconied two-story houses of the type seen in southern Spain.

Among the churches the largest complex is that of the cathedral (*Pl. 4, fig. a*). This structure was erected upon the ruins of the temple to the Inca god Viracocha, with the uniformly cut brownish stones of the pagan buildings furnishing the material. During the construction, as frequently happened, the functions of the cathedral were carried on in a nearby hall, a *galpon* of the last Inca.[44]

Work on the cathedral was begun in 1560. The first architect is said to have been the Basque Juan Miguel de Veramendi, who was called from Chuquisaca, now Sucre, Bolivia. He seems to have accomplished little, for some twenty years later new plans were drawn up by Francisco Becerra, already mentioned as having provided plans for the cathedral at Lima. Judging from the similarity of the two layouts it would appear that Becerra's drawings were used as a working basis for the Cuzco building also. Here too, however, they had to undergo modification. In 1603 Bartolomé Carrión, known for his design of the cathedral portal at Tunja, was called in as *maestro mayor*.[203] More than forty years later a new bishop, Alonso Ocón, found the walls at barely half their projected height and he attacked the problem with great zeal. To raise funds, a levy was made on the king's income, on the landowners, and on the Indians of the

diocese. The floor of the structure had become buried in the intervening decades under an accumulation of rubbish, which, according to legend, the chapter of the cathedral now began to haul away in leather sacks. Shortly the *corregidor* and his aides came to their assistance, and soon all the religious in Cuzco and the Spaniards—even the ladies—joined them, providing a noble display of Christian co-operation and industry.[195] In 1650 occurred one of the most destructive earthquakes in the region's history, but the partly finished cathedral fortunately survived. A year later the bishop could report that fifty masons, "all Indians," were at work on the façade. In 1654 the structure was completed, and within four years even the towers were finished. It was a very costly edifice, consuming nearly the equivalent of two million dollars. Like many Latin American cathedrals it is dedicated to the Assumption of the Virgin Mary. An important name throughout the period of final activity is that of Miguel Gutiérrez Sencio, who was *maestro mayor* of the project for at least thirty-two years; it was probably he who coordinated the various plans and who, together with Canon Diego Arias de la Cerda, a zealous administrator, is responsible for the cathedral as it now stands.

The weather-beaten andesite façade of this structure presents an aspect of unaffected nobility. Decoration is centered around the main portal, which projects somewhat from the face of the wall. Over the doorway two steeply curving sections of a broken pediment open to give space to the window and the crowning decoration above it. This early Baroque build-up is a favorite one in Peru and will be seen later in both façades and retables. Heavily rusticated masonry emphasizes the two lesser entrances; their peculiarly rounded pediments enframe the coat of arms of Spain. Open belfries and the irregular lines of their cornices alleviate the undecorated mass of the two towers, and the evenly spaced pinnacles in place of a balustrade lend dignity to the effect.

The general restraint in its line has caused

the edifice to be associated with the Herrera style of Spain. Herrera's work in toto has an aloofness, a subtlety, and a general academic tone, little of which can be felt here.[35] This has different weight, different proportions—in short a different spirit. It is American in its primeval power when compared with the courtly and sophisticated suavity displayed in the Escorial. In this building the traditional ability of the Indians of the region in stone construction manifests itself eloquently; the powerful walls may even suggest to some the solidity of the ancient citadels.

If the exterior of the cathedral, as viewed across the imposing esplanade, provided a most eloquent backdrop for colonial Cuzco, the interior conjures up the life of the period in full three dimensions for the visitor. Monumental cruciform pillars of stone sustain the Gothic brick vaulting—now painted in lighter tones; there is no dome. The tall gilded grilles of the side chapels, numerous polychromed statues, fading oil paintings, and bizarre wood ornamentation record not only the work of the Spaniards but also the originality and creative spirit of the many mestizos and Indians who contributed the unique flavor to the whole complex. When the horizontal rays of the afternoon sun strike in through the open doors and penetrate into the upper sections a peculiar golden dust seems to vibrate through the arches.

Early in the nineteenth century the main altar was removed and an imitative baldachin-type silver structure was erected. One of the discarded retables (*fig. b*), now placed against the end wall of the building, shows a variety of fantasy detail and an unusual richness in the caryatides and the number of niches. It probably dates from mid-eighteenth century.

The cathedral, an expression of colonial Cuzco at its height, served as an unfailing source of inspiration for the entire region throughout that epoch. In the earthquake of 1950 its right tower fell, but little of the interior was damaged.

Two smaller churches flank the cathedral, stepped back somewhat from the line of its façade but having direct access to it. The church of El Triunfo, or the Sagrario (*fig. c*), to the right of it occupies approximately the site where the adobe structure which served as a temporary cathedral is said to have stood. This building too was reconstructed after the completion of the great cathedral. The present structure, which dates from 1729 to 1732, was designed by the Carmelite friar Miguel Menacha[203] in the form of a Greek cross, at the center of which rises a cupola of stone unusually perfect and airy. In its façade can be seen a rarely successful blending of Renaissance and Baroque elements. Singularly effective is the frieze which alternates corbel-like scrolls with cartouches containing the monograms of Mary and the Saviour. Similar cartouches are used above the door and even in the angles of the pediment. The severe faceted design of the stonework in both the portal arch and the niches at the sides finds a fanciful variation in the rosettes that frame the upper window. An even fish-scale pattern entirely covers the spandrels, and a related motif is found on the lower part of the columns. Specially cut interlocking stones, visible on both sides of the portal, show a manner of wall construction characteristic of the Inca. High above the portal a decorative niche holds a wooden figure of Santiago.

On the other side of the cathedral stands the church of Jesús y María (known also as the Sagrada Familia), built between 1723 and 1735. Like the cathedral it has powerful piers set close together and solid brick vaulting. Although this building matches the others in style and material it fails to achieve fully their noble lines.

Cajamarca, situated at an altitude of nearly 10,000 feet on a slope overlooking a fertile Andean valley, is another prominent name in the history of the Conquest. Here the Inca Atahuallpa was taken prisoner in 1532 with his retinue; his soldiers were slaughtered, and a fabulous ransom was exacted. Despite the fact that he was complying with the Spanish demands and had already gathered an unparalleled golden hoard (what a treasure trove for today's archaeologists) a pretext was found for his execution.

The town retains its colonial character and boasts many picturesque houses with elaborate portals. Like other buildings of the old city, the cathedral (*Pl. 5, fig. a*) was constructed in part from material that was salvaged from the destroyed Inca palaces and temples. According to Harold E. Wethey, eminent authority on Peruvian colonial art, it was begun about 1682 and consecrated in 1762. The side portal, carved with the coat of arms of Spain, bears the date 1686; the façade, however, remains unfinished. The persons standing by the door in the illustration give an idea of the scale of the building.

Over-all decoration characterizes the façade. Basically the plan is serene and uncomplicated. A study of the detail reveals a tremendous richness in the carving and a combination of motifs that would be unusual in Europe. The columns are wound with spiraling garlands of Eucharistic grapes; the heavy fruit clusters are exaggerated in relation to the leaves and vine, a characteristic of Andean Baroque. Figures are scattered among the foliage, serve as caryatides, or, poised above the niches, support flaming hearts that sprout with flowers. Angels adorn the spandrels of the main doorway. Many of these elements belong to the vocabulary of wood carving as used in retables, especially the birds among the grapes, the zigzag decoration on the columns, and the elegant and complicated scroll which serves to bind the carving of the portal to the plainer masonry (*fig. c*). Somewhat less ebullient is the carving of the broad entablature and the delicate pattern framing the central window. A waffle design around the bell arches provides contrast. Even unfinished this façade makes a definite contribution to Spanish colonial art, through both its quality and its manner of decoration.

Within, the barrel vault of the central nave is built entirely of stone and rests on an arcade so heavy that it gives the appearance of a wall. There is no dome. The interior is spacious and austere in spirit although a number of Baroque altars lighten the effect. In the main altar (*fig. b*) the functional character of the elements is lost and a riot of ornamentation dominates. A Corinthian-type capital can be discerned, but the shaft has become a gilded fantasy reminiscent of a flower stalk—as if elements seen in a drawing or perhaps in the chasing on some piece of jewelry had been translated by the local craftsmen into a three-dimensional composition in wood. Cleflike scrolls, similar to those on the façade, and a variety of shell-shaped medallions are further additions to this bizarre *comparserie*.

Those who interpret Spanish American colonial architecture as merely a shadow of the motherland's frequently use this façade to argue their point. But in Spain there is an engraving-like clarity, laden with conscious three-dimensionality; further a rich and varied iconography is incorporated. In the New World an unsophisticated artistic imagination has selected decorative motifs from the vast vocabulary of European styles and applied them in a highly picturesque manner regardless of their traditional contexts.

In colonial times the Viceroyalty of New Spain included Mexico and Central America; to those who travel today from the Mexican capital to Honduras—whether by road or by plane—the difficulties of communication which existed in that early period become apparent. The Honduran town of Santa María de Comayagua, founded in 1537, was destroyed almost at once by hostile Indians; it was re-established, however, with a handful of hardy Spanish settlers, and in 1557, when the nearby silver mines began to produce, it was elevated to the status of a city. In 1573 it became the capital of the province and five years later boasted one hundred Spanish settlers, with fifty-eight Indian villages in the vicinity and twenty-six hundred subjects who paid tribute.[146] One of the last stands of the Maya took place in the adjacent hills under the chief Lempira, and descendants of these people still inhabit the region.

As early as 1559 a route between the Atlantic and the Pacific with Comayagua as its center was under discussion as an alternative to the dangerous and unhealthful passage across the Isthmus of Panama. The city lies at an altitude of 4,000 feet, almost equidistant between the two oceans and also midway between Guatemala and Nicaragua. Because of its favorable location it retained its importance until the nineteenth-century struggles for independence broke Central America into many factions. Some of its population, however, still live in the glory of that bygone era when the city was called Nuevo Valladolid de Comayagua.

The present cathedral (*Pl. 6, fig. a*) is said to have been erected between 1703 and 1724; the church of La Merced (*see Pl. 73*) served as the first.[152] The cathedral tower is more or less independent and, like other belfries in the town, it neither conforms to nor conflicts with the rest of the complex; on the other side of the façade it is counterbalanced by a buttress which has half the bulk of a tower.

The cathedral façade (*fig. d*) is unusual in its general aspect as well as in the details of its decoration. As is evident in the distant view, vertical vies with horizontal; single engaged columns extend through all four orders, crowned above the undulating line of the pediment with vases pyramided with flowers, while the heavy lines of the cornices cross the façade furnishing the horizontal emphasis. In the first order the combination of stylized palm trees and Eucharistic grapes is unique in Latin America, and the palm-leaf arrangement in the spandrel shows a strong local adaptation of an imported decorative motif. In the first and second orders the capitals of the columns are worked out in highly original designs. Unusual also is the placing of the circular window in a rectangular Baroque frame, which is like those around the niches on

either side of it. This kind of frame is used to relate the first order with the second. The second and third are connected through the broad deeply undercut band that enframes the niches; sun, moon, and stars are carved in the spandrels. The third and fourth orders both bear palm-tree medallions. The reliefs here, however, with their garlands and other decorative detail, speak a classicizing language, so much more liquid and precious that one wonders whether those portions are not of a later date. The doorway, with its recessed arch, belongs to a type that will be seen repeatedly in Chapter 8.

The rather squat major dome of the cathedral rests on a sturdy octagonal drum and is flanked by two smaller domes. Covered with green and yellow tiles, it shimmers like gold in the sunshine; similar tiles are applied to the slanting tops of the buttresses at the sides of the building. These tiles are close in color and quality to colonial pottery which is preserved in the local museum and is known to have been made in the region.

Within, a bright and even lighting is achieved by rectangular windows in the side walls. Barrel vaults cover the nave and the side aisles.

The main retable (*fig. c*) shows the same restraint that characterizes the exterior of the cathedral. This is all the more apparent when it is compared with the retables at Cajamarca or Tegucigalpa (*see Pls. 5, 11*). The central figure, the Virgin of the Immaculate Conception, is markedly in the tradition of Juan Martínez Montañés, the Sevillian sculptor, and further investigation may prove it to be one of the few imported pieces that have come down through the centuries. In its entirety, however, the retable shows a limited vocabulary of motifs, so that it could well be ascribed to regional craftsmen. (One of the highly original side altars, considerably different in style, is illustrated on *Pl. 175*.)

The Sagrario chapel, standing at the left of the cathedral almost like an annex, boasts a deep dome, fine in its proportions and rotundity. On the inside (*fig. b*) the palm tree is again used as a motif, together with a flower that closely resembles one of the petaled medallions seen on the façade. To this author's knowledge such emphasis on the palm tree, both on the façade and inside the building, is encountered nowhere else in Latin America. The large sun at the zenith also is striking and unusual. The rigid angels in the pendentives are descendants of those impassioned mobile creatures that uphold the Dome of Heaven in Byzantine frescoes, from Hagia Sophia to the Catalan chapels of the twelfth and thirteenth centuries. This idea, revived in the Counter Reformation, took special hold on the imagination of Central American builders.

According to record, Philip IV of Spain (reigned 1621–1665) sent a retable and other ecclesiastical objects to Comayagua in 1644, at which time the church of La Merced was serving as the cathedral. This single document has been responsible for accrediting to Spain innumerable works of art in the town. It has been suggested that the retable mentioned might be the one in the present Sagrario, a portion of which is visible in the photograph of the dome. The one here, however, is definitely later in style and bears the mark of the regional school.

In contrast to the cathedral of Cajamarca, which demonstrates originality in paraphrasing an imported style, the cathedral of Comayagua manifests the powerful creative forces of local mestizos and Indians.

Mexico has a wealth of colonial architecture and her various states have produced such fascinating regional artistic work that each of them deserves individual study. A most scholarly beginning has been made in that direction with a series of monographs, but in this volume, the aim of which is to present artistic highlights from all over Latin America, only a few examples can be included. The group illustrated here (*Pl. 7*) emphasizes the great divergency which existed within the present territory of Mexico.

Among these the cathedral of Oaxaca (*fig. c*) bears the earliest date. It was founded in 1535 and subsequently went through the usual transformations and enlargements. Late in the seventeenth century it was practically demolished by earthquakes; after rebuilding, it was reconsecrated in 1733. It has been pointed out that the ground plan employed a geometrical system set forth in Simón García's architectural compendium, published in Spain in 1681, but this apparently was modified to take advantage of some sections which had survived.[86]

In the exterior, simplicity of basic line contrasts strikingly with an elaborate façade that has the effect of a retable. The main entrance is flanked by niches with statues, which are framed by single classicizing columns. Sculptured panels in high relief, noble and somewhat cool, fill the space above the doorways. Among the Baroque features are the irregularity of line—accentuated in the overhanging cornices—the coupling of the columns at the corners so as to divide the façade vertically into three parts, and the daring break in the cornice above the two lateral doorways to accommodate oval windows. In the slim twin columns of the belfry, with their deeply cut spirals, we meet for the first time a characteristic embellishment that was lavishly developed and used during the eighteenth century in Mexican Rococo. On the side can be seen one of the massive buttresses of the structure.

The soft green tinge of the local stone employed in the building and the colored tiles that cover the roof, domes, and towers bring a cheerful warmth to the somewhat soberly composed façade. The interior has suffered from earthquake, revolution, and neglect; but even so, this cathedral, standing on the busy sunlit plaza of Oaxaca, remains the mightiest colonial landmark in the valley from which Cortés, the Marqués del Valle, derived his title.

The cathedral of Puebla, though founded later than that of Oaxaca (1552), was finished earlier and dedicated in 1649. Its main façade —the portal is dated 1664—reflects a cold academic design, but the many additions give the building as a whole considerably more of a Baroque character, mirroring the change of taste during the colonial era.

Structurally it is closely related to the cathedral of Mexico (*see Pl. 2*), and for that reason some authorities feel that Claudio de Arciniega may have been connected with it, although Becerra claimed to have drawn plans for it.[203] Like the cathedral of Mexico it is thought to have been projected with four towers; the two which were built are unusually tall, slender, and airy. One is dated 1678 and the other was completed in 1768. The side view (*fig. b*) shows the lines of the nave, transepts, and aisles, and of the vast tile-covered dome, impressive in its proportion. Since Puebla produced what are probably the finest *azulejos* and other ceramic ware in the New World, it is small wonder that it furnished something exquisite for its cathedral. The deeply set star window toward the rear, the many finials, and the protruding scrolls that mark the buttresses are enriching late-Baroque additions. An idea of the lofty noble lines of the interior can be gained from the illustration of the organ (*see Pl. 158*).

More homogeneous than the cathedral of Puebla and less bulky in appearance is the cathedral of Morelia, also shown from the side (*fig. d*). It should be mentioned that both of these buildings lie with their length on the plaza. The cathedral at Morelia was begun in 1640, dedicated in 1706, and, with the exception of the second tower—added in 1768—it was completed in 1744. Compared to the cathedrals of Puebla and Mexico, the building proper is low, though the great stress laid on the towers gives an impression of height. It would seem that this structure was laid out on a free plan (not plotted according to geometrical proportions), with many problems and details left to be worked out as the building progressed.[86] Baroque balustrades, finials, and oval windows lighten the design, but many details manifest an academic spirit. The general decorative effect is greatly aug-

mented by the pinkish stone used. Here thin translucent plates of native marble used as windowpanes are still preserved—a rare occurrence.

The construction of the cathedral of Zacatecas dates according to one source [127] between 1718 and 1752 and according to another [111] between 1730 and 1760. Somewhat later than the others on this plate, it surpasses them in the richness of its façade (*fig. a*). It is the third church to be built on the site, and although it was not elevated to cathedral status until 1862 it was constructed "in the style of a cathedral," plotted exactly according to one of Simón García's plans for a church "with three naves" in his *Compendio*. Originally only one tower was erected; its twin went up in 1906. Zacatecas ranked high among the silver cities of Mexico. Its mines are credited with yielding before the end of the colonial period a fifth of the world's entire silver output.[123]

In this façade is displayed an elaboration of stone carving and an inventiveness with locally favorite motifs which make one wonder who the carvers were, where they acquired their proficiency, and what other buildings they executed (*compare Pl. 47*). Rare is the grouping of the columns with three on either side framing two niches. In the second and third orders each matching pair of columns is decorated with a different motif, either wound with grape vines, encrusted with shells, one heaped on another, or (upper center) crowded with caryatides. The theme also is unusual, a presentation of Christ and the twelve Apostles; the four Church Fathers are depicted in relief beside the window, which is encircled by a heavy garland. At the very top, over all, God the Father is enthroned, surrounded by a group of eight angels playing musical instruments. The pretensions of this church to a cathedra are manifest in the incorporation of the bishop's paraphernalia— miter and keys—in the carving (upper left).

The virtuosity of the sculpture—with the deep undercutting and sharp edges reminiscent of embossing—is set off by the golden brownish stone used, which was locally available and of fine quality. It lends itself when freshly quarried to precise carving and presents a finish almost metallic in its brilliance.

The colonial capital of Guatemala, today known as Antigua (the ancient), was originally named Santiago de los Caballeros de Goathemala. More detail about the town will be found in Chapter 8. Though once forced to move because of a landslide, the city was again located in the very lap of a volcanic region and is constantly subject to earthquakes. It was heavily damaged in 1717 and almost totally devastated in 1773, after which the seat of government was removed to its present site, Guatemala City. Throughout its colonial existence Antigua was a center of learning and art and its architects, sculptors, and painters were invited to contribute to many an edifice within the viceroyalty.

Renovation and enlargement of the cathedral was begun in 1663 and completed about 1680, but the work of embellishment went on and may not have been finished when the catastrophe of 1773 befell the city.[137] It was dedicated to St. James and must have been a superb building (*Pl. 8, fig. d*). It had seven entrances. Its stone atrium overlooked the main plaza, the scene of many a grand spectacle (processions, tournaments, bullfights) staged against the backdrop of the church and the volcanic peaks beyond. The exact appearance of the cathedral before the great havoc is somewhat problematic; early drawings show it with two rather low flanking towers, the heavy bases of which still stand. Columns, slender and plain even as to base and capital, extend through to the cornice, effectively framing the statues. This use of the colossal order and the repetition of the arch in the recessed portal and the windows lend serenity to the whole. Both broken and unbroken pediments are used over the niches, and the volutes on the espadaña are without much verve. Between the lower and the top

sections of the façade there appears to be a slight stylistic difference, and indeed the latter is said to have been rebuilt in the nineteenth century.[70] The frame of the center doorway is decorated with fine tracery, and the Virgin of the Immaculate Conception in the niche above has an elaborate background of arabesques.

Today the former Sagrario serves as the church. The vast nave of the original building which stretches beyond suggests, even in decay, its former grandeur (*fig. c*). Ruined walls reveal the structure of the brick vaulting, with its thick mortar. (In pre-Columbian times the Maya Indians, aboriginal inhabitants of Guatemala, were adept in the manufacture of a most durable cement.) Patterns in stucco, tastefully selected and infinitely varied, were applied on the moldings and friezes. In one of the pendentives which once supported the dome stands the figure of St. John the Evangelist, his symbolic eagle at his feet and above him an angel in relief swinging a censer. The considerable differences, in both design and gesture, between this angel and the one in Comayagua attest to the individuality of the regional artists even within the same captaincy-general. In the background an over-all stucco pattern, strongly reminiscent of the Mudéjar, harmonizes with the lacy embellishment of the window frame.

Early reports described the richness of the interior. The baldachin above the high altar was supported on sixteen pillars sheathed in tortoise shell and decorated with finely wrought bronze medallions; and on the cornice stood marble statues of the Virgin and the twelve Apostles. A great many gold and silver ornaments are listed in the church's treasury. Tradition has it that the Conquistador of Guatemala, Pedro de Alvarado, and his wife, Doña Beatriz, were buried here, and that here also was laid to rest that picaresque character, Bernal Díaz del Castillo, Grand Captain, *regidor* of Guatemala, and in addition the author of the immortal history of the Conquest which was written in this city. However, excavations in the vaults under the main altar and the *Capilla Real* in the 1930's failed to uncover any remains. It must be assumed that the bodies of the notables of Antigua were removed but when and where no one knows.[138]

By interesting coincidence, León, the colonial capital of Nicaragua, also bore the name Santiago de los Caballeros, and like Antigua it lies in a volcanic earthquake region, though in a tropical climate and practically at sea level. It was founded in 1610 after an earlier capital of the same name had to be abandoned because of constant floods.

The present cathedral building is the fourth to stand on the same site. The second, a modest structure, was burned in 1685 by pirates under Dampier, and the third, according to tradition, was erected shortly afterward under the supervision of an English architect who had been captured from among the invaders.[136] This third structure is described as a fine stone building with brick arches and a roof of wood and thatch; its interior was brightly painted and studded with gilt stars. But it was narrow and ill lighted, and about 1747, under Bishop Isidro Marín Bullón y Figueroa, the construction of a new and larger cathedral was undertaken. For more than thirty years work on this ambitious structure either forged ahead or stagnated, as the available funds and the enthusiasm of successive prelates rose or waned. Another illustrious name connected with the project is that of Juan Vilchez y Cabrera, a native of the Nicaraguan town of New Segovia. It was he who, first as dean and later as bishop, drove the work to its conclusion, appealing to the captain general in Guatemala and even donating funds from his own pocket. He died in 1774 and therefore did not live to witness the consecration of the building (about 1780). Diego de Porras is named as its chief architect, and the Mercedarian friar Pedro de Avila was called in from Guatemala by the bishop as a consultant. Its solemn dedication[143] as Basilica of the Assumption did not take place until 1860.

This massive structure (*fig. a*), built of cut stone and impressively placed on a low platform, extends the full width of the vast plaza and back an entire block. It is the largest ecclesiastical building in Central America, though the population of the capital at the time of its erection was less than ten thousand. Its façade and towers (which date from early nineteenth century) form a five-part composition. The rounded pediment is compact and severe, the decoration sparse, and the aspect strongly neoclassic. Today its proportions are disturbed by the modern steel supports which link the towers and the central section.

The lateral walls of the cathedral, dating from around mid-eighteenth century, give a clearer impression of its colonial character (*fig. b*). Here can be seen the bulk of the towers and the sturdy buttresses, which counter the thrusts of the stone vaulting within. Rectangular recessed windows high up in the thick walls are framed as in Comayagua with flowing stucco garlands, and a tastefully harmonizing stucco motif is applied below the cornice. The stout Baroque balustrade pushed out to include the tops of the buttresses holds the mass well together.

In the interior instead of lateral chapels an additional aisle is provided on either side, producing what the Spanish phrase describes as a church of five "naves." It is interesting to note that the plans of the cathedral which are in the Archive of the Indies, dated 1767, differ considerably from the actual building.[45]

Because of its massive construction and commanding position, the cathedral of León was predestined to be used as a fortress; in 1823 no less than thirty pieces of artillery were mounted on its roof. Such incidents did not help protect the building or preserve its architectural features, and on its most exposed side pock marks of shot can still be seen.

Riobamba lies at an altitude of nearly 9,000 feet on the sloping side of Chimborazo in a fertile sun-baked valley of Ecuador, surrounded by snow peaks. Even in pre-Inca times this valley was an important center of agriculture and home industry; one of the famous Inca rope bridges was flung across a chasm nearby, connecting the region with the south, and in colonial days the *Camino Real* followed the same route. In 1797 the city was overwhelmed by an earthquake and landslide and all the survivors were removed from the original site to the plains of Tapi, twelve miles distant. Little remained from the holocaust; some religious objects were salvaged and taken to nearby estates, and carved stones from the cathedral façade were transported to the new site.

The cathedral of Riobamba (*Pl. 9, fig. a*), though an unpretentious structure, displays much charming naïveté and originality. The façade is not of the retable type. It has only one doorway, small windows, and neither niches nor a tower. The bells are hung in arches that form a modest espadaña. There are no columns here, only slender fluted pilasters, vaguely reminiscent of the early Renaissance. In the frieze a garland of angel heads alternates with a conventionalized floral motif, and above it is a "blind" balustrade, kept very flat. Two angel trumpeters in *contrapposto* position stand at the foot of the small rose window. Peculiar interest is lent the façade by the beautifully balanced and unusual relief medallions with their story-telling content—chiefly from the life of Mary—which are placed in quatrefoil or oval frames between the pilasters (*fig. b*). The balls within the frames might well have been suggested by the escutcheons that adorn illuminated missals and other books of the Renaissance, but they are here applied in a different dimension and medium and with a completely different effect. The motif on the piers of the portal arch and on the shortened pilasters below the windows, though it recalls the palm trees of Comayagua, seems best interpreted as a stalk of maize, an indigenous plant in the New World. In the rectangle below the four medallions is shown Peter's sword and the ear which

it cut off. The round deeply undercut stones on either side of it are quite Mudéjar in pattern. Fine details in all the carving have been obscured by much whitewashing.

The cathedral in Córdoba, Argentina (*fig. c*), carries practically no figural decoration; the effect is derived largely from the bulk and the accented architectural lines of the building. The sober and classicizing lower section of the edifice is attributed to José Gonzales Merguelte, a native of Granada, Spain, who was called to Córdoba in 1697 after he had designed the cathedral at Sucre in Bolivia. Accustomed to the munificence of the rich mining regions, he, reportedly, soon lost interest and returned north. Work in Córdoba then stagnated until taken over in 1729 by the Italian Jesuit Andrés Blanqui, who was joined three years later by his compatriot Juan Bautista Prímoli. Together they are believed to have executed the main part of the cathedral.[213] It was inaugurated in 1758, but the towers were not finished until 1787.

These towers, unlike some seen earlier, do not serve as buttresses to the façade; they are hollow and with the classical portico form a wide vestibule. It is the build-up of the upper portions which gives this cathedral its individuality: the lanterned dome flanked by turrets, the arcaded balustrades, and the twin belfries with their sculptural embellishment. The Mudéjar appearance of the towers, the classical lower section of the building, and the Baroque elaboration of detail all combine to form a most unusual blend.

A drawing of this cathedral, as projected, was made in 1758 by the Franciscan Vicente Muñoz, of Seville, and is now in the Archive of the Indies.[45] In it the main emphasis is placed on an enormous central dome, which dominates the structure; the two towers, featuring many columns, are set well at the sides of a broad façade which contains all three doorways and is topped by a classical pediment. This drawing presents a cathedral that is quite suave and European, entirely without the fierce contrasts and the almost top-heavy quality which give the actual building its dynamic character. Here is revealing insight into the theory and practice of architecture in colonial Latin America.

The cathedral of Sucre, Bolivia, was originally finished about 1600; it was later enlarged and in its present form dates from the end of the seventeenth century. José Gonzales Merguelte, who was connected briefly with the cathedral in Córdoba, Argentina, constructed the nave and the side aisles.

Like the cathedral of Córdoba, it does not reflect in any way the regional style that was developing around it. In its composition it is generally horizontal; its roof is flat, and the surface of its vast walls for the most part is unrelieved, except at the portals. The building is so placed that its length extends along the main plaza, an orientation which has already been noted in Puebla and Morelia and will be met also in later chapters.

Thus the side portal (*fig. d*), dated 1683, was given considerable importance.[220] It is built around the door like a retable. The niches, the coupled and garlanded columns, the open pediment with twin columns placed uniquely inside its "wings," and the scroll-like ornaments which bind the whole composition to the plain masonry at the sides—all are retable elements. Tight spirals, many finials, and other motifs that play with curves and angles are superimposed one on another or are developed on several planes. Nevertheless, the effect is singularly formal and unindividual for such a wealth of detail. (Compare with the church of San Francisco in Lima, Peru, shown on *Pl. 92*.)

As has already been mentioned, earthquakes, landslides, and volcanic disturbances in the New World caused the removal of entire cities to other sites, but there was still another plague—man-made—which forced the shifting of whole towns to new locations. In some regions the buccaneers and their ilk were as great a menace as all the destructive forces of Nature.

In 1671, during the infamous siege of the freebooter Henry Morgan, the old city of Panama was plundered, fired, and razed to the ground. Two years later Panamá la Nueva, the present city, was founded some five miles distant. As the inflammability of the wooden, thatch-roofed houses was partly responsible for the total destruction earlier, it was decreed that the new city should be built of stone and brick. Whatever stone could be salvaged from the old site was transferred to the new, except for the tower of the old cathedral—named for St. Anastasius—which still stands as a reminder of the violent events of the seventeenth century.

The fortifications of the new city were the strongest in all the Americas and, considering the difficulty of providing stone for the vast defense system of walls, turrets, and bastions, the costliest. After auditing the construction account, the Council of the Indies is said to have inquired whether the fort was made of silver or of gold. However, the city resisted successfully all subsequent attacks.

Although the new cathedral (*Pl. 10, fig. b*) was founded at the same time as the city, construction on it did not get under way until 1690. Almost a half-century later the military engineer Nicolás Rodríguez made a survey of the work still necessary and calculated its cost. He found the building practically completed except for the façade and the towers—the foundations of which were laid. Finally in 1796 it was consecrated.[49]

Like León's, the cathedral of Panama is constructed with five aisles. The free-standing twin columns in its broad façade are kept classically simple; the niches in the second and third stories, though related to them, are unconventionally arranged—perhaps to accommodate the figures of all twelve Apostles. The espadaña, with its swelling curves and bulbous finials, is Baroque, while the section below it has a post-Renaissance placidity. Striking are the many openings—the arrangement of the windows suggests a palace rather than a church. Seemingly little effort was made to integrate the towers; their covering of marine shells is a late addition and may have been a substitute for tiles or majolica.[76]

Nobler in design, more distinguished in execution, but also suggestive of a palace is the cathedral in Salvador, the capital of Bahia, Brazil (*fig. a*). Its three doorways and many windows, rhythmically spaced, contribute to this impression—a quite common one in Brazil as will be seen in Chapter 14. This structure was built by the Jesuits between 1652 and 1672 and at one time housed the most important church and college in Brazil; not until the demolition of the old cathedral in 1935 was it elevated to its present rank.

Prior to 1763 Salvador was the capital of the entire Portuguese viceroyalty, but the removal of the seat of government to Rio de Janeiro in that year had little effect on the affluence of the town. It had already grown immensely rich because of its proximity to large sugar plantations and its advantageous commercial situation on a fine harbor. The Jesuits, the first missionaries in Brazil, are closely connected with the development of its colonial art. Their threefold program aimed at the conversion of the natives, general education, and the training of the oncoming priesthood. But they were expelled from Brazil in 1759—eight years earlier than from the Spanish colonies—and their institutions disintegrated rapidly.

The cathedral of Salvador, which stands close to the sidewalk, shows a façade that is far more cosmopolitan than any presented thus far. The lines of the pilasters, with their unobtrusive paneling and subtle emphasis at the corners, extend from the ground to the upper cornice and even beyond into the belfries and the center gable. Here the belfries form an integral part of the façade in an arrangement met frequently also in Central America. The pediments above the openings are broken, but the insertion of a classicizing niche or an obelisk keeps them within the spirit of the late Renaissance. Baroque volutes fill in the space between the gable and the belfries, but they

are so untemperamental that they pass almost unnoticed. A coolness of spirit pervades the whole building, in marked contrast to the tropical environment; this is partly explained by the fact that its design leaned heavily for inspiration on Jesuit buildings in Portugal. Eighteenth-century travelers describe the interior as magnificent; its imposing sacristy displayed a painted ceiling, altars and floors of colored marbles, furnishings inlaid with tortoise shell, and walls brilliant with tile pictures.[229]

In Europe no valid claim can be made for a definite Jesuit style, its canons precisely laid down in Rome, and in the Americas there is even less justification for such a statement. The various regions adopted certain stylistic features, according to the exigencies of the time and place and the abilities of the builders, and out of them they created something original. A comparison of the cathedral in Havana, Cuba (*fig. d*), with that of Bahia, just discussed, will illuminate that fact. This also was a Jesuit church, begun, as was the other, in the seventeenth century and completed in the eighteenth. It was not elevated to the rank of a cathedral until 1789, more than twenty years after the expulsion of the order from the Spanish colonies, and work on the interior continued into the nineteenth century. Although dedicated to the Virgin of the Immaculate Conception, it is today better known as the church of San Cristóbal, the patron saint of Havana. It was built of native limestone, which has darkened in the damp salty air of tropical hurricanes. Its façade, dating from 1777, shows a decided individuality in design and texture. The columnar sections on either side of the main portal are brought forward obliquely as if hinged near the door. Single, doubled, and even tripled columns are used in effective variety. The niches, pediments, and capitals suggest the late Renaissance, whereas the balustrades and volutes at the sides, the temperamental lines of the cornices, and, above all, the foliated windows, so felicitously placed, are all Baroque. The towers, similar in general design but unalike in proportion, are successfully integrated into the composition.

No two places in the Spanish colonial world could be more different in climate and background than Havana and Potosí, in Bolivia: the one, a major harbor, the gathering place for the fleets of the Indies, prey to the attacks of corsairs, tropical in climate, and with a numerically strong Negro population; the other, remote behind snow-blown passes of the Andes, high on a treeless plateau at an altitude of 13,600 feet, with an overwhelming majority of mestizos and Indians. Yet the cathedral of Potosí (*fig. c*) shows a certain kinship to that of Havana. But what was rugged and contrasty in Havana appears here in an aerified version; the columns are more slender and the decorative scheme is confined to the portal. The plain expanse of the upper section is enriched with three windows, of which only the center one has the suggestion of a star shape in its framing. The vibrant line of the overhanging scalloped cornice connects the two towers. Their pepperpot shape is set off by the lines of the pilasters, which are carried through to the dome. In contrast to the niches in the Havana church, these are small, and the plastic decoration lies close to the wall.

Potosí reached its apex in 1611, at which time, as one of the most important mining centers of the world, it had 150,000 inhabitants. Its cathedral was erected at the very end of the colonial period, long after the city's most glorious epoch. The first stone was laid in 1809 on the site of an old church, dating from 1573. The Franciscan Manuel Sanauja prepared the plans, the most outstanding figure in Bolivian architecture in this period.[220] It is reported that, disturbed by the rising revolutionary atmosphere about him, he requested permission to return to his home in Arequipa, but the prefect insisted that he remain to complete his work; it was not finished until 1836. For an architect so closely associated with the neoclassic as was Sanauja, the cathedral façade manifests a rare blend of stylistic elements.

At this point the term "espadaña," already encountered, should receive some further explanation. It is a Spanish word often used to denote a belfry or a bell-wall in the upper façade. Apparently it is derived from the verb *espadañar*, "to spread the tail feathers," and in this volume it is used in a broad sense to define the ornamental extension of the façade above the roof line, a feature that found a most interesting application in Latin America. This architectural member is related to the ornamental gable that masked the peaked roofs of medieval buildings. Later, even in roofs constructed at less steep angles it was retained as a decorative screen—frequently a free-standing wall—and added greatly to the impressiveness of a building. The Maison de l'Ancien Greffe (1537), in Bruges, Belgium, now part of the Palace of Justice (*see Appendix, Pl. 190, fig. a*), is a Renaissance example of the ornamental gable.

In Latin America, where buildings usually were kept low, the espadaña received special emphasis. Through it the façade achieved greater height and dignity. Sometimes it was constructed entirely of stone, but more often a combination of stone and brick was preferred to keep it lighter in weight. An espadaña—as the term is applied in this volume—might be decorated with niches in keeping with the rest of the façade, or it might be perforated with arches to hold bells or occasionally even statues.

On this plate three different treatments of that crowning member are shown. In the cathedral at Salvador it is close to the European prototype, even to the attic window and peaked roof; in Panama it is a free-standing wall with niches and statues; and in Potosí it takes the form of a masonry parapet that screens the outline of the low roof.

Since most of the New World cathedrals took generations to complete, it is not surprising that many of them display a variety of styles and decorative motifs—milestones, as it were, in the taste development of the different colonial cities. The cathedral of San Miguel de Tegucigalpa, in Honduras, one of the exceptions, was built within a relatively short period and consequently shows unusual unity of style both inside and out.

The name Tegucigalpa has been variously explained: it may be derived from the native *teguz* or *teuz* (hill) and *galpa* (silver) or from another dialect, as meaning "Place of the Pointed Stones." Either interpretation applies, for the town lies along a rocky river bank among hills rich in silver deposits which jut up several thousand feet on three sides. The greatest silver mine of the country, the Rosario at San Juancito, is near Tegucigalpa.

The town began as a mining settlement. It did not achieve the rank of a city until 1824 and succeeded Comayagua as capital of Honduras only in 1880. But it was not unusual during the colonial period for the wealth of local mines to provide the impetus for the creation of gorgeous churches in remote and sparsely settled regions (*see Pl. 41*); some of the seventeenth-century churches near Cuzco and in the High Andes stand today without any apparent economic hinterland to explain their magnificence. The fact that Tegucigalpa has always been difficult of approach—even today it has neither a railroad nor an international highway—is one of the reasons why some of its colonial architecture is so well preserved. Nineteenth-century travelers described the city as pleasant, clean, and with a salubrious climate—impressions which still hold today; the neat houses were painted after the owner's fancy in blue, rose, cream, or white and boasted grated balconies, evenly tiled roofs, and paved patios.[162]

Its cathedral (*Pl. 11, fig. a*), erected as a parish church and dedicated to the archangel Michael, was built between 1756 and 1782 on the site of an earlier church, which had fallen victim to fire in 1746. It is recorded that this earlier building was of wood, to which the magnificent pines of the region offered themselves. For the new edifice artists, architects, and craftsmen from Guatemala

as well as from Comayagua worked together with local labor. The material accounts in part for the grace and lightness of the structure; it is built of burned brick—manufactured locally—plastered over and whitewashed.

According to an inscription on the façade, that portion was completed in 1765 under Gregorio Nacianceno Quiróz as chief architect.[155] Almost a half-century later, in 1809, and again in 1899 it was damaged by severe earthquakes. Fortunately, however, subsequent repairs were not disfiguring, and the cathedral remains among the few colonial edifices that are sufficiently well preserved, both within and without, to permit a just appraisal of their original beauty.

Retable elements are used in the façade but without producing the effect of a retable. Coupled pilasters, somewhat smaller in the second order than in the first, constitute the chief decoration. In impression, their deeply cut horizontals recall the stepped cascades of a Rococo garden. Such deep grooving is found frequently in Central America and will be discussed more fully in Chapter 8. A blind balustrade divides the belfries and espadaña from the heavier lower section. A statue of St. Michael occupies the center niche above, and the other figures represent his companion archangels.

The two gateways, which lead to garden patios, are harmonized successfully with the cathedral façade, though differences are evident in their design. One of the church's side portals is illustrated in Chapter 8 (*see Pl. 70*). The broad atrium, which extends across the entire front of the complex, served as an open-air stage for the religious ceremonies and processions for which Tegucigalpa was justly famous.

The expectations awakened by the Rococo charm of the exterior are abundantly fulfilled within. Not intended originally as a cathedral, the building has a single nave, covered by barrel vaulting; a cruciform effect is achieved by chapels that open off the apse, and an ample dome is placed above this "crossing." Covering the entire surface of the end wall and illuminated directly by side windows stands the main altar (*fig. c*). Its unity of style, great figural and decorative richness, and the superb quality of its carving immediately capture the attention. The figure of the Virgin stands in the center. Guarding her are St. Michael in a grotto below—a fountain suggested at his feet—and on either side his companion archangels, all of whom are represented also on the façade. The statues are exquisitely carved and expressive, but still more remarkable is the ornamentation on the retable. This great gilded screen of carved wood is embellished with serpentine undulations, arabesques, and other caprices of the imagination; the columns are turned into fragile, tenuous members, highly Rococo in effect. Especially noteworthy is the treatment of the side pieces; usually these are composed of scrollwork, more or less conventionalized, but here the design culminates in the figure of a winged siren, very originally conceived (*see Pl. 188*).

At one side of the retable and matching it in spirit stands the pulpit. Never reworked or even retouched and veritably sheathed in pure gold, it preserves a fascinating local Rococo. A detail of the staircase (*fig. b*) which leads up from the altar side shows an excellent feeling for the functional as well as the decorative. Its flowing patterns are applied with a sense for the curved surface and, in true Rococo manner, with due regard for empty spaces. Fantasy in concept is revealed especially in the scrollwork on the upper panel, where a human head is carved at one end and at the other a graceful bird, vaguely reminiscent of the symbolic pelican. As a crowning embellishment, on top of the canopy stands a miniature chariot of elaborate detail, all of gilded wood. It has been interpreted as symbolizing the chariot of Elijah but it might also represent the triumphal car of either Faith or Truth, which was drawn in the religious

processions. With its baldachin like a wisp of cloud, it has a movement seldom seen in an inanimate object. According to one source the pulpit is the work of the sculptor Vicente Gálvez, who came from Antigua, Guatemala.[163] It may well be surmised that his hand also worked on the main retable, so homogeneous are they in spirit. In this amazingly refined work, an inventive imagination is coupled with an impeccable technique.

These New World cathedrals which outrode the earthquakes—whether seismic or political—stood at the fulcrum point of the white man's authority. It was intended that they should embody not only the power and dignity of the church but also the might of the mother country. But even in these administrative centers, where the inclination to turn toward or imitate the homeland would be strongest, regional differences sprouted from the beginning.

Numerous factors were responsible for this condition. There was the matter of distance, with the attendant difficulties of sending plans back and forth. In many cases construction was supervised by friars, carpenters, masons, and others who were not professional architects; and labor was recruited from the mestizos and the Indians of the district. Moreover, a building always had to be adapted to local conditions; the possibility of earthquakes, the problem of ground water, the presence or lack of certain materials all led from the very start to modifications of European types. Wethey demonstrates that in Lima and Cuzco the Gothic type of vaulting, with brick, was resorted to early in the seventeenth century not as a matter of style but as a practical solution, for brick construction appeared to withstand the earthquakes most successfully; from there this method spread at even later dates throughout Peru. Proportions of line and bulk were changed of necessity, and towers often had to serve for buttresses as well as for belfries.

It is apparent that different regions solved

similar problems differently. Local preferences asserted themselves; for instance, Mexico has a great number of ingeniously constructed domes while Central America, where domes are less frequent, achieved superb lighting in their churches by other means. Out of an immense artistic vocabulary various regions selected their favorite motifs and by applying them with different techniques created new effects.

4

CHRIST IN THE NEW WORLD

THE formative period of the early Christian church took place in the Near East, which at that time was the vortex of many influences from pagan and monotheistic religions. The first books of the New Testament were written in Aramaic, a Hebrew dialect. The earliest versions now extant are in Greek, the language then generally spoken in the Near East, and about the end of the second century the Latin text appeared. The symbol IHS, derived from the Greek monogram of Jesus' name, provides one example of the transformation of ideas which accompanied the change of language; *Jesus Hominum Salvator* (Jesus Saviour of Men) is the Latin interpretation, said to have been used [4] first by Savonarola (1452–1498).

Christ in early art is largely a representation of the Eastern ideal, a bearded figure with the emphasis laid on the symbolic and transcendental. After the Roman Empire was Christianized, he was sometimes depicted as a beautiful Roman youth, clean-shaven. Christian art as taken on by Central and Western Europe shows both of these trends. The mosaics of Ravenna present an Orpheus-like figure as Good Shepherd, the crucifixes of the Trecento have a dark tonality in face and flesh and the body has little in common with the anatomical studies of later centuries. When the Renaissance reached its peak and national schools of art emerged, Christ was portrayed in two manners: one as the sublimated ideal, spiritually refined, an aristocrat in body and soul; the other as a suffering human being, inward-turned, broken, bloody, and realistic in agony.

Both of these tendencies came to the Indian in the New World. In the first decades the missionaries made a swift and perceptive appraisal of the spiritual inclinations and the traditional concepts of the Indian, and it soon became evident that certain ideas could not penetrate the minds of even the most willing pupils because the intellectual and spiritual background—the climate in which the religion flourished in Europe—was completely lacking here. Recognizing that the Indian could advance only at a slow pace, his teachers took several steps in his direction. They learned various Indian languages into which they translated the Scriptures, prayers, the catechism, and even parts of the Mass; they invented pictographs for the interpretation of the ideas of the new religion. The story was dramatized to the full, made present by pageantry and personal by the participation of the Indian. Here began a metamorphosis, a process taken over later by the natives themselves—all within the dogma. The Indian chose the ultra-realistic representation of Christ, but, as we shall see, in his search for the transcendental, he turned it into what today would be called surrealistic or expressionistic.

The representation of Christ as an unattended child is rather rare in Latin America. A Mexican carving (*Pl. 12, fig. a*) depicts him in a pensive pose. His expression is childlike, smiling and half-remote, as if he were aware of his destiny. The position of the right hand suggests that he originally held some object, perhaps a T square. A popular subject of contemporary European engravings was the youthful Christ carrying a carpenter's tool which formed a cross either in shape or in shadow. Throughout the centuries in Europe a succession of art works can be discerned in which the predestination of Jesus is implied. This piece is said to have come from the state of Puebla and to date from the eighteenth century. It is made of a corklike wood, probably *zumpantle*, which was native to that region and a favorite material for carvings because it was easily worked and easy to carry about. Such light-weight woods are found frequently in carvings and even in furniture from Puebla and Oaxaca, whereas in the state of Mexico heavy woods are more common. This statue, as is apparent in the lower portion, was covered with a very thin canvas, which was glued to the wood and then coated with gesso and painted. Despite the crude repainting and its somewhat dilapidated condition, the figure is touching and makes a warm appeal.

A canvas that hangs in the Abbey of Graça, in Salvador, Brazil (*fig. b*), dated in the seventeenth century, shows the youthful Jesus seated in one of those richly embossed chairs which the folk artist was accustomed to associate with colonial civil and ecclesiastic dignitaries. His head bent, the Child is contemplating his pricked finger, directing one's gaze to the crown of thorns which rests on his lap. The glow from his halo is reflected on the under side of the heavy encircling clouds, beyond which cherub faces, full of cheer, look on with an earthly childish curiosity.

Another variant of the "Baby God" is the polychromed wood carving in the Salguero collection in Quito, Ecuador (*fig. c*). To date it is the only known signed work of the great Indian sculptor Manuel Chili, or Chil, better known as Caspicara, who will be discussed at length in Chapter 9. Even the lettering of his signature (*fig. d*), exquisitely carved, shows a master who had full command of his tools. Both statue and signature are published here for the first time.

The theme of a little boy asleep, his head resting on his arm, goes back to classical times. Italian sculptors of the Renaissance revived it, one of Murillo's paintings was inspired by it, and the outstanding master of the Murcia school, Francisco Salzillo (1707–1783), carved several versions of the subject in stone. Sometimes the Child is clasping a crown of thorns. Even in such company Caspicara holds his own. His genius gives his statue a pleasing individuality. The softly closed eyes, the angelic mouth, half-opened—so like any child enjoying sleep—and the finely proportioned little body all radiate life. Note the handling of the arms, hands, and hair, like those of a *putto*. The delicate tones of the enamel-like finish—the encarnación—can be imagined even from the black and white print.

In contrast to this interpretation of the Christ Child, universal in its idiom, the last of this group (*fig. e*) is pure Aymara Indian. Wearing a poncho around his shoulders and a knitted cap inscribed *Yo soy Jesús* (I am Jesus), this figure stands in the church of San Juan in Juli, Peru, on the shores of Lake Titicaca. The road over which the riches of Potosí, Bolivia, were carried across the Andes to the sea passed through this town. Here, 12,500 feet above sea level and far from any center of white people, a large group of Aymara Indians still lives. They worship in colonial churches, within which a wealth of colonial art is disintegrating because of poverty and the lack of appreciation. But the Child Jesus, warmed by a native shawl such as any Aymara boy would wear, is well kept; the face has been repainted and the handmade lace on the sleeves is clean. This Divine Child is of the people and through him they come nearer to the spirit of the distant God whom the white conquerors brought to their mountainous land.

[49]

The four representations of the Christ Child on this plate—from Mexico, Brazil, Ecuador, and the Bolivian border of Peru—date from either the seventeenth or the eighteenth century. Three show derivation from a different epoch of European art: the first is an expression of the Baroque; the second has Byzantine prototypes; the third can be traced back to the classic. And the fourth is a flower of folklore. Through the different artistic sensibilities and the traditions mirrored in them they reveal how creative was the soul of colonial Latin America.

Other figures of the youthful Christ are generally found in scenes from the life of Mary and St. Joseph. Representations of the suffering martyred Lord are much more numerous. The Indians, now degraded to the lowest caste in their own land, might well have found release for their emotional tension by embracing the realistic agonizing Christ. Prints with scenes of the Passion were favorite subjects for translation into the plastic and pictorial mediums. As will be discussed in Chapter 7, the flesh was represented on carved wooden figures by an enamel-like finish called "encarnación," and garments were decorated after the Spanish fashion in a manner known as "estofado." As in Spain, glass eyes and long lashes, real hair, and textile costumes oftentimes were employed to heighten the realism of statues.

A carved figure of Christ (*Pl. 13, fig. a*), which bears the cross in the Good Friday procession, occupies a niche in the church of San Francisco in Comayagua, Honduras; the cross itself is kept in the sacristy and placed on the shoulder of the figure only when the complete sequence of the Passion and the Crucifixion passes through the streets of the town. The gesture of the sensitive hands, the position of the shoulder, and the stoop of the body all transmit the impression of exhaustion beneath a great weight. The penetrating eyes seem to seek out each onlooker with an expression unusually personal. Long,

real hair hangs below the waist—the offering of some zealous believer.

Into the crown of thorns, here wrought in silver, are incorporated the emblems of the *tres potencias* (three powers). The representation of the three powers seems to have had its origin in the cruciform halo, the Greek cross within a circle, which has been used to designate divine personages, especially Christ, ever since Byzantine times; thus it is sometimes called the divine nimbus. The Renaissance dropped the outer ring, and some painters, notably Tintoretto, indicated the halo merely by rays of light or tongues of flame in the form of a cross. For statuary these were fashioned out of metal, especially in Spain, and in Latin America they were developed into a major decorative motif. Often they lost the cruciform shape, as here, but nearly always the suggestion of rays was retained. The *tres potencias* were given renewed significance by the Spanish mystics. St. Ignatius urged meditation with the "three faculties" of the soul: memory, understanding, and will. St. Theresa and St. John of the Angels also used the term in this sense.[33]

If possible the atmosphere of impending tragedy is still more strongly expressed in the Ecce Homo from the Santa Prisca church in Tasco, Mexico (*fig. b*). Here there is no gesture in the hands; they hang straight, though not without expression, bound at the wrist with a coarse rope. The face streams with blood, and the thorny crown casts its shadow on a wan and pallid countenance. The eyes no longer look out into the crowd; the gaze is turned inward. The rich background of the gilded retable, with its garlands and ebullient angels of true Baroque, contrasts startlingly with this somber and majestic figure.

Both of these statues are clad in purple velvet. The breast of the Tasco Christ is covered with *milagros*, or votive offerings, and the flowers, both real and artificial, are gifts of the flower-loving populace.

The seated Man of Sorrows (*fig. c*) is in the church of Santo Domingo at Popayán,

Colombia. Physical torture is portrayed by the flowing blood, the wounds from falling on his knees and elbows, and the left cheek bruised by the blows of the mockers. Nevertheless the sculptural expression here is less dramatic; the pose of the whole body is somewhat conventional. A subtle symbolism is evident in the crown of silver thorns: the three powers are fashioned in the form of wheat and grapes, emblems of the sacramental bread and wine. More local associations are revealed in the reed in Christ's hand—a leafy stalk of sugar cane wrought in silver. This rendition could be popular only in the New World, where sugar cane abounds; by the folk, the statue is called the Christ of the Cane.

More complex in its symbolism and quite transcendental in idea is the Christ of the Globe, from the church of San Sebastián in Cuzco, Peru (fig. d). Here Christ is kneeling on a flattened sphere that represents the world; on it is pictured the overspreading Tree of Paradise, with Eve offering Adam the apple. The sacrifice is complete: in addition to the rope, the double stripes of the scourge, the bruises, and the crown of thorns, Christ bears the mark of the nails and the spear wound. His hands are upraised and his eyes turned toward Heaven, as if in the very act of offering himself in redemption. The whole concept here is rare in European as well as Latin American art; one other such portrayal is found in the church of San Agustín in Popayán, Colombia.

All of the statues illustrated on this plate, as well as many of those which follow, were carried out from the churches to take part in religious processions.

Out of the vast repertory of cruel scenes from the Passion of Christ, the Mexicans often seem to have selected those in which their breath-taking realism could express itself to the point of paroxysm; in South America, on the other hand, a somewhat different approach prevailed. In the Christ at the Column from San Miguel Totocuitlapilco, Mexico (Pl. 14,

fig. a), both face and body show infinite suffering and brutal torture. Large wounds gape in the chest and side, blood streams over the body, and the features are twisted with pain, agonizing. Even in the arms and legs the stiffening of death is forcefully expressed. For the moment the shocking impact of this portrayal completely overshadows the story-telling and the spiritual contents of the theme.

A less startling version of the same scene (fig. c), also from Mexico, is said to have come from Toluca. Here the expression is rather one of meditation; the gaze of the glassy eyes is turned inward. The crown of thorns, now only implied by the drops of blood on the forehead, has been removed, and the large *tres potencias* of silver, which show sophisticated workmanship, may have been added later. Unusual is the detailed execution of the swollen veins, worked out to a degree very rarely seen; the effect is that of a flayed body. Here is an attempt at realism but the result is expressionistic.

When the two preceding figures are compared with the Christ at the Column from the church of Santo Domingo at Cuzco, Peru (fig. d), the difference in approach touched upon above is more obvious. Physical torture is apparent at first glance, but the portrayal has also a measure of composure—to a certain degree a philosophical quality. No attempt is made to awaken even fleeting sympathy. Christ stands; he has not fallen, and it is evident that within himself he has another world. The lack of proportion between the upper and lower parts of the body may indicate that this work was inspired by a drawing; much that can be represented in the flat without arousing criticism seems exaggerated when translated into three dimensions. (*Compare Appendix, Pl. 190, fig. b.*)

Prior to the seventeenth century the Christ of the Flagellation was depicted as bound to a tall column. Later this representation was used to symbolize the scene in the temple portico on the night before the Passion, while the short column came to be associated with the scourging ordered by Pilate.[12]

Closer to the interpretation favored in South America is a Mexican version of the Man of Sorrows which is in the parish church of Tehuilotepec, near Tasco (*fig. b*). He is seated in meditation, his head resting on his hand. The angular position of his arms and legs produces a gripping effect. Though much of the paint has flaked off and the attributes are gone, this Christ has inner drama, nobility, and perhaps the deepest spiritual quality of the four examples pictured here.

In Europe, by the time of the Conquest, the crucifix had long been accepted as the greatest symbol of the Christian world. To the New World it came as a new and powerful symbol, to banish idols and to push out other pagan practices. Inspired by it the mestizo and Indian craftsmen produced astonishingly varied and sometimes unique artistic manifestations.

A crucifix in the church of La Recoleta in Cuzco, Peru (*Pl. 15, fig. b*), shows Gothic trends overlaid with the strong realism of Spanish Baroque. Both the face and the body are powerfully sculptural. The "Biblical" landscape in the background has a rustic colonial atmosphere. Unusual is the cross-shaped wound on the figure's left side. The nailing of each foot to the cross brings to mind that the painter Francisco Pacheco (1564–1654), father-in-law of Velázquez and arbiter of the Spanish iconography of the Counter Reformation, advocated a return to the medieval representation of the Crucifixion, using four nails.

Caspicara is said to have carved the crucifix in the church of El Belén in Quito, Ecuador (*fig. c*). Its realism makes a strong appeal through the excellence of its craftsmanship. The large aureole that encompasses the entire carving harks back to the Gothic. Entwined silver bands here replace the thorns as crown, and the *tres potencias* are flamelike in shape. The refinement of the figure is brought out

by the contrast with the crudely carpentered cross.

The crucifix from Xochimilco, Mexico (*fig. a*), is an expression of folk art. Christ's crown is of beads, and the real hair, matted to his brow, is straight. His hands are bound to the wooden crosspiece by strips of white cloth, as if to ease the weight on the pierced palms. His loins are wrapped in a figured textile of native weave like the garments worn by Indians on windy mornings and cool evenings in the high Valley of Mexico. The weight of the sagging body as it hangs on the cross is movingly expressed in the bend of the knees. Both the color of the skin and the anatomy of the figure suggest that this also may be the work of an Indian artist; he infused into the carving something of his own blood. The intellectualized Christ of Europe, draped in diaphanous veils, has indeed traveled a long way.

In the church of La Concepción in Lima, Peru, is an aristocratic Christ with a nobly proportioned body, portrayed with assurance and an expert naturalism (*fig. d*). It has been identified by Wethey as the work of the famous Spanish sculptor Juan Martínez Montañés.[204] The contract for it, as well as for other carvings for an altar dedicated to St. John the Baptist, is dated 1607, and it is certified as delivered in 1612. This crucifix offers an opportunity for a comparative study with works of possible European origin in the colonies and also with those that are outspokenly American. Here the dramatic in the subject has been filtered out. The blood and wounds have received little emphasis; the loincloth is kept subordinate as a detail and provides no separate sculptural interest. The tension and the gripping subjectivity are less acute than in the other portrayals. It should be kept in mind that this is an early sculpture of Martínez Montañés; besides, documents reveal that the masters in Spain gave less attention to pieces destined for the colonies than to those which stayed in the motherland and immediately enhanced the prestige of their creators.

Not merely was a fresh interpretation given to the iconography of Christ's figure in the New World by the mestizo and the Indian but in addition in certain regions a new material was used. America brought the maize, her own autochthonous plant, into the service of God. The use of a light and pliable mixture based on the pith of the corn had a deep significance, for in many areas corn was the staple food and in pre-Columbian times it had its special god; particularly in Mexico ancient idols were formed of grain or seeds and dough.

An excellent example of this type of figure is shown in a crucifix belonging to the Franciscan Third Order in Pátzcuaro, Mexico (*Pl. 16, fig. a*). It stands in the center of the main altar of the church of San Francisco there and is highly venerated as miraculous. On July 28, 1656, an earthquake shook the town and in the afternoon the church bell began to ring of itself. This figure of the Christ on the Cross, which had recently been put into position, was seen to move; the head slipped to one side, the left arm stretched, and later the whole body shifted itself into its present expressive position.

The figure is larger than life-size—an unusual feature but characteristic of this type of statue—and has a soft, yielding plasticity. The rib system is brought out clearly here, an illusion made possible by the pliant material of the under-structure; for statues made of maize were not sculptured but modeled. In spite of the beard the impression is strongly Indian. Light-colored glass eyes produce a striking contrast to the darkened flesh, and real hair falls over the shoulder. A certain rigidity in the features, as of approaching death, is distinctly conveyed.

The great bishop of Michoacán, Vasco de Quiroga, encouraged the modeling of such statues under the direction of an aged Tarascan convert, a former pagan priest who knew the ancient technique. Many of the images now extant were manufactured in or near Pátzcuaro and seem to date between 1538 and 1565 (in

which year the bishop died), though doubtless figures continued to be made by this method. They are vivid in their coloring and extraordinarily light in weight; one figure over six and one-half feet high weighs scarcely thirteen pounds.

To make one of these statues, first an armature or skeletal foundation was constructed of dried maize leaves fastened together with fibers of the agave cactus; for fingers and toes turkey feathers were used. Then this framework was roughly covered with a paste composed of the pith of cornstalks mixed to a spongy mass with the ground-up bulbs of a local orchid. To ensure strong joints and extremities, these parts were bound with strips of cotton or agave cloth. After the figure was dry a fine coating of the paste was spread over it in the manner of stucco, and later the coloring was added in its proper tints. To give luster a quick-drying oil, known to the natives, was applied. The profuse blood was simulated by a compound of cochineal and lampblack. Hair and beard were made of human hair or were modeled and stained black.[92]

An image of the Virgin of Salud, still in Pátzcuaro, was probably the first piece constructed under Quiroga; an Immaculate Conception of the same material is in the church of San Juan de Lagos in the state of Jalisco. A crucified Christ made in this technique hangs in a church in Telde, Las Palmas, Canary Islands. It was presented by the colonists and purchased, according to a historian, out of income from wine and sugar produced in the New World. Among others are figures of the entombed Christ in Las Monjas Catarinas, Morelia (*see Pl. 21*), and in the sanctuary of Amecameca. More may be found in Mexico when the village churches have been inventoried.

In the crucifix of the San Cristóbal church in Nexquipaya, Mexico (*fig. b*), echoes of the early Renaissance may be found. The quiet plastic composition of the head gains strength from the dark tone, which gives the piece the monumental character of a bronze. As in the preceding example the glass eyes, with their "real" eyelashes, are half-closed but the effect is different: this Christ appears to be still conscious while the other is expiring.

A broader humanism is evident in the crucified Christ from the monastery of San Francisco in Quito, Ecuador (*fig. c*), a small carving attributed to Caspicara. In this piece attention is directed to the face by the converging lines of the large *tres potencias* of silver, represented here as emanating directly out of the head.

Earthquake, fire, revolution, and neglect have all taken their toll of colonial art. But even some fragments of figures bespeak the power of the artists who made them. Large dark eyes of glass add depth and realism to the expression of the Christ head in the museum at Morelia, Mexico, perhaps from a Man of Sorrows (*Pl. 17, fig. a*). The encarnación has largely disappeared, but the pallor that results intensifies the emotional appeal.

An Ecce Homo (*fig. b*) offers a rare example made in terra cotta, a craft much practiced during the colonial period, although few pieces have survived. The small statue here (only about a foot high) is said to have been made in or around the Mexican capital and to date from early eighteenth century. By the simple but effective means of using slits for eyes and mouth the folk artist produced an enigmatic expression. The rope is disproportionately large, a method of emphasis occurring also in pre-Columbian pottery.

The third Christ head (*fig. c*) is attributed to Caspicara, although the carving does not show the subtlety of the crucifix on the preceding plate. The immediacy of the portrayal, however, is evident even in the fragment. Blood streams down the face, but the effect is not shocking; the piece has too much spiritual content and artistic integrity for that. Death masks of Christ are found in certain regions of colonial South America, and this may be one.

The hurried visitor who sees in Tasco,

Mexico, only the enchanting scenery and the picturesque exterior of the church of Santa Prisca (*see Pl. 41*) misses the deeper satisfaction that awaits him within. By the time the lavish Baroque ornamentation of this building was created, the population had developed a religious folk art of their own and had found their favorite themes. The consummate skill of some regional craftsman is shown in the Christ at the Column which stands in one of the side chapels of the church (*fig. d*). This figure is life-size, with real hair. A coarse rope binds the hands. So masterly is the delineation that the incongruous addition of a pair of drawers can be overlooked. The beard and mustache have a rich and metallic plasticity. This region also produced the Ecce Homo that stands in the same chapel and the Man of Sorrows at Tehuilotepec some fifteen miles away (*see Pls. 13, 14*).

The martyred Christ in the last illustration on this plate (*fig. e*), from Mexico, is akin to the Christ at the Column from San Miguel Totocuitlapilco. His staring eyes and drawn lips are morbid expressions of suffering, and his head and body are spotted with blood. The absence of hair and crown gives the piece an especially haggard appearance. The angular ridges around the eyes, ending on the protruding cheek bones, are truly expressionistic.

A statue that may have been inspired by a drawing has already been shown (*see Pl. 14*); but statues in turn inspired paintings, which then underwent various changes.

The Christ of the Earthquakes (*Pl. 18, fig. a*) stands in a special chapel of the cathedral of Cuzco, Peru, and is associated with miraculous powers. It is said that when this crucifix was brought out of the cathedral during the devastating earthquake of 1650 the temblor subsided. It is still carried out for religious processions on the shoulders of men, as can be seen at the bottom of the photograph. Intact after the catastrophe of 1950 it was placed in the center of the main plaza. In spite of the tradition that the figure was sent from Spain it has the marks of a colonial work. Usually the statue is clothed in a short lace garment as in the paintings on this plate; the long one of satin is reserved for holy festivals. Special prayers were said before this figure whenever an earthquake occurred, and since it could not be carried to distant regions requests for reproductions of it came from far and wide. Thus paintings of the crucifix were made as it stood in the Cuzco cathedral, amid flowers, candles, hanging candelabra, and mirrors.

One such painting is in the church of Santiago in Cuzco (*fig. b*). Many others have been seen by the author in distant earthquake regions—even as far as Guayaquil, Ecuador— and always they are consciously identified by the name "Christ of the Earthquakes."

In the example now in the Prado collection near Lima, Peru (*fig. c*), to the miraculous crucifix, clearly recognizable, were added the figures of Mary and John, making it a part of a Calvary group. These two figures have no pedestals; but the crucifix is depicted as a statue. The vases of flowers at the feet of Christ are decorative motifs that are frequently encountered, painted on the walls of colonial churches, carved in gilded wood and in stone, and also woven in textiles.

Seemingly it was thought that the addition of other favorite saints might augment the miraculous power of the representation. In one such variant from Cuzco (*fig. d*) the crucifix is again represented as a statue, but here Mary also is placed on a pedestal, a clear indication that this figure too is a statue. On the other side of Christ stands St. Francis of Assisi, contemplating a small crucifix. From an iconographical point of view a revealing anomaly results: the saint is gazing upon a small crucifix, Mary is holding the Baby Jesus in her arms, and between them is the miraculous crucifix, the raison d'être of the painting. The mourning angels may remind one of those which hold back the curtains at either side of an altar niche; it is noteworthy that in the preceding illustration they have been turned into medallions of gold lace.

On all three paintings shown here, but especially on the last two, the metal trim of the cross is painstakingly copied from the original statue of the Christ of the Earthquakes, and in the last illustration the wooden scrolled loops on the base are reproduced through which poles were inserted when the statue was carried in a procession. Such small details faithfully copied by the folk artist now furnish a link to the original. This type of statue-painting was popular among the colonial folk artists. In Europe grisailles and other painted reproductions of statues were also common in the fifteenth and sixteenth centuries (*see Appendix, Pl. 191, fig. e*).

For the Indian the Cross was the first great symbol of Christianity, but he often turned it into a fetish. His pre-Columbian past was full of idols, and the Cross of the missionaries served as the chief substitute for the images which were destroyed. Even in the life of the Spanish conquerors the Cross held a unique place. One need only recall scenes from the Inquisition in which the victim, already half-consumed by flames, was offered one last look at a crucifix, or remember the death of Francisco Pizarro, who, mortally wounded by his Spanish rivals, traced with his own blood a cross upon the floor.

The Mexican Indian, out of his non-European traditions and using his proven skill, carved crosses of stone in which his peculiar reaction to this new symbol is apparent. Such carving is now known as *tequitqui* (Nahuatl for "tributary"). One example is in the atrium of Acolman (*Pl. 19, fig. a*) and another in the Atzacoalco cemetery (*fig. b*), not far from Mexico City. In both cases the face of a living Christ, with wide-open eyes, is placed at the center of the composition. It takes little imagination to see the horizontal piece as the arms, the ornamented ends as hands or fingers, and the vertical as the body. Both shafts bear symbols of the Passion—the cock, pillar, ropes, ladder, sponge, spear, and Eucharist cup—but differently arranged. The crosspiece of the

Acolman carving is decorated with floral sprays that are typically indigenous in outline and asymmetry; a similar motif is entwined in the letters of the inscription. In the second example the collar of thorns and the ribbon wound about the arms are both unusual; and still more unorthodox is the heavy stone ornamentation that tops the piece like a feathered headdress.

These crosses date from the second half of the sixteenth century and come from Indian communities that were articulate and strong in artistic traditions from pre-Conquest times. Elizabeth Wilder Weismann has devoted considerable study to such colonial sculpture.[135] To seek out the sources of the various decorative elements here involved would indeed be an interesting excursion into the fantasy world of the pre-Columbian past. It should be remarked that no evidence of this type of stone cross has been found in South America, but plain wooden crosses with the instruments of the Passion attached to the shaft are common.

The crucifix known as Lord of the Tree (*fig. c*) is said to have grown in the shape of a cross in a forest near Morelia. According to the story the folk in the locality gathered in the open before the wondrous mesquite until it was removed to a small chapel. It is covered with canvas and stucco and painted. There is Romanesque starkness in the mask-like oval face, sharply emphasized against the black of the body. The transposition of the lance thrust from the dark body to the right cheek of the figure is an ingenious device of the folk artist.

Vestiges of realism can be found in the three examples just seen, although they are predominantly symbolic. In the next illustration, a wooden crucifix from the Indian mission church of San Javier at Mocovi, near Santa Fé, Argentina (*fig. d*), the portrayal is expressionistic. No attempt was made to cover the wood or to disguise the joints in the crosspiece. This whole figure is carved with an amazing linear economy: the arms are a wavy line, a circle represents the head, and crude,

radiating lines indicate the halo. The shallow diagonals suggesting the ribs are paralleled in the lines of the loincloth. The flaring "knot" at the waist may indicate the spear wound, which quite frequently is depicted on the heart side by folk artists in Latin America. Below the many diagonals the two sharp lines that terminate the drapery and separate the legs repeat the shape of the cross—a detail in which a maximum effect is achieved with a minimum of plasticity. One wonders if the person who made it could have created a more realistic figure or whether it was his technical limitations that were responsible for this uniquely conventionalized yet revealing work of art.

The Aztec crosses of stone are magnificent examples of the "primitive" artists' incredible grasp of symbolism; in the last cross a symbol long familiar is expressionistically portrayed.

The Biblical inspiration for the allegory of the Mystic Vintage comes from Isaiah 63:3: "I have trodden the winepress alone; and of the people there was none with me. . . ." A representation of this subject is encountered as early as the twelfth century in an illuminated book; a sketch by Dürer, a mural attributed to him, and a few Italian paintings of the Renaissance and Baroque periods also present the theme. These interpretations show the metaphorical subject realistically rendered, producing story-telling pictures such as the artists of those centuries loved to concoct for many abstruse passages from the Bible.

A print of the Mystic Vintage (*Pl. 20, fig. a*) was made by Hieronymus Wierix,[5] the famous Flemish engraver who in association with his brothers contributed thousands of engravings for the illustration of religious books (1552–1615). Here the saints are shown bringing in the grapes. The winepress, handled by God the Father, is an authentic depiction of a contemporary device (*see Appendix, Pl. 190, fig. c*); most representations, however, show a press with a horizontal beam, as in Mainardi's painting on the high altar at

Cremona, Italy, dated 1590 (see *Appendix, Pl. 190, fig. h*). The blood of Christ flows into the vat, from which it is collected in a chalice by two angels; the paten under the cup completes the symbolism of the Eucharist. Beside the winepress sits the Sorrowful Mother, while in the foreground is a child-like company of saved souls, adoring and rejoicing.

This engraving, or reproductions of it, must have circulated widely in the colonies. One painting that is obviously based on it hangs in the church of San Miguelito in Puebla, Mexico, a canvas by Diego de Borgraf (*fig. b*). This Flemish artist, who worked also in the Puebla cathedral, was born in Antwerp and about 1652 emigrated to Puebla,[85] where according to the records he married three times and died in 1686.

While in its general composition the seventeenth-century painting remains similar to the sixteenth-century print, the Dolorosa has been brought forward to figure more prominently in the scene. The action has undergone considerable transformation: a small soul kneels on the paten receiving baptism in the holy blood and at the left the donor is introduced, dressed in splendor and placed in an attitude of utmost devotion, an interesting and lively portrait.

An eighteenth-century canvas in Quito, Ecuador (*fig. c*), clearly derives from the Wierix engraving. It is signed "A. S.," initials which might indicate Antonio Salas, active about 1760, or eventually Antonio Silva, one of the painters chosen in 1786 to help complete the illustrated work of the great Colombian botanist José Celestino Mutis.[183] In this canvas the position of Christ's body is basically the same, as is the Holy Ghost which hovers above his head. The composition is greatly simplified and one significant detail in the symbolism is omitted: the blood does not flow from the vat into the chalice. Thus the reason for the two angels kneeling before the press is lost. In contrast to the engraving, the attention here is sharply focused on the Mater

Dolorosa, especially by the gold tooling on her garment and halo.

That the theme of the Mystic Vintage must have been widely popular during the colonial period is shown by the fact that other versions exist in the Prado collection, probably from the Cuzco school, and in Salta, Argentina; a somewhat altered interpretation hangs in the estate chapel at Conapaya, not far from Potosí, Bolivia.[215]

And long after the colonial era this theme seems to have intrigued the imagination of José G. Posada (1851–1913), a Mexican artist who, in his woodcuts, caricatured the corrupt politics of his period and portrayed lusty, often vulgar scenes of everyday life. In his Christ of the Pulque (*fig. e*) he too touches the abstruse symbolism of the Mystic Vintage. Here Christ is seated on a wine skin; behind him is a keg and at his side the cactus plant from which is made the popular drink *pulque*. In his hand is a cup of liquid, which he is spilling onto the earth. As Dionysiac as the picture appears, it still presents the original symbolism: the libation of Christ's blood to atone for the sins of the world.

In not one of these representations does Christ show anguish. This might be explained by the transcendental character of the subject expressed in the Flemish prototype. But that the tortured and agonizing face did exist in painting as well as in sculpture is shown in the fragment of a canvas from Peru (*fig. d*). It is from a Christ on the Cross and despite the limitations of the medium measures up to the carved examples.

The arrangement of statues into a group was an exacting but satisfying task for the dramatic and strongly plastic talent of the colonial artist. One such scene, the mourning over the crucified Christ (*Pl. 21, fig. b*), is set forth with sincerity and story-telling naïveté. This group occupies the center of the main altar in a small Calvary chapel isolated on a hilltop near Pátzcuaro, Mexico. In the background looms the cross, a reminder of the

[57]

events which led up to this scene. Both of the Marys and John touch the body of Christ—a close composition of line and gesture. Only the heads and hands of these three figures are executed plastically, carved of wood, and finely polychromed; their garments are of real silk, velvet, and lace and probably are more or less recent since from time to time they are refreshed and replaced by devoted hands. A sense of gesture is conveyed in the drapery, however, and through it the composition is integrated. This is one of the rare cases anywhere in which John is depicted with a mustache.

While a certain realism pervades the three mourners in this tableau, Christ is represented in an expressionistic manner. Despite the delineation of anatomy, the wounds, the blood, and the crown of thorns, his figure is already changing into a symbol. One characteristic of pre-Columbian art is the effective combination of the realistic and the abstract.

A rocky path leads up to the Calvary chapel and no settlement is around it. The courtyard is overgrown with weeds and the whitewash everywhere is peeling off. Near the door is a plaque inscribed with the date 1666. The overseer's family were the only people about, and a young son helped us as we photographed the group. Just as the peal of the noon bells was floating up from the town the head of the family returned from the fields. He was a pure-blood Tarascan, squat but strongly built. His long angular face was characterized by stiff upright graying hair and a sparse mustache that merged into a square-cut beard. He wore his old-fashioned garb of white cotton drawers and loose shirt with the dignity of a shaman. We praised the idyllic location of the chapel and the beauty of the mourning group. He listened with pride and asked us to contribute toward the upkeep of the chapel, which we did. Then with a lift of the hand, he gave us a blessing in the Tarascan tongue.

The Christ Entombed in the church of Las Monjas Catarinas, Morelia (*fig. a*), had long

been familiar to us. Its expression of divine calm brings a new note into this collection of suffering and tortured Christ figures. The nobly sculptured face, with its brownish matte *encarnación* and real hair, is framed by a white headcloth and coverlet, which serve to contrast and lift the plastic and spiritual qualities.

Our last visit to Morelia was on the Saturday before Passion Sunday, at which time all altars, statues, and holy pictures are veiled, in accordance with the traditional mourning for Christ's road to Calvary. We knew from experience that during these two weeks before Easter almost no photographs could be made of church interiors, but we wanted a last glimpse of this figure. From a bright sunny street we stepped at midday into the church but stopped instinctively just within the door; the building was filled to the last bench with members of a mestizo sodality, deep in prayer although no priest was visible. All the women were dressed alike, in uniform black with black *rebozos* over their heads, their only decoration the purple silk ribbon about their necks on which hung the golden badge of the order. This gathering of prayer-murmuring women surrounded the *Cristo del santo entierro* in his glass casket; he was their divine hero, laid to rest. Several turned inquiringly in our direction—somewhat inimically, we felt, for our intrusion. Then we realized how much this Christ—made out of the pith of the corn and wearing the headband that was the mark of distinction in pre-Columbian times—is the product of this soil and how much he remains the exclusive property of this people.

Christianity had traveled far from its point of origin to conquer and embrace the second largest continent in the world. It underwent changes in iconography, ritual, and philosophy. Not only geographical and psychological distances but spiritual and artistic capacities also were involved in creating the Indianized Christ.

5

COLONIAL COLOMBIA

THOUGH the Kingdom of New Granada of the Indies was one of the more remote territories which the viceroy of Peru had to administer, it was not cut off to form the Viceroyalty of New Granada until 1717. The new viceregal seat was at Santa Fé de Bogotá, and the administrative area included present-day Ecuador, Colombia, Venezuela, and Panama. As heretofore, for the sake of easy identification modern geographical names are used.

With three high mountain ranges running through this region and deep river valleys between them, flowing northerly, it was in some ways more accessible from Europe than from Lima. Its fine harbor at Cartagena was the first authorized port of call on the American mainland for the fleet of licensed merchant vessels from the motherland; in fact, this region was known as Tierra Firme, the mainland.

Cartagena, called Pearl of the Indies, was made a city in 1575. For a long time it vied with Mexico City and Lima in wealth and importance. The annual arrival of the Spanish galleons was an outstanding event for the populace, and when the trading fleet was riding in the harbor the city was a giant fair. Muletrains laden with Spanish wines, cloth, tools, and other manufactured goods made their way inland, while precious metals, pearls from Venezuela, emeralds from the highlands of Colombia, indigo and dyewood, tobacco,

cocoa, tropical spices and resins were loaded for Europe. In the hinterland was excellent farming country, where tropical fruits and vegetables, cereals, and cattle and swine were raised for the town's markets. But this city was also the victim of its fortunate position, for English, French, and Dutch freebooters made it their goal. The capital of Mexico was high on a mountainous tableland far from the coast, and Lima, though near the Pacific, was difficult of approach from Europe. Cartagena, on the other hand, lay exposed on the Caribbean shore, easily accessible from the many islands where pirate bands had their hideouts and whence clear sailing was possible with luck—and loot—to the safety of any European port desired.

For this reason the very existence of the town depended on its defense system. Fortifications were started by the order of Philip II (ruled 1556–1598), which for two centuries were in the process of building or of enlargement. At strategic positions in walls that were sixty feet high and forty feet thick, assault towers and lookouts were constructed, and beneath them were built underground passageways and dungeons. Thousands of Negroes were imported to work on these bulwarks, as well as on the breakwaters which protected the harbor entrance and the low-lying town from hurricane damage.[182]

One section of the fortification, called La Tenaza (the pincers), was constructed on the breakwater toward the northwest under the supervision of the Spanish engineer Antonio de Arévalo between 1765 and 1771 (*Pl. 22, fig. a*). A drawbridge and subterranean passage connected it with the land. With its back to the inner city of Cartagena it commanded a sweeping view of the sea.

The old city lies enclosed within the ramparts. It was first established on a sandbar but soon spread over its bounds. By early seventeenth century its population numbered fifteen hundred Spanish inhabitants, in addition to mestizos, mulattoes, and free Negroes.[81]

Even today, bleached by tradewinds and blazing under the tropical sun, Cartagena retains something of the staunch and indomitable air of the important colonial stronghold it once was. Whole sectors of streets are lined with colonial houses with grilled windows, behind which the womenfolk could sit for hours and see and be seen without leaving the home (*fig. b*). Below, along the wall, a benchlike base of brick provided a place for the menfolk to rest as they conversed, without ceremony, through the windows. Up and down the street the anvil-shaped corbels below the grillework alternate with the blocky steps that lead to the doorways. Most of the houses here have two stories and the wooden balconies are open, not shuttered as in Lima. Wood was preferred to iron in some parts of the colonies, for iron was apt to corrode in the moist tropics. This type of house, well-adapted to the hot climate, is common in southern Spain in the district of Jerez and in the Western Hemisphere in Cuba, Nicaragua, and coastal Peru.

Philip III (reigned 1598–1621) ordered the erection of a building to house the Holy Office of the Inquisition, which was established in Cartagena in 1610 with jurisdiction over present Colombia and the island of Santo Domingo.[57] The Palace of the Inquisition as it stands today (*fig. c*), facing a palm-lined plaza of the old city, was finished in early eighteenth century. Constructed of stone and brick and whitewashed, it is a dignified edition of the typical balcony dwelling of the city.

The stone portal, dated 1770, extends through the two stories and is distinguished by a projecting pediment with heavy, undulating sides. In the center, between two spirals, were the arms of Spain, now effaced. Deeply coffered panels flank the arched entrance, and, as frame, a ropelike molding begins at the top in two tight spirals and drops down on either side to the base.

Tunja, known also as the Emblazoned City, was one of the few colonial centers that had not yet felt the full force of the modernization craze at the time of our visit in 1945. While here and there an image with the spirituality of the bygone epoch may have been replaced by an impersonal, factory-made statue, or some chapel redecorated in execrable taste, much of the city's colonial splendor still remained.

Nearly 9,300 feet in elevation, Tunja overlooks a bleak mountainous landscape and is swept the year round by cold harsh winds. In the second decade of the seventeenth century the city itself had over six hundred Spanish residents and the entire district was described as one of the most thickly settled sections of the country, partly because of its gold and silver mines. The façades, in harmony with the surrounding country, are austere, almost without exception lacking the playful exuberance of the Baroque. Like the cathedral of Tunja, they bespeak a frozen Renaissance (*see Pl. 1*).

Thus all the more astonishing is it to find the interiors of certain churches displaying pomp and ebullience in their decoration. Among the most notable of these is the church of Santo Domingo (*Pl. 23*). The Dominicans arrived on the American shores with the Conquistadores, and together with their rival mendicant order, the Franciscans, they took a prolonged and effective part in the pacification of the New World and in the conversion of the Indians. The Inquisition was in the hands of the Dominicans—not in vain did the Castilian St. Dominic fight with zeal and decision against heathen and heretic.

The Dominican monastery in Tunja was founded by 1551, and in the first decade of its existence the order received additional land. In 1568, upon the death in the city of the Conquistador García Arias Maldonado (Capitan General, Regidor Perpetuo, and Justicia Mayor), much of his property was received by bequest for a chapel to the Virgin of the Rosary, Dominican patroness.[181]

This Brotherhood of the Rosary was established by friar Pedro Bedón, a sculptor and painter born in Quito who reached Tunja between 1591 and 1595. Bedón was an enthusiastic devotee of the Virgin of the Rosary, and he was active also with the Rosary *cofradía* in Lima.[65] It is possible that the actual construction and decoration of the chapel in Tunja proceeded under his direction: some detect Quito influence in its interior decoration; and, as will be seen later, Quito as a major spiritual and artistic center did exert considerable influence on many of its neighbors. Details now surviving here, however, can hardly be said to be directly connected with it.

The Rosario chapel (*fig. b*) opens off the left aisle of the church of Santo Domingo. A sheathing of wood painted a deep red and encrusted with gilded medallions softens the outline of the architectural elements, and large-patterned wooden ceilings, decorated with pendent knobs, like fruits, lend the effect of a grotto. On the side walls are panels carved in low relief, framed like paintings and separated by pilasters which, though they probably date from mid-seventeenth century, retain a feeling of the Renaissance.

The main retable (*fig. a*), possibly the latest work in the chapel, is mentioned as nearly finished in 1689. It occupies the entire end wall. Lorenzo Lugo contracted for the eight reliefs from the life of the Virgin, and the sculptor José de Sandoval undertook the tabernacle. To make sure of a good gilder the administrator sent to Bogotá for one Diego de Rojas, and the sculptor Gonzalo Buitraso is recorded as furnishing eight small angels.[172]

The reliefs are placid and somewhat international in tradition; in contrast the framing decoration around them has a remarkable regional flavor. The columns are arranged in sets of threes, with the foremost one in each case composed of figural and floral elements sprouting out of a candelabrum base; interesting also is the very original native version of the spiral column.

The Virgin of the Rosary stands in the center in her *camarín*. This term, meaning "little chamber," sometimes denotes merely her niche and sometimes a small sacristy behind the main altar where the image is tended and decorated. The Colombian interpretation, however, is quite specifically a masonry oriel, built with windows (*see Pl. 29*). Thus the figure stands behind the main line of the altar and is illuminated by natural light from the outside. The effect is highly dramatic.

In this chapel the Virgin's bower is encrusted with heavily gilded flowers and medallions, reflected in fancifully framed mirrors. Here and there little angels—perhaps those furnished by Maestro Buitraso—are playing on musical instruments. At the center of the great gilded medallions are bowls of blue and white porcelain; other ceramic ware is used in the same way in the church nave. The chapel as a whole has a strong Mudéjar feeling, and the retable exemplifies the high quality of the regional craftsmanship here.

One of the side altars in the church of Santo Domingo is inscribed to the effect that Francisco de Ocampo, sculptor, made it in 1609 and Blas Martín Silvestre painted it. This, then, is an authentic Spanish retable; the contract for it, written in Seville and dated 1608, is preserved in that city. It was intended for the Rosario chapel in this church.[27]

It has been asserted repeatedly that the Chibcha Indians, excellent pre-Columbian gold workers of this region, made no significant artistic contribution after the Conquest; the detail of the lower part of the altar in the right aisle of the same church (*fig. c*) makes one wonder. The sun, a symbol of the Godhead, is here as much Indian as Christian; though carved of wood it appears as if cast in pre-Columbian gold. The framing of the face in a rosary, with the cross placed at the top like the emblem in a coronet, is unusual. In the square medallions on either side and in the flowing decoration around the border a finer feeling for the medium—wood—is evident. Both the design and the proportions suggest that the patterns may have been seen on a reliquary or other small object and enlarged to fill the space, a not uncommon practice among native craftsmen, who had no tradition to guide them as to which patterns were more appropriate for a large space and which for a small.

On the red pier of the *arco toral* (triumphal arch) a decorative pillar is outlined in gilded wood, with flamelike motifs darting out at the sides (*fig. d*). Here familiar decorative elements became exotic through the touch of the native artists. Canephorae, or basket carriers, bearing pineapples, grapes, pomegranates, and melons figure prominently in the design, and above the pedestal are two fanciful satyrs seated *contrapposto*. The "tongues of flame" may be an Indianized version of the acanthus that is applied around the arches leading to the Rosario chapel. The dog at the bottom of the pier is fashioned of stucco, an amusing rendition of St. Dominic's symbol.

The Franciscan monastery in Tunja was founded in 1550, and within a quarter of a century a building was standing. This structure caved in and a new one was begun which, despite usual financial difficulties, was finished in the first quarter of the seventeenth century. The church of San Francisco has a high broad nave (*Pl. 24, fig. b*). Two side aisles, much lower in height, lie the other side of the heavy supporting walls. Below the trough-shaped wooden ceiling are beams showing Mudéjar interlacing, and in the corners are ornamental braces in the Mudéjar tradition.

As is frequent in Colombia, the apse is separated from the nave by a wide arch, some-what suggestive of a proscenium arch. Here the polygonal outline of the piers is Mudéjar but the type of the ornamentation is characteristic of Tunja. A great five-part retable fills the entire width of the apse. In the outer panels are figures of the four Church Fathers carved in relief, and in the two inner rows saints of the Franciscan and the Dominican orders stand beneath their respective emblems; statues of the Saviour and the Virgin occupy the central section. Judging from its style this retable probably dates from only a little later than the building; as in many early altars, most of the figures stand out in three-quarters relief from a flat and plain background, heavy with gold.

The pulpit (*fig. a*), which is suspended from the wall, bears polychromed figures in relief against a gilded wood background, and its canopy—no doubt reworked—is carved to imitate drapery, with even tassels suggested. On top, in an ornate circular frame, is a crucifix, so placed that one can look up from the nave and see the face of the gilded stucco Godhead on the wall shining through the circle. The inspiration for this extraordinary symbolism is found in John 3:16: "For God so loved the world, that he gave his only begotten Son, that whosoever believeth in him should not perish, but have everlasting life." The Dove, symbol of the Holy Ghost, poised beneath the canopy above the head of the preacher in reminder of the Pentecost, completes the Trinity. It would seem that the composition was more elaborate before the canvas at the back was added. A Franciscan cord, decorated with the fleur-de-lis, another symbol of the Trinity, is used to frame the entire unit. Below the canvas in the stucco relief can be seen a human figure with upraised arms; it has lost much of its colorful appearance through unskillful repainting.

The church of Santa Clara in Tunja belonged to the first nunnery that was founded in the Kingdom of New Granada. Its cornerstone was laid in 1571, and three years later construction was well under way, with both funds and land provided by the Conquistador Mongua Francisco Salguero and his wife. Like the Rosario chapel of Santo Domingo, this church preserves a remarkable blend of styles in a local interpretation of the Mudéjar. Its interior (*fig. c*), decorated during the seventeenth century, shows a pointed triumphal arch sheathed in gilded wood, Mudéjar rather than Gothic in its effect. Canvases in large frames cover the walls so completely that not an inch of undecorated surface remains. The ceiling is studded with gilded medallions and painted stars. Especially splendid are the medallions on the spandrels of the arch, composed of bunches of grapes and leaves with spiraling tendrils. The rinceau on the arch, with its birds and grapes, has a Byzantine feeling, whereas the type of ceiling and the squinchlike bracket that occupies the corner are strongly Mudéjar. But the double-headed eagle on the bracket is not Mudéjar; nor are the plumelike ornaments that fringe the arch or the composition on the ceiling above, which depicts an angel-guarded Host with a painting of the Crucifixion. Even more original is the apse ceiling (*see Pl. 181*).

The outspoken Hispano-Moorish features apparent in Latin America—the shape of some domes, the manner of construction and decoration of many ceilings, and certain ornamental designs—cannot be explained wholly by the presence there of Moorish artisans, even though the Spanish soldiery shortly after the Conquest is said to have included as many as two hundred converted Mohammedans, some of whom may have been craftsmen.[76] The deep-rooted Moorish tradition of the motherland was still alive also in the minds of those who guided the construction in the New World. Every master carpenter had to be as familiar with Mudéjar interlacing as he was with a coffered wooden ceiling of the Renaissance. An extant book of architectural drawings by the friar Andrés de San Miguel—a Spanish-born architect active in Mexico between 1598 and 1644—contains a comprehensive treatise on Mudéjar joinery.[78] And the regional craftsman of the New World adapted

the Mudéjar style to his need, according to his own taste and technical ability.

In the house of Juan de Vargas, which stands near Santa Clara in the same quarter of Tunja, frescoes are preserved dating from the last third of the sixteenth century. Figures from classical mythology framed in arabesques decorate one hall, and in another room is a display of exotic animals, including the elephant, in the manner of early tapestry work.

The richness of the Tunja district and the importance of the city are borne out by the fact that by 1623 all the major conventual orders had their own establishments here. At that time the archbishop of the colony divided the town into three parishes, the total Spanish population of which was six hundred. It had five large churches, two nunneries, and five small churches and chapels.

The parish church of Santa Barbara was founded in 1599. Its triumphal arch, like many others in this city, is sheathed with gilded wood. These piers also are divided into sectors, each with its own motif. At the spring of the arch is a canephora, which is similar to those on the preceding plate; here the representation of the body is comparatively flat, less emphasized than the various elements that flow above and below it—as if the carver was unaccustomed to bringing out the human figure in such an arrangement. On the broad surface of the pier at the left a column is outlined by spiraling garlands. The triple columns of the altar are a Baroque feature, but otherwise its general spirit is again a frozen Renaissance.

At the time of our visit extensive repairs were in progress. A hole in the ceiling revealed the original type of roofing, a construction of reed and clay (*see Pl. 188*), and a completely new façade was being constructed, disfiguring the colonial beauty of the building.

Little more than fifty miles across the chilly *páramo* from Tunja, in one of the highest valleys of the Cordillera Oriental, lies the village of Monguí at an altitude of over 9,500 feet. Its valley and the surrounding hills were populated long before the Conquest. This region was assigned for evangelization to the Tunja Franciscans.

The first establishment there was comprised of a chapel for the Indians and a rest house for the missionaries who worked in the region. Later, in the first half of the seventeenth century, it would seem that a church was erected, but this fell into such disrepair that in 1702 a royal permit was issued for a new church building and an adjoining monastery. It took about three decades, however, before the work was started (the contract was signed in 1733), and the natives of the valley as well as the friars contributed money and labor. Martín Polo Caballero was the master architect,[168] and under his direction the complex was completed in the 1760's.

The vast church has an impressive approach by reason of the stairways which ascend from three sides (Pl. 25, fig. a); this type of entrance will be seen on the more pretentious church of San Francisco in Quito (see Pl. 98). The central part of the façade, flanked by two massive towers, is composed with restraint, its low heavy scale recalling the Romanesque. A bit of fine stone tracery fills the small round window between the segments of the broken pediment, and a crucifix is placed at the apex. The coats of arms at the sides of the arched windows show the insignia of the Franciscan order of Spain combined with that of the proud city of Tunja. This section of the façade, which is built of stone, terminates in a peak like a gable. The upper section, of brick, appears to be of a later date. The builders probably followed a prototype for the lower part, but in the remainder they seem to have developed the plan on the spot as work progressed.

One of the great heraldic shields on the towers gives 1699 as the year when they were begun. Their stone bases furnish an interesting contrast in texture and color to the brick of the belfries. The projecting stone brackets were seemingly intended to support a gallery (see Pls. 92, 109). Noteworthy is the use of twin columns on the belfries, a contemporary Baroque element in a structure which is rather retarded in its general style.

This matter of time lag is still more pronounced when we look down on the building from the rear (fig. d). A cruciform plan is evident. Note the extended nave and the manner of constructing the transepts, the lantern, and the apse, which is like a separate lean-to.

In the interior the church is divided by three aisles. A number of large paintings by the famous Colombian Gregorio Vásquez, signed and dated 1671, decorates the walls. An unusual picture in this church is presented in Chapter 12 (see Pl. 149).

That this is not an isolated instance in which devices from earlier periods were employed in the eighteenth century is shown in the architecture of the parish church at Leíva, like Monguí in the department of Boyacá (fig. b). Lying in a valley between two mountain ranges which separate the towns of Tunja and Chiquinquirá, this community boasted a lively market place even in pre-Columbian times. In 1573 the Indian chiefs who held sway over the region were asked to gather contributions for the erection of a church. At that time the town had about one hundred and fifty Spanish residents, who owned large cattle ranches and sugar plantations; cotton and henequen also were grown in the protected valley. The façade of the present building is extremely simple, almost without ornament, and the tower massive. Seemingly space was left on the other side for a second tower. The platform, reconstructed with cement, unfortunately has completely lost its colonial character.

The rear section in this photograph provides an illuminating study of the manner of construction. A roof of heavy tile covers most durable timber, and the dome, flanked in Byzantine manner with half-domes on the transept sides, is constructed of wattle and daub.

In the capital city of Bogotá the Jesuits started building their church and college in 1605, one year after their installation there. Among the first friars was the Italian Juan Bautista Coluccini, born in Lucca. He is described as a man of literary talent, versed in the astronomy of the day; his observations were the first recognized studies of the starry heavens above the colonies. He also had a knowledge of architecture, and to him is credited the construction of the church of San Ignacio, seen here from the patio of the former college (*fig. c*). The main part seems to have been under way by 1625, and the building was dedicated in 1635, before its completion. By 1639 the side chapels were in the process of building, with some of them even then serving as mausoleums for the city's aristocracy.[169] In this church stands the celebrated altar carving, the Ecstasy of St. Ignatius (*see Pl. 56*). The main retable, the pulpit, and the choir stalls are mainly the work of the Jesuit friar Luisinch, whose Slavic name is a revealing bit of evidence that different national strains contributed to the blend that is colonial art.

According to tradition the plans for this structure came from Rome—a statement made about nearly every Jesuit building in Latin America. But only a glance is needed to convince one that this shallow cap above a high drum has little in common with the elegant hemispherical domes of Roman Baroque. In contrast to the European Baroque churches, which were constructed mainly of stone, San Ignacio in Bogotá is of brick. Together with the examples shown from Monguí and Leíva, it calls to mind those early small churches in the Balkans and the Near East which still survive from a pre-Baroque era. Such a linking with Rome serves only to blind one to the true values of local achievement. It is to the everlasting credit of the colonial builders that with the labor and material available they were able to raise such substantial and tasteful

edifices; they had to modify—sometimes radically—the building methods which they knew and often had to invent new ways and means to satisfy their needs.

Bogotá was founded in 1538 by Gonzalo Jiménez de Quesada, a man of letters as well as one of the most daring figures of the Conquest. He came up from the coast in search of the head waters of Colombia's largest river, named by the white men the Magdalena. After months of hardship, during which three-quarters of his army perished, he arrived with one hundred and sixty-six ragged and starving men on the plains of Bogotá—or Bacactá as it was originally called, after the Chibcha chief of the territory—8,660 feet above sea level. One year later two other famous Conquistadores arrived, Sebastián de Belalcázar, coming from Peru, and the German Nicholas Federman, who followed a branch of the Orinoco from Venezuela. The settlement grew rapidly, enlarged by the newcomers and the colonists who followed after them. By the end of the sixteenth century Bogotá was already regarded as a cultural center, especially after 1564, when it became the seat of the captaincy-general for this region of South America. In 1717 it was made the capital of the newly formed Viceroyalty of New Granada and achieved even greater prominence. However, Bogotá was the most difficult of the viceregal centers to approach and the time lag, general in the arts throughout the colonies, is even more noticeable here.

Few examples of the first century of the city's colonial architecture still exist. For this reason its church of San Francisco is of great importance, especially so because it has preserved sculpture in wood and paintings from that period. The letter of endowment for this church is dated 1569, but a half-century passed before the work was finished inside and out. Like most of Bogotá's churches it is serene in spirit and its brownish stone exterior carries restrained decoration (*Pl. 26, fig. a*). It has only one tower—stepped slightly forward—which was erected in late eighteenth century to replace the original one that fell in the earthquake of 1785. The single entrance is flanked by coupled columns bearing medallions in very low relief at the base of the shafts and on the pedestals and is topped by a large window that lights the choir. The scalloped espadaña is finished with a heavy coping surmounted by finials.

Within, the nave is broad (fig. b), with an aisle on the right and a deep side chapel on the left near the sacristy. The choir gallery—from which this photograph was taken—still retains its fine ceiling of Mudéjar tracery, and the gilded pendant at the top of the illustration is a remnant of the elaborate decoration that once covered the nave. In 1751 glass windows were installed in the roof, an ingenious solution for increasing the light.

The use of two large pulpits, one on either side of the apse, is rare; their heavy domed baldachins are surmounted by life-size statues. The apse itself, which gives the appearance of a separate room behind the triumphal arch, is lined with gilded and polychromed reliefs in wood; only the central section above the altar has statues in the round placed in niches. This vast work was contracted for in 1623, after the design of Ignacio García de Ascucha, a native of Asturias, Spain, and was created under his supervision.[170] Ascucha, born in 1580, arrived in the New World at the turn of the century, fleeing from Spain because of a marital scandal. His design for the altar in the cathedral won for him, in 1620, a commission for work on one of the side chapels of the Franciscan church and, finally, the contract for the great retable. He had an atelier in the district of Las Nieves, the artists' quarter of the city, with creole masters as assistants and slaves as apprentices. In 1629 he died suddenly, long before the work was completed, and he now lies at the foot of his own masterpiece. A deposition made a year before his death to the guardian of the Franciscan monastery has preserved his story. Lorenzo Hernández de la Camara, a native of Argamasilla,

in La Mancha, contracted for the polychroming of the retable in 1633.

One section of this famed retable shows its general build-up (fig. c). Biblical scenes make up the bottom row of panels, including the Flight, the Baptism of Jesus, the Martyrdom of St. Catherine, and Jerome in the Wilderness (see also Pl. 58). It is a question whether Ascucha himself carved these or only designed them and executed some of the architectural decoration. The second tier is devoted to women saints—a rare occurrence—which were carved by Ascucha's followers, and the third contains the Apostles, in half-length, attributed to a Franciscan lay brother of the seventeenth century. The marked simplification of the content, as well as the reduction in size, of the upper carvings sets off the rich and lively plasticity of the lowest group. The double columns that separate the reliefs are classically cool, showing a spiral fluting rather than the Baroque twist.

In the sacristy of this church stands an altar dedicated to St. Joseph (fig. d), which is quite different in concept. The wardrobes and other furniture there are dated 1618, but the retable appears to be later. A figure of St. Joseph holding the Christ Child, his flowering staff in his hand, occupies the only niche. Angels are seated in the broken pediment, and above, in a sweeping semicircular band, is an unusual composition of the Annunciation, showing Gabriel on the left, Mary on the lower right, and in the center God the Father, who is turned toward her. Paintings by Vásquez of the annunciation to Joseph and of his death are incorporated into the piece. While a classicizing tendency can be discerned in the decoration of the apse just discussed, this retable bears the impress of colonial Baroque. It is, however, a rather literal application of the Baroque, for although prescribed elements of the style are present they do not produce the rich complexity and the sweeping drama which are apparent in examples to be seen later in this volume.

At the time of our visit in 1945 the demolition of this colonial landmark—unique in all Latin America—was being considered to permit the widening of the street. Rather than harm a recent building across the way, aesthetically of no value, it was proposed to tear down the church and transfer the more important works of art to the colonial museum. In 1948 a revolutionary mob attacked and destroyed several monuments of the city, but fortunately the church was harmed little. Doubtless, however, it will be endangered periodically until the general public is educated to take pride in it as a precious legacy from the past.

Although permission to found the first Dominican monastery and church in Bogotá was granted in 1550, the earliest portion of the complex (*Pl. 27, fig. a*) probably does not antedate 1619. In 1761 a fire destroyed the interior of the church and also parts of the monastery. The work of restoration, under the direction of the Capuchin friar Pérez de Petres, took from 1792 to 1817. In the latter year, during an earthquake, the dome collapsed; it was rebuilt on the original drum in neo-Renaissance style by Pedro Cantini and Eugenio López.[49] It was in this church that the Great Colombian Congress was held upon the return of Simón Bolívar from Venezuela in 1827; the building is still in use. Sections of its walls, some of them visible in the photograph, survive from the early epoch.

The seventeenth-century cloister, with its wide arches and slender coupled columns, has a Mudéjar feeling. In the nineteenth century the monastery became the property of the state and was used to house the main post office. Situated as it was in a densely settled portion of the city, at the junction of the busiest thoroughfares, its central location sealed its fate, and in the 1930's it was demolished to make way for a large modern building. Newspapers, magazines, and cultural societies all protested in vain; for seldom are humanists victorious over commercial and political interests anywhere on earth.

The much smaller monastery of San Juan de Dios—the Hospitalers—with its church (*fig. d*), was finished as early as 1635, but it was twice enlarged in the first half of the eighteenth century after being damaged by earthquakes. Friar Juan Antonio de Guzmán is noted [169] for his untiring efforts in the refurbishing of the building (1729-1757). Today the church boasts several good paintings as well as sculpture and, despite neglect, a well-preserved ceiling, barrel-vaulted in wood and studded with gilded ornaments. The cloister, which was being torn down at the time of our visit in 1945, had a colonnade that recalled the Mudéjar, like the Dominican cloister above. Dormer windows, unusual in that they were constructed of glass on three sides, made the attic floor livable; they must have been added when glass was plentiful, perhaps even manufactured in the colony. A similar type of construction can still be seen in the convent of Santa Teresa in Cuzco, Peru.

In Bogotá, as in Tunja, some church interiors have preserved an opulence of gilded woodwork, even though the exteriors have been modernized. Usually the ceilings show a characteristic ornamentation, with diaper patterns echoing Renaissance designs. The church of La Candelaria, or Purification, which has such a ceiling, stands in a quarter as yet little disturbed by modernization. It is surrounded by one-story colonial dwellings that boast imposing stone portals and spacious inside patios; on the same square is the house in which Vásquez lived, worked, and died. Most of the interior decoration of this church is said to have been finished in 1703; in impression it is late Renaissance. Diego Sánchez de Montemayor was in charge of the work.[170] The detail of the ceiling illustrated here (*fig. e*) is the under side of the unusually deep choir loft, which is located just above the entrance. In the pattern a leafy motif is effectively paired with a compact medallion. (From this church comes the Pietà that is shown on *Pl. 88*.)

The construction of the church of San

Diego was begun in 1607 as a Franciscan *recoleta*, or retreat; it was dedicated to San Diego de Alcalá.[169] Built on the site of a summer villa it lay some distance from the capital in an idyllic spot on the Tunja road. In its plain walls and unornamented portal is revealed the intention of modest and contemplative living. The church came to public notice when miraculous powers were attributed to a small unfinished statue of the Virgin there, sculptured by Juan de Cabrera. A chapel was dedicated to the image—called the Virgin of the Fields—and the people flocked to the place, bearing valuable gifts. The worldly viceroy Solís y Folch de Cardona, who took office in 1753, lavished his devotion upon this figure. He ordered elaborate silver vessels from Quito for the chapel, donated Brussels lace and splendid garments for the Virgin's adornment, and into the seventeenth-century altar had a *camarín* constructed, an exquisite Rococo salon.

A detail from this chamber (*fig. c*) shows a palm tree in gilded wood as principal motif placed against a lacquered cream-colored background. The spacing is airy, and the individual motifs are kept separate in accordance with Rococo taste; mirrors are used as part of the design. The palm tree as a motif—here suggestive of the phrase "Quasi palma . . ." from the Psalms—has already been encountered in stone on the façade of Comayagua's cathedral and in stucco on the dome of the Sagrario there (*see Pl. 6*).

The Marqués de Solís, an intimate friend of Ferdinand VI, continued to lead as profligate and adventurous a life after he was appointed a viceroy in the New World as he had in Madrid. So firmly entrenched in royal favor was he that the king, though admonishing him publicly to avoid further scandal, privately sent him assurances of confidence and friendship. The most famous of his love affairs, that with the creole María Lutgarda de Espina (called La Marichuela), was the talk of two continents.[41] After her heyday Doña María retired, in 1758, to the nunnery of Santa Clara.

And three years later the viceroy withdrew to the Franciscan monastery nearby, abandoning his high office and living out his days as the friar José de Jesús María. He made the donations described above in the year of his retirement from public office.

In the list of Solís' gifts are mentioned porcelains taken from his own house. At that time such ware was an object of great interest and the possession of it a mark of distinction. Majolica and porcelain were all the rage in the early eighteenth century; in Europe and even in some colonial centers excellent and frequently original ware was produced. It was used for both exterior and interior decoration, as well as for the table. If whole rooms could not be lined with it, as in the porcelain salons of Aranjuez, Dresden, and Schönbrunn, plaques and single pieces were featured, framed in panels of gilded wood. Such medallions are found in Colombia, especially in *camarines*, where the decorative effect of the colored design is enhanced by brilliant illumination.

In the example illustrated here (*fig. b*) a bowl in two shades of blue on white is set off by an elaborate frame of carved and gilded wood; allegedly this piece came from a Tunja church, now demolished (*see also Pl. 23*). It is not of Chinese, Spanish, or colonial provenience, as was variously suggested; the brush mark on the back is unclear, but the Delft Museum in Holland has identified it as delftware of the type called "little pancake" and dated it as from mid-eighteenth century. It is not hard porcelain but earthenware with a tin enamel glaze.[165]

Articles of majolica, including all kinds of tile, were produced in the Low Countries as early as the sixteenth century. About 1560 or 1570, potters from Antwerp, as Protestant refugees, fled to Holland and England, and within a hundred years the Dutch city of Delft had become famous for its pottery. Until the end of the eighteenth century the thriving export trade of the Delft potter supplied a large market. Designs were borrowed from contemporary Chinese work, which was imported in quantity by the Dutch East India Company. A close imitation of Chinese patterns characterizes many types of eighteenth-century delft, and often as many as five colors appear in a single piece. Holland had then long been a leader in commerce and her trade relations with the Iberian Peninsula were already centuries old. Although Portugal produced a high-grade ware of its own, Dutch tiles were used in that country to such an extent that a student of Dutch tile pictures must visit there to obtain a comprehensive view of the subject; contemporary Italy also, though a prolific manufacturer of ceramic objects, imported Dutch ware. For often an article created in a foreign land has a greater fascination than a home product. As early as the reign of Philip II the Spanish crown granted to a number of Dutch, Genoese, English, Flemish, and French merchants the privilege of establishing trading agencies in Cadiz; and that port held the monopoly of commerce to the New World from 1720 to 1765. Dutch merchants carried inexpensive delftware to Latin America as ballast for their nearly empty outward-bound ships also from the home harbors of Rotterdam and Delfshaven and sold it there for any good offer they could get. Thus this blue and white bowl attained such a splendid and exotic application in a remote corner of Latin America, so distant from its place of origin. Declared "Talavera" in the catalogue of the Bogotá museum, it provides another clear instance of non-Spanish artistic influence in the colonies.[179]

Popayán lies in the fertile Pubenza Valley in southwestern Colombia and enjoys a broad view of mountain peaks—some of them volcanoes—veiled in a dark blue haze. This was a rich territory and its climate pleasing, but so remote that up to mid-seventeenth century most bishops refused an appointment to the see or managed to stay away from it. Though a main station on the overland route from Cartagena to Lima, it was separated from

both capitals by a dismaying series of mountain ridges and deep valleys. Today the visitor walking about the streets finds white marble tablets on numerous houses, inscribed with names prominent in its colonial history or in its struggle for independence.

This city was founded in 1536 by the Conquistador Balalcázar, and four years later it became the administrative seat for the whole province. Since it belonged to Peru until 1717, it is not surprising that artistic influences came first from Peru, by way of Quito, and only later from Bogotá. But throughout its entire colonial existence the city manifested a degree of artistic independence.

Popayán's extant colonial monuments date, in the main, from mid-eighteenth century, for in 1736 a severe earthquake all but destroyed it. Apparently the rebuilding of the church of Santo Domingo (*Pl. 28, fig. d*) was started soon after the catastrophe, since the keystone in the entrance arch carries the date 1741. Its monolithic solidity, heavy tower base, and deep portal reflect the caution born of the disaster. With lighter material and more modest bulk, the structure was completed in 1750.

The gray-brown stone of the portal stands out sharply from the whitewashed walls. It has a double broken pediment: the central one, with its heavy engaged columns, is echoed by another on a recessed plane. A central window with a flaring frame fills the space in the curve of the pediment, seeming to depress it. The candelabrum effect of the columns—a Platersque feature—is most unusual at that late date. Simple but powerful regional motifs are carved in the stonework, each one set off by itself and thereby given individual emphasis. Today the University of Cauca is housed in the former monastery adjoining it at the right.

The church of San Francisco in Popayán was begun in 1775 under the regional architect Antonio García and was completed about twenty years later; the tower, joining the church with the former monastery, is a twentieth-century addition. In its bell is fifty pounds of gold, the gift of early benefactors.[178]

A blend of styles can be observed in the façade (*fig. a*). It is not the retable type. It has sets of twin columns, but they do not frame niches and their ornamentation—medallions in low relief—is confined to the lower portions of the shafts. The pilasters are even more subdued in line, and the niches are shallow and few. Obelisks top the two tiers of plain columns. In general the façade lacks the protruding or strongly curving masses of the Baroque. The undecorated panels and the touches of ornament above the niches and on the column shafts, as well as the elliptical windows, lean toward the Rococo. Note that there are three doorways.

In the outlines of the façade is revealed the plan of the interior: a very high nave, with clerestory and excellent lighting, and low side aisles roofed over with domical vaults. The spacious effect is augmented by the barrel vault of the vestibule (*fig. c*); above it masonry brackets, clean in construction and varied in outline, support the curving edge of the choir loft.

The pulpit in this church (*fig. b*) has the shape of a chalice. It is exquisitely homogeneous in detail throughout, its canopy matching it like the cover of some goldsmith's masterpiece. On the top stands a statue of St. Francis, and smaller figures of Franciscan saints, preaching with book and gesture, occupy the niches around the sides. The monotone coloring of their habits accentuates the shining richness of the gilded surfaces. Among the many felicitous details perhaps the angel heads connected with the leafy volutes in the canopy and on the lower section of the pulpit are the most outstanding. In the style of its carving this pulpit is closely related to one in the church of San Diego in Quito, Ecuador (*see Pl. 183*), and might date, with it, from the second quarter of the eighteenth century. The balustrade of the Popayán pulpit is shown in a later chapter, as is also the statue which stands in the *camarín* of the main altar (*see Pls. 182, 79*).

That architectural feature so often encountered in colonial churches in Colombia, the *camarín*, has already been discussed and illustrated as a part of a church interior (*see Pls. 23, 27*). An outside view of the *camarín* of La Encarnación (*Pl. 29, fig. c*), the church of the Augustinian nunnery in Popayán, shows how ingeniously the oriel was devised to illuminate the main statue on the altar; sunlight shines through one or another of the three windows nearly every hour of the day. This nunnery was founded in 1590 and reconstructed in 1743. To what extent such *camarines* were used in the other colonies is not definitely known—evidence of one, its windows cemented over in the twentieth century, was found by this author in La Merced at León, Nicaragua. In Spain *camarines* constructed in this manner are rare today.

The Moorish spirit is manifest in the buildings from Cartago and Cali shown on this plate. Until early in the twentieth century Cali was just another quiet colonial town populated by prosperous landowners. It lies about a hundred miles north of Popayán, its ancient colonial rival, in the fertile Cauca Valley. Early in the seventeenth century it had one parish church and Mercedarian and Augustinian establishments.

The Augustinian house was founded in 1581 and within two decades a monastery was functioning. In mid-seventeenth century the monks began the construction of a chapel to Nuestra Señora de la Gracia (*fig. d*). Originally a tower stood on one side, but in 1925 it was in such disrepair that it had to be pulled down. The chapel was built of adobe and had a façade of large uneven bricks, the irregular courses of which produced an unusual play of light. In the three niches were statues of the Virgin, Augustine, and St. Thomas of Villanueva, all of which, like the medallions, are of terra cotta. Probably the sculpture was once polychromed and glazed, and glazed tiles may have embellished the dado. Note the wrought-iron grille in the center window and the Augustinian arms above the door. This façade shows an interesting manifestation of the Mudéjar which is greatly accentuated by the material—brick. The exotic line of the arch over the door is sharply defined by the ceramic molding, increasing the stage-design effect of the whole.

This Augustinian establishment functioned for years as an educational center under the colonial regime, and afterward it continued as a college under the name of Santa Librada, the patroness of national independence. Upon our visit in 1945 the building still stood as here pictured, but a few months later it, like so many others, gave way before the advance of city planning. Fortunately its statues and medallions were rescued by Manuel María Buenaventura, in whose private collection at Cali they are now preserved.

With the passing of the craftsmen who had had direct contact with the Mudéjar tradition in the homeland—roughly after the first century of the more substantial construction in the New World—interest in Mudéjar forms and decoration lapsed. But by mid-eighteenth century, when a well-established colonial society was requiring new buildings and beginning to enlarge and refurbish old ones, designers with an enriched imagination and hands technically less restricted not only reached out for Rococo patterns but also revived the Mudéjar, which blended colorfully into the cityscape of the day. A contemporary revival of Mudéjar was also taking place in some of the affluent cities of southern Spain.

This neo-Mudéjar style is recorded in the tower of San Francisco at Cali (*fig. b*). To that town in the 1740's came a friar from Quito, one Fernando de Jesús Larrea (who signed himself "Rhea"). So eloquently did he preach that he was implored to stay and help with a Franciscan foundation.[185] In 1757 a royal permit authorized the establishment of a mission college, and by 1764 a new convent was ready and the church was more or less completed. Its tower of rosy brick picked out with glazed tiles of peacock-blue and green

is one of the notable examples of the neo-Mudéjar in the New World. Especially fine is the pattern of the tiles, which around the belfry window suggests columnettes and above, in a honeycomb design, provides a contrasting background for the light-colored multifoil arch. The church itself, finished later than the tower, was built from plans said to have been made by Pedro de la Cruz Herrera; the interior is modern.

Cartago was founded in 1540 by Jorge Robledo, a subordinate of Belalcázar and a Spanish gentleman of high rank. Perhaps it was because of his breeding and education that he showed an uncommonly humane attitude toward the natives. These natives were of the Quimbaya people, who ranked among the finest of the pre-Columbian workers in cast gold. From them Robledo's men obtained quantities of the precious metal in breastplates and ornaments without the violence and bitter coercion so often employed. This region drew upon mines as well as alluvial gold deposits, and it grew even wealthier from its cattle husbandry and its cocoa, sugar, tobacco, and—later—coffee plantations.

The church of Guadalupe in Cartago (*fig. a*) was finished in 1810 under the direction of Mariano Ormuza y Matute, a hero in the fight for independence.[171] Its façade presents certain familiar elements and exhibits the romantic attitude—especially in the feeling for nuances in light and shade—which produced the neo-Mudéjar. Its plain wall surface and the absence of ornament bear witness to the fact that the Baroque age was past. Deeply set round openings as well as arched doors placed into rectangular frames, in the Mudéjar manner, have already been seen; but their arrangement in this façade is quite individual. Unusual, too, is the angular build-up of the espadaña; the very thick middle section virtually forms a central tower.

Ecuador, Colombia's neighbor to the southwest, was also a part of the Viceroyalty of New Granada; but the highly original colonial art of this country swings more toward the Peruvian—if indeed it can be linked with that of any neighbor—because of a long association under Lima's authority. Its architecture therefore will be presented in Chapter 10.

Colombia's eastern neighbor, Venezuela, was also called Nueva Andalucia in colonial times. According to one explanation the name Venezuela (little Venice) was given to this land because the natives' dwellings around Lake Maracaibo were set over the water on piles. This region boasted no great mineral wealth or high indigenous culture in pre-Columbian times, and the development of its colonial art never reached the full tide of splendor found in some of the other colonies. Its churches, like those of provincial Colombia, are generally mild and serene.

The participation of non-Spanish Europeans in both the Conquest and the colonization of Spanish America is an interesting side path that has never been fully explored. In the open as well as behind the scenes many foreigners loosened their purse strings and in consequence were in a position to demand favors. Among these were two great German banking houses. The first, the Fuggers of Augsburg, was connected with the network of the Medicis. Another family, the Welsers, also operating in that Bavarian city, became their rivals in both banking and trade. In 1473 four Welser brothers founded a trading company, and by 1490 they were the sole lessees of silver mines in Tyrol. As business prospered, they established a house in Lisbon, Portugal. Then, interested in the East India spice trade, they invested twenty thousand florins—to the Fuggers four thousand—in a vast expedition undertaken in 1505, which seems to have been equipped by German and Italian merchants.[46] The story of their rise and fall gives an insight into the way the New World monopolies operated.

With the ascendancy of the Habsburgs to the Spanish throne both of these German banking houses entered the scene, providing money for the opening and exploitation of the colonies across the sea. Charles V of the Holy Roman Empire tried to keep Portuguese and French participants out of his overseas enterprises, but for many reasons he welcomed the nationals of other countries. The immense resources of the New World came to the Spanish crown somewhat as a surprise; at the end of the fifteenth century Spain was not the most eminent of the seafaring nations nor were her bankers and traders the most skillful at playing the high international stakes of their professions. Through Habsburg connections entrepreneurs from the Low Countries and the German provinces often were able to reach out and with their long, greedy, and sometimes bloody fingers turn the machinery which—though creaking and inordinately wasteful—ground out vast wealth from the New World.

At that time the Welser family had houses or factories in Nuremberg, Danzig, Venice, Milan, Rome, Genoa, Fribourg, Bern, Zurich, Lyons, Seville, and Saragossa; they even owned land in the Canary Islands. In due time they opened an office in Santo Domingo and acquired an interest in the silver mines of Mexico. Further, they had a share in the Pedro de Mendoza expedition, which resulted in the discovery of the Rio de la Plata, Argentina. For a loan of a hundred thousand ducats they obtained the right to explore and settle the territory of Venezuela. Thus they secured footholds in the Tierra Firme, where they hoped to find wealth to outrival Mexico's. Already the pearl fisheries off the coast of Venezuela were being ruthlessly exploited. In 1529 a Welser agent in Santo Domingo is reported to have bought for 450 gold pesos a pearl the size of a pear, which had been taken from Venezuelan waters. Shortly after, at their own expense, the Welsers outfitted the caravels that were to go to Venezuela. Fifty skilled German miners were included in the expedition so that gold and silver could be extracted as efficiently as possible. The leader, Ambrose Alfinger—actually Ehinger—a creation of the Welsers, was appointed governor and captain general for life with a high salary. In 1529 he took over the command from one Juan de Ampiés, who until then had been the head of the small Spanish settlement in Coro, founded only about two years earlier. Relations between the local Indians and this Spaniard had been peaceful, and much help had been given his administration by them.[173] But the zeal with which the new German governor exploited the district made him so hated by Indian and Spaniard alike that by the time the grant to the Welsers was canceled in 1556, the name of Alfinger had become synonymous with unspeakable cruelty. For the sake of rounding out the story it should be added that Alfinger was killed by a poisoned arrow in Colombia, having just missed the fabulous lands of both Colombia and Peru, and the Welser "empire" collapsed in bankruptcy before the end of the sixteenth century.

Coro, Venezuela, lies on a secluded bay of the Gulf of Maracaibo, and not without reason was it given its name: wind. But the ceaseless trade winds were the least damaging of the many turbulent experiences that were visited upon these hot sun-beaten shores. The town finally was burned by the English privateer Amyas Preston, who, in 1595, also sacked Caracas. It never fully recovered, and in the first quarter of the seventeenth century it is described as on the down grade. At that time it had only about a hundred Spanish residents, a Franciscan monastery, and a cathedral which even then was about to be transferred to the rising city of Caracas. Thus in the accelerating tempo of colonial life Coro was left behind.

In this ancient town the Casa de las Ventanas de Hierro (house of the iron windows), dating from about mid-eighteenth century (Pl. 30, fig. a), delights the visitor with its individuality. On the portal of this rambling one-story building interesting provincial echoes of Baroque are evident in the twin columns that flank the door and in the shell design, which, spread out like a fan, crowns the whole. The projecting decoration on the extrados of the arch is both unusual and picturesque.

Unusual too are the huge lively volutes at the corner of the same house (fig. c). The illustration shows a grilled window with an anvil-shaped base, somewhat like those at Cartagena (see Pl. 22). It is this iron grillework which gave the house its name. Caracas also, as well as Trujillo, Peru, and some coastal towns of Brazil, is notable for its ironwork, a contrast to the usual wood.

In Venezuela, as elsewhere, tall espadañas were favored to give a church façade greater height and dignity. In the parish church of Turmero (fig. b) we encounter an espadaña of two stories, largely free-standing and remarkably thin, with niches for statuary (compare Pl. 71); especially striking are the curves of the side sections. The three doorways here, each with a window above it, occupy nearly all the space of the lowest tier, a tendency that will be noticed later in Brazilian architecture.

Like the Coro house, the Turmero church was constructed by local labor. An account of Bishop Mariano Marti's visit to these regions in 1781 reports that it was then in the process of building, a structure of adobe and rubble with a timber roof covered with tiles.[175] For Alexander von Humboldt, who traveled through this village in the first years of the nineteenth century, it was a fine edifice but overloaded with architectural ornament, an observation that shows how taste has changed in the century and a half since his neoclassic period.[59]

Humboldt describes Turmero as set among plantations of sugar, indigo, cotton, and coffee and laid out with a regularity in plan which reminded him that it owed its origin to monks and missions. The village is near Maracay in a district rich in memories of Bolívar.

The purely decorative use of columns applied tight against the wall, without pediments, can be observed not only in various parts of Spanish America but also in the Philippine Islands, as the church in Laöag shows (fig. d). Here the columns, terminating in small urns, are ranged across the façade like giant candles.

The low drawn-out plan suggests somewhat the church in Subtiava, Nicaragua (*see Pl. 75*), but close observation will reveal differences, especially in the treatment of the openings and the angle of the roof.

Spanish colonial architecture in the Philippine Islands has been little photographed and still less studied. During the three centuries and more of Spanish occupation there, immense wealth was accumulated, partly through the development of agriculture and still more through commerce with the Asiatic mainland and Europe, most of it via the Americas. Manila was founded in 1572, and in 1815 the last of the privileged Spanish merchant ships sailed out of its harbor. In the interim Spanish Baroque spread through the islands, but it was much modified. Native building methods introduced change, as did also the use of wood, cane, thatch, and other tropical materials. Tropical flora furnished new motifs to be ornately carved in stone. The sumptuous church interiors were decorated with treasures, many of them brought from China and Japan, so that local artisans could draw for inspiration not only on their own land and on Europe but also on their Oriental neighbors.

An early study of the great number of colonial buildings that once stood on the eleven large islands and the hundreds of smaller ones which make up the Philippine archipelago would have greatly enriched art history. It is to be hoped that the damage wrought by World War II was not so extensive that this phase of Spanish colonial art will pass into oblivion, unexplored and unrecorded.

6

SOME MEXICAN GEMS

Mexico is a world in itself, varied in its topography, climate, and peoples. Before the arrival of Cortés the territory belonged to a number of Indian nations, including the Maya, a people who attained the highest level of artistic development in the Western Hemisphere. The individuality, refinement, and technical skill revealed in the pre-Columbian art of this country are beginning to be recognized and appreciated in ever-widening circles.

Of all the mainland colonies, Mexico—which, with much of Central America, comprised the Viceroyalty of New Spain—was perhaps the most closely connected with the motherland and Europe. Hither in the wake of the Conquistadores came craftsmen and artists and with them artistic influences from the Old World. The road up to the capital from Veracruz, Mexico's great fortified port on the Caribbean, was only 265 miles, and the distance from the capital west to Acapulco, which boasted one of the best harbors on the rocky coastline of the Pacific, was only a few miles more. Thus the city found itself a midway station on the trade route between Spain and her colonies in the Philippines. And to the artistic language of Christianity—which here from the beginning incorporated slumbering impulses of pre-Columbian cultures—were added influences from the Orient. Small wonder that from a meeting of these civilizations, each virile and distinctive, an artistic blend evolved which, through its vitality and

diversity, enchants all who come in contact with it. Though the art here mirrors several stages of European styles it always retains its definitely Mexican temperament.

The vast mineral and agricultural wealth of this viceroyalty induced a spectacular achievement in architecture and the other arts during the colonial period, an adequate discussion of which would require a whole series of volumes. For this book, examples revealing the wide variety of artistic activity were selected, either because they are highly characteristic of Mexico or are stunning displays of Baroque and Rococo. Our first illustrations were drawn from the sixteenth-century styles, in which the later manifestations had their roots.

The Indian did not yield peacefully either to the customs or to the persuasions of his conqueror. Countless is the number of civil and ecclesiastic workers for Spain who lost their lives during the period of pacification. Every growing town had its garrison, but even then violence and outbreak could not be prevented. The arid plateaus which radiated from the capital were a wilderness, topographically as well as spiritually. There monasteries began to rise, often under the supervision of only a handful of friars. The actual labor was performed by Indians from the subjugated regions, while beyond the unexplored hills the eyes of fierce and unconquered blood relatives watched.

In that stark landscape the sturdy stone

walls and massive towers of these religious establishments constitute a rare artistic manifestation. Something of the atmosphere of medieval Europe envelops the visitor who stands in their now abandoned cloisters. Built in a style often compounded of Romanesque, Gothic, and Renaissance elements, they evoke, even as empty shells, a spirit of the asceticism, self-sacrifice, and fanatic zeal which characterized the lives of the missionaries who once lived there. It should be remarked that many monasteries as mighty as fortresses were erected in Mexico around mid-sixteenth century; in South America few traces of this "fortress" type of building can be found, although parallel circumstances existed in certain regions, especially in the Andean Highlands, where large groups of Indians were only superficially converted and remained recalcitrant until the end of the colonial period.

The Augustinian order was one of the first three to evangelize Mexico, and their monasteries, erected in regions assigned to them by the crown, attest to their artistic as well as their religious activities. Not bound by a vow of poverty, as were the Franciscans, they were famous for the grand scale of their buildings.

The Augustinian monastery of Yuririapúndaro, founded in 1550 in the colonial province of San Nicolás de Tolentino de Michoacán and now lying in the state of Guanajuato, was an outpost among the bellicose Chichimec Indians. The place takes its name—Lake of Blood—not from any sanguinary battle but because of the brilliant flowers that float on the waters in the spring. The conventual church and its monolithic tower (Pl. 31, fig. a) dominate the landscape; adjoining it (on the left) is the huge complex that was once the monastery. The buildings were constructed somewhat after mid-sixteenth century under the supervision of the friar Diego de Chávez, a relative of the Conquistador Pedro de Alvarado. Pedro del Toro, from the same region in Spain—the Estremadura—is mentioned as architect.[127] The magnitude of the

undertaking was protested in the Mexican capital but apparently to little avail. On several occasions the massive structure provided refuge for Spaniards and faithful Indians.

Forbidding and sober, the crenellations along the top of the church wall and on the tower contrast sharply with the playful overall decoration of the main façade (fig. b). Out of the verbose Plateresque, the contemporary style in Spain, a limited number of motifs was chosen here; expanded and blown up, they were applied with a highly decorative effect. Flanking the door are pairs of ornate candelabrum columns. Sirens with women's heads and the bodies of birds are carved on the lowest sections; this symbol, a favorite with the Augustinians in Europe, is rarely found in Latin America. At the sides stand statues of Peter and Paul, not in niches but on corbeled bases and under baldachins in the Gothic manner; the carved scrolls bear Latin inscriptions. The spandrels contain round medallions carrying the type of cherub head already seen. A projecting cornice separates the lower story from the section above, though the vertical lines of the columns are continued in the four canephora figures. Musicians stand in the triple niche above the doorway. On either side of the single window a large quatrefoil medallion, sprouting leaves and flowers, features an angel carrying a bow and arrow. The ribbon-like tracery reminds one of Gothic *phylacteria* (message scrolls) or the cloisonné work on some bejeweled reliquary. Similar ornamental sprays are carried to the top of the façade, where the center niche contains a statue of Augustine.

At the side entrance (fig. c) motifs similar to those on the façade are utilized, but with restraint. Such rosettes as those on the portal arch and the frieze became popular as colonial architectural decoration, while filleted columns like these here are rarely seen in later structures. The statue above the doorway depicts a miracle associated with St. Nicholas of Tolentino, an Augustinian saint and the patron of the province. It is said that he never ate animal flesh and once, when weakened by a severe illness, he made the sign of the cross over a dish of doves which was set before him and the birds came to life and flew away.

Like most "fortress" churches, the building is lofty. Inside, it boasts groined vaulting in the Gothic manner and an impressive transept.

The decorative scheme of this church, as well as that of the Cuitzeo edifice on the succeeding plate, is a rustic interpretation of a European style. The presence of just such folkish overtones was a deciding factor in the selection of the illustrations for this chapter.

Less than twenty miles south of Yuririapúndaro lay the Lake of Cuitzeo, which today has for the most part vanished; only the fata morgana visible during certain hours calls up a vision of water. The fisherfolk living along its shore at the time of the Conquest were converted by a Franciscan friar, but shortly thereafter the district was assigned to the Augustinians. Although their establishment at Cuitzeo is contemporary with that at Yuririapúndaro and the name of Diego de Chávez is connected with it, the complex shows considerable differences both in plan and in decoration (*Pl. 32, fig. a*). The church, its great height more pronounced because of its severe, narrow façade, has a single nave.

The ornamentation on the façade is a native version of the Plateresque. Here is the nucleus of a regional art that by the seventeenth century had established its taste preferences; the decorative motifs were conditioned by the ability of the craftsmen and indicate the psychology of the builders. In many of the details the hand of the Indian is revealed. An abbreviated phrase on the façade has been interpreted as "Francisco Juan Metl me fecit," proof of Indian participation. The tower, with its open belfry arches, was built in the early seventeenth century by Jerónimo de la Magdalena.[110] A reservoir constructed in the early days under the supervision of the friars—the lake has always been notably brackish—still supplies the village with water.

The fortress character of the construction is even more evident at Cuitzeo than at Yuririapúndaro: both church and monastery walls are crenellated, the large enclosed atrium could have served as a first line of defense, and the buildings themselves are sturdy enough to have withstood siege. Entrance to the monastery was gained through the arcade; in the center (behind the third arch from the right) was built a large niche or recess which served as a chapel. Here, even before the church building was finished, Mass may have been celebrated for a crowd of Indians assembled in the atrium.

The open chapel, a version of the "Chapel of the Indians," was an ingenious solution to meet the immediate task of the early missionaries: the instruction of great masses of people by a very few. Just after the Conquest a mere handful of friars was faced with the problem of converting and teaching thousands of Indians in an unfamiliar tongue. Upon reaching their field of service they had to provide themselves with safe living quarters; but as evangelization was their aim, they also had to begin preaching and teaching at the very outset. The chapel for this purpose might take the form of a nichelike recess, sometimes within an arcade—as at Cuitzeo—and sometimes constructed into the façade of the church above the central door; or it might be a great hall-like structure. Meanwhile the converts could manifest their faith by working on the erection of more substantial buildings for the order. But even after a church was completed, it could not always contain the crowds that came on Sundays and holy days during those early decades. In pacified regions the Indians were gathered for the service, group by group, the roll was called, and the absentees marked for severe punishment.[102] Essentially a structure of the pioneering age, the open chapel ceased to be used about the end of the sixteenth century, except in Yucatán, where a tropical climate favored its continuance, and in Tlaxcala, where the population enjoyed special privileges for their support of Cortés and did not fear to congregate. By that time considerable depopulation had occurred in the colonies; thousands of Indians had died prematurely, either in epidemics of diseases imported by the white man or from overwork, and many others had fled to the mountains trying to escape forced labor, exacted under various pretexts. Also, as more towns sprang up more churches were established, and many more friars and secular clergy were arriving in the New World; in addition, individual churches were erected to minister to separate groups.

Later the open chapel was more or less incorporated into the building complex, but a number are still extant. The existence of its equivalent in several monastic structures in Central and South America has been suggested by certain authors, but definite identification is still a matter of argument. However, in the Old World a somewhat parallel solution to a similar problem can still be seen, for example in the sixth-century church of Sant' Apollinare in Classe at Ravenna, Italy, and especially in Milan's Sant' Ambrogio, from the eleventh and twelfth centuries; here in the spacious colonnaded atrium and wide narthex was provided a gathering place for the uninitiate and those temporarily excluded from the church proper because of misdemeanor. In medieval Europe, an open-air pulpit constructed on the façade of a church was not uncommon, providing the priest with a commanding podium from which to exhort the crowd in the square below. A Gothic exterior pulpit on the church of Notre Dame at Saint-Lô, France, survived the bombardment of World War II, and an exquisite example from the early Renaissance can be seen in the Duomo at Prato, near Florence, Italy. An illustration from a fifteenth-century Flemish book[21] shows pilgrims kneeling before a structure with three arches, which resembles an open chapel.

Occasionally in the early part of the colonial period in Mexico the entire monastery complex was placed on elevated ground and the atrium—a spacious churchyard—was approached by a flight of steps and through an imposing gateway (see Pls. 36, 51). At the four corners of such a churchyard sometimes four chapels, or posas, were erected. The posa here illustrated (fig. c) is one of those at the Franciscan monastery in San Miguel Huejotzingo, in the state of Puebla. A compact little structure (dated 1550), it stands against the atrium wall.[134] Crude but powerful angels on the spandrels awaken echoes of the Romanesque or Gothic. The decorative application of the Franciscan cord, a carry-over from Spain, was much used later in the colonies, not always in Franciscan establishments.

The posa has been explained as a stopping place for the out-of-door religious processions which marched in the enclosed atrium; the term is supposed to derive from the Spanish and to indicate the spot where the Sacrament rested—i.e., se posaba. In Roman Catholic countries today religious processions still halt before out-of-door chapels, crucifixes, and shrines—often temporarily constructed at the corners of prescribed routes—where, though Mass is not celebrated, prayers are said and benedictions offered. Posas are extremely rare in South America but some are preserved at the shrine of Copacabana—likewise an Augustinian establishment—on Lake Titicaca (see Pl. 123).

Civil architecture from this period also foreshadowed the originality and the great regional variety of the later centuries here. The Casa de Montejo (fig. d), which stands on the main plaza in Mérida, Yucatán, at an angle from the cathedral, was built in 1549, only seven years after the founding of the town. It was ordered by Francisco de Montejo, the younger, for the use of his conquistador father. Stones from wrecked Maya edifices were used in its construction, and it was built after a Spanish design by an Indian master mason, with Indian labor from Maní. Its peculiar combination of styles is distinctly regional. The lower section, with its paneled jambs, fluted columns, and round portrait medallions, is Plateresque in effect, whereas the upper section recalls the Gothic. Two gigantic halberdiers stand as atlantes, their feet on human heads—a symbol of the subjugation of the natives.[121] Wild men dressed in skins and carrying clubs guard the sides, a crouching figure upholds the corbeled balcony, and a variety of figural motifs, vines, and mythical animals is spread all over the composition. The building extends to the right and has four large grilled windows, also adorned in monumental fashion.

This house was occupied by the old Conquistador for only a short time before he was dislodged from office; he returned to Spain to protest his dismissal and died there in 1553. The son then lived in it until his death twelve years later, and from that time to 1914 it had twenty-one owners; today it houses the British vice-consulate. Over four hundred years old, it still stands in sturdy dignity, a romantic and dominating landmark.

The house of the dean of Puebla cathedral (*fig. b*) is dated 1580 and reflects that quiet Renaissance style which persisted long after new fashions had been introduced. But at the very top the ornamental vases, the scrolls suggesting a broken pediment, the lambrequin between them, and the placing of shells within the pediments over the windows all bring new life to the design. Note the peaks in the lines of the window frames. The words *Placa Decanus* on the pediment indicate the residence of the dean, and the Latin text above the door bids those who enter to "Let coming and going be in the name of Jesus."

The northern part of the island on which stood the Aztec capital, predecessor of Mexico City, in a saline lake, was occupied by the suburb Tlatelolco (also spelled Tlaltelolco). Here was situated that famous Aztec market which Bernal Díaz proclaimed as greater and richer than any he had ever seen in the Old World. Even after the Conquest this section remained densely populated by Indians. On the platform base of a pagan temple there, and using some of its stones, the first church of Santiago Tlatelolco was erected as part of a Franciscan college for the education of children of Indian nobles. In this church preached Sahagun (1499?–1590), venerable chronicler of the Aztecs, and here prayed Juan Diego, the humble Indian to whom appeared the Virgin of Guadalupe. The present edifice, which replaced an earlier provisional building, was finished in 1609; in 1660 and again in 1701 it was repaired and refurbished, and in 1763 it was whitewashed and regilded. Its lofty main retable—four and one-half stories high and filling the apse completely—was discarded in the late nineteenth century.[120]

Fortunately the four pendentives still remain more or less untampered with. Composed to fit into the curving triangular spaces are powerful reliefs of the four Evangelists, Indian work modeled in clay. Matthew, holding a quill in his right hand and a book in his left, is represented as riding on the shoulders of an angel of heroic size (*Pl. 33, fig. b*). Mark occupies the pendentive opposite (*fig. a*). His lion's long mane, to the left of the saint, is coifed like a wig. All four reliefs are remarkable for the force of their conception; such a sense of upsurging inspiration in the depiction of the Evangelists has seldom been achieved.

In the city of Oaxaca the Dominican order, established there in 1535, built a new church during the last quarter of the seventeenth century. In 1731, through the munificence of one of the friars, Dionisio Levanto, the Rosario chapel was added to the sprawling complex.[103] It is a large cruciform building, and its interior, like that of the main church, is covered with figural and plant motifs in stucco, heavily gilded. During the War of Reform (1858–1861), when the city was a turbulent center of strife, the main altar of this chapel was destroyed, and not many years later the French soldiery of Maximilian's following chipped the gold leaf off the walls and damaged whatever interior decoration remained.[107]

The interest in the present altar as it now stands (*fig. c*) lies in its statues, which like mounting steps direct the eye to the Trinity enthroned—at the left, Christ with the Cross, at the right, God the Father, and in the round window between, the Dove, or Holy Ghost. The arrangement of the radiating gilded rays emanating from this high point is very effective. All this religious statuary extends beyond the apse to the very top of the dome (*fig. d*), where the Virgin and Child hold court amid a host of saints. In the pendentives appear again figures of the Evangelists, designated as "S. Joan" and "Sant Matheus"; compare the latter's disproportionately small angel with the monumental, almost apocalyptic creature at Tlatelolco.

Especially awe-inspiring is this interior at night in the mystic light of candles. Though all the figures have been over-painted, they are still appealing in their sincerity. The imported Christian iconography has here undergone a process of simplification; yet the regional artists have produced a moving display of folk art.

In the Christian church the individual Indian had closer contact with his religion than had his ancestors in pagan times, when most of the ritual was in the hands of the priests and the humble man or woman stood remote from the rite, a spectator among the multitude crowded into the great square before the high temple platform. As a Christian he could enter the church, light a taper himself, and remain close to his favorite saints.

For nearly three hundred years the state of Chiapas, neighbor to Guatemala and related to it racially and topographically, belonged to the Captaincy-General of Guatemala, but in 1824 it joined the Republic of Mexico, then in the process of formation. The town of San Cristóbal de las Casas, in Chiapas, was founded in 1538 under the name Ciudad Real, or Royal City. After five changes, in 1844 it adopted its present name in memory of the friar Bartolomé de las Casas, Apostle of the Indies and an early bishop and benefactor of the region.[101] The town lies at an altitude of 7,000 feet, and partly because of its inaccessi-

bility it has retained much of its colonial character; it has been called a small edition of Antigua, Guatemala, from which it received many artistic influences when that city was its colonial capital.

The doorway of a residence in this town (*Pl. 34, fig. b*) shows an interesting adaptation of the Plateresque. Because the arms in the shield have been defaced, the identity of the early owner of the building is uncertain, but it is thought to have belonged to the family of Andrés de la Tobilla. Rustication lends dignity to this entrance. The lower columns end, with little logic, on a level with the lintel and are then surmounted by other columns which continue beyond the molding. Atop these are seated two lions, the tails of which are executed in relief, laid flat against the wall. Plateresque elegance is achieved in the carved panels to the right and left of the upper window, where a pair of griffins, *contrapposto*, stand guard. This fantasy animal was very popular in medieval as well as in later heraldry, but here, as interpreted by the local stonecarvers, it is somewhat difficult to recognize.[126]

The Dominican monastery in San Cristóbal de las Casas was founded shortly after the arrival of the first friar in 1545, but the present Dominican church there (*fig. a*) probably was not finished until about 1700; it was emblazoned with the Habsburg double-headed eagle on the third-story panels just when that bird was taking flight from Spain's royal coat of arms. An impressive stairway of fifteen steps leads up to the church. The façade, remarkably high, is rich and shows originality, displaying a combination of jutting cornices and twisted columns with a flat over-all pattern of stucco work like bobbin lace. In every story the pediments break through the cornices. The thick espadaña, crowned with sturdy obelisks reminiscent of crenellation, is divided into two parts, making five horizontal fields in all, each embellished with a different pattern. A pair of mermaids adorns the topmost member.

Within, solid paneling of gilded wood—rare anywhere—sheathes the walls and gives to the interior a luxuriously warm tone (*fig. c*). The side altars, placed in shallow nichelike recesses and marked with twisted gilded columns precisely carved, are unusually homogeneous. On the left, near the main altar (all too obviously modern) stands a pulpit that will be shown in a later chapter (*see Pl. 182*).

John McAndrew points out that already in the second half of the seventeenth century in Mexico vigorous regional styles were developing and that in the eighteenth the ideas flowing from the mother country were accepted or rejected as they suited the artistic temper of the land, which by that time had a dozen regional styles.[113] In the area between Oaxaca and Puebla the folk idiom became highly articulate. As has been seen, the advance of technical knowledge in construction brought with it the urge for additional ornamentation. While in the northern parts of Mexico stone played a substantial role in the decorative scheme, in the south the use of stucco, often reinforced with stone tenons, was more general. Great dexterity was acquired in this medium, and a manner of decoration developed which featured capriciously curving detail, extravagant line, and complicated shapes. Especially in the Puebla region, which produced the finest ceramic ware on this continent, stucco fantasies combined with tiles reached a most demonstrative expression.

An unusually original and exquisite example of this regional art stands on a hill about a mile from Tlaxcala (*Pl. 35, fig. a*). MacKinley Helm describes [107] this building as "the most delicious church in the world." Its two lacy sculptured belfries, shining with the whitest whitewash, rise on curving bases covered with red-orange hexagonal tiles. Between them, framed within a shell-shaped arch, is a fascinating potpourri of sculptured decoration, like the entrance to a fantasy grotto, peopled with angels and saints. Above the doorway stands a figure of St. Francis supporting the three globes that signify his three orders, on which the crowned Virgin is poised.

This building is the Sanctuary of Ocotlán. Its name—from the Aztec *ocote* (pine) and *tlán* (place)—denotes the great pine trees that surround the hill where once the palace of an Indian ruler is said to have stood. The spot has been a famous pilgrim place since early in the Spanish rule, when, at a time of drought and plague, a miraculous spring gushed forth. The church dates from about 1745 and is constructed of stucco and bricks which were manufactured in Puebla. In its façade the play with ever-changing planes is fascinating. Within the deeply recessed arch of the portal, the columns, cornices, and statuary are all thrust forward. The bulge of the tower bases is followed and accented in the molding of the belfries. At the right in the photograph are visible the first two arches of the conventual building which in colonial days housed the Franciscans in charge of this shrine.

The interior was finished in mid-nineteenth century, and alteration, decoration, and regilding went on into the 1940's.[114] Its sanctuary and the adjacent side altars, however, have been left more or less intact. Also, except for the retouching of the colors, the octagonal *camarín*—in this case a small chapel behind the main altar—is still in its original state. With its stalactite decoration in polychrome stucco, it resembles the setting for a large manger scene. This little chamber is richly furnished with cabinets, benches, and tables of carved wood. Quatrefoil windows light the place, and one of them opens into the main altar directly behind; probably the famous golden statue of the patroness once stood there. The walls are encrusted with broad gilded spirals of ribbon and thick garlands of flowers and foliage. The dome, upheld by archangels, contains niches in which saints in rich vestments are set among intricate and fanciful arabesques. On the ceiling, within a ring of gold, are represented Mary and the Apostles at the Pentecost, and poised above their heads against a background of bright blue is the Holy Ghost (*fig. b*). Many of the colors have a metallic luster, which lends unusual brilliance to the scene. The Indian artist Francisco Miguel is said to have spent more than twenty years in the execution of this lavish composition, probably around mid-eighteenth century.[84]

In the Casa del Alfeñique (*fig. c*), in Puebla, the blend of decorative stucco work and tiles was carried further and a proportionately greater space was given to the tiles; *alfeñique* means "almond cake." This building is said to date from the last quarter of the eighteenth century, when Puebla tile and other ceramic work had attained artistic and technical maturity. Glazed blue and white tiles, set into a background of unglazed red tile, cover the main part of the façade; the trim and ornaments are of stone and whitewashed stucco. The black of the wrought-iron balconies stands out in striking contrast. Antonio de Santa María Incháurregui is named as the architect of this palace, and according to tradition it was used as a guest house for high officials. Any viceroy must indeed have been satisfied with its splendor when he rolled in his Rococo coach through its wide portal (visible on the left).

The word *poblano*, which in Mexico denotes an inhabitant of Puebla, is used here in a broader sense to designate the earthy, virile folkloristic art of this region. The stucco work in the interior of San Antonio chapel in Puebla (*Pl. 36, fig. c*), situated at the left of the church of Guadalupe, displays the same articulate workmanship that characterizes Puebla pottery. This interior is covered with stucco motifs, floriated in character and executed with precision and finesse. Narrow leafy fillets rather than grapes entwine the twisted columns. As in most *poblano* decoration, the figural abounds. Compare the archangels on the pendentives with those at Antigua and Comayagua (*see Pls. 6, 8*); these are more plastic, and perhaps, like the carved wooden angels frequently seen in Andalusian churches, they once had lamps dangling from their out-

stretched arms. Two other angels stand on the spandrels of the choir arch and figures are placed even between the windows, high in the drum of the dome. The main church of Guadalupe was redecorated by Luis Osorio in 1758, and its façade presents a specimen of eighteenth-century tilework in brilliant colors, incorporating picture panels; the chapel interior, however, may have been left little changed since its construction (1694–1714), for it has a feeling rather of the turn of the century.

San Pedro de Atlixco lies in a picture-postcard valley—known in colonial days as the Val de Cristo—not far from the old road from Mexico City to Oaxaca and less than twenty miles from Puebla. Its northern horizon is filled with the gigantic snow-crowned profiles of Popocatépetl and Ixtacchihuatl. Built around a steep sugar-loaf hill, on the slope of which lies an early Franciscan monastery, it is one of the few towns that still retain their walled character. It has a delicious climate and warm mineral springs that made it famous even in pre-Columbian times. Its importance as a market center extended into the colonial epoch. As early as the first quarter of the seventeenth century the valley had over a thousand Spanish residents and the town, founded in 1579, could boast seven monasteries, a parish church, nunneries, and hospitals, as well as other churches and shrines. Its wealth was derived from the extraordinary fertility of the region, which is free from frost and enjoys an abundant water supply; here were harvested yearly over sixty thousand bushels of the best wheat raised in all New Spain.[81]

The Rosario chapel (*fig. a*) stands on the town's main plaza and is part of the large, much-renovated edifice which today functions as the parish church. Its great dome, however, with colorfully patterned tiles, is unchanged. Note the sun, a favorite tile motif in the decoration of domes in Mexico. A stencil-like design in stucco frames the rectangular central window and its shell-shaped arch. The first-story columns remind one of those in Puebla's San Antonio chapel, just discussed, while those on the more prominent second story carry a different type of decoration—as if braided pastry had been translated into stucco. The large medallion, too, which contains a representation of the chalice, rampant animals, two archangels, and the double-headed eagle, looks as if it might have come from the mold of some eighteenth-century honey-cake baker.

A feeling for the doughlike quality of stucco is revealed again in the façade of the former Mercedarian conventual church in Atlixco (*fig. b*). But here is a more daring exhibition. A lively flow of motifs cascades down the façade. In addition to the varied assortment of nonfigural ornament, well spaced for clarity, the group around the Virgin of Mercy in the central niche calls for special attention (*compare Pl. 136*). Little angels uphold her sweeping cloak, and typical *poblano* figures, their lower limbs lost in leafy spirals, hold a crown above her head. The upper section of the niche suggests an aureole, while the elliptical window above is fluted like a pastry mold. On either side are smiling siren figures, half mermaid, half leaf-sprite, wearing feathered headdresses. In the opening of the broken pediment stands a statue of the Virgin and Child. The whole composition has a malleability that suggests wax or marzipan.

The Indian population of the wide circle of villages which encompass Puebla found ample outlet for their artistic energies in the various guilds of arts and crafts established in that region during the colonial period. For this reason often a small village was able to erect a church many times more imposing than one would expect to find. An example is the church of San Francisco in the village of Acatepec, some seven miles from Puebla (*fig. d*). It was finished about 1730 and displays a most lavish use of tiles.

Approach to it is through a dramatic neo-Mudéjar gateway, which probably dates from the same time so felicitously does it harmonize with the church. The façade stands well forward from the building line and curves outward at the sides like the hinged sections of a screen. Glittering with variegated detail, it is a gem of ceramic work. Glazed tile—much of which must have been manufactured expressly to fit a particular place in the design—not only is applied on the wall surfaces but also makes up columns, pilasters, moldings, and vases. Especially splendid is the topmost section, where volutes flow downward as if to define a pediment. A statue of St. Francis stands in the eight-pointed star window. The belfry at the left is placed somewhat pertly at an angle. On the other side, the tower is built up of delicate elements, such as might adorn a great jewel box; blue and yellow majolica bands spiral around its columns, and the shimmering tiled dome forms a beguiling cover.[83]

The interior of San Francisco in Acatepec—a mass of stucco carving, polychromed and covered with gold leaf—in design and execution is a most excellent example of eighteenth-century *poblano* art. A composition as luxuriant as a jungle vine frames the baptistry door (*Pl. 37, fig. c*). Scattered about are small heads, perhaps derived from the canephora motif, but the baskets here turned out to be more like crowns. The finials were nearly lost when a huge canvas painting was fitted around them, but the manner of combining the painting and the sculpture leaves little doubt of the regional craftsman's preference for the three-dimensional. Traces of a dado on the wall suggest that the canvas was placed over a colorful pattern painted in outline on the surface. In the late 1930's the interior of this church suffered from fire, and at one of our later visits the Indian parishioners and artisans were working with great zeal on its restoration; the grace and sparkle of the eighteenth-century craftsmanship, however, could not be duplicated and the effect had become rather rustic.

Expert modeling of clay and stucco can be observed also in colonial façades just outside the Federal District of Mexico in that complex net of villages which were connected by causeways and canals radiating toward the capital. The pre-Columbian Indians here were highly skilled in arts and crafts, as well as in agriculture. With the coming of the Spaniard the population was favored because its co-operation was desired in the construction of the new capital, but later, when the colonial administration was pursuing more distant goals, these hamlets were left in a backwater.

The village of Huexotla (place of willows) is situated only a few miles from Texcoco, a former Indian capital and during the Spanish Conquest an important administrative center. Huexotla lies within an archaeological zone and has several large pyramidal structures as yet unexcavated. On the platform of one of these, with a broad view of Mexico's two giant volcanoes, a Franciscan monastery was established within a decade of the Spaniards' arrival. In pre-Columbian fashion, steep stairs have to be ascended before the complex is reached. The monastery in Huexotla, finished about mid-sixteenth century, consisted of only a few narrow cells and a small cloistered patio. Its massive rubble walls are supported on staunch wooden beams. Here Jerónimo de Mendieta, who arrived in Mexico in 1554 and died there in 1604, began and finished (1596) his monumental work, *Historia eclesiástica indiana*.[119]

The conventual church as it now stands (*fig. b*), of a later date than the monastery, has a golden yellow façade, which carries both stone and stucco ornamentation. In build-up its columns differ markedly from the classical concept. In the first order they are cut in half by moldings which break the decorative scheme; just above the moldings angel faces alternate with masks that are pre-Columbian in spirit. The design of the central section of the façade also is unconventional. The two angels which usually occupy the spandrels are floating in decorative if somewhat stiff positions above the arch; two others flank the choir-light, and pilasters rise

above them as if from corbels. Scallops of masonry, in imitation of drapery, ornament the upper edge of the window. A sharply projecting molding in stepped and arching lines crosses the entire façade. The arrangement is worked out in terms of a more or less flat design—like those to be found on the title pages of contemporary books—and little consideration was given to bulk and plastic form. As at Yuririapúndaro (*see Pl. 31*), Plateresque elements were taken out of their customary context and applied by the regional artisans according to their different artistic imagination; but in the upper section the mild *estípites*, or inverted obelisk shapes, and the oval medallions bespeak a far later period than that building. The tower, into the decoration of which ceramic bowls are incorporated, bears the date 1721, and the year 1745 is carved on the choir gallery; these, however, may denote later restoration work.

Somewhat more organized in the academic sense is the façade of the church at Coatlinchan (house of the serpent), a neighboring village of Huexotla. Dedicated to St. Michael, whose statue stands in the top niche, this church (*fig. a*) also was once connected with a monastic order. In its lofty and narrow proportions and its few openings it still shows the tradition of the "fortress" church. The façade, however, is Baroque. Long stucco "aprons" hang below the niches, which are placed unusually high, and a stucco garland upheld by angels encircles the choir-light. A rose-colored wash enhances the lacy effect of the bold flat designs. The tower is covered with *azulejos* that show a fine patina; note its many statues and the peculiar use of a short twisted shaft placed at each angle. On the choir loft is inscribed the year 1724, and the façade, as well as the tower, bears the date 1731.

San Pablo Ostotepec, in the region of Milpa Alta in the Federal District, was another ancient Indian settlement. There, in the sixteenth century, a shrine to the Lord of Chalmita (*fig. d*) was erected on the base of a pagan temple, high above a lovely valley.[119] A Via Crucis extends before it, with entrance gateways at both sides; the small gabled niches in the wall, which give the appearance of crenellation, once held tiles marking the fourteen Stations of the Cross. Its paved court and stairway are said to be survivals of pre-Columbian days, and they bulge from age and earthquake shocks. To the right lie the crumbling remains of a large early stone church.

This shrine was altered in the seventeenth and eighteenth centuries and was completely made over in 1871 without any feeling for its historical atmosphere. Colonial objects, however, were preserved in its interior and some colonial tiles were incorporated in the tower and around the portal. In passing through the archway below the tower one first comes upon the friars' quarters, and then across the wide terrace a sweeping view opens into the picturesque valley, where myriad flower and vegetable patches converge upon Xochimilco. One is struck with the thought that though generations may come and go, this fertile earth will hold forever the flavor of its long past.

The first church of the Mercedarian order in the Mexican capital was finished in early seventeenth century. But it soon proved too small to accommodate the faithful, and in 1634 a new church was begun, which was completed a few decades later. Around that time also can be placed the construction of the lower arcade of the monastery cloister (Pl. 38, fig. c); the upper story was completed in the early eighteenth century.[127] In this unique cloister—all that now remains of the once vast complex—virile imagination and solid craftsmanship produced an unusual decorative scheme. The ground-floor arches are accented with plain squarish stones, which alternate with carved rosettes; on each keystone is a shell-shaped medallion with a figure. Floriated designs, each one different from the others, fill the spandrel space. On the second story the number of arches is doubled and the column shafts are elaborately carved with

crisscrossing reminiscent of that on a shepherd's staff. The use of sharply faceted stones on the arch lends a Mudéjar touch. In the plaza in front of the monastery a noisy market still thrives; an ancient canal formerly terminated there upon which for centuries the Indians brought in their produce.

The nunnery of Santa Mónica in Guadalajara, founded as the Incarnation of the Indies, was established[98] under the Jesuits in 1720. It covers a city block, and the conventual church stands at one corner at the intersection of two streets. Here a monumental figure of St. Christopher (fig. b), carved of two large pieces of stone, stands at just the right height and angle to watch over the traffic, in keeping with the saint's tradition as the patron of travelers. The church's ornate façade (see Pl. 47) is in marked contrast to the archaic rigor expressed in the statue. Toussaint suggests that the Christopher may well belong to the century preceding the church.[127]

Long before the custom of naming and numbering streets was introduced here, the statues of saints, or symbolic figures, or even paintings which decorated the buildings came to be used to identify streets or districts. This accounts for the puzzling and often seemingly fantastic appellations that still cling to some sections of colonial towns.

In many conventual churches, the choir loft, placed at the end of the nave opposite the main altar, was built out to unusual dimensions and served as a special private enclosure for the devotions of the secluded residents. It was carefully screened from the view of the public, who were admitted to the building only during certain hours. In nunneries frequently the main entrance below the choir loft was blocked off and used as a lower choir. The public entrance was then placed on the side of the building and was often designed as twin portals. These have been explained as primarily utilitarian: such throngs were attracted by the lavish services, the specially fine music, and the tasteful decorations—for which the nuns grew famous—that one door was needed for entrance and the other for exit.

In the city of Morelia—known in colonial times as Nueva Valladolid but later renamed for the hero Morelos—the nunnery church of Las Rosas presents a felicitous design of twin side portals (*fig. a*). Renaissance elements of northern Europe appear in a Baroque interpretation, remarkable for its tasteful balance of ornamented and plain surfaces. The first story shows an application of the lambrequin, which was popular throughout northern Mexico in the second half of the eighteenth century. The relief work under the windows and in the medallions has the softness and fluent line of wax. A statue mounted on the central column helps tie the twin pediments together. Work on the church was finished between 1746 and 1756, and the names of Nicolás López Quijano, José Medina, and Martín Eliza Coechea are mentioned in connection with it.[87]

This nunnery was founded on the site of a fulling mill donated by a munificent citizen; the making of textiles was at one time an outstanding industry in that region. The convent maintained a music school (see Chapter 13) and was dedicated to Santa Rosa; from her name the populace came to call the nuns the Roses.

The placing of the portal within an arched recess is an interesting architectural feature that is encountered in several regions of colonial Spanish America. The builders in Mexico produced their own version, which suggests a niche but is built on such a monumental scale that it sometimes occupies the entire wall of a building and extends the full height of the façade. In Europe the niche had received great attention since the Renaissance, and from mid-fifteenth century on, colossal archways were constructed as portals, forming an open vestibule—S. Andrea in Mantua, Italy, for instance, designed by Alberti about 1460. Among Mohammedan builders emphasis of the portal had long been favored: they, too, placed a door

in a niche which extended to a great height, framed it elaborately, and sometimes crowned it with a dome (*see Appendix, Pl. 190, fig. d*).

In Mexico the use of the monumental niche appears in widely separated sectors. The oldest one shown here is from the church of San Juan de Dios in Mexico City (*Pl. 39, fig. b*). This edifice, which occupies the site of an earlier chapel erected in the last third of the sixteenth century, was finished in 1727. Its façade, entirely of stone, is designed with a deep porch—architecturally the most interesting of the whole group—which is rounded at the sides like an apse and covered with an airy half-dome, ribbed like a shell. The niches in the first story, grouped into quartettes to the right and left, blend with those above them in amazing harmony. In the center stands the patron saint, San Juan de Dios, who was not canonized until 1700; his niche echoes the line of the whole façade. The stonework throughout shows considerable technical skill, especially in the flame-shaped lines of the undulating pilasters.

In the town of Cuernavaca (an Indian name corrupted into the Spanish for "cow's horn"), west of the Mexican capital, the Franciscans founded an establishment in 1529. They enclosed a large tract with crenellated walls and, within it, erected their various buildings. What was once the main church of the monastery now functions as the cathedral. Flower beds and vegetable plots, watered by fountains and tended by Indian gardeners, flourished in the central area. *Posas* may once have occupied the corners where today three churches stand.[106] The most impressive of these is the church of the Third Order (*fig. d*). Here the nichelike porch was designed for the lateral entrance that overlooks the garden. The sides of the recess open out at an angle. An image of the Virgin stands in a shallow niche above the arched doorway. Large panels carved in relief flank the figure, and the flat surfaces are enlivened with a fluent overall embossing that is very effective in the golden yellow stone of the building. This church may have been finished in the first third of the eighteenth century; its main altar is dated 1735. Probably the greater part of it is the work of Indians; in this region they not only were numerous but also held high positions in the colonial administration.

San Miguel el Grande, known today as San Miguel de Allende, was founded in mid-sixteenth century as a military outpost against the Chichimec and Otomi Indians. Near the market place, where much of the merchandise and the methods of business still hark back to customs established in a bygone age, stands the chapel of Our Lady of Health (La Salud) (*fig. c*). It was built toward the end of the eighteenth century, mainly at the expense of the friar Luis Felipe Neri Alfaro;[112] he spent a great part of his patrimony on the construction. Its portal of dark stone, once painted in a variety of colors, brings new details to this now familiar type. Here, too, the line of the portal recess is angular, producing a hinged shape that doubtless complicated the placing of the rounded shell above. A small shell is set at the base of the large one and from it the "Eye of God" gazes out on the plaza. A number of details bespeak its late date: the pilasters taper downward in the form of *estípites* and carry a minimum of decoration; in the spandrels of the neo-Mudéjar entrance, nondescript abstractions take the place of the floating angels so frequently encountered earlier. The use of two rectangular windows instead of one in the upper tier above the entrance is unusual. S-scrolls, drawn out large enough to fill the area, provide the only ornamentation above them.

This Baroque shell design is found in Yucatán also. The church of San Cristóbal in Mérida (*fig. a*), which replaced an earlier primitive chapel, was erected on property once owned by the Franciscans. The royal permit for this structure is dated 1757, but the inauguration did not take place until 1797. In its high arch, plain wall surfaces, and lofty turrets, it carries some strong suggestions of Mérida's cathedral (*see Pl. 2*). The recess in San Cristóbal curves

from the outside wall to the entrance. Noteworthy is the Mudéjar window, with its multifoil arch and heavy ornate frame. All the decoration around the door and window—as well as the entire surface of the shell, which is finished with great elegance—is of stucco. Some writers consider the two towers to be out of proportion to the recess, whereas others find that this very factor, together with the rustic finish of the rest of the church, tends to point up the refinement of the whole portal. Among the bells in the right tower is one dated 1591, probably a survival from the earlier building. This church became a parish church for the purely Indian population that lived in the district and it remains so to this day. A monograph published in 1945 on the religious structures in Yucatán lists thirty-five churches for Mérida, twenty-three of which are situated in the city proper.[95]

In the four shell portals on this plate note the difference in the treatment of the shell itself: in two cases it radiates from the center of the base line; in Cuernavaca it is centered above, like a half-dome; and in Mexico City it is centered on a window and has only a slight splay.

On *Plate 40* are presented Mudéjar doorways of various periods in Mexico. In the door to the cloister of the Sagrario of Pátzcuaro (*fig. b*), formerly the Hospital of Santa Marta,[130] stone was cut in subtle Mudéjar lines suggestive of the Gothic. The pointed arch rests on the modestly paneled piers, as fluid and graceful in line as if it were made of stucco or wood; points dart out from both the extrados and the intrados, the outer independent of the inner. Today the building is in a poor state of repair and, together with other architectural remnants of the early seventeenth century in this town, pleads for attention.

In the eighteenth century Querétaro, a city southeast of the silver cities of Guanajuato and Zacatecas, enjoyed a period of great prosperity. Agriculture, industry, commerce, and nearby mines all contributed to a life of plenty. Before the middle of the century it had grown to be the third largest city of the viceroyalty.

The first church of La Compañía there, founded by the Jesuits in connection with their college which adjoined it, was finished in early seventeenth century. Later it was enlarged several times and about 1755 it was practically rebuilt. In 1771, after the expulsion of the order, it was made a parish church and dedicated to Santiago.[117] Now the cloister of the former monastery (*fig. a*), once made friendly and cheerful by flowers and running water, is occupied by the little-disturbed office of the parish priest. The arcades, one above the other, are built entirely of stone. The lower story has round arches and cloister vaults. All the doorways leading into the building show Mudéjar lines. Here the arch, its inner line multifoil and its outer one ruffled, seems to spring from the center of the fluted jamb.

As might be expected in a city where ecclesiastical edifices displayed such elegance, the civilians sought splendor in the designing of their houses. An upper gallery in the mansion of the Count of Sierra Gorda, in Querétaro, gives a glimpse of an interior (*fig. d*). A narrow arcade showing neo-Mudéjar decoration surrounds the entire patio, and in the ceiling of the upper corridor this style is blended with the Rococo; the elaborate combination of stucco spirals and shell-rosettes gives an unusually lively and pleasing aspect to the place.

The main patio of another Querétaro mansion, that of the Marquis of Villa de Villar de Aguila (*fig. e*), shows extravagant fantasy in its design; here the various current modes were combined to produce a highly theatrical setting.

Contrast is offered in the palace of the Count of Santiago in the Mexican capital (*fig. c*). Built entirely of stone, it breathes reserve and dignity. The founder of this family, the first Count of Calimaya, was a cousin of Cortés, the Conquistador. He began to build

his house on this site in 1528, with stones from the main *teocalli;* a block carved with the plumed serpent was used as a cornerstone. In 1779 the building was considerably remodeled and changed in style under the supervision of the famous architect Francisco de Guerrero y Torres (*see also Pl. 49*); the mermaid fountain in the court probably dates from this time.[93] By then the family had intermarried with the Altamirano y Velasco, the Catilla, and the Mendoza families, all distinguished throughout the colonial epoch; a coat of arms mounted high above the portal indicates the noble lineage. On the cornices of the house are gargoyles in the shape of a cannon, a symbol of privilege.

Quite unique is the dentil above the door. The Mudéjar curves of the lintel are carefully plotted and suggest drapery. Rococo taste is visible in the console-like decoration on the pedestals—the ball and claw familiar from the furniture of the period; however, the engaged columns at the sides, fluted and with small capitals, approach the neoclassic. On the massive wooden doors, two coats of arms occupy the medallions carved above two heraldic lion heads; the design is so divided that one sector may be opened, to permit entrance, without disturbing the balance.

The Churrigueresque style of architectural decoration derives its name from the Madrid-born José Churriguera (1650–1723), whose most telling work stands in Salamanca, the seat of Spain's most ancient university. In his first works he held to a degree of classicism, into which he injected Plateresque elements. But his was the age of expansiveness, of pomp and an inflated monumentality, and in this world he found his own individual manner when, about 1689, he came to Madrid. There he won the competition for a catafalque for Queen Maria Louisa, the first wife of Charles II. The greatest of Spain's painters, sculptors, and architects had competed, and Churriguera's victory indicates that his manner well expressed the times. His prize-winning design breathes a broadly theatrical atmosphere, melancholic and emotionally high pitched. Most elements of that style which was later named for him are apparent in this project: wreaths and garlands, columns, scrolls, carved drapery, medallions, candelabra, flags, vases, obelisks, balustrades, and religious and mythological statues.[36]

Churriguera had two sons, a grandson, and a nephew, all of whom followed him in his profession; thus the name covers considerably more in time—as well as in production—than could be encompassed in one life span. In the use of estípites, pedestals, busts, and other motifs that have come to be accepted as characteristics of the style, his pupil and disciple Pedro Ribera was more Churrigueresque than Churriguera himself. It should be recalled, however, that the estípite was used in Italy in mid-sixteenth century (see Appendix, Pl. 190, fig. f).

It is interesting to note that, according to a writer and archivist in Barcelona,[40] Churriguera was of Catalan origin and his family name originally began with an "X." If this is true, it is all the more ironical that Churrigueresque became more elaborated and more widely used in Mexico than in Spain, for Catalans were not at first permitted to emigrate to the New World and even later permission was suspended at various intervals, when Catalonia stood in opposition to the crown of Castile. Churrigueresque is said to have been introduced into Mexico by the Spanish sculptor Jerónimo de Balbás. He came over to carve the Altar de los Reyes (begun in 1718) in the cathedral of Mexico City, after having won fame with his work in Seville.[37]

In this volume the term Churrigueresque is applied not to all exuberant eighteenth-century Baroque in the New World but to that style, predominantly Mexican, which is closely related to de Balbás' manner. The use of the estípite and the lambrequin is characteristic. Often the total effect is of a stalactite mass, with countless pointed elements hanging down from above, producing a verticality that has nothing to do with structural requirements.

The style was welcome in the colonies, where buildings usually were designed on a basically simple ground plan, partly because of the absence of virtuoso architects and partly because recurrent earthquakes conditioned the manner and type of construction. Thus, despite the fact that not one of the five Churrigueras was ever in the American colonies, Churrigueresque became a characteristic expression of Mexico; for here was a style which could endow a simple structure with a highly alive and ostentatiously elegant air. The Sagrario Metropolitano in Mexico's capital (see Pl. 2) is a key example of Churrigueresque, and many others can be found throughout the land. In the examples selected for this chapter, attention is directed especially to regional variations.

On this earth are certain spots which have become so famous for their beauty that the sensitive traveler approaches them with timidity, in doubt whether his impressions will measure up to his expectations. Tasco belongs to the group that will not disappoint him if he outstays the midday tourist scramble. In the light of the subtropical afternoon, the houses, washed white or pink, above terraces brilliant with flowers, begin to shimmer in golden dust. The church, with its rose-colored stone, white stucco, and bright tiles, stands radiant at the heart of an arena-like valley.

The Nahuatl name Tlachco (where ball is played) implies a shrine, but little is known of the pre-Columbian past of this place. It is said that Cortés saw minerals that were discovered here and that Franciscans from Cuernavaca were the first evangelizers. But fame came later, with José de la Borda. That young Spaniard left Spain in 1716 to join his brother Francisco, who for about eight years had been mining in Tasco with little luck. However, under José the enterprise soon prospered. He exploited mines in other parts of the country and amassed great wealth but always showed a preference for the place where fortune had first smiled upon him. He effected improvements in Tasco's water supply and carried out many building projects, among them the erection of a parish church. According to the story, José de la Borda was anxious to retain near him his son Manuel, who was about to enter the priesthood, and wished to provide the young man with a church worthy of the Borda name. To this end he obtained permission from the archbishop of Mexico to demolish the old parish church and erect a new and greater one, his sole condition being that he alone should direct the work and control the funds. Construction began in 1751, and seven years later the building was finished (Pl. 41, fig. a). It was dedicated to St. Prisca and St. Sebastian; the former was a virgin martyr of Roman times and a fitting companion to the youthful Christian soldier. Diego Durán and Juan Caballero are named as the architects. The altars are the work of Isidoro Vicente de Balbás, believed to be the son of Jerónimo, the master of Churrigueresque mentioned above.[127]

This building, one of the most eloquent landmarks of the golden era of Latin American colonial art, embodies in its heaped floral ornaments and stalactite elements a special interpretation of the Churrigueresque. The single doorway in the retable façade is flanked by slender columns with figures jutting out from between them. Interest is concentrated on the second order, where a monumental sculptured medallion depicting the baptism of Christ occupies the space usually allotted to a central window. Above it, a multifoil choir-light extends up into the arched pediment, which suggests an espadaña but does not rise beyond the roof. The exquisite manner of stone carving, the placing of statues on top of the façade, the many balustrades, and the distribution of finials—arranged like festive bouquets —all invite comparison with the Rococo churches in the mining towns of Brazil (see Pls. 169–173).

The tower bases protrude beyond the portal, and four variform windows in each, with Rococo framing, enliven the mass. In the belfry sections the towers are more ornate: decorated columns are playfully fashioned and heavy corbels are carved with grotesque faces. The dome in its sprawling bonhomie is as Mexican as the lapis lazuli sky and that dazzling sun which gilds its own image in the blue and yellow tiles.

In the interior are found some extraordinarily expressive statues. An idea of the homogeneity of its execution can be gained from the illustration of its organ (see Pl. 160).

Humboldt, who visited Mexico in 1803, remarked upon the prosperity that accrued to all branches of the economy in an agricultural district when mines were discovered. He made mention especially of the high tableland of Anahuac, which extends as far as San Miguel de Allende and at that time belonged to the Intendency of Guanajuato. At the center, situated in a mountain gorge at the meeting of several valleys, lies Guanajuato (a corruption of the Tarascan name which meant "hill of the frogs"). The richest mines of the district—Las Rayas, La Valenciana, and La Cata—are close to the city. Much unrest has plagued this region: miners early struggled for their rights against the crown and even fought one another; Indian uprisings continued here late into the eighteenth century; and the region was a revolutionary center during the war for independence.

But such disturbances did not hinder the newly rich from erecting lavish churches or from building seignioral mansions for themselves. Only a small portion of their fabulous incomes was needed to purchase titles and coats of arms from the crown, and new aristocrats, with only a brief lineage behind them, appeared on the scene to become patrons of the arts. Vicente Manuel de Sardeneta y Legaspí, the first Marquis of San Juan de Rayas and the son of an already famous minero, or mine operator, was such a silver magnate. Humboldt mentions the mine of Las Rayas as one of the most lucrative. In his opinion it produced from the same vein as did La Valenciana. But in addition Las Rayas had amethysts in crystal form; furthermore the silver ore here was nearer the surface than that at La Valenciana and also of a higher grade.[58] Though much the smaller and less than a fifth as costly to operate, Las Rayas brought nearly the same net income as the other.

At the mouth of this mine the new marquis built, about mid-eighteenth century, the church of San Juan de Rayas (*fig. b*). In style it represents a local version of Churrigueresque and is distinguished by its well-organized ornamental units, the finesse of its execution, and the sobriety of its general plan. The molding of the *estípites* is here like ruffles. The entrance has a clean-cut multifoil arch, and a sculptured lambrequin, draped below the choir window, brings out the Mudéjar spirit of the design.

After mid-nineteenth century the mining industry here fell on evil days, and the crumbling walls of this graceful building, as it stood at the edge of a ghost town, made a pathetic sight. But in 1946 the Guanajuato Rotary Club, in a most praiseworthy act, had the façade transported stone by stone and reassembled to form the front of the church known as Pardo Templo, a half-block from the city's main street.

About three miles above Guanajuato is situated the church of San Cayetano, popularly known as La Valenciana because it was built at the mouth of the mine by that name. It is dedicated to the Italian St. Gaetano (1480–1547), founder of the Theatine order. This church is larger than the one at Las Rayas, is more lavish in execution, and is still preserved in its full splendor on its original site. Further details are presented in subsequent plates.

The doorway that leads from the sanctuary to the sacristy (*fig. c*) shows the same scheme of decoration in stone carving which was applied to façades; here are the lambrequin and the Mudéjar arch, the divided pediment developed into three separate units, the medallions, the delightfully ruffled moldings, and the deep and closely filled-in spaces above the arch. An edge of the high altar, carved of

wood, gilded, and polychromed, is visible at the right. All these details bear witness that by the last quarter of the eighteenth century, Baroque, Churrigueresque, neo-Mudéjar, and Rococo were blended in Mexico into an operatic and ebullient style, which was expressed with equal felicity, regardless of the scale, in stone, stucco, or wood.

Humboldt also tells of a poor and simple Spaniard named Obregón, who in 1766 was working in the Guanajuato region at a depth of over 240 feet, but with little success. His enthusiasm for mining was so great, however, that rather than abandon his enterprise he accepted privation. A year later he entered into partnership with a small Las Rayas merchant by the name of Otero, and before another year had passed, the mine—later famous as La Valenciana—was producing silver. Between 1787 and 1791 the value of the extracted ore reached nearly two million marks, and by the end of the first sixty years the total production amounted to some $22,000,000. Among the barren rocks above the Ravine of San Javier, where, only a few years before, Obregón had started to prospect, a town of some seven or eight thousand inhabitants arose; by the end of the eighteenth century thirty-one hundred mestizo and Indian laborers were working in the Valenciana mine, nearly half of whom descended daily to a depth of over fifteen hundred feet. Obregón himself—better known as the Count of Valenciana—is said to have retained his simplicity of manner and unpretentious customs in spite of his vast fortune. Guanajuato then had reached a population of some seventy thousand, and here and there on streets that were fringed with the miserable huts of Indians stood the mansions of the mine owners, which, according to Humboldt, could have held their own in the great European capitals. Especially magnificent was the neo-classic palace built by Francisco Eduardo de Tresguerras for the Count de Rul, who married the third Countess of Valenciana and thus came into possession of the renowned mine.[115]

Just as the church of Santa Prisca in Tasco attracts the eye from the first moment that the town can be seen, so the church of La Valenciana immediately strikes the traveler as he rounds the mountain ridge and looks into the gorge where Guanajuato lies. The surrounding hills are more or less treeless and the deep green of the copse contrasts with patches of slag that form frozen pools or fantastic boulders. In the former mining settlements, sprawling over hills and *barrancas*, many of the houses are empty; their roofs have caved in and the sun pours into forsaken and crumbling rooms. But high on a promontory, La Valenciana stands intact, its stones tinged with a rosy tan and its shining dome reared against a deep blue sky (*Pl. 42, fig. a*).

This church, begun in the 1760's on the site of a chapel, was dedicated in 1788. The peons who labored in the mines for a pittance gave part of their daily wages toward its erection and furnishing and in addition spent their holidays working on the edifice without pay. It is said that silver was built into the foundations and fine wines were brought over from Spain to be used in mixing the mortar.[99] When it was completed, every miner donated to it a piece of ore the size of a man's fist. At times its income amounted to fifty thousand pesos yearly. The names of its architects and any details in the history of its construction perished with its archives during the struggle for independence.

As at Tasco, the central part of the façade is stepped back somewhat from the towers. Here also the entire central composition is homogeneous, drawn together under a pronounced arched cornice. In the tower bases the windows with neo-Mudéjar arches might well belong to a secular building; with the more modestly framed openings below them and the small star windows above, they lend a friendly aspect to the imposing front.

The *Gaceta de México* of 1788 describes this church as having two towers; the second one, however, was never finished. As the

building was going up and its projected magnificence was unfolding, the jealousy of the parish priest down in Guanajuato was aroused. He protested that the royal license had been granted for the erection of a hacienda chapel, not a basilica. The ensuing controversy held up the work until finally a compromise was reached and the rank of the church was lowered by completing only one of its towers.

The interior has a single nave, and a broad arch supporting the choir loft spans its entire width (*fig. b*). The spandrels, ceiling, pilasters, and even the walls carry stucco patterns in a soft creamy tone, which range from figural motifs to abstract designs. Similar pattern treatment is carried out on the wooden *mampara*, or entrance screen, so successfully that the various materials blend with exceptional harmony. A companion to the sacristy portal seen on the preceding plate is the entrance to the baptistry on the right under the choir loft; all the doorways within the building are of stone and are ornamented in the same manner. Over the side door, which leads out into a garden, is a molded shell of stucco, exquisitely shaped and fancifully decorated. In the corners of the ceiling a Gothic device is imaginatively applied with a highly Rococo effect. The inlaid pulpit, said to be made of exotic woods, is strongly Oriental in line. Two details from the retables will be seen on the following plate.

For all the variety they reveal, the lavish retables presented here (*Pl. 43*) are not far removed from one another geographically or chronologically.

Manuel Tomás de la Canal, a great patron of San Miguel de Allende, defrayed the expenses of the Loreto chapel there, and had a *camarín* constructed behind its altar. That small chamber is laid out on an octagonal plan, and above it four great arches cross to form a cupola with a central lantern, in the Mudéjar manner; a similar construction is found at Tepotzotlán, which also enjoyed the generous patronage of Don Manuel.[112] Here the walls are practically sheathed in gold, applied either on the carved wood of the retables or on the stucco decoration between them. A section of the side altar at the right of the entrance (*fig. c*) shows a most original arrangement—a sequence of huge leafy scrolls, with an angel head surprisingly worked in at the lower right. Protruding from this plastic composition, a scalloped baldachin hangs like a great blossom from a spray, suggesting a design on a Chinese wallpaper or screen. Judging from the space beneath the canopy, a statue larger than the present one may have stood here originally. This retable, dated 1735–1740, is the earliest of the group on the plate. Another interesting feature in this chapel— the panels painted above the two doorways— shows pages from some didactic book, greatly enlarged.

As mentioned above, de la Canal also made large contributions at one time to the rebuilding of the famous Jesuit college and church dedicated to St. Francis Xavier at Tepotzotlán; the college was endowed by an Indian cacique[129] as a seminary in 1582, and in early seventeenth century further gifts were received. In the eighteenth century the complex underwent several alterations, which terminated only in the 1760's a short time before the expulsion of the order.

Three typically Churrigueresque altars, inaugurated in 1755, are placed in a group at the apse end of the nave. Shown here is a detail from the left side of the main retable (*fig. d*). The *estípite* shafts are encrusted with flowers, medallions, shells, and various capricious shapes. Noteworthy are the depth of the retable and the many planes, a scheme that increased the saturation point for ornamental detail. Attention is focused on the expressive and well-executed statue of St. John the Baptist in the niche. Two angels ride on a spiral ornament above him, and cherubic figures in appealing gestures are balanced throughout the composition. Beneath the carved drapery, stepped back under a turret-like baldachin, is another saint, looking out from a medallion.

The façade of the church carries a design in stone very similar in spirit to this retable.

A comparison of the Tepotzotlán detail with one from the lower left of La Valenciana's high altar (*fig. a*)—of a somewhat later date (1788)—shows a different interpretation within the same style. In the first instance a complex scheme with an amazing variety of decorative elements was kept geometrical and cold but highly plastic; the second has a pictorial quality and greater clarity. Here the rhythmic and the linear are emphasized, and an immediacy and a softness in the composition are apparent. A Rococo element is noticeable in the slender spiraling garlands on the half-columns. The estofado on the statue of St. Joseph has a fluency which is also Rococo, and the panel behind him is enlivened with a scattering of bouquets like that on eighteenth-century wallpaper.

In the upper section of the retable in the left transept of the same church (*fig. b*), the Mother of Charity sits enthroned, a rather rare representation, clasping a second child in her arms. Two angels at her feet seem, from the positions of their hands, to have once held lute and harp. Before the window stands a heroic figure of St. Michael, holding a large cross as spear (*see Appendix, Pl. 191, fig. a*); the light pouring in from behind surrounds him like an aureole. Companion archangels are poised on massive corbels at either side of him. Although the figures here, all deeply symbolical, are no longer primarily story-telling, they are thoroughly ingratiating in their exquisite apparel and romantic carriage. The backgrounds behind the statues are sprinkled with painted nosegays, and the spiraling garland is seen again on the pilasters as well as on the arching gilded frame. Even the ceiling and the masonry walls tie into the composition through the vibrant lines of the molding.

Before the Conquest the city of Salamanca in the state of Guanajuato was a pre-Columbian settlement of the Otomi Indians, called Xidoo.[131] After the arrival of the Spaniards the brothers Juan and Sancho de Barahoma established there a hacienda, and in honor of the chaplain of the Conquistadores, who was a native of Salamanca, Spain, the Indian name was changed to that of the proud Old World city. It was officially founded by the Spanish in 1603. Blessed with abundant water for irrigation, the region supported many prosperous farms and orchards, and lush meadows provided pasture for the extensive cattle, sheep, and hog ranches owned by the Spanish gentry. Also in the district were many large Indian villages. The old parish church of the town is reproduced later in this chapter (see Pl. 47).

The Augustinians established themselves in Salamanca in 1616. Their church, San Agustín, unlike Santa Prisca and La Valenciana just seen, stands modestly on one side of a minor plaza. The building itself is tall and narrow, recalling the early type of church structure in Mexico. Its façade (Pl. 44, fig. a) is unpretentious, giving no hint of the splendor within. On either side of the single entrance are severe columns grooved with a widely spaced spiral. This portal has little of the Baroque in it; lambrequins decorate the square choir window and niches. Unusual is the placement of the crucifix at the very top of the building, where a flaring shell breaks through the cornice.

On entering, the visitor finds himself in a single-nave church which is virtually lined with polychromed and gilded paneling; vibrant gold sweeps from floor to vaulting and from choir gallery to crossing (fig. b). In the ceiling, lighted from the side entrance, bosses of gilded wood bring a strongly Mudéjar touch, and Mudéjar also is the pattern of the wooden choir-loft railing.

Passing this entrance—called the Portal Purísima because of the relief above it—one ⌐omes upon a side altar (fig. d), which is dedicated to St. Nicholas of Tolentino, the Augustinian friar of the fourteenth century whose statue was seen at Yuririapúndaro (see Pl. 31). Episodes from the life of the saint are dramatized with half-life-size figures set on corbeled platforms on the retable. The illustration here shows him with a beggar before him and two kneeling children pleading at his feet, all of them worked out in varicolored estofado; the beggar especially, in his theatrically picturesque rags and patches, is a truly Rococo figure. Above the group a boldly designed arch and shell effectively mark off the scene from the other decoration. But the most immediately striking element is the masterly executed mesh design forming the background. Like the great volutes, it is metallic in the precision of its workmanship and in its sheen.

Opposite that altar is one called La Consolación, dedicated to Santa Rita del Cassia, who is known as the Saint of the Impossible on account of her many miracles. The section pictured (fig. c) shows both the variety and the harmony which distinguish the decoration of this church. Against a carved and gilded linen-fold panel and below a lively valance stands the figure of the saint, while in the oval medallions are presented scenes from her life. For all their size these representations, carved in relatively low relief, are eclipsed by the shining and varied paneling which surrounds them. A basket-weave pattern spreads across the surface, interrupted here and there by leaves which are placed with great virtuosity, as if they were floating downward.

The main altar in this church was replaced in 1832 by a dull neoclassic construction, otherwise the interior has undergone no large-scale renovation. In deep transept-like bays at the "crossing" are two companion altars (Pl. 45), one dedicated to St. Joseph (fig. a) and the other to St. Ann (fig. b), mother of the Virgin. (The Christ in a velvet robe in the foreground, carrying the cross, is a modern statue which could not be removed at the time of photographing.) These magnificent altars are unique in both conception and execution; neither has much of the conventional retable about it. As if in deliberate contrast to those in the nave, which were kept relatively flat, emphasis was laid on the three-dimensional. Five scenes from the life of each saint are presented; the figures, almost life-size, are enriched with a colorful estofado, which sets them off against the golden background. In both cases the main tableau in the sequence is staged in a curtained niche under an immense crown, opulent and majestic. Atop each is poised an archangel, ablaze in the light that pours through the window behind him. Smaller crowns are placed like baldachins above other scenes to the right and left.

At first glance these two retables appear very similar; in general plan they are definitely companion pieces, with the dividing columns, the niches, the crowns, the drapery above the scenes suggested by voluted cornices, and the window, all substantially in the same arrangement. And both have exquisite but different interlacing patterns as background—a Mudéjar device used throughout this church. Upon closer scrutiny, however, differences are discernible, particularly in the details of the decoration. In the St. Joseph altar a greater spontaneity is evident. The motifs are larger and there is much more figural decoration; also several characters participate in the action. God the Father occupies the central position just beneath the arch, while in the other a purely ornamental garland is festooned across this space. In the St. Ann altar a hint of the neoclassic is noticeable; a greater restraint characterizes this retable and there is less variety in the motifs. Except for the Presentation (upper left) the drama is subdued. Only a single figure occupies the central niche, standing against an enchanting flowered pattern.

According to local information considerable work was done on this church interior in the last quarter of the seventeenth century (1683). It is claimed that the last refurbishment [107] of the church was begun in 1744 and finished in 1771. In the choir are large canvases signed by Juan Baltasar Gómez and dated Salamanca 1768. A gilded bench also is preserved from this period (see Pl. 187).

The confessional at the foot of the St. Joseph altar shows similarity in its heart-shaped garlands and frame to that in the church of Santa Rosa in Querétaro (see Pl. 185); indeed, the high quality of craftsmanship and the resemblances in the artistic idiom suggest a relationship between the working groups. The interior of Santa Rosa was completed in 1752, and it is possible that after the successful reception of the Querétaro nunnery church some of the masters connected with that building, as well as their craftsmen, were hired for the Salamanca church less than sixty miles away.

Some time after these stylistic observations were written they were corroborated by a contract discovered in the Querétaro archives and published by Heinrich Berlin.[48] According to that document one Pedro (Joseph) de Roxas was signed to carve and gild a lateral altar dedicated to "the Lady St. Ann" for the church of San Agustín in Salamanca. The tabernacle of the saint was to stand above the sagrario, and the window was to be integrated into the design. Mysteries from her life were to be incorporated into the work, as well as seven "Principals"—four on the four pilasters, two on the pediments, and the other, "who is the Lord St. Gabriel," in the Annunciation scene—each to be fitted into its proper place. The altar was to be carved within ten months and brought down to Salamanca where it would be assembled by the master and gilded by his own hand. He signed the contract on May 4, 1768. With the exception of the archangel figures, this contract seems to have been carried out more or less as drawn.

As yet little is known of the sculptor Roxas. He is mentioned in the notes of Tresguerras, the famous neoclassic architect born in Guanajuato, as claiming to have come from the capital and leaving only a number of side altars in Celaya, Salvatierra, and Querétaro; these works, in Tresguerras' opinion, were almost alike and were characterized by an intemperate extravagance. The same notes [127] mention that Roxas was known for his use of the figures "called from the Italian de Alquilé" and for a type of nymph "always useless, idle." The term *alquilé* might be derived from the Italian *a chiglia* (as on a keel or prow of a ship).

Fortunately taste has developed far beyond the academic norms of the neoclassic epoch. Travelers of the early nineteenth century recommended Salamanca as well worth a visit for the remarkable altars in its Augustinian church.[133] Today, off the railroad and tourist route, it is rarely mentioned in guidebooks, though it has retained one of the best preserved church interiors in all the country, a monument of North Mexican Rococo.

Certain façades in Mexico are striking for the detail work in their decoration and others attract attention through their irregular ground plans and the manipulation of their wall planes. Of the latter group the façade of the church of La Soledad in Oaxaca (*Pl. 46, fig. b*) is an excellent example (*see also Pls. 10, 66*). Its walls are brought forward obliquely on either side of the door, section by section, like the wings of a paneled altar screen, with the outermost panels standing parallel to the recessed portal. In general the decoration is conservative and shows fine details. Different treatment was accorded the columns and niches in each tier, and an interesting variety was achieved through the two reliefs in the central section. The statuary, which is in an amazingly good state of repair, has dramatic expression. This church and its nunnery were constructed for the Recolet nuns of Santa Mónica between 1682 and 1695, when they branched out from their convent in Puebla. Its greatest benefactor was Pedro de Otálora, a statue of whom appears in the top frame at the right.

In the same city stands a former Jesuit church, now known as La Concepción (*fig. c*). The Jesuits arrived in Oaxaca in 1576. Their house and church underwent considerable repair after the earthquakes of 1607, 1787, and 1801. At the time of the second catastrophe the order had already been expelled, and in 1790 the complex was given in the name of the king to the nuns of the Immaculate Conception.[103]

The church is built on a platform and is approached by a flight of steps, a position which emphasizes the monumentality of the structure. In contrast to La Soledad, the portal here protrudes and the two sides turn back to connect with the towers (*see also Pl. 169*). The engaged Plateresque columns stand on high pedestals, and especially noteworthy is the stepped molding on the receding wings. The restraint noticeable in the decoration may be explained in part by the straitened circumstances of the order here when it started.

From the very beginning of the Conquest Oaxaca was important as a main station on the Royal Highway to Central America. The town's population increased from 120 in 1522 to 2,000 in 1626 and to 14,000 in 1790. It derived a considerable income from the production of cochineal, a clear red dye manufactured from a tiny insect that feeds upon the cactus. All Oaxaca churches are noteworthy for their stonework; the Zapotec and Mixtec Indians, natives of the region, were excellent masons, as their nearby pre-Columbian ruins testify. In colonial days Oaxaca early had her own school of craftsmen; over forty local carvers of the period between 1680 and 1800 are known by name from their contracts.[48]

The region around Zapopan, only about three miles northwest of Guadalajara, came into prominence much later than Oaxaca. As one of the missionary centers from which friars pushed on into California, it is intimately connected with the development of our own West. In the early seventeenth century Zapopan had a primitive Marian sanctuary in charge of Franciscans, which was taken over by secular clergy in mid-century and a new building raised.[98] The present edifice was dedicated in 1730.

This Sanctuary of Zapopan (*fig. a*) stands in an immense flagstone atrium that can hold a multitude of pilgrims. The façade of the building is on one plane, but the set-back of the lofty octagonal towers (they are more than 120 feet high) and the protruding masses of the grouped pilasters at the sides break the line. Giant volutes make the transition between the piers and the towers, producing a highly Baroque effect. The portal section is mild, in the mid-seventeenth-century style of Mexico, and the espadaña is extravagantly high, richly ornamented. When viewed from a distance the Sanctuary beckons with a kind of rustic joviality, the yellow plaster of its façade blending with the rose-colored stone of the towers and the sparkling majolica on the melon-shaped domes.

Within this Sanctuary is a miraculous statue of a crowned Virgin in praying pose, at her feet a crescent moon with a human face. On Sundays and especially on the fiesta of the patroness in October, this quiet monastic place teems with people, who come on foot and by bus for prayer and a leisurely outing. Then the gray flagstone patio is enlivened by the happy hubbub of children and the gay colors of Indian tribal costumes.

In this northwestern sector of Mexico, where a prosperous mining industry brought general economic well-being, architecture in the eighteenth century reached a high level of craftsmanship. Many of the façades display a strongly regional manner of decoration; unusual undercutting, the close grouping of motifs, and the combination of shallow and deep relief all blend to give an effect of tapestry or embroidery. The examples shown here (Pl. 47) are taken from towns that have already been encountered in this work.

In Guadalupe, a suburb below Zacatecas, a college was founded in 1707 by a friar sent out from Querétaro, and its adjoining church, dedicated to the Virgin of Guadalupe, was opened in 1721. An old guidebook (1887) describes the trip from Zacatecas in the nineteenth century, when tramcars ran out by gravity at a high rate of speed, winding through streets and past mine heads, slag heaps,

and primitive smelters. On the return trip the car was dragged up the steep slope by six mules, harnessed three abreast.

The façade of the church of Guadalupe (fig. b), stepped forward, resembles the familiar retable type, but only in the first story. Its columns are divided into three sections, one showing figural decoration, one twisted, and one covered with a basket-weave pattern. Above the angular arch a high relief shows the miraculous Virgin of Guadalupe being painted by the Apostle Luke. Francisco de la Maza points out that his eyes are of obsidian and his palette is inlaid with colored stones—a practice that recalls the early *tequitqui* work.[111] The upper section of the façade is marked by two somewhat extended columns, which lift the espadaña well above the roof line, while the two outer columns are little more than stumps. The carving on this portal is so specifically regional that it may have been executed by members of the school—perhaps even by the same team—which worked on the cathedral of Zacatecas (see Pl. 7).

The tower on the right is contemporary with the rest of the building and, crowned with multicolored tile, harmonizes with it. That on the left is an addition from the late nineteenth century and justifies the sharpest of the criticism directed at the many similar architectural atrocities which have been committed in Latin America during the last hundred and fifty years.

The church of Santa Mónica in Guadalajara, said to have been established in 1720 for nuns brought from Puebla,[98] was mentioned earlier in connection with its gigantic statue of St. Christopher (see Pl. 38). On the twin portals of this building (fig. a) the regional sculptor again made use of a tapestry-like treatment. Grapevines spiral about the twisted columns and maize cobs can be distinguished among the dense carving on the walls. In the wide frieze above the doorway, two angels—suggestive of mermaids—hold a heraldic device which features a heart with arrows, a miter, and other emblems of the order, and on the face of the pedestals at either side of them a caryatid is wreathed in vines. The composition is without the undulating lines, the sweeping curves, or the swelling masses of the Baroque; in spite of its late date and rustic cadence it has much that derives from the Plateresque.

Salamanca's old parochial church exhibits still another aspect of the regional manner. Its rustic façade is more or less contemporary with the others on the plate; Churrigueresque *estípites*, with niches between them, and an elaborate star window place it in mid-eighteenth century. But the section here reproduced (*fig. c*), showing a niche and pillars at the right of the entrance, presents regional forms and motifs that are strongly folkloristic. Small screw-shaped columns terminate in canephorae, and below the niche two masklike heads end in fishtails or leaf spirals. The arch is angular, like that in the Guadalupe portal. Here the shafts of the bulky columns are divided into two sections, the lower cut with a zigzag pattern. In the upper portion the fantastic twisting spiral, half shell and half flower, brings to mind pre-Columbian carved serpents. Cherub heads look out between the coils. At the base of the right-hand column is a group of little atlantes, nearly concealed under their decorative guise. A human figure stands on a console at the edge of the façade, dressed in a jerkin and high boots and carrying objects in both hands; the large shell behind his head could be a gloria or even a feather headdress. This old church is now in a run-down sector of the town and a high solid wall hides most of its first story from the street. But for those who seek it out, it has much to reveal even in its neglected state.

For an illuminating comparison one should turn at this point to the illustrations of Arequipa and Puno, in Peru, and La Paz and Potosí, in Bolivia. There too a regional dialect in stone carving was developed, roughly contemporary with Mexico's. Guatemala also found its regional expression about this time,

but in polychromed stucco work. The differences in the various manners will become more evident as these chapters proceed.

Guadalajara, founded by one of Cortés' officers as a base for conquest toward the northwest and along the Pacific coast, is described in the early seventeenth century as having six hundred Spanish residents, exclusive of the servant class. By that time the region already could boast a well-developed agriculture and animal husbandry; sugar mills were in operation, and the preserves made from the native and Spanish fruits of its orchards were famous. In colonial times the city achieved an importance second only to that of the capital, a position it has retained to the present day.

The Palace of the Audiencia of Nueva Galicia (*Pl. 48, fig. a*), in Guadalajara, now houses government offices. An extravagant, somewhat swaggering edifice, it gives character to a bustling plaza in this modern city. It was constructed between 1751 and 1775, apparently under the architects Nicolás Enríquez del Castillo and José Conique; a tablet in the spacious hall bears the date 1774. Churrigueresque elements, such as the monumental *estípites*, were used in the two upper tiers. But the suggestion of statues in the armor racks applied as finials, the illusionistic play in the rustication, and the simulated drapery under the overhanging cornice are all delightfully and richly Baroque. The columns on the ground floor, with their crisscross pattern, are also in the Baroque tradition, as are the huge volutes. The window framing, so quiet in line, and the plain wall surfaces lean toward the Rococo—some might say the neo-Mudéjar. From such diverse styles could the imaginative architect in eighteenth-century Mexico choose his decorative motifs.

In the espadaña many of the same elements are repeated. A hanging garland falls on either side of the protruding clock, and a highly decorative use is made even of the metal clock springs; in the double spirals just below the balcony, carved in stone, the position is reversed. The waterspouts have the shape of cannon, a sign of privilege.

The Ecala Palace (*fig. b*), one of many seignioral mansions in Querétaro, dates from the last decades of the eighteenth century. It is said that its proprietor, Manuel L. de Ecala, and his next-door neighbor began to renovate their houses at the same time and were soon involved in a building race. The adjacent façades were pushed farther and farther into the plaza, until finally the city authorities intervened and stopped them where they stood.[117]

Little decoration was used on the broad banded arches. The continuation of the pier lines through the pilasters to the roof is extraordinarily effective (*see also Pl. 40*), and an interesting use of scrolls was made on the modest capitals. As was general at that time, the second floor was made more elegant than the first; all of its openings are doors letting onto balconies, a scheme common in Venetian palaces as early as the thirteenth century; the deeper balcony conforms to Spanish practice. In the highly ornate grillework (signed by the local master Juan Ignacio Vielma) the central place is given to a double-headed eagle. Although some fifty years had passed since the Habsburgs stepped down from the throne of Spain, Mexican folk art was still clinging to a motif with which it had become enamored —and indeed it has not yet discarded it.

Much of the wall space was left plain. Even the framing of the windows shows restraint; but the independent and massive stone pediments above them are sufficient to ornament the whole. Such heavy and elaborate decorative members distinguish public and private buildings of the same epoch in Pátzcuaro and Morelia. (*See also Pls. 166, 171.*) A twisted rope of stone frames the wide frieze of blue and white tiles under the roof cornice. The small opening at the left, surrounded by carved drapery, once held the family coat of arms. In 1862, when the display of heraldry was suppressed by edict, the center of the

stone emblem was effaced and a window broken through.

In general in colonial architecture the decorative features were refined while the structure itself remained rather heavy and uncomplicated. Some edifices, however, show much play with sophisticated form. The jewel among these is El Pocito, the Chapel of the Little Well (*Pl. 49, fig. a*). It stands in the suburban village known as Guadalupe (the Arabian name of a city in Spain) some three miles northeast of the Mexican capital. Here occurred, before the Indian Juan Diego, the first appearance of the Virgin in the New World; the miraculous likeness of her on his cloak is enshrined in the vast basilica, a favorite pilgrimage place for all Latin America. The chapel, adjacent to the basilican complex, is built above the spring that is said to have gushed forth from the rock on which the Virgin stood. All day long Indians can be seen filling their pitchers with the water, which is credited with healing powers.

Construction on the chapel was begun in 1777, with funds provided by some large private contributions but chiefly by alms from the populace. Workmen donated their services on Sundays and holidays, and it is said that even ladies and gentlemen of fashion helped carry construction material with their own hands. The work took fourteen years, and in 1791 the *Gaceta de México* published the plans, the cost, and the names of the contributors.[129] The architect, serving without remuneration, was the famous Francisco de Guerrero y Torres, who also remodeled the palace of the Count of Santiago (*see Pl. 40*) and designed that of the Marquis of San Mateo de Valparaiso, now the National Bank of Mexico in the capital.

It has been pointed out that a drawing by Sebastiano Serlio may have inspired the ground plan. This great architect, born in Bologna in 1475, wrote a number of architectural treatises, which were published between 1537 and 1583; a Spanish edition of his works first appeared in Toledo in 1552. But though a two-dimensional Renaissance plan may have provided the inspiration for the layout, the talent and imagination of Guerrero y Torres conjured up into three dimensions this fairy-tale Rococo building. Covered with blue and white Puebla tiles, with the ribs of chrome yellow, the three domes seem to vibrate in space above the dark maroon-washed walls. Contrasting white effectively sets off the star windows and lacy portal. Its proportions, its domes with their airy lanterns and ring of frilled cornices, its portal with the fantasy stucco panel and multifoil neo-Mudéjar arch—all are highly original.

It is interesting to note that Mudéjar decoration featured the six- or eight-pointed star and that this shape was favored by the Rococo for windows. While it became fashionable in Europe to cover domes with overlapping slate in a fish-scale pattern, in Mexico the system of laying tiles flush over domes, arranged to bring out a polychrome pattern, was retained to the end of the colonial period. (*Compare Appendix, Pl. 190, fig. e.*) Noteworthy also are the size and variety of Mexican domes, which often were raised over even smaller and less important churches.

Zacualpan-Amilpas, in Morelos, is best known for its sixteenth-century Augustinian "fortress" church and conventual foundation; adjoining that edifice is a chapel which is also well worth a pause (*fig. c*). This building appears to have been erected early in the second half of the eighteenth century, but since the archives in Morelos were destroyed during the revolution, nothing definite is known about its history. It shows a delightful play with elliptical forms and Rococo details. In the view printed here the curved lines of the plan are apparent. The bays with their semicylindrical connecting members and the scalloped cornice of brick and stucco are as unusual as they are genial in effect. Note that the ribs of the dome are not extensions of the pilasters at the corners of the drum but that they end above the windows. Probably the building was once painted in various hues. With its many planes and different levels, it still makes an arresting picture.

In the eastern part of the Valley of Toluca is a large spring-fed swamp, out of which flows the Rio Lerma, Mexico's most important river. In colonial times the city of Lerma, situated on the edge of this swamp, was a prosperous community, though now the population is less than twelve hundred. It was granted a city charter in 1613, and for a short time during the struggle for independence, it was the capital of the state of Mexico.

Near this town two haciendas were maintained by the Carmelite order. One of them, now named San Nicolás Peralta, has within its building complex the church of San Miguel (*fig. b*), constructed in mid-eighteenth century. A scalloped wall encloses the modest atrium. The façade seems small in proportion to the dome and tower; it has, however, a subtly shaped star window and is decorated with plain *estípites* and lively moldings. The majority of the workers on this farming establishment were mestizos and Indians—probably only a handful of religious lived here. For that isolated group this church with its affable lines must have been a source of great pride; it evidences the devoted care lavished upon it. After secularization the hacienda passed into the hands of the Peralta family, and in the present century it changed hands again. The church now stands empty and abandoned. Despite the distance between this building and certain Jesuit *reducciones* in Argentina (*see Pl. 128*), they have in common a friendly, rustic aspect.

As a prologue often sets the mood of a play, so a portal frequently gives character and spirit to an entire building. Six examples of such portals, ranging in date from the second half of the sixteenth century to the end of the eighteenth, are illustrated here (*Pl. 50*). Many others, equally pertinent, could have been chosen from the immense variety still to be found in Mexico.

It has been suggested that the panels on the portal of the colonial house in Puebla called the "House of Him Who Killed the Animal" (*fig. c*) were copied from some hunting scene on a Flemish or French tapestry of the fifteenth century; indeed its tight composition and interlocking masses are distinct characteristics of tapestry. The lintel panel shows a somewhat compressed rinceau featuring pomegranates and, in the center, a basket of flowers, a favorite subject in colonial art. The design on the simulated capitals is strongly reminiscent of pre-Columbian carving.

In the remote village of Angahua, in Michoacán—a Tarascan district only recently brought to public notice through the volcano Paricutín—the Franciscans built the church of Santiago, dated 1577. The portal (*fig. a*) is strongly Mudéjar in general composition, but in its detail it is permeated with the Indian spirit of the regional artist. A deeply undercut relief of Santiago, as a pilgrim figure on foot, occupies the central position, and a metal cutout of the saint on horseback is nailed to the wooden door. The representation of Santiago as a pilgrim occurs in Latin America and Spain much less frequently than in most parts of Europe; found here, it calls to mind that this region of Mexico was evangelized by one Jacopo Daciano, perhaps a native of Dacia (Rumania) though called a Dane by the chronicler Mendieta.[118] The original doors of the church, now part of the garden portico, are carved with reliefs of Biblical scenes and saintly figures.

Just outside Pátzcuaro, likewise in the Tarascan region, is preserved a wayside crucifix that was venerated by the Indians in the early decades after the Conquest. Besides inscriptions, a coat of arms, and religious symbols, it bears the date 1553, making it no doubt the oldest cross in the vicinity.[130] Early in the seventeenth century this shrine was enclosed within a small chapel, which is known as El Humilladero (*fig. b*). In design its portal is Renaissance, but a strange and local interpretation of that style. The slight break of the pediment

is filled with a cross carved in relief, and at the sides are pinnacles which seemingly some regional artist translated out of a two-dimensional drawing as best he could. On the face of the pediment are the figures of Father Sun and Mother Moon, symbols common to many religions. The pattern around the archway reminds one of a chased silver band, but enlarged in the manner of the Indian and infused with a vigor and an immediacy which sprang from the soil of this place. This chapel and its garden are enclosed by a high masonry wall. Another cross, dated 1628, stands among the cypresses in the idyllic atrium.

These three examples fall approximately within the first century after the Conquest—at least before 1650—and show Indian versions of medieval, Mudéjar, and Renaissance models, respectively. The three to follow are of later date but no less revealing.

The church of San Francisco at Ayotusco, in the state of Mexico (*fig. d*), shows a type of pilaster that reached a highly characteristic development in Guatemala and Honduras (*see Pl. 70*). In this example the pilasters seem to be divided into segments by a series of sharp-edged moldings and various symbols are carved in the narrow fields between. The two windows with their octagonal frames and cruciform grilles of cut stone are powerful in their simplicity. Two vases inserted into the wall on either side of the central niche act as finials, naïvely executed but decorative. The broken pediments of the side niches bring out the triangular build-up.

During the century preceding the Conquest Texcoco rivaled in importance the Aztec capital of Tenochtitlán, and its people enjoyed a high level of culture. Their material wellbeing was seriously impaired by civil war, however, even before the arrival of the Spaniards, and Cortés took advantage of the existing feuds to use Texcoco as a base in his attack on the other city. Here the flat-bottomed boats propelled by sails and oars, which had been fabricated in Tlaxcala and brought across the mountains in sections, were re-assembled and launched upon the canal that led to the Aztec island capital. After the Conquest, pending the building of Mexico City, Pedro de Gante founded the first Franciscan mission here. This establishment remained strong in the region and continued to be enlarged and refurbished well into the late eighteenth century. The church of the Third Order in Texcoco stood at the edge of the Franciscan property, its portal facing the great atrium (*fig. e*). Above the neo-Mudéjar arch floating angels uphold a crown, and on the heavy cornice stand finials, like vases on a shelf. Regional preferences are evident in both the lining and the framing of the star window. Also characteristic is the ease with which the stucco garlands are applied at the sides, here composed of fruits, some of which look like bananas, rather than flowers. Surmounting them are two larger angels, each of whom is standing on two cherub heads pasted against the wall. Floating angels were used prominently in the decoration of the main church, erected in an earlier century, and it is not surprising that the lay brotherhood should choose the same motif. A pattern simulating brickwork, such as framed the side niches in the preceding illustration, decorates the pilasters. When we revisited Texcoco in the late 1940's this charming composition, full of the spirit of folklore, much to our dismay was gone, a victim of "renovation."

Long and proud is the history of Mexico's Royal and Pontifical University. Functioning under the aegis of the Jesuits, it possessed large tracts of land, on which numerous buildings were grouped about cloisters and gardens. In mid-eighteenth century the order consolidated its various seminaries into a single institution. The portal illustrated here (*fig. f*) is elegant in build-up. Its piers are decorated with stone filigree work carrying Churrigueresque motifs, and that style is evident also in the lambrequins in the center and in the console aprons on the bases. The heraldic emblem in the rounded pediment is the Bourbon coat of arms. When the old university building was demolished, early in the twentieth century, this portal was transferred to the School of St. Peter and St. Paul. The tile panel and the composition which surmounts it are additions from that time.[108]

As was mentioned earlier, the atrium, sometimes a large area, remained important throughout the colonial era; even today much of the village life takes place in the plaza on which the main church stands. Here is the market place, where on holidays peddlers and itinerant showmen converge with their tents. Usually the fireworks and rockets which constitute an important part of a fiesta are set off here. Many churches have kept their yards separated from the public square, and because a parochial church was an object of special pride, such enclosures—especially around Texcoco—also reflect the peculiar artistic imagination of the regional craftsmen. The parish church at Chiconcuac, an ancient Indian village known even today for its weaving, has an atrium with three gateways. The three arches of the main entrance (*Pl. 51, fig. a*), which opens on the town's main plaza, are decorated with modest stucco moldings; considerable ornamentation, however, rises above the heavy cornice. A figure of St. Michael, the patron of the village, occupies the central niche, which is flanked by massive scroll buttresses. To the right and left stand two stone slabs pierced with star-shaped openings, and ornamental vases provide further decoration and height. On the curving wall beside the pier is a large lion, inspired perhaps by a heraldic emblem or possibly by a Chinese porcelain figure treasured in some eighteenth-century home. An occasional human figure and tall ornamental finials are placed at intervals along the coping. Finials occur on many walls in nearby villages, sometimes taking the shape of an elaborate pottery incense burner reminiscent of pre-Columbian work.

Papalotla, a few miles beyond Chiconcuac, is another old Indian settlement. The present parish church there was begun in 1719 and finished in 1733. Its atrium gateway (*fig. b*), here seen from within the enclosure, carries the date 1733 on the keystone. The profuse *argamassa* (plaster) ornamentation which covers both sides of the arcade shows a powerful regional spirit as well as strong influences of the Mudéjar.[78] Atop the cornice again appears a statue of a saint, blocks with star-shaped openings, and giant urns. The forms which buttress the central niche here are unmistakably animal, and for this reason the scroll pieces leaning against the niche at Chiconcuac can also be interpreted as derived from heraldry.

The portal to the Hacienda de Cristo Grande (*fig. c*) shows an example of neo-Mudéjar decoration used on a private dwelling. This estate, situated near Atlixco, is said to have been named for a great crucifix that stood in its chapel in viceregal times. The building itself is a sprawling one-story structure, with a chapel at one end, and the portal shown opens into the patio of the master's rooms. In design it resembles the ornamentation around a fireplace. On the top, carved in much deeper relief to make it stand out, is a huge coat of arms, boasting a crest of helmet and plumes. The adjacent spirals, occupying a similar position to those at Chiconcuac, might well hark back to a rampant animal of heraldry. With their fluting, the unusual chimney-like blocks suggest column shafts or pedestals and may once have carried ornamental finials (*compare Pl. 32*). A wide triple-arch gateway leading to the estate is embellished in a similar manner with stucco decoration, and still preserved in one of the rooms is a broad plaster frieze with a strongly Moorish flavor.

This manor house stands on a knoll, its vast rich lands spreading around it. As one looks out from the terrace, giant snow-capped volcanoes fill the sky, while in the foreground lie the multicolored houses of Atlixco and its Franciscan monastery. A little below the house is the hacienda's reservoir, which catches all this beauty in its sparkling surface. In such an Arcadian spot one can understand why some

still think with longing of the life of the colonial centuries.

Before 1903 Marfil was the last station on the railroad that now runs on to Guanajuato, and the few miles up to that city were covered by mule-drawn tramways through the Canyon of Marfil. So long as the mines of the district were being worked intensively, Marfil was a thriving settlement supporting two churches—one for the upper section and the other for the lower. Today, however, it is a ghost town, with here a house crumbling into a heap of rubble, overgrown with riotous flowers, and there a bridge, its noble Baroque balustrade half in the river bed, leading to nowhere.

The region has always been subject to water famine in the dry season and catastrophic washouts when the rains begin, but during the prosperous days a system of reservoirs was built to restrain the floods and store the water supply. On the eastern slope of the gorge stands the Presa de los Santos, the Dam of the Saints (*fig. d*). The buttresses of this stone and brick construction were utilized as bases for a series of stone shafts—plain except for moldings and lambrequins—which, in turn, served as pedestals for a row of elegant Rococo figures. These statues, each in a different pose and costume, are as dramatic as actors in an open-air theater. Although the structure is greatly damaged, its suavity and perfection are still delightfully real. In Congonhas do Campo, Brazil, is another example of statues digested effectively into the out-of-doors (*see Pl. 173*).

Some of the Baroque in Mexico, working with volume and shadow play, brings out the animated rhythms of the style. Much of it that was selected for this chapter is characterized by lavish surface ornamentation, which had a strong appeal for the regional craftsman and often carries reminiscences of the Plateresque and the Mudéjar. Occasionally some of the façades remind one of the architectural inventions which appeared as frontispieces in

European books; in the New World the colonial artisan made of them structural realities, creating a style more Baroque in its daring than the Baroque of Europe.

Only in a land with Mexico's heterogeneous background, in which both tradition and a constant renewal of art influences operated, could such varied interpretations appear so close together in time and place. Like the anonymous builders of the Romanesque and Gothic cathedrals in Europe, the people here were emotionally involved in their architecture. As long as Renaissance models were put before these neophyte Christians, they remained, in general, copyists. But by the time the Baroque arrived, their pagan past was well behind them and they carried on under the power of their own imagination, giving to this style a new significance. Their names may long have been forgotten and many of their creations may be neglected, but enough remains to demonstrate how a talented people made Baroque their own exuberant language.

Mexico's vast repertory of colonial architecture unfolds as one stands on the main plaza of a large city, walks along the single street of a small town, and, traveling in the country, catches sight of a distant church off the highway. Even far across the cactus-hedged fields the rich façades beckon; after centuries of exposure the tiled domes still have enough color and glaze to reflect the sun. Against a brilliant sky they blend in dignity and beauty with the ever-changing, yet changeless landscape—forgotten jewels of a magnificent epoch.

7

RELIGIOUS DRAMATIS PERSONAE

Drama has served religion as handmaiden from time immemorial. Much of the ceremonial accompaniment of the medieval church was adopted from earlier religions; music, chanting, the dance, allegories in elaborate costume, the offering of flowers both real and artificial, and statues adorned with precious materials were all drawn in to tell the Christian story. The Passion play, instituted in Gothic times, has survived into the twentieth century, and the macabre rite of the *penitentes* continues in such disparate regions as Belgium and New Mexico. The occasions seized upon for ceremonial display are legion. On St. Hubert's day hunters carrying their horns march into church in their red coats and caps for a special service. In numerous countries the sea is blessed with appropriate rites for the safety of seafarers and fishermen, and in certain regions of Europe all household animals and vehicles—now even the automobile—are paraded to the church steps to receive a blessing. The marriage of Venice and the sea, during which a ring was flung into the waters in the presence of ecclesiastic and civil splendor, was celebrated even into the twentieth century. Numerous saints were—and are—honored with festivals on their respective days, and through the visits of the multitude to their chapels these places often have developed into popular shrines. Many other saints are venerated throughout the entire year, among them St. Anthony, for bringing back things lost,

including lovers and husbands; St. Christopher, for his protection of travelers; St. Gaetano, for promoting business; St. Filomena, for warding off evil; and St. Roch, for healing the sick. Today over two hundred Virgins and saints are popular in Spain, counting only the major ones.

Spectacular processions celebrated religious holidays in many European countries. Court, military, and civil functionaries, in addition to the clergy, marched in gala, while the dazzled populace framed the pageant. Religious statues, reliquaries, banners, lanterns, and candles were carried by gorgeously caparisoned knights of the church, as well as by lay orders in austere robes. Masters of the guilds participated with their emblems, and the sound of orchestras and the chanting of choirs mingled with the incense rising from heavy silver censers. In Spain such processions were especially magnificent. The Spanish church retained much Gothic mysticism, added to it the illusionism of the Renaissance, and staged the pageantry with devices created by the Baroque. Even today spectators from foreign lands crowd into Seville, Toledo, and other Spanish cities at the various holy seasons to witness the celebrations there.

In Spain the religious statues, which were the chief protagonists of such ceremonies, changed during the sixteenth and seventeenth centuries, and the appealing and warmly human expressions of the Renaissance gave place to asceticism, agony, and ecstasy. The sculptors who carved these statues belonged to a professional guild. They received their training by apprenticeship and had to pass strict examinations before they could work independently or take on pupils. They were required to submit their plans and sketches to experts for approval, not only with respect to the artistic concept but also to make sure that the iconography or manner of representation was acceptable; such experts were specifically named in the contract.[26] Small wonder that Pacheco's *El arte de la pintura, su antigüedad y grandeza*, first published in Seville in 1649, was the painter's standby for more than a century, for it describes with authority not only the methods of mixing and applying the various colors but also the manner of representing the countless figures of saints and allegory.

In the carving and coloring of holy imagery, sculptor and painter worked hand in hand. Generally all wood statuary—and much of the stone—was painted. The *imaginero*, or carver of images in the round, executed a figure with all the finesse of his craft before it was given to the painter. In the coloring, a waxy tinted finish, called encarnación, was used to represent flesh. At first this was executed in oils, which produced a porcelain-like translucency that was lifelike and dramatic, especially so under the flickering light of candles and tapers. Encarnación could be either high gloss or matte. Pacheco himself much preferred the latter and presented many arguments in its favor, but the glossy type persisted in many colonial centers where wood sculpture was of exquisite quality.

The figured textiles for the garments were depicted with elaborate patterns worked out in color on a gold or silver base; this technique was called estofado—significantly enough, a word that also means "quilting." ("Encarnación" and "estofado" are technical terms for which no English equivalents exist; they are taken over here from the Spanish in the hope that they will be admitted into the English vocabulary.) Three different crafts were involved in the decoration of a statue: that of the painter, the *encarnador*, and the gilder. Pacheco was a master of all three and collaborated with such great sculptors as Juan Martínez Montañés and Pedro Roldán. In discussing techniques, he advised that first the carving be de-resined with hot substances, then all the knots and cracks be filled, and finally a thin plaster base be applied for the colors. Sometimes layers of gold leaf were then laid over the entire surface of the statue, but more frequently the flesh tones were painted on a carefully sized base and only the garments were gilded. Pacheco executed his estofado work in tempera, which was spread in layers over the gilding and then removed in sections with a fine instrument to reveal the metal, as the pattern required; sometimes color predominated and sometimes metal. The gold might be burnished, or given a dull finish, or damascened; work in relief and tooling in lines, dots, and crosshatching offered endless possibilities for variety. With the increase of production, less extravagant methods were devised. Occasionally contracts specified that oil paint was to be used exclusively.

Pacheco also furnished instructions for applying color to silver gilt and for painting with oil on stone and on the various silks used for banners, horse trappings, and the like. He discussed, too, the proper varnishes for the preservation of the work.[32]

Religious statuary in wood shows three distinct types: statues carved entirely of wood and finished with encarnación and estofado, as just described; those dressed in garments made of a cloth which was stiffened and molded and then painted; and the "candlestick" figure. This last type has head, hands, and sometimes feet of carved and painted wood, but the body consists only of an armature or is stuffed like that of a doll; such figures wear real robes of velvets, brocades, or other materials richly embroidered with gold and pearls. It should be noted that as early as the sixteenth century sculptors were urged to deliver their figures complete with carved garments so as to spare the community the expense of costuming and re-dressing them; most of the costumed armature figures extant, however, date from mid-eighteenth century if not later. Frequently the religious figures of the Baroque period are life-size, or even larger, and have eyes of glass, human hair, and long applied eyelashes.

Not only the type of religious statuary in Spain but also the pageantry there was transplanted in the New World. In this hemisphere the Roman Church intensified all its activities. In Europe it had only heretics to fight, but here a heathen continent had to be brought within the realm of the Cross. The Indian had a great artistic past of his own, but his concepts had been developed in isolation and along completely different religious and social lines. He was ignorant of Christian iconography; his pantheon was populated by numerous gods—of rain, wind, maize, flowers, war, and death, to mention only a few. He had, however, been accustomed in his former religion to colorful celebrations—processions, dances, and plays. Spectacular rites had been ingrained in the lives of these peoples for too many centuries to be easily uprooted.

The complexity of the problem facing the early missionaries is revealed not only in the strict discipline meted out during the conversion period—and even later—but also in the art of the Spanish colonies. In interpreting for the Indian the life of Jesus, the exemplary behavior and authority of the saints, the drama had to be reiterated and the spectacle often over-emphasized. Thus was created, in great measure by anonymous artists, statuary with an amazing story-telling quality, which enabled the unlettered neophyte, by observation alone, to grasp the idea behind the material. Whether the figure was plastic or pictorial, whether the representation was calculated to be moved about or shown in a fixed arrangement, it had to have dramatic impact, and in most cases it was loaded with it.

A great number of stirring Baroque and Rococo statues executed in Latin America have survived and show the richness of the plastic *comparserie* which played an important role in the religious life of the colonies.

Before the Renaissance the Eternal Father was represented frequently in the art of Europe, but with the coming of the Baroque, the subject was rather neglected. In Latin America, on the other hand, innumerable Baroque altars carry the figure at the apex, and in the eighteenth century it appears also on the carved stone façades of many churches, especially in the High Andes.

The God the Father here presented (*Pl. 52, fig. a*) is in the seminary church of San Antonio, in Cuzco, Peru. It is of polychromed wood, except for the garments, which are textile, starched and painted. The second sculpture (*fig. b*), from Quito, Ecuador, is of miniature size, carved from a tagua, a native nut of South America which is soft when fresh but becomes as hard as bone; for this reason it is used for small carvings as a substitute for ivory. In both examples the Eternal Father is represented as rising out of a cloud, his right hand raised in benediction as iconographically prescribed. In the Quito piece he clasps a sphere, emblematic of the world, and his triangular halo symbolizes the Trinity. It has been suggested that the triangle—a survival from the earliest Byzantine period—having the shape of the Greek "D," also proclaims him *Dios*, God; here, however, the significance of the shape seems to have been lost, for the aureole rather looks like a bishop's miter.

The two statues of St. Christopher (*figs. c and d*) come from Mexico. The first is in the cathedral at the capital and the second in the cathedral of Cuernavaca. These carvings show Christopher in the full vigor of manhood; both figures have their trousers rolled above the knee, which makes them appear taller. In the life-size Cuernavaca piece the muscular and robust are emphasized, even to the point of clumsiness. The drapery, with its heavy-patterned estofado, is massive, and the staff is an actual sapling. The Christ Child, too, is a sturdy figure. The expressions of surprise and delight which pass between the two is tellingly communicated. The other Christopher, which measures only about three and one-half feet high, has little of the heavy-blooded heartiness of its companion piece. Here the garments are painted in flat light colors, without gold, and the treatment of the drapery—indeed the whole figure—conveys the striding through wind and water. While the Cuernavaca statue has the jolly air of provincial Baroque, the smaller one has a pastoral quality in the spirit of Rococo. (*See also Pl. 146*.)

St. Sebastian has been a favorite subject with artists ever since the Renaissance, not only for its artistic possibilities but also because of its emotional content. Sebastian was an officer in Diocletian's army who was condemned to be shot to death with arrows. However, when St. Irene and other Christian women came to bury him, they found him still alive and nursed him back to health. He is venerated as a protector against pestilence, symbolized by arrows. Usually he is represented as bound to a tree, either surrounded by his persecutors or deserted and unconscious, left for dead; more rarely he is shown with ministering women or angels.

Pictured here (*Pl. 53*) are four portrayals of this figure from as many countries. The painting (*fig. a*) hangs in Cuzco, Peru, and the relief (*fig. b*) is in the sacristy of a chapel dedicated to the saint in León, Nicaragua. Both probably trace back to the same origin. Van Dyck painted St. Sebastian at least seven times, with either one or two angels removing the arrows (*see Appendix, Pl. 191, fig. b*). This artist also made engravings of his own canvases, which in turn inspired popular prints. The two compositions here show basic similarities: the position of the saint, the cord tying him to the tree, the fall of the hair and drapery, and the placement of the arrows. Even the tree is developed in the same manner, though in the relief it is a palm. The angels,

however, are quite different, in position as well as in dress. Another painting of this subject, very similar to the relief, hangs in the Convento de los Descalzos in Lima, Peru, and is signed Carreño.

Of the two statues shown here, the first (*fig. c*) was carved by Juan de Chávez and stands in the cathedral at Guatemala City. With the upcast eyes and open mouth, it has a *larmoyant* realism. Allegedly it was made in 1737 for the cathedral of Antigua, and subsequently it was transferred to the new capital. The wood, from an orange or a lemon tree, has a firm and even grain.[145]

The second statue (*fig. d*) is in the church of San Sebastián in Quito, Ecuador. This figure shows a deviation from the traditional posture: the right arm is upraised and bound to the tree trunk instead of the left, the usual pose in European iconography and that in the Guatemala carving. The somewhat cool and intellectualized expression given to the Quito statue and the delicate pattern of the estofado would place it in the second half of the eighteenth century. It is sometimes attributed to Caspicara.

A studied elegance is evident in both pieces —the one from Guatemala has a certain preciosity and the one from Quito, placidity. In each the estofado has its own characteristics and the encarnación shows differences in coloring and texture. A more intensive study of the traditional representation of St. Sebastian will be found in Chapter 12 (*see Pl. 138*).

The tableau of the manger scene harks back to the grotto where Christ was born. The earliest Christian art depicts it, and it was a part of the Christmas festival in medieval churches, probably posed with living figures. Gradually, to the first simple group—the Babe adored by the Holy Pair under the mild gaze of ox and ass—were added the shepherds responding to the angel choir; the visit of the Wise Men following the star came later and waxed important because of the pageantry it furnished. Such tableaus were the core of the

Nativity plays and were held inside the church; even dances were executed in the vestibules and atriums. Gradually comic relief and extraneous episodes became so numerous in the performances that in the thirteenth century the pope banned them from consecrated buildings; driven into the streets, they continued to expand, sometimes playing different scenes in different parts of a town and thus varying the settings. Artists of note assisted in the staging and costuming of the dramas, putting into them the talent and originality customary in all the celebrations of those days.

Sculptured Nativity groups appeared in Florentine churches in the early Renaissance, and Naples also began making them at this time. Again the picturesque and dramatic possibilities led to an elaboration of the simple story. One early contract called for—in addition to the Holy Family, the ox, and the ass—three shepherds, twelve sheep, two dogs, four trees, eleven angels, two prophets, and two sybils.[17] In southern Italy the shepherds soon developed into representations of all the humbler classes of that heterogeneous society, from street vendors to strolling players, peasants, and laborers, while the entourage of the Three Kings might comprise Eastern princesses with their entire retinues of slaves, entertainers, and luggage trains, including camels and drivers— all coming to pay tribute to the Holy Child.

In the seventeenth century some four hundred churches and many private homes in Naples were displaying elaborate manger groups at Christmas time, and by the eighteenth century the carving and costuming of the figures constituted an industry. Naples used terra cotta or wood for its figurines, which varied in size from very small miniatures to those a foot high; later even costumed marionettes were used. Magnificent Baroque palaces and landscapes, as well as the humble cottages and inns of the countryside, were constructed of wood, cork, and stucco. Sicily's manger groups were generally carved of wood and painted; sometimes, however, Sicilian figures were dressed in real textiles, which had been stiff-ened with plaster, then molded on the figures and, when dry, painted. Here the drama of the Nativity was expanded to include other Biblical sequences, among them the Massacre of the Innocents, the Flight into Egypt, and even scenes in the carpenter's house in Nazareth.

During much of the sixteenth century and all of the seventeenth, Naples and Sicily together formed a viceroyalty of Spain, and even in the eighteenth century they were still closely connected with that country. Many of the Neapolitan sculptors of miniature figures were employed in the ceramics factory of Capodimonte, which was later transferred to Spain. Manger figures and the later genre figurines in wood and porcelain, being small, were easy to transport and may well have constituted one of the channels through which European artistic currents were introduced into the New World, especially from mid-seventeenth century through the eighteenth. The Latin American *pesebre* (manger group) reveals European influences, but in each area regional taste preferences and individuality also are evident.

From an early date the Christianized Indians participated personally in various religious plays. An eye-witness account from 1587 tells of a mystery play about the coming of the Wise Men which was acted out by the Indians of the region around Tlajomulco (Jalisco), Mexico. Booths of green boughs on two sides of the plaza represented Herod's palace, where a feast was going on amid much buffoonery, and the humble stable of the Nativity. An angel in the church tower notified the shepherds on the adjacent hillside of the Holy Birth, and they came down singing in the native tongue and shouting "Goria, goria . . ." in their strange pronunciation. Meanwhile, following a star which ran on two ropes from the tower, the Wise Men could be seen making their way on horseback down the mountain, from such a distance that it took them two hours to arrive. They were accompanied by an ancient Indian, the oldest man in the region, and after they laid their gifts before the Child, he knelt and told Him in his Indian dialect that he himself was poor and had nothing to present save his labor and suffering. A handful of Spanish friars and laymen attended the performance and over five thousand Indians flocked to it from the region round.[123]

Two kneeling figures of Mary and St. Joseph that were carved for a manger group are in a private collection in Querétaro, Mexico, where they have been preserved for over half a century in perfect condition (*Pl. 54, figs. a and b*). According to local information they were formerly in the possession of the last Mother Superior of the convent of Santa Clara and had been handed down in her family from the eighteenth century. Although at first glance they might appear to some as rather sweet, their relatively small size and their purpose—part of an intimate and elaborate manger group—prevent them from being in any way saccharin. In them the true drama of the scene can be sensed, transmitted with great sincerity. The drapery is handled with clean-cut precision and the estofado is masterly; the all-over, rather loose patterns accord with the stylistic preferences seen in the Rococo churches of Querétaro. Meticulous care is revealed in the variety of the coloring. Mary is robed in a white gown flowered with gold. Her dark blue cloak has, on the outside, a golden pattern brought out by different kinds of tooling and is lined with palest turquoise delicately striped in gold. Joseph's color scheme is olive-green, with red flowers outlined in gold and dark blue; his cloak is golden, lined in coral-red crossed by slender stripes of blue and gold.

The encarnación on the two figures has preserved its especially fine waxy texture and appeared somewhat pale when the statues were brought out into the patio to be photographed. But as they were warmed by the sun, the cheeks actually began to take on a blush. It seems that the sun's rays affect certain ingredients in the colors, bringing out richer tones.

Rubens once wrote to the painter Sustermans that he was afraid that the colors in a picture of his, long crated, had suffered, especially the reds and the white, and reminded him that this could be remedied by exposing the painting to the sun at intervals.[13] The red paint used in the encarnación of the Querétaro statues apparently began to show the same reaction.

Two examples of the Guatemala school of sculpture are shown in the figures of the Virgin and Child and the statue of St. Joseph. The group carving (*fig. c*) is somewhat earthbound by the cumbersome robe, despite its exquisite estofado. Interesting are the angel heads at Mary's feet, not too common in seated representations of this subject; their presence and the fussiness of detail indicate a desire to heap on as much decoration as possible.

More spirituality is evident in the figure of St. Joseph (*fig. d*), which, from the pose, probably belonged to a manger group. Reverence and loving concern are expressed in the face and in the inclination of head and body. A conscientious realism is manifest in the carving of the hands. The eyes are Indian, but not so the beard and curly hair. In its large widely spaced pattern, the estofado is typical of Guatemala work. The variety of color and pattern in the cloak, robe, and tasseled tunic, the elegance of the burnished gold, and the carving of the drapery as it hangs over the arm all attest to the hand of a master.

As the sense of security and the wealth increased in the colonies, rivalry ran high in both civil and ecclesiastical circles. It was a matter of pride—indeed, often a measure of it—as to which sector of a town had the larger choir in its church, the more instruments, the finer vestments, the heavier silver, and the larger and better statuary. From this atmosphere of expansion and competition, especially noticeable from mid-seventeenth century to the end of the eighteenth, the arts profited greatly. In the decoration of a private chapel it enkindled much splendor. The monasteries—and even more the nunneries, to which often the daughters of nobility retired —showed particular zeal in sponsoring the fine arts and the applied and folk arts.

The Mary and St. Joseph from a manger group in a private collection in Quito (*Pl. 55, figs. b and d*) are said to have come from Cuenca or its vicinity in southern Ecuador. They are carved of balsa wood and are so light in weight that one is surprised upon lifting them. Balsa, a corklike wood native to Ecuador, is extremely buoyant and has a velvety texture; when freshly cut it is easy to shape, and because of its porous character it holds glue and coloring remarkably well. It was used for furniture as well as for statuary. These figures have hooks affixed to the backs, which are not entirely worked out; apparently they were intended to be secured against a background, perhaps in a niche. The armature is of wood and the garments are of woven materials, stiffened and painted; such drapery could be executed most easily with textiles, for then the many angles could be arranged before the starch applied had set. The coloring is rather dark, and the estofado pattern differs from that in the preceding examples. Though these figures, like those just shown from Querétaro, have glass eyes and "real" eyelashes, there is nothing dollish about them. They are typical of the high standards of workmanship in Quito toward the end of the eighteenth century.

The Nativity scene in the Guadalupe basilica near Mexico City (*fig. a*) contains a contemporary figure of the Christ Child, rarely preserved in such colonial groups. These statues are all of wood and show great delicacy in the carving of curves and folds; brilliant craftsmanship is evident in the estofado. It has been suggested that they belong to the Guatemala school of carving, examples of which were illustrated on the opposite plate; for they too have in their estofado a large repeated pattern, such as was popular in that country.

The last group (*fig. c*), part of a private collection at San Miguel de Allende, Mexico,

probably dates from the end of the eighteenth century. In general impression, the estofado has the somewhat diluted pattern—in keeping with Rococo taste—which is apparent in the Querétaro figures just mentioned. A detail of Mary's cloak is illustrated later (*see Pl. 84*).

Since so many of the main altars in colonial churches have fallen victim to the modernizing rage of the last century, it is fortunate that side altars and side chapels survive —some of them with little over-painting or structural change—in which the art standards of the period can be studied and enjoyed.

One such chapel, in La Compañía of Bogotá, Colombia, has a group of life-size figures just above the altar which depicts the Ecstasy of St. Ignatius Loyola (*Pl. 56, fig. b*). The tableau, framed by a heavy proscenium arch, shows the saint in the arms of a ministering angel during his trance, which lasted for eight days. In the middle distance stands an archangel with one foot resting on several tomes, the topmost of which is entitled *Heresis Lutheran.* . . . He is flanked by two globes showing the New and the Old World and is exhibiting a page emblazoned with the phrase: "The sword of the spirit, which is the word of God." Angels on the other side hold the cardinal's hat and robes which the saint in his humility refused. The encarnación, with its ivory sheen, is especially beautiful. On the background at the left is painted the bare room of a hospital and on the right, a landscape with a ship; the center panel, like a backdrop, carries a columned altar and a figure of the Virgin. A triangular arrangement, classically correct, prevails for the main figures, and the lines lead to a vision of Heaven, full of Baroque exuberance. Here a riot of little angels bearing mottoes, a shield, and other emblems, centers on the symbol of the Almighty, brilliant with gold—a triangle bearing Jehovah's name in Hebrew. Below the clouds, golden trumpets proclaim: "Through all the earth. . . ."

The tableau is inscribed in the left corner

as the work of Pedro de Laboria, an Andalusian sculptor who carved several single statues for this and other Bogotá churches. It bears the date 1749.

A statue of St. Joachim (*fig. a*), part of an altar dedicated to the Virgin of Chiquinquirá (*see also Pl. 149*), stands in a chapel of the church of San Diego in Quito, Ecuador. The saint is dressed in stiffened and painted textiles. But perhaps more important than the figure in this case is the setting. Subtlety is revealed in the framing of the niche, shell-shaped as was the tradition. Its upper section is carved with leafy motifs, which emanate from behind the head as if from the halo and appear again outside the arch; flowering garlands and scrolls, lightened by basketry work, frame the sides. These same motifs are varied on a larger scale and with great elegance of detail in the vertical garlands of the altar wing. The two shields, placed against the pilasters, are survivals from the Baroque, but here they have little weight and blend into the general composition. Color comes into its own in this altar. The surface of the panels has a most unusual metallic luster, probably produced by the application of transparent coloring over a base of silver or gold. Bright floral sprays are well spaced to enhance the relief work, and nosegays dot the background of the niche and the estofado of the statues. Gold is used only to bring out the composition. The colors are vivid and varied, a brilliant green predominating. So high was the general standard of workmanship in Quito that even this less important establishment could boast such an exquisite interior.

Some religious statues were carved to fit into a definite place, often as part of a larger composition, while others were created to participate in the various outdoor processions of the church year. In the statue of John the Evangelist (*Pl. 57, fig. a*), said to have come from Ayacucho, Peru, only the head and hands were sculptured of wood; the body is a mannequin, clothed with a robe of woven material. This figure of the friend of Christ is carried beside the Dolorosa during Holy Week. Fine encarnación is visible, and the hair is interestingly carved in a rather classical manner. The head is fifteen inches high, and the features are large and sharply delineated to convey the expression to the crowds along the way.

The bust of San Pedro de Alcántara (*fig. b*) is a nearly life-size polychromed wood carving from seventeenth-century Mexico. This Spanish saint of the sixteenth century was a conscientious Franciscan who lived a rather unmolested life, without torture or martyrdom. Tradition has it that his love of God was so intense that it caused him actual pain and frequent ecstasy. Thus it is a spiritual experience that is communicated here, though with such power as to suggest physical suffering. The transfixed eyes of glass, the exhausted open mouth, the cheeks haggard from inward torment, and the distended veins of the throat all give the piece a disturbing fascination.[109]

San Raimondo de Peñaforte was a thirteenth-century Spanish nobleman who became a general of the Dominican order. Uncompromising in his crusade against the Moors, he even dared to reprove the King of Aragon, who then banished him to the island of Majorca. But when he miraculously returned home the king yielded, and Raimondo died in Barcelona in his hundredth year. In this portrayal of him from Argentina (*fig. c*) vehemence and a fighting conviction dominate the visage, with its windswept beard. Movable arms are fitted into sockets at the shoulders, and over this construction is hung a velvet mantle.

The next statue (*fig. d*), three-quarters life-size and carved of a very heavy wood, stands in Lima, Peru. It probably represents St. Joseph. Especially noteworthy are the drape of the mantle, the easy-lying fold in the collar, and the fine execution of the veined hands and fingers. The gestures are quiet and show great dignity. Probably the upraised hand once held a staff. The other one, like the gaze of the figure, is directed downward, as if guiding the Child on the journey out of Egypt. Seemingly this figure is unfinished, for it has neither gilding nor paint.

In contrast, the wood carving of St. Francis of Assisi in Ecstasy (*fig. e*), from Mexico, shows a perfect finish. The large pattern of estofado, in burnished gold against the dark brownish tone of the robe, is evenly distributed; a different design decorates the edges of the cowl and sleeves, and the cord has a flowing line. Glass eyes and long eyelashes add realism to the somewhat *larmoyant* gesture. There is no feeling of weight—the figure seems to be floating, even to move upward. Zurbarán painted St. Francis kneeling thus with wide-open arms.

The last statue in this group, probably of St. Bernardino of Siena, stands in the church of San Francisco in La Paz, Bolivia (*fig. f*). Bernardino, a great and persuasive Franciscan preacher of the early fifteenth century, founded the Monte di Pietà, an organization which lent money on small pledges. He is often represented as carrying a tablet surrounded by rays and inscribed with the monogram IHS. Here again only the head and hands are plastically executed; the brown habit edged with gold braiding covers an armature, but a positive sense of the body is present. As is often the case with colonial sculpture, the sensitive hands—which probably clasped his emblem or a crucifix—convey much of the mood. The eyes and mouth have unusual beauty, and the whole face has a mystic, inward-turned expression. There is something eerie in the sheen of the smooth-falling silken robe as it catches the reflections from the shiny encarnación of the face and casts them back again.

A comparison of the three heads in the upper row and the three figures below them reveals different manners of representing hair. In two instances baldness adds to the characterization.

Jerome, born in the fourth century and one of the four Latin Fathers of the church, is the patron of students and scholars, especially theologians. For years he lived as a hermit in the Arabian desert, where he was subject to temptations and visions and heard the trump of doom. In penance for his love of earthly learning he studied Hebrew and made the Latin translation of the Bible known as the Vulgate. A lion became his companion after he had fearlessly drawn a thorn from its foot. Jerome's symbols are his lion, his cardinal's hat, and the trumpet of the Last Judgment. He was a favorite with artists in the colonies. His story has many picturesque details and the tame lion especially must have been a fascinating subject at a time when the zoology of distant continents was awakening intense interest. The variety in pose and gesture accorded to this saint is amazing, even in the six examples reproduced here (*Pls. 58 and 59*).

The first statue (*fig. a*), from an eighteenth-century chapel in El Tejar in Quito, Ecuador, again illustrates the high standard of execution in the Quito school. The saint's cloak is unusually ample and his cardinal's hat is of fine red leather.

A high relief of this saint (*fig. b*) constitutes one of the series of magnificent wood carvings which line the apse of the church of San Francisco in Bogotá, Colombia (*see Pl. 26*). The trumpet, hat, and lion—here with the face of an old man—are all represented, as well as the stone with which the hermit saint was wont to beat his breast. The wilderness is pictured as a fantastic forest, all the trees of which, like the saint's cloak, are studded with flowers. In the frieze below the panel, strange birds and heaps of fruit partake of the same exuberant fancy; the masks with rings in their mouths might have been taken from some design where such rings served a really functional purpose.

The next statue of Jerome (*fig. c*) stands in the church of San Pedro in Juli, Peru. It has lost much of its paraphernalia and the colors are somewhat dulled, but it nevertheless has an appealing quality, augmented by the unnatural but effective presentation of a gaunt aging body. This carving has been compared to the famous work of the Italian Pietro Torrigiani (1472–1522) in Seville, Spain. The gestures differ somewhat, however, and in addition the European piece places the main emphasis on realistic anatomy rather than emotional content.

Still another interpretation is seen in the carving from Guatemala (*fig. d*). Here the saint leans over a book, under which lies a cloth wonderfully executed in the best estofado. The lion has almost human features —the popular concept of that animal was far from realistic. Note also the treatment of its mane in the various illustrations. The influence of Flemish and Central European engravings on the art of the colonies, which will be discussed more fully in Chapter 12, is strikingly demonstrated here. This statue is a translation into the three-dimensional of an engraving by Justus Sadeler after an oil painting by Jacopo Palma the Elder (*see Appendix, Pl. 190, fig. g*).

Of the two Jeromes pictured on the next plate, one (*Pl. 59, fig. a*) formerly stood in the chapel of San Andrés in Cuzco, Peru, and is now on a side altar of La Compañía there. The body is dark from smoke and repeated varnishing. The expression here is perhaps the most dire and dramatic of the six and the emaciated body transmits best the asceticism of the hermit.

Greatly simplified in gesture and anatomy is the statue of Jerome from Argentina (*fig. b*). This figure shows a new posture and a somewhat different expression. The treatment of the beard and hair, the twist of the body, the position of the legs, the hollows in the cheeks, and the drapery all point to later and different sources. The lower half of the carving has a ceramic-like brittleness. Besides his halo this Jerome wears the sign of the *tres potencias*, an attribute of Christ. (*See also Pl. 148.*)

A depiction of father and daughter is most unusual in the roster of religious statuary. A feeling of joy and freshness—even briskness—

emanates from the Mexican statue of St. Joachim carrying the child Mary (*fig. c*). Virtuosity is revealed in the sweep of the drapery, which effectively points up the delightful mood.

The carving of John the Evangelist (*fig. d*), from Brazil, was made to be viewed in profile and to stand at the foot of the Cross. As in the statue of Joachim, the mood of the portrayal—here one of intense emotion—is accentuated by wind-blown draperies. The whole body seems swept toward the left, that is, toward the crucifix. The estofado is built up of large patterns; little gold is visible. This sculpture is an example of Rococo rhythm; beside it the Baroque statue has an earthbound joviality.

The head of St. John the Baptist—prize of Salome's dance—has intrigued the imagination of artists, writers, and even musicians into our own day. It was a favorite subject in Spanish art. Murillo—whose work is unjustly catalogued as "sweet"—depicted it, and it was a vehicle for a number of other Spanish painters and sculptors. In a subject so iconographically circumscribed, the characteristics of a particular artist or school reveal themselves.

An example from Mexico (*Pl. 60, fig. a*) shows the martyr's eyes all but closed and a sagging jaw, in a realistic expression of death. But realism is not carried through; there is little blood, the hair does not fall as it would for a recumbent position, and the head is most effective when standing upright. The mark in the forehead should be noted. It has been suggested that this might represent a caste mark seen in some Hindu or East Indian figure; but it rather derives from Maya and Aztec traditions, in which semiprecious stones were set into the faces of statues.[125]

A carving from Peru (*fig. b*) represents the head on a platter. A terrible gauntness is depicted, the eyes are half-open, and bloody hair flows over the dish. This stark portrayal makes a rare impact; it sounds only a note or two, but they are struck with full force.

In contrast what elegance has the head just below (*fig. d*). This comes from the retable of Martínez Montañés in La Concepción (*see Pl. 15*), in Lima, Peru, and demonstrates the suavity of the imported style. The lips are serene and the eyes softly closed. The hair is carefully arranged, with attention to the effect produced, which above all had to be beautiful. Through its calculated finesse, this carving achieves a touching quality, whereas the piece above it—the expression of the land—conveys the story in all its violence.

Another version of this subject is presented in a polychromed wood carving in the church of San Juan de Dios in Granada, Spain (*fig. c*); it has been attributed to Juan Alonso Villabrille, or a contemporary eighteenth-century sculptor.[31] In it the attempt to portray the gruesome and the horrific is so obvious that it all but misses the mark. The mouth—open, as if shouting—is hardly that of a dead man, and the Medusa locks are arranged primarily as decoration; indeed at the top they lose any vestige of realism. The virtuoso routine of the sculptor is most evident in this piece; but it conveys neither conviction nor a spiritual message.

The two lower carvings show extreme interpretations of the Old World approach; the upper ones present the reaction of the New World to the same story. All are studies of violent death, and in their differences they reveal the artistic and psychological chasms which existed between the two civilizations.

The saints of Heaven were not the only figures to take part in the religious drama, for earthly mortals, too, are found in the holy company, preserved for posterity. The colonies offered a fecund soil for religious fervor, and often the entire fortune of a family was left to the church.

Francisco de Villacís, a royal commissioner of the Quito district, in Ecuador, defrayed the expenses of a whole chapel (1661–1662) in the church of San Francisco. His statue there represents him in the traditional pose of devotion (*Pl. 61, fig. b*). The costume of the period is depicted in detail, showing the full heavy cloak with its tasseled cord, the boots, and the trousers with buttons up the leg.

More individuality is perceptible in the kneeling figure of García Sarmiento de Sotomayor, the Count of Salvatierra, in the Peruvian capital (*fig. d*); his full titles contain nearly fifty words.[199] Born in Spain, he was appointed a viceroy of Mexico in 1642 and of Peru in 1648. Upon his retirement, some seven years later, he did not return to Spain because of the perils incident to the war with the English, and he died in Lima in 1659. His statue, carved entirely of cedar, has considerable realism. The eyes are of glass. The hands, in their conventional pose, show much character. Noteworthy also is the careful execution of his wig.

In the church of El Carmen Moderno in Quito is the praying figure of Andrés Paredes y Almendaris, bishop there from 1735 to 1745; he was responsible for the construction of this building, which was completed in 1743. The statue is attributed by some to the great mestizo sculptor Bernardo Legarda, who will be discussed more fully in Chapter 9; the date of the donation would fall within the period of his activity.[176] Others assign it to one of his best pupils, Jacinto López y Gregorio, who worked somewhat later.[183] The features are striking, and despite a stiffness in the carriage, there is living individuality in the piece. The lace edge of the bishop's surplice and the cloak are of starched textiles.

Manuel Tomás de la Canal was the benefactor of the agricultural, commercial, and industrial center of San Miguel de Allende. He was born in the Mexican capital in 1701 and at the age of thirty was admitted to the Order of Calatrava, a military society second in importance only to that of Santiago. He was alderman and mayor of Mexico City and held the same offices later in San Miguel. He sent to Rome for the measurements of the Santa Casa of the Virgin of Loreto and at his own expense had a reproduction of it built in the Oratorio de San Felipe Neri, in San Miguel. The Santa Casa is the cottage in Nazareth where the Annunciation was made to the Virgin; twice, according to the legend, it was miraculously translated to escape the advancing Turkish invasions and finally reached the vicinity of Rome. Both side walls of the Mexican interior are hung with fine damask, giving the impression of a mundane salon of warm elegance. Here, in a niche, is placed a portrait statue of de la Canal (*fig. a*), holding a votive lamp in his aristocratically slender fingers. The frame and the lamp are nineteenth-century additions. In a similar frame on the opposite wall of the chapel is a portrait statue of his wife. The carving of him is made of a single hollow piece of wood, even to the fine edge of the long coat; only the silk scarf is of real textile. His costume shows the familiar style of mid-eighteenth century. The date 1735 above the niche refers to the construction of the chapel; it is easily possible that the statue is of a later date—even by several decades —for often such a portrait, whether carved or painted, was executed after the death of the person. Both Don Manuel and his wife died[134] in 1749.

To create the endless procession of religious figures in the New World, all available resources were drawn upon. European models and methods were modified not only by the ingenuity of native talent but also by influences from the Orient. One of the main routes by which exports from the Far East reached Europe after mid-sixteenth century was via the Philippines to Acapulco, Mexico, and thence, after reloading and transshipping, from Veracruz across the Atlantic. Missionaries introduced European Renaissance and Baroque art into Japan and China, as they did into the New World, and it is recorded that art objects were sent as gifts from Macao on the Chinese mainland and from Japan to the Americas.[14]

The appealing figures which make up the Holy Family group with St. Michael (*Pl. 62, fig. a*) are such gifts, carved in China in the late seventeenth century under the supervision of Portuguese missionaries. Except for the arms and the wings of the archangel, each statue is carved of a single piece of ivory; in the larger figures, about twenty-seven inches tall, the curve of the ivory tusk is clearly visible. They are surprisingly heavy. On close inspection the drapery, especially that of Mary and St. Joseph, and the gold ornamentation are reminiscent of work on Chinese porcelain. This scene suggests the return from Egypt; both of the adults are extending a hand toward the Child, a large pilgrim hat hangs down the back of Joseph, and he may have once carried a staff.

The Michael originally did not belong to this group. It was found by the author amid a jumble of miscellaneous paraphernalia in a storeroom of the cathedral in 1933, when he had these ivory statues photographed for the first time.

Behind the altar in the Sala Capitular of the Dominican monastery in Lima, Peru, is a series of carved ivory plaques set in wood. One of them depicts the Resurrection (*fig. c*). An alien air pervades the whole composition, and it would seem that this piece, too, came from the Orient. Ivory as a medium was unfamiliar to the New World craftsmen, as was also the technique of undercutting as it appears here. The clouds surrounding Christ are executed in the flat manner of Chinese work and the angels' skirts fall like Chinese drapery. The angels hold a crown as for the coronation of the Virgin and carry the palms of martyrdom —attributes seldom associated with the Saviour. Perhaps the most striking detail is the sun in the upper left—with a short beard and mandarin-like mustache—which probably symbolizes God the Father. The pale matte surface of the ivory plaque contrasts pleasingly with the elaborate gilded woodwork into which it is set.

These were instances in which objects from the Orient, exposed to the view of local artists in the New World, brought powerful and direct influences from a different civilization.

But such Oriental pieces were limited in number here, and since fashion favored them, the native artist sometimes adopted Oriental motifs and mannerisms. For the plaque showing Santa Rosa or St. Catherine (*fig. b*), Huamanga stone was used, a variety of alabaster found in the Andes. Skill in composition as well as in technique is revealed by the gradations in the relief, which emerges in some details into the full round. But what makes the piece extraordinary is that the pedestals, upon which the saint, the angel with the attributes of martyrdom, and the church are placed, are red lotus blossoms, common in Chinese art.

Such tablets bearing religious or symbolic reliefs have been found in various regions of the High Andes; this one is now in La Paz, Bolivia. They may have been made for votive offerings or perhaps for individual gifts. They recall the carved jade plaques of contemporary China, which were set in ornamented wooden stands for use as table screens.

A fascinating blend of Christian legend comes out in the small polychromed wood statue of San Juan de Dios from Pátzcuaro, Mexico (*fig. d*). The saint here is carrying a wounded man. That this figure represents Christ (as in the story of St. Martin) and not merely some poor traveler is revealed by the nail marks on the hands and the fact that the faithful have fitted him with a pair of tiny silver sandals. The headband also may signify something more than a simple bandage; in pre-Columbian times it was a mark of authority. He is clothed in blue and gold patterned trousers and a white shirt ornamented in gold. The saint wears a brown habit, relieved with fine gold striation, such as is seen often in paintings and estofado work. One might think that the saint's head and Christ's figure were of ivory, so striking is the encarnación and so precise the carving. Worm holes throughout the piece, however, prove that it is entirely of wood. The disproportionately large bald head in itself might be considered an Oriental feature. Pátzcuaro, a Tarascan town, was an important center in colonial times and had a number of local sculptors and *estofadores*.

By mid-seventeenth century in many colonial districts a vigorous folk art was thriving in which European iconography was adjusted to regional tastes and talents. Certain subjects that were popular in Europe never became favorites here, whereas others, which appealed to the fancy of the regional artists and the populace, were much repeated. As the neophyte became better acquainted with the hierarchy of Heaven, the folk artist expropriated many religious symbols and used them in an unorthodox way. In 1600 an edict prohibited crosses, heads of Christ, figures of the Virgin and saints, and scenes from sacred history to be carved, engraved, painted, or embroidered on furniture, utensils of any kind, and bed and table linen. Molds for pastry and sweets, however, in the shape of sacred hearts and other such symbols were allowed, since, being edible, they were not treated irreverently. Many other folk customs persist here to the present day. Wishes are still written on paper and dropped into a well in one cloister dedicated to Santa Rosa in Lima. Paintings of miraculous escapes adorn the walls of many pilgrim shrines; religious statues are hung with miniature arms, legs, crutches, and the like, called *milagros*, in token of wondrous healing. If a household saint does not comply readily to an appeal, he may be reminded of his obligations by being shut in a dark place, turned upside down, or made to face the wall.

Among the favorite subjects of the folk artist in the colonies were the archangels and Santiago. In the cathedral of Cuzco, Peru, the side chapels are closed off with gilded wooden grilles and the semicircle of each archway is filled with figural groups. In one of these St. Michael and four other archangels are represented (*Pl. 63, fig. a*). In the second figure from the left, St. Raphael is recognizable by the fish dangling from his hand; the others have lost their distinguishing symbols. All are armature figures dressed in stiffened textiles that are gilded and colored—a veritable plastic ensemble, especially effective at the great height of the arch. The visitor has only to move about to have protagonists of the religious drama brought to life before his eyes.

Santiago, or James the Great (the Apostle of Spain), was one of the most popular saints in the colony. Historically he was James the son of Zebedee, whose brother was John the Evangelist. According to the Golden Legend, he journeyed to Spain to preach and later returned to Judaea, where he was the first of the Apostles to be martyred. His body was miraculously transported to Spain and, after performing many wonders, it finally found rest at Compostela. The Visigoth and Mozarabic liturgies of the early Christian era in that land call him the "Evangelist of the Peninsula." Because he assisted the Christians several times in battles against the Moors, he became the patron saint of Spain.[30] His first appearance is recorded as in A.D. 939, when he was seen on a white charger bearing a white banner and leading the troops of the King of Castile in the great victory at Clavijo. Thereafter "Santiago" became the Spanish battle cry. The same saint was made the patron of a military order of Spanish knights, whose *ejecutoria*, or patent of knighthood, always carried a picture of that battle scene at the head of the parchment. Knights of this order, among them Hernán Cortés and Pedro de Alvarado, six viceroys, and several other notables, came to the New World and helped spread the popularity of the dashing figure. In 1805 in Peru alone 138 such knights were counted, and 155 cities and villages in Spanish America carried Santiago in their names.

For the Indian, Santiago must have epitomized the Conqueror, who, bearded and pale-skinned, was borne on a marvelous steed and possessed invincible weapons and supernatural power. He is said to have appeared in the New World fourteen times between 1518 and 1892, the first instance being in Tabasco, Mexico, during the fight at Centla before the taking of the Aztec capital.[30]

The three carved statues of Santiago pictured here (*figs. b, c, and d*) are processional figures from Argentina, Peru, and Mexico, respectively. The first is dressed in starched textiles, painted, the second in actual clothing, embroidered, spangled, and trimmed with lace, and the third is of polychromed wood. Variety can be observed in the expression and execution of all three; simplification is carried farthest in the Mexican piece. The steeds have the verism of a rocking horse or a carrousel figure. The Moor on the ground beneath the horse's hoofs was so universal that it may be assumed that he has been lost from the example in the middle. A sham battle between Spaniards and Moors was a part of the religious drama and a standard feature of certain fiestas in the New World. It may have derived from the medieval mystery plays that depicted the battle between the forces of light and darkness; the masks of the Moors often have the aspect of the Devil. Usually it was staged in a humorous vein, with much clowning and roughhouse. Today it has passed into folklore. (*See also Pl. 139.*)

The Holy Family group on this plate (*fig. e*), represented as resting on the flight to Egypt, is from San Miguel de Allende, Mexico. The bodies are stuffed and dressed in real materials. The heads and hands, of wood, attached to the bodies like those of a doll, are finished with a porcelain-like *encarnación*. It has been suggested that the group was made either by Mariano Perusquía or by Mariano Montenegro, well-known mid-nineteenth-century sculptors. An angelic sweetness is in the expression, and a naïveté characterizes the arrangement. Small birds are perched in the palm tree, and on the ground are gathered numerous miniatures. The sheep, some of which are made of wax, bear the names of parishioners long since dead.

Also taking part in the Holy Week processions—and sometimes in the dances that follow —are people dressed in masks and appropriate costumes to impersonate with as much illusion as possible other characters from the religious drama. Two eighteenth-century masks are shown here (*Pl. 64, figs. a and c*). The first, from Toluca, Mexico, represents a centurion, one of the soldiers who drove Christ upon the Via Crucis. It rested on the upper part of the wearer's head, making him very tall, and he looked out between the fierce teeth. Notable is its strong resemblance to a jaguar, revered in pre-Columbian times. This mask is a tawny gold with some metallic coloring on the helmet.

The carved wooden mask of Judas (*fig. c*), from Michoacán(?), shows excellent modeling, brought out by the shiny encarnación—blue and mauve on a pasty white ground. Both mouth and nostrils are cut through, and slits above the eyes make vision possible; this solution, together with some of the plastic treatment, reminds one of certain pre-Columbian jade masks. The carving shows true plastic talent and real joy in the work.

The human skeleton recurs in art through various periods. To the Middle Ages it was a reminder of man's mortality; then it found favor in the Renaissance, when emphasis was laid on the study of anatomy; and later the Baroque adopted it as a subject of whim which could be presented with the bravado inherent in that epoch. Death with a Bow and Arrow (*fig. b*) is the work of the mestizo Baltasar Gavilán, of Lima, Peru, who is acclaimed by many as the best Peruvian sculptor of the whole eighteenth century. He executed polychromed portrait statues and busts of several notables, figurines for manger groups, life-size altar figures, and also the famous bronze equestrian statue of Philip V, now destroyed. His wood carving of Death was made for the monastery of San Agustín in Lima and was carried in Maundy Thursday processions. An inscription on the piece states that the sculptor failed to deliver it as promised and that upon seeing it unexpectedly when he awakened one night he was so terrified by its aspect that he collapsed and died penitent.[41]

In this bizarre subject, created in the lavishly living, Rococo town of Lima, a time lag is evident. The prototype which first comes to mind is the wood carving of Death, a life-size skeleton, by Gaspar Beccera (1520–1570), which is now in the Valladolid Museum, Spain. It too is draped with a winding sheet, but it carries a ram's horn to signal the final hour. Gavilán gave a special swing to his figure; it has more action and shows more attack than Beccera's. The bow and arrow, Indian weapons, are unrealistically portrayed; the arc is shaped for its effect in the design.

Whether Gavilán in Peru had seen any of Beccera's work, including his anatomical studies, is a question that may never be answered. Such a book as the *Epitome* of Andreas Vesalius might have come to his hand. This work by a Brussels physician (1514–1564), which went deep into the study of the skeleton and human anatomy, was very popular throughout the western world.

In the sacristy of the church of Santa Rosa in Querétaro, an outstanding example of Rococo in Mexico, is an assemblage of various symbolic scenes from the religious drama. Life-size statues of Christ and the twelve Apostles (*fig. d*), evidently made to be seated at a table, are placed on the top of a long chest. Behind them, like a backdrop, is a large canvas. Its heavy gilded frame gives the impression of a proscenium arch. The painting is the *Hortus Conclusus*, or Enclosed Garden. Illusionistic effects are well carried through in a rather dogmatic spirit. Within a rusticated gateway sits the Virgin in the role of Good Shepherdess; with the late seventeenth century she increasingly became the intermediary between sinful humanity and Christ, the Judge of Mankind. Above her is a symbolic representation of the Sacrifice, showing the faithful flock at his feet and an archangel gathering the sacred blood in a chalice. The depiction of the Cross as a tree recalls the legend that a branch of the Tree of Paradise was planted on Golgotha, eventually to be used in the Crucifixion. Nuns of the convent stand tend-ing the walled garden, with its life-giving fountain, its roses, and its lilies. The religious symbolism of the age had grown so abstruse that the Gothic *phylacterium* was revived to clarify the various didactic points.

The painted gateway and wall provide a good background for the carved figures of the Last Supper. The statuary here assembled shows technical facility and considerable individuality in expression and pose; it was probably the product of the Querétaro school of sculpture. The sheep at Christ's side was not there when Sylvester Baxter published a photograph of the scene fifty years ago. A suggestion for its presence may have come from the canvas. Such an extraneous addition shows how the iconography changed, upsetting tradition.

One of the greatest religious spectacles in Latin America, as well as in many parts of Europe, is the festival of Corpus Christi. In Cuzco, Peru, this event is celebrated with extraordinary pageantry. During the week preceding the feast, which generally falls in June, when in the Andes it is clear and cold, statues from the churches in outlying districts are brought down the narrow streets to visit with those in local churches; the Virgin of Bethlehem (Belén) is the hostess in the church of Santa Clara. On the feast day they all are carried in procession to the cathedral, where they remain for the octave.

Even more magnificent was the display in the colonial period. Since every strata of society then belonged to one religious association or another, the preparation of statues and floats commanded the active interest of the entire population. The lay brotherhoods and sodalities vied with one another, sometimes even going into debt, to have the name of their affiliated church in the mouths of the assembled spectators. The embossed silver bases of the images were heaped with real and artificial flowers, the figures were arrayed in special clothing and jewels, and festive dress was provided for the carriers. Trium-

phal arches were erected, garlanded with flowers and banked with silver objects, altars were constructed in the streets, tribunes were raised from which the select could view the spectacle, and private houses were made gay with tapestries and rugs hung from windows and balconies. People traveled great distances to witness the celebration.

In the church of Santa Ana, situated high on a hill in a suburb of Cuzco, a series of twelve large canvases preserves an excellent record of the colonial Corpus Christi procession. The *Carro de San Sebastián* (Pl. 65, fig. b) shows the saint borne in a four-wheeled chariot. His coach might be compared with that on the canopy of the pulpit in the Tegucigalpa cathedral (see Pl. 11); note the figure emerging from a leafy scroll at the front. The statue depicted here can be recognized as the one which still stands in the church of San Sebastián near Cuzco; it is also reproduced in a painting (see Pl. 138d). Live birds are perched in the tree above his head, as is still the custom today. Before the chariot walks a high Inca functionary in gala costume, which includes a patterned poncho with a large sun worked on the breast, worn over breeches of the Spanish type; full lace sleeves are attached to the poncho at the shoulders, and the headdress is decorated with both jewels and plumes. It is interesting to note that Indians held prominent positions as late as the second half of the seventeenth century and that in these paintings they are sometimes identified, with the title "Inca" preceding their names. Behind the chariot move the priestly attendants. Spectators line the street— an official in native headband, Indians, even a Negro—and ladies watch from the decorated balconies.

Another canvas (*fig. c*) shows the procession passing in front of an altar which had been erected outside a church, recognizable as La Merced. The central figure here is the Immaculate Conception; below her, archangels wearing lace garments and headdresses of curling plumes are carrying tapers. The various sections of the altar are paneled in embossed silver, and mirrors with wide frames are set in it. At the top are paintings of saints, and in front, on a special table that stands on a rug, incense is smoking from an elaborate dish. At the right, extending across the street like an arch, is a baldachin—with twisted columns —under which noblemen and their ladies are passing. Two litters carrying the figures of St. John the Baptist and the Apostle Peter are passing by. The bearers of the first seem to be artisans in Spanish dress, of 'the second, Indians. Both saints wear garments of textiles and stand on characteristic Baroque bases with the familiar scroll decoration. In the foreground again is a row of spectators, whose varied headgear gives a faint idea of the dress worn by the various classes of society in that day. Note the bearded Spanish figure in the center with the large hat.

José Uriel García believes that these paintings were executed before the earthquake of 1650 because the cathedral façade shown differs from the present one.[190] Wethey, however, favors late seventeenth century, an opinion with which this author agrees.[203] Judging from the materials and techniques, the canvases are probably the work of mestizos and Indians of the local school. The real development of Cuzco painting began in the second half of the seventeenth century and reached its zenith in mid-eighteenth, when it attained its greatest originality and charm.

Statues played an important part also in the dedication of new churches and in the reinstallation of beloved figures upon the refurbishment of an edifice or its restoration after some catastrophe. Processions commemorated military victories—even though the battles occurred on distant continents and were reported months after they were won —the marriages of royalty, and the birth of a royal heir. The demise of a ruler gave rise to special ceremonies that centered around a catafalque in the main church of each town.

In the sketch for such a *tumulo*, designed in 1701 for the Spanish king Charles II, the anonymous artist in Coatepec, Puebla,[45] a faraway corner of the Spanish colonial empire, worked up the skull-and-crossbones theme to a showy climax (*fig. a*). Skulls and crossbones were important symbols in several pre-Columbian cultures in Mexico, as is attested by stone carvings in Chichen Itzá and Uxmal, as well as by the infamous skull rack in the Aztec capital, described at the time of the Conquest. The tradition of the Indian cult of death survives today in the cakes and sweets which are formed like skulls and skeletons and sold in the markets, even of Mexico City and Puebla, on All Souls' Day.

In the drawing illustrated here, Death at the pinnacle, crowned and holding a scepter and shield, stands on two globes; on the shield is a bird pierced by an arrow. The skull and crossbones, crowned, make up the candelabra. The pilasters are decorated with them, and the same elements adorn the frieze. They are embroidered on the cope of the priest. Even the crowns of the heraldic eagles at the sides are topped with the motif as candle holders, and it appears again under the feet of the bird. The halving of the heraldic eagle of the Habsburgs to form side garlands was perpetrated by a designer whose psychology was as far removed from that of the European as was Coatepec from Madrid.

The break of the symbol here occurred just when Habsburg power in Spain was broken. Charles II was almost imbecile from his cradle to his deathbed. He was brought up under the tutelage of an Austrian mother and was married first to a princess of the House of Orleans and after her death to the daughter of an Austrian nobleman. Always weak in mind and body, he made a will under pressure in favor of Philip, Duke of Anjou, a grandson of Louis XIV of France; thus the Spanish Habsburg crown passed to a son born of the union of French and Bavarian royal families. The new king ascended the throne under the name of Philip V, the founder of the Spanish Bourbon dynasty, whose last reigning descendant went into exile in 1931.

8

EARTHQUAKE BAROQUE

FROM the southern border of Mexico to the Isthmus of Panama lies a land of rocky mountain ranges, volcanoes, high plateaus dotted with lakes, and tropical lowlands, known today as Central America. The territory which now comprises Guatemala, Honduras, El Salvador, Nicaragua, and Costa Rica was formed by the Spaniards into a captaincy-general and audiencia under the administration of the Viceroyalty of New Spain. To this also belonged Chiapas, which cast its lot with the Republic of Mexico during the struggle for independence. Panama—important as a connecting link between Spain and South America —was governed first from the island of Santo Domingo, then by a local audiencia, and finally by the Viceroyalty of New Granada.

The Captaincy-General of Guatemala— called at one time the Kingdom of Goathemala—had in its domain a large part of the territory once inhabited by the ancient Maya peoples, as well as a number of other Indian tribal groups, among them the Pipils, Chorotegans, Chiriqui, and Nicoya. The name Guatemala is said to derive from that of the Indian chieftain Juitemal. At various times during and after the Conquest, Indian populations were shifted and resettled; for instance, Pedro de Alvarado brought with him Indian soldiery from Tlaxcala and Cholula which remained near the early capital. It will be seen that wherever the artistic seed imported from Europe fell on a rich cultural soil that had been productive in pre-Columbian times, the result was a blend that is as fascinating to many observers as the overseas prototypes.

Although this whole territory was under the jurisdiction of the viceroy in Mexico and final decisions and the most important personnel problems were carried to him, many questions had to be settled locally because the Mexican capital was so far away. The more distant provinces were ruled in the name of the king by governors, who were responsible to the captain general. In practice, owing to the difficulties of communications, each province functioned largely as an independent unit, cherishing its private jealousies of its neighbors and all sharing a mutual hatred for the capital, upon which they visited their indignation over the monopolistic and wasteful practices of Spain. Guatemala was cut off from legal trade with the Orient and even from traffic with the other American colonies; not a single vessel was owned by any resident of the province.[160]

The first stable capital of this area was established in 1527 on the slope of the extinct volcano Agua. Led by the dashing Alvarado, one hundred and thirty Spaniards signed the founding documents. Among these was a Hernando Pizarro, whose relationship to the famous Francisco is unclear.[161] The town was named for Santiago, and as the ceremony took place on the festival of St. Cecilia, patroness of music, she became its secondary guardian.

Franciscan friars accompanied the Spanish troops. Within seven years Guatemala had a bishop, who at his own expense sent for four Dominicans from Nicaragua; one of them, Bartolomé de las Casas, was already launched on his mission as Protector of the Indians.[157] Shortly Mercedarians and Franciscans established their orders in the province; the Jesuits, who were later to grow so powerful, did not arrive until 1582.

By 1539, with the aid of an unlimited supply of Indian labor, the first cathedral was completed. Within two years, however, the entire settlement was wiped out by a landslide, a river of mud that followed torrential rains. The capital was then removed to a spot a few miles distant—the site of the present Antigua —but it still retained its name, Santiago.

The church at Almolonga (Pl. 66, fig. a), near Antigua, is generally believed to stand on the ground of the first cathedral. Recent excavations indicate, however, that the site of the early capital was farther up the slope of the volcano and that the district under discussion, which was occupied by Mexican allies of the Conquistadores, was little damaged. The edifice illustrated is a Franciscan foundation from the eighteenth century.[141] Noteworthy is the plan of the angular façade, like a triptych, somewhat reminiscent of La Soledad in Oaxaca, Mexico (see Pl. 46). On it are ranged all seven archangels and, below them, the four Evangelists. A number of decorative elements appear here which will be encountered in considerable variety throughout the area. Superposed "urns," one inverted on the other as if its mirrored reflection, make up the pilasters; the column is found only as a frame for the topmost niche, which holds a flaming heart.

By mid-seventeenth century the capital alone had more than fifty places of worship, including chapels in colleges and hospitals as well as retreats. A century later, shortly before the earthquake of 1773 which brought the place to ruin, the white population amounted to at least seven thousand (not including the clergy and conventual orders), and the mestizos, mulattoes, Negroes, and Indians there numbered some sixty thousand more.

One of the last churches to be erected in the city was La Merced (fig. b). The Mercedarian order, with respect to its activities as well as its wealth, was comfortably ensconced in the Viceroyalty of Peru, but in Guatemala this brotherhood lived in modest and frugal quarters from the time of their arrival in 1534 until the completion of their church and monastery just prior to 1760. Whereas the monumental establishments of their rivals, the Franciscans and Jesuits, continuously expanded, the roof over their heads remained thatched with straw.[151] It was one of the ironies of history that the two rival churches toppled to the ground in the catastrophe of 1773, while the strong new church of La Merced was little affected. Responsible in part for its stability were its massive walls, which in places are as much as ten feet thick.

Here, too, characteristics appear on the façade which run through the colonial period of this land. Among them are the immensely heavy undecorated tower bases, with their polygonal windows, and also the Baroque layout of the façade, in which coupled columns are spaced to leave room for niches with statues and less emphatic decorative elements. Arches in the central section stress the vertical. A statue of the Virgin of Mercy stands in a large splayed niche before the choir-light; the stucco decoration about her, showing a vase with a spreading bouquet, is among the finest in all Guatemala. The shallow stucco design covering the façade employs fruit, flower, and fantasy motifs; baby angels, or what Verle L. Annis calls "celestial urchins," are posed on the bases of the upper columns. Note also the spiraling garlands on the stalwart shafts of the first story. Marking the corners of the towers are the horizontally grooved pilasters that are so characteristic of Central America.

The entrance to the former monastery, which boasts some of the best stucco decoration in the country (seen at the left in this photograph), is shown in greater detail later (*see Pl. 69*).

Antigua is said to have been planned by the engineer Juan Bautista Antonelli (died 1588), a native of Italy; his younger brother of the same name (died 1616) designed the great fortresses of Morro Castle in Havana, San Juan de Ulúa at Veracruz, and others in Puerto Rico, Cartagena, and elsewhere in the New World.[43] The city, laid out on a rectangular plan, was conceived on a seignorial scale, with space provided for vast gardens and patios and broad shaded avenues. It was oriented to make use of the slope between two rivers. Because of its valley location and the proximity of mineral springs, it had superb water facilities. Every private house and conventual establishment had their fountains, often very decorative; the Capuchin nunnery in 1735 could boast running water in every cell.

Although the first bishop of Guatemala, the redoubtable Francisco Marroquín, bequeathed funds for a university in the late sixteenth century, the country had to wait until 1676 for the royal seal on its establishment. But before that, colleges were functioning under the supervision of the Jesuits, Dominicans, and Franciscans; in fact, it was partly opposition from this quarter which delayed the use of the bishop's legacy. At first the university occupied the edifice of the Dominican College of St. Thomas Aquinas, which had been restored for the purpose and was reopened under the name Royal and Pontifical University of St. Charles Borromeo. In 1687 it was granted all the privileges enjoyed by such institutions in Mexico and Peru, among them the right to award degrees and the permission for graduates to wear hoods. No person who had been convicted by or who had a forebear punished by the Inquisition could gain admittance; and to satisfy the objection of the various orders that such an establishment would foster heresy and free-thinking, each graduate was examined on his beliefs upon the completion of his courses. For a time the aristocracy tried to limit the enrollment to students of Spanish descent, but this was finally overruled.[160]

After the earthquake of 1751 made the old building untenable, a new edifice was erected (1763) on the south side of the cathedral and next to the Colegio Tridentino.[160] The main façade lost much of its original aspect when it was reconstructed in the nineteenth century, but the patio colonnade and the side walls still retain their colonial appearance.

In planning the edifice, the architect and military engineer Luis Díez Navarro was influenced by the Moorish style of southern Spain, which was being revived with such elegance in many sections of eighteenth-century Spanish America. The neo-Mudéjar finds expression here not only in the multifoil archways—seven on each side of the patio and all twenty-eight of them lined with terra cotta—but also in the stylized decorative elements (*Pl. 67, fig. b*). In the bubble-like lantern (upper left in the photograph) the lines of a large dome are combined with the grace of a miniature. The fountain in the center of the court is traditional. A Mudéjar effect is achieved also by the manner in which the vertical line of the piers runs through to the finials that top the blind balustrade. Note the horizontal grooving on the pilasters between the arches and beside the heraldic medallion of the free-standing pediment.

The street side of this building (*fig. c*) shows deep octagonal windows in the massive walls. Heraldic medallions and large conventionalized lyres as consoles break the monotony of the stucco surface, which is painted a bluish gray. Above a strip of blind balustrade, pyramidal finials are synchronized with the ornaments on the wall.

This popular revival of the Mudéjar was widespread in Central America. In the village church at Santa Cruz el Chol (*fig. a*), in Guatemala, on the road to Cobán, a Mudéjar-Gothic arch enframes the single doorway and the niches echo its lines. The whole building is without pretension, but it contains a number of original details. The paired columns flanking the niches, according to Baroque formula, are much farther apart than usual, although they are coupled at the base. Skill is manifest in the execution of the archway moldings and the splayed star window. Intermediary moldings below the cornices hold together the central section, leaving the two outer edges free, as if to recall the flanking tower masses so frequently used. In the two-story espadaña, bell openings, happily placed, furnish a transition from the lower niches to the central figure at the apex.

The popularity of the neo-Mudéjar style is again documented in the side portal of the church of La Merced in León, Nicaragua (*fig. d*). Here the pyramidal finials, the blind balustrade, the spirals in the pediment, and even the angel heads in the spandrels betoken an artistic vocabulary related to Guatemala's. This structure is said to have been built in 1685 and reconstructed in 1723 and 1820–1821. Behind the apse are the remains of an oriel *camarín*—now sealed up—a type extremely rare in this region but frequently encountered in Colombia (*see Pl. 29*).

The ruins of the church of Santa Cruz in Antigua (*Pl. 68, fig. a*) stood abandoned in a field of a coffee plantation until this author first published photographs of it.[149] Now the place has been cleared and has become a favorite excursion spot. Since early in the seventeenth century a hermitage has occupied this site. Before the great earthquake the Indians of the district took pride in its upkeep and constant refurbishment. A restoration is recorded in 1731 which was celebrated amid much festivity.[145] This façade has great refinement. A varied over-all stucco pattern covers the flat surfaces. Renaissance elements are retained in the low candelabrum bases and the triangular pediments which couple the columns in each tier. Note how the break in the pediments in the first order effectively integrates the upper and lower panels. The many scrolls and the balancing of the various niches

are Baroque, as are also the figural elements throughout the façade. Infant atlantes, playfully applied, decorate the friezes and the capitals of the larger columns. On the spandrels are "rampant" angels—another motif favored in a number of regional styles in colonial Spanish America—and on the pediment heraldic lions guard the stucco Calvary group that gives the church its name. Horizontally grooved pilasters are again used with effect. A wealth of invention is evident also in the interior, which once must have had an elegance comparable to that of the cathedral (*see Pl. 8*). The low choir vault can be seen through the arch. This church faces on an atrium in which stands a stone cross; at one side of it is a fountain, dated 1732.

The church of El Carmen at Antigua (*fig. b*) is also in ruins. It was founded by the Brotherhood of the Holy Scapulary in 1686, but the first building was practically destroyed in the earthquake of 1717. Reconstructed on an improved plan and reopened in 1728, it soon became one of the favorite churches of the capital, famous for its orchestra and choir.

While coupled columns are a regular feature of the Baroque, the multiplication of them as seen here is unusual. Each pair in the lower tier has its own pediment, except in the case of the innermost four, which are united by the ogival pediment that extends over the doorway; at the peak of this stands a stucco statue of the Virgin. In the upper tier, the whole group of columns on either side of the Virgin is successfully drawn into a single unit within a larger pediment. The tempered simplicity of the lower shafts brings out the pomp of decoration in the upper story, where a loose garland around the choir-light makes a fine contrast with the meshed pattern on the columns. This façade is of brick, as is evident where the stucco has fallen away. The whitewashed wall section and the corrugated iron door under the arch were added recently to prevent further collapse. Inside, the walls were covered with arabesques and carved festoons of gilded wood.

Guatemala had its full share of the earthquakes which harassed much of Spanish America. As tremors damaged one building after another, construction methods were conditioned more and more by the ever-recurring calamities. In different regions of the colonies, as has been shown, different structural solutions were essayed; tremendously heavy masonry, monolithic with cement, was resorted to in Central America. Arches were given extravagantly calculated support, buildings were kept low, and vaults grew thicker. The number of openings was reduced to a minimum, and even espadañas were seldom perforated but were thick-walled and carefully tied into the body of the masonry. So apprehensive became the builders that, according to tradition, they mixed their mortar at times with milk, honey, wines, crushed pearls, and even blood.[151] It is worth while to contrast the churches of this region with those of Brazil, where façades having many doors and windows were in the tradition even before the spread of Rococo.

The former parish church at Panajachel, Guatemala, near Lake Atitlán, is a good example of a façade that is drawn out horizontally and treated as a single surface (Pl. 69, fig. a). The usual emphasis upon the central section, with the portal, is absent here. There are no towers at the sides; bell openings are provided in the third story on a line with the niches and on the topmost member of the espadaña. The whole façade, soberly restrained, shows that inclination toward the classic which runs throughout the seventeenth and eighteenth centuries. The pediments are unbroken, even in the uppermost tier of niches, where often the Baroque trend is most in evidence. Note the engaged columns, without bases, which seem to hang like long straight garlands from the pediments. It is said that a church stood on this site as early as 1641; in the late eighteenth century the town had five churches and ten *cofradías*.

In the parish church at San Antonio Aguas

Calientes (*fig. c*) the primary impression is one of solidity. The square towers, on a line with the rest of the façade, and the thick columns, perhaps even somewhat over-proportioned, contribute to its robust air. Here the retable build-up is evident; the frames around the niches, especially in the first order, might well have come from a sixteenth-century tabernacle. The fact that this village is only four miles from Antigua may account in part for the taste apparent in the design.[150]

Although inaugurated in 1743, when Baroque was in full flourish, the *Real Cabildo*, or Town Hall, of Antigua (*fig. f*) adheres strictly to the established style for governmental structures, incorporating Renaissance traits. Colonial buildings of this type still survive throughout Spanish America, from Mexico to Argentina. Antigua's city hall was built entirely of stone and without stucco embellishment; but the double colonnade—with its series of arches on each floor—has functional beauty. Opposite it on the main plaza stands the Palace of the Captain General, similarly arcaded. It is dated 1763 and is the work of Díez Navarro, who was mentioned in connection with the university and also won the composition for the Casa de Moneda in the Mexican capital in 1733, now the National Museum.[90]

Twisted, or salomonic, columns are not too common on colonial façades in Central America. The remaining illustrations on this plate present three examples from Antigua. The House of the Lions (*fig. d*) appears to have been built in the first half of the seventeenth century, when Antigua was already enjoying great wealth, and was owned at one time by the high-ranking Toledo family. It is laid out as a single-story structure with a series of patios beyond the main entrance, a favorite and practical plan for a colonial dwelling. The portal is of stone, unusual later when brick became the chief building material. This façade was badly damaged at one time, perhaps by the earthquake of 1717. The original stone walls, three feet thick, rise only to about six feet and above them are *tabique* walls, half-timbered and stuccoed over, which are only eight to ten inches thick.[188] Although the composition here is not on a grand scale, it possesses considerable vigor. Annis suggests that above the lintel there was once a more monumental ornamentation which was never rebuilt. The heavy hand of the local carver simplified the pattern on the piers and the adjoining panels. Romanesque charm lies in the rampant lions, which look as if they might have been copied from a patent of nobility. Heraldic animals were displayed on many private dwellings (*see Pls. 34, 126*), and these may earlier have adorned the pediment. One of the first houses to be built in Gracias a Dios, Honduras, in the same captaincy-general, has two lions on its lintel; it, too, is known as the Casa de los Leones.

The walled-up side gateway behind the Hospital of San Pedro Apóstol (*fig. b*) is flanked with richly plastic coupled columns that spiral in opposite directions. In the niche is a polychromed stucco statue of the Assumption. A Mudéjar touch is noticeable in the line of the main cornice, which, curving, forms the platform for the figure, and volutes of Baroque proportions descend on either side of the niche to provide a finish for the free-standing pediment. (Compare the portal of El Carmen at Cuenca, Ecuador, illustrated on *Pl. 102*.)

The decoration of the entrance to the former Mercedarian monastery in Antigua (*fig. e*) is even more exquisite than that of the church itself. A fine calligraphic design flanks the niche above the arch, giving the effect of a pilaster, and a variety of delicate patterns in stucco adorns the friezes. The vigorous scrolls on the pediment and around the niche add greatly to the lively impression of the whole. Compare this niche with that in the illustration above it.

One of the cloister corridors in this building is roofed by heavy cemented corbeled

vaulting, a method used by the Maya in ancient times.

Characteristic of the Baroque are the changes that can be noted in the treatment of the column; it was variously adorned, grouped in pairs, twisted, engaged in the wall, and often used as a purely decorative element. In Central America a type of engaged column or pilaster occurs frequently which to many may appear to have grown out of a playful fancy. A number of these are grouped on *Plate 70*.

El Calvario (*fig. b*), a hermitage in Antigua, stands on the site of an earlier building, finished in 1655 and destroyed by the earthquake of 1717; it was inaugurated in 1720. In the pilasters the horizontal grooving is so deep that they have all but lost their basic shape and convey no sense of support; but their shadow effect is rich and ever changing. This hermitage lies at the end of a tree-framed promenade, along which Franciscans once erected the wooden crosses of a Via Crucis; later these were replaced by small domed chapels, where the Good Friday processions stopped in their march.[157]

A side portal of the cathedral in Tegucigalpa, Honduras, which leads into a religious garden, shows another example of such grooving (*fig. a*), also notably used on the façade. Mermaids function as caryatids, and a skillful handling of stucco is apparent in the ornamentation.

The weather-stained village church of Camotán, Guatemala (*fig. d*), is situated on the plaza of this lifeless little hamlet, the last settlement before the Honduran border. John L. Stephens, traveling on a road that had been used in pre-Columbian times, once spent a night in jail here when on his way to the ancient Maya city of Copán. This unusually tall, two-story espadaña has bell openings, a niche, and powerful voluted buttresses. In outline the engaged columns in the second order suggest superimposed squat Indian jugs; those below give the effect of a tight spiral but actually they are grooved horizontally, somewhat in the manner of those in the detail at the left.

Colohete, Honduras, situated only about twenty-seven miles southeast of Copán and not far from Camotán, also has a parish church with deeply grooved columns (*fig. c*). In both these façades multifoil arches are used in the niches and the original statues survive, a rare occurrence. As is often the case in Central America, the figures crowd their allotted space. Colohete's church is unusually broad, with two niches in a row on either side of the portal, and the entire surface is decorated with a lacelike pattern in stucco, a type of ornamentation which was executed also in stone in that region (*see Pl. 6*). At the base of the wall, much disintegrated, the structural brick and stone are visible. It is to be feared that soon the whole fanciful pattern will be chipped off, the wall cemented and whitewashed anew, a procedure that the author witnessed in a number of less remote villages. The interior of this church is illustrated later (*see Pl. 73*).

Horizontally grooved columns and pilasters are found on colonial buildings removed from one another in both distance and time. It is possible that those on the mid-seventeenth-century church at Cobán, Guatemala, were among the earliest examples and those on the cathedral in Tegucigalpa, Honduras (*see Pl. 11*), completed about 1782, among the last. Many suggestions have been offered as to the origin of this feature. Some claim that it developed from an exaggerated rustication, others that it derives from the spiral column, and still others trace it to the woodcarvers' virtuosity. The Spanish term for it is *almohadillado* (cushioned), suggesting a pile of little pillows heaped one upon another. Some examples are preserved on mid-eighteenth-century houses in Jerez and Cadiz and thereabouts in southern Spain. But whatever or wherever was its model, the horizontally grooved pilaster in Central America developed with **individuality and a rare virility**.

Other types of pilaster favored in Central America are illustrated here in three churches from three provinces of the Captaincy-General of Guatemala, all dating from the first half of the eighteenth century (*Pl. 71*). The most original of them (*fig. a*) is the church of Los Dolores in Tegucigalpa, Honduras. This edifice was founded in 1732, according to the inscription, but was not finished until 1815 and was later (1910) restored.[155] Its pilasters in outline are somewhat like those just seen but are flat on the front; they are decorated with rosettes, each studded with a ball. The towers are relatively slender. Their star windows have angel heads above and swags of fruit below, unusual touches. A blind balustrade was applied on the towers and above the main cornice. This motif was a favorite in Central America; on such a modest mission church as the Franciscan establishment at Orosi, Costa Rica, it was used as the sole ornament and only on the tower.[144] Emblems of the Passion, a flaming heart, and, within the round opening, a sun disk, pierced to show the light through, adorn the two-story espadaña of the Tegucigalpa façade. Pendent knobs under the cornices cast lacy shadows. Most of the decoration, including the tiles on the tower roofs, a large finial at the rear of the church, and the four women saints standing on consoles before the shallow niches, are ceramic work, once lustrous and brilliant-hued. Rarely does one find today such large statues in that material well preserved. Inside the building are remnants of a splendid timber ceiling, executed in the Mudéjar manner.

Related in general design is the façade of the parish church at Chiquimula, Guatemala (*fig. b*), a town which lies on the pilgrim route to Esquipulas (*see Pl. 72*) and at the head of the road to Copán. This church, restored after the damaging earthquake of 1765, shows one type of peripheral earthquake Baroque. Little attention was given to variety in the ornamentation. The statues stand in conventionalized poses, all somewhat alike and with the dignity of the rustic. The main pilasters are shaped like stereotyped urns, and in the central panels above the arch, vertical grooves ending in convolutes hark back to engaged columns. This façade, too, has the two-storied espadaña that can be observed in many churches of these regions. In the rear a low, flattened dome is visible. The door at the side, which opens upon a wide garden—perhaps once part of an atrium—also received considerable emphasis.

Masaya, Nicaragua, formerly the chief town of a powerful Indian tribe, lies on a ridge between two lakes, Nicaragua and Managua, and is most fortunate in its climate. In colonial days its Indian inhabitants manufactured quantities of cordage and cotton sailcloth for the ships that sailed the Pacific. Its parish church (*fig. c*), dedicated to St. Ferdinand, may have been begun in the late seventeenth century. It was enlarged in the eighteenth and the façade dates from about 1800; further repair work was done, according to an inscription, in 1833. It is notable for its three entrances, in contrast to the general tradition in Guatemala. The modest stucco decoration that still remains and the lacy design over the lesser doors connect it stylistically with Granada, Nicaragua, which is not far away, while its single squat tower—a separate unit—recalls those in Comayagua, Honduras. Its pilasters, like the ones on the church above, are built up with undulating lines, giving the appearance of urns, one placed upside down on another; even the pedestals carry the urn form.

The pilgrim church of Esquipulas (*Pl. 72, fig. a*) is unique in its architectural build-up and is surpassed in religious significance by few churches in Latin America. This village lies in the southeast corner of Guatemala, near the borders of both Honduras and El Salvador and one day's journey on foot from the ancient religious center of Copán. From indications the two sites were once linked by a direct road. Five stones carved in a Maya style similar to that of Copán stand on the bridge leading to the Sanctuary. Early chroniclers record

that the natives thought nothing of journeying many days on foot to some famous religious center to participate in the ritual, as well as in the trading which followed it. Shortly after the Conquest a Calvary was established in Esquipulas. In 1595 a chapel is mentioned here as having a miraculous statue of the crucified Christ; this carving, of balsam or orange wood, blackened with incense and candle smoke, is the work of Quirio Cataño, whom some sources call a Portuguese.[142] The present massive edifice was completed in 1758 to house that figure.

Raised on a vast platform the basilica is dazzling in the subtropical sunlight. Four ponderous towers, all of equal size, anchor the structure, their bases broken only by small windows at the sides. Each succeeding member is smaller in size and more elaborately embellished; the topmost belfries are octagonal, crowned with bell-shaped cupolas and many finials. Noteworthy is the staggering of the cornice across the entire front. The façade proper is not the retable type—the horizontals are too strong, the openings too large, and the niches too subordinated. Major decorative emphasis is laid on the deep multifoil arch in the second story, with its openwork railing and double tier of flanking niches. Above stands a statue of the Virgin. The variety of arches, pediments, and moldings in this building, its obelisks, spirals, and other ornamentation make up a Baroque which is strongly flavored with the Mudéjar. The lateral portals also are ornate, with heavy, freestanding pediments, and the large tiled dome at the rear reminds one of contemporary churches in Antigua, Guatemala. In some places the walls measure ten to twelve feet thick.

Inside, the vast size of the church is apparent. It is paved with large red tiles and is lighted by silver chandeliers. In some sections the walls are covered with hundreds of *ex votos* in gold, silver, wood, or wax as thank offerings. On others hang colonial paintings and primitive sketches depicting scenes of miraculous healing, presented by grateful pilgrims.

The parish churches in both Jinotepe, Nicaragua, and Heredia, Costa Rica, are good examples of how much towers can do for a barnlike structure, besides buttressing it against earthquakes. Jinotepe, which lies near Masaya, was important for its cattle ranches and farms, to which, later, coffee plantations added their wealth. The simplicity of the neoclassic design in the façade of its parish church (*fig. b*) is underscored by the plain dark stone employed. The towers are square and solid, without openings except in the belfries, revealing their function as buttresses. A small dome, cautiously low and supported on two sides by short barrel vaults, can be seen at the rear. (Compare this church with the cathedral at León on *Pl. 8*.)

The Heredia façade (*fig. c*), broader than the body of the church, is thrust forward far beyond the towers and is itself very thick and buttress-like. With its three portals and sparse decoration, it suggests a theater entrance. The towers are nearly independent units and might well have been added to the building later. They are more powerful than those in the Jinotepe edifice just shown and have openings in all three sections. This church has no dome.

Heredia lies only six miles from the present capital of Costa Rica and is said to have been settled by Andalusians.[81] The district thereabouts was noted for its sarsaparilla—"the best in all the Indies"—a superior henequen fiber, and many medicinal fruits, gums, and other extracts, and roots. It had rich ore deposits of gold, and gold grains were found in the stream beds; the pre-Columbian inhabitants of this region were excellent metalworkers. During much of the colonial period the town was known by its Indian name Cubujuqui. In 1763 its residents petitioned for the status of a *villa*, incorporating into its title the name of the president of the Royal Audiencia of Guatemala, one Don Alonso Fernández de Heredia; thus the place became Inmaculada Concepción de Cubujuquí de Heredia. After Costa

Rica became a republic, only the last part of the name was officially retained.

The barn-shaped church with a plain gable roof was a natural structural solution during the early evangelization of Latin America, when many churches had to be erected as quickly as possible with, chiefly, local labor. Later many of these simple structures were altered, added to, or replaced. But the early plan persisted late into the colonial period, and examples can be found in regions where the pace of life was slow or where the mania for modernization has not totally destroyed the colonial design.

Honduras has a number of churches of this type. La Merced in Comayagua (*Pl. 73, fig. a*), one of the earliest buildings still extant there, is known to have been under construction in 1611. Further additions were made during the seventeenth century.[152] It served first as the main parish church and later, before the new building was completed in the early eighteenth century (*see Pl. 6*), as the cathedral. At one time it had a sagrario chapel and a baptistry;[155] but even with those additions it must have been an unpretentious edifice. The graceful stucco scallops of the cornice molding only slightly modify its barnlike appearance. Besides the central statue the sole ornamentation on the façade consists of flat garlands and the insignia at the top. No horizontal breaks the architectural surface, no intermediary cornice. Two feline creatures are perched at the ends of the pediment, and conventionalized pineapples form some of the finials.

Inside, the church has a single nave and a timber ceiling. The carved frontal of a side altar (*fig. c*) suggests silver repoussé work, but actually it is of wood, ungilded. The relief has the spirit of folk art; while a certain angularity characterizes the angels, the trees and flowing ornamentation show artistic freshness. Some see a Maya glyph in the sharp V-shapes in the upper corners.

In 1644, while this church was serving as the cathedral, Philip IV sent a retable for the main altar, a number of statues for side altars, a large crucifix, missals, chasubles, and various ornaments. Local tradition would like to identify the altar in the present cathedral sagrario with this gift. But that altar does not appear to be so old; furthermore it fits perfectly into the space it occupies and it is not notably Spanish in style.

Similar in construction to La Merced, although in its present form of a later date (1730), is La Caridad, also in Comayagua (*fig. b*). This photograph, taken in the first quarter of the twentieth century, is presented to show the early type of construction; the building has since been heavily restored. Its façade, like the preceding one, was unbroken by an intermediary cornice. S-spirals and a low crenellation framed the espadaña. A raised panel extended from the pediment of the doorway to the bell arches above and was decorated with an ornamental vase from which a bouquet branched in a widespreading arrangement. As is clearly evident, the tower was constructed separately, grafted onto the side wall; its roof and cornices are little related to the rest of the building. Today all floral decoration has been hammered off and the entire front cemented into an empty surface and whitewashed.

The parish church at Colohete (*fig. d*), in Honduras, presents an example of interior construction that was typical of many early colonial provincial churches and is strongly Mudéjar in derivation. An exterior detail of this building has already been shown (*see Pl. 70*). Huge beams resting on wooden pillars carry the weight of the timber roof; the broad brackets form the outline of Mudéjar arches, and standard Mudéjar interlacing is applied on the crossbeams. An exceptionally rich multifoil arch of brick and stucco separates the sanctuary from the nave.

That this method of construction and, to a certain degree, the manner of decoration were once fairly general is suggested by the chapel of San Francisco in Uruapan, Mexico (*fig. e*). Here painted panels conceal the open timber construction. A horizontal ceiling covers the aisles, as in the adjacent example, but there is no apse.[78]

Although the mines in Honduras are not so famous as those in Mexico, Peru, or Bolivia, some of them produced a vast wealth of gold and silver in the last colonial century. Less than thirty miles east of Tegucigalpa lies the mining village called La Mineral de San Antonio del Oriente. It is mentioned as early as 1720 and in mid-nineteenth century its mines were still producing;[146] the grade of ore is said to have been so high that, though a third of its value was lost by the crude methods used, one proprietor was affluent enough to throw silver pieces to the populace by the handful on every feast day.[162]

Today those mines are abandoned, and the few villagers go out for daily or itinerant labor, mainly into the broad valley of Zamorano. Only a path wide enough for a single beast leads to the village, and any visitor journeying from the capital to the foot of the range and then riding up to the settlement experiences first hand something of the transportation difficulties in colonial times, when Tegucigalpa itself was only an outpost. The few buildings nestle against the mountainside, with scarcely two of them on the same level along the steep winding street. In the colonial period the surrounding hills were completely denuded to facilitate prospecting, but the beneficent tropical sun and rain are slowly restoring the natural cover of tall pine.

All the houses, small one-story structures, are still roofed with red tile—a sharp contrast to the defacing corrugated iron common where modern commerce has made its inroads. Standing out among them, the freshly whitewashed village church, dedicated to La Merced, catches the eye immediately from afar (*Pl. 74, fig. a*). It is reported that the Mairena family, who owned one of the richest lodes, built this church out of the proceeds of their mines. Its designer, with limited facilities but an eye for grandeur, produced a façade full of naïve charm (*fig. b*), using decorative elements borrowed from more pretentious edifices. The plastic features are flat and thin; niches are only outlined. Pierlike pedestals, flanking the entrance, carry urns. Below the pediment, with its turret and coupled engaged columns, a blind-balustrade motif forms a frieze. Green majolica urns, cemented on the undulating cornice and the towers, echo ornaments on Los Dolores in Tegucigalpa (*see Pl. 71*); some of them have been whitewashed.

Inside, the nave is covered by an open timber ceiling; the apse has an octagonal cupola with steep sides and, at the corners, squinches—a common method throughout the region. A disregard for the functional—a mark of the Baroque—is carried to the extreme in the main altar (*fig. c*). Columns look like the undulating bodies of sea horses; although they end in capitals that extend through the cornices, they support nothing and seem almost to be suspended from above. Tropical vines, shells, fish, and other figures of caprice spread over the background, shining with rich gilding. Doubtless the two ovals—a fashionable shape at that time—were designed for paintings. The statues are new, out of harmony with the articulate craftsmanship which shaped the altar.

When one asks in such an out-of-the-way place as this who built the church and decorated its interior, the prompt reply credits the mestizo—the regional—craftsmen. But in a large town the answer to the same question all too often brings up the name of an artist in Spain, sometimes completely anachronous, or claims that an object was sent from Spain as a royal gift. As was discussed in more detail in Chapter 2, the foreign artists and craftsmen who could have had a hand in the building of the countless edifices of colonial Spanish America comprised only a small percentage of the total number employed, and not much larger is the percentage of furnishings imported from Europe, whether paintings, statues, or bits for interior decoration. The contribution made by regional talent to

the less accessible churches is evidenced by a side altar in the cathedral of Tegucigalpa (*fig. d*). In conception and general impression this altar shows a strong affinity to the one pictured beside it, although its carving is somewhat more delicate and elaborated. Note the peculiar shape of the baldachin above the central panel in each case, suggestive of an open animal jaw.

As mentioned earlier, León, Nicaragua's colonial capital, was removed from its original site in 1610 to where it now stands. Through this move the pre-Columbian settlement of Sutiaba was incorporated into the capital and today forms the suburb Subtiava. León is situated in a fertile valley, somewhat cooler than the surrounding countryside—the Indians always chose their sites well. In colonial days it had the additional advantage of lying directly on the Royal Highway. Besides agricultural produce, it supplied indigo and cordage made from the maguey cactus.

The parish church at Subtiava, dedicated to St. John the Baptist, was started in mid-sixteenth century to serve the needs of that prosperous Indian settlement, and according to some sources [143] it was completed by the seventeenth (*Pl. 75, fig. a*). Bartolomé de las Casas is reputed to have preached here, but since the Protector of the Indians made his final departure from America in 1547, his visit probably occurred before the present building was finished. In E. G. Squier's book on Nicaragua this church is illustrated with tiles intact on a rounded belfry atop the tower, its façade complete with finials and statuary and its wide atrium enclosed within a turreted wall.[158] But it deserves attention even in its dilapidated state. Its façade has a basic simplicity and dignity. From the *comparserie* of saints that once filled the niches, only St. Peter and a Virgin and Child remain. Effective is the grouping of the engaged columns, carrying the vertical line from base to top cornice. The two lower windows light side chapels. A timber roof, tiled, covers the long nave. Over the apse is a squat, cautious dome of stone, reinforced on the sides by stone barrel vaults, beneath which are side chapels—a solution seen also at Jinotepe. The church has no transept; the blocky buttresses at the corners which carry the final thrust of the dome contain chapels and the sacristy.

Inside the three-aisle structure the superb height of the native trees is apparent. Each column, some forty feet high, with considerable length also extending underground, is the trunk of a single cedar. Though the system of construction here is typically Mudéjar, the decoration on the crossbeams does not make use of the familiar geometric interlacing and the eight-pointed star; instead, an intertwining floral pattern, executed in a light-colored wood, fills in the space (*fig. b*). Medallions are applied in the ceiling where Mudéjar pendants would normally be suspended, and in the center is a full sun with spreading rays (*compare Pls. 6, 181*). The lower end of each column (*fig. c*) carries interwoven floral elements, as does the upper molding of its mortar base.

The decorative scheme in the side altar (*fig. d*) also leans toward an interweaving of floral elements. This altar does not appear to be as early as the building itself and may have been constructed of fragments.

The conventual church of San Francisco in Antigua, though now largely in ruins, offers a splendid example of regional earthquake Baroque (*Pl. 76, fig. b*). Because the Franciscans came with the Conquistadores, or soon afterward, they often acquired a choice location for their establishment. Work on their Antigua complex was begun in 1544, when the Franciscan friar Toribio de Benavente—better known to history as Motolinía (poor), the notable opponent of Las Casas—arrived from Mexico with twenty-four of his brethren. They made their monastery one of the leading institutions in the community. Extensive refurbishment was undertaken in 1692; the timbered ceilings were changed and murals

were painted in the cloisters. By that time the complex was immense. It occupied several acres and was surrounded by high walls with a number of gateways. It had its own printing press, library, stables, and gardens and patios. Buildings of the Third Order, a chapel, and the College of San Buenaventura were then already annexed to the main conventual church.[160]

This church once had two towers. Its façade, which was probably finished by early eighteenth century, is of the retable type; the variety in the pediments and the recessed portal and choir-light make it a rewarding study. Note the horizontally grooved pilasters in the belfry and, on the base, the Franciscan cord. No major pediment is to be found on the entire façade; but then the upper sections are gone. Ten of the twelve polychromed stone statues of Franciscan saints which originally occupied the niches have survived. A Virgin and Child stand within the arched entrance, above them a coat of arms bearing a double-headed eagle. Through the doorway and window can be glimpsed the broad arch of the choir gallery. The ingenious brick construction of the twisted columns is visible at the lower left.

This façade stood almost intact until the earthquake of 1917. The disaster of 1773, however, had badly damaged the rest of the complex. Only the chapel of the Third Order then warranted reconstruction, and when shortly afterward the establishment itself was transferred to Guatemala City, this chapel was kept up by lay members of the order who remained in the ruined town.

In its general composition the façade of La Recolección at León (*fig. c*), probably dating from late eighteenth century, echoes that of Subtiava's parish church. Its columns are grouped in the same manner, emphasizing the height of the espadaña, but are wound with spiraling garlands. Stucco ovals containing the instruments of the Passion decorate the spaces between them. At the top is a relief of the risen Christ. The large rectangular choir-light—the only opening besides the entrance—is ingeniously framed by a continuation of the cornice molding, which draws it into the lower tier and causes the espadaña to appear even more soaring. A single tower buttresses the façade. Outlines of urn-shaped pilasters can be discerned at the corners of its lowest section, while just above them rise the horizontally grooved type. Rounded corners in the belfry tend to lighten the massivity. Very effective are the balustrades, the zigzag beading, and the uneven edging of the espadaña, all of which catch and break the brilliant sunlight. The last extensive work on this building in colonial times was completed in 1795.

In the church of La Merced in Granada, Nicaragua (*fig. a*), the classicizing tendency evident in La Recolección is even more marked. The Baroque, however, is still apparent in the finials, the spirals on the espadaña, and the two flanking pediments. The bulk of this structure was drawn out horizontally and there was little striving for height. An ornamental motif derived from the Franciscan cord outlines the façade. Note the three entrances.

La Merced was completed around 1781. In 1856 it suffered in the war with the Walker filibusters; the tower especially was heavily damaged, but according to an inscription on its base it was restored in 1862. The graceful draped curtain on the belfry is a neoclassic motif which might have been there before restoration.

Some examples of the barn-shaped church have already been shown; the façades of the four illustrated here (*Pl. 77*) are comparatively plain. The columns, drawn up through at least two orders, are severe and straight. Wherever niches are applied, they are sober; and the ornamental gables are kept low.

The pilgrim church of La Candelaria at Chiantla (*fig. b*) stands in a village inhabited by Mam Indians, in a picturesque spot in western Guatemala near Huehuetenango. Every year this shrine, founded by the Dominicans in the sixteenth century, attracts one of the largest pilgrimages of the country.[158] Stylistically it shows a considerable contrast to the churches in the more eastern regions. Its architectural interest lies primarily in its series of arches; the broad arc described in the main pediment is especially effective. Columns define its towers and lead the eye upward to the belfries. The high roof line indicates an unusually lofty nave.

El Salvador is represented in this group by two parish churches, one from the town of Jocoro, in the southeast corner of the country near the Honduran border, and the other from Panchimalco, about nine miles south of the capital. In the first (*fig. a*) a Baroque stucco relief on the upper half shows graceful sprays of fantasy flowers arranged in great vases and, around the niche, decorative leaves ending in sunflowers that remind one of Comayagua cathedral (*see Pl. 6*). As is usual in this type of church, the towers are small and are kept about on a line with the pediment.

In Panchimalco (*fig. c*) towers are only suggested. A belfry may once have stood on the left corner. The whole façade is very thick, a solid block with no opening except the wide doorway. Note the peculiar shape of the pinnacles. All eight niches have retained their statues. Inside this church are some fine wood carvings. The village of Panchimalco is inhabited by Pancho Indians, descendants of the Pipils who migrated in pre-Columbian times from Mexico; they still observe many of the customs of their forefathers.

In the two Salvadoran churches the accent is on the horizontal; the Guatemala example emphasizes the vertical. The church at Ajuterique, Honduras (*fig. d*)—another predominantly Indian village and not far from Comayagua—shows a blend. A large palm branch in relief, finely executed, is preserved on its espadaña. Judging from the other churches in the region it can be surmised that once the lower part of this façade also carried stucco ornamentation. Note the buttresses of the side walls, showing the method used in such churches. The second tower was never constructed; a pier takes its place. The interior is Rococo, gilded and white. One door near the altar is painted, on canvas over the wood, with a scene from the Apocalypse and two Evangelists in traditional Byzantoid style. Two-toned tiles in mellow harmonized shades, very similar to those on the cathedral cupola in Comayagua, cover sections of the floor.

In the neighboring village of Lejamaní at the time of our visit in 1947, the brutal hand of modernization was chopping away at an intricate stucco design on the church façade, effacing archangels and garlands to make a cold and plain cement surface. Another folkloristic display was being obliterated which can never be reconstructed, the more tragic because such buildings were seldom recorded or even photographed, so little have they been appreciated.

With the coming of the nineteenth century the trend to the neoclassic grew increasingly stronger and many façades reflect the change. No longer of the retable type, they are designed without the decorative effect of statuary in niches and often are rather flat. In El Calvario in León (*Pl. 78, fig. a*), Nicaragua, finished about 1810, the figural decoration consists of story-telling scenes executed in stucco relief, later much repainted. In addition, medallions, garlands, and rosettes were applied in a neoclassic manner, leaving much of the surface plain. The triangles of the pediments are closed and the columns are drawn out and unadorned. The effect is placid and aloof.

Granada, Nicaragua, was founded by Francisco Hernández de Córdoba in 1524 and named after his birthplace. It had a most advantageous location and, through Lake Nicaragua and the San Juan River, was a major link on the Atlantic–Pacific traffic route. Even though the earthquake of 1663 reduced the flow of the river, Granada, surrounded by sugar plantations, became the richest city in eighteenth-century Nicaragua; in size it was

second only to León. In 1780 a young British naval officer, Horatio Nelson, came up the river in command of a party intent on capturing both Granada and León. He was recalled the day before Fort San Juan fell to the English and the party never gained its goal. But in 1856 the Walker filibusters succeeded in sacking the city, leaving it in ruins.

The church of San Francisco in Granada (*fig. b*) was originally part of a fortress and commands a splendid view of Lake Nicaragua and the surrounding countryside. In mid-sixteenth century a structure occupied this site which was intended to house the Spanish treasure gathered thereabouts. In one of the adjacent adobe buildings of the Franciscan monastery, Hernando de Soto, explorer of Florida and discoverer of the Mississippi River, was once imprisoned, and Las Casas, Protector of the Indians, preached here often. The present church façade, last repaired in 1862, presents a strongly neoclassic aspect. Its three entrances and the unusual and graceful spacing of the windows first attract the eye. Tenuous pendants of the *corizo*—a local flower with a powerful perfume—are the only ornaments in the large square panels, and the palm leaf provides the decorative motifs for the lower oval windows and the main entrance. Since the columns are not carried above the second order, the emphasis is transferred to the horizontal. A large portion of the tall espadaña is completely free-standing. Three open arches at the right serve as the belfry.

The vast church of Santo Domingo in Guatemala City (*fig. c*) was erected between 1792 and 1802 by Pedro Garci-Aguirre. It is much weightier than the other examples here, but like them it has three doorways and is approached by a flight of steps leading to a paved landing; it too has attenuated stucco ornamentation. Its numerous openings are of various shapes and sizes. The outline of its façade is made irregular by the jutting clusters of columns which divide the sections. Its pediments are closed, whether they are placed above openings or crown the central section.

Besides the balustrade, three heroic statues ornament the top. This church was ruined by the earthquake of 1917 and doubtless its original design was somewhat befogged in the reconstruction.

Colonial architecture in Central America started out with few pretensions; at the close of the period it again had little decoration but the scale was grand. In between these two phases the retable type of façade went through considerable modulation. Sections of it were recessed or thrust forward. Its columns and pilasters were twisted, horizontally grooved, and urn-shaped. Towers were stressed and varied. If the plan for the structure was too ambitious, it fell victim to catastrophe and can no longer be studied. When the architecture of this area is compared with that of its neighbors to north and south, it is evident that seismic conditions, regional labor, and local building methods, some of them dating back to pre-Columbian cultures, all contributed to the special character of earthquake Baroque in Central America.

9

SCULPTORS OF QUITO

On a quiet sunlit plaza in Popayán, Colombia, stands the church of San Francisco; occasionally footsteps echo along the sidewalks against its high stone walls or a platoon of pigeons decides to change position and with a loud flapping of wings alights on the roof of the monastery. To leave the semitropical glare of the plaza and enter the church is a pleasant relief. In it are preserved distinguished art works from its colonial past. The pulpit ranks among the best surviving examples of its kind (*see Pls. 28, 183*); the side retables shine with their original gold and colors untouched; canvas paintings hang on the walls in their Baroque frames, rich with gilded patterns and corner ornaments. The main altar here has been considerably changed, though some of its statues remain from colonial times. It spreads across the entire end wall of the nave like a great screen; in the center, filling the upper arch, stands a huge cross, behind which a stiff canvas curtain closes the *camarín* off like a stage.

Seen from the outside, this *camarín* is a separate bay, built of brick, so large that it might be mistaken for an apse. Access to it is through a narrow passage behind the altar, over the catacombs of the monks, and up a narrow dark winding stair cut into the thick brick walls. Inside the spacious friendly upper chamber, bathed in crystalline light from the lantern of a dome, is a life-size winged figure (*Pl. 79*). She seems to float, weightless, on a silver crescent moon. The base is a great silver globe, some three feet in diameter, bound with gilded lacelike bands. Out of these sprouts an immense silver lily. A serpent winds about the moon. One foot of the figure rests on its body and the other seems poised to tread on its neck. With her right hand she aims a golden javelin at its head, and her left arm and the cloak swing out, responding to the movement. Her powerful outspread wings are of silver, and a silver crown in filigree rests on the slightly bent head; heavy star-shaped earrings hang from her ears. The figure is clothed entirely in gold, each garment—robe, surplice, and mantle—differentiated by the manner of tooling in their large flowing patterns, tinged with color.

This splendid statue is revealed only at certain seasons, and there are some who even after a prolonged stay in Popayán do not know of her existence; the photograph shown here is the first taken of her. She is called by the faithful La Inmaculada, the Immaculate Conception.

Indeed, she has some of the attributes of the Immaculate Conception, but the representation is by no means orthodox. Although the Immaculate Conception was not defined as dogma until 1854, the idea of Mary the Immaculate was propounded in Palestine as early as the seventh century and was supported especially by the Franciscans. Later it was championed by the Jesuits against the Dominicans, who in 1483 and again in 1661 had to be admonished to cease their opposition to it. In 1511 the Portuguese Beatriz de Silva founded the order of the Purísima Concepción.³⁹ In 1760 the Virgin of the Immaculate Conception was declared the principal patron of all Spanish possessions, particularly of those in America.

The iconography of the Immaculate Conception developed very slowly. In the Middle Ages, Mary and the Christ Child were pictured at the top of the Tree of David. Later the figure of a young girl was favored. The painter Pacheco, erudite lay theologian and arbiter of religious iconography in the employ of the Inquisition, gave detailed instructions on "how to paint the Immaculate Conception": She should be represented in the flower of youth, some twelve to fourteen years old, clad in white with a mantle of blue; she should be crowned with stars, under her feet the moon, and the rays of the sun should encircle her. Pacheco argued that the crescent should be represented with its points turning downward, to indicate a spherical shape and to place its shadow properly on the side opposite the sun. He traced the iconography of the Immaculate Conception from the mysterious Woman whom John beheld in his apocalyptic vision in Chapter 12 of Revelation and stated that he preferred to depict her, as described in the first verse, before her Child was born. As for the dragon, he felt that such a monstrous creature should not appear at all in the presence of such perfection.⁸ Nevertheless at least once he painted her with a bat-winged monster beneath her feet, on either side of which was a demon in human form, the one clutching a bow and the other an arquebus; in that depiction she is upheld by angels and surrounded by the attributes of the rosary. The Immaculate Conception is perhaps best known from paintings by Murillo (1617–1682). On his canvases she floats on clouds surrounded by angels, she always has a halo about her head and sometimes a chaplet of stars, and her hands are clasped in prayer or crossed on her breast.

In Murillo's work the monster seldom appears; in no case is Mary winged or does she wear a crown, and neither does she stand with open gestures nor wield a weapon.

The Woman of the Apocalypse, as depicted in fifteenth-century blockbooks, follows the text from Revelation more closely. Dürer's woodcut is one of the best-known versions of this figure; similar representations by contemporary artists are found in the Low Countries and Germany. Crowned with stars and winged, she floats on the crescent moon, her hands clasped. Her Child is being caught to Heaven by angels, while St. Michael and his legions rush in to battle the seven-headed dragon, which is spewing forth a flood; John sits on the other shore, recording the awful scene. This portrayal can be found frequently in paintings of colonial Spanish America, especially in Mexico. But again, this Woman is not the militant figure at Popayán.

It may occur to some that the South American statue portrays the Church Triumphant. But in that case she would wear a papal tiara, and heresy, beneath her feet, would be symbolized by a demon in human form.

As the Virgen del Socorro, or the Virgin of Aid, popular in eighteenth-century prints, Mary adopts the dart and can be seen with her Child on her arm, flinging the weapon at Satan, sometimes a dragon and sometimes in human form (see Appendix, Pl. 191, fig. b). A representation seen more frequently is one in which the Virgin is piercing the head of the monster with a long lance. But in neither case is she winged.

All these depictions involve the idea of Mary as the New Eve, the one soul untouched by original sin, through whom the Redemption was made possible. Thus the dragon of Revelation turned into the serpent of temptation, sometimes even holding the apple in its mouth. The Virgin was envisioned as existing before time; in the church of Aracoeli, in Rome, a sixteenth-century mural shows her battling against Satan's hosts at the side of St. Michael before the creation.¹² In Italian and Spanish paintings especially, Virgin and Child are depicted with Adam and Eve imploring at their feet; sometimes the latter are represented as bound to the dead Tree of Knowledge and sometimes they are shown in the anterooms of Hell or looking out from a skeleton, surrounded by supplicating prophets, kings, and priests.[10]

The outstanding example of Mary as the New Eve is in the Church of SS Michel et Gudule in Brussels, the work (1699) of Hendrick Verbruggen (*see Appendix, Pl. 191, fig. a*). There she stands on the baldachin of the pulpit. Under her feet is the upturned sickle moon and about her head are the twelve stars of Revelation; but she has no wings. Jesus, as a young boy, stands before her, his foot as well as hers planted firmly on the serpent's neck. Her hand above his guides the long lance—topped with a cross—as it strikes the creature between the eyes. At the base of the pulpit Adam and Eve cower by the gnarled Tree before the avenging angel; above them is a shield bearing Mary's monogram and a Latin phrase in which the name "Eva" is modified to become "Ave."

In Würzburg a somewhat similar representation can be seen in a statue by Claude Curé, dated 1728. The German verse on its pedestal might be translated:

> What through the apple bite
> Brought Evil on the world
> Was through the Ave sweet
> And through the Cross transformed.
> So accept the Ave
> Mary full of grace;
> And all pay service unto thee—
> With Jesus protect us from harm. . . .

From this discussion it becomes evident that while European prototypes parallel in one detail or another the composition at Popayán, that statue expresses a still more complex symbolism. From the Middle Ages on, all Scripture, but especially Revelation, was subject to various interpretations—as referring to Christ and the Redemption, to the Virgin, the prog-

ress of the soul, the history of the church. Treatises were written upon the many aspects that resulted, and symbolic meanings, often of deep philosophical significance, came to be attached to them. Perhaps one of the most familiar of such interpretations comes from the Song of Solomon, where the Christian church is personified as the Bride (of the Lord). As we shall see in later chapters, phrases from this book were applied to Mary also.

In the Popayán figure we meet the apocalyptic vision of John from Chapter 12 of Revelation interpreted with reference to the Virgin, and she appears not only as the Woman crowned with stars and provided "with two wings of a great eagle that she might fly into the wilderness," but also as an active participant in the "war in Heaven." How consciously and conscientiously the apocalyptic symbolism was followed in this representation is evidenced by the inclusion of the "flood" that "the serpent cast out of his mouth after the woman," painted on the dome of the *camarín* and identified unmistakably by the ark floating on the limitless waters beyond her head.

In this aspect the Virgin, if looked upon as the protagonist of striving mankind, corresponds with the Vision of the Fifth Seal in mystic lore. She may be said to embody the fifth stage of mankind's progress, which Augustine defined as fear overcome and full confidence in the contemplation of truth. She would then be killing darkness with the arrow of spreading light; indeed, her zigzag javelin is the thunderbolt from Heaven itself. Her statue is so placed in Popayán that the sun falls on the golden weapon and the open hand seems only to guide it toward its goal. Through its human charm and the superb rendition of the symbolic act, the statue makes a great appeal even to the onlooker who has no religious interest in it or iconographic curiosity.

So far as this author has been able to ascertain, this aspect of the Virgin in statuary occurs only in South America. That its symbolism was understood and tolerated within the Roman Church is clear from the fact that it was often repeated; a number of such statues are still extant.

Several other examples are found in Popayán. One, a small carving, is in the sacristy of San Francisco. Another, life-size and nearly as striking as the great statue just seen, stands in the long reception hall of the archbishop's palace (*Pl. 80, fig. b*). Here there is no lily, and the Woman is enclosed within a vast silver aureole, some nine feet high; the bands on the silver globe are very similar in pattern to those on the work in the *camarín*. Stars are placed at the lower edge of the rays behind her head, and the encircling aureole is designed to accommodate her crown, held by small angels. In this case the serpent carries a red apple in its mouth. The angels scattered about would appear to be later additions, and the whole composition has lost some of its expressiveness through over-painting: a matte encarnación makes the face doll-like, and the estofado of the mantle is daubed with stars in two different sizes; also, real lace has been added at the cuffs, endangering the dignity of line.

A lay brotherhood owned this statue and in the 1930's, in their zeal to assist the church, sold the original crown. Shortly afterward the magnificent piece, of gold set with large irregular Colombian emeralds, was exhibited in the United States.[174] The statue is carried in Popayán's famous Corpus Christi procession on the shoulders of sixteen men and is, with right, a favorite of the town's inhabitants.

Another example of this subject stands on a side altar in the church of Las Monjas de la Concepción in Popayán. Though iconographically the same, this carving seems to be of a later date; it is half life-size and the globe is indicated by only a hemisphere.

A statue in Quito on the main altar of the church of San Francisco (*fig. c*) offers a clue to the authorship of this remarkable interpretation. Here a halo has replaced the crown and the globe is absent, but she still has the new moon under her feet, and like the others she looks down at the serpent's head. The weapon is gone, but the gesture is similarly open and swinging. In its estofado and general line this statue shows relationship to the one in the archbishop's palace, despite retouching.

The heads and hands of such images were made separately—for the better application of the enamel-like encarnación—and then fitted to the body. Both hands of this figure can still be taken from their sockets (*fig. d*). On the tenons are two inscriptions, placed as if on two medallions—"*Bernardo Legarda*" on the one and "*se acabó en 7 de diciembre d año de 734*" on the other ("Bernardo Legarda finished this on the 7th of December, 1734"). This is the only signed work of the great mestizo sculptor known to date.

In the choir of the same church is still another statue, smaller in size and somewhat marred but unmistakably of the same type (*fig. a*). Here the estofado, very fine in quality, has not been tampered with.

The Franciscan monastery in Quito has in its possession similar statues in various sizes. Particularly ingratiating is a little figure mounted on a miniature pedestal (*Pl. 81, fig. a*); it is shown here set within a decorative niche called an *urna*, or shrine. The frame, exquisite in detail, is emblazoned with Mary's monogram, and the background is strewn with painted flowers.

In all these Quito examples the globe is omitted and the moon rests on a few curly clouds—a detail which was elaborated in larger compositions. Although most figures of the Vision of the Fifth Seal are associated with the Franciscan order, a small example (*fig. b*) is in the chapel of San Juan de Dios in Quito, placed against the back panel of the pulpit. This chapel is part of the building complex that houses the oldest hospital in the city. Now closed to the public, it is entered from the hospital court, and few have noted this carving, which, like the Popayán statue, was photographed for the first time for this volume. Its special interest lies in the fact that it is adapted as a relief. The moon is disproportionately large—she rides in it as if in a boat—and a globe is suggested by the mass of clouds, which form a segment of a circle.

Still other representations of the subject survive in Quito. One is in the church of El Belén, which was built in early eighteenth century.[183] This author found another, half life-size, as far north as Tunja, Colombia, in a corner of the Mancipe chapel in the cathedral, and a miniature, about a foot high, on a side altar of the church of Jesús y María in Lima, Peru. All of these have the bent knee, the pose of treading the serpent, and the upflung hands—never the praying gesture of the Immaculate Conception—and the head is bent to look down on the monster, though in none of them has the javelin been preserved.

The period of Bernardo Legarda in Quito, and most probably the sculptor himself, can be credited with the creation of this unique version of the Virgin. The figure's full symbolism, however, is revealed only through those examples in Popayán in which the javelin has survived—the key to its identity. The wide radius within which these statues have been found shows the extent of Quito's trade in art pieces in the eighteenth century.

In the infirmary of the Franciscan monastery in Quito is a small carving of the Virgin standing on a new moon and holding the serpent leashed on a chain—a heavy affair of gold links and beads which may have replaced a simpler one (fig. c). She has many of the attributes seen earlier—the wings, moon, and open gesture. Also in the possession of the same Franciscan establishment is a graceful figure about whose wrist a coarse rope is looped, bound at the other end to the monster—doubtless a replacement but still carrying out an iconographic tradition (fig. d). Her posture is somewhat different. She bends her head still lower as if to fix the monster with her eyes; her whole pose is less active and she has no wings. Clouds are carved on the globelike base, and she stands poised above them on the moon. A clue to the identification of these two figures is provided in Revelation 20:1-4,

which describes an angel, "come down from heaven, having the key of the bottomless pit and a great chain in his hand. And he laid hold on the dragon, that old serpent, which is the Devil, and Satan, and bound him . . . and set a seal upon him." In mystic lore these statues represent the Vision of the Sixth Seal, which carries the implication that Evil itself will finally be forced to do the will of God. (Compare Appendix, Pl. 191, fig. c.)

Here might be mentioned a painting of the Cuzco circle from the seventeenth or eighteenth century, which shows St. Thomas Aquinas as the defender of the Eucharist, brandishing a flaming sword—such as is usually associated with the Archangel Michael—and holding the seven-headed dragon of the Apocalypse on a heavy chain. On a fountain in Puebla, Mexico, Michael himself performs these acts.

To understand the amazing flowering of the plastic arts in Quito, its earlier history should be reviewed. The province of Quito—so-called after the pre-Columbian Kingdom of Quitu—occupied roughly the territory of present-day Ecuador. It lies at the north end of that high Andean plateau which in pre-Columbian times developed into the backbone of the vast Inca Empire. The region is broken by deep gorges and precipitous slopes, falling off on the east to the rain forests that feed the Amazon and on the west to steaming equatorial jungles, inhabited even today by savage Indian tribes. Ten magnificent volcanoes, among them Chimborazo, loom up from turbulent valleys. Only a few decades before the Conquest, the city of Quito was made the Inca's second capital (the other was Cuzco). Lying at an altitude of nearly 10,000 feet, it is remote and difficult of access. It enjoys a temperate climate, though nearly on the equator, and is situated amid fertile valleys of volcanic soil on the slope of the volcano Pichincha, down which flow unceasing streams of purest water. So hilly is the site that even in the pretentious eighteenth century practically everyone went on horseback or on foot—the gentry distinguished by large umbrellas borne by servants; only the president of the audiencia and the bishop rode in coaches, the navigation of which through the steep, uneven streets was a special art.[61]

As early as the 1530's three Franciscans founded an establishment there, led by the friar Jodoco Ricke (or Rijcke) de Marselaer, a Fleming from Ghent.[166] An illuminating side light is provided in the fact that his uncle was secretary to the only Flemish pope, Adrian VI, who had once been a tutor to Charles V. Ricke was allotted Indian labor to erect the first buildings, and according to tradition he himself placed the first stone. He began at once to teach the Indians to plow with oxen and build roads, to count in Spanish, read and write, and bind books.[164] Like his more famous compatriot Pedro de Gante in Mexico, he established a college for the instruction of the Indians in the arts, and like the Colegio de Santa Cruz in Tlatelolco, the Colegio de San Andrés in Quito trained the sons of distinguished natives in the services of the church, the playing of musical instruments (including the organ), and also in the techniques of sculpture and painting. The first professor of painting here was one Pedro Gosseal, a native of Mechlin (halfway between Antwerp and Brussels) and one of the monastery founders. Ricke also established the Franciscan monastery of San Bernardino in Popayán, where he died about 1574.

Thus Quito had from its colonial beginnings a monastic atmosphere, which was conducive to mystic contemplation, and a rare artistic tradition. The flowering of Christianity on new soil there might be compared in some of its expressions to the spirit of the Trecento or early Quattrocento in Italy. This was the more remarkable because even in the early eighteenth century colonial artists lacked many implements and materials deemed necessary in Europe for fine workmanship.

Little is known of the Quito sculptor Bernardo Legarda. He was a mestizo and tradition has it that he lived on the great plaza opposite the monastery. His atelier was large and a number of apprentices worked under him; the names of some pupils have come down in connection with works begun by the master but finished by them.[183] He signed the statue on the main altar of San Francisco and may have been the creator of the Vision of the Fifth Seal. Legarda must have been a true initiate of Marian lore at a time when the visions and ecstasies of saints were part of religious life and artists prepared for their work with prayers and fasting.

The drama of Mary's life culminated in her ascension and her coronation in Heaven—the last of her Glorious Mysteries. The Assumption of the Virgin was a popular subject among artists everywhere, especially after Titian executed his magnificent canvas in the Frari church in Venice. It was also a favorite with the sculptors of Quito.

The figure shown here (*Pl. 82, fig. b*) can probably be assigned to Legarda. It stands in a private collection, not in a church; but even as a separate piece of polychromed wood sculpture, its appeal is immediate. The sublimated expression, the gesture of the delicate hands, the delineation of the three mystic garments—each different in its fall and folds—are all the work of a master. Note the graceful bow of the girdle. The manner of tenoning the hands to the wrist can be seen in this carving.

Besides the mestizo Legarda, who was active in the first half of the eighteenth century, another Quito sculptor, Caspicara, produced work of outstanding quality. The only known date [183] in connection with him is 1792, when he is mentioned in a document as "contemporary." He was born of Indian parents, and his real name was Manuel Chili or Chil, but like many artists—even in Europe—he is better known by his nickname, "Rough Face," which referred to his pock-marked skin. The only signed work of his that has come to light so far was illustrated earlier (*see Pl. 12*).

Caspicara's manner is related to Legarda's, but it is not likely that he studied directly with the mestizo master, as fifty-eight years separate the two known dates for them. It seems more probable that the artistic tradition in Quito, established by the first third of the eighteenth century on an extraordinarily high level, was kept vigorous in various workshops. Caspicara lived in the Rococo period, when porcelain and ivory figurines were cherished possessions in many a colonial household, and most of his statues are only half life-size, in contrast to those of Legarda's era. But Caspicara's is no dainty playful talent; in some of his work he might even be called Donatello-esque. He is especially noteworthy for his group compositions; until he appeared, single statues were generally the order in Quito.

His Assumption (*fig. a*) tells a complicated story. The group occupies the topmost part of the transept altar dedicated to St. Anthony in the church of San Francisco in Quito. So high is it placed and so heavy is the goldwork around it that the scene is almost lost, but when considered apart from its surroundings, it comes to full life and has the power of a much larger composition. The upward movement of the Virgin's figure is emphasized by the strong horizontality of the astonished earth-bound group below. Her expression is sublime but at the same time warmly human. The cherubs bearing her heavenward are delightfully unconventional; one even seems to support her with a hand under her elbow. The curly clouds, by now familiar, recall the representations of Heaven in early manuscripts and woodcuts. Despite the vehement gestures of the Apostles gathered below, they are not playing theater; they are the ecstatic eyewitnesses of an overwhelming drama. Although each is portrayed with a certain independence, together they convey a single sweeping impression. The five huddled figures beyond the coffin produce a contrast that strengthens the effect of the whole—a minor chord between two major ones.

Mary's gown has the small metallic all-over pattern of the Rococo, and the estofado of the Apostles' robes shows considerable variety;

the colorful flower motifs in the right foreground could have been copied from a porcelain.

Another Assumption figure by Caspicara (*Pl. 83, fig. c*) is in the Franciscan monastery at Quito; note again the liquid pattern in the estofado, a characteristic of that master's work. Very similar in posture is a carving in the church of El Carmen in Popayán, Colombia (*fig. a*). Both have a transfigured gaze and finely proportioned outstretched hands. Small details, such as the flying scarf and the bow of the girdle, are worked out in both. There are differences, however, especially in the arrangement of the cloaks and in the estofado; in the one, glowing red roses are widely spaced on a silvery base, in the other, *mille fleurs* are scattered over a white ground. The former has a remarkably fine encarnación, enamel-like in its sheen. Similar bowknots can be seen on Chinese ivory figures shown earlier (*see Pl. 62*).

In the Tota Pulchra (all beautiful)—the phrase is from the Song of Solomon—we have an authentic Legarda piece (*fig. b*); it too is in the monastery of San Francisco in Quito. Compare it with the Caspicara beside it. The effect of Legarda's work is generally more massive, the figure is fuller, and the hands are heavier. The carving is executed with longer lines and bolder angles, and there are no flying or sharply protruding sections—the cloak enfolds the figure. Legarda's estofado has more verve; larger motifs are used, spaced farther apart.

As has been suggested the estofado on a statue may furnish a clue to its general provenience and epoch. The manner of its application has already been described in Chapter 7. On this plate are gathered samples of estofado from eight statues to show the wide range in style (*Pl. 84*).

The examples from Bogotá and Tunja, Colombia (*figs. a and b*), are probably among the earliest in this group. Both have much of the traditional Spanish manner—for instance, in the fine lines drawn across the surface to reveal the gold beneath; but even in the first sample, with its black and gold striation, the flowers are unusually large for the Spanish style. In the second, mild tints bring out the variety in the motifs, which however remain carefully subordinated to keep the total effect serene. (*See also Pl. 174.*)

The example from Querétaro, Mexico (*fig. c*), is decidedly original. The cloak carries deeply indented tooling, and the white field of the gown is scratched with lines to expose the metal base and painted with numerous motifs. The pattern is stiff, not fluent as in most of the others; some may see elements suggestive of pre-Columbian characters in it. Note the painted lace edging.

The next three examples come from statues from the Quito circle. Contrast the manner of tooling on a gold ground from the Vision of the Fifth Seal in Popayán, Colombia (*fig. d*), with the more simple and spotty punchwork pattern in the Mexican example just seen. Though complicated in design and execution, the Popayán estofado has clarity and fluency, calling to mind a rich, heavy brocade. (*See also Pl. 79.*)

A predilection for large spreading flower patterns is noticeable throughout the colonial epoch. This type of work was not too popular in contemporary Spain but is found in early- and mid-Renaissance Italian wood statues, which are polychromed, with little or no metal. The next robe (*fig. e*) shows such a varicolored flower design applied on a silver ground. Tooling appears here only in the foliated medallions, best seen in the lower center. Painting instead of tooling decorates the edge of the mantle, which seems to have been retouched. (*See also Pl. 87.*)

The last detail from Quito (*fig. f*) has no tooling; the motifs which lent themselves so well to that technique in the two others—the large medallions and the edging—are both painted here. On the skirt (lower center) small bright flowers are scattered directly on

gold; the surplice has deep and rich-toned Rococo bouquets on white, and the medallions are outlined in ochre. The scarf is Roman-striped in soft colors. Coarse irregular stars—later additions—stud the mantle, out of harmony with the rest of the distinguished piece. (*See also Pl. 82.*)

The sample from Honduras (*fig. g*) is characterized by a large diapered pattern formed by a chain of golden leaves; within it are painted nosegays of bright flowers. The gold ground is roughly striated, and the whole little piece is full of sparkle. It is outspokenly Rococo, recalling porcelain or ivory figurines. This detail is taken from a small Dolorosa which may be a product of the local school or may have been brought down from Guatemala.

Our last sample of colonial estofado (*fig. h*) comes from a late-eighteenth-century figurine in San Miguel de Allende, Mexico, possibly from a Querétaro atelier. The tooling produces a staccato line, somewhat like that in the preceding piece, but there is no garland to hold the design together and the painted pattern is large, loose, and free. Colors stand out from a dark ground and little metal is visible except in the punchwork. The impression is of subtle but rapid work which has dash and vibrancy, strongly on the coloristic side.

The quality of such carvings and the perfection of detail depended to a certain extent on the price paid for them. Extant contracts show how precisely both size and coloring were specified. The artist who contracted in Seville to paint and gild the Martínez Montañés altar for the church of La Concepción in Lima (*see Pls. 15, 60*) guaranteed that gold and not half-gold would be used in his work and that the garments would carry estofado in all manners —with the point of the brush, on open fields, engraved with a gimlet, eyeleted, prinked, hatched, and wrought with scales or wavy designs, as in watered silk; also that the encarnación would show differences in tone, conforming to the character of each figure, with the mouth, eyes, eyebrows, the roots of the beard, and the wrinkles done in fresco.[27] The same careful craftsmanship is evident in the work of many colonial masters.

Santa Rosa of Lima (1586–1617) became a favorite subject in the colonial art of the eighteenth century. She was an accomplished musician and was known also for her charming and gay temperament, in spite of the acts of penance which she had practiced even in youth. Against the wishes of her family she entered a Dominican convent at an early age. Catherine of Siena was her ideal and, like her, she had a vision of the "mystic marriage." According to her legend she was seen walking in the nunnery garden with a radiant child of about twelve, who instructed her in the healing of the sick and whom she called her "little doctor."

The commemorative prints issued upon the canonization of a saint provided the iconography for later representations. At the splendid ceremony which accompanied Santa Rosa's canonization in St. Peter's at Rome (1671), the basilica was hung with painted banners displaying scenes from her "true life," one of which pictured her, for the first time, with the Christ Child in her arms.[12] In two engravings (one is dated 1711) she is holding a miniature portrayal of the Infant Christ as an emblem, such as was used by professing nuns, encircled by a sheaf of roses. In Spain she was painted with the Child floating before her on top of her workbasket.

In Quito, Santa Rosa is depicted with especial affection, as is evident from the three figures illustrated (Pl. 85), all of them made there within an eighty-year period. The first statue (fig. a) occupies a lower niche of the altar by Caspicara in San Francisco, Quito—on which the Assumption is the central group (see Pl. 82). In this version Rosa, radiating inner serenity, is represented as a heavenly figure kneeling on clouds.

The smaller carving in the center (fig. b) shows a happy young girl, reserved and shy, somewhat astonished at the miracle unfolding before her. This work is said to be a Legarda. However, new light is shed on its authorship by the recently found Baby Jesus (see Pl. 12) signed by Caspicara. That infant and the one in Rosa's arms have so much similarity —in the extended left arm and the bend of the leg—that the attribution to Legarda is subject to considerable doubt.

The third Santa Rosa (fig. c) presents a statuesque woman in full command of beauty, within and without. Although this powerful figure stands in the Quito cathedral practically at the crossroads of the town, no one until now has taken enough notice of her to photograph or study her. The estofado here has a rich pattern of deep red roses, in contrast to that on the other figures, which is mild and silvery, with little color.

All three carvings show the saint dressed in nun's robes, with a wimple and dark mantle. But they differ not only in general interpretation but also in such details as the modeling of the hands and the arrangement of the drapery. The Christ Child in the last portrayal wears a new silk dress and even kid baby shoes.

Caspicara is the sculptor of all the statues on the next plate except the first; the carving of San Pedro de Alcántara is said to be by Padre Carlos, who was active in the second half of the seventeenth century (Pl. 86, fig. a). A dramatic representation of this saint, from Mexico, was shown earlier (see Pl. 57). The Quito carving presents a less ecstatic but more humanly touching figure and is more realistic all round. He is the only one in this group to wear a robe of textile.

Caspicara's angel (fig. b)—probably one of the band that stood in wonder before the manger—speaks for himself in his gracefully endearing pose. Even in this small piece the estofado is worthy of study. Different textures are brought out in the different garments, in both the carving and the painting; the surplice could not be finer in its delicacy and floral decoration if it had been painted in Botticelli's studio.

St. John Nepomuk (*fig. c*) is portrayed in ecstasy. As is characteristic of most Quito sculpture and especially of Caspicara's work, the hands by themselves convey much of the mood. The estofado is quiet but varied; the technique as well as the composition relates this figure to that of the first Santa Rosa on the preceding plate, its companion piece on the altar. Nepomuk was the patron saint of Bohemia, and his presence in Ecuador is significant, calling to mind the nationality of some of the friars there.

Three aspects of St. Francis of Assisi are presented in the lower row. In the first (*fig. d*), the saint is shown in penance, stripped to the waist, with iron bands and chains about his waist and upper arms like the San Pedro above him. Of the two carvings, Caspicara's is the more idealized. There is a gentleness in the portrayal, which characterizes many works of this Quito master. Note the superiority of wood over textile in the representation of the garment.

Another episode in the life of St. Francis shows him supported by angels as he receives the stigmata (*fig. e*). In the upper left is a vision of the Crucified, clasped in the sixfold wings of a seraph—an early mode of depiction used by Giotto and revived in the Counter Reformation.[12] The saint's body is in a rather cramped position, and the entire carving suggests the two-dimensional, in the tradition of some of the early altars (*see Pl. 24*).

As the Seraphic Father (*fig. f*) the saint himself wears sixfold wings, which, like his halo, are of silver. His robe has a tapestry-like pattern and a real cord is bound about the waist, a real rosary pendent from it. The sheep, symbol of the congregation, is a later addition; note its separate base. Metal loops are fastened on the pedestal of the statue through which carrying poles were slipped when it was borne in processions. A resemblance in the features can be noticed in all three carvings.

In contemporary European representations —especially the Spanish—the Mater Dolorosa frequently appears with a strongly theatrical presence. In the costumed figure from Quito (*Pl. 87, fig. a*), the face and hands of which are said to have been carved by Caspicara, we see a composed though suffering woman; the bent head and the gesture of the hands are sentimentally touching. This representation reminds one of certain fifteenth-century Flemish paintings, which were imbued with a rare intensity and even showed pearl-like tears but had no suggestion of the *larmoyant* so evident here. The Quito statue, half life-size, is dressed in a brocaded damask gown and a taffeta cloak; real pearls adorn the veil, the gold and silver threads of the edging and medallions are of pure metal, and precious and semiprecious stones are strewn on breast and girdle. It is regrettable that the statue is not better protected, for the textiles are crumbling and the threads which fasten the jewels are breaking.

Mary mourning in solitude between the Crucifixion and the Resurrection—La Soledad —was also a favorite subject in Latin America, and many churches there are dedicated to her. In the seventeenth century the Spanish sculptor Pedro de Mena carved a famous statue of this Virgin, in which her whole figure is enveloped in a cape edged with gold lace; she is wringing her hands and her expression is one of deepest anguish. That Spanish depiction may have influenced the artist who created the Soledad in Oaxaca, Mexico (*fig. b*), but only remotely. Here also the figure is completely enveloped in a cloak; gold braid edges the entire garment, giving a pronounced vertical emphasis. But the hands, thrust out very slightly, are held in the calm pose of prayer. The pale face, partly covered with the somber cloak, has a withdrawn expression. The Mexican example uses a different artistic language, and for many it may be more immediate.

A carving of Mary Magdalene, kneeling, the work of an unknown artist (*fig. c*), is part of a Crucifixion group in the church of El Tejar in Quito, Ecuador. Although grief and pain permeate the figure, again the gesture is controlled; the look and clasped hands tell the story of suffering. Remarkable is the estofado of the gown, showing a large floral pattern on a silver ground, one of the rare examples untouched in later centuries. The shiny encarnación also is well preserved, the type of finish which Quito seems to have specialized in throughout her colonial greatness. The bold and vigorous lines of this carving indicate another master, as yet unidentified but quite different in manner from either Caspicara or Legarda.

Caspicara's ability to convey the drama of a scene without hyperbole comes out eloquently in his Pietà, a group composition in the cathedral of Quito (*Pl. 88, fig. a*). The three mourners gathered around the Christ furnish emotional background. The body of the dead Christ has an ivory-like quality. He is stretched on the ground, his head resting against his mother. This is post-Reformation iconography; in earlier representations Mary is holding her Son on her lap, as in Michelangelo's famous statue in St. Peter's at Rome. The two other mourning women here are Mary Magdalene and Mary Salome, mother of Santiago and John the Evangelist. As in all Caspicara's creations, the hands are communicative; those of Christ, still strong, hang like relaxed wings. The various gestures of the three women form a rhythmic pattern. Like many of the Quito master's carvings, these figures are only half life-size, but they have monumentality. In this group the effects of unfortunate repainting are apparent.

Another Pietà (*fig. b*), executed by an unknown artist, stands in the church of La Candelaria, Bogotá, Colombia. It is said to date from the early eighteenth century.[170] Here, in the older tradition, Christ lies more in the lap of his mother and hers is the more dominating figure. The estofado seems to be untouched, but the large halo and silver heart pierced with a dagger are probably later additions.

A third Pietà (*fig. c*), in the left transept of El Calvario in Antigua, Guatemala, has been attributed by one writer[141] to Julio Urruela

and by another[159] to Manuel Cuéllar, who was active in the second half of the seventeenth century. In this sculpture the position of the Christ is reversed; Mary's right hand holds his arm, while the left is placed so that it could clasp a sword piercing her heart.

In these three compositions—from Ecuador, Colombia, and Guatemala—the Christ figures show considerable variation; still greater differences of approach are manifest in the portrayals of Mary. Caspicara, perhaps through the addition of the two other Marys, has produced the fullest drama. The Bogotá piece is fervent and sincere, somewhat transcendental in its feeling. In the Guatemala sculpture the mystic bond that unites mother and holy Son finds moving expression. (*Compare Pl. 21.*)

When in 1760 the Virgin of the Immaculate Conception was declared the principal patroness of Spanish possessions, she was already beloved in the New World. Two interpretations of this subject are shown here, both from late eighteenth century (*Pl. 89*).

For over two hundred and fifty years the cathedral at Quito, Ecuador, was enriched by the works of artists and craftsmen of high attainments. In 1793 a suit over the estate of a wealthy man was settled by the king in favor of the cathedral, and the reigning bishop, the Quito-born José Eliodoro Mariano Díaz de la Madrid y Unda, used the money to redecorate the building. He put in windows and an elaborate portal, presented the old Baroque altars (alas!) to rural parishes, and installed new ones executed on more classic lines, adorned with paintings.[164] The choir, which in this building occupies a semicircular space behind the main altar, must have been redone about this time. In its midst the archbishop's throne, upholstered in red velvet, stands under a shell-shaped baldachin. To right and left are four statues attributed to Caspicara. He may also have cooperated in the general embellishment, for his only known date (1792) coincides with the time of this work.

A figure of Mary stands on the new moon

at the top of the throne, a section of her mantle flying beyond one shoulder and her hands in the praying pose of the Immaculate Conception (fig. a). Two angels, above horns of plenty, grasp the points of the crescent, and, below them, framing the chair back, are two peacock-like creatures, their feathered bodies highly decorative. In early Christian art the peacock symbolizes eternal life. The arrangement of the creature, divided and used in a conventionalized form, reminds one of the double-headed eagle, perpetual favorite in Spanish-American art. The columns and the applied motifs on the choir walls are gilded, but the entire background is a smooth cream color, in keeping with the changing taste of the era.

The other Immaculate Conception (fig. b) originally stood in the chapel of the Hacienda Purísima de las Flores, near Guanajuato, Mexico, but in 1894, when the descendants of Count de Rul sold the Flores mine, it was removed to the church of La Valenciana.[99] Though contemporary with the statue beside it, this carving shows very different taste preferences. The crescent moon is absent, and the figure floats above a cluster of cherub heads—a popular arrangement ever since Raphael's time. What healthy unsophisticated faces they have! While in the Quito statue a restraint is noticeable in the lines of the drapery—only above one shoulder is a sweeping movement allowed in the mantle—here it billows about the hips and is blown outward on either side of the figure. The estofado has a floral pattern, mild in color. This figure, polychromed in true Rococo spirit, stands in its own niche and is framed by a fantasy garland of leafy fronds. Wooden candelabra emerge from a shell at the bottom, and two others branch at the sides from the garland. Compare the heavy volutes in both compositions. Quito's strong spiritual heritage shows itself in the gentleness and refinement of the first carving, while the Mexican figure has the dash and fluency characteristic of that land.

The legendary fame of Charles V, the first emperor of the New World and sovereign of the Conquistadores, lingered in the colonies long after the Bourbons replaced the Habsburgs on the throne of Spain. A small statue of him—twenty-eight inches high—was made in Quito probably in the first half of the eighteenth century (fig. e). Two European likenesses of him, both posthumous, are placed beside it (figs. c and d), the first a painting by Peter Paul Rubens (from 1634–1635) and the second an engraving by the Flemish master Pieter Balten (1580). Such representations circulated in the colonies and doubtless passed from generation to generation. In certain details the statue is similar to them—the white neckband, the armor and mail shirt beneath, the greaves, the sword, and the orb with its cross; absent are the gloves, the crown or wreath (which may have disappeared), and also the Golden Fleece, so meticulously included in the European depictions. In general a simplification is noticeable. The long face with its heavy Habsburg chin and protruding under lip are not represented, and the mantle that hangs in dignified folds in both European portraits is carved in the Quito sculpture with verve, much like that of the Inmaculada above. Commemorative statues and paintings of bygone rulers of Spain, beginning with Ferdinand and Isabella, were common in Spanish America; some still survive today in remote corridors and dusty attics.

By mid-eighteenth century the fame of Quito's art had become widespread. Between 1779 and 1788 over two hundred and fifty chests of art products—sculpture and painting—were shipped out by way of Guayaquil. The technical methods that were so well exemplified in the larger statues were applied in the manufacture of figurines. Oriental trade, legal and illegal, had already made the colonial household familiar with Chinese porcelains and ivory figures, and traffic with Europe was bringing into the New World finely colored Rococo statuettes. Quito itself had a ceramics factory, established in 1771, which turned out not only Nativity groups but also genre pieces and its renowned basket arrangements of native fruits and flowers.

The next two plates present miniature figures and groups in which naïve realism blends with deep sentiment, creating a religious folk genre.

The popularity of the manger scene has already been discussed. Quito specialized in such groups and exported them widely in the Spanish colonial empire. The three doctors (Pl. 90, fig. a)—not quite six inches high—show the same virtuosity in their carving and coloring as the larger statues. The archangels (figs. c and f), charming in gesture, are also carefully detailed as to feature, hair, and drapery. Both have a certain pastoral air, characteristic of the Rococo, somewhat like the kneeling angels on the archbishop's throne just seen. Noteworthy are the gilded and tooled patterns of the estofado, in each case different.

The figure of St. Peter (fig. d)—without the base only a little over three inches high—also might have belonged to a Nativity group. His bright yellow gown and rose-colored cloak are finely harmonized, and the quality of the encarnación recalls ivory figurines. The kneeling shepherd, on the other hand, has the softness of a Rococo porcelain (fig. e). The coloring is generally light, the plastic detail masterly. A delightful story-telling atmosphere pervades all of these carvings.

In comparison, another group, the Magi (fig. b), from San Miguel de Allende, Mexico, has a more folkish touch. One is a white man, one is a mestizo, and one a Negro. Dürer was among the first European artists to introduce the African king into the Adoration scene; soon in the Spanish colonies, particularly in Mexico, another of the kings was turned into a mestizo, or sometimes an Indian.

These three statuettes, about twelve inches high, are remarkably light in weight. The costumes, with their broad collars, are made of starched material, in contrast to those in the Quito group, which are entirely of wood. The eyes, though as lustrous as glass, are painted, and eyelashes of hair are attached. Though Querétaro, with its distinguished studios of sculpture, was near, it is easily possible that these pieces were made locally. In colonial times San Miguel had its own mint, and the silver coins of Charles III (1716–1788) issued there show a beauty in design and execution which leaves little to be desired.

A slight digression with reference to Charles III of Spain offers a revealing study in the intricate international relationships that colored art as well as politics around many a Rococo ruler. His father was the Bourbon Philip V of Spain and his mother, a Farnese of Parma. Through the rights of his mother, he was the Duke of Parma and Tuscany. Later (1738) he ruled over the Kingdom of the Two Sicilies; after he inherited the throne of Spain (1759), his relationship with Naples and Sicily continued, for his son succeeded him there. During his rule in Naples he built the famous San Carlos Opera House. When he left, he transferred the Capodimonte porcelain factory from Naples to Buen Retiro in Spain. His wife was a daughter of the king of Saxony, who was also king of Poland. Thus again with Charles III artistic influences from France, northern and southern Italy, and Central Europe came into Spain, and eventually into her colonies.

From the naïve story-telling Nativity groups produced in Quito it was only a step to the portrayal of scenes from the lives of the saints. Like a stage in a doll's theater is the *urna* which presents St. Anthony in his chamber with the Christ Child (Pl. 91, fig. a). This miniature stage, about fourteen inches high, is framed with light balsa wood into which mirrors with a chased pattern are set in the Venetian tradition. A provincial eighteenth-century interior provides the setting. The figure of the saint is carved entirely of wood and bears a fine estofado. The Christ Child lies on a real lace coverlet. The tiny candelabra are of glass, but the books on the wall are painted. Slippers stand under the bed, a skull rests on the shelf, and a pilgrim hat and staff are placed in the corner.

The relief (*fig. b*), only two and one-half inches in diameter, tells the story of the Nativity amazingly well within a very limited surface. Its material is tagua nut, called vegetable ivory because it takes on an ivory-like hardness and tone when dried; it is not easy to carve even when green. Three halos in strong relief direct attention to the main characters. Space was found, behind the cradle, for even an archangel and the Dove. To provide the atmosphere of a manger two engaging cattle are carved in the lower section. Rays radiating from the Eternal Father above fill the background. In this diminutive composition each element is picked out with polychrome or gilt.

A spirit of intimacy is conveyed in the group showing St. Ann, St. Joachim, and the child Mary (*fig. c*), which stands on a side altar in San Diego, Quito. These figures are half life-size and are dressed in starched textiles, polychromed with care. Again especially expressive are the gestures of the hands. The setting displays the best tradition of Quito Rococo, with painted patterns of widely spaced flowery vines; note the column at the right, encrusted with grapes and grape leaves, carved with virtuosity.

The little scene of the Flight into Egypt (*fig. d*) makes its appeal through its simple humanity. It shows a mestizo or Indian couple very much as they appear today traveling along the road home from the market in town. The costumes are, in part, of starched textiles; the rest is of wood, painted. Thousands of such pieces were produced. They never lost their grace because they never lost their sincerity.

Wax also provided a medium for the colonial artist. The domestic scene of Mary watching over the sleeping Christ Child (*fig. e*) was fashioned of that material around mid-eighteenth century by Toribio Avila, a sculptor known for his wax portraits of nuns.[176] Here the stage is set in a shadow box. A silver halo is placed behind the head of the Child, and his hand clasps what may be a crown of thorns. Mary is making pillow lace, while a cat sits at her feet and pigeons peck at the floor, just as they might in some local peon's house.

In the stimulating artistic atmosphere of Quito, in which a Legarda was inspired to create the Vision of the Fifth Seal, there was room also for the production of such delightfully original pieces of religious folk genre, each in its place and in harmony with its surroundings.

10

VICEREGAL PERU I

From the Pacific to Arequipa

Aᴌᴌ Spanish territory in South America, from the fog-enveloped rocks of the Strait of Magellan to the steaming jungle of Panama and from the sylvan bay of the Rio de la Plata to the bleached sands of the Pacific, at first was formed into the Viceroyalty of Peru, with its capital at Lima (1544). Not until almost two centuries later (1717) was the Viceroyalty of New Granada established at the north, comprising present-day Panama, Colombia, Venezuela, and Ecuador; still later (1776) the Viceroyalty of Rio de la Plata was carved out, embracing Bolivia, Argentina, Paraguay, and Uruguay.

The original Viceroyalty of Peru was eighteen times as large as the mother country, and in climate and topography it showed even greater diversity than the northern viceroyalty, Mexico. The official who tried conscientiously to review his domain—or even had to traverse a part of it on his way from Spain—could not fail to observe the enormous distances and differences, which for us fall into pictorial focus from a high-flying plane. It took weeks to travel from one administrative center to another. The official himself rode on horseback, accompanied by a packtrain of mules—those most reliable live engines used even today. The ladies and those who were unable to sit in the saddle rode in palanquins or horse litters, lying on mattresses and protected from the sun and dust by awnings and curtains. In the Andes and the Cordilleras, roads climb up and down and frozen *páramos* alternate with fertile stretches of emerald-green, traversed by rushing torrents; in some spots during the day the equatorial sun beats hotly down upon the traveler from almost directly overhead, while at night puddles freeze.

The diversity in environment and population in the various regions of the Peruvian viceroyalty is manifest in their colonial art, the outstanding remnants of which date from mid-seventeenth century to the end of the eighteenth. An accumulation of strongly local characteristics can be observed, explained in part by the fact that the distances separating the cities were so great that outside influences, whether European or colonial, often were filtered not merely by space but by time. Furthermore, by mid-seventeenth century the artistic inclinations of the Indian and the mestizo had stamped many imported ideas with a native mark; in such regional work the traditional ideology of European art can be detected at first glance, but a strangeness, sometimes even a barbaric touch, is evident in many examples.

Lima, the Peruvian capital, in contrast to Mexico City, had no hinterland with large Indian settlements to draw upon for labor. Along the sandy Peruvian coastal plain, Indian towns were sparsely populated and widely scattered, existing only where rivers brought down from the Andes life-giving water for irrigation. Through Callao, Lima's harbor town, common laborers and artisans soon began to enter—newcomers from Spain and her other American colonies, as well as Negro slaves and even Asiatics, by way of Manila, from her Far Eastern colonies. Thus a cosmopolitan atmosphere developed early in the Peruvian capital and is reflected in its colonial art. The conditions there were not conducive to the full development of the Indian's artistic talents—he was crammed into a community in which he had no roots. Eighteenth-century Lima presented a brilliant spectacle, drawing for its color on the tradition and talents of all layers of its varied society.

The city's supremacy in South America remained unchallenged during the entire colonial period, and it made the most of its unique position. Its ecclesiastic and civil buildings inside and out still reveal a grand scale of living.

Rustication, fashionable in the Baroque period in Europe, is common in viceregal Peru, executed in stone in the High Andes, where stone is abundant, and on the coast in stucco over brick. Such extensive use of it as is seen in the church of San Francisco in Lima (Pl. 92, fig. a) is quite rare in Latin America. The Franciscans established themselves here in 1535 on land granted by Francisco Pizarro, and later viceroys added to these holdings; the actual foundation of the monastery, however, did not occur until 1546. By mid-seventeenth century it had grown to be the greatest religious establishment in the capital, housing more than two hundred friars and sustaining a hospital as well as an adjoining building of the Third Order.

The present church was designed by the Portuguese Constantino Vasconcellos,[192] but its side portal bears the name of Manuel de Escobar, who took over on the death of the first architect and finished that section in 1674. The interior contains early specimens of cane and plaster vaulting and considerable Mudéjar ornament in plaster.

The church itself is constructed of brick and plaster, painted gray, but the portal is of stone. Despite the horizontal lines that cross the towers—belfries as well as bases—there is a verticality in the façade as a whole, emphasized especially in the doorway. Here the columns are paired according to Baroque tradition. Above the lower broken pediment stands a statue of Mary between two Franciscan saints and above them rises another pediment, broken to give space for the oval window at the top. Wethey calls this the first important retable façade in Lima.[203] In composition it is somewhat similar to La Compañía in Cuzco (see Pl. 109). Note the two stone lanterns above the outer columns, almost Oriental in their effect.

A general rebuilding of the living quarters in this monastery was effected between 1669 and 1674. The cloister (fig. b) shows the simple and high arches on the ground floor from the earlier epoch, and the fine picture tiles, imported from Seville, which cover the walls of the lower corridor, are dated 1620. A majestic stairway of brick leads to the upper gallery, where in a more elaborate fashion large and small arches alternate. Here is an early use of the oval in Peru, a favorite shape of both the Baroque and the Rococo.

The sacristy with its imposing stone portal (fig. d) is a most characteristic example of Lima's ecclesiastical splendor. On the entrance is inscribed the name of the architect, Lucas Meléndez, and the date 1729. This inside portal, which is approached through an impressive antechamber, presents an architectural composition, heavy with plastic emphasis; a niche and statue occupy the space in the center of the flaring segments of the pediment, and rustication echoes the pattern of the façade.

Through the half-open door the elaborate woodwork within the sacristy is visible. Chests line the walls; above them stand thirty-five Franciscan saints framed in niches (fig. c). From their style these statues appear to be earlier than the hall where they stand. Though the cartouches, directly above the saints, and the fluted columns are classicizing, the total effect, especially with the additional medallions at the top and their winglike scrolls, is Baroque.

Two of the three altars from Lima churches illustrated here (*Pl. 93*) stand in the conventual church of Jesús y María, which occupies the site of an earlier chapel. It was finished in 1721 but after the earthquake of 1746 was considerably rebuilt.[192] The side altar dedicated to St. Ignatius (*fig. a*) is so designed that the missing segment of the heavy broken pediment below seems to have been placed on top the second tier. The columns are sturdy and rather squat; their twist is emphasized by heavy garlands of flowers. This altar and its unusually homogeneous companion pieces in the same interior must have come from the same workshop.

The main retable in this church has finer and lighter lines. Again the columns are wound with flowers (*fig. c*); compare the side garlands in the two altars, the first compact, the second graceful and more lacy. Below the statue of St. Francis a blind door in the shape of a panel has as its main ornament a decoratively developed vase of flowers. José de Castilla designed this retable,[203] which was commissioned in 1708.

A product of the Rococo period, the main altar of La Concepción (*fig. b*) was finished in 1783, the work of the sculptor Llorente. It is painted a pale gray, and much less gold was applied than was customary in Baroque times. Here again a protruding pediment closes off the lower section, which might almost be a unit by itself. A general upward movement is achieved through the many undulating lines and the flaring wings; also, each section of the central panel pushes above the horizontals of the wings, a tendency frequently encountered in the High Andes. What were once columns have been turned into fanciful urn shapes, some of them carved with attributes of the rosary. Vertical side garlands are present here, too. but very liquid and uncomplicated in

design; and the two doors flanking the altar table carry only inscriptions within typical Rococo panel frames.

The earliest church of San Carlos in Lima, named for San Antonio Abad, was started in 1606 as part of a Jesuit college for novitiates, but the earthquake of 1746 severely damaged this complex and a new church went up between 1758 and 1766. The exquisitely carved wooden tribune (*fig. d*), one of a pair on the side walls near the main altar, provided a loge from which the superiors and visiting dignitaries could witness the Mass unobserved. About twelve feet long, it has the swinging line of a Baroque coach, but the lucid decorative motifs in the grillework and on the solid body are Rococo. The wood, extremely hard and of a very fine quality, is almost ebony in color. The matching pulpit is illustrated on *Plate 183*. Johann Rher, the Austrian Jesuit, was connected with this work, as well as with the reconstruction of the cathedral.

With the expulsion of the Jesuits only a year after the completion of the building—during the viceregal administration of Amat —both college and church were closed. In 1770 the college was reopened as part of the Royal College of San Carlos, but it was soon closed again because it became a center of the independence movement. The monastery now houses part of the University of San Marcos, and the church serves as the national Pantheon.

The Dominicans, the administrators of the Holy Inquisition, were present at the founding of Lima and by the beginning of the seventeenth century already had an imposing establishment there. Their church has been a victim of various neoclassic and modern restorers, but their chapter house, dated about 1730, has fared better (*Pl. 94, fig. b*). The large shell vaults above the entrance and the niche have a magnificent plastic quality; their scallops are finished in the neo-Mudéjar manner. Baroque are the massive volutes applied as consoles and the rustication, executed in plaster. The wood carving is excellent throughout, especially in the tribune over the doorway. Scenes from the lives of St. Dominic and St. Thomas are depicted in the paintings. Antonio Vázquez de Espinosa, an early-seventeenth-century traveler, remarks that this monastery contained works by the Italian Mateo Pérez de Alesio (or Alecio), who established a school of painting in the viceregal capital.

The church and monastery of San Agustín also were laid out on a grand scale. The first church on the present site, erected during the last quarter of the sixteenth century, was replaced late in the seventeenth. Work proceeded slowly because of several destructive earthquakes; the façade was completed in 1720 but was restored in the early twentieth century and is now totally stiffened with modern cement. (For the richly gilded coffered ceiling in the antesacristy of this monastery see *Pl. 181.*)

San Agustín's sacristy has great artistic merit (*fig. a*). Lowboys with squarish Rococo panels line the sides, and above them is a series of thirty Augustinian saints. Among these may be the twenty-eight statuettes contracted for by Diego de Medina in 1643; the surrounding lacelike woodwork, however, is in the style of 1760–1770 (*see also Pl. 179*). Note the richly carved table in the center of the hall.

The *lavabo*, or washstand, behind the sacristy (*fig. e*) is formed of three shell-shaped marble basins, upheld by angels, and the shell motif is repeated in the niche above. With colored tiles on its base and the side walls, the whole piece has a sunny radiation. It is dated 1669.

Another of Lima's wealthy monasteries is that of La Merced. Its monks, many of them sons of Spanish aristocracy, lived in considerable luxury. In the seventeenth century this monastery boasted five cloister patios, some with fruit trees and flowering shrubbery. Embellishments were added throughout that century and the one following.[192] In the sacristy (*fig. d*) one of the bulging Rococo chests

bears the date 1776, which may apply to the entire woodwork, as the earlier sacristy was ruined by fire in 1773. At that time the growing spirit of worldliness, fanned by books and prints from Rococo Europe, was bringing new stimulus to colonial artists in Peru. Without the religious paraphernalia, this place could be an elegant drawing room. Note the neo-Mudéjar in the ceiling pendants.

Above the chests, instead of statues are a number of paintings interspersed with mirrors. They are painted on glass and set in wide mirror frames, Rococo in outline and chased in the Venetian manner. Illustrated here (*fig. c*) is a scene from the life of Jacob—probably his meeting with Esau—executed with folkloristic charm. Others depict a Rake's Progress with the verve of a Hogarth.

Torre Tagle Palace (*Pl. 95, fig. b*), a unique civil building in Lima, stands in the old section of the metropolis. It was more or less finished in 1735 as a city mansion for José de Tagle y Brancho, a Spanish knight who came to the New World as captain of the lancers. After successful exploits in Chile against the Araucanian Indians he was elevated to Marquis of Torre Tagle and given the highly lucrative position of Permanent Paymaster of the Royal Armada of the South Sea—the Pacific silver fleet. Two cannon barrels placed beside the gateway signified the right of asylum within. Despite favors from the crown, the fourth marquis of this line supported the cause of Peruvian independence and for his rebel activities died a royal prisoner. The edifice has since served as the presidential residence and the headquarters for several commissions; today it houses the Ministry of Foreign Affairs.

Hard palm, cocobolo wood, and the best cedar and mahogany from Central America went into its construction. Bronze and iron of fine workmanship were used for the railings, locks, and hinges, and glazed tiles were ordered from Spain for the courtyard, corridors, and staircases. The façade is strongly neo-Mudéjar, the most striking elements of which are the ornately carved closed wooden balconies. Such latticed enclosures were in keeping with the Lima custom that required ladies to go fully veiled in the streets—a Moslem tradition against which repeated edicts were ineffectual. The stone entrance, splendid with the flaring segments of its broken pediment and the large grilled window, rises above the roof level. On the ground floor subtle stone and stucco frames encase the windows.

Inside, the main patio was once paved with colored tiles from Seville, now replaced with modern ware. Monumental in its daring yet graceful in line is the Baroque molding around the principal doorway (*fig. c*), which opens on an elegant stairway leading to the seignioral rooms on the second floor. The upper galleries carry a series of trefoil arches; only after the earthquake of 1746 were the tall wooden pillars added for support. The beam ends, all carved, rest on elaborate brackets (*fig. d*). Torre Tagle Palace has a certain similarity to the Palace of the Inquisition in Cartagena, Colombia (*see Pl. 22*); the Lima structure, however, is much more elegant and complex in its architectural decoration.

Few buildings in all South America approach in romantic association the Quinta de Presa (*fig. a*), a country seat across the river from the city yet near enough for its owners to spend many leisure hours amid its gardens. It was built on the property of Count Fernando Carrillo y Albornoz early in the second half of the eighteenth century (1766–1767), and legend would have its plans drawn up by the contemporary viceroy, Manuel Amat y Junyent Planella Aymerich y Santa Pau, who reigned in Lima between 1761 and 1766; besides his administrative and military talents, this Catalan possessed notable ability as a draughtsman. His amorous relations with the seductive dancer and actress Micaela Villegas —better known as La Perricholi—are immortalized in several exquisite works of literature. Around her life Jacques Offenbach built

one of his light operas, entitled *La Périchole*. She was born in 1737 and is described as lively and charming. According to political commentators, she influenced the viceroy in affairs of state. Her forthright disposition and charitable spirit have received almost unanimous praise.[41]

Quinta de Presa, with its rustic Rococo (*fig. a*), reminds one of provincial manor houses in contemporary Central Europe. It is built of brick and adobe and trimmed with stone, fine woods, and tile. Its large bay windows, painted in a dark color, are remarkably effective against the pink and white plaster surface of the wall. Once water ran through the open stone basins in front of the building, making bridges of the walks just beyond the low steps.

The great reception room on the second floor (*fig. e*) has many Rococo features—its shape, undulating moldings, paneled doors, mirrors, and gilded ornaments. At the back of the villa a covered veranda, almost as spacious as the interior, looks out on the garden and a charming view. With its tall slim columns and its many floor levels, it makes one think of sixteenth-century Persian pavilions.

Quinta de Presa was never owned by the mestizo actress; her property—today part of a brewery—lay nearby. But considering the friendship between the count and the viceroy it is probable that she attended many a garden party and candle-lit dinner there. This villa was no more her home than the House of El Greco was that of the great Spanish master; just as that reconstruction in the quarter of Toledo where the artist lived calls up the atmosphere of his epoch, so Quinta de Presa preserves the last flourish of viceregal Peru.

In 1557 an Indian cacique donated to the Franciscan order a plot of ground and an adjoining irrigated vegetable garden, then lying well outside Lima but now a pleasant suburb of the city. Here the church of Magdalena Vieja was erected (*Pl. 96, fig. b*). After the earthquake of 1746 it required considerable repair, and its present façade dates from 1931 —one of the better examples of Peruvian neo-colonial style. Its reconstruction was made possible through the munificence of Victor Larco Herrera, a member of a distinguished Peruvian family which has done much to further archeological and historical research in that country. Typical of the smaller churches in and around Lima, it preserves, both inside and out, certain qualities of local Baroque from the late seventeenth century and the early eighteenth.

Its dark portal, standing out against the plain white walls, is fairly elaborate, and the application of the twin belfries is ingenious. Eight windows of Huamanga stone—a sort of alabaster—still survive from a time when glass was not available. The church contains six magnificent eighteenth-century side altars, one of which will be shown later (see Pl. 175).

Stylistically the façade of the church at Surco (fig. d), near Lima, differs from the others on this plate. A close series of pilasters provides the vertical in the design, and multiple moldings in the cornices and base furnish the horizontal. The side niches are placed very high, as are also the two circular windows, framed like pictures. The window in the espadaña is notable for its gracious line. Johann Rher has been suggested as the architect of this building also, which was once part of a Jesuit college. Many members of the various religious orders in the New World—especially Jesuits—came from Central Europe, and Central European Baroque and Rococo influence can be detected in Latin America more often than has been generally realized. (Compare Pl. 171.)

Pisco, a city one hundred and fifty miles south of Lima, originally was built on the Pacific shore but because of disastrous floods was later relocated farther inland. Thus the town itself now lies at a distance from its port, which is the most important between Lima's Callao and Mollendo. The region is well known for its vineyards; as early as 1620 the traveling friar Vázquez remarked on the abundance of its fruit, both Spanish and native, the sumptuous houses among the vineyards, with their winepresses and storerooms, and the many chapels for the Negro plantation workers.

The former conventual church of the Jesuits there (fig. c), finished about 1723, is a characteristic example of the coastal type: a relatively small structure with an elaborate portal. A sheltering arch is formed by a projection of the barrel-vaulted roof, fashioned here, as it often is along the coast, of cane and plaster. As at Surco, shadow play is produced by a reduplication of the pilaster lines—a favorite device in colonial Spanish America. The portal section is encrusted with lacy stucco work; note the heraldic shield flanked by lions over the entrance between the segments of the broken pediment. The ornamentation on the belfries draws the twin towers, with their wooden galleries, into the composition. (See also Pl. 25.) A right-angle arrangement of the entrances to church and convent was frequent in Spanish America, especially in the eighteenth century.

El Belén in Trujillo (fig. a) dates, for the most part, after the earthquake of 1759. The photograph reproduced was taken before the rebuilding of the second belfry, which fell during a recent shock. In design the entire portal recalls that of the city's cathedral. Note the rustication in the upper section and the deep niche, which contains a Nativity group.

In coastal Peru most of the buildings were constructed of material locally available, such as adobe—either in bricks or in *tapia* (clay poured into a form)—reed, and cane. Though the exteriors of ecclesiastical buildings here sometimes show restraint, inside is a lavish display. Documentation is lacking for the two gilded and polychromed retables from Trujillo churches illustrated here (Pl. 97), but stylistically both would seem to date from late seventeenth century or very early in the eighteenth.

The first (fig. d), which is devoted to scenes from the Passion, stands in the left transept of the church of San Francisco (for the companion piece opposite depicting the life of Mary see *Pl. 184*). It is dedicated to St. Nicholas, a relief of whom appears in the oval at the top of the central panel. He was a contemporary of Constantine and is the patron saint of many seaports as well as the protector of children, travelers, and sailors. Other reliefs present, in the center, the Last Supper, to the right, the Crowning with Thorns, and below it the Flagellation; in the lower left is the Ecce Homo (with Pilate's wife waking from her dream) and above it, Christ Carrying the Cross. Over the altar table is Christ Crucified, carved in the round against a painted background.

In the composition of all five panels the influence of prints and title pages from books —largely of Flemish origin—can be felt; this subject, already touched upon, will be discussed at greater length in Chapter 12. The work of translating and enlarging a small two-dimensional picture into a larger relief and keeping a proportional arrangement is in general successfully carried out; there is much movement, even in the poses of minor persons, and an archaic touch, produced unconsciously through technical limitations, gives added appeal. The decorative frames which set off the story-telling scenes are designed with exquisite clarity.

The other retable (*fig. e*) is dedicated to the Virgin of the Rosary and stands in a chapel of Santo Domingo, which was presented by devotees of the Rosary in 1641. This retable, with its several planes, its niches, and its statues in the round, produces a quite different effect. Grapes and leaves alternate in the squares of the diapered background, and domes crown the lower niches, decorated with great scrolls of carved and gilded wood which once served as candelabra. The panel on the lower right is a door that leads into the sacristy. At the very top, between angels blowing trombones, are a crown and Mary's monogram held by two angels, tipped forward to follow the curve of the arched ceiling

and projecting even beyond the altar table. The use of enormous crowns was widespread in the involved cult of Mary (*see Pl. 184*). Several other instances of such crowns above retables occur in Trujillo; one is over the main altar of El Carmen, where the date 1759 is inscribed and the Indian Fernando Collao is named as the sculptor.

The triangular surface of the pendentive furnished another opportunity for sculptural decoration; traditionally, four archangels—or sometimes the four Evangelists or the four Latin Fathers of the church—filled this space. However, on the pendentives in the nunnery church of Santa Clara in Trujillo, angels support group scenes from the life of the patron saint. In one she is taking her vows before St. Francis (*fig. a*), and another (*fig. c*) shows the angelic meal. These reliefs, executed in stucco and polychromed, carry a number of persons effectively composed into the curving surface. Some of their charm has been lost through repainting. This church was founded in 1743.

Trujillo, after the capital, was the most important city on the Peruvian coast and enjoyed a favored position in the viceroyalty. A seignioral manner of living was engendered by the wealth of the surrounding ranches and plantations. Local poets eulogized the beauty of local ladies, and the many fiestas and balls, occasions of intense preparation, were the subject of animated correspondence for weeks ahead and months afterward. While the romantic and gallant life here was pursued by most young men, others left the town for greater adventures and their Dulcineas retired to the nunneries. The manor houses tell much of this lavish and picturesque epoch. Usually they were rambling structures, one story high, with several patios, one beyond the other. The first—reached through a short passageway which a coach might enter with ease—opened onto the reception rooms of the house; the second, more intimate, was reserved for the family, and the third and subsequent courts belonged to the kitchen, the servants' quarters, the wash house, and the stables.

Such a colonial mansion was that of the Ganoza Chopitea family (*fig. b*), situated directly opposite the monastery of San Francisco and a few blocks from the main plaza and the cathedral. Its portal carries above it an ornamental gable flanked with heraldic lions. Iron grillework screens the windows, above which, in stucco, are draped curtains. At the right is a closed wooden balcony, where in this tropical climate the ladies, eager to see, though not dressed to be seen, could watch the passing show.

The high valleys comprising the Kingdom of Quito (present-day Ecuador) saw much fighting even after the Conquest. Indians battled with Spaniards and the Spaniards fought among themselves, Conquistadores against viceroys, until finally in 1569 Francisco de Toledo, an enlightened viceroy, established peace and strengthened the power of the Quito audiencia, which had been functioning somewhat hesitantly since 1563. Twice this high court was abolished and the whole province transferred to New Granada, but each time it was reestablished. After 1717 the Kingdom of Quito was administered from Bogotá instead of Lima, but by that time its artistic foundations had been laid and the art of the region had already developed the special character and powerful contours which it never lost. The artistic and cultural background of colonial Quito can be gleaned from the preceding chapter.

In 1581 the Franciscan church here is mentioned as one of the noblest in the kingdom. It was built of limestone and brick and had a ceiling of richly carved cedar paneling covered with gold. Conquistadores and landed gentlemen endowed its private chapels.[167] Mid-seventeenth century saw the establishment complete. It was an elaborate complex, covering four city blocks and boasting four cloisters adorned with altars and hung with many paintings. In 1755 a convulsive earthquake severely damaged a large part of the church interior. The nave from the crossing to the entrance had to be restored, a work which took more than a decade. At the end of the eighteenth century even travelers who were not interested in the fine arts mention it as the showplace of the town. And such it remains today. Many of the treasures presented in the chapter "Sculptors of Quito" stand within its walls or in the monastery.

The church façade (*Pl. 98, fig. b*) shows a somewhat austere, late Renaissance design, given a Baroque touch by the paired columns and the bands of rusticated stonework that extend even across engaged columns and pilasters. Notable are the large rectangular windows, grilled with heavy iron. The choir-light section, with its powerful arching cornice and curving lines at the sides, is treated as if it were a gable. There is very little sculpture; decoration is provided by the great variety in the stonework. In the earthquake of 1868 the towers again fell and only recently were replaced.

This façade, built of a local gray stone, is greatly enhanced by an impressive stone atrium, which stretches across the entire front of the complex, and by the stairways, especially the broad flight of elliptical design which leads up from the vast sloping plaza below. The dark stone contrasts sharply with the mass of whitewashed brick masonry on either side of it.

As is so often the case in colonial Latin America, the architect who drew the plans and the various persons who directed the construction during the years are not known. Except for the participation of a few European friars, the work was carried through by natives. An Indian from the Peruvian highlands, Jorge de la Cruz, "builder of houses in the Spanish manner," and his son Francisco Morocho took part as master craftsmen for more than twenty years in the construction and decoration of this establishment.[166]

Within, the church is magnificent (*fig. a*). So much remains of its undiluted colonial splendor that few churches in Latin America outrank it in grandeur, not merely in size but in the quality of its artistry. Mudéjar work has survived in the ceilings above the transepts and the choir (*see Pl. 180*) as well as in the octagonal cupola, which rests on squinches at the crossing. Not at all Moorish, however, is the frieze around the cupola; here polychromed wooden reliefs of saints remind one of the panels in some enameled Byzantine tabernacle. The lower part of the nave is sheathed with gilded wood carving, richly polychromed, and above the cornice, figures of the Apostles are placed at regular intervals; large canvases fill the spaces between the high windows. An inscription on the arch facing the nave states that the restoration of this part was completed in 1770. Low transverse arches divide the side aisles into separate chapels. Light from a large dome centers upon the sanctuary, which here is raised to an unusual height on a stone foundation. The high altar fills the entire apse and even flows around the corners into the cross aisle; some of this is said to be the work of Legarda and thus would probably date from the second quarter of the eighteenth century. In the arrangement an exquisite balance of Baroque elements is evident, as well as a tasteful counterbalancing of sculpture and canvas paintings. (*See also Pl. 80.*) A donation is recorded in 1792 from the bishop José Eliodoro Mariano Díaz de la Madrid y Unda towards the altar of the Immaculate Conception in this church, together with a thousand yards of crimson damask for hangings.[164]

Two smaller churches, San Bonaventura and —on the extreme left in the photograph—the Cantuña chapel are included in this massive Franciscan complex. The former building is believed to stand on the site of the first church erected by Friar Ricke. Cantuña was constructed in mid-seventeenth century and was named for the wealthy Indian whose bequest provided the funds. It was the headquarters of the painters' guild, and when the confraternity took it over as their own in 1781 it was redecorated and made the center of their religious festivities. The names of Caspicara and other notable artists of the epoch are perpetuated in the work. (*See also Pls. 86, 101.*)

The Jesuit church of La Compañía, constructed later, shows greater homogeneity. The Jesuits came to Quito at the end of the sixteenth century, the last of the religious orders to arrive there. Their primitive church, built in 1595, was razed in the seventeenth century, and in its place the present sumptuous edifice was erected. Work on it commenced in 1605, but it was more than eighty years in the building.

The present façade (*Pl. 99, figs. a, d*) has an unusually dramatic build-up. It was begun in 1722 by the German friar Leonard Deubler and was completed, after a destructive earthquake, in 1765 by Venancio Gandolfi, an Italian from Mantua who had recently (1754) come to the New World.[183] Spanish and Italian Baroque are fused in its decoration in an amazing and original blend. The edifice itself is set back slightly from the monastery beside it, and the pedestal bases of the columns and pilasters protrude, so that an uneven line is presented. There are no towers; a large dome on a high drum marks the meeting of the nave and transepts, and a lower one rises over the apse.

The interior (*fig. b*) is constructed entirely of stone. A barrel vault pierced by lunettes covers the nave, and domes with lanterns are placed over the side aisles, which, like those in the church of San Francisco, are partitioned into separate chapels. Unlike the shadowy atmosphere of the Franciscan church, the light here is even and bright. Subtlety is revealed in the treatment of the great piers, the railed gallery, and the frieze, which runs not only the length of the nave but also on into the upper story of the main altar. A lively interlaced pattern, cut in stone on the piers and continued in stucco across the walls and ceiling, embellishes the nave. The Mudéjar character of the design is brought out by the coloring—gilded strapwork on a red background. Baby angels enliven the frieze; the pendentives carry the figures of the Evangelists.

A richness truly Baroque characterizes the side chapels (*fig. c*), where figural elements abound. Above the arch seen here is a curious blend of Mudéjar and classicizing motifs, reminding one in their continuity and pattern of a tile-covered surface. Paintings on canvas are incorporated into many of the retables, framed by and blending with the general decoration of stucco and polychromed wood. (The massive composition of the *mampara* below the choir loft at the entrance is illustrated on *Pl. 101*.)

La Compañía at Quito is often said to be a blend of two Roman Jesuit churches—Il Gesù and Sant' Ignazio.[177] The first of these Italian churches dates from late sixteenth century (1584), the second, from mid-seventeenth century (1626–1673)—that is, it was begun later than La Compañía and was being built at the same time. A comparison with either will point up the great individuality of the Quito edifice. Whatever similarity exists is found mainly in the ground plan, which is not surprising since both of the Roman structures are recognized prototypes of Baroque churches in general. Both of them have on their façades a rigidly academic pediment, drawn out to include the entire upper section, and straight classicizing lines throughout. Neither of them is enlivened with statues. Within, their apses are shallow and low, domed in the back, their aisle separations are less massive than those in the Quito church, and the side chapels are more open. The interior of La Compañía is more intimate in its proportions; it has a restrained yet positive exuberance, in distinct contrast to the lofty and cold lines of the two Roman churches.

It is worth while to point out that the twisted columns on the façade of La Compañía have the fluted section in the center and a thin garland spiraling up the crevices (*fig. d*), whereas those in the Bernini baldachin at St.

Peter's in Rome, so often referred to as prototypes, have the fluted section at the bottom and the ornamentation is spread over the bulging sides of the columns. Further discussion of the salomonic column will be found in Chapter 15.

Both the Franciscan and the Jesuit church at Quito have time and again received additional decoration; yet each has retained its own individuality. One might say that San Francisco embodies the inspirational in the colonial church, and La Compañía, the intellectual.

The America into which Christianity was transplanted was a different world from Europe. Cities were few and separated by great distances. A social life comparable to Europe's did not develop until the eighteenth century, when greater security was enjoyed and better roads made communication easier. The population of a colonial town tended to become ingrown; the Spanish and creole circles were small, and all aspects of its life were circumscribed and interwoven. Even the monasteries and nunneries acquired additional importance in the New World. As in Europe during the Middle Ages, they became cultural centers, and they were headquarters for missionaries and educational work. Their social prestige increased. In addition, they provided a retreat for the wealthy, protection for the woman alone, either young or old, and retirement for the official after a life of activity and adventure.

It is understandable that the main cloister of such an establishment became its pride. Invariably a fountain with statues stood in the center. Pure water was all-important for the life of the population, and the play of water, refreshing to look upon. Flower beds in great variety as well as fruit trees and fragrant shrubbery flourished here in the warm climate. Since the ground floor of the main patio usually was open to visitors, they could admire the luxurious growth nourished by loving care.

The cloister of La Merced (*Pl. 100, fig. a*), adjoining its church, was built in the first half of the seventeenth century in the heart of the town. But the complex repeatedly suffered from severe earthquakes—in 1645, again in 1660 when Pichincha erupted (upon the slopes of which the city lies), and still again in 1698 when Riobamba was engulfed. Thus much of the present structure dates from the first half of the eighteenth century. In the photograph the plain gable of a transept of the church is visible, the rectangular windows of which, inside the church, are deftly incorporated into one of the retables. The second and lower dome over the apse, as in La Compañía, provides ample lighting for the sanctuary. Also discernible is the lantern above one of the domed side chapels.

An interesting effect is produced by the doubling of the cloister arches in the upper gallery. Large paintings decorate the walls of the patio.

Above Quito, with a thrilling view across the housetops to snow-crowned peaks, stands the Mercedarian retreat of El Tejar; beyond lies a blue-toned eucalyptus grove. The brick and tile kilns that were once in this vicinity gave the place its name. El Tejar, founded in mid-eighteenth century, underwent considerable reconstruction in 1832, but the outline of the cloister proper was little changed (*fig. b*). The sturdy columns of the lower arcade are somewhat squat and without pedestals. A connecting wall of masonry constructed between those above them produces a rhythmic line in its counterplay with the curves of the arches.

Early in the seventeenth century the Franciscans founded a retreat, La Recoleta de San Diego, on the other side of the city on land donated by Marcos Plaza and his wife Beatriz de Cepeda, a niece of St. Theresa of Avila. Enclosed by high walls with a heavy gate, it offered a quiet place for meditation and penance. It is said [167] that the friar Antonio Rodríguez was the principal architect of the building in mid-seventeenth century and that the second cloister was constructed under the direction of the Negro architect José de la Cruz between 1698 and 1705. The structure (*fig. c*) is barnlike in shape and has a heavy base for its belfry. The façade shows us an early portal designed in a sober Renaissance style and recessed within an arch. Its pediment is broken for the insertion of a niche, which in turn is topped by a smaller broken pediment and a stone ball. The door, with its iron nail heads, hinges, and heavy lock, is in character with the rest of the portal, and the small atrium of native stone, typical of early colonial rigidity, harmonizes with the serious mood of the retreat. Though the interior was refurbished in the eighteenth century, remnants of a Mudéjar ceiling are preserved. The raised choir roof, visible in the illustration, may date from this later period.

Like many other religious establishments, the nunnery of Santa Clara, founded in 1593, first had an adobe church; a new church was completed in 1657–1658, according to plans by Antonio Rodríguez.[177] In this place were gathered members of Quito's most distinguished families, and it was furnished and decorated, outside and in, with rare artistry; the embellishment continued into the second half of the eighteenth century. Its two doorways, which are placed in a lateral wall as in many nunneries in Mexico (*see Pl. 38*), are surmounted by rounded pediments, within which are clay reliefs, almost like retable scenes. One of them (*fig. d*) presents the Coronation of the Virgin; its once tasteful polychrome today is roughly whitewashed over. Note the tight spirals used to represent clouds —a manner found also in wood sculpture in Quito and reminiscent of the depiction of clouds in medieval manuscripts.

The Dominican monastery in Quito occupies an immense tract. Its buildings were laid out around four large patios arranged in the form of a cross, and the whole conventual area—gardens, orchards, and the various buildings—were protected by high unbroken walls.

Francisco Becerra drew plans for the Dominican church about 1580, but no traces of his participation remain in the present construction, which was completed around 1640.

As early as the seventeenth century, chroniclers paid tribute to the magnificence of the Rosario chapel here, which belonged to an Indian lay brotherhood. In 1733 the municipality granted the Dominicans a piece of land for the addition of a *camarín* for the Virgin of the Rosary. To prevent this addition from blocking a public thoroughfare, a large stone arch was erected over the street, and on that foundation the necessary extension was constructed.[183] In keeping with Quito's colonial tradition this chapel is paneled almost throughout with gilded wood carving, set off by touches of carmine (*Pl. 101, fig. a*). Mirrors and candelabra are incorporated in the design, and here and there an oil painting adds to the artistic variety. The sanctuary is raised unusually high even for Quito, doubtless because of the arch upon which it stands. The low heavily embellished proscenium arch and the light focused upon the altar produce a theatrical effect. In the center stands the patroness, depicted in painting as well as in sculpture, and above is carved a Trinity group. Especially noteworthy are the two great scenic doors of gilded wood at the sides of the altar table, carved with a Baroque boldness that makes them fit for a palace. The four tall columns, entirely non-functional, hold the composition together splendidly. Note the fanciful shell shapes, the volutes and curves in an unusual arrangement.

The small church of Cantuña, already described within the Franciscan complex, was erected about the middle of the seventeenth century, after plans, it has been suggested, of Antonio Rodríguez, the architect of San Diego and Santa Clara.[166] It was dedicated to Our Lady of Sorrows, in whose honor a *cofradía* already flourished. The wealthy Indian who financed the project, Francisco Cantuña, is buried in the chapel—his tombstone bears the date 1699—and somehow in the mouth of the folk his name has replaced that of the patroness. Highly original details are evident in the gilded main altar (*fig. b*), a masterpiece of wood carving and design. Powerful columns twist in opposite directions, and the pediment is completely lost in convolutes. Note the doors at the sides, leading into the sacristy. Seldom does one see such a well-preserved lacy frame of gilded wood as that around the arch of the recess into which the retable is fitted. This retable is considered by some to be the work of Legarda, but it may have been altered when the chapel was redecorated in 1781. (For statues of polychromed wood in this church see *Pl. 86*.)

The *mampara*, a screen which shuts off the interior of a church from the entrance way and usually stands directly under the choir loft, provided another vehicle for the extraordinary wood-carving talent in Quito. The sagrario, adjoining the cathedral, was erected in the seventeenth century; work on its portal was finished in early eighteenth century, but its *mampara* (*fig. c*) was not ready until around 1747. Technical mastery is evident, and a rare virtuosity characterizes the design, a filigree pattern of fine small leaves and elegant detail. Again red and gold are combined, giving a warm rich effect. Especially felicitous is the ebullient side garland (left) with its human figure.

More architecturally conceived is the *mampara* of La Compañía (*fig. d*), the gilded sections of which are set off against a white lacquered ground. The section immediately above the cornices echoes, in gilded wood, the stucco strapwork seen on the walls of the church. Both screens have heavy volutes on the pedestals of their columns. Both use broad overhanging cornices, central niches with curving pediments, like baldachins, and corbels ending in smooth medallions. Yet each embodies a different concept of decoration, executed with assurance.

It would be difficult to overestimate Quito's contribution to the spiritual and cultural life of South America. It was a center of vigorous missionary work throughout the colonial epoch, sending men as far away as the Central American wilds and reactivating establishments such as those at Popayán and Cali. Its art works were exported all over the colonies.

Cuenca, in southern Ecuador, was founded in 1557 on the site of a pre-Columbian settlement and took its name from the Castilian city. It lies at an altitude of 8,640 feet on the Royal Highway to Lima. The nearby mountains, rich in gold and silver, also produced the invaluable quick silver, so important for extracting metal from ore. Fine marble in several colors was quarried here and exported as far as Lima.[180] The unpolished stone was used for building in Cuenca and gives the cityscape a special warmth.

In the early seventeenth century Cuenca had some five hundred Spanish inhabitants, who were attended by countless mulattoes, Negroes, and Indians. It boasted a large parish church and five monasteries and nunneries, served by more than fifty clerics—mostly creoles born in the vicinity. A torrential stream coursed through the city, supplying power for the numerous mills along its banks and water for agricultural projects, even the growing of sugar cane. Cinchona bark, from which quinine is extracted, was another source of wealth. At the end of the eighteenth century one traveler reported its population as near ten thousand exclusive of the Indians, whom he numbered as some ten thousand more.

Cuenca gentry were criticized for their arrogance, their hot-tempered feuds, and their showy pretentiousness, which led them to erect two- and even three-storied houses in an earthquake region. Here as elsewhere in the colonies, white people considered it beneath their dignity to work, and many are said to have preferred to live in proud bankruptcy. The folk of this region were famed for their excellent weaving; today the best straw hats—known to us as "panama"—are produced here. In colonial times the nuns instructed their young pupils in the making of artificial flowers, delicate lace and embroidery, delicious confectionery, and dried fruit.[77]

In the façade of the nunnery church of El Carmen at Cuenca (Pl. *102*, fig. *a*) we see the simple barn type of structure, with towers which may have been added later. The Baroque twin columns of the doorway twist in opposite directions. No real pediment tops the entrance and the upper niche, which contains a relief of the Virgin of Carmen; rather, the lines of a pediment are indicated by the side scrolls, decorated with grapes and pomegranates. Note the two small figures below the spring line of the arch and, in the spandrels, the double-headed eagles. (*Compare Pls. 50, 69.*)

Las Monjas (*fig. b*), another nunnery church, is known also as El Campanario (the belfry), from its perforated espadaña where hang a number of bells. Its façade retains a suggestion of flanking towers. According to local information there was once a doorway in the end wall; at present the only entrance is at the side, visible on the extreme right. Although doubtless this building was altered in post-colonial times, its turret-like pinnacles, the ceramic work in the green balls and balusters, and the bright tiles around the central pediment give it enough colonial character to warrant its inclusion here.

Even more individual is the treatment of the lateral entrance to this church (*fig. d*). The decoration, in stucco on brick, now painted bright red and white, probably was once enhanced by polychrome. From the high pedestal bases of the twin pilasters to the bold pineapple finials the designs are strongly regional. Above the arch is the suggestion of a pediment, serving to connect the simple rectangular window with the pilasters; this section has been whitewashed and repainted too often to carry more than a hint of its original effect. The heavily carved wooden door seems to be of a later date.

The doorway of a colonial dwelling in Cuenca (*fig. c*) speaks a rugged and rustic language. Its pilasters are single but, framed and protruding, are powerful enough to pro-vide adequate support for the heavy frieze. A spool pattern—like the Mudéjar cane weave—extends the length of the shaft, while a zigzag motif decorates the horizontal band above. The pediment here is treated still more inter-estingly, for the apex is completely separated from the two sides, as if pressed down from its logical position by the circular window im-mediately above it. Both doorways display the power of unsophisticated craftsmanship. (From Cuenca comes one of the cathedral organs shown on *Pl. 155*.)

Much farther south along the Royal High-way—which here, as often, follows the Inca Royal Road—lies Cajamarca, Peru. This city, though not far from the Pacific shore, lies at an altitude of 10,000 feet, high in the Sierra del Norte. Here again the superimposition of Spanish culture on the Indian produced a fascinating blend, revealed in many facets of the old town's art. Its cathedral, discussed earlier (*see Pl. 5*), was under construction between 1682 and 1762, a period which also saw the erection of several other impressive buildings.

A strong local flavor is evident in the rich ornamentation of the church of El Belén. Its retable façade (*Pl. 103, fig. d*), tall and narrow, is flanked by massive undecorated stone sur-faces. Some will be reminded of Inca stone cutting in the squarish uneven blocks, and material from that earlier epoch may have been reused here. In the decoration a rustic idiom is applied, a hold-over from the Plater-esque and similar to that seen on the cathedral. Unusual is the third tier, with its three niches drawn up high, producing an espadaña squared off at the sides. Note the shell-shaped niche below the choir window, almost too small to have contained a statue (*compare Pl. 168*). This building was commenced about 1699, but, as an inscription states on the façade, it was not finished until 1744, under José Morales. Thus it was more or less contempo-rary with the cathedral. The belfry is dated

1761. Connected with the church was a men's hospital.

The interior of the church shows no less originality. Bands of the waffle-iron pattern seen on the exterior adorn the nave. The deco-rative scheme culminates in a large stone cupola (*fig. c*). Windows all the way round the drum furnish the main illumination for the church. Above is a ring of angels, their upper bodies human, their lower limbs lost in a leafy fantasy. Although all hold up their arms in a stereotyped gesture, they support nothing, documenting again how single ele-ments were applied in a purely decorative manner. The result has a naïve charm. In the upper part of the dome, chainlike garlands of double spirals alternate with two rows of cherubim, carved in the large ring to look downward and in the smaller to face the sky. (For other cupolas decorated in a folkloristic spirit see *Pls. 33, 35, 107*.)

An inscription over the doorway of the former Women's Hospital, now used as a col-lege, dates this building as of 1763–1767. Its portal (*fig. a*) also reveals the indigenous idiom. Floral and fantasy motifs are inter-woven, tapestry-like, and the familiar waffle-iron pattern covers the surface of the belfry.

The church of San Antonio (*fig. b*), a Franciscan establishment, presents another un-usually tall façade. In its whole design it shows considerable similarity to El Belén and perhaps even more to the cathedral, which stands directly across the plaza. The main portals of these three buildings have no pediments and in their spandrels are carved two angel trum-peters *contrapposto*. San Antonio's columns carry rich carving in all three tiers; nude babies among the leaves provide an original touch. There are indications that the carving was planned to extend across the entire front. The side sections, with their cold rusticated sur-faces, distract attention from the virile center. In the two side entrances, inspired by the lateral portal of the cathedral, broken pedi-ments are suggested. The sloping roof on the right, the upper section of the gable, and the belfry were added in 1941; formerly the tower had three bell arches, like the cathedral. San Antonio is larger than the cathedral and has a dome. There is little interior carving, but the stonework is extremely fine throughout.

The plans for this church were drawn by Matías Pérez Palomino about 1699, and work on it continued into the middle of the following century, at which time José Manuel and Francisco de Tapia are mentioned as architects. According to edicts preserved in the Archive of the Indies, both the king and the viceroy urged that the edifice be turned over to the Indians "who built it." This is one of the rare instances where documents definitely mention the contribution made by natives to colonial architecture.

Wethey points out that these two churches, as well as many others in the central Peruvian valley, incorporate interesting features of both the coast and the Andean plateau: the heavy wall-like piers dividing the nave from the side aisles derive from Trujillo, while the structures were built entirely of stone, the material favored in the Andean region.

Cajamarca in the north of Peru and Ayacucho in the central valley are important names in Peruvian history. At Cajamarca, Inca power received a fatal blow in 1532; at Ayacucho (the Quechua for "corner of death"), a plain near the town of Huamanga, a decisive battle was fought in the war for independence in 1824. After freedom was won, that city adopted the Quechua name for the nearby field of victory. Huamanga—or Guamanga—was founded in 1540 by Pizarro at the halfway point between Lima and Cuzco. In the first quarter of the seventeenth century Vázquez described its buildings of excellent brick and cut stone as among the most sumptuous in Peru. Its population then numbered about four hundred Spanish residents and mestizos, besides the native and imported mulattoes and Negroes, and the Indians. In addition to its cathedral, the city had at that time six conventual establishments and several other churches and shrines. It is reported to have always been full of transients, for it lay on the Royal Highway and enjoyed an active trade, furnishing an abundance of excellent supplies.

Ayacucho's colonial buildings, with dignified portals but no ebullience of carving on the façades, are characterized by a sort of provincial Renaissance. Typical of their sturdy sobriety is the portal of a small chapel which stands to the right of the Jesuit church and probably dates not later than 1583 (*Pl. 104, fig. d*). Its patrons were the Orue family, as Wethey proves, for emblems from their coat of arms—griffins and an elephant—guard the monogram of the Virgin in the central medallion. The adoption of a heraldic symbol out of context for decorative purposes can be observed throughout Spanish America in the use of the Habsburg double-headed eagle. We have also seen heraldic animals separated from the family shield and used as finials on the Plateresque portal of a family mansion (*see Pl. 34*). In Ayacucho a number of dwellings show such an arrangement. The elephant, though not among the most frequently encountered animals of heraldry, appears in medieval bestiaries as a symbol of Christian morality. It was known in Europe after Hannibal's march across the Alps and is immortalized on Trajan's Column in Rome. Elephants are depicted in a procession on a Flemish tapestry from the first decade of the sixteenth century, illustrating a Petrarch poem, and in a mural in the Cuzco cathedral the Virgin herself sits in a tower mounted on an elephant's back.

The church and nunnery of Santa Clara in Ayacucho were inaugurated in 1568, built through the generosity of Antonio de Orue, *corregidor* of the district, who derived his wealth largely from nearby silver mines; his family arms are emblazoned also on the choir wall. This small conventual structure has as its greatest attraction a Mudéjar ceiling over the sanctuary (*fig. b*), composed of interlacing and gilded medallions and said to be the earliest of its kind in Peru. This type of octagonal cupola was probably common in much of Spanish America in early colonial days, as is indicated by survivals in Colombia and Central America (*see Pls. 74, 181*). The main altar, though quiet in its effect, has several noteworthy features. Its columns, fluted obliquely at the base, its massive cornice over the first order, and the whole ornamental build-up, terminating in a central cartouche, retain the dignity of the Renaissance; these parts date from around 1670. Its protruding central section, on the other hand, shows a Baroque spirit, with playfully twisting columns, encrusted with carving, and ornate garlands along the sides. The four angel figures supporting convex mirrors, which magnify and reflect the lighted candles, belong to the eighteenth century. Above the niches typical Peruvian scrolls, auricular in shape, flank small oil paintings, and beneath the uppermost arch is a larger painting, the Coronation of the Virgin.

The church of Santa Teresa was founded by three Carmelite sisters[196] who came from Lima in 1683. Twenty years later the building was consecrated; the main retable (*fig. a*) also may date from about that time. This church, like Santa Clara, has a single nave, the unusual height of which emphasizes the major characteristic of the retable, its striking depth. A dramatic overhang is achieved through staggering the mass of ornament. At the top God the Father looks down between two angels. The cornices thrust far beyond the columns, and the many niches are considerably recessed, their upper parts worked out in shell designs that in some cases are repeated just above on the next plane forward. Sprays sprouting from the capitals combine with fruitlike pendants to form graceful baldachins. The single columns are twisted and ornamented with floral garlands. Statuary, convex mirrors, and paintings on canvas all add to the unusual effect. (*Compare Pls. 5, 97.*)

In a comparison of these two retables, the restrained early Baroque of Santa Clara's contrasts with the joyful spirit of Santa Teresa's, a later work. In the latter all classicizing motifs are dissolved into a playful symphony of truly regional Baroque. The scale is enlarged, sobriety is exchanged for exuberance, and reserve for volubility.

At the other end of the nave in Santa Teresa, above the entrance with its shell-shaped archway, is the enclosed nunnery choir (*fig. c*). The perforated wooden choir screen, gilded and inlaid with shell and mother-of-pearl, is unique. Fortunately, despite its fragility, it is well preserved. (*Compare Pl. 178.*)

Arequipa was an important Inca city between the Pacific coast and Cuzco on the route over which relays of runners in pre-Columbian times carried fresh sea fish to the royal table. According to legend, when the runners asked their leader to let them make a halt at this point the reply was, in the Quechua tongue, "*Are quepay*" ("Yes, rest"). In 1540 the Spaniards established a stronghold on this site, called the Villa Hermosa de la Asunción, but the name derived from the Indian has persisted throughout the centuries.

Arequipa, today the second largest city in Peru, lies at an altitude of 7,500 feet on a vast open Andean slope, which falls in about sixty miles to sea level. Unforgettable is the landscape; at the horizon rise the volcanic cone of Misti and the ranges of Pichu-Pichu and Chachani. The climate is mild and dry, flowers bloom all year round, and fruit and even excellent wheat are grown. It is an earthquake region and many disasters have befallen the city; especially tragic were those in 1582, 1600, 1687, 1715, 1784, and 1868. The last one was the more devastating because by the time the colonial buildings were being reconstructed a railroad existed, which brought, in quantity, horrid examples of French, Italian, and Central European nineteenth-century church art, disfiguring the taste with a mirage of pseudo Gothic. Nevertheless, the colonial remnants are powerful enough to give a grand impression.

First among these is the Jesuit church, La Compañía (*Pl. 105, fig. c*). That it survived the later catastrophes is a high tribute to its builders; only the tower has toppled, and the present reconstruction is of recent date. The entire façade has great vitality. It contains numerous decorative motifs from the repertory with which the mestizo artisans in the Andean area worked, whether in stone, wood, silver, or textiles. The lines of both the lower and the top sections are amazingly fluid; the central section is more static, put together like a sampler of patterns, one above another.

The Jesuit fathers established themselves in Arequipa in 1578, and two Jesuit churches preceded the present one, which was commenced in mid-seventeenth century. The façade bears the inscription *"EL AÑO"* in the medallion on the left, and in that on the right, *"DE 1698."* An arch in the adjacent cloister, now partly in ruins, is inscribed with the date *1738*, though its decoration is quite similar to that on the façade—proof of how tradition persisted.

To designate this region's indigenous style, in which the original contribution of the Indian far surpassed that of the white man, the term "Indo-Hispanic" has been used and also "creole," implying native-born. Wethey calls it "mestizo style." The phrase is apt indeed. "Mestizo" denotes a person of mixed white and Indian blood. Generally the father was Spanish and the mother, Indian, and since the mother usually brought up the children of such a union, they absorbed her traditions and reflected her psychology. How powerful was the mother's influence is evident in the originality manifested in the art. As we have seen, similar conditions prevailed in nearly all areas where Spanish colonial art achieved a character of its own. Therefore Wethey's nomenclature might be modified to read "Andean mestizo style." In the Puebla region of Mexico, *poblano* covers about a similar blend.

In the roof of La Compañía in Arequipa (*fig. a*) the distinguished stonework of these regional craftsmen can be studied—in the domes, the barrel vaulting over the nave, and the huge buttresses which support it. Domical

vaults that cover side chapels are visible in the foreground. The open stairway is customary in this district, the treads here worn not merely by those on official business but by the many who knew that the roof offered a sweeping view of Arequipa's unequaled skyline.

The sacristy is roofed by a deep and intricately coffered dome, which rises from very low pendentives. The walls are whitewashed, but all the curving surfaces are painted with fluent gaily colored designs (*fig. b*); birds pick at bowls of exotic fruit, and baby angels climb among flowering vines. The coffers carry more conventionalized floral patterns, similar to those applied to wooden ceilings or on stone portals. Carved busts of saints occupy pedestals on the cornices, and paintings of the four Evangelists fill the pendentives. The effect of the mural is like that of a native tapestry from the same epoch.

The side portal of La Compañía in Arequipa (*Pl. 106, fig. c*), together with certain other portions of the structure, was contracted for by Simón de Barrientos in 1654. The relief above the doorway shows Santiago Matamoros (killer of Moors), the patron saint of the church, whose legend is told more fully elsewhere (*see Pl. 63*). Here he brandishes a sword with a wavy blade. His garments, his hair, and the horse's mane and tail are all stylized to harmonize with the framing garland. Pomegranates and grapes are recognizable amid the tight swirls and curls, which are characteristic of Andean carving. The saint's halo is developed to imitate a shell, a motif often carved in the top of a niche. Sustaining the figure are two mermaids, provided with wings. These creatures appear with surprising frequency in the mountain-locked region of the Andes, as well as in sections of Mexico, notably the state of Puebla. Usually they are associated with either the Virgin or Santiago. Of interest in this connection is the costly litigation between the Portuguese crown and the Grand Master of the Order of St. James as to who should have the possession of any mermaids cast up on the shores of Compostela, Spain. The suit was settled in favor of the crown, but seemingly mermaids had some special relation to Santiago.[51] Perhaps they were involved with the mysterious translation of his body from Palestine to the shores of Spain. The association is also borne out in his aspect as protector of sailors.

The main façade of the church of Santo Domingo in Arequipa faces a narrow side street, while the lateral portal (*fig. a*) opens on a broad atrium and thus gains importance. A plaque on one of the piers inside gives the date of consecration as 1680. In this side portal the heavy arching pediment rests on two pilasters, the unornamented panels of which stand out against the relief work on the walls. In the medallion, rays which form a shell provide background for the figure of the patron saint; on either side of it grapes hang, like giant berries, and spirals are turned into leaf-sprites wearing feather headdresses. The two *contrapposto* trumpeters in the spandrels are more like elves than angels. Masks in profile are carved in the side garlands at the level of the main cornice; nude babies stand upon them, and toward the bottom others clasp the twining vines. The human elements blend perfectly with the floral—a good example of how the local carver worked over the models put before him into an expression of his own. Note the squarish rosettes—seven different designs—around the arch, another feature strongly Andean.

In and around Arequipa a number of other examples of this mestizo style of carving survive, covering about three-quarters of a century. The parish church at Yanahuara (*fig. b*), dedicated to St. John the Baptist, is dated 1750. Here we see a three-lobed pediment, such as that on La Compañía, and a medallion in the center, as in the side portal of Santo Domingo. The paired columns, however, are divided in their decoration; cherubs wearing flowing feather headdresses and leafy collars adorn

the upper part of the shafts. Niches fill the second story. Of the many figures on this façade, note especially the statues of St. Anthony of Padua and St. Vincent Ferrer silhouetted against the sky, as if on a great Baroque balustrade. The framing garland at each side contains a profile mask (center) and down-swooping angels holding cornucopias. Through sloppy and frequent repainting, this façade has lost much of its plasticity. Probably it was painted in several colors originally, which gave it still more folkloristic charm.

About the same artistic vocabulary was used in the decoration of Arequipa's seignioral houses. In the Casa de Moral (*fig. d*) the nobleman's coat of arms fills the tympanum over the portal, and the monograms of Jesus and Mary are incorporated into the design over the windows. Note the effective use of the vase shape in the corbels beneath the window ledges. The inner patio, filled with flowers and palm trees, has beautifully carved ornamentation in the same manner on the door and window frames.

This type of one-story house is thought by some to be closer to the civilian architecture of the Canary Islands than to that of Spain.[194] Indeed in the early seventeenth century Juan de Mesa y Lugo (1605–1665), a councilman of Tenerife in the Canaries, became the governor of Arequipa, and in 1803 an archdeacon from the Canaries was made bishop of the colonial city. Doubtless both of these officials brought with them a considerable following, with pronounced taste preferences in art. The stylistic relationship between the Canary Islands and Spanish America has been little investigated, but a comparison of photographs from the two regions reveals many similarities. Tenerife was the main harbor where ships from Spain bound for the New World called to take on final provisions and fresh water and to round out their crews—one way for many to make the passage who could not obtain a clearance on the mainland. In Arequipa's Compañía this author photographed a large canvas entitled the Virgin of the Canaries. It pictures at her feet a galleon, flying an immense streamer, as it sets forth under full sail, while a procession of angels bears her statue along the shore.

Of the three colonial nunneries in Arequipa, Santa Catalina was the first to be established (1576). The massive wall of the convent church (*Pl. 107, fig. a*) has a rugged monumentality, dramatized by the shadow play on its evenly cut volcanic stones. Buttresses and walls have a fortress-like quality, and its tower is the only colonial tower in Arequipa which survived the earthquake of 1868. The dome resembles somewhat that of La Compañía.

The cloister entrance (*fig. b*) shows the same austerity as the rest of the complex. Unusual are the two arches, one above the other, on the same plane. Except for the flower band that flanks the niche of the patron saint, there is little decoration. At the end of the seventeenth century this establishment probably stood more or less as it is today, though it was restored in mid-eighteenth century (the choir gallery carries the date 1758). Its walls are washed with golden yellow, its entrances and dome with white—producing an uncalculated yet striking impression. As it stands, almost medieval in its massivity, amid the Baroque buildings of the city, it rounds out the picture of colonial Arequipa.

The church at Chihuata, a more distant village in the Arequipa district, was a Dominican foundation, like that of Yanahuara. It is dedicated to the Holy Ghost. Though small, poor, and undistinguished on the exterior, within it has a highly unusual sculptured dome in stone (*fig. d*). The pendentives carry, instead of the Evangelists or the four Latin Fathers so often seen, reliefs of St. Francis, St. Dominic, St. Anthony of Padua, and St. Vincent Ferrer. The surface of the dome is divided into twelve segments by twelve vases with tall stylized floral garlands. In each segment is carved an angel in a flounced skirt

with arms upraised, so posed that it seems to have flown up from the corbel beneath its feet in the ecstasy of some "Gloria." Above each figure is Mary's monogram, and beyond it is a stylized crown that resembles a flower. A tight garland of cherubs, grapes, and pomegranates encircles the open center of the dome. White sets off the reliefs from the lively blue background. The local artist must have been allowed considerable liberty in choosing the motifs from the standard vocabulary and in arranging the decorative elements.

Before considering the region of High Peru, where the Andean mestizo style had further manifestations, the village church of Huata is presented (*fig. c*) to show how decorated portals were treated in some mountain valleys farther north. Huata lies south of Cajamarca, some 9,000 feet above the sea in the Callejon (strait) of Huaylas, a sort of lane between two major Andean ranges about four miles across at the narrowest point and twelve at the widest. From the floor of the valley twelve snow-capped peaks are visible, including Huascaran over 22,000 feet high. Despite the altitude, parts of the valley have tropical vegetation and an abundance of fruit, poultry, and fish. According to an early-seventeenth-century description it contained seven Indian villages, under the charge of the Dominicans. Rich gold and silver deposits were already being worked there at that time, and, before the end of the century, textile mills were producing blankets, cloth, grosgrain, and other woolen fabrics; the raw material came from the sheep and llama ranches which flourished in the higher regions. This valley, very much isolated, was far from any center of the Andean mestizo style, but it too had an ancient culture and a numerous Indian population with considerable artistic skill.

The elaborate, retable portal of Huata's village church is placed in an arched recess, a manner of building encountered frequently in the High Andes. The building is constructed of adobe bricks, with thin bricks lining the

recess. Only the base of the portal is of stone
and much of the rest is of stucco. Small figures
placed on the extensions of the twin twisted
columns uphold segments of the broken cornice, and two others decorate the pilasters that
flank Mary's niche.

In Arequipa we have seen powerful and
articulate examples ·of the Andean mestizo
style. As we continue our architectural pilgrimage in the following chapter, considerable
differences within that style will become
evident.

11

VICEREGAL PERU II

From Cuzco to the Atlantic

THE city of Cuzco, rebuilt after the earthquake of 1650, preserves a unique colonial atmosphere despite the catastrophe of 1950. Perhaps only Antigua in Guatemala can offer the visitor such a telling colonial picture. Some of Cuzco's history was given earlier (*see Pl. 4*). Its Incaic past strikes the eye wherever one goes, for many of its colonial buildings were constructed of stone from former Inca edifices or were built on ancient Indian walls. The steep narrow streets catch the sun for only a short time during the day, and the shadow harbors the penetrating chill of the city's great altitude—11,000 feet. Thus doubly welcome are the small plazas, frequented by children who frolic among telephone and electric-light poles against a background of pre-Columbian remnants.

Upon such a square stand the nunnery of Las Nazarenas and the church of San Antonio Abad (*Pl. 108, fig. a*). The former (left), originally a military school for Inca scions, was not made a nunnery until late in the seventeenth century. Inca serpent symbols decorate a section of ancient stonework incorporated into its walls. The heraldic composition above the doorway is practically identical with one on the "Broad Street of the Smiths" in Antigua, Guatemala.

The church of San Antonio Abad (right), connected with the seminary, was rebuilt about 1678 under Cuzco's munificent bishop, Manuel de Mollinedo (held office 1678–1699),

whose arms adorn the entrance. The belfries on both buildings are similar. What a din must have filled the air when on festive occasions or in emergencies all the city's bells were rung at once. The doorway has little Baroque character. A large splayed oval choir-light fills the broken pediment, dwarfing the niche, which is flanked with auricular motifs.

The interior (*fig. d*) shows the typical single-nave church structure of the High Andes, roofed with timber; though windows are few, the lighting is satisfactory because of the brilliant sun. In the upper corners of the photograph the carved and tooled beams of the choir gallery are visible. Large canvas paintings line the walls, their heavy gold frames ornamented with twisted columns. The open timbers of the roof were once concealed by woven material, stuccoed and painted with scenes or geometric patterns. A richly gilded retable fills the end wall, and at the left is a pulpit exquisitely carved to harmonize with it. Thus a modest structure was transformed into an impressive interior.

The detail work displayed in this small church reveals the high standards of Cuzco's colonial craftsmen. The pulpit (*fig. b*) is topped by a crownlike baldachin, and twin columns twisting in opposite directions frame its carved reliefs. Note the row of gilded wooden candelabra under the painting at the right.

In the retable the closed niche, or sagrario,

in the center (*fig. c*) usually guards the cult image behind its sliding doors. Here the convex shape, very difficult to carve, is embellished with a delicate relief of the Annunciation. The Apostle Peter stands in the panel on the left and St. Paul on the opposite side. The dividing columns carry a pineapple pattern, while the heavier twisted shafts of the retable (left) are entwined with garlands of blossoms.

Despite legal steps taken by the canons of Cuzco's cathedral in the sixteenth century and after the earthquake of 1650, the Jesuits erected their Compañía (*Pl. 109, fig. a*) on the plaza obliquely across from the cathedral and later rebuilt it on that site. Many declare it to be the most artistic and impressive church in Cuzco, if not in all Peru. Its unity of style is explained partly by the fact that it was erected in less than twenty years (1651–1668), a relatively short time in the colonial era for such a vast edifice. Its ground plan is a Latin cross; a large dome covers the crossing, and shallow niches form side chapels—both new features to the Cuzco of that period.[203]

The building is constructed of the same rich brown andesite as the cathedral; but the cathedral shows a horizontal emphasis, and in La Compañía the vertical prevails. Its towers are an integral part of the composition, tied in by means of the massive shelflike platforms and the heavy cornice. Its portal, of the retable type, is stepped back somewhat and is composed under a trefoil arch. The niches, the many openings, and the different planes in the façade produce a finely proportioned articulation, seldom encountered in this region.

Inside, the pendentives are carved with heraldic designs framed by a cord, and the Evangelists—in this illustration, Mark and his lion—occupy niches at the top of the piers (*fig. c*). A balustraded gallery runs around the building above the broad cornice, facilitating the decoration of the church on holidays, when much drapery and the apparatus for special illumination have to be arranged. Note the multiplication of corbels below the cornice —an Andean feature. The vaulting, ribbed in the Gothic manner, is of brick.

Stylistically the main altar, the upper portion of which is shown here (*fig. d*), is singularly harmonious with the rest of the building. The columns stand away from the general plane of the retable, and paintings and statuary alternate in a meticulously balanced design. Moldings, surface decoration, scrolls, and volutes all are immensely varied. Especially the open segments of the broken pediments and the shift of horizontals in the central section produce an upsurging effect, leading the eye to God the Father at the top. Particularly ornate, yet kept in the spirit of the whole, are the portrait medallions at the sides, surmounted by carved heads crowned with fruit.

The grille enclosing the tribune to the right in the sanctuary (*fig. b*) has an exquisite interlacing pattern cut out of wood, strongly Mudéjar in feeling, with even a suggestion of tilework in its lines (*compare Pl. 178*). At the right, as a side garland, is an excellent example of the winged scroll—another favorite motif of the Andean region—which was used in considerable variation also on the retable.

After the earthquake of 1650 little was left of the Mercedarian establishment in Cuzco. Within twenty years, however, both church and monastery were again standing. The lines in the monastery entrance (*Pl. 110, fig. b*) are elegant, classicizing, and severe; even with its curving broken pediment it could be early-sixteenth-century Italian. Bullet marks on the left call to mind political upheavals in recent times.

In La Merced's elaborate main cloister (*fig. d*) the arcades are carried on rusticated masonry piers, and slender carved columns stand before them. The vaulting in the lower gallery beside the church as well as in each corner is of stucco; otherwise the ceilings are fine examples of carved and gilded woodwork (*see Pl. 181*). Two sides of the upper gallery are covered with corrugated iron sheets, visible in this illustration—an inexpensive and rapid modern method of roofing, ugly but practical. Large paintings, in quite good condition considering the two centuries or more of exposure, hang on the inner walls. Two magnificent stairways connect the upper and lower stories.

The church of San Sebastián (*fig. a*), founded in 1572, stands in an Indian suburb of that name about three miles from Cuzco. This village is said to be populated with descendants of the Ayllos, families of Inca blood, who were assigned this spot after the Conquest.[200] Originally the church had a single nave, with adobe walls over six feet thick. In 1696 arched openings were broken through each side wall and side aisles added. Influence of both the cathedral and La Compañía in nearby Cuzco can be seen in the build-up of the towers and façade. The elliptical window frame in the center and the architectural ornament above the cornice are individual features. Even from a distance the portal has a definite elegance and clear sharp outlines. On closer observation it can be seen that it is ornamented with dense carving. Effective and original use was made of the winged scroll and large medallions. Some of the sculptors who worked on the cathedral choir stalls (about 1657–1678) may have carved the portal, as similar motifs occur there. Noteworthy is the raised atrium, which lends distinction to the structure. The right tower carries two inscriptions, the one giving 1664 as the date of its completion and mentioning by name seven caciques, and the other bearing the name of the Indian Manuel de Sahuaraura as the architect of that section. The left tower is dated 1799. Bishop Mollinedo's escutcheon is placed above the central window. His interest and munificence were felt throughout this region; in 1678 he wrote that the façade of San Sebastián was finished and was as beautiful as if it had been worked in wax.[203]

At the southeast end of the Franciscan establishment in Cuzco stands a monumental gateway, the Arch of Santa Clara (*fig. c*), raised to commemorate the Peru-Bolivia Confederation in 1836–1839. It is constructed of the same rich brown stone as the colonial monuments, cut into blocks in the Indian manner, and bears extenuated single columns, finials, and statues still in colonial tradition. Until the railroad connected Cuzco with the outer world in the 1870's, carrying in the products of the machine age, the skill and style of her craftsmen preserved much of her great heritage.

Venice, Bruges, and Toledo each had its poets; Cuzco is still waiting for some worthy pen to eulogize its unique beauty.

One is apt to visualize the land of the Incas as a barren wind-swept region, inhabited by a stubborn and starving people. A quite different picture unfolds for the traveler as on his way to Cuzco he traverses the fertile valley of the river Vilcanota through fields of yellowing grain and patches of green pasture. Here, before European animals were imported, the llama and alpaca grazed. The villages of the valley, populated by mestizo and Quechua people, energetic and cheerful, lie near the river, and strips of cultivated land run up the steep deforested mountain sides. Checacupe, one such village about sixty miles from Cuzco, goes back into prehistoric times, according to some sources before the Inca regime. Its population counts, besides the Quechua, members of the Aymara nation, who are numerous in the Lake Titicaca region and farther on into present-day Bolivia. The name Checacupe is said to derive either from the Quechua word *chchecca*, meaning "union," and *kope*, an Aymara word for "road," or from *checca*, meaning "right" in Quechua, and *kupe*, meaning "left" in Aymara.[187] Francisco Pizarro resided in this village at different times, and his second will was dated there June 22, 1539. The name of the able viceroy Francisco de Toledo—one of the few administrators who inspected his realm thoroughly —also is connected with Checacupe; by royal grant he presented the village and the territory belonging to it as an *encomienda* to the widow of his good friend Diego de Silva. In colonial times a prosperous gold mine was worked nearby; and even today the dance of the Tucumanos there commemorates the muletrains that kept this region in contact with Bolivia and northern Argentina.[202]

Small wonder that Checacupe's parochial church mirrors its favorable economic position. This adobe building (*Pl. 111, fig. b*) lies with its long side on the main square. Its stone portal has simple columns and carries no figural decoration. The bell tower stands separate, an arrangement not too usual in this region, and the ample raised atrium is closed off by an adobe wall.

All the more striking is the richness of the interior. The walls of the nave are covered with large murals in tempera, which are frequently interrupted by superimposed retables or by broad canvas paintings in ornately carved and gilded frames. Near the entrance door at the end of the nave is an immense wall painting of Santiago in battle (*see Pl. 139*). It would appear that the murals, cane ceiling, and painted beams date from the last quarter of the sixteenth century, at which time the whole interior was decorated in this manner. Probably the tray ceiling of the apse survives from this early period. It is covered with textile fastened to a reed base, the whole smoothed with gesso, and this surface painted with figures which have the character of enlarged book illustrations (*see Pl. 144*). Though Mudéjar in construction, the beams carry decorative portrait medallions in the center.

About a century later (1690–1700) a refurbishment, which brought in the canvases and wood carvings, replaced the main retable with the one that stands there today (*fig. a*), though some of its details seem to be of a still later date. The amazing skill revealed in the wood carving throughout this interior is especially evident in the main altar. Its columns are decorated with garlands of grapes, heavy and protruding. Variety is gained by placing

the statues within niches in the first order and, in the second, on corbels against an intricate golden grillework. The crownlike baldachins above these figures recall the pulpit canopy in the seminary chapel in Cuzco. Paintings on canvas also are incorporated into the composition.

The communion rail, seen in its full length in the foreground, presents the figures of the Apostles, a poignant reminder of the Last Supper. In some medieval churches (such as the Duomo at Torcello, near Venice) the Apostles were depicted on the screen before the sanctuary, and they are still to be seen on the iconostas in Greek Orthodox places of worship. Apparently these figures were later placed on the communion rail in European churches, until the Renaissance supplanted the railings of wood with bronze and marble balustrades. One such panel from Lombardy, gilded and polychromed, is preserved in the author's collection (*see Appendix, Pl. 192, fig. e*). The full series of Apostles on the altar rail of Checacupe's church is probably a unique survival. In the detail (*fig. c*) Mark is depicted on the right and beside him, Andrew. On the left panel, the gate opening into the sanctuary, the figure is that of St. Paul, who sometimes replaces Judas among the Twelve.[187]

Andahuaylillas, another Andean village, lies about thirty miles from Cuzco. Squier remarked on the rich mountain-locked valleys in this region suggesting the beds of former lakes and on the number of extensive haciendas here, with their comfortable houses enclosed by heavy walls. The parish church of Andahuaylillas is shown on *Plates 112 and 113;* the lettering of the two plates runs consecutively for the sake of clarity. Founded in 1580, this church is said to have been built on the ruins of an Inca temple. Today it appears too large for the shrunken population of the village, but more people and greater prosperity existed here in colonial days. Constructed with adobe walls and a pitched roof of cane and timber, with a separate bell tower of stone, it belongs to a type met frequently in the high-lands and found also in other, widely scattered mission districts. The portal is of brick (*fig. c*). The four Latin Fathers are painted in the niches, and a monogram of Mary—thick with repainting—is over the door above an inscription which seems to contain phrases in Quechua. Murals line the second-story gallery, which is accessible from the choir loft.

The general view of the nave (*fig. e*) shows the barn shape of the interior, the sloping roof, its surface plastered over and painted, and the long beams, which are not entirely Mudéjar in their decoration. On the walls are large canvas paintings mounted in wide lavishly gilded frames with crests that reach to the ceiling. There are two pulpits, now in disrepair.

The lower part of the walls, as well as the entire choir loft, is painted in tempera with elaborate designs (*see Pl. 153*). The large mural beside the entrance (*fig. d*) seems to derive from a book illustration. It shows a man in his prime leaving the feast of this earthly life—note the fruit pie, the planked fish, the scattered flowers, and the fork. He is bidding farewell to his companions before he passes through the narrow gate to enter the Mansion of the Lord. Angels are assisting souls over the final hazardous bridge—even performing last-minute rescues—while three young men exactly alike, a symbol of the Trinity, lean from their high rampart to encourage the newcomers, and the Apostles and Mary watch from windows. Roman letters are strewn over the composition as in didactic books where various figures are explained in the text; but the quotation below the painting contains verses from the Psalms and seems to have no direct connection with it.

At the left of the entrance beyond the mural is the door to the baptistry (*fig. f*), inscribed with the text "I baptize thee in the name of the Father and of the Son and of the Holy Ghost, amen"—in Latin in the medallion held by angels, in Spanish across the painted frieze, and, over the arch, in Quechua. A statue of Peter stands beside the door. Like nearly all of the statues at Andahuaylillas, it is an armature figure, made out of the pulp of the maguey or century plant, covered with plaster, and dressed in starched and painted garments.

The sanctuary of this church, raised somewhat, is set off from the nave by a wide toral arch, embellished on the altar side with clusters and swags of fruit; in the frieze is a lively series of *putti* (*fig. e*). A splendid ceiling in the Mudéjar manner covers the apse (*fig. b*), painted in the clear tones that characterize the decoration throughout the building and liberally gilded. Especially striking is the shell that curves above the main retable. This retable presents a number of unusual motifs (*fig. a*), notably the baskets holding three elements, like thistle blossoms, repeated here again and again. Small squares of mirror are composed into an arch about the Virgin and above her into a crownlike canopy. In style the retable appears to be late. seventeenth or early eighteenth century, and the mirrors were probably added somewhat later.

The toral arch was decorated in 1631 at the expense of the parish priest of Andahuaylillas, Juan Pérez de Bocanegra.[187] He was a great linguist who published a Quechua dictionary, which may account for the Quechua inscriptions over the entrance and baptistry doors. Probably the beginnings of the rich interior date from this period. The earthquake of 1650, however, must have caused damage here also and occasioned considerable repair. Note the crack in the adobe arch. Some of the silver objects in the church are dated 1765, whereas the wooden screen behind the Coronation group at the top of the altar has the following inscription: "Through the veneration of an Indian devotee 1843."

A comparison of the churches which dot the countryside of High Peru reveals the great architectural variety that occurs in districts not far distant from one another. The parish church in Mamara, department of Apurimac (*Pl. 114, fig. a*), dedicated to St. Michael, follows the twin-tower type seen in Cuzco. It is said to date from late seventeenth century or early eighteenth.[203] Most unusual is the division in the decoration of its twin columns that flank the narrow niches. The suave ovals in the belfries and the choir-light recall Cuzco's Compañía and San Sebastián. As in the latter, an all-over decoration, extremely rich, covers the portal section. Flat fanlike shell motifs alternate with fanciful rosettes, and cherubim fill the spandrels. The massive gateway also is elaborate; stone finials are placed along the wall as well as at the corners, and above the arch stands a figure of St. Michael dressed in Baroque costume.

In the interior, unusually well-integrated woodwork is preserved in the railing and beams of the choir loft, which rests on a heavy arch (*fig. b*). The main retable (*fig. d*) has vigorously twisted columns, divided into sections by broad rings. These features, together with the use of much mirror and glass, suggest that at least portions of the retable might be a few decades later in date than the building itself.

In the portal of the hermitage of Oropesa (*fig. e*), dated 1685, fairly flat rosettes are used in rows, each on a separate stone. The only figural elements are the two archangels in the spandrels, executed and arranged with the charming simplicity of honey-cake sculpture (*compare Pl. 107*). The columns should be noted for their leafy bases and the puma masks carved in the blocks above the capitals. The side garlands are simplified, composed of an auricular scroll alternating with flowery crosses. On his trip in 1875 Squier found the principal quarries of the Incas still in use in Oropesa; from here Cuzco, some twenty miles away, received its chief supply of the reddish stone which went into its edifices. Immense piles of stone blocks of every size and in every state of processing were scattered over an area covering more than half a square mile. Close to the site stood the rough stone huts of the workers and the more pretentious dwelling house of the overseer.[200]

East of Cuzco, in the department of Quispi Cauchi, a gold-mining district, lies the village of Huaro. In the first quarter of the seventeenth century it had a population of about seven hundred. Its church, enormous for the size of the village today, follows in type the barn-shaped structure of the Cuzco region, built of adobe and with a pitched roof of cane. Within, the lofty choir gallery rests on three arches, forming a vestibule beneath (*fig. f*). Murals cover the arcade walls: above the arch on the right are the Annunciation of the Virgin and the Baptism of Christ; over the center arch are the Coronation of the Virgin and St. Michael Conquering Death. The sculptured medallions apparently portray the four Latin Fathers. Larger murals decorate the vestibule and the choir; the ceiling and even the railings are painted. Two skeletons are depicted here, another example of the occupation of these people with the representation of death—one beneath the feet of St. Michael and another, a large one, on the side wall under the choir loft at the right in the illustration (*see also Pl. 116*).

Probably different persons with varying degrees of talent contributed to this religious miscellany; some of the scenes are painted with considerable knowledge of composition, while others are rather crude attempts at religious story telling. In Europe such naïve murals survive from pre-Renaissance times, turned into folk art by the repeated retouching of itinerant painters.

To the southeast of the Cuzco plateau, across a 15,000-foot pass, lies the immense expanse of Lake Titicaca. On the eroded sun-parched slopes around it neither tree nor shrub will grow, and the mountains—strangely two-dimensional in this thin atmosphere—are transformed into the green-brown shapes of a fantastic stage setting. The town of Juliaca is situated at an altitude of nearly 12,500 feet, where the route from the Pacific joins the road which connects Cuzco with Puno, on Lake Titicaca, and continues on to Potosí, Sucre, and, finally, Buenos Aires. In the first quarter of the seventeenth century the town's population numbered almost twenty-five hundred; today, a railroad junction, it has some seven thousand inhabitants.

Juliaca's parish church (*fig. c*) has some features that remind one of Cuzco—notably the handsome tower; others, such as the placement of the main portal within an arched recess and the use of stone throughout the structure, are characteristic of the Puno-Potosí area. Especially imposing is the dome with its many finials; finials are distributed also on various levels of the roof and on the corners of the building. Vigor and strength are expressed in the lines of the transept, but apparently the chapel just off the entrance was added with little regard for the general effect. Splendid barrel vaulting in stone—rather than brickwork, as was commonly used for Cuzco's ceilings—distinguishes the interior. The church is dedicated to St. Catherine, and the façade carries the date 1774.

Only fifteen miles from Juliaca and less than thirty miles from the northeast point of Lake Titicaca lies the small village of Lampa, in the valley of the river by that name. In early seventeenth century its inhabitants numbered nearly thirty-four hundred souls; both silver and copper were then being mined nearby. An eighteenth-century visitor noted that cochineal was prepared here and traded by the Indians to provinces that used the red dye in their woolen mills.[61]

The parish church at Lampa (*Pl. 115, fig. b*), built between 1678 and 1685, is constructed of the reddish stone of the region. It has a chapel opening off either side just beyond the entrance, barrel vaulting in stone, and a large dome. A bell tower is set at some distance from the main building. Again the portal stands within a shallow arched recess. Influence from Cuzco, especially from its Compañía, can be seen in the steeply flaring segments of the pediments, the columns with their leafy capitals, and in the absence of figural ornamentation—except for the mermaids upholding Mary's monogram above the door—in a re-

gion where a play with figures was favored. Note the horizontal accent in the numerous moldings on the double pedestals. This portal shows a suavity in design and treatment—especially when compared with the façade illustrated beside it—rarely encountered in this region.

Asillo, a small village north of Lampa and about forty-seven miles from Lake Titicaca, is guarded by peaks nearly 14,000 feet high and is close to several pre-Columbian ruins. In Vázquez' day it had no mines; nevertheless it boasted forty-four hundred people, occupied with agriculture and animal husbandry, and paid more tribute than either Lampa or Juliaca. Today the population numbers only about eight hundred.

The church here, of red stone, started in 1678 and finished in 1696, has a broad raised atrium, twin towers, and a cane cupola raised on an octagonal masonry drum.[203] Originally it was covered with thatch. Like several other churches in the Titicaca region, it has powerful transepts and two side chapels near the entrance, which in this case are beautifully integrated into the building. The amazing feature of its façade (*fig. c*) is the strongly Indian interpretation of the architectural decoration. Here through the grouping of triple columns a forward thrust is achieved, as of clustered piers. Much of the peculiar Baroque quality of the whole derives from the columns, which are of various sizes, tapered, and banded with leafy crowns and broad medallions. Mermaids hold Mary's monogram above the door. Flaming hearts, so strongly stylized that they look like fruit and the flames suggest shells or plumes, are placed over the three second-story niches. They are inscribed *Sanctus Deus, Sanctus Fortis,* and *Sanctus Immortalis*—phrases which are found in abbreviated form also on the façade of La Compañía in Arequipa (*see Pl. 105*). Angels, some with feathered headdress, flank the various medallions and the relief at the top—a seated figure of God the Father which has a touch of the archaic.

Most of the churches just seen, whether near

Cuzco or in the Titicaca region, stand in once-powerful Indian villages and manifest a common—non-European—spirit; each expresses in an original and articulate way the regional idiom.

Ilave, on the shore of Lake Titicaca, figured prominently in Inca history after the twelfth century. The façade of the church of Santa Barbara here (*fig. a*), in contrast to the others on this plate, has no carving whatever, although it too is built entirely of stone. Originally the portal may have carried modest columns, but decoration now appears only on the gateway. In the center (at the top), flanked by twin twisted columns, stands a statue of the patron saint; reliefs of four saints, carved in a flat cutout technique, make the gateway unusual (*inset*). Carved rosettes are distributed evenly over the piers and arch, and a lacy decoration fills the friezes. The austere architecture of the building and the Byzantoid manner of the reliefs evoke the sober spirit of early Christianity; indeed, such a spirit was in keeping here where the Christian religion had not yet been established two hundred years. (For a painting discovered in this church see *Pl. 131c.*)

Lake Titicaca, the highest navigated body of water in the Western Hemisphere, covers an area of 3,200 square miles. Beyond the surface of its wind-swept waters, playing now green now dark blue, rise the endless snow fields of the dazzling Cordillera Real of Bolivia. Since before the Conquest the Titicaca region has been the heart-land of the Aymara Indians, a powerful and individual people. Here there is little mixture of Spanish and Indian blood. Indeed, the colonists shunned this infertile soil and wearing climate, where the average altitude is 12,500 feet and the temperature rises during the day to summer heat and sinks below freezing at night, where, because of the scarcity of wood, llama dung is used for fuel and hardly burns for lack of oxygen.

Until mid-seventeenth century the administrative center for the Titicaca region was Chucuito, the residence of the governor as well as the main station for the traveler who had to cross that section of High Peru. Some silver mines were worked near the western border of the province, but great prosperity arrived only after 1660, when exceptionally rich deposits were discovered. A veritable silver rush followed; Andalusians, Basques, Castilians arrived in numbers, carrying their Old World antipathies even into the highest Andes. Such anarchy ensued that the famous viceroy Conde de Lemos (governed 1667–1672) came personally to quell it.[198]

Around this time (1669) the town of San Carlos de Puno was founded about seven miles from Chucuito on the site of the pre-Columbian Indian village Laicacota. The prosperity of this place continued well into the following century, when the present cathedral (*Pl. 116, fig. a*) was erected. Built entirely of stone, it is noteworthy for its excellent masonry as well as its apselike *camarín*, unusual in this region.

The sculptured retable façade, placed between two solid towers, is inscribed as finished in 1757 by Simón de Asto. While certain elements in the structure suggest the Cuzco type, its decoration places it among the Baroque examples of its region. Here niches appear only in the first order. Above, the short flaring segments of an open pediment recall those in Arequipa's Compañía. The upper half of the façade contains panels carved in high relief surrounded by interwoven straplike decoration. At the top is a figure of God the Father, reaching far out beyond the plane of the wall; note also the overhang of the cornices. The towers with their many pinnacles and drawn-out corbels remind one of Juliaca. In this area a number of large crosses still survive, erected outside various churches against the front wall. They are decorated with the instruments of the Passion and the Crucifixion —a strange bit of realism among so much obscure religious symbolism.

In the next illustration one of the niches of Puno's façade can be studied in greater detail (*fig. b*). The columns are not twisted but are wound obliquely with garlands of grapes, wide-open flowers, and nut or melon shapes; their capitals are complex and heavy. Above the niche is carved a mermaid playing a *charango*, a native version of the guitar, and, below it, a bird pecks at a bunch of grapes which resembles a huge berry. The statue has an archaic immobility, and its halo, developed into a shell, stops at the top of the head instead of extending high into the niche, as in Arequipa. The iron bands on the right-hand column are recent additions to hold the cracked sections in place.

The north door (*fig. e*), dated 1754, reveals the same type of decoration. Small caryatides with upraised arms seemingly hold the heavy corbels of the niche and the cross above. Within the panels of the pilasters twisted columns are carved, almost flat—a good example of a three-dimensional member translated into the purely decorative.

The great divergencies to be found in Andean regional carving are seen in the transept portal of the church of Santiago Pomata (*fig. c*). While the Puno side portal has an embroidery-like pattern, Pomata's carries a bolder design—a single spray of flowers to each unit—executed with a strong feeling for the sculptural. Note also the differences in architectural build-up.

Less than a mile south of Puno lie the town's cemetery and mortuary chapel, a building surprisingly large even when compared with the unexpectedly pretentious edifices found throughout this region. It has the dimensions of a church, and in its general lines it bears a strong resemblance to the Puno cathedral. However, its portal (*fig. d*) carries little decoration. Plain columns support a powerful cornice. The central window, placed within a niche, is flanked by singularly appropriate carvings: on the left, Jerome, who envisioned the Last Judgment, and on the right a skeleton, crowned and holding a scythe. The skeleton occurs also on a tapestry from this region,[206] dated around 1621. Death in human

form intrigued many European artists. One wonders whether Holbein's woodcuts of the Dance of Death ever reached here, in which a skeleton is shown consorting with all classes of society, from pope and emperor to the modest burgher.

The town of Juli lies at about the center of the southern shore of Lake Titicaca on a bay at the delta of the Juli River. Copper and silver mines in the vicinity made it important immediately after the Conquest. It has been said that the native population yielded more readily to the Dominican friars than to the Spanish soldiery. By mid-sixteenth century, monasteries and houses of this order had been established in all the large Aymara settlements around the lake. The Dominican missions rapidly became so rich that they aroused the jealousy of other orders and were expelled from the region on the charge that they had exacted excessive tribute; in 1569 the Jesuits took over. In those early days in Peru, Chucuito and Juli were outranked in the number and splendor of their churches only by Cuzco and Lima.[201] In 1612 an Aymara dictionary was printed in Juli.[188]

In 1579, Juli and its suburbs had an Indian population of about fourteen thousand souls; thus, understandably, several churches were necessary. Of the five or six great churches erected there, four remain today, which, as the inhabitants point out, are so arranged as to form a cross; according to tradition they were built to accommodate the different dialects of the region.

Perhaps the retarded Renaissance spirit of this early period is most tangible in the church of La Asunción, finished in 1620, now used as a depository. It is a lofty cruciform structure of adobe and brick and has an unusual polygonal apse. One of the side retables is still in good condition (*Pl. 117, fig. b*). Built of masonry and covered with stucco, into which delicate Plateresque details were worked, it was painted over and, in parts, gilded. Masonry retables are extremely rare in Latin America today, and this one, probably dating from the beginning of the seventeenth century, may be among the earliest extant examples. A time lag is perceptible not only in the piece as a whole but also within the work itself, especially between certain architectural members and the figures. The statues, quite stolid in expression, have the stiffness of tomb figures; even the angels at the top stand as if congealed in this frigid atmosphere. At present the building is roofed with corrugated iron, visible above the piece; though completely out of tradition, it provides the safest roofing in a region where the principal hazards to buildings are earthquake and lightning.

On the inner surface of a transept arch are panels painted in tempera, bearing the phrases *Quasi Cedrus*, *Quasi Oliva*, and *Quasi Palma* from the Psalms, attributes of the Virgin (*fig. c*). Archangels holding the various trees are depicted, framed in stucco relief work, thickly gilded and lacquered. One is reminded of pages from illuminated books, with their great initial letters and phylacteria, brought into this wilderness by the friars. (For a large relief from the main altar of this church see *Pl. 174*.)

Although the tower (*fig. a*) probably dates from the late seventeenth century or perhaps the early eighteenth, it also has a certain Plat-eresque feeling. It stands independent, its huge bulk made up of the brownish stone found in the region. The two arched bell openings at the top were partially destroyed by lightning not long ago. Single columns with a mild twist form the main decoration and star-petaled rosettes are evenly distributed over the intervening panels. Highly dramatic are the two cornices with their many moldings and their tapering entablature blocks, which end in knobs shaped like blossoms or bells.

From the Zavala mansion (*fig. d*) one gains an idea of a colonial manor house in this region. It is somewhat weathered, but the decoration of its two portals is in good condition. The motifs include grapes, open flowers, and

hanging melon shapes; a spiraling band gives the columns a twisted effect. The carving above the doors, characteristically undercut, recalls houses in Arequipa. On the larger is a detailed heraldic transcription; on the small one are religious symbols, flanked by animals probably intended for lions. (*See also Pl. 126*.) To many the thatched roof above such elaborate portals may appear incongruous, but thatch belongs to the traditional building materials of the region. Large timber was very scarce here, but reeds from the nearby lake were available in unlimited quantity; *balsas*, the unique boats on Titicaca, are constructed entirely of them. Besides, thatch keeps the interiors warmer—an important consideration in this icy climate. Pre-Columbian temples and palaces had thin hammered sheets of gold or silver laid over their thatched roofs.

The parish church of San Pedro Mártir in Juli (*Pl. 118, fig. b*) stands on one side of the main plaza, opposite the Zavala mansion. A contract dated 1590 calling for the erection of three churches in Juli was let out to two carpenters and a mason with the common names of Gómez, López, and Jiménez.[203] In 1592 money was collected through taxation for an altar for the parish church. This building, however, has gone through many transformations; the Jesuits are said to have rebuilt the entire nave at the end of the seventeenth century or the beginning of the eighteenth. It was constructed of brick and a mixture of adobe with small stones. At one time the façade may have had more extensive stone facing. With its plain Doric columns and the shells in the spandrels, the entrance—today cruelly whitewashed—has the stark simplicity of an austere Renaissance, while the Rococo small-paned window in the tier above it, decorated with flowers and leafy garlands, suggests mid-eighteenth century. In the walled-up opening at the left of the door are remnants of a similar decorative frame, showing that the structure has undergone several changes. The tower dates from the eighteenth century.

A tiled arcaded wall, a very decorative element, once enclosed the atrium.

San Pedro Mártir is a cruciform church with a broad nave and side chapels set in bays. The upper part of one of the side altars (*fig. a*) shows the intricate cutout pattern of the gilded retable and the matching sheathing of the arch. Mural painting covers the wall space between. Here we have an unspoiled example of the eighteenth-century regional school, which combined angels, fruits, flowers, and vines into a tapestry-like covering, whether in carving or in painting. Sharply drawn outlines emphasize the contours of each element, giving the effect of appliqué needlework, popular in that period (*compare Pl. 105*).

An architectural design painted on the wall (*fig. c*) frames the grille and the gilded wooden pediment of the baptistry door (*compare Pl. 113*). The two angels at the sides of the arch are both flying in the same direction; seemingly they were copied without a knowledge of their traditional treatment, *contrapposto*. In the baptistry is a marble baptismal font of early date. The mural painting on the dome of this chapel is illustrated later (*see Pl. 137*).

Within the church of San Pedro Mártir pointed arches meet at the crossing, above which is a cupola constructed of reed and plaster. Statues of the Evangelists occupy the "pendentives." Shown here (*Pl. 119, fig. c*) is Mark, dressed in textiles, starched and painted. The fanlike cluster of three gilded stucco shells, repeating the shell motif on the façade, is an original arrangement. Note the figure used as corbel. The angel at the side—an excellent carving—doubtless once held a hanging lamp, like figures so placed in Spanish churches.

At the time of our visit (1945) a large rug, in its last shreds, lay in front of the high altar. Mermaids playing *charangos* were depicted among floral arrangements on a yellowish background—an exquisite sample of colonial weaving very rare today.

The church of San Juan in Juli (*fig. a*), also originally Dominican, was built about 1590 of adobe, rubble, and wood. At the end of the following century it was greatly transformed by the Jesuits, who added the lateral portal and constructed a new apse and transepts, a domed baptistry, and a vaulted sacristy—all of stonework, richly carved. The severe lines of the tower, the main portal, and the low cupola—made of wood on a masonry drum—hark back to earlier types. Stylized flowers and other favorite elements in the regional idiom are carved on the elaborate side portal. Note the walled-up arches.

On the inside, the walls of the long nave are covered with large oil paintings on canvas representing scenes from the life of St. John the Baptist, patron saint of the church (*fig. d*). They are placed in elaborate frames—if indeed the word "frames" can do justice to the carved and gilded compositions in wood which line even the recessed windows, giving the church interior an extraordinary richness and warmth. In the paneling around the window are creatures which resemble peacocks and monkeys amid tropical fruits, such as the papaya, pineapple, and banana. This wood carving is executed in a rather flat strapwork technique, similar to the tapestry-like stone carvings seen in the region; there is scarcely an attempt to come out in the round and make use of the depth of the third dimension. It would seem that the European idea of plasticity was not fully digested by the craftsmen; a rare folk art resulted from the transplantation of European illusionistic styles. An alien psychology is evident in all this work, whether the composition is carved in stone or wood or painted on a wall.

The window panes are not of glass but of alabaster. Even in the Old World before glass was reinvented in medieval Europe, window openings were covered with translucent materials—semiprecious stones planed very thin, parchment, or fine cloth, bleached, oiled, and stretched on wooden frames. In Peru such panes began to be replaced with glass in the seventeenth century.[186] The ceiling at Juli was covered with woven material, coated with gesso and painted; today much of it has rotted away or hangs down in strips, revealing the method of roof construction general in the region, with reeds and small poles bound together (upper left).

The retables with their polychromed figures, competently executed, probably date from the time when the Jesuits did over the interior. The main altar, a section of which is illustrated (*fig. b*), is another of those rather rare pieces built up of panels in relief. Though Baroque in its design, the work as a whole is somewhat cold. Columns decorated with small painted patterns over gold frame the reliefs, here the Vision of St. Ignatius. Little rapture is to be felt in the scene; rather it is humanly simple, almost matter of fact. As is the case in many statues in the High Andes, the estofado pattern is too small to lend dash to the total effect. Of all the carving, freest in line is perhaps the side garland at the right.

As the traveler leaves Juli and continues along the southwestern shore of Lake Titicaca, the road winds across brown-red patches of grazed-down land and tops a slight rise, from which the town of Pomata comes into view in the distance (*Pl. 120, fig. b*). It is situated on a promontory at an altitude of nearly 13,000 feet and offers a broad view over the lake. The name is said to derive from the Aymara for "House of the Puma." Pomata seems to have been one of the stations on the relay road into Bolivia in pre-Columbian times. It, too, was first assigned by the Spaniards to the Dominicans. Within five years of their arrival (1540) they had built a chapel. Their establishment was probably still small when the viceroy Francisco de Toledo transferred this region to the Jesuits (1569). After the turn of the century, the Dominicans again were permitted to take over in Pomata, and they remained there until 1754, when the church was secularized and given into the hands of a parish priest. In 1606 the "house" serving as an abode for the friars was elevated to the

rank of a monastery, and less than two decades later Vázquez mentions it as a priory. Of the entire complex nothing remains today except the great church, which is dedicated to Santiago and the Virgin of the Rosary.

Its main portal (*fig. a*) is placed within an arched recess between two tower bases, only one of which now has a belfry. A large, deeply splayed choir-light emphasizes the austerity of the façade. Except for a rather flat relief of God the Father, placed tight under the arch, only the columns and moldings are decorated. In contrast, ornament is lavished on the lateral portal, which also has an arched outline but it does not stand in a recess. Its columns are beribboned, and its surface is covered with a virile pattern of grapes, palmettes, canephorae, birds, and animals carved in such low relief that one is reminded of an etched design. In the repeated use here of puma heads and the sun disk, the old pagan religion of the region comes close to the surface—although these symbols had ostensible justification in the name of the town or in Christian iconography.

Outside and in, the church is built of native stone, a deep rose in color. The barrel-vaulted nave (*fig. c*) has a steely perfection of line. The side arches form niches for altars, and the windows in the vaults are deeply splayed. Tasteful and well-spaced carving accents the architectural elements. Throughout the building the carved ornamentation of the stone is shallow but characterized by vigor and assurance. Star-shaped flowers and a vase with a spreading bouquet are the principal motifs, used also on the pendentives of the lofty semispherical dome. The development and origins of this dome, one of the most famous in Latin America, have been studied in detail by Wethey.

The same decorative motifs appear also in the apse windows beside the main altar (*fig. d*), at the top of which is Mary's monogram upheld by angels. The pattern again recalls tapestry, with not an inch of free space. This illustration shows one of the heavy ornate corbels, extending down the wall, and immediately beside it a portion of the main altar, composed to fit into the allotted space. The combination here of rose-colored stone and brilliant gold wood carving is stunning. The upper columns of the retable are cut with gemlike facets. A scaly dragon makes up the main part of the side garland, and the capitals of the twisted columns—just below the small niche with its statue—are developed into dragon heads.

The dating of this church is far from definite. Inventories in the sacristy mention the completion of the high altar in 1722 and repairs to the vaulting in 1729 and 1732. The arched gateway to the atrium is inscribed 1763, but stylistically it has little connection with the church building. On the base of the left tower, which is now only a stump, is inscribed, in Spanish: "Quiroga finished this, 1794." In the proportion of its parts and the homogeneity of its spirit, this church ranks among the most distinguished in the region.

The sacristy door in Pomata (*Pl. 121, fig. a*) also demonstrates how well wood and stone blend in this strange artistic idiom, not only through a similarity in motifs but also to a certain degree in technique. In the paneling of the door proper, two alternating motifs vary an eight-petaled flower; the stone jambs and low frieze each carry a single flowering stalk. Heavy cornices accent the horizontal. Above, in a heraldic arrangement, two angels, with a remarkable hairdo, hold Mary's monogram and a crown; their wings blend into the scrollwork of the pediment. A vase stands on each side as a finial, holding three stiff stylized flowers. Note the animal head in the side garlands.

Compare that doorway to the one leading into the sacristy of San Juan at Juli (*fig. c*). Here the carver worked with a larger vocabulary (though still regional) and a more complex design, which is so thoroughly integrated that the stone seems to lose its hardness.

The third sacristy doorway illustrated here (*fig. b*), in the church of San Pedro in Acora, shows a different composition, carried out in a more rustic manner, with painting playing an essential role. Acora, which lies on the road between Puno and Ilave, also was a settlement in pre-Columbian times and has several churches preserved from the colonial era, though now only one is kept up for the use of the small parish. Here the entrance is flanked by two thick engaged columns ornamented with grapes. The lintel, with its peculiar Mudéjar shape, repeats the same subject as at Pomata, and angel heads are placed at the right and left. Basically the design on the wooden door is similar to that at Pomata; but it possesses nevertheless an individuality of its own. Note the tassel-like ornaments at the height of the capitals—elements which in Juli are exquisitely digested into the composition; it has been suggested that these were bases for candelabra.[203] In addition to much gold and the flesh tone of the angels, the outstanding colors are a brilliant red, silver, and green.

Pomata's two other churches even in neglect reveal how much artistic fantasy was expended on such buildings in this town. To the simple thatched structure of San Miguel, finished in the first decade of the seventeenth century, a choir loft was added probably some hundred years later. The piers (*fig. d*) are of stone, carved with great skill and plastic feeling. On either side of the niche mermaids playing the *charango* are so exactly balanced that one has to perform left-handed. Under the arch is carved a masklike face, surrounded by deeply undercut motifs. Two profiles can be discerned on the sides in the turns of the scrolls, and in the side garland a caryatid supports with one raised arm the scroll above it. The columns are covered with a chain-mail pattern, the links of which diminish in size as the shafts taper upward.

All four examples of regional carving lie within thirty-five miles of one another, and all were created within half a century or less. A comparison shows with what originality and exuberance the Indian and mestizo made use of the forms and patterns which the Spaniards put before them. The Juli portal has subtlety of composition and a certain monumental quality. In Pomata's sacristy door the design is simplified and the arch absent; but it is executed with plastic clarity and remarkable verve. The Acora doorway, the least articulate and the latest, by reason of its naïve composition and its lively use of color, is undiluted folk art. In the free-standing columns and the decisive undercutting on the pier of San Miguel Pomata a much stronger feeling for plasticity is apparent than in any of the others.

The virility of this regional art has left its imprint on monuments all along the lake. One of the masterpieces survives in the tiny settlement of Zepita, close to the Bolivian border. This is the church of San Pedro (*Pl. 122, fig. a*), set on a platform at the top of a sloping grass-grown plaza. Its tower, its dignified dome, and especially the broad arched recess of its portal strike the traveler's eye, even at a considerable distance, above the thatched roofs of the hamlet. And again the question comes to his mind, how was it possible in mid-eighteenth century in a remote and sparsely populated region to erect a building that required so much constructional knowledge and embodied such an artistic flair.

The church has the shape of a Latin cross and is without side chapels. Its end portal carries practically no decoration; all attention was given the lateral entrance (*fig. d*). As is common in Andean Baroque, its niches are flanked by two smaller columns, with pedestals and entablature effects of their own, comprising almost isolated decorative elements. A comparison of familiar motifs—the large medallions with supporting angels and the carving in the spandrels—with those at Cajamarca (*see Pl. 5*) and Arequipa (*see Pl. 105*) will demonstrate how differently the same schemes were carried out.

In the Zepita portal the carving on the wall surfaces, which is delicate and complicated, reminds one of the work in the church of Santiago in Pomata. On the other hand, that on the columns and pedestals, which is bold and monumental, shows a relationship to the choir-loft ornamentation in San Miguel there. Zepita's columns, however, carry considerably more variety of motif, and grotesque masks are introduced among the meshes of the chain mail. It is worth noting that though technical mastery is evident in all this stonework, the column is not twisted; salomonic columns in stone, features of contemporary Baroque elsewhere in Spanish America, are infrequent in the High Andes.

Great originality distinguishes the side garland of the portal (*fig. c*), an unusually wide and involved composition, where a half-figure wearing an enormous headdress is resolved into the inward-turned spirals of the frame. Probably it will never be fully established from what sources these regional stonecarvers drew their inspiration. Their imaginations might have fed on engravings, woodcuts, pages from illuminated books—secular as well as religious—on designs in tapestries or embroideries, and even on costumes and ritual objects still preserved from pre-Columbian times. There seems to be no justification for the claims of some circles, who, disdaining the Indian, go out of their way to explain such strange sculptural details as derived from the Hindu or other Asiatic peoples rather than appreciate an artistic phenomenon autochthonous to this soil.

Today the interior of the church (*fig. b*) is practically bare. A few canvas paintings hang on the wall, and along the base runs a narrow masonry bench. Such a construction, a hold-over from the sixteenth century, is rare in an eighteenth-century building—another example of the clinging to tradition. A sweeping arch resting on corbels supports the choir gallery and, as is frequent in Andean churches, the ribs of the stone barrel vaulting terminate in corbels. These are massively developed and decorated with wide leaves, but they have been so cruelly whitewashed that much of the finer detail work is lost. Just below the cornice, patches of wall painting can be detected, forming a sort of border of thistle and pomegranate-like motifs. (For a detail of the main altar see *Pl. 189*.)

The village of Copacabana is set on the slope of a rocky promontory overlooking a lovely crescent-shaped bay and the sacred island of Titicaca, dedicated to the sun god of the ancient Aymaras. Its name derives from the Aymara *kgopa* and *kgwana* (rock from where one sees).[217] Protected from winds and open to the sun it has a genial climate, which seems an impossibility to one remembering Puno, the harsh, at the other end of the lake at the same altitude.

Copacabana's famous shrine, like the one in Esquipulas, Guatemala (*see Pl. 72*), was a religious pilgrim place long before the Spaniards took over. In both, large basilicas replaced the pagan temples, and both still attract visitors from distant places. Here the cult centers about a statue of the Virgin which was carved around 1576 by the Indian Tito Yupanqui, a native of Copacabana who worked in La Paz. A few years later the figure was brought to Copacabana, and soon miraculous powers were attributed to it. At that time a Via Crucis led up from the lake to a Calvary with three crosses, much revered. The royal permit to build a sanctuary was issued to the Augustinians in the 1580's, and shortly afterward they commenced a custodianship that continued for almost two hundred and forty years. During the early decades of independence the place was in the hands of various religious orders; by 1842 the Franciscans from La Paz had assumed the guardianship, and they still hold it.[216]

The large chapel, begun in 1614 and finished four years later, is now incorporated into one of the transepts of the basilica. Its capacity proved inadequate for the masses of pilgrims, and in 1668 a truly monumental building complex (*Pl. 123, fig. b*) was started under the architect Francisco Jiménez de Sigüenza and the patronage of Viceroy Lemos; it was inaugurated in 1678, but construction continued.

The material of the church is brick—with occasional stone—painted to resemble stone masonry. The lateral portal, its chief entrance, is placed within an arched recess. This complex has features common to some other Augustinian foundations, notably those in Mexico (*see Pls. 31, 32*): the atrium walls are crenellated, as was also the edge of the church roof before restoration, and four *posas* stand in the atrium corners. There is also an open domed structure, like a huge outdoor baldachin (at the right of the gateway), which doubtless functioned as an open chapel. It contains an altar and a large cross, and a few statues of an *apostolado* remain around the cornice of its dome.

The lanterns and cupolas are covered with modern jade-green tiles, probably in the tradition of earlier decoration, and pottery vases of the same color are placed as finials along the edge of the walls. Colonial ware from nearby Pucara has a beautiful green tone, and even today that village and its neighbor Ayaviri manufacture earthenware animal figures, toys, and candlesticks, often colored a fine green though crudely painted and glazed.

Especial interest attaches to the side altar (dated 1618), which stands at the left of the principal entrance (*fig. a*). Seemingly this was the main altar of the earlier chapel, and it continues to be a favorite of the Aymara Indians today. Stylistically it resembles some of the work in Juli. It was made by the friar Juan Viscaino and painted by Dionisio Sebastián Acosta Inca, an Indian as his name implies. A Donatello freshness marks the entire plastic composition. Angels adorn the spandrels of the central niche; the classical egg-and-dart pattern is rather originally applied above the edge of the shell. On either side of this niche medallions in polychromed stucco portray sibyls, studies in costume and hairdo. Of the thirteen ancient prophetesses, the six who appear here seem to be, starting at the upper left: the Erythraean, who spoke scornfully of pagan wisdom; the Cumaean, prophetess of the Golden Age of Christ's coming; the Cumanian, often depicted with a cross; the Samian, who sometimes carried a cradle; the Lybian, who proclaimed the Light of the World; and Agrippina, who foretold the conversion of strange lands. The Virgin's statue in the niche is dressed in modern garments, but the crown and the silver basket, appurtenances of La Merced, appear to be of colonial workmanship.

The main retable (*fig. d*), finished in 1684, is unusually high, filling the apse completely. Its columns are heavily encrusted with carving; broken pediments, heavy scrolls, and ornate medallions bespeak the Baroque. The earlier type of images in wood is found, carved half in the round against a plain gilded background, together with canvas paintings and statues placed in deep niches. Note the atlantes beneath the overhanging cornices in the first order, thrusting boldly forward and extending beyond the line of the moldings (*see also Pl. 189*). The central silver frame and the tabernacle are out of harmony. No doubt some changes occurred in the latter half of the nineteenth century and again in 1924, when large-scale restoration was undertaken on the occasion of the first centenary of Bolivian independence. Nevertheless the retable retains considerable individuality as a result of the fusion of local and imported motifs. (*Compare Pl. 109.*) The decorative ribbed vaulting of the interior, in late Gothic tradition, is visible in this photograph.

More homogeneity can be observed in the retable that covers the corner pier at the right of the apse (*fig. c*), below one of the pendentives of the large dome. Here the columns are twisted and garlanded with grapes. Especially the relief of the penitent Magdalene and the elegant spirals exhibit the high standard of late-seventeenth-century craftsmanship.

Copacabana's single-story cloister, with its air of meditation, harks back to the earlier period; it is important because most colonial cloisters received a second story in the eighteenth century, or even before, obliterating the original aspect (*Pl. 124, fig. c*). The photo-

graph shows clearly the domical vaults that cover the arcade, as well as the battlement-like crenellation on the roof.

This basilica is the scene of pilgrimages on holy days, when Mass is said every hour and columns of pilgrims, coming and going, people the landscape. The environs are dotted with wayside crosses and shrines, many of which are temporary, erected specially for the great processions of the fiestas.

As the traveler proceeds southeast toward the outlet of Lake Titicaca, the road follows about the same route as was used in pre-Columbian times. On the border between Peru and Bolivia lies the village of Desaguardero. Here passage across the river was early effected by means of a floating bridge, first constructed in 1160 on the order of the Inca Capac Yupanqui. It was in service in the first quarter of the seventeenth century, made of heavy strands of reeds bound together, much in the manner used for the native *balsas*, and was renewed and strengthened twice a year by local Indians.[81] As the lake is left behind, the land descends and a broad view of a vast arid plateau opens ahead. The slanting rays of the afternoon sun bring out strange shapes of yellow, red-brown, or gray in sand and stone. On the horizon of this Martian landscape stand, like a gigantic screen, the snow-covered peaks of the Cordillera Real. The road winds toward the most lofty and fantastic in shape, the Illimani, more than 21,000 feet high. As the details of this giant emerge, the traveler comes upon the city of La Paz, lying in a deep and sudden ravine, its electric lamps glittering in the dusk of the narrow valley, eclipsed by the towering mountain tops still red with the setting sun.

La Ciudad de Nuestra Señora de la Paz was founded in 1548 as an important rest station on the journey to or from Potosí. Its history is full of struggle and bloodshed, battles between Indians and Spaniards and later between political factions within the independent nation. Since the turn of the present century La Paz has developed into the active center of government, finance, and society, though Sucre is still the legal capital of the country.

The La Paz River—originally called the Choqueyapu—runs through the canyon, dividing the city. In the early seventeenth century the Franciscans, Dominicans, Augustinians, Mercedarians, and Jesuits all had establishments here. Construction on a Franciscan church and monastery was started in 1549 in the Indian quarter—which still surrounds it—but the buildings were not finished until the first years of the following century. In 1612 the church collapsed. The present edifice probably was begun around 1743. According to an inscription, the dome was finished in 1753; another date, 1772, is found in the choir vault. The building was consecrated in 1784.

More than a decade ago the distinguished scholar Mario J. Buschiazzo noted similarities in the ornamentation of this church and that of certain churches in the Titicaca region. In the façade the central doorway (*fig. b*) shows relationship to Santiago Pomata in the undulant spray on the two jambs, the fronds on the multifoil arch, the puma heads below the columns, and notably in the monster heads among the fernlike leaves on the spandrels. Wethey points out that the columns wound with spiral bands suggest carving at Puno and Juli (*see Pls. 116, 121*). On the other hand, the second story offers a different scheme—bold medallions that include grotesque figures. In ground plan, too, the Franciscan church at La Paz is quite different: it is rectangular, a three-aisled basilica, while the others mentioned here are cruciform.

Inside, the carving, though much less elaborate, is even more closely related to that of Santiago in Pomata. The dome is constructed in a similar fashion and divided into four major and four minor fields for decoration. In both churches the pendentives carry great flower-filled vases almost identical, and some of the bosses bear the same irregular star-shaped flower.

Panes of translucent alabaster, used instead of glass, are still preserved in the windows of the central vault. Several benefactors of this church are recorded, especially one Diego Baena y Antipara, a wealthy mine owner who contributed more than half a million silver pesos towards its erection.[208] But not one name of the artists and craftsmen connected with the work has come to light.

The church of Santo Domingo, lying in the northern portion of the old town where the Spanish and creoles lived, shows a façade strongly regional in style (*fig. d*). It served as the cathedral for more than a century (1830–1932) while La Paz, like many other Latin American cities, was building a Greco-Roman imitation.

The Dominicans set up a priory here and began to build their church in the first decade of the seventeenth century; reportedly the architect of the Copacabana sanctuary, Jiménez de Sigüenza, later assisted in the work.[220] Within an arched recess are a trefoil portal and four niches, the latter today unfortunately closed with cement. Larger elements are used in this carving than on the façade of San Francisco and in a warmer and more sweeping manner. The grape design seems almost rambling, and many of the motifs have a vagueness of line, especially in the second story. Most unusual are the large parrots pressed into the space on either side of the choir-light, flat and unrealistic but highly decorative. Every protruding angle of the cornices is developed into a puma head, reminiscent of pre-Columbian carving. Mid-eighteenth century is suggested as the date for this building; the tenor of its decoration suggests palaces in La Paz and Potosí (*see Pl. 126*).

Sucre, southeast from La Paz, lies in a broad valley at an altitude of over 9,000 feet. The place is often called the City of Four Names, for in the course of its history it has been known as Chuquisaca, Charcas, La Plata, and finally Sucre, in honor of General Antonio José de Sucre (1795–1830), a lieutenant of Bolívar. Founded in 1538 on the site of the Indian village of Chuquichaca (golden bridge) the city was the oldest Spanish settlement in this region and was destined to be an important station between Lima and Buenos Aires. Its proximity to fabulous Potosí added to its prosperity and its prominence. As the capital of the province of Charcas and the seat of the audiencia, it had full administrative, military, and religious staffs. A mint dating from 1572, a spacious well-outfitted town hall, and an impressive archiepiscopal palace are mentioned by Vázquez. Indian artisans plied the trades of silversmiths, silk weavers, potters, tailors, shoemakers, and carpenters; and more than a hundred mulattoes and sambos lived in the city.

Sucre's University of San Francisco Javier was founded in 1624, the fourth in Spanish America, and was under the charge of the Jesuits in 1767 when they were expelled from the Spanish colonies. Soon after it became a royal academy, and later some of its members played important roles in the movement for independence. Its buildings have been modernized with the exception of the cloister (*fig. a*). This section, constructed largely of stone, has two different orders of columns in the two galleries of its somewhat somber arcades; through a doubling of the arches in the upper story a change of rhythm was achieved. The tower beyond, which belongs to the former Compañía, now the church of San Miguel, is imposing in outline, though today it is repainted to imitate stone—a questionable refurbishment.

The story of the city of Potosí, situated in the Bolivian Andes at an altitude of more than 13,600 feet and four hundred miles from the nearest seaport, is perhaps the most incredible in the Spanish colonial world. According to legend, silver was found here in Inca times but was not exploited because a thunderous voice forbade it, saying that the precious metal must be kept for a later comer; thenceforth the place was called Potosí (noise). The Spaniards founded the city (1547) on discovering the ore. Fifteen years later, in recognition of

some 350,000,000 gold pesos paid to the Spanish crown as the royal fifth assessed on the metal from its mines, it earned the title of Very Loyal Imperial City. In the first half of the seventeenth century the population reached its maximum, 160,000—one Spanish household for every 10,000 souls.[186] Thereafter it slowly declined, until in 1825 there were no more than 8,000.

It lies at the foot of the famous Cerro Rico (rich hill) in a harsh and restless landscape full of jagged rocky hills, fantastic in the sharp light of the overhead sun and the weird perspective of this altitude (*see Pl. 127*). No crops grow within some twenty-five miles of the city; in its most prosperous days it was a paradise for merchants. Supplies poured in from outlying valleys, from Cuzco, and even from Arica on the Pacific coast. It is reckoned that at the end of the sixteenth century more than two thousand Indians were requisitioned yearly from the region around Chucuito for forced labor in the Potosí mines. They furnished their own supplies, each coming with a packtrain of fifteen to twenty llamas, most of which eventually were slaughtered for food. In 1573 the "patio" method of processing the ore with mercury was instituted and traffic began to deliver this precious material to Potosí from Huancavelica eight hundred miles away. The safest route for its delivery, as finally decided, ran from Huancavelica down to Chincha on the Pacific, then by ship to the port of Arica, and finally by llama train again into the mountains to Potosí; in 1603 over three hundred Indians and five thousand animals were required for this traffic. Mercury had priority for shipment; when the year's supply was safe, the transport of merchandise was a sure and lucrative investment. A return of 1,000 per cent was not unusual in this market, the most unscrupulous in the New World.[210]

Potosí was situated, roughly, midway between Lima and Buenos Aires, some 1,200 miles from the former and around 1,600 from the latter. Although Lima controlled the monopoly of commerce for the whole viceroyalty and ships were forbidden to enter at Buenos Aires, as time went on the Atlantic port served more and more as a "back door" for profitable trade in both directions.

In Potosí the Andean mestizo style reached its last impressive station. Of the thirty churches, monasteries, and nunneries here when the great past was the living present, some are today in ruins, others are closed, and one has even been converted into a moving-picture theater. Most of the ecclesiastical and many of the civil buildings are decorated in the regional style, manifesting variations in accordance with changing tastes and the talents of the craftsmen; a notable exception is the nineteenth-century cathedral (see Pl. 10).

The Carmelite church of Santa Teresa was founded in 1685, and the tympanum over the nunnery door bears the date 1692—a few years earlier than Arequipa's Compañía—but the façade of the church (Pl. 125, fig. a) may be somewhat later.[214] It is constructed of brick and stone, whitewashed, and is not the retable type. The portal is ornamented with small all-over patterns, and the more ornate upper section is connected with the lower through lambrequin-like corbels. The belfry—a true flying façade—almost doubles the height of the building. Single twisted columns flank its bold arches and small carved stone tablets enrich the walls. The scroll-like wings at the sides, vaguely suggestive of towers, make an effective transition to the belfry.

Scrolls and leaves, carved in low but clean relief, adorn the frame of the nunnery doorway (fig. c). The pediment above it seems somewhat detached. Three ornamental stone panels display the arms of the order and probably those of its local founders and supporters.[214]

The decorative tendency seen in the façade of Santa Teresa comes to a more ebullient effect in La Compañía (fig. d); its portal and tower are dated 1700–1707. The carver was the Indian Sebastián de la Cruz, who was also connected with San Francisco Potosí. La Com-

pañía's plastic elements stand out with special vigor against the plain wall of rose-colored stone, unmarred by whitewash. The repertory of motifs is richer than at Santa Teresa; in places its columns are coupled and its niches are framed with petaled rosettes. The tympanum above the entrance is semicircular and is flanked by two semicircular bases topped with large leafy finials. Human faces are woven into the side garlands. The two-story espadaña, rising 115 feet above street level, is a monument in itself, decorated with twisted columns even inside the largest bell arch.

No documentation has yet been found for the dating of La Merced (fig. b), but generally it is placed in the last quarter of the seventeenth century. The retable arrangement of the façade, with two niches one above the other in the first story and a small niche under the window, reminiscent of San Francisco in La Paz, is not unusual in Potosí. It is a question whether the portal originally stood under an arch or, as today, beneath a protecting gable. Its restrained ornamentation contains a blend of various familiar motifs, rather suggestive of wood carving, and makes its contribution to the variety offered here. At the left the tall belfry, which dates from a considerably earlier time, stands separate, without ornamentation—an infrequent occurrence.

As has already been seen, civic buildings also displayed the regional style. The House of the Corregidor in Potosí (Pl. 126, fig. a) immediately captures the eye with its lacelike carving, which even several thick layers of whitewash do not obscure. This was the office of the town's mayor in colonial times, and the carvers outdid themselves in producing a pleasing aspect. Two of its three portals—all different—are visible in the photograph. The more distant has peculiar pilasters with undulating profiles. Short columns and sections of pilasters on different levels produce an effective play of light and shadow. Note the large windows with iron grilles above each doorway and the beautifully carved panels of the wooden balcony in the foreground. In the third entrance, which stands to the right of the balcony, the pilasters with undulating lines are repeated and a massive carved pediment carrying a heraldic device rises under the gable.

Imposing in its primeval quality is the portal of the National Bank in Potosí (*fig. d*), built (1750–1785) as a residence for the Marquis Otavi.[214] Here, as elsewhere in this area, spiraling bands give the columns a twisted appearance (*see also Pl. 116*). The arch is framed with blocks containing large four-petaled rosettes; similarly uncomplicated are the patterns of the side garlands. In the heraldic composition the two lions seem to be hanging from the shield instead of upholding it. Especially noteworthy are the moon with a star and the full-faced sun on the blocks above the capitals; between them the frieze is filled with stars and a cherub head. This ornamentation as a whole is developed in the same way as on church portals; compare the three-cornered fern motif in the spandrels with that on La Merced just seen.

Another sun face occupies the center of the lintel in the doorway of the Herrera mansion (*fig. c*), now a part of the university in Potosí. The carving here, with its double outlines, is extremely delicate throughout, reminiscent of work in wax. The motifs emerge from two vases at the bottom; two birds are worked in among the foliage. The design above the neo-Mudéjar arch is skillfully composed into its limited space. A medallion in the upper right-hand corner carries the date 1781.

The former city palace of the Marquis Villaverde (*fig. b*), in La Paz, is judged as somewhat earlier, about mid-eighteenth century. The photograph shows one corner of the patio, just at the right of the stairway of honor, which leads up to an open corridor in the second story. The stone columns of the arcade are carved with festoons that end in bunches of grapes, and the balustrade carries a broad-leaved garland spreading out from a central vase, its undulating stem suggestive of a ser-

pent; in the spandrels are abstract figures, also with pre-Columbian echoes. The tall column (one of two flanking the stairway) is banded with a medallion featuring a heraldic bird, and above the capital the mask on the block in the frieze section may be a puma head.

These palaces bespeak authority, culture, and wealth. At the same time they reflect, perhaps more clearly than many of the ecclesiastic edifices, the powerful differences of the region—racial, climatic, and material—as well as its remoteness from the motherland.

The church of San Lorenzo in Potosí has two towers and a central pediment; the latter was struck by lightning in 1896 and later restored. In ground plan it is a cruciform structure, with a dome at the crossing and three half-domes over the apse and transepts.[212] According to history a church dedicated to San Lorenzo stood on this site as early as 1547–1552. Many scholars regard the façade of the present church (*Pl. 127, fig. a*) as the culmination of Hispano-American art—the masterpiece of the Andean mestizo style. Its portal stands within a sheltering arched recess. The pedestals of the columns are high and slender, each carrying a panel of small motifs; the moldings protrude sharply, isolating this lower section somewhat from that above. Ornate finials on semicircular bases top the main columns (*compare Pls. 105, 125*). We have seen columns divided by crowns or rings and sometimes each section differently treated; usually the heaviest decoration has been placed in the lowest third. In San Lorenzo the upper portion is transformed into a caryatid with arms akimbo, exotically costumed in a flounced skirt. Below it more of a twist is attempted than is usual in this region, though here too the effect is augmented by a spiraling band. Masks look out from among the leaves of the entwining garlands. Two other caryatides, with leafy bases as pedestals, are worked out on the piers of the arch, taking the place of inner columns. In the second order the single niche, containing a statue of St. Michael, harmonizes in build-up with the doorway below it. On the flat surface of the background an opulent yet homogeneous effect is achieved by a repetition of motifs in many separated fields. One of the richest and most varied of side garlands is to be seen on this façade; the favorite vases of flowers are included, but much subordinated.

Above these side garlands are two mermaids playing the native *charango*. The sun is carved over the head of one, the moon over the other, and the space around them is studded with stars. In these symbols Marco Dorta sees reminders of the redemption on Golgotha and the promise of Heaven. Herein lies perhaps an explanation for the presence of those mysterious creatures, the mermaids, so favored in certain regions of Spanish America yet seemingly out of context amid a galaxy of holy figures. The same symbolism is borne out in Milton's lines from "At a Solemn Musick": "Blest pair of sirens, pledges of heavenly joy. . . ."

The façade is dated 1728–1744 in an inscription at the very top, above the images of the patron saint and St. Vincent. It speaks the same regional idiom as many other colonial buildings but with greater eloquence. José Kondori has been named as its sculptor, but no documentation has ever been offered in substantiation. It has also been suggested that he must have come from the tropical lowlands of Mojos, in Bolivia, and have been expert in carving and inlaying wood in the production of furniture.[219] Be that as it may, it is clear not only that he had fully digested the idiom of the Andean mestizo style but also that he added certain flourishes out of his own talent and imagination. The section of the city in which the building stands has always been an Indian quarter, and there can be little doubt that the carver was a mestizo if not an Indian. To this author it seems that he was not so much imitating the manner of wood carving —though he probably worked also in that material—as he was approaching his task with a different tactile sense from that of a Euro-

pean. The quality of the stone itself—soft when quarried and hardening upon exposure—contributed to this difference, for a sculptor could use his tools on it in a very different way or perhaps even employ tools which in Europe were more commonly applied to wood carving.

By now it is obvious that the term Andean mestizo style includes a wide variety of regional characteristics. On La Compañía in Arequipa (*see Pl. 105*) the motifs are shallow-cut and cover a broad surface; one is placed beside another in a somewhat casual sequence, as on a sampler. A larger variety of motifs, made up of small elements, and much more figural representation can be seen at Zepita (*see Pl. 122*); here the patterns are more closely interwoven and the carving is more deeply undercut. On Puno's cathedral (*see Pl. 116*) powerful architectural members—free-standing columns and shelving cornices—are placed against a background of fine continuous tracery. The portal of San Lorenzo in Potosí shows an all-over covering and a preference for small elements; its effect is that of filigree, sometimes even approaching the appearance of work in wax, and its design is among the best integrated in this group. The lower sections of the cathedral and El Belén in Cajamarca are comparable in the virility of their regional manner (*see Pls. 5, 103*).

Through the present-day demand for tin, Potosí has recovered some of its former importance. Mining in silver, copper, and lead also is carried on here, and the population has increased to about thirty-five thousand. Its tile-roofed houses of one or two stories, facing one another across narrow and often crooked streets, have preserved in stone the great epoch when Baroque was a living expression. In the cityscape (*fig. b*) one can see the cathedral (right center); toward the left is La Compañía, and somewhat farther rise the flat domes and arched roofs of the Casa de Moneda, the famous mint. Against the mineral color of treeless hills, the various cupolas and towers, the clustered roofs, and the outlines of patios all combine into a picture that stays with the traveler long after the colonial bridge has been crossed on the way south. Before the Argentine border is reached, the landscape becomes milder. One passes haciendas, vineyards, and orchards; but the massive range of the Andes still marks the horizon.

San Salvador de Jujuy, capital of the northernmost province of Argentina, is situated where the rough country ends and the great plains begin. The terrain, desolate and semiarid in places, is populated largely by mestizos and Indians. Jujuy was founded in 1593 on the site of a Quechua village.[81] In the early seventeenth century it had about a hundred Spanish residents, most of them muleteers who freighted flour, grain, cheese, and other foodstuffs to the Potosí mines high above. Thriving mule and cattle ranches lay nearby. Ox-drawn carts traveled not only into the mountains but also as far as Buenos Aires, about 1,500 miles.

From this province down to the Atlantic two tendencies can be noticed in the arts: trends brought in direct from the Old World by way of the Atlantic ports—especially by Jesuits in the eighteenth century—and the autochthonous influence from the High Andes. In the latter case local flora and fauna were stylized in the archaizing art of the people. (For an example see the eighteenth-century pulpit from the Rosario chapel at Jujuy on *Pl. 182.*)

Although the colonial monuments in Argentina may not show the range in originality which is to be found in certain other Spanish American countries, scholars there have investigated the field with praiseworthy thoroughness and illuminated many significant points. (The reader with a special interest in this area is referred to the Bibliography.)

Southwest of Jujuy, in the Calchaqui Valley, lies the small settlement of Molinos (the mills). In this smiling country the somberness of the *altiplano* is broken and even oranges are cultivated. The parish church of Molinos (*Pl. 128, fig. b*), of adobe brick, shows characteristics of the Andean area: two towers, an arched

recess, turret-like pinnacles and a dome, as well as a small atrium enclosed in an adobe wall. In this church, which faces the highway still called *Camino de los Incas*, is buried the last royal governor of the region.

As in Mexico the large estates, whether civil or ecclesiastical, each had its chapel, the quality of the architecture depending on the prosperity of the land. Sugar cane, wheat, corn, and grapes were grown here, and cattle and mules were bred for the mines in the High Andes—an old industry. Here also were gathered as many Indians as possible from the surrounding country to be instructed in the Christian religion; their settlements were called *reducciones*, or missions. Since the area was sparsely populated, the center of one estate lay far from the next and post stations or relay houses were established to provide the traveler at the end of a full day's journey with shelter and food for his party and his animals. Many of these stations had existed in Inca times, called *tampus*, with a caretaker on the premises and supplies of firewood, blankets, corn, and water. Indeed the *tampus* greatly aided the advance of the Conquistadores in Peru. During colonial days the administration kept up these inns and built new ones where the need arose. The system began to fall to pieces only in the first half of the nineteenth century, when it was no longer of pressing interest to the separate republican governments to maintain such close and relatively easy connections.

The inn at Sinsacate (*fig. c*), not far from Córdoba, is such a colonial rest house. This drawn-out single-story building, constructed of brick, adobe, tile, and wood, has high spacious rooms to insure coolness, one large dining room, and quarters for servants. A chapel with a free-standing belfry adjoins it, entered through an arched recess which constitutes a vestibule. Square columns support the slanting roof, forming the colonnade to a wide brick-paved corridor which runs in front of the rooms for shade and cleanliness.

This type of chapel, modest in size and built of local material by local labor, can be found in many areas of the Spanish colonial empire. One example (*fig. a*), on the other side of the Andes, is situated near Huarás, Peru, about 220 miles northeast of Lima at an altitude of nearly 11,000 feet. But while the outer shell of these buildings more or less follows a general scheme, the interior decoration usually reflects local talent.

The *reducciones* near Córdoba were connected with a vast chain of missions in a territory which was then entirely under Jesuit control and is now part of Paraguay, Argentina, and Brazil. Members of the order circulated freely and with them went their architects and artists, instructing the Indians how to build, carve, and paint. Young ecclesiastics just out of seminaries came hither to gain experience with land and people.[213] Upon the expulsion of the order (1767) many of these missions fell into disrepair and ruin.

Santa Catalina (*fig. d*) is perhaps the most elaborate of the Jesuit establishments in the hills around Córdoba. It was founded in 1622 for the maintenance of a novitiate; but the complex as it now stands was not completed until after mid-eighteenth century.[213] The portal of the residence bears the date 1726, and it is believed that the church was commenced about 1754 and finished shortly before the expulsion, with the assistance of Anton Harls, a German. In this region the influence of the two Italian Jesuits, Andrés Blanqui and Juan Bautista Prímoli, who were active in the completion of the main part of Córdoba's cathedral (*see Pl. 9*), must be taken into consideration. A somewhat protruding portal enlivens the two-towered façade of the church. The central pediment is characterized by graceful undulating lines, which are echoed in the espadaña above it. An imposing approach leads up to the atrium, as if to a Baroque theater. Emphasis on rounded shapes is evident—in the finials, the balustrade, the decoration on the espadaña, and the deep quatrefoil windows in the towers.

A view of the one-story cloister (*fig. f*) shows the bulging dome, with its large lantern and scrolled buttresses—strongly simplified devices of European Baroque—somewhat out of proportion with other parts of the complex. The single-nave interior manifests a certain stolidity, which, however, is neither crude nor awkward. Today the ranch buildings are in ruins, overgrown with destructive subtropical vegetation, but they still show massive high arches and other remnants of substantial construction.

Alta Gracia, at an altitude of only 1,920 feet, also near Córdoba, was another settlement for converted Indians. Juan Nieto had an estate there in 1588, called by its Indian name Parauachasca. His successors improved the property and in 1643 presented it to the Jesuits. That order installed a system of irrigation and set up a mill for the weaving of wool and cotton cloth to provide apparel not only for the inhabitants but also for members of the Jesuit college in Córdoba. The following workshops were active: a carpentry shop, an iron foundry capable of casting bells, a lime kiln, a brick kiln, and five looms; in addition there were printing presses, an apparatus for soap making, a dispensary, and a barber shop. Among the peons and personnel were numbered 140 Negroes and 170 Negresses. The estate—by no means the largest in the region —owned nearly 4,000 head of cattle, over 5,000 sheep, 1,300 mules, and nearly as many horses, besides goats and several thousand domesticated fowl.[213] As is clear, these *reducciones* raised much more produce than they—or even the mother church in the city—needed and the surplus was traded in commerce. In 1810 Alta Gracia was bought by the viceroy Santiago de Liniers y Bremond, a Frenchman who had commanded the Spanish fleet in the defeat of the English in Argentina.

The church at Alta Gracia (*fig. e*) was finished about 1762 after designs drawn by Andrés Blanqui. Curving stairways provide a dramatic approach. The long-drawn-out nave is covered with barrel vaulting. Again the dome is massive and provided with large windows and a tall lantern. Twin pilasters, undecorated, extend the full height of the façade. There is no free-standing espadaña, but a section of the wall curves down on either side, making the upper story seem part of a decorative gable. The gateway also is worthy of note, with its flaring stairway and espadaña-like crown. The belfry is at the rear of the church.

Both Santa Catalina and Alta Gracia evoke reminiscences of rustic churches in Central America and Mexico (*see Pl. 49*). It is regrettable that their interiors, like others still to be discussed in this chapter, were so thoroughly restored in the last century that much of the original flavor disappeared.

Across the eastern range of the Andes lay the Captaincy-General of Chile. Comparatively little art from the seventeenth and eighteenth centuries has been preserved here.[207]

Córdoba de la Nueva Andalucia, located in the center of Argentina at the heart of a vast and immensely rich agricultural area, was founded in 1573 by Spaniards crossing the Andes.[211] It was named for the Spanish town where the governor's wife was born. The Jesuits established themselves there in the first third of the seventeenth century and finished their "domestic chapel" about 1670. The mother church for the whole region (*Pl. 129, fig. a*) also may have been commenced at that time. It was dedicated in 1671, and its towers bear the dates 1673 and 1674.

Recently the high angular façade of the building was reconstructed to recapture its colonial aspect. It is built of irregular stones tinged a faint rose; the archivolts around the doors and windows are of brick. Above the stark horizontal of the cornice rise two belfries. Three widely separated entrances indicate the three aisles within. The arrangement of the second-story windows is similar to that in some Brazilian churches; in Spanish America at this date such a design was rare. (*Compare Pls. 10, 171.*) It is a matter of dispute whether a sheathing of stone was originally intended for this façade or not.

Inside the building, the entire ceiling is of cedar brought from Paraguay, the exclusive mission territory of the order; it is said to have been constructed by the Belgian friar Felipe Lemer.[213] The barrel vaulting and the cupola (*fig. c*) have remarkable elegance and warmth of line, enhanced by the rich tonality of the painted decoration, which suggests some manuscript border. Representations of the Evangelists occupy the pendentives. (For the pulpit in this church see *Pl. 183*.)

Buenos Aires was the eastern terminus of the Royal Highway. Pedro de Mendoza, with a contract from Charles V for the settlement of the lands bordering the Bay of Rio de la Plata, founded the city in 1536 and named it Puerto de Santa María del Buen Aire (the port of St. Mary of the Good Breeze), patroness of sailors. But quarrels among the settlers, harassment by Indians, and fires all led to the abandonment of the site five years later for Asunción in Paraguay. In 1580 Buenos Aires was refounded. Forty years later local government was granted and in many matters the settlement became independent from western Argentina. At this time it is described as having about two hundred Spanish residents; wheat, corn, various fruits, and wine were produced nearby, and the country was full of game—partridge, quail, pheasant, turkey, guinea hen, rabbit, and deer. Around mid-eighteenth century, though it had a population of over ten thousand, its administrative jurisdiction was still confined largely to local affairs. Its sea trade was restricted in favor of Lima's, and ruthless duties were imposed even on overland commerce. To such unfair treatment may be attributed, in part, the disinclination of Argentina to co-operate with her sister republics in Latin America. But in spite of restraints the colonial city throve. Goods smuggled in from Spain and other European lands, with or without the consent of corrupt officials, made up a lucrative business. The traffic was profitable enough in the second half of the seventeenth century to invite attacks by French, Portuguese, and Danish freebooters. By 1770 Buenos Aires ranked as the fourth city in the Viceroyalty of Peru, surpassed only by Lima, Cuzco, and Santiago de Chile. In 1776 it became the capital of the Viceroyalty of Rio de la Plata, the last in the New World, comprising present-day Argentina, Bolivia, Paraguay, and Uruguay.

It prospered especially under the viceroy Juan José de Vértiz y Salcedo (ruled 1778–1784), who was born in Mexico, one of the few viceroys not a native Spaniard. He was active in effecting the exploration and settlement of outlying regions. He introduced street lighting into the capital—by oil and candles—and had the streets paved and even sidewalks laid. Under his direction the liberalization of the teaching in the university came under discussion. He was an enthusiast of the theater, which he considered the best school for the purity of language and for manners, and he granted permission for a slave market to be transformed into a house for comedies; as may well be imagined, the sophisticated and biting tone of some of the Rococo plays was not always to the taste of officialdom and the clergy.[79] Buenos Aires then had nearly twenty-five thousand inhabitants, and in the country round about were thirteen thousand more. But its days as viceregal capital were too disturbed and too short for the erection of monuments comparable to those in Mexico, Lima, or even Bogotá. Furthermore, throughout its whole existence it lacked the mineral wealth which brought spectacular prosperity to cities like Potosí.

One of the least changed of the capital's colonial churches is San Ignacio, or La Compañía (fig. b), an important Jesuit center that enjoyed wide influence until the expulsion. The large three-aisled edifice was commenced in 1710 by the Jesuit Juan Kraus, a native of Pilsen, Bohemia, and it was consecrated about twenty-two years later. Among the architects who worked on this church were a number of Germans and Italians, including Prímoli, already mentioned in connection with Córdoba. The façade underwent changes even into the twentieth century. Its three entrances,

all the same size, lead into a vestibule. Protruding scrolls used as pilasters—echoes of the Italian Baroque—serve as central columns. On the second story the two panels to the right and left of the window contain, in stucco relief, vases of flowers, true Rococo in design. The espadaña, somewhat dwarfed by the towers, is high and narrow, again like those along the Brazilian coast; it has even a balcony before the arch and, at the top, a large cross. An inventory made shortly after the Jesuit expulsion shows that the embellishment of the church was then far from complete; altars were ungilded and many of the statues and paintings were makeshift.[218]

Pausing at this Jesuit church one might well ponder again on the validity of the term "Jesuit style" as applied to Latin American architecture, in the face of the diversity found in the Compañías of Córdoba, Salvador, Havana, Bogotá, Quito, Cuzco, and Juli (see Pls. 9, 10, 25, 99, 109, 119).

The former quinta, or country villa, of General Juan Martín de Pueyrredón (fig. d) stands in the suburb of San Isidro, overlooking the Rio de la Plata, twelve miles from Buenos Aires. It has much of a posta about it. A solid and unpretentious edifice, it reflects the sociable air of the nineteenth-century bourgeois, with the emphasis on hospitality. A small cottage stood here at the end of the eighteenth century. In the early nineteenth a wing was built by a new owner, the wealthy Spanish merchant whose daughter married General Pueyrredón. As a loyal Spanish colonial official, Pueyrredón fought valiantly at the side of Liniers against the English, but later he became a champion of liberation under José de San Martín. The estate remained for some time in the hands of this family. About 1840 a son who had studied architecture in Europe added the colonnade. Carefully restored in the last decade, the quinta is now a museum.[209]

Our architectural pilgrimage, which started on the Pacific coast of Peru, mounted to the high valleys of the Andes, and then crossed the pampas, comes to an end at the Bay of

Rio de la Plata on the Atlantic. We have seen churches of basilican dimensions and modest adobe chapels of forsaken missions, orientally lavish palaces and thatched-roof houses with mud walls. In spite of ground plans, structural elements, and decorative motifs which derive from Europe, most of these edifices have an individuality of detail and a rugged rusticity which set them apart from the architecture of the Old World and differentiate them also from buildings seen in Mexico and Central America.

12

UNKNOWN PAINTERS

THE sails of Columbus' ships had holy symbols painted on them, and banners bearing pictures of Christ, the Virgin, and the saints landed in the New World with the Conquistadores. Thus painting in the European sense appeared on the American scene with the first Spanish invaders, to run a spectacular course. To make such emblems was part of the Spanish painter's trade; Pacheco as a young man (towards the close of the sixteenth century) decorated standards of crimson damask, thirty to fifty ells in length, with the royal coat of arms and the figure of Santiago Matamoros for the voyagers to the "Indies." The earliest chroniclers of the Conquest of Mexico relate that pagan idols smashed by the Spaniards were at once replaced with an engraving or a woodcut of the "gentle figure" of the Mother of the Christian God.[94] Later, as the pacification of the colonies proceeded, paintings were needed not only to decorate churches but also as a story-telling medium for the instruction of converts.

The highly developed technique of painting in oil as practiced in sixteenth-century Europe was novel to the Indian. In certain pre-Columbian cultures mural painting was used to depict historical events and calendrical and religious symbolism. Sometimes human and animal forms were painted on pottery vessels or woven into textiles. The Maya and some of the Mexican cultures had illuminated manuscripts. But in none of these artistic manifestations was the three-dimensional approached as in contemporary Europe. The Indian, who showed such a mature sense of three-dimensionality in his sculpture and modeling, had not come upon the manner of creating the illusion of depth in painting by foreshortening and the application of shadows. For that matter neither did Chinese, Egyptian, Indian, and Persian painting use it. How strange and unnatural the chiaroscuro of a Rembrandt appeared to a Chinese connoisseur of art, newly arrived in Europe, is manifest from his remark that the old man in the portrait must have been very poor since he had soap enough to wash only half of his face. Even in Europe that ingenious combination of design and color which produces perspective was not achieved until the Renaissance.

Oil painting is the flower of luxury among the arts, and the European master painter of the sixteenth, seventeenth, and eighteenth centuries was a prince of society. One has only to call to mind Titian's luxurious studio at the edge of the Venetian lagoon, where the wits of the sophisticated city gathered and musicians performed in the background, or the philosophizing circle that surrounded El Greco, high in the hills of Toledo.

The subtleties employed in the manufacture of oil colors, the blending of pigments, the fixatives, varnishes, and other related technicalities are described at length by Cennino Cennini about 1439 and later by Pacheco and other contemporaries of famous European colorists. In Europe a highly developed trade brought in the raw materials that were used in the secret formulas of the great studios from Antwerp to Naples, from Nuremberg to Seville. Merchants specialized in dyes, oils, powders, liquids, and gums; another group handled the hair and bristles for brushes, taken from a variety of animals.

From both the inspirational and the technological points of view the situation in the New World was quite different. The typically European commerce mentioned above never developed to any extent in the colonies. Few could afford the most select of the imported materials, and the New World relied to a considerable degree on its own products. Some of these had excellent possibilities, such as the red from cochineal, the blue from indigo, and the various tones of other vegetable juices and special earth colors available here. But their suitability for oil painting was largely untried, and the choice was limited.

A firm and evenly woven canvas is essential for painting, and to augment the profit of the royal treasury—the Spanish crown held the monopoly on linen—the law required that a new canvas freshly cut from the bolt be used for each picture.[94] Cotton cloth, however, was often employed instead of the scarce and expensive imported linen, for cotton was native to many of the New World regions. The great Quito painter Miguel de Santiago (active 1655–1706) and his best-known pupil, Nicolás Javier de Gorívar, frequently resorted to it.[183] But cotton cloth, no matter how tightly woven and firmly spanned, absorbs the pigments and dulls the colors; a completely different grounding would have been necessary to preserve the top tones of the paintings. Also, cotton shrinks unevenly and soon sags. Under such conditions it was not easy for the colonial painter to develop a coloristic talent. Moreover, whether a layman or an ecclesiastic, he lacked the stimulating atmosphere and free exchange of ideas usual in European ateliers.

For such reasons colonial painting in general does not show the brilliance in color and the blending of tones achieved by European masters. And it is these shortcomings which make suspect many of the so-called Zurbaráns, Murillos, Van Dycks, and others so proudly displayed to visitors in Latin America.

At this point two trends in colonial painting which developed side by side should be differentiated—the one following European tradition as closely as possible, the other coming close to folk art.

The first always looked to the Old World, importing, copying, and imitating. In this category belong the numberless canvases (and how many have been destroyed or sold away) which show positive influence of leading European painters, as well as of lesser artists who were fashionable in their time. It should be kept in mind that in Europe certain favorite poses of a figure or of a group created by some master were copied again and again without any feeling of a breach of artistic integrity. Many painters kept sketches of their successful themes, which were repeated on order by their studios at the scale required, with as many touches and changes by the master's hand as came within the contracted price—often including a portrait of the "donor" who ordered it. These practices held among painters in the New World as well as the Old. But for the former few of the great originals were accessible; second-rate productions and, as we shall see, especially reproductions served as models.

Despite the many handicaps, some colonial painters rose to eminence. The Echave family in sixteenth- and seventeenth-century Mexico furnished three distinguished painters, and members of the Juárez and Rodríguez families, among others, attained wide recognition somewhat later. In Colombia, Gaspar de Figueroa and Gregorio Vásquez Ceballos became famous; in Ecuador the aforementioned Miguel de Santiago and Nicolás Javier de Gorívar, as well as Manuel Samaniego y Jaramillo. Engaging paintings from Peru by Diego Quispe

Ttito and from Bolivia by Melchor Pérez Holguín will be shown in this chapter.

The better-known names in colonial painting have by now received some attention from scholars and connoisseurs. Monographs have appeared on some, and others have been treated more or less intensively in general studies. But all too often their work has suffered from a comparison with European art. It is a product of unparalleled circumstances and should be evaluated as such on its own merit—which is considerable.

The second trend found in colonial Latin America is among those painters—generally mestizo or Indian—who knew no other land than that of their birth and had little Old World tradition in their background. Though in some cases they may have learned their craft from artists with European traditions, the examples set before them from a remote and unrelated world brought forth a different response. The work of the unknown—and frequently anonymous—painter mirrors a naïve soul, contending with handicaps both technical and compositional. Nevertheless his creation is illumined by a spirit as compelling as an earthy folk tale. Indeed the story-telling quality in such painting is as unique as the psychological background which produced it.

Folk art throve in many European countries, especially before mid-nineteenth century; numerous articles, from furniture and household utensils to wagon ornaments, received the characteristic decoration. The United States, too, had its "primitives" and unknown if not completely anonymous artists—frequently itinerant—who painted portraits, family groups, and landscapes or carved ornaments and ship figureheads to order.

"Primitive" art and folk art tend to be non-realistic, for they deal with what the artist feels and knows rather than with what he sees. Thus the forms, since they are not studied from life, tend to abstraction and conventionalization; the backbone of the work is its design, not its realism.[63] Moreover, even when the intention is to produce a realistic piece,

through technical limitations the result may be conventionalized or unconsciously expressionistic. In folk art the impression of three-dimensionality often is attained by placing different scenes one above another, as in the paintings of pre-Renaissance Europe; shadows appear only occasionally and lack subtlety and effect, recalling the Italian masters of the Trecento.

Painting in the European sense made its entrance into the New World as an adjunct of the new faith, and in many of its aspects it is closer to early Christian art than to contemporary European Baroque art, even though it makes use of the latter's sophisticated iconography and mannerisms. Frequently the unknown colonial artist seems to have been drawn to the transcendental and mystical aspects of his religion. As in Byzantine art, personal characteristics are submerged—resolved, as a chord in music—in the expression of the general devotional attitude. And the subject is repeated over and over again with little variation because the prescribed representation of the theme was the primary objective.

The pronounced Byzantine air in certain regional paintings may be traceable to more direct influences. With the fall of Constantinople and the Mohammedan invasion of the Roman Empire in the east (including the Greek Islands), artists, philosophers and writers, along with merchants, bankers, and professionals, were driven into Western Europe. They brought with them their own culture and provided a great stimulus to intellectual life there. With this new impetus, the Italo-Byzantine school of painting persisted into the late seventeenth century in Venice, centering in the Scuola dei Greci. A conservative taste characterized leading economic and political classes even there where life was pulsing faster than anywhere else. It is recorded that when Titian was at his zenith the patricians of Venice still showed a preference for panels by Domenico Veneziano and the elder Bellini.

Conservatism in Spain was especially complex. At the time of the Conquest, Spanish churches, convents, and castles were still full of Byzantine and late Gothic art. Greek refugees in their exodus reached even the hills of Toledo, and some of them formed a circle about El Greco. It will never be known how many panels of the early Spanish and Flemish schools came over to the New World in the first hundred years to fructify the imagination of local artists. Also, the time lag was accentuated in certain regions there; as late as the eighteenth century some paintings in Spanish America were executed in what might be termed a Byzantoid manner.

Besides favoring the rather hieratic figures of saints and holy personages, the indigenous painter in Spanish America turned his talent to group scenes and often depicted various actions on the same canvas, each in a different section. Here perhaps he approached most closely contemporary European models, especially the genre scenes of the Low Countries. Such paintings, through their special handling of perspective, their characteristically proportioned figures, and above all through their touching naïveté and delightful irrelevancies, form a group by themselves, best called "religious genre."

Among the great influences which shaped the iconography of painting in the New World were imported prints and illustrations from books. These woodcuts and engravings were by no means exclusively of Spanish origin; in fact many of them came from Flanders.

One of the early Flemish printers to bring out books in Spanish was Nuyts Van Meere,[15] better known as Martin Nucio, who was active in the first half of the sixteenth century. His workshop in Antwerp was taken over by Guillermo Simon and then came into the hands of Christophe Plantin (1514–1589). Plantin undertook an ambitious enterprise: the publication, in five languages, of the *Biblia Polyglotta*, which was intended to clarify the translations and interpretations of Holy Scripture. Despite opposition by some of the clergy, he

was supported in the project by Philip II of Spain, who sent to him a learned Benedictine to superintend the work. The publisher earned little immediate profit from this undertaking (1567–1572), but he later received the privilege of printing all the liturgical books for the realm of Philip II, an empire upon which the sun never set. Philip was then enjoying a monopoly granted by Pope Pius V, giving him the right to print and distribute the religious books for Spain and her colonies, and he made Plantin his chief printer—*prototypographus regius*.

Plantin's business soon grew very large; of twenty presses manned by seventy-three workmen, fifteen were run exclusively for the Spanish trade, domestic and colonial. The first parcels of his books left Antwerp late in 1571, and an order was agreed upon for 6,000 breviaries, 6,000 diurnals, and 4,000 missals quarterly.[18] Besides this contract, he brought out, in 1576, the monumental opus of Clusius Carolus, the first basic work on the flora of Spain and Portugal, illustrated with many woodcuts. He even published music.

His trade with Spain was organized through the Jeronymite order of San Lorenzo in the Escorial, which held the privileges of sales and distribution of Plantin publications and sold them exclusively in their Madrid and Seville shops. By 1581 two of Plantin's associates had established in the Spanish university town of Salamanca a branch of the firm, which handled—besides religious subjects—classics and books on history, geography, and science.

After Plantin's death his son-in-law Joannes Moretus took over the workshop. He was succeeded by Baltasar Moretus (born 1605), who devoted himself to keeping up the vast enterprise established by his forebears. In 1680 Baltasar Moretus III made a trip to Madrid to confer with his clients and agents, the Jeronymite friars, because their payments had been falling into arrears. There he discovered that the monks had been ordering religious books from Lyons, France, copying his firm's products and distributing them under the imprint of the Plantin press. Finally an agreement was reached which upheld the rights of the Antwerp publisher and compensated him in part for his losses. In 1692 he was made a nobleman by Charles II of Spain, with the privilege of continuing as a printer.

The Plantin press export to Spain included eleven types of breviaries, missals in three sizes, Books of the Hours in four sizes, hymnals, and other religious works in various editions. This trade flourished for nearly two hundred and fifty years; by mid-seventeenth century it had taken on such dimensions that the press printed hardly anything else. Toward the second half of the eighteenth century, however, it began to slacken. Yet in 1757 in a single month 1,820 books were exported to Spain, and the invoices of 1785–1786 show that 260-odd volumes per month were still being shipped there. In 1804 direct trade with Spain ceased; but as late as 1844 Spanish America received a number of religious works directly from the Plantin press.

One of the great attractions of all these books was that they were copiously illustrated. The list of artists and master engravers who worked for this press and others in Antwerp is well-nigh endless. To mention only a few from the sixteenth century, there were Pieter van der Borcht, Martin de Vos, Philip Galle, and the Wierix brothers. Rubens' studio collaborated closely with the Plantin firm when Baltasar Moretus I was its head. Among the later artists were Jan Collaert, Abraham van Diepenbeek, Richard Collin, and, in the eighteenth century, Richard van Orley and Cornelis Joannes d'Heur.[11]

One chapter from the important but little-known story of the adventures of Flemish engravings in the Spanish Empire deserves recounting. Ignatius Recalde Loyola, founder of the Jesuit order, planned a book presenting episodes from the lives of the Evangelists with pictures, an explanatory text, and pious meditations. The Jesuits requested Plantin to recommend engravers to illustrate the work. In a letter[5] dated November 5, 1585, Plantin relates his unsuccessful attempts, naming several craftsmen who were either unwilling, or under contract elsewhere, or out of the city. He mentions, however, that the Wierix brothers were excellent engravers and available but were reprehensible characters, living in debauchery. After years of negotiations from Rome to Antwerp and back across Europe, the Jesuits finally solicited Anton, Hieronymus, and Jan Wierix, together with several other craftsmen, to design and execute the plates. The book, *Evangelicae Historia Imagines,* appeared in 1593.

The Wierix brothers—also spelled Wierx and Wiericx—were Flemish designers and engravers, active in Antwerp between 1552 and 1615. Their output totaled several thousand engravings; 2,055 separate sheets from their hands are named in one catalogue. They engraved paintings of the Flemish and Italian schools, including many of the works of Martin de Vos (1536–1603), and also designed plates of their own. In addition they were much sought after for book planning. Their consummate skill and immense productivity were responsible in part for the copperplate supplanting the woodcut.[5]

It is apparent in the correspondence that Plantin was reluctant to undertake the project —particularly under Jesuit surveillance—because of the unsavory reputation of the Wierix brothers. This reluctance is all the more understandable when it is known that Plantin himself was once under the suspicion of heresy. It is now established that though outwardly a faithful son he was till his death a member of a mystic sect banned by the Roman church; it has also been proved that the Plantin press published, without the printer's name, books and pamphlets which never would have received the imprimatur of the religious authorities.

There were many ways for such nonconformist literature to reach both Spain and her colonies. Antonio Pérez, the rich and powerful secretary of Philip II, became head of the Calvinist Consistory in Antwerp in 1566 and had 30,000 copies of Calvin's *Institutes of the*

Christian Religion smuggled in barrels into Spain. Other Protestant tracts followed.[64]

The thousands of prints that were issued—in black and white or carefully illuminated by hand, reproducing the favorite paintings of the time or presenting original "inventions"—soon became an inexpensive substitute for paintings and were favorite collectors' items. Around 1650 the painting and engraving studios in Antwerp outnumbered the bakeries and meat shops about 300 to 169 and 78 respectively.[7] A Flemish connoisseur traveling in Spain in the seventeenth century recognized with surprise that engravings from his homeland had been used as prototypes for a number of Spanish religious paintings.[5]

A wealthy merchant house of the mid-seventeenth century and early eighteenth in Antwerp, the Forchoudt family, arranged for the shipment of many consignments of engravings, as well as oil paintings, fine furniture, tapestries, and maps, all over Europe. Each country had its preference—Spain for religious subjects, Portugal for pagan and secular scenes, and the Germanic countries for landscapes and battle scenes. Orders from the branch of this firm in Cadiz, then the main port of export to the New World, include wool, hides, lace, brandy, and leather tooled in gold; only occasionally is there mention of art works, but in 1671–1672 two hundred pictures are listed as shipped to the Spanish colonies.[6]

In the rapidly expanding world of that era, maps had a great and sustained vogue. Two of the most famous cartographers of all time were the Flemings Gerard Mercator and Abraham Ortel or Ortels—better known as Ortelius—a good friend of Christophe Plantin. When Ortelius published his magnificent *Theatrum Orbis Terrarum* (1570), the first geographical atlas in the modern sense of the word, the Low Countries were seething with revolt. He had been cautioned by a Lisbon friend as to the type of material that could enter Spain: there should be no pictures that might be construed as obscene, and special care should be taken that the coat of arms of some family in

disfavor should not appear on any of his maps.

On maps, as on the title page of a book, the text was at first placed within a standardized cartouche, which somewhat later came to be enclosed by a cord, an emblem often used to frame the coat of arms of the pope or some member of a royal family. Gradually the cartouche became increasingly elaborate, with heavy strapwork and rolled edges composed into intricate patterns. Such strapwork was taken over by the engravers, who invented all kinds of variations on it. Sphinxes, sirens, cherubs, and busts that resolved into leafy swirls began to adorn the cartouches and even the empty spaces on maps; figures dressed in contemporary costume were drawn so accurately that today they serve as sources of information.[2]

Of this vast output of publications a percentage certainly reached the New World. Besides the Spanish merchant navy, privileged ships of the English, Dutch, French, and other nations brought into the colonies at least tokens of the artistic and intellectual life of Europe. Secular literature came in, as well as illustrated Bibles, catechisms, Books of the Hours, calendars, and lives of the saints. There were treatises on architecture—such as works by Vitruvius and Serlio and later Palladio and Piranesi—books on perspective and stage design, on hydraulics and gardens, descriptions of voyages, emblem books, albums of samples with floral and geometrical decorations, designs for jewelers, and the like. Some were ordered and others arrived in the private libraries of travelers, from the entourage of the viceroy down to the nameless friar.

The colonies themselves were full of enterprise in publishing. Pedro de Gante (1480?–1572), Flemish-born Franciscan lay brother, who was among the first missionaries to reach Mexico, wrote a little catechism in the Nahuatl tongue for the Aztecs, which was brought out in Antwerp in 1528. The first book was printed in Mexico in 1539 by Juan Cronberger, a German from the Holy Roman Empire. Another printer, Antonio Ricardo, a native of Turin, Italy, was working in Mexico in 1577; three years later he appeared in Lima, and in 1584 he obtained royal permission to establish a press there.[57] In 1600 Santo Domingo had a press; in 1607, Cuba; three years later, Bolivia; and in 1660, Guatemala. By the last third of the seventeenth century a significant number of locally produced prints, especially woodcuts, were in circulation, presenting in a popular vein holy figures and events. However, no book treating American subjects, whether published in Spain or the New World, could circulate in the colonies until approved by the Council of the Indies.[66] This explains in part various manuscripts still lying forgotten in library corners both in Europe and Latin America.

The field of printing also includes the manufacture of playing cards. It is known that cards brought in by the Spanish soldiers excited the interest of the Aztecs. By the time of the Conquest many designs were in use in Europe and some card games had been turned to didactic and instructive purposes. In 1572 the viceroy in New Spain forbade the domestic printing of playing cards in order to protect the royal monopoly on imported items. A decade later, however, nine thousand packs were being produced yearly in Mexico and the local cards were preferred to those engraved in Spain.[94]

As has been pointed out, the colonial painter did not have the opportunity of his European contemporary to enrich his knowledge and craftsmanship through travel. Generally he sat in some isolated town on a high plateau or in a mountain valley and had to rely for instruction and inspiration on what he could find there. The Italian painter Mateo Pérez de Alesio, a resident of Lima, signed a promissory note in 1587 to pay the librarian of the main church at Seville 520 ducats for a large album of drawings and one containing "all the prints" of Dürer and other masters.[27] In Quito an album of Flemish and Dutch engravings is still extant which once belonged to the mestizo painter Miguel de Santiago.[183] A contemporary

traveler remarked on the fact that this artist had never left his native city, though his paintings were widely admired and some were sent as far as Rome. One instance of the far-reaching influence of engravings on colonial painting was shown in Chapter 4 in connection with a Wierix print; others will be seen in this chapter. Even in the Far East there is evidence of Wierix prints, brought in by the missionaries, influencing painting and sculpture.[14] The leaf-sprite and mermaid—favorites of folk art in many regions of Spanish America—may have entered the New World on maps and the title pages of books, where they are commonly found.

The work of the colonial painter is permeated with devotion, intensity, and a folkish stylization—and nearly always with a disarming naïveté. Often a peculiar inward-turned spirituality is perceptible, which is more akin to the spirit of the Christian catacombs than to that of the brocade-hung studio of a Velázquez in the royal palace at Madrid.

A detail of the Codex Monteleone (Pl. 130, fig. b) presents one of the earliest renditions of the Virgin and Child by an Indian. For a time after the Conquest such tribute rolls, with their pre-Columbian picture writing, were made use of by the Spaniards, who accepted temporarily certain devices from the pagan past so as not to disturb too much the rhythm of native life. It is clear that the Indian scribe was adept in rendering his ancestral ideographs. He also simplified the representation of the Holy Mother and Child to a remarkable degree. Executed on cloth and with local paints—not in oil technique—the picture has all the fundamentals of the conventional representation, but cut to the bone. Probably the most novel details for the Indian artist were the portrayal of a head *en face*—the pre-Columbian painter invariably depicted it in profile—and the delineation of the relationship of Child to mother in the prescribed pose.

In a canvas of the same subject in the Behrens collection (*fig. c*), in Mexico City, the composition is outlined with a thin brush stroke and more detail is shown on the larger surface, but linear economy and coloristic restraint are again evident. The Baby has a crucifix in his hands, and the position of his head is almost the same as in the other example. The Virgin's left arm, as she holds him, subtly closes the circle. Her right hand holds a flower with a daintiness and an emphasis amazingly well expressed. This painting is reputed to have come from around Toluca and to date from the second half of the eighteenth century.

A panel in the Orihuela collection (*fig. a*), in Urubamba, near Cuzco, Peru, belongs spiritually and pictorially to the two preceding depictions; here, however, greater depth is achieved and there is more color. More formalizing is to be seen in the handling of the neckline and head covering, picked out with a gold stitch. This painting has about it something of certain Catalan panels. Though in spirit it suggests the early Christian world, it may date as late as the second half of the eighteenth century—when Europe was cajoling Tiepolo, Watteau, and Gainsborough. All of these paintings in their simplification of line and color show a definite relationship to the style of the *santos* panels of our Southwest which has survived into the present century.

The Virgin of Carmen from Mexico (*fig. d*) is seated in a chair, her feet on a cushion, and the curtain arrangement above suggests a niche. Both mother and Child hold the Carmelite scapulary in their hands. On the two columns at the sides stand two saints, with decorative ribbons of golden text emanating from them. In the lower right-hand corner, completely outside the rich atmosphere of the center, is painted a small figure in praying pose, perhaps the donor. Despite the lavish brocade dress of the Virgin and the theatrical setting, she is basically similar to the others illustrated here, notably in the position of the head, the small stylized mouth, the drawing of the hands, the veil, and the calligraphic line of nose and eyebrow.

Miraculous power was attributed to some of the paintings in the colonies, and the churches where they hung became the goal of masses of pilgrims. One such canvas is that of the Virgin of Guadalupe, which occupies a chapel of its own in the cathedral of Sucre, Bolivia (*Pl. 131, fig. a*). The Virgin of Guadalupe was introduced into the New World when in 1493 Columbus named an island in the West Indies after the Santa María de Guadalupe in Estremadura, Spain. In 1531 she is reported to have made a miraculous appearance near the Mexican capital. The name Guadalupe was used to designate several towns and shrines in Spanish America.

The Sucre canvas was painted by the friar Diego de Ocaña about 1601.[221] It can be locked behind a door, an understandable precaution in view of the valuable gifts of the faithful hung upon it. Hieratic in expression to begin with, it has taken on the appearance of an icon through its covering of jewels; pearls outline the pattern in the cloak, and precious and semiprecious stones fill the spaces in between. An inventory made in 1784 enumerates her valuables, including several elaborate chatelaine watches, pinned to the front of her gown, and miniature animals fashioned of irregular pearls and other precious stones. Note the diamond swallows flying toward her crown and the bird at the right carrying a pearl (*fig. b*). Her scepter alone presents a veritable display of jewelry, and her crown, affixed through a slit in the canvas and sewed on at the back, has a base of silver, completely covered with pearls and stones. The faithful, it is said, presented her with so much jewelry that the friars had to rule that the pieces be given them to attach. *Milagros*, votive offerings shaped like human heads, arms, and legs, hang all over the painting.

Like the Guadalupe of Mexico, this figure was so popular that it was reproduced again and again, growing more formalized the more it was repeated. One version of it, a statue-painting (*fig. c*), was discovered by this author in the village church of Santa Barbara at Ilave, Peru. The Virgin stands on a base carried by two angels, and two others hold back the folds of a curtain which might have been copied from some altar. The outlines of the Child blend into the geometrically developed decoration of her robe; the pearl rectangles seen on the Sucre painting are recognizable here. A special light falls from above, and the edges of the curtain are outlined with staccato white dots in an amazing stylization, Byzantoid in its effect.

In 1487 the city of Malaga, in Spain, was retaken from the Moors after a protracted siege by the troops of Ferdinand and Isabella, and that battle is celebrated in the figure of Our Lady of the Victory of Malaga. A painting of this subject from Cuzco (*fig. d*), now in the Freyer collection, at Denver, Colorado, shows the Virgin standing in a gilded niche. Exquisite tooling in gold, a characteristic of the Cuzco circle, covers her robe and crown in intricate and varied patterns. The new moon, small and dark, has become part of her costume. Two small angel musicians are placed at the spring of the arch. Carefully painted and enamel-like, the flesh tones of all the faces stand out of the surrounding decoration.

The Sanctuary of Quinche, situated in a smiling, luxuriant valley not far north of the Ecuadorian capital, is one of the pilgrim places most frequented by the country's Indians. The statue of the Virgin of Quinche, venerated there, is carried out on special holidays and possesses a complete travel wardrobe, including a raincoat and an umbrella to protect her in inclement weather. The statue-painting of her (*fig. e*) represents her as she is borne forth on the shoulders of lay brothers. No light shines down from above or beyond her, nor are angel figures present, indicating that a more or less realistic depiction of the statue was intended. Perspective is meticulously expressed, especially in the canopy. Both crowns are emphasized, which is not the case in the other representations on this plate. Note the face on the new moon.

A much more romantic setting surrounds the Virgin of the Rosary (*fig. f*), also from Ecuador and now in the village church of Lican, near Riobamba. She is painted as standing on a processional base and in a niche, which is decorated in an illusionistic manner with angels, vases, and garlands. Little gold is used on the gown, but all the more delicate is the flowered pattern of the textile.

In Spanish South America three distinct centers of painting existed in colonial times, usually designated as the "schools" of Cuzco, in Peru, of Quito, in Ecuador, and of Potosí, in Bolivia. "Circle" might be a better term, for the influence that emanated from these three centers spread out in an ever-widening circle, like the ripples made on a pond when a stone is dropped into the water.

The three paintings next illustrated (*Pl. 132*) —one from each of these circles—show three different interpretations of the crowned and seated Virgin holding the Christ Child on her arm. In the first (*fig. a*), the Virgin of Belén, or Bethlehem, from Cuzco, the colors are almost entirely red and gold except for the flesh tones. Gold tooling is evenly applied against the background in varied but well-harmonized patterns. The stalk of lilies is naturalistic, but the figure of the Child is stylized and blended into the composition. The round halo, elaborately tooled, has a three-dimensional effect and resembles that of the Virgin of Malaga just seen. This Virgin has an enigmatic dignity, Byzantoid in her hieratic aloofness—a truly royal personality.

From the Potosí circle comes the Virgin of Carmen (*fig. b*), a canvas stretched on an oval panel of wood. Patroness of the Carmelites, she holds in her right hand a scapulary bearing their emblem, which is also embroidered on the front of her gown. The Child is portrayed with one hand on the globe and in the other a red rose. Both faces have the whiteness of a doll and a star-eyed expression. However, the loving care lavished on details—the ornamented veil, the pearls and earrings, and the flowery robes (the stars traditionally scattered over the Virgin's cloak are here transferred to her dress)—will bring this painting closer than the others to many hearts, for through its unspoiled and charming naïveté it speaks the most direct language. It should be mentioned that the Aymara Indians have a special fondness for ear-bobs, a sign of prosperity among them even today.

Many small colonial paintings, especially those of the Quito and Potosí circles, were painted on metal plates and wood panels, as well as on canvas, and were executed not on an easel but lying at an angle on a table, like a manuscript for illumination. The result is a flat and "bookish" representation.

In the circle around Quito, a district unsurpassed in its sculpture, the style of painting was perhaps the most literal of the three—it adhered more strictly to the letter of the iconographical formula; even emotion was filtered through this literalism. The Virgin of the Rosary (fig. c) comes from the church of Santa Rosa in Riobamba, Ecuador. The gold tooling in this painting differs markedly from that in the Cuzco example. The arrangement of the cloak, especially at the right, suggests a statue, and the crescent moon with a human face has already been encountered in the picture of the Virgin of Quinche.

Among the three compositions on this plate the Quito painting reveals most clearly its relationship to the printed page. The one from Potosí possesses the playfulness and loving detail of a fairy-tale illustration, while that from Cuzco has spiritual impact and the sweep of monumentality. Despite the fact that Cuzco and Quito were twin capitals of the Inca Empire—connected by a three-day runner service, increased to eight days in the colonial epoch—the two cities retained their individuality.

The Jesuits favored the Immaculate Conception surrounded by attributes of the rosary, a representation which sometimes is called [9] the "predestination of Mary." In the sixteenth and seventeenth centuries, particularly in Spain, paintings of her followed the prescribed iconography strictly; engravings and woodcuts made after famous canvases were carried far and wide. An example is the Immaculate Conception by Baltasar de Echave Ibía (Pl. 133, fig. a). A son of the famous colorist Baltasar de Echave Orio, young Echave (c. 1582–1650) had the advantages of living at the viceregal seat. The canvas shown here, signed "Echave ft. ano 1620," shows clarity of arrangement and considerable success in representing the three-dimensional. Though it is somewhat didactic in composition, it makes a sympathetic contact with the onlooker.

Iconographically the representation is the most complete of those on this plate: the Virgin is "fair as the moon, clear as the sun" (Song of Solomon, 6:10); the little angels have intelligible symbols of the rosary in their hands— the ladder to Heaven, the mirror without flaw, and the gate of Heaven. The landscape is carefully delineated according to tradition, including the walled city, the tower of David, the well of living water, and the lily. The Virgin stands in a praying pose looking upward. A rosy orange radiance surrounds her. Rays emanate from her figure, and the Holy Ghost is poised above her head. At her feet is a new moon with its points turned downward, following Pacheco's preference (discussed in Chapter 9) though not the solid body which he advocated; between its horns is placed that iconographically problematic figure, the mermaid. Care is given to the detailing of the Virgin's heavy robe, wind-blown to reveal the lining. The colors are brilliant and fresh, and the plastic quality is remarkable.

At first glance the anonymous painting from a private collection near Cuzco (fig. b) appears not too different from the Echave beside it; its iconographical details, however, are blurred. It is not clear whether Mary stands or sits; her hands clasp a book, and she looks out of the canvas, not upward; as for the angels, it would seem that the artist was more concerned with grouping them into a decorative garland than with a display of symbols. In the lower center is pictured a pedestal with handles, such as the processional bases for statues are wont to have —indeed, the figure has a certain rotundity which suggests that a statue served as model. It has been remarked that the pedestal might represent a coffin, thus involving the Assumption of Mary with her glorification.

Gold tooling played a prominent role in South America, where often it was an integral part of the composition, while in Mexico it was sometimes used only to touch up the decoration and sometimes omitted.

Another Cuzco painting (*fig. d*) shows the Virgin as a young girl, seated, her hands outstretched. The stars in her halo are accented. Two angels floating on high hold her crown, and little angels without symbols form a ring around her. In this picture there is more economy of color, and the tooling as well as the large spreading pattern in the gown is quite different.

Mary with a Distaff (*fig. c*), also from Cuzco, gives the impression of a dressed-up child. Her figure fills the entire canvas as she sits in a straight-backed chair, late seventeenth century in style. Under one arm she holds a distaff, and with her right hand she twists the thread, weighted with a spindle whorl. This process of spinning by hand can be observed today as Indian women prepare their wool while they walk to or from market. The features here are Indian, especially the eyes, and the jeweled headband holding the lock on the forehead is an Indian touch. She has been interpreted as an Inca princess in her finery, and it has been noted that the first Inca empress, "Daughter of the Sun," was supposed to have brought the art of weaving to her people.[189] However, it should also be mentioned that Italian and Spanish painters selected the child Mary performing various household tasks as a subject, and many Flemish books depicted the youth of the Virgin. The painting here reproduced is very close to a canvas by the Spanish artist Juan de las Roelas (1559–1625), even to the flowered robe and the large brooch on the breast. But through the new interpretation the whole impression is changed.

Not angels but flowers surround this figure. Breughel and Rubens especially popularized the fashion in Europe of framing a portrait with a colorful garland; often special painters were called in for this part of the work. It is possible that in the colonies, too, specialists supplied the flowery frame just as they applied the gold tooling. Sometimes it is so loosely and carelessly executed that it covers details of the main subject.

Even as late as the eighteenth century, Spanish and Portuguese painters seldom represented the human body in the nude, and this conservatism was even more pronounced in the colonies. Nevertheless the colonial painter often found a way to transmit a sense of physical beauty. A large canvas of the Inmaculada (*Pl. 134, fig. a*), in the cathedral of Cuzco, shows a young woman dressed in an elaborate velvet costume. The conical contour of the figure holds the eye from the first. No attempt was made to present the iconographically traditional three mystic garments in three colors. Bodice, skirt, and cape are all of the same material, worked in amber on a gold background. The collar and cuffs are a creamy shade, and even the veil over the hair, studded with large stars, is kept in a mellow tone. The costume is in the style of about 1660–1670 in Spain, but there the line of the bodice was pointed. Considerable plasticity is given the bows on breast and sleeves. The eyes in the pale face are downcast but nevertheless have an intense gaze, and the small but alive mouth is lightly closed. Her hands, with their heavy rings, are in a praying gesture. No halo is visible; did she not wear the crown usually associated with Mary Queen of Heaven, she might be, in her gala costume, a young noblewoman attending Mass—and not without accelerating the heart beat of many present at the service.

Though the creoles of Cuzco deprecatingly dismiss this canvas as the work of some mestizo whose name is not worth searching for, the portrayal has become a favorite of the Indians. The large picture hangs high on one of the columns on the left side of the nave amid more spectacular objects, and the visitor might even pass it by without noticing it. But the Indians call her *Mamacita*, dear little mother, and come in to kneel before her on the bare stone blocks of the floor. Occasionally one of them places a burning candle or flowers at the foot of the column, and the next day another lump of cold wax or handful of wilted petals remains to annoy those who know how to offer their oblations with propriety. This painting of *Mamacita*, intensely human but with a certain aloofness, has a psychological relationship to a portrait of a Mexican nun (*see Pl. 150*).

Melchor Pérez de Holguín, a son of a prominent Potosí family and a Bolivian painter of considerable individuality, is reputed to have studied with Diego Quispe Ttito, a Cuzco Indian, but the disparity between the dates of these two artists makes this claim highly improbable. It is also said of him that he later went to Spain and became a pupil of Murillo, but, to date, his association with the Spanish master has not been documented. Another report, quite possible, describes him as an albino, whose eyes were so badly affected by the brilliant light of high altitudes that he worked only at night. Neither the year of his birth nor that of his return from Spain is known, but this author has seen canvases by him dated between 1705 and 1712. The latter year appears with his signature in the lower left of his Rest on the Flight to Egypt (*fig. b*), now in the Cuenca collection at La Paz, Bolivia.

In this painting Mary, dressed like a lady for travel in the fashion of the early eighteenth century, is washing out clothes, while St. Joseph and a cherub are wringing them; one small article has already been hung up to dry. The Baby Jesus lies sleeping under a blanket, with angels at his head and feet, one of them admonishing silence and the other moving off with a pottery jug in his hand. A romantic landscape fills the background. Holguín's alleged apprenticeship to Murillo is not corroborated by this picture. Any European influences that may be found in it are rather in the anecdotal spirit of the Italian Baroque or the Flemish genre. This work by Holguín proves how strong the popular vein was in Spanish America; whatever he may have learned while abroad was absorbed by and blended into the powerful folkloristic atmosphere here. In its well-arranged composition, its lively hues, and the underlying charm of its unpretentious story-telling, this painting is a fascinating example of Andean Rococo.

No region in the Spanish colonies in South America was more densely populated by virile Indians articulate in the arts than was the area around Cuzco. During the Conquest the once cheerful and friendly folk here turned into grim fighters, but when peace returned, in general they settled down to a life that in many ways was not too different from that of pre-Columbian times. The unknown painter of upper Peru gave expression to the religious image which his folk formed in their imagination. In all probability he had never been out of his own district, where shamans still practiced magic with ritualistic objects of the pre-Columbian religion. Even the Sunday Mass was said only partly in Latin; the rest was in Quechua or Aymara.

A miraculous image of the Virgin of the Rosary is recorded in Pomata in mid-sixteenth century, made after she had twice appeared there, and the main church of the town is dedicated to her (*see Pl. 120*). The Virgin of Pomata as illustrated here (*Pl. 135, fig. a*), several versions of which survive, is in the Osma collection, near Lima. For her costume the artist drew on two very different civilizations for inspiration. Rose is the predominating color and there are touches of sky-blue in the plumes. In her right hand is a lily (or is it an Inca *kantuka?*). Her robe has a courtly elegance and is tooled so thickly that the gold stands out from the canvas. Her crown, as well as that of the Christ Child, is in the shape of a papal tiara, but they both have feathers rising from them. Feathers are also suggested by the radiating rays, which terminate in cherub heads. The spectacular headdresses still worn by the Aymaras when they impersonate legendary heroes in dance and pantomime are very similar,[202] with their flowers and long feathers shooting upward, to the two crowns on the canvas.

In this painting the pyramidal contour is again encountered. Such treatment might arise from the ambition of the artist to decorate the figure with an abundance of ornament, disregarding realistic proportions. But one also might find here an intention to make the figure as imposing as possible, even superhuman; by its sheer mass it evokes awe. Note that the painted garland does not belong in the composition and covers some of its details.

The painting of the Virgin of Merced in Cuzco (fig. b), one of the most revealing and beguiling examples of the Cuzco circle, looks like a colored fashion plate from around the end of the seventeenth century. The social and religious life of the topmost strata of Spanish and creole society in the New World was accompanied by considerable pomp and circumstance. The ladies of high officialdom were kept informed by friends in Europe of changes in fashion, and by mid-seventeenth century, when travel had become less strenuous, even they crossed to and from Europe. Also, sometimes the family of an official accompanied him on his visits in the colonies, and, as the seasons changed, the landowners with their families moved to or from their haciendas, often at some distance from their winter quarters. Thus fashion was spread. But the Baroque and Rococo costumes created for European elegance stood out here strangely, for the overwhelming majority of the people wore either the untailored garments of the Indian, little changed from pre-Columbian times, or the drab clothing prescribed for the lower classes. When the viceroy's wife in gala dress passed in her palanquin or caleche, to the simple folk she must have been close to a vision. The hats of both mother and Child indicate travel, perhaps even a pilgrimage. The Virgin is seated; the chair is visible above her left shoulder. She holds the Child on her right arm—usually it is on the other—and in her left hand she carries flowers and the Mercedarian emblem, which is also on her brooch. Note the crosses at her neck and girdle. Two bottles of flowers stand at her feet, and across the front are ranged a row of candles in an elaborate silver holder. Columns and curtains frame the scene, suggesting another statue-painting.

The Order of Mercy, whose members are known as the Mercedarians, was founded by St. Peter Nolasco and the King of Aragon in 1218 for the purpose of ransoming Christian captives in the hands of the Moors. Their white habit bears the arms of Aragon as their badge. Their patroness, the Virgin of Mercy, is a favorite figure throughout Spanish-speaking countries. She is represented with angels holding her mantle protectively above a group of kneeling figures.

In the three paintings of her here, the pope is on her right and the king on her left. Delicate gold tooling was applied to the canvas from Arequipa (Pl. 136, fig. a), in Peru, and special attention was paid to the folds in the drapery, while in the one from Quito (fig. b) the coloring is emphasized. In the third example (fig. c), also from Quito, the mantle has become a veritable canopy and two additional small angels hover about the crown. Here particularly one can sense the adherence to some printed source, frequently a characteristic of Quito paintings. The two small children kneeling close to the Virgin may represent those of the donor. This canvas, which hangs in the refectory at El Tejar, a Mercedarian retreat, is signed Francisco Albán, 1772. Albán was one of the very few artists who, even in that late period, signed and dated their paintings. He was a native of Quito, is reputed to have been an Indian, and worked especially for the Dominicans and the Mercedarians.[76]

The wood relief of La Merced (*fig. d*), also from Quito, is a small traveling piece and has doors that can be closed over it, like a triptych of earlier times but here the wings are left plain. From the multitude represented on the canvases, room was found on this carving for only two persons. Perhaps the Tejar composition influenced the carver to include two small children at the feet of the Virgin, a not too frequent addition. Above, the tympanum is given over to a figure of God the Father, iconographically not necessary in this case but much liked by the folk artist.

In the parish church at Cuautitlán, Mexico, a large colonial painting of La Merced shows a group of white men in eighteenth-century laces and silks on her right and, on her left, Indians in gala serapes and headbands. This church also contains two of the rare Martin de Vos canvases still extant in the New World.

Soon after the invention of oil painting, some painters directed their imagination to what would be called today abstract or surrealist art. It was an age in which a king might occupy himself with astronomy, or astrology, or perhaps with the invention of *perpetuum mobile*. Interest was developing in chemical and physical experimentation. Yet it was an intellectual climate, too, in which the fantastic, the grotesque, and the visionary had a great part. Holbein's *Totentanz* and Bosch's surrealistic landscapes are creations of a period in which monsters, witches, and distortions of both humans and animals played important roles. That age was interested not only in physics but also in metaphysics.

In spite of the vigilance of the Inquisition to prevent any but orthodox representations of religious subjects from reaching the colonies, artistic and literary material survives there today which does not conform to the regulations laid down by the Council of Trent. This extended church convention forbade, among other iconographical practices, the depiction of the Holy Trinity either as three identical figures or, because of its grotesque appearance, as one head with three faces. Nevertheless, both of these prohibited versions were repeated in Spanish America to the very end of the colonial period.

A Peruvian version of the latter representation (*Pl. 137, fig. d*), probably dating from late seventeenth century or the early eighteenth, shows a figure with three faces holding a geometric symbol of the Trinity. Along the edge of the triangle the text reads "Father is not Son," and toward the center, "Father is God." The figure wears churchly vestments, and the pendulum-like end of the triangle is suspended directly above a papal tiara held by two angels. In the four corners of the picture are busts of the Evangelists. Lettering along the bottom of the canvas indicates that again an illustration from a book was used as model. It is difficult to trace the beginnings of this delineation, but it appeared in 1491 as a woodcut in a Florentine edition of Dante's *Divine Comedy*, in 1506 on the title page of Lynwoodd's *Canon Law*, brought out in London, and 1524 in a Book of the Hours printed by Simon Vostre.[4]

A mural painting on a pendentive in the baptistry of San Pedro in Juli (*fig. e*), Peru, reminds one of a woodcut. Two of the Latin Fathers, Augustine and Ambrose, are depicted in a Byzantoid manner, as if enlarged from a page of some book. The flowers and strawberries in the frame are typical marginal decorations in illuminated manuscripts.

The simple Indian folk of the mountain valleys in the High Andes, accustomed to use the material at hand, sometimes painted religious pictures on animal skins that had been prepared with a chalklike sizing as base, not unlike that for a fresco. Such pictures can be found in regions as far apart as New Mexico and upper Peru. The example here (*fig. f*) shows St. John the Baptist, dressed in skins, and John the Evangelist holding a quill pen in his hand. Their features are drawn in much the same way as those of the Trinity on the same plate. The ribbon on the staff of the Baptist bears his name, though the letters are garbled to read "Johino." At the saints' feet are numerous scenes from pastoral life—weaving, spinning, milking, and grinding corn. Both saints are barefoot, as are all the other figures in the painting. The village artist who made this picture in the Peruvian Andes at the end of the colonial epoch is related through his manner to the painter of the Codex Monteleone (see Pl. 130), which dates from the very beginning of the era. Whether a Mexican or a Peruvian, each was working with a language of which he knew only the most basic words.

Metaphysical passages in the Bible also provided an outlet for the painter. The sixteenth-century Franciscan church at Tecamachalco, in the state of Puebla, Mexico, has a number of oval paintings in its choir vaults, among them the Four Horsemen of the Apocalypse (fig. a). One rider brandishes a sword, another an arquebus, and a third carries a scale. The fourth, Death, is below them, pushing the damned with a triton toward the jaws of Hell. A strong bookish atmosphere emanates from the whole series, which is dated 1562 and is the work of the Indian painter Juan Gerson. The series of paintings was copied from a Bible printed in Lyon in mid-sixteenth century, fragments of which were discovered recently in a Mexican library and were identified by this author. Certain iconographical formulas seem to have been fixed at an early date and carry over even into the work of such masters as Martin Schongauer (1453?–1491) and Dürer.

A portrayal of the tortures of the damned (fig. c), from Cuzco, presents a terrifying scene, a chained victim being gnawed by seven monsters (the seven deadly sins?). Below the picture are several lines of text, showing that it was taken from a book. But only a very small percentage of those who saw the painting could read, especially Spanish, for in the Cuzco Valley even today the common language of the Indians and many of the mestizos is Quechua. This Cuzco painting might be placed in the second half of the seventeenth century; Manuel Villavicencio, a printer of religious woodcuts in Puebla, Mexico, reproduced a somewhat similar version toward the end of the eighteenth century (see Appendix, Pl. 191, fig. g), evidence of the continued popularity of this subject.[116]

In the painting of the Carmelite martyr San Anastasio (fig. b), also from Cuzco, demons are being exorcised. This saint, a native of Cordova, Spain, was condemned to death in 853 and beheaded for publicly professing the Christian faith. Despite the gruesome details of severed head and dripping blood, the face has a warmly human expression. In the lower portion of the canvas, kept in somber tones against the brilliance of the center, two tailed demons crouch in terror; the text describes their overthrow by the saint. The coloring in this picture is unusually subtle. The radiant light encircling the saint's head accentuates the darkness around the demons and also illuminates a city in the distance; thus in the one picture are suggested the celestial, the terrestrial, and the infernal worlds.

The immense role played by prints in the diffusion of iconographical concepts and pictorial compositions in the New World has been noted repeatedly in this volume. In Europe sometimes a famous painting was reproduced as a print in the atelier of its creator, but usually it was engraved by a specialist. From late sixteenth century on, engravers were attached to one publishing house or another, which in turn had its agents in distant lands. On the next plate are shown two engravings executed by members of the Sadeler family. Jan Sadeler, born in Brussels about 1550, appears to be the first of this name to enter the recorded history of art. At the beginning of his career, while living in Antwerp, he engraved Martin de Vos's Christ Child Treading on the Serpent (1576), as well as other works of that artist. He later traveled and worked in Mainz, Frankfort, Cologne, Munich, Verona, and Venice (where he died in 1600)—a revealing list, the route of the northern artists as they moved southward and of the Italians when they traveled northward.

Raphael Sadeler made an engraving of the Vision of the Cross (*Pl. 138, fig. a*), another work by Martin de Vos, in Munich in 1614. In this print the translucent and mild colors of the Flemish master are translated into the exacting and sober medium of copperplate. Nevertheless the characteristic late Gothic atmosphere of the original is preserved.

A painted version of the same subject (*fig. b*), executed in Cuzco, is illustrated beside it. This canvas is said to bear the signature of the Indian Diego Quispe Ttito, one of whose works is dated 1631. Thus in the first half of the seventeenth century a theme by Martin de Vos reached Cuzco in the form of an engraving by Raphael Sadeler—made only a decade or so earlier—and inspired a painting by a pure-blood Indian of the Andes. The likeness is apparent at a glance. The Baby Jesus, the cross borne by six angels, the background, the house with its garden—all are identical in the two. The Virgin's pose is the same; even the fold in the garment breaks at the same point on her left shoulder. But while her hair hangs loose in the print, in the painting it is completely covered by a head cloth. The bed has acquired four large buckles, a Baroque touch.

However, in the Cuzco version not only were buckles added to the curtain and loose strands of hair put out of sight; important new elements were introduced that have a real significance—at the left the kneeling St. Joseph and at the right the youthful Baptist. By the addition of these two figures the traditional representation, iconographically correct in the engraving, is so changed that the painting is entitled *Sagrada Familia* (Holy Family). This raises the question as to whether the Indian painter understood the Latin text at the top of the engraving (omitted by him) —"*Augustissimo Crucis Trophaeo, Foelicissi-*

mae Arbori, dicatum"—which points unmistakably to the message of the original: Christ as a baby choosing the Cross instead of his mother's breast. The Cuzco painter has put on the canvas a warm earthy group scene. Except for the Christ Child, whose visionary trance is still perceptible, the whole picture takes on a dark-blooded undertone. Some time after this chapter was written, Martin S. Soria found in Quito, Ecuador, a similar painting, also closely related to the engraving, and signed by Antonio Montúfar, a painter of Guatemala who was active around mid-seventeenth century.

The engraving of the martyrdom of St. Sebastian (*fig. c*) was made after a painting by Jacopo Palma the Younger (1544–1628) by two Sadeler brothers—Egidius the drawing and Marcus the engraving. The "inventor's" name appears on the quiver in the right foreground. The martyr is shown as he is being fastened to a tree by two men. In the background are pictured two episodes from the story, and in the sky is an angel bearing the crown and palm branch of martyrdom.

This Sadeler engraving was doubtless the prototype for the anonymous oil painting in Cuzco illustrated beside it (*fig. d*). But the Sadeler work went through an intermediary transformation, for somewhere along the way the composition was reversed, a quite frequent occurrence with engravings in general. Perhaps one engraving was traced onto another plate, or perhaps the original was copied by another engraver directly onto the new plate. Another reversed version of the same theme was executed [132] in Mexico by the painter José de Ibarra (1688–1756). The unknown Cuzco artist, like Quispe Ttito, transcribed quite literally, though his figures are all brought forward, the facial expression of his saint is more *larmoyant,* and his background scenes are more pedestrian. In the oil, the trees and vegetation have taken on a lushness and the costumes a more tactile quality.

This painting strongly resembles the St. Sebastian statue being carried in a religious procession in Cuzco illustrated earlier (*see Pl. 65*), while a statue from Guatemala (*see Pl. 53*) may have been inspired by the engraving.

Santiago Matamoros, as discussed in some detail in Chapter 7, was the patron of Spanish knighthood. Each newly anointed knight of the Order of Santiago received a parchment decorated in polychrome miniature technique, his *carta ejecutoria de hidalguía*, which bore the figure of the saint. The scene on one such patent of nobility (*Pl. 139, fig. a*), granted in 1610 to Gaspar Guerta de Cañamal of Seville by Philip III, is somewhat condensed within its wide frame. The Spanish lances are visible beyond the saint's white charger; to the right are the fleeing Moors, and in the foreground is a group of fallen heathen. These parchments, proudly displayed by their owners, must have been a source of inspiration for the regional artist in Spanish America. Even the decoration on the frame provided ideas for various motifs —note the leaf-sprites, favorites in the colonies.

A large mural in the nave of the village church at Checacupe, Peru, presents the same subject in an arrangement more or less identical (*fig. b*). The routed Moors occupy about the same proportion of the available space; but here because of the rectangular shape and the larger area Santiago has more breathing space, more Moors were included, and the Spanish soldiery behind the saint received more detail. A bit of empty surface in the background is filled with a lone rider, placed against a little landscape with houses; in a cloud in the sky is another miniature, showing Christ holding the cross and at his feet the Virgin. The frame is painted in the local tradition of fine dadoes, and the beam ends above show how harmonious was once the decoration in such a village church (*see also Pl. 111*).

The three canvases on this plate (*figs. c, d, f*) come from Mexico, Quito, and Cuzco, respectively. They reveal characteristics of these three circles of painting; in size they range from 64 inches by 50½ (on the right) to 36 inches by 24 (on the left). The Quito example (*fig. d*) was taken directly from a missal

printed in 1737 for the Spanish trade by the Plantin press in Antwerp (*fig. e*). A copy of this book is in the Museum of Religious Art in Mexico City. Its title page carries a Latin text to the effect that it is the proper holy missal of Spain in general use in that country and carries the apostolic concessions by four popes; it was printed in the "*architypographia Plantiniana*, M.D.CC. XXXVII." From the representation of the saint in profile, with all his paraphernalia—including his shell symbols on the saddle blanket—to the placement of the two fortresses in the background and the array of the soldiery in the two camps, the Quito painting is a faithful copy of the Flemish page. The regional artist added one detail—the angel in the sky pointing his lance toward the enemy and sounding the victorious charge. The repeated use of a popular representation through decades is proven by other missals from the Plantin press. One published in 1693 has a picture of Santiago on the appendix leaf. Another Santiago, with slight variations, engraved by Louis Fruytiers in 1756 after a drawing by Cornelis J. d'Heur, appears [11] on the title page of a missal issued in 1761 (*see Appendix, Pl. 191, fig. i*).

The Santiago from a Peruvian collection (*fig. f*) is said to be in the image of Philip IV, but it is the costume of the epoch that it reproduced rather than the king's likeness, familiar through portraits by his favorite painter, Velázquez. In the liveliness of its color this painting is the best among the colonial examples illustrated here, and the tooling, so thick that it stands out from the canvas, is exquisite. The three Moors on the ground, unmistakably identified by the double crescents on their turbans, are all alive and looking up at the rider with admiration. In certain paintings of the Cuzco circle the saint is represented as killing Indians, recognizable as such from their patterned Inca ponchos and headbands.

In some ways the Mexican picture (*fig. c*) is the crudest. Both hands of the saint are occupied—the right with his swinging sword and the left with a standard—a difficult feat for a rider. The armor is picked out by gold tooling. In the lower right the words *Sr. Sn Tiago* (Señor Santiago) label for the country-folk their favorite hero.

The horses in every instance have the unnatural posture of the animal trained in the Spanish riding school, as seen in the paintings of Velázquez, Van Dyck, and others.

In European art this aspect of James the Apostle, as slayer of Moors, occurs chiefly in Spain, and even there it is rare among the works of great masters from the seventeenth century on.[30] However, the militant figures of St. George and the Archangel Michael as riders—the latter on a winged steed—appear frequently in Byzantine painting and in other countries into the eighteenth century.

One archangel as the subject of a painting also was rare in Western Europe; some notable exceptions are representations by Guido Reni and Zurbarán and that by Martin de Vos at Cuautitlán, Mexico. In this case, too, the colonial mentality established its own pictorial preferences; statues and paintings are common throughout Spanish America in which an archangel, usually St. Michael, is the principal actor if not the only one.

Both pictures of him shown here come from Peru. The first (*Pl. 140, fig. a*) presents him among clouds, brandishing a flaming sword with a wavy blade as he subdues the Devil. The composition has immense swing. The centrifugal whirl beginning with the downsweeping weapon is intensified by the flying cloak and the heavenly radiation behind him. The textures are well differentiated, and the gold tooling emphasizing the figure of the archangel is varied and carefully done.

In the depiction at Zepita (*fig. b*), on Lake Titicaca, St. Michael has lost much of his metaphysical radiation but in exchange has become more immediate and human. He stands against a dull-colored background. His garments are elaborately patterned and tooled. He wears the costume of a mid- to late-seven-teenth-century gentleman; the large feathered felt hat, the knee breeches, the shoes with bow ties, the laces, and the long wavy hair are all in the mode of the day. He carries not a saber but a gun, which he is loading. This must have been a mystifying weapon, almost supernatural, to a people who at that time were still using arrows and spear throwers.

The penitent Magdalene in a theatrically *larmoyant* pose doubtless appealed as a subject to many sentimental Spanish ladies. A canvas from a church near Riobamba, Ecuador (*fig. c*), shows her in the finery of her repudiated mundane life contemplating the Cross. The interpretation here has a certain literalism that was typical of the Quito circle; all the attributes of the story are carefully recorded. This composition might have illustrated a mid-eighteenth-century romance. It undoubtedly had a famous painting as prototype which circulated in the colonies as a print.

The placing of the figure in an exquisitely detailed landscape suggests the manner of Manuel Samaniego y Jaramillo, a native of Quito active during the last quarter of the eighteenth century and in the early nineteenth. Samaniego left a compendium,[183] called *Tratado de pintura*, which contains sections copied from Pacheco's *El arte de la pintura* and notes from a book on the precepts of painting which he says was written "*en Lengua flamenca [por] Carlos Bexmandes, Natural de la Ciudad de Hadem en Olanda.*" After some research this artist was identified as Carel van Mander, a native of Haarlem, whose notes Pacheco had appended to his own volume. Such confusions result from the repeated copying of cherished works.

Samaniego's notes throw light upon some of the characteristics and procedures of colonial painting. For the artist who lived out his life in his native colonial town, traveling little if at all, the technical observations and artistic interpretations of his predecessors were all-important. They constituted a *vade mecum*, furnishing him not only chemical formulas but also directives on how to represent certain established subjects. Samaniego gives exact proportions for drawing a head in profile or full face, explains how to bring the arms and hands into the composition, discusses the size of feet and the different tones of encarnación to be used, and how to paint a gloriole or color the living or the dead Christ. He gives the attributes and manner of representation of allegorical figures from Prudence to Ignorance —a fleshy, strongly painted, and richly bejeweled woman of deformed features—and offers a recipe for Chinese ink.[183]

As late as 1782 it appeared necessary in Spain to publish instructions reiterating the resolutions of the Council of Trent. This work, written in Latin in the early part of the century by the Spanish monk Ayala and then translated into Spanish, bore the descriptive title, *The Christian and Erudite Painter, or a Treatise of the Errors Frequently Committed in Painting or Sculpturing Sacred Images*. It gave exact norms—the degree of nudity permissible without danger of scandalizing the sensitive—as well as the proper age, stature, and gestures for numerous saints and Virgins.[94]

In the portrait from the Cuzco circle (*fig. d*) we see a definite leaning toward the sentimental type illustrated beside it. Distinctly a socialite, the lady is dressed up in her best for her sitting. A quadruple string of pearls extends across her shoulder like a sash, and in addition she wears many rings and earrings, hairpins and feathers. On the table are more of her valuables. Through the long window are visible the palm and the cedar, recalling the attributes of the Virgin. Her head, eyes, and tearful pursing of the mouth are similar to the Magdalene's, and her right hand has the same pose. The essence of this portrait lies in the dolorous expression of the sitter as she turns away from her earthly possessions and, with her left hand indicating the cross at her throat, raises her eyes to Heaven.

The two paintings on the left are somewhat sophisticated interpretations of European prototypes; in those on the right much of the academic has been lost, but special attractiveness was gained through the infusion of the folkloristic.

Though the artist in Spain was conditioned in the selection of his themes by the life about him, which was surcharged with religion, from the last decade of the sixteenth century he began to produce for the taverns (*bodegas*) still-life paintings, the flowers and foods of which are often exotic in provenience.[38] During the first half of the following century such *bodegones* became popular. Further impetus for non-religious painting came from the picaresque romance, peculiarly Spanish, and from secular books and prints from other lands. In addition tapestries with secular subjects, often allegorical, first from the famous Flemish workshops and later from the French and Spanish, exerted their influence; these wall hangings were welcomed for their decorative effect and, in chilly climates, to help keep the rooms warm.

All of these sources stimulated the art of the colonies. The bringing forward of a landscape out of the background, the compact defined shapes of a woodcut, the tight composition of a tapestry, and the sharp thin lines of an engraving—all can be perceived in its pictorial language. By including common folk in a landscape and emphasizing the flora and fauna, the supporting details of a religious painting often were so strengthened that its Biblical message was obscured. This tendency is exemplified in the canvas from the Cuzco circle representing St. Anthony preaching to the fishes and birds (*Pl. 141, fig. a*). Though the saint standing among his finny and feathered congregation is the largest figure in the picture, our eye is first attracted to the stage-design landscape with its lush vegetation and is then led on up the broad expanse of the river. The scene in the right foreground is so full of descriptive detail that it could well be an illustration for a story. In this composition especially, the influence of landscapes by Joachim de Patinier (1480?-1524) and the atmosphere of woodcuts from Central European travel books can be felt.

The inclusion of the worldly often gave to a religious or symbolic theme the appearance of a painted romance. In the Prodigal Son (*fig. d*), also from Cuzco, less than half of the canvas is devoted to the main subject—the merry-making with banquet and music. For this section Murillo's Prodigal Son might have served as inspiration; even more similar are details in Raphael Sadeler's Amor, engraved (1591) after Martin de Vos. The loving couple in the foreground seems a separate story, and still more independent are the idyllic groups at the left, divided by the stream. Note the deer-hunting scene in the background; hunting with spears was still usual in that age. Thus a composite arrangement of several episodes was presented on one canvas, as if to make the picture as entertaining as possible.

Without apparent religious content but probably with allegorical significance is the carnival scene from the Cuzco circle (*fig. c*). The greater portion of the foreground is given over to seven masked dancing figures, familiar from Venetian prints of the second half of the seventeenth century. Farther back, the figures on the bridge, in the water, and on the shore and the sailing ship on the horizon tell their own stories. The presence of animals emerging from the forest, as if charmed by the music of the banqueting party at the edge of the woods, suggests a knowledge of the Orpheus legend, which was popular in that period. Since the eighteenth century knew many romantic stories now long forgotten, it is difficult to comprehend all the literary allusions in these paintings.

The well-stocked booth in the Market Scene from Mexico (*fig. b*), dated 1766, is easier to understand. The viands displayed range from vegetables and fruits to shrimp and other fish. Judging from the marked difference in their dress, the two men at the right are employees, while the others are customers. Note the fine pottery jars, the beautiful tightly woven baskets, the bottles and boxes, all depicted in loving detail. The inherent artistic sense of the natives which made this shop scene so attractive continued beyond the colonial period, for even today the lively exhibitions of many Latin American markets are real spectacles.

In the vast repertory of Biblical scenes few subjects have the enduring charm of the Flight into Egypt. The imagination of countless artists—from the greatest of the Italian masters to the unknown colonial painters of Latin America—was fired to tell the oft-repeated story. The Flight hanging in the museum at Querétaro (*Pl. 142, fig. a*) is signed in gold "*Joannes Rodríguez Xuárez fc.*" Four painters from this Rodríguez family came to the fore in colonial Mexico: Antonio, José, Juan (1675–1728) and Nicolás. Juan's father was Antonio and his mother was the daughter of José Juárez, a noted artist.

The Querétaro canvas is 7 feet by 5½. Maturity is manifest in the composition, and a rare delicacy of sentiment pervades the work. The scene is set in a romantic landscape that has much of tropical Mexico about it. Mary is depicted with the tenderness of devotion; St. Joseph is portrayed as solicitous and dignified. The two cherubs leading the ass by its halter rope reveal an exquisite feeling for plasticity. The same artist executed another Flight, still larger in size (about 13 feet by 6), as one of a series of eight canvases for the cloister of Tepotzotlán. Whether the success of that painting caused him to repeat the subject or whether the example here was the earlier has not yet been established.

Juan Rodríguez Juárez signed his paintings in several ways: as "Juan," then again as "Ioannes," or even as "I," and often Juárez was spelled "Xuárez"; *fecit* was written out or variously abbreviated. The dates in his signatures range from 1693 to 1714; the painting shown here carries no date.[132] A self-portrait of this painter hangs in the San Carlos Gallery in Mexico City. It is executed in an amazingly impressionistic style and shows a youngish man wearing a braided mauve-gray coat, which contrasts with his dark hair. Sensibility is revealed in the narrow face, the finely wrought nose, and the mobile fingers. It is interesting to note that he was a contemporary of Holguín, active in Bolivia. (*Compare Pl. 134.*)

An unknown Cuzco painter tells his story of the Flight (*fig. b*) with charming naïveté. While in the Rodríguez painting the couple is traveling light, here both St. Joseph and the mule are heavily loaded. Joseph in the Mexican rendition is looking at Mary and her face is turned toward husband and Baby—all three are enclosed within a single circle of affection; in the Peruvian, each gazes in a different direction. The minor scene in the background refers to the apocryphal story that relates how the little group in their flight came upon a man sowing wheat, whom Mary begged to answer to all who might inquire that he had been planting when they passed; overnight the field sprang to full maturity and the next day when the soldiers of Herod heard the man's truthful reply they gave up the pursuit as futile.

The Return of the Holy Family from Egypt (*fig. c*), another Cuzco painting, has the atmosphere of a fairy tale. Jesus, now a young child, is walking, and flowers spring up before his feet. The mule at St. Joseph's side has become a shadowy background figure, and no incidents of the journey are recorded. Little subtlety is evident—either in compositional rhythm or coloristic display; all the brilliance lies in the rich and careful tooling in the several patterns. A single large tree is pointed up as center and background, and before it the group is placed almost as if in a *tableau vivant*.

The tropical trees have a considerable massivity in all three canvases, and birds are given an important place. Note the different treatment of the halos.

In a Cuzco depiction of the Rest on the Flight (*Pl. 143, fig. a*) most of the canvas is devoted to the Holy Family; the remainder shows a fantasy landscape with mountains, buildings, birds, and vegetation, very much subordinated in spite of its many details. The grouping, with St. Joseph occupying the center, is somewhat unusual. All of the figures, elaborately tooled, are outspokenly two-dimensional. Note in the foreground the two birds kissing—a folk motif—and the parrot eating grapes. Highly decorative in quality, this painting belongs to the best of the Cuzco circle—a sublimation of folk art.

The Return from Egypt (*fig. b*), from Quito, has a landscape background made up of elements basically similar to those in the Cuzco paintings shown here and on the preceding plate. But it is more integrated into the whole, especially through the general mellowness of its coloring. The Quito circle never applied gold tooling as lavishly as the circles of Cuzco and Potosí, and thus the main figures were not lifted out of context in the same way. In contrast to the Byzantoid aloofness that pervades the preceding group, a subdued rhythm is perceptible in the movement of the Holy Family, and the little angel leading the mule is full of action. The painter is said to have been Manuel Samaniego.

With the next two pictures from Quito we reach the best religious genre. Both are attributed to Samaniego, and they are close to each other in their evenly distributed interest and their touching atmosphere—primary requirements of this type.

The Carpenter's Shop (*fig. c*) shows the Holy Family at home in Nazareth. Nine little angels are busy about them, two sawing a board, one carving on a spoon, and two others gathering chips; in a second group, as two blow the fire a companion recoils from the rising smoke; the last one is scattering food for the chickens. The Child Jesus is holding the spindle from which Mary winds a ball of thread, and St. Joseph is planing. Framed in the window is a landscape very similar to that in the Cuzco painting above it—a stairway leading up a hill where stands a chapel, an arched gateway at the left and a cliff on the right. In the Quito piece this detail is brought out with the clarity of a Rococo wallpaper, while in the Cuzco canvas it has the rather fat chiaroscuro quality of a seventeenth-century Dutch or Flemish work.

A composite character is again evident in another Quito painting, the Rest on the Flight (*fig. d*). One angel is offering Mary food, two are in the fruit tree, and a fourth is laying a fire in a hollow. Somewhat farther away three little angels are occupied in guiding the ass to water, and in the distance the story of the soldiers and harvesters is repeated. Flemish emblem books and albums of sketches contain many small engravings featuring a jolly company of baby angels about the child Mary or the Infant Jesus.

The mystically beautiful theme of the Annunciation was treated with great diversity by colonial painters. The first painting of it shown here (*Pl. 144, fig. a*) is on the ceiling of the apse opposite the main altar in the church at Checacupe, Peru (*see also Pl. 111*). Again apparently the subject matter was translated and enlarged from a book illustration. The scene takes place in a bedroom depicted in the matter-of-fact Gothic tradition of Schongauer and Dürer. Mary kneels at a prie-dieu; the angel, standing before her on the patterned floor, carries a staff with a phylacterium inscribed with his greeting, "*Ave Maria Gratia Plena.*"

The second example (*fig. b*), an oil painting from Cuzco, has a strong Baroque character in its display of chiaroscuro. The third Annunciation (*fig. c*) is one of the countless art pieces belonging to the monastery of San Francisco in Quito. Here Mary kneels at the right and the angel floats in above her from the other side; thus their positions are reversed. The words of the Annunciation, in Latin, are most decoratively used in a band of gold lettering, and her reply, "Behold the handmaid of the Lord . . ." (Luke 1:38), is in mirror script, indicating the direction from which the communication comes. Grace and a genuine sweetness are in Mary's bearing.

In spite of the general monotone coloring, a transparent veil-like quality gives the canvas especial attraction. Note the vase of flowers in the foreground and the sprays scattered over the floor, which is drawn in careful perspective.

Luis Juárez studied with Baltasar de Echave Orio and was engaged to furnish paintings for the Mexican cathedral.[132] Canvases which he signed and dated place him in the first half of the seventeenth century. His Annunciation (*fig. d*) brings some new details. Mary here is placed on a low podium and the angel stands on an even lower level, but since the Virgin is kneeling, he is still the taller.

Upon comparing these four Annunciations, one finds that in two of them the angel stands on the floor in a simple and quiet scene that is typical of early European representations; in the other two he floats in greater splendor, a concept of the Counter Reformation.[12] Mary's figure and that of the Dove are depicted differently in each case, and the halos and heavenly radiance show considerable variety. In the two Cuzco paintings the angel points upward to the Holy Ghost, a gesture found also in Mexican works. In the Quito and Mexican examples God the Father is sending down the Dove, and in the latter he wears a papal tiara. These similarities and differences reveal how manifold were the sources from which the painters could make their choices.

Colonial families of standing had house altars if not house chapels, for which at least one large religious picture was required. Among their favorite subjects were the Virgin and Child (*Pl. 145, fig. b*) and St. Joseph with the Child (*fig. a*). In these two paintings from Cuzco the arrangement, pose, and gestures are identical, and the existence of a common formula can be presumed, although they are distinctly executed by different hands. The figures are drawn as large as the space permits, and garlands of flowers frame the canvases, a popular feature, as has been noted. The Joseph picture is somewhat glassy, while the other, though less skillful in composition, has considerable warmth.

Already it must have been observed that in Latin America St. Joseph is not the old man —frequently a bit doddering—depicted in the Middle Ages and occasionally in the Renaissance. From late sixteenth century on, especially in Spain, he was portrayed as a younger man, for his was a figure particularly reverenced by St. Theresa, who regarded the Holy Family as symbols of the Trinity on earth. According to the Apocrypha, to signify that he was to become Mary's husband his staff flowered in the wilderness. This staff as pictured on the canvas in the sagrario chapel of the cathedral in Comayagua, Honduras, is as thin as a pipe stem (fig. c), evidence of the refining influence of the Rococo. The build-up in this painting differs from that above it, and the tooling—exquisitely done in that work—is here limited to golden flowers on the garments and the edging of Joseph's robe. The composition and clear transparent coloring indicate a good tradition. This painting bears the name Gómez and the date 1778; the same artist (José Manuel Gómez, born in Honduras) painted the dome and pendentives[163] in the cathedral of Tegucigalpa in 1786 (see Pl. 11).

Numerous examples in this volume have shown the vast influence of Flemish and Central European art on that of colonial America. The second Virgin and Child from Cuzco (fig. d), in the warmth of its atmosphere and the manner of its gold tooling, harmonizes with other eighteenth-century works of that circle. It gains additional interest when it is compared with the Dürer Virgin and Child painted on wood in 1512 (see Appendix, Pl. 191, fig. f). Reproductions of the Dürer panel served as prototype in the distant New World, whose pre-Columbian treasures that artist admired[62] on his visit to Brussels in 1520.

The translation from Dürer to the Cuzco canvas reveals much of the compositional method of colonial artists. The original painting, an important item in the Habsburg collection, may have been reproduced in woodcuts

and engravings by several hands before it reached the high valley in the Andes. The Gothic spirit in the blonde femininity and the translucent headdress was translated here into Baroque ebullience; the dark hair and massive head cloth are in the fashion of Latin America. But nearly all of the purely compositional details are retained. The Holy Child's pose is copied even to the folds in the cloth about his loins. Mary's square décolleté and the fall of the head cloth also are drawn from Dürer's panel. Taken over exactly are the line of the eyebrows and nose and the mouth. But the hair, which with its hanging strand was observed with a keen eye and daringly depicted by the European master, has been changed; here every lock is under control, conforming to the prudery of the time and place. Dürer's much-discussed tuft of cloth, or "pear," in the Christ Child's hand has been turned into a rose, and the intricacies of the drapery beneath his arm have been obscured in shadow. The widening of the eyes, the darkening of the pupils, and the nearly imperceptible rounding of the faces contribute to the fascinating transformation.

St. Christopher was so generally beloved that the Council of Trent tried to curb his popularity, though with little success. Even today he attracts painters and sculptors, for, in this subject, revealing contrasts can be portrayed—between the tall and small, the old and young, the one striving and the other serene and assured.

The present church of Santiago in Tlatelolco, Mexico, erected in the first half of the seventeenth century, was refurbished in mid-century. In the decoration of the whole complex a strongly Indian interpretation of European forms occurs (see Pl. 33). Above the side entrance of the church a mural of St. Christopher (Pl. 146, fig. a) fills the vast arched space. Here is the legendary giant of a man, presented in heroic proportions, his staff a veritable tree trunk. His halo has the shape of a metal disk, such as is often pinned on the heads of statues. Note the new moon with a human profile in the right corner. At the bottom of the mural stands a hermit, framed in the mouth of a cave—a detail which accentuates the Byzantoid atmosphere of the scene. In their compositional approach some modern Mexican frescoes parallel this wall painting which goes back to a century or so after the Conquest.

Another St. Christopher (*fig. b*), dating from around the end of the seventeenth century or the early eighteenth, comes from Cuzco. Here he is seen wading through a river full of fishes; his two garments are differentiated by the patterns of the tooling. Jesus carries a large globe topped with a cross, as in the Mexican mural, but here it is like a toy balloon and the Child's leg is wrapped around it. He returns the giant's gaze mischievously, as if enjoying the situation. The position of the palm tree used as a staff is unrealistic but reinforces the oblique lines that give movement to the figure. At the left is the chapel of the hermit. This painting also must have been made after a prototype that was repeated fairly often in South America, for nearly an exact replica hangs in the presbytery of San Francisco in La Paz, Bolivia.[208] (For other Christophers see *Pl. 52.*)

To Holguín is attributed the canvas of St. Francis de Paul, La Paz (*fig. c*). The figure of the saint is flatter than that in either of the two paintings above, and detail is emphasized. The face has innumerable wrinkles in pseudo realism, the nose and beard are carefully delineated, and amazingly warm and expressive are the eyes. The hands are a study in themselves, isolated from the rest of the body by the gold tooling. A flat geometrical stamped pattern, applied to the garments without any attempt to show folds, offers startling contrast to the three-dimensionality of the crucifix, skull, and books and to the charming conventionalized landscape. The cock on the church roof symbolizes the preacher.

A sweeping brush stroke, covering much surface, was employed in the depiction of St.

Paul that hangs near the baptismal font in the church of Santo Domingo in La Paz (*fig. d*). For many the static quality and the general Byzantoid atmosphere will evoke memories of Catalan frescoes. This work, executed on cotton cloth, is one of a pair which once formed the outside wings of an organ; musical subjects painted on the other side were discovered under a heavy layer of dust and dirt by this author when the pictures were removed for photographing (*see Pl. 153*).

Eligius, later St. Eloi, born in 588 near Limoges, France, gained prominence as chief coiner to the king. Though appointed Bishop of Moyon, he continued to hold his former post. He died after 650. A wealth of legend arose around him and he became the patron saint of jewelers, metalworkers, and kindred trades.

St. Eloi was portrayed infrequently in eighteenth-century Europe, but his figure evidently caught the fancy of an unknown Cuzco painter. This conception of him (*Pl. 147, fig. a*), strongly in the spirit of religious genre, shows him, dressed in elaborate flowered ecclesiastical robes, as he is working on a crown. A large silver candlestick stands on the table, and some of his tools are lying about. His chair has not the stiff straight back so often depicted but the bulging line and gilt ornaments of the Baroque; the drapery held back by a heavy tassel also is Baroque. A twisted column divides the canvas in two, and on the other side unrelated picturesque groups are presented. The European tradition for such a division harks back to the woodcut pages of fifteenth-century block books and even to Byzantine manuscripts. Though the figures here are dressed in Rococo costume—note the three ladies and the men clustered around a spy glass in the background—the scene has the atmosphere of a Chinese wallpaper.

A delightful representation of the Adoration of the Shepherds was realized by another unknown Cuzco painter (*fig. b*). The naked body of the Christ Child is set off by the voluminous gold-tooled garments that form a kind of background for it. For the four shepherds—all bearing gifts—the tooling is less elaborate. Miniature animals in the foreground help provide the atmosphere of the traditional scene. Seated on a distant hilltop a Rococo shepherd, like a porcelain figurine, is blowing on his pipe. Sheep are grazing in corrals close by, and an angel is emerging from lively-colored clouds. The large angel above the stable, with a phylacterium inscribed "*Gloria in Excelsis Deo,*" though iconographically not prescribed, is an enriching detail. The subordinate plein-air scenes in both pictures are infused with a graceful Rococo touch.

In much colonial painting, especially that executed by folk artists, the absence of coloristic brilliance and contrast can be felt. Technical limitations and the paucity of available colors account for this in part; but many of these paintings—often on cotton cloth—were prepared with red ocher, a damaging ground color which, though it produced a vibrant tone at first, ate through and with time obliterated the more varied and brilliant hues applied as upper layers.[94]

The depiction of saints was everyday work for the colonial painter. Many canvases were needed, and the larger the picture, the more impressive it was to the illiterate masses. Cuzco produced the over-life-size portrayal of Gregory (Pl. *148, fig. b*), one of the Latin Fathers, who became pope. He is crowned with his triple tiara, and, as a symbol of divine inspiration, the Dove flutters at his right ear. Books make a picturesque background.

The painting of Augustine (*fig. a*), from the Potosí circle, is one of a set showing all four of the Latin Fathers. The Eye of God in a triangle is his symbol; his bishop's miter is painted with much detail and two pens are visible on his table. The tooling differs from that on the Cuzco canvas in its engraving-like cleanness and widely spaced pattern. A more advanced knowledge of both technique and design is evident in the Potosí work and more

attention was concentrated on the coloristic. The lingering tradition of the Byzantine can be felt (*compare Appendix, Pl. 191, fig. d*).

This painting retains its original wood frame with a bishop's miter incorporated into the decoration. Note the flowing ribbon motif twisting among the flowers and foliage, carved in filigree that has the exactness of metalwork.

The Mexican painting of Jerome (*fig. c*), another of the Latin Fathers, is attributed to Juan Tinoco, active in Puebla in the second half of the seventeenth century.[182] Signed works of his dated 1683 and 1685 are extant. The saint is seated in his study at a table covered by a velvet cloth with a gold border and tassels; two pens again are evident. A large library provides an effective backdrop, calling to mind what a proud thing was the possession of books in those days. Jerome's lion has a somewhat human face; probably few natives of Puebla had ever seen the actual animal. A rather expressionistic detail is the trumpet thrust through the ceiling. The emphasis on the checkerboard pattern of the floor and the perspective of the arches on the left remind one of the interest of early Flemish and Italian painters in such studies.

Bordering on the sweet but not offensive in its sentimentality is the representation of the young Italian Jesuit, St. Louis Gonzaga, from the Quito circle (*fig. d*). His youth makes him especially appealing. The crucifix he holds seems somewhat out of proportion to the rest of the composition, but this was one method of securing emphasis. Book, lilies, cord, and cherub heads—all are present as iconographical accessories, but they add no particular pictorial interest. Through the inclusion of arches and the angles of a few steps this painter displays sound knowledge of perspective.

The strength of these Cuzco and Potosí paintings lies in their monumental line, in a powerful sense of decoration, and in their folkloristic imagination. Intellectual mannerism permeates the Mexican and Quito canvases, resulting in bookish overtones.

The colonial artist, with his flair for the decorative, recorded textiles in loving detail. Sometimes he went further and applied real textiles, working them into the composition. The Holy Family in Monguí, Colombia (*Pl. 149, fig. a*), shows this technique. Velvet, silk, linen, cord, and tassels make up the garments affixed to the painted figures. Metal stars stud the Virgin's cloak and the new moon is a piece of silver. Crown, chains, and rings are all creations of the jeweler's art, inserted into slits in the canvas and sewed on at the back. The effect is not so much that of an icon (*see Pl. 131*) as of low relief.

A painting of the Virgin of Chiquinquirá and her attendant saints Anthony and Andrew (*fig. c*) occupies the center of a side-chapel altar in San Diego, Quito. These figures are dressed—as were many statues—in clothing which was stiffened and painted. In its stage settings the Baroque epoch often combined painted surfaces with real materials. The Virgin's cloak shows a fine small-patterned *millefleur estofado*; the two saints in dark garb have enough gold to give them distinction. Andrew, leaning on his cross, holds a book that protrudes from the canvas. Delicately carved and gilded latticework frames the group; artificial flowers are hung across the top and votive paintings fill the Rococo frames at the bottom. (For a wing of this altar see *Pl. 56*.)

The original painting of the Virgin of Chiquinquirá—the one here is a replica—hangs in the town by that name in Colombia; but the figure was much venerated throughout the Kingdom of Quito also. Bernardo Recio (1714–1791) writes that when he stopped at Cartagena on his way from Spain he received from the Dominican provincial there—in return for some little devotional books which he had brought with him from the motherland—a painting of this Virgin, which subsequently he presented to another monastery on his route.[180]

A somewhat different combination of materials is seen in the panel of the Miracle of the *Matriz* in the church of Santa Clara at Cuzco

(*fig. b*). According to legend Indians attacked the Spaniards, who had sought refuge in their first small church, and set fire to the roof, but the Virgin, descending, smothered the flames with her robes. Her costume is made of starched textiles, painted, and her jewelry is real. Through repeated over-painting, the fabric has become so stiff that it now has the appearance of a lacquered relief. The expressions of the angels also have suffered through over-painting. The clouds are executed in spirals, like those seen in Quito sculpture. Compare the defenders in their coats of mail with the poncho-clad Indians.

The Inca Princess (*fig. d*), from Cuzco, is important because it offers a painted record of Indian textiles, today very rare. She is depicted in the stiff, stereotyped pose familiar to the artists from the many pedestrian "portraits" of Spanish nobility displayed throughout the colonies. Most of the canvas is given over to her; other details—the fortress, the high cliff with its shrubbery, the attendant Indian dwarf and his macaw—are crowded into the margin. The lady's untailored garments, still pre-Columbian in cut and pattern, are delineated in great detail. In her right hand she holds the sacred flower of the Incas, the red bell-like blossom of the *ñukchu*, and in her left, a spindle—perhaps a reminder of the goddess queen who introduced spinning to her people, but it also recalls Mary with a Distaff (*see Pl. 133*).

This Inca princess probably was painted in the second half of the seventeenth century. In a scene from the Corpus Christi procession in Cuzco, an Indian cacique of about the same period marches in native gala attire before the chariot of St. Sebastian (*see Pl. 65*), and a painting in La Compañía there records the marriage of an Inca princess, also in Indian costume, to a relative of Ignatius Loyola.

For the convenience of the reader the four portraits from Mexico on *Plates 150* and *151* are lettered consecutively.

By mid-eighteenth century luxurious living

had become more general in Mexico. Beginning with the viceroy Francisco Fernández de la Cueva, who reached Mexico in 1702, influences from Versailles, via Madrid where the Bourbons had succeeded to the throne, began to enter New Spain. The services of dressmakers, shoemakers, ribbon and silk weavers, and corsetières were at the disposal of the fair sex and medicinal baths and beauty treatments were available to enhance or to preserve their charm. Though some noble family's house might be in dire need of repair and the servants' pay long in arrears, on public occasions the ladies had to appear in full elegance of dress and jewelry.

The portrait of Doña María Romero (*fig. a*) was painted by Ignacio María Barreda in 1794. According to the inscription she married Don José Manuel García Aurioles de León at the age of sixteen and is portrayed here at the age of thirty-four, after having had nine births and three miscarriages—the last only the year before the portrait was made—from which, the text goes on to say, it is clear that she has fully recovered. One cannot begrudge her the gay life implied by her finery. Her gown is of black and gray, with a velvet stripe and silver embroidery, and her tall coiffure, powdered gray, is adorned with ribbons and plumes; the metal disk at the temple adjusted the wig. Her two chatelaine watches, prominently displayed, her collar of pearls, and the trinkets laid out on the table (note the scissors) recall the affectations of Quito and Cuzco (*see Pl. 140*). A saffron curtain lined with peacock-blue, draped across the background, carries a coat of arms executed as precisely as that on a patent of nobility.

Doña Josepha Rosa de Sardeneta, Legaspi, Oxeda, Espejo, Torres Luna (*fic. c*), painted by Joannes Fernández in 1770, bears the name of the first Marquis de la Rayas, the owner of the silver mine near Guanajuato (*see Pl. 41*). Her family was a distinguished one from Jalisco and Zacatecas, and some of its members held high ecclesiastical positions. Seated in a red lacquer chair—somewhat similar to that of

St. Eloi—she is shown holding a large book; a rosary and the scapulary of a sodality lie on the table beside her. She wears no wig; apparently the artist's intention was to portray her informally as she appeared in her home, without pretensions, reading and relaxed. Nevertheless her gown is a brocade of dark peacock-blue, finely wrought in gold, scarlet, and white. Though there is no display of jewelry, a modest double string of pearls and her earrings show affluence. In the first portrait the materialistic prevails, here character. A real personality is delineated, who is no longer a young woman but a shrewd and clever one, wise in the ways of life.

In eighteenth-century Mexico, where viceroys, church dignitaries, and high society were immortalized in decorative fashion, the young girls of distinguished families who were about to take the veil also sat for their portraits. Several such paintings exist in Mexico, exhibiting considerable individuality of feature and costume and all dating from about the same period. The likeness of Sister María Ignacia of the Blood of Christ (*fig. b*) is signed by José de Alcíbar. An inscription states that she was the daughter of Don Manuel de Uribe y Sandoval and took her final vows in Mexico City as a Clarissa nun on May 1, 1777, at the age of twenty-two years and three months. Over her dark habit is hung a rich blue cloak, heavily embroidered in silver. Her crown and the emblems in her hands (note the shield with a wax? figurine of the Woman of the Apocalypse) are of colorful beadwork; similar examples of this craft, a specialty of colonial nuns, still survive in Mexico.

The portrayal of religieuses was not entirely unknown; Velázquez painted a Franciscan nun before she left Spain to found a Clarissa convent in the Philippines.[38] But that Spanish painting, which is dated 1620, is kept a monotone—in browns with only a touch of white and red—and concentrates on the character of the reverend mother, who carries a puritanical wooden cross in her hand. Colorful portraits of nuns, such as survive from eighteenth-century Mexico, have not been found by this author either in Spain or in other areas of colonial Latin America.

A young "donor" by Juan Correa occupies the lower right-hand corner of a large canvas of the Virgin from Zacatecas (*fig. d*); a fold of Mary's skirt and a part of a tall candelabrum are visible in the background. In contrast to the hieratic representation of the holy figure, a statue-painting, the young girl's portrait is realistic, full of personality. No detail of her highly decorative dress and rich jewelry has been overlooked. Two colonial artists of this name are recorded, probably father and son.[132] The signatures of the older date from 1686 to 1714, of the younger, from 1731 to 1760. In this portrait the costume suggests the early part of the eighteenth century.

Colonial painting in Latin America has several peculiarities which this author has never found noted. Very frequently the canvas or cotton cloth was glued onto the strainer, not nailed. In South America often the picture was painted over the entire surface to the very edges; also, no strip was left unpainted for folding over on the sides of the strainer. When the strainer had a crosspiece, as was sometimes the case for a large picture, the fabric was usually glued to it, too. One explanation of this practice may lie in the fact that nails were scarce in the colony whereas firm and lasting glues were conveniently at hand.

Certain differences can be noted between paintings from Mexico and those from South America. In Mexico composite landscapes are rather infrequent. Gold tooling is more rarely encountered there and never attained the same compositional importance as in South America. Also, less cotton cloth was used. The Mexican artist often left the edges of his canvas unpainted to be folded around the strainer. These various characteristics can furnish clues to the provenience of a painting.

The production of paintings in the colonies was a widespread industry. To estimate its size accurately is impossible. But to attempt an approximation—one source [127] states that colonial Mexico alone had 15,000 churches; another [57] places the total number for the New World at about 70,000. If each of these had only ten paintings—and some cathedrals, basilicas, and convents boasted hundreds—the number of colonial paintings could be put at three-quarters of a million without danger of exaggeration. Both fate and time have been cruel to them; thousands are gone, and with them doubtless many excellent works. But those that remain form a vast and revealing panorama, one which could unfold only here in America where many diverse artistic streams converged.

THE SPLENDOR OF COLONIAL ORGANS

THE history of the organ can be traced back to the third century before Christ, when Ktesibios in Alexandria is said to have constructed the first one. The Romans knew the instrument as a *hydraulus* because it was driven by water power, and its loud and penetrating tone offered an appropriate accompaniment to the robust entertainments of their circuses. But they also used an organ equipped with bellows. Parts of such an instrument from early in the third century after Christ were found on the site of Aquincum, a Roman city in the province of Pannonia (West Hungary), in a cellar among the ruins of the fire brigade's chapter house; seemingly it was a custom at that time to have at least one singer, with organ accompaniment, to entertain the firemen on duty during the night to keep them from falling asleep.[242] The importance of the organ in classic times is evidenced by the fact that to date it has been found represented in some forty reliefs, paintings, and manuscripts.

The early Christian church was reluctant to make use of any musical instrument, and the organ especially was looked upon with disfavor as too suggestive of gladiatorial battles, the blood of the martyrs, and other pagan customs of the recent past. But before long it took its place in the service of the church, and religious writers mention it with praise. Byzantium was the first organ-building center in the Middle Ages and sent craftsmen and treatises on the subject into Europe. About the time of Charlemagne (742?–814), the organ began to be used widely in Western Europe.[243]

By the year 1000, the organ had grown very large and sometimes was so powerful that the townsfolk are said to have had to plug their ears when it was played. It was still primitive, however, with only a few notes—held down by the fist—each of which probably sounded a number of pipes simultaneously. Smaller instruments were used to accompany plain song. It was not until the thirteenth century that projecting levers, the forerunners of keys, were invented, which could be worked by the fingers. There were then about three octaves on the manual. The organ was the first instrument to become entirely chromatic, although at first not all the half-tones were present.[238]

Organs were made in Spain as early as the fifth century. It should be noted that this country developed its own liturgy, independent of the rest of Europe, from the time of its conversion to Christianity and that it can also boast its own tradition of music, in which the peculiarities of the Arabic melody line can be felt.[245] As early as the thirteenth century Alfonso X established a chair of music at the University of Salamanca. Philip the Fair of Burgundy, when he came to Spain in 1501, brought with him an "orchestra" of Flemish musicians, consisting of fifteen singers, nine trumpets, three musettes, and two tambours.[232]

In 1517 Charles V, Philip's son, enlarged this orchestra into the *Real Capilla Música*, which he took with him when he retired into the monastery at Yuste, Estremadura, in 1557.

During the Renaissance a number of technical improvements made on the organ effected a greater ease in handling and a finer quality of tone, so that by the time it was introduced into the New World it was already the queen of instruments. The great organ in the cathedral of Seville, dating from the sixteenth century, had 5,300 pipes and 110 stops, or sets of pipes of different timbre, arranged in musical progression. The list of organ builders in Catalonia in the sixteenth century contains German, French, and Flemish names, notably one Pedro Flamench (Fleming), who is described as being singularly expert and without an equal in the whole Kingdom of Aragon.[241]

Flemish organ builders were invited to construct the famous organs in the Escorial, each of which has two manuals as well as a pedal work, rather unusual in Spain.[244] Antonio de Cabezón (1510–1566), the Spanish organ virtuoso, born blind, traveled in England, Flanders, Italy, and the Germanic lands, and was influential in the establishment of the Neapolitan school of virtuoso playing. He exercised considerable influence on the English composer William Byrd; Cabezón was a member of Philip's retinue in London when the Spanish crown prince married Mary Tudor. He published several books on the art and technique of organ playing, which were re-edited by his three sons after his death. Also worth noting is the fact that the Neapolitan Domenico Scarlatti (1685–1757), who was pitted against Handel himself in Rome in a competition of harpsichord and organ playing, spent the last thirty-seven years of his life in the Iberian Peninsula. About 1720 he came to Lisbon as music master to the Braganza princess, and when she married the Bourbon king Ferdinand VI nine years later, he followed her to Madrid.

Spanish organs had certain individual features. Emphasis was placed on the reed stops, especially the various trumpets.[239] The tiers of projecting horizontal pipes—with their inevitable suggestion of fanfare—are quite peculiar to this country, appearing here in late seventeenth century. Also typical are the grotesque faces which utilize the slits in the pipes as open mouths, found frequently on even the most ornate and suavely decorated instruments; bizarre decoration of organ pipes occurred on Gothic and early Renaissance instruments from the Low Countries, but it was out of fashion there by late sixteenth century.[250] The pedal organ, which probably developed from the drone note peculiar to pneumatic instruments (notably the bagpipe), was neglected in Spain until well into the eighteenth century, as indeed it was everywhere except in the Low Countries and Germany; in general, early organs in the United States also were without pedals.[246]

As to the type of music performed in Spain, the forms of the Flemish school of religious music, which became the official style in the fifteenth century, persisted until the eighteenth century, and then, when the rest of the world was being carried away by the operatic, Spanish religious music returned to the plain song. Various accompanying instruments, each with its own part, appear in the church about this time; among them, harps, strings, clarinets, flutes, and sackbuts.

Italian, French, and Spanish organs were at their best in the sixteenth and seventeenth centuries, while the organ of the Low Countries kept its high technical level longer. German and Latin American instruments reached their highest development in the eighteenth century. The latter, however, show pronounced architectural and mechanical differences from the former and seem to have been influenced little by this parallel flourish; they had no pedal work, an important part of German organs, and they rarely had their small stops built into the choir organ, which stood at the front of the choir gallery. In Latin America the instrument itself was not noticeably incorporated into the church architecture but was embellished as a separate unit.[236]

The few extant Baroque organs that can be heard today have a mild sweet tone, usually quite reedy, like a great choir of woodwinds. Polyphonic effects are amazingly clear and untangled and have none of the "smear" and stridency occurring in motor-driven mechanisms. Serene and rich in timbre, they present a straightforward musical line.

One of the greatest contributions which the white man's civilization made to the New World was music. Although musical instruments were part of pre-Columbian life and no ceremony among the higher Indian cultures was carried on without an accompaniment of shell or clay trumpets, flutes of pottery or reed, drums of various types, and singing and dancing, potentially the Indians had far more musical ability than had been brought out by their own civilization. Just as they seized upon steel tools to further their talents in carving, so they appropriated the new musical instruments and modes to their joy and elevation.

The first missionaries to land at Veracruz in 1523 observed that music was one of the most effective means of interesting the Indians in Christianity, and therefore they requested that new missionaries if possible be men who could play some instrument.[248] The school established before 1527 at Tlatelolco, Mexico, by the Flemish Franciscan Pedro de Gante gave special attention to the training of musicians. Prayers and responses, it was found, could be learned more easily by the Indians when set to some simple chant. Soon orchestras as well as singing and the dance were employed to serve the new religion. The first mention of an official organist in Mexico City is in 1539.[234]

Jodoco Ricke, another Flemish friar, also installed a music teacher in his school in Quito, Ecuador. A list of musicians and singers from there (1568) does not contain a single Spanish or creole name; all were Indians from the various districts of the Kingdom of Quito, proficient in singing, in reading and writing music, and in playing the flute, the *chirimía* (native

flageolet), and the organ, as well as other keyboard instruments.[183]

In 1576 Bernal Díaz, looking back on the first decades of colonial life, remarks on the many bells in Guatemala and the part-singing of the chapel choirs. He reports that several churches had organs and most places had at least an orchestra, with flutes, oboes, sackbuts, trumpets both large and small, and dulcimers, many of which accompanied the festive processions. When the friars entered our own Southwest, music went with them, and as early as 1590, organs were transported hither, going overland from points as far away as Mexico City, in those days a six months' trip.[247]

Under the supervision of Spanish and Flemish experts the Indians soon were able to construct organs and other instruments for use in their churches; Vázquez observes that the Indian easily learned to make everything that he saw the Spaniards making. At the beginning of the seventeenth century, Colombian Indians constructed a rustic organ with pipes of bamboo and some other large cane. Guillermo Hernández de Alba found the records of local organ construction in Bogotá in the seventeenth century, among them the contract for an instrument for the church of Santo Domingo (*see Pl. 27*). Julián López is documented as an organ builder in Antigua, Guatemala.[240]

The instrument maker, or *violero*, of colonial Mexico belonged to the same guild as the fine cabinetmakers and woodcarvers. In 1568 a master *violero* had to know how to make an organ and other keyboard instruments—harpsichord and clavichord—a harp, a lute, and various kinds of fiddles and guitars; he also had to pass an examination on their form and decoration as well as on their tone. Berlin observes that he has found no clerics among the organ builders mentioned in the Mexican archives from the eighteenth century; apparently organ construction belonged to the regular crafts. Many of the names are definitely Indian, and often the skill was passed from father to son.[91]

In Latin America, as in Europe, the organ

was used in church services to accompany other instruments as well as voices and to fill in the periods of silence; there evidently was much less virtuoso solo performance than in Europe—at any rate practically no manuscript for the organ alone has been found here, though organists were doubtless excellent in improvisation then as now. The first music book published in the New World seems to be Juan Pérez Materano's *Canto de organo y canto llano*, printed in Cartagena, Colombia, in 1554. At least seven "gradual antiphonals" and similar works appeared in Mexico before 1600, and in 1604 Juan Navarro brought out a book of Passions for use during Holy Week.[246]

Organ music was forbidden at any service —even funerals—from Maundy Thursday until the Gloria on Easter Saturday, although singing was allowed. While strings and such woodwinds as the flute, clarinet, and bassoon were permitted in the church, the use of clamorous instruments—the drum, *chinesco* (bell-tree), tambourine and cymbals—as well as the guitar, mandolin, and even the harp was frowned upon. In certain parts of the New World attempts were made to bar the panpipe, clay trumpet, *chirimía*, and other instruments of the pre-Columbian past, but the testimony of the chroniclers suggests that such efforts were unsuccessful. The author has heard the Indian flute and small drum playing on the ground floor of El Oratorio de San Felipe Neri in San Miguel de Allende, Mexico, while the organ was sounding in the loft; and, as will be seen, at Pisac in the Peruvian highlands conch trumpets are used in the celebration of the Mass.

In this chapter a number of colonial organs are illustrated. A full musicological appraisal of them lies outside the scope of this work; they are included here because they reveal another colorful facet of colonial art.

A fair idea of the small primitive organ used in the earlier centuries in the colonies can be gained from the examples still extant in remote places. One such instrument (*Pl. 152,*

fig. d), in the village church at Pisac, Peru, might be called a portable, for it is small enough to be carried about from chapel to chapel.

Even in pre-Columbian times Pisac was a famous market town; it lies on the shores of the Urubamba River about forty miles across a mountain range from Cuzco and is surrounded by fertile fields, many of them terraced in the Inca manner. Sunday Mass brings the Indians from their distant villages to the weekly fair on the church plaza. Their costumes, bright with red and blue and elaborated with compact multi-colored designs, lend a rare picturesqueness to the scene. The church is a seventeenth-century structure with evident eighteenth-century alterations. On one side is an arcade painted with murals, and in its shadow the Indians are wont to take their Sunday meal, brought with them from home.

Within the barren whitewashed walls the congregation turn their strong clay-red faces toward the altar, where the priest conducts the service partly in Latin but chiefly in their own Quechua tongue. The floor is tamped earth— there are no benches—and a primitive character prevails throughout. The small organ stands on an adobe podium against the left wall of the nave, its two bellows attended by two young Indians dressed in their native best; their stoic expressions are in keeping with the automaton movement with which they steadily work the levers. The organist brings out a labored somewhat wheezy tone, and, at the elevation of the Host, the sonorous penetrating roar of conch trumpets is added to the instrument's fortissimo. Similar shell trumpets are used today in the pagan ceremonies of the Lacandon Indians, a fast disappearing Maya tribe in the depths of the Chiapas forest.

This primitive organ at Pisac is most unusual in the graduated arrangement of its pipes, set according to size in chromatic sequence, so that the case which encloses them looks like that of an upright harpsichord.[250] Its bellows are small, but then they have only a few pipes to feed. This example also shows the disposition of the key connections—the trackers—in a radial scheme that is rare in Europe but not infrequent in Latin America. All these atypical points suggest that the organ was made in the region.

Another primitive instrument is found in the church of Valle (*fig. a*), a Peruvian village situated at an altitude of 6,600 feet in the Huanuco Valley. This organ stands in a loft at the rear of the nave. It has Rococo lines; the doors are decorated with graceful paneling, and the shell is treated as an independent ornament. Here both keyboard and radiating trackers are visible. The arrangement of the pipes is again curious: an even row extends across the front and all of them seem to have the same diameter, a fact which suggests that the instrument has no stops and is capable of few changes and combinations of timbre.

More the type of a "portative" are the two small organs from Mexico (*figs. b, c*). Convenient for choir practice, mission work, and the plain song of the monks, such instruments were widely used, even in communities which boasted larger and more lavish ones. The first stands in the choir loft of the monastery church of Santo Domingo in Zacatecas, Mexico. Silver mines early made this place an important center; its rights as a township were established in 1585. The church was not erected until the eighteenth century, but it does not necessarily follow that the organ is contemporary with the building. The second example, now at the Conservatory of Music in Mexico City, appears to be somewhat later in date.

Both rest on simply carpentered stands. The bellows are visible behind them, heavily weighted to compress the air. Their several rows of small tubes, like series of panpipes, contrast interestingly with the gigantic show pipes of the larger organs on the following plates. The keyboards cover about three and one-half octaves, and the half-tones are raised and placed as in the modern manual. A lever for the manipulation of a stop or of some special sound effect can be seen in the Zacatecas instrument, and the horizontal rods and many threads above the keyboard give a glimpse into the complicated mechanism. Both cases are modesty itself.

The Andean village churches at Andahuaylillas and Checacupe, near Cuzco, were discussed in some detail in Chapter 11 (*see Pls. 111, 112, 113*). The interiors of both churches were complete by mid-seventeenth century, and much of the early decoration still survives, though considerable refurbishment took place just before the eighteenth century.

In each the organ is placed at the front end of one of the arms of a U-shaped choir loft (*Pl. 153, figs. a, b*). M. A. Vente, a Dutch authority on ancient organs, believes that these two instruments date from about 1630, or at least within the first half of the seventeenth century.[250] He calls attention to the few trackers—denoting a small number of keys—as well as to their primitive construction. Also, the tall center sections of the cases show the early type of arrangement, with the longer pipes in the middle. Both organs are closed by means of painted canvas doors, following a tradition that goes back to the Gothic organ, which had folding wings like a triptych; Hans Holbein the Younger (1497?–1543) painted the wings for such an organ in the Münster at Basel, still preserved.

A group of angels adorns the Andahuaylillas organ, all playing musical instruments which are in the tradition of the seventeenth century. The guitar at the lower left has a shorter neck than the European type and resembles the native *charango*, a favorite instrument of Andean mermaids (*see Pl. 116*). In its shape the portable harp suggests the native adaptation which is still the backbone of Indian orchestras in the High Andes. The fiddle beside it seems an invention of fantasy, but the bass viol and the lute—in spite of the peculiar placement of their sound holes—and the little drums are all more or less realistic.[251]

The spacious choir loft at Andahuaylillas opens onto an outer gallery. Murals cover both ceiling and walls; note the flower vase at the right of the organ. A detail of the dado beside the instrument shows a bust of St. Paul enclosed within a medallion held by two cherubs (*fig. c*). Its heraldic scrolls, framing bands, and Medici "balls" placed at regular intervals recall illuminated manuscripts of the Quattrocento, particularly those from the Attavante studio. A series of anthems celebrating the Incarnation of the Word were discovered here; Juan Pérez de Bocanegra, the priest who had much to do with the embellishment of the building, was an excellent poet and wrote verses in honor of the Virgin.[187]

At the left of the Checacupe organ is another dado, different in style but also containing *putti* (*fig. b*). The wings of this instrument bear paintings of Peter and Paul and a few angelic musicians. Again the *charango* type of guitar and the portable harp are in evidence, both popular in the region.

Portrayals of Peter and Paul, painted on two long narrow strips of cotton cloth, hang in the nave of Santo Domingo in La Paz, Bolivia. When they were removed by this author for photographing and cleaned of their inch-deep accumulation of dirt, they were found to have pictures on both sides; apparently they were once organ wings. St. Cecilia at the Organ (*fig. d*) became visible on the lower part of the panel representing Paul (*see Pl. 146*), and above her, separated by the crosspiece of the flimsy strainer, was an angel playing a shawm-like instrument, very similar to the alto recorder popular in Elizabethan England. These paintings show a certain Byzantoid manner, and from their style they probably date from the second half of the seventeenth century.

The cathedral in Cuzco, Peru, boasts a pair of organs, placed opposite each other above the high partition which encloses the choir. Pipes that differ in height and caliber are decoratively grouped across the front in a manner common to Renaissance Europe,[250] and gilded wooden scrollwork screens the upper open spaces (*Pl. 154, fig. a*). Small paintings have been fitted into the console. There are only a few stops, each of which affects only half the keys of the single manual.

Tradition has it that the works of the organ shown—on the right as one enters—were of Flemish construction, and several features bear this out. Its pipes are massive, unpainted, and without the bizarre decoration which both Spanish and colonial organs carried prior to the nineteenth century. Also, the various ranks of the cornet stop are placed just behind the large front pipes in a typically Flemish arrangement introduced in late sixteenth century (*fig. b*). Vente dates this instrument according to its style between 1600 and 1625, by which time in the Low Countries its compass was already outmoded. Since there are no records of organs being shipped directly from Flanders to the New World, probably the works were manufactured in Spain by a Flemish organ builder. The case, however, may have been carved in Peru.

The two fluelike wooden pipes at one side of the instrument (left, in the illustration) may be drone pipes, or sub-octaves, which sustained the richness of tone in the tenors and basses. They must have been connected by a special stop, for there are no pedals. This organ is equipped with two other special sound effects: in the lower corner of the left pipe compartment the small cistern with a few tiny pipes issuing from it is so designed that when filled with water and manipulated by a special stop (not a key) it gives out a high trill—hence its name "nightingale"; the other device, at the extreme right, is called a lyre.

The position of these organs above the cathedral choir can be seen in the illustration showing the second of the pair (*Pl. 155, fig. a*), which is reported to have been constructed in the colony to match the imported instrument. The choir stalls here, perhaps the most interesting and elaborate in all Peru, carry forty-three full-length figures carved in relief and above them a row of women saints and martyrs. These stalls are dated[203] between 1657 and 1678. Thus quite an interval separates the date assigned by Vente to the works of the older organ and that of the choir stalls or even of the building, which was erected soon after the earthquake of 1650. Possibly the imported instrument was used in an earlier structure and refurbished when moved to its present location. The wings, one of which shows a St. Cecilia in a flowered and beribboned gown, are painted in the style of late seventeenth century. Fruit and flower bowls in the same style decorate the locally made instrument.

The organ in La Merced in Cuzco (*fig. b*) stands, as in most conventual establishments, on one side of the choir loft and well toward the front; so deep is this loft that it forms a secluded room where the monks can participate in the service unseen by the congregation. At the left of the instrument are visible the arches of the nave and the windows above them, framed in canvas paintings. These choir stalls, too—dated by Wethey about 1710—have a double row of figures, somewhat as those above; a detail is presented in Chapter 15 (*see Pl. 176*). The organ may be one or two decades earlier: it has the same shape as the cathedral organs and like them has undecorated pipes, grouped conservatively. Special sound effects, such as the nightingale and lyre, rest on the heads of the carved grotesque figures at the base of the dividing columns.

In a book published in Europe in 1773, Bernardo Recio, a Jesuit chronicler, describes conditions in Ecuador before the expulsion of that order from the Spanish colonies. He praises the musical talent of the natives and remarks that many churches as well as cathedrals there had their own orchestras. The violin had become popular with the Indian—reportedly through the efforts of a German friar—and also the harp, ten to twelve of which were sometimes played together at festivals with a marvelous effect. Bells were the pride of those communities which possessed them. Quito had its own foundry, but many bells were imported from Spain and carried up the arduous jungle-covered slopes on the shoulders of the Indians. The manufacture of organs

was a flourishing industry in the colony, and even less important churches had very beautiful instruments, for the craftsmen, besides being expert, were also clever at selecting good materials at a low cost. In addition to the grand organs little portatives were used in combination with stringed instruments—so as to comply with the letter of David's Psalm: *in chordis, et organo*—making as harmonious music as anyone could desire.[180]

To the author's knowledge no one had ever photographed for study the great cathedral organ at Cuenca, Ecuador, before his visit in 1945. It occupies the center of a deep choir loft (*fig. c*), and its elaborate decoration suggests that it was designed for that position. Excellent feeling for the architecture of the instrument is revealed in the columnar grouping of the pipes; even the vents were put to decorative use. The curious application of small paintings, irregular in shape, recalls the wings on earlier instruments. Two mermaids *contrapposto* are reclining against the central column, holding bunches of pale blue grapes, and ten small carved figures—paired, girl and boy—are blowing *chamade* pipes. Their costumes are delightfully varied; those at the top wear pink and gold garments and pale green hose, while the others show such combinations as green and pink with blue hose, blue and pink without hose, and yellow and green, also without hose. A clear blue covers the background of the large gilded medallions in the lower section of the case, and some rose is used about the pipes, bringing out their silvery color.

No documentation on this organ exists except for the inscription just below the pipe compartments: the instrument, dated August 30, 1739, was made by Antonio Estevan Cardoso when Gregorio de Vicuña was the rector of the church and Campo Domingo Gonzáles the treasurer. Cardoso himself, a resident of Cuenca, supposedly designed the organ. In 1924 it was carefully repaired and the colors were touched up.[235] Though more than a hundred pipes are said to be missing, it is still played regularly at the services. Four large bellows feed it, two on either side, so that each pair can be worked by one man. Its single manual has only two and one-half octaves and fourteen stops, seven on a side, arranged as follows:

Left	Right
voces humana	cromornos
lleno menor	lleno mayor
rte mayor	quintas
vinuenas	tda segundo
ova avierta	mdio rde corta
tda primera	ata do primero
angeles	(unnamed)

La Merced in Quito, Ecuador, manifests the same solidity in its interior construction as was observed in its cloister, dome, and outer wall (*see Pl. 100*). Its organ (*Pl. 156, fig. a*) might be dated within a decade or so of the completion of the edifice (1736). Like others shown here, it occupies the front end of one arm of a U-shaped choir gallery. Its loft is a riot of wood carving, in gold on a deep red background; small figures placed against the pilasters keep the whole fluid mass from commingling like a jungle vine.

The instrument itself is rather boxlike. Its pipes are grouped in a conservative pattern, with the tallest ones in the center, and are topped by a heavily gilded balustrade, contrasting with their silver. There is no series of horizontal pipes above the manual, but three appear on either side in the hands of boys, which end in leafy scrolls. Set amid honey-cake arabesques in stucco, which cover walls and ceiling, this organ is another telling example of the decorator's art in Quito.

The Minas Gerais district in Brazil was not opened until early in the eighteenth century. Its art, as will be seen in the next chapter, had no indigenous stylistic past, and by the time substantial edifices were being erected there, the century had passed the halfway mark. Into this artistically virgin territory the Rococo swept like a prairie fire, with no traditions from earlier centuries to block it. The *matriz* (parish church) of Tiradentes offers a charming example of that late Rococo style which prevails throughout the district. The organ (*fig. b*), like its companion on this plate, is so placed that the organist can watch the service and at the same time direct the choir. According to report, its pipes were imported from Porto, Portugal, and assembled in a case that was constructed in the mining town.[226] They are grouped in a columnar design and garlanded with scrollwork. Much of the case is painted, in keeping with the Rococo style. The angel trumpeters on the top are less forceful than those in the Quito piece but more ingratiating. This section of the choir loft, enclosed by an airy balustrade, tapers into a slender, elegant console, which carries a medallion painted with a Biblical scene in a Rococo setting. Supporting the gallery are pilasters of a delicate *estípite* form, exquisitely harmonious with the rest of the interior (*see also Pl. 172*).

Unpublished music manuscripts from the eighteenth century, found by Francisco Curt Lange in the cellar of an abandoned colonial house in Ouro Preto, in Minas Gerais, testify to the musical activity there. They were mainly sacred works written by mulattoes and Negroes for use in local churches. The scores include a motet and other forms in the style of contemporary Europe.[249] Here is stimulating proof that much may still exist to add to our limited knowledge of musical life throughout colonial Latin America.

The Jesuit establishments in Argentina and Paraguay were famous for their music. Among the nationalities represented by friar musicians in the missions around Córdoba, Argentina, are the Austrian, Belgian, French, German, Italian, and Swiss. The Tyrolese Anton Sepp taught (1691) the Indians of these regions to make organs and other instruments. It is indicative of the versatility of such friars that in addition Sepp practiced painting and carving; he also discovered lime in Paraguay, a real contribution to architecture there. Domenico Zipoli, born in Prato, Tuscany, in 1688, gave up his outstanding position as organist of the Jesuit mother church in Rome and in 1716 entered the novitiate of the order in Seville. A year later he joined an expedition to Rio de la Plata as a missionary and became the organist of the principal church in Córdoba. He died there in 1726, a highly respected figure in the musical life of colonial Argentina. Among his pupils was an Indian named José, who followed in his footsteps as a music teacher.[233]

As early as the beginning of the seventeenth century the Italian-born José Dadey held a distinguished place as a musician in Colombia. The Neapolitan Cármine Nicolás Caraccioli, Prince Santo Bueno and viceroy of Peru from 1716 to 1720, brought many Italian musicians to Lima who spread music everywhere.[72] By mid-eighteenth century every administrative center in Latin America could boast a roster of capable musicians.

The Dominican establishment at Tlacocha-huaya, in the Valley of Oaxaca, Mexico, was founded late in the sixteenth century, but much of its interior decoration dates from the seventeenth and even the eighteenth. A strongly folkloristic all-over design characterizes its church organ (*Pl. 157, fig. c*), in harmony with the charming provincial style of the painting on the walls. A lively floral pattern covers the front and sides of the instrument and even the vertical show pipes; the only figural element is an angel with a viol, placed in a medallion on the side panel. The carving is confined to the garlands which relieve the boxlike contours of the piece. This instrument has a row of horizontal *chamades*, favored in the Viceroyalty of New Spain more than in Spanish South America. The keyboard is open to view and seven stops can be counted on each side.

In contrast to this instrument, which makes its effect largely through painting, the organ in the lower choir of Santa Rosa in Querétaro, Mexico, depends on sculptural ornamentation (*fig. a*). Here the verticals are broken by

angles and protruding curves in an animated rhythm. The pipes are prominently displayed, and decorative use is made of the varying calibers and lengths. Nevertheless, this organ remains a big box for music: the carved case, though gloriously Baroque, reveals little of the instrument's structure; the opulent cornices, shells, and medallions, the garlands, and the figures all attract the eye first. When not in use, the keyboard is closed by a panel bearing a heart-shaped medallion, like those on either side, to produce an unbroken pattern. The double tier of horizontal pipes that once projected between the great shells above the keyboard must have constituted a harmonious unit by themselves; photographs from the late 1920's show a few still remaining then, but at the time of our visit in 1947 all of them had disappeared. The organ is sixteen to eighteen feet high, and its colors are chiefly gold and blue, with some touches of coral. It has three and one-half octaves, with four separate keys in the bass for sounding *g, a, b, c*, without accidentals. Its twelve stops are all placed on one side.

An inscription dated 1759 in the lambrequin at the base of the long pipe states that the chaplain of the "college" met the cost of the instrument and Ignacio Casas, a native of the town, built it. This sculptor, Ignacio Mariano de las Casas, is credited also with the plans for the church of Santa Rosa (finished in 1752) and with some of its altars. In the Querétaro archives a contract, dated 1758, signed by him gives detailed specifications for an organ for the nunnery church of Santa Clara there.[91] But the only old organ to be seen in that church today is a pitiful shell of painted canvas and flimsy wood braces; the works may have been transferred to another case. Two other eighteenth-century organs stand in the choir gallery of La Valenciana near Guanajuato (*see Pl. 42*).

Although the strong new church of La Merced in Antigua, Guatemala, withstood the catastrophic earthquake of 1773 with minor damage, nevertheless, when the abandonment of Antigua was decreed, the Mercedarians with all the other religious orders had to follow the administration to the present capital. The new Merced there was not dedicated until 1813, and then the interior decoration was transported from ruined Antigua. The great processions of images and treasures over a route of more than twenty-four miles were among the spectacular events of that period. Most of the altars of La Merced were in place by 1815, and probably the organ also was transferred about that time. Juan de León and his son are named as its builders in the memoirs of the Guatemala-born archbishop Francisco de Paula García Peláez (1785–1867). The same source mentions a number of native organ-makers who provided instruments for even small and distant towns. It is worth noting that some of these craftsmen were also skilled as clock-makers.[139]

Merced's large organ has an elaborate case of gilded wood (fig. b). This system of columnar grouping for organ pipes was used in Europe in the first quarter of the eighteenth century, but, considering the time lag that is often manifest in the New World, this instrument is probably contemporary with the final decorative touches given the church in Antigua around 1760. Especially striking is the bulging ornamentation at either side, which might be interpreted as a conventionalization of either the "ship's figurehead" or the bust placed on a leafy base, a favorite motif in Latin American wood carving. The grotesque masks once held *chamade* trumpets, huge panpipes protruding from their wide mouths. A fragment from Antigua (fig. d) served a similar function. The headdress especially, composed of floral elements, has plasticity.

As can be seen from these and the following illustrations the Viceroyalty of New Spain, much more than that of Peru, evinced a constant interest in the "up-to-date." Its organs employed such typically Hispanic features as the ranks of horizontal trumpets and grotesque faces painted on the pipes, but applied them

with much originality. Spanish South America, on the other hand, kept in general to the more conservative Flemish practices, developing in its own way that which had been implanted at an early date.

Four organs from Mexico show the variety achieved there in the eighteenth century. The neo-Mudéjar choir stalls of inlaid woods in the Puebla cathedral were constructed between 1719 and 1722, and the two imposing organs above them probably date from about that time. The instrument shown here stands at the left as one enters the nave (Pl. 158, fig. a). It has all the attributes of the monumental organ, which reached its height in Latin America in the eighteenth century. The storied columns of vertical pipes, used architecturally, overpower the single bristling line of those arranged horizontally below them. Sham pipes are added, mainly in the upper tiers, some of them placed upside down with their vents above, to give balance to the composition. Angelic musicians playing the flute, bassoon, and trumpet are perched about the structure as if on a retable; especially noteworthy is the one with a violoncello (upper left), an instrument which just about this time was approaching its present-day form. The wood carving on the framework is restrained, in keeping with the dignified atmosphere of this cathedral, in which the sheen of gilded grilles contrasts pleasantly with the many canvases.[238]

The church at San Martín Texmelucan, part of a Franciscan foundation, carries the date 1782 on a tile tablet on its façade. The organ here (fig. b) manifests perhaps more than the others on this plate a powerful folkloristic spirit. Curious and most original is the design of its pipe compartments, as well as the placement of the two large bass pipes, one on either side of the instrument.[250] Two cherubs in the upper corners are playing coiled horns, and two mermaids, lying along the top of the main pipes, are blowing long tubular trumpets —to the knowledge of this author a unique pastime for them. Just below the organ loft, near the main entrance, are ranged on leafy pedestals a series of busts of mermen, playing *chamade* trumpets.

Another Franciscan establishment, in San Miguel de Allende, includes four churches, all founded in the eighteenth century. The license for the erection of the largest of these, El Oratorio de San Felipe Neri, was issued in 1712, and two years later it was completed.[112] However, its interior represents various stylistic epochs. The organ (*fig. d*) bears carved decorations in brilliant gold, and a delightful painted Rococo pattern covers the two side doors that lead into the mechanism. A large instrument, it has twelve stops on either side, five auxiliary slides, and even a small pedal connection. On top is a series of sham orchestral instruments: a cello, French horn, and trombone on the right and, on the left, a clarinet and a viol of a peculiar oval shape. This unusual organ was played as late as the 1930's. It has retained a more complete set of horizontal trumpets than most; all too frequently the supports were not sturdy enough to hold up the heavy constructions of tin and lead.

The cabinet organ on this plate (*fig. c*), about eleven feet high, is at present in the Bello collection, in Puebla. Though its case is less typically colonial than the others, with their strongly regional decoration, the front pipes are painted with faces and arabesques, touched up with gilding. The native cypress of the woodwork was left in its original silvery color. A petaled medallion decorates each panel, and a lacelike side garland brings out the beauty of line in the instrument. This organ is believed to have been built around 1700 and to have stood originally in the nunnery of Santa Rosa in Puebla; indeed, it has the delicacy and intimacy appropriate to a nunnery. Its manual comprises three and three-quarters octaves, and it has sixteen stops—but no heavy basses—and nightingale and trumpet effects; the horizontal pipes issue from the sides. Concerning its maker, the story goes that he was a humble carver in Guadalajara,

an organ master who wandered about, nameless, intent on constructing beautiful instruments.

Music was closely tied into the life of nunneries. Crowds of appreciative listeners flocked on holy days to hear the nuns singing behind the curtained grilles of their upper and lower choirs, and many nunneries conducted schools of music, forerunners of our conservatories. Documents from the College of Santa Rosa de Santa María in Valladolid, now Morelia (*see Pl. 38*), reveal how carefully its young pupils were chosen; even though the tuition of an orphaned or poor girl was usually paid by the bishop or some wealthy benefactor, she nevertheless had to show a certificate of legitimacy and "purity of blood." The archive of the convent contains music composed in the eighteenth century for performance in the church or by the pupils. Numerous cantatas for various occasions exist, written for solo or chorus and strings. Arias, motets, and carols have been found—in general much Christmas music—and several Masses, including a Requiem Mass for four-part choir, violins, and trumpets. The instrumental compositions include sonatas, suites, and fugues, and several overtures.[236] It has been remarked earlier that there is very little music for organ among such manuscripts. But as in many of the smaller European courts, the organist probably was the leader and supplied the *basso continuo* throughout, either on the organ or on the harpsichord.

Some nuns achieved fame as accomplished musicians. St. Rosa of Lima could play the harp and the guitar and sang "to rival the birds." Thomas Gage recounts with malicious glee the scandal that surged around the beautiful Juana de Maldonado, a youthful nun of La Concepción in Antigua whom a wealthy father and an indulgent bishop tried to force into the position of abbess. But out of this story emerges also the picture of an unusually cultivated and talented young woman delighting her companions with witty improvised verses and entertaining them with music on the several instruments at her command, among them an organ which stood in her chamber.[55]

The cathedral of Mexico, unique in size and importance (*see Pl. 2*), preserves two colonial organs, worthy of the building in which they stand (*Pl. 159*). They bring to a majestic culmination Mexico's long tradition in musical performance as well as composition. Like the pair in the Cuzco cathedral, these organs are placed in galleries above the partition that separates the choir from the side aisles. Also like those in Cuzco, one was imported, the other was built later, and adjustments were made to harmonize the two. *La Gaceta de México* reported their dedication in October 1736, praising their exquisite cases of unvarnished cedar and calling attention to their great size. Each has more than 3,350 pipes, and five large bellows, efficiently connected with the entire range of stops, are hidden away in the interiors. José Nasarre is named as the builder of the organ on the gospel side (*fig. a*)—the right as one enters the building.

A document dated May 31, 1688, in Mexico, gives the specifications for the organ on the epistle side (*fig. b*), which the venerable dean of the cathedral requested to have made in Spain:[128] it should consist of a great organ, a *cadareta*, or small choir organ, and pedal work. The great organ should be pitched somewhat lower than was the custom in Spain because the voices in the viceroyalty did not have the compass of the Spanish choirs; but since the choir organ was intended especially to accompany the winds in their natural pitch, it was to have the same pitch as the Spanish organs so as to avoid constant transposing. These peculiarities were stressed in the specifications as essential to the requirements of this church. As for the stops, very suave and full diapasons were requested with all the doubles, or suboctaves, to sustain tonal richness; then, flutes in all their diversity, all sorts of trumpets with their tremolos, "birds," and echoes; the vox humana stop and the one called "nazarete" should be included, together with the custom-ary mixtures of quints, octavos, fifteenths, twenty-seconds, and twenty-fourths to achieve a balanced tone. And any novelties of which Mexico had no experience would be acceptable if passed on by someone competent to judge. Easy key action also was specified.

The measurements of the gallery it would occupy were given so that it could be harmoniously proportioned to this space. As for the general exterior design, the "modern" organs of the Spanish court were suggested as models. The instrument was ordered complete with case and bellows, and accompanying personnel was requested to assemble it in Mexico. The document notes, however, that if for any reason the case offered difficulties it could be supplied in the viceroyalty, which possessed both exquisite woods and excellent carvers.[128]

As a sequel to these specifications, a paper, undated, presents an appeal for payment from Tiburcio Sanz, who states that he came from Spain to assemble the Spanish organ; he had been given the commissions to make the case and to construct the bellows and another register of *contras* (lowest basses), as well as four hundred mute pipes for the adornment of the organ's façade. After he had carved the first story of the case, added an octave to the cornets of the echo, and readjusted the basses and when the tone of the instrument had been adjudged select and very sonorous, Sanz requested final payment and the permission to return home.

The cases of the two monumental organs, though not identical, are well harmonized, framing the metallic beauty of the pipes with a wealth of carved ornament. They are also carefully proportioned in relation to the choir stalls, a detail of which will be shown in Chapter 15.

The illustration of the newer instrument (*fig. a*) shows the choir organ, placed behind the organist on the edge of the gallery with a large angel on either side of it; a rather rare feature in Spanish America, it is found only with the more monumental organs there. In such old instruments the tone of the grand organ is characterized by its strength and richness, while that of the choir organ is sweet and somewhat colorless.

The other photograph (*fig. b*) shows the towering height of the older instrument as seen from the side aisle opposite. A gigantic bracket, ornamented with compact Baroque motifs of angel figures among dense foliage, forms an appropriate base for the whole bulk. With its extraordinary dimensions, its doors leading into the interior, and its suggestion of grilled windows, this huge organ looms over the spectator like some galleon destined to ride the waves of music.

While the majority of the organs illustrated in this chapter are more or less Baroque in style, the instrument in Santa Prisca at Tasco, Mexico (*Pl. 160, fig. b*), leans toward the Rococo. In the design of its case it is close to the example at Tiradentes. It, too, has a column of long pipes in the center, garlands draping the dividing piers and the upper section, and angels perched on top. However, it has more stops and is more monumental also as a decorative piece. Note the charming treatment of the choir organ at the front of the gallery and the lantern-shaped bell racks, all in harmony. The cherubs that seem to be leaping out of the side of the case once held long trumpets.

Fourteen stops are grouped on the left and thirteen on the right of its single manual. There are no pedals, but ten large wooden bass pipes are ranged behind the case.

The first organ in this parish church is said to have been installed in 1759, two years after the building was completed. Reparation and alterations were effected in 1806. The fact that this date is inscribed on a painted cartouche on its case probably is responsible for its being attributed to the early nineteenth century. The inscription states clearly, however, that the great organ work was at that time "aggrandized" by the addition of a new "mixture," which was installed by José Antonio Sánchez, a native of "Yxmyquylpan." (Ixmiquilpan is a town in the state of Hidalgo, known for its sixteenth-century Augustinian establishment.) Strictly interpreted, the term "mixture" denotes a stop or set of pipes which, by sustaining the trebles and strengthening the harmonics, adds brilliance and richness to the fundamental tones of the diapason; in this instance perhaps the new stop was a new and special effect. Changes may have been made on the case at the same time, for the neoclassic is discernible in certain motifs, particularly in the bust medallions. A great flowery rug from the Orient is said to have once covered the entire nave of this church. With the magnificent altar here, the sparkling crystal chandeliers, and the glittering garb of the priests, the pomp of a High Mass must have been superbly operatic, a scene for a Mozart or a Cherubini.

Since Tasco is on the route from Acapulco to the capital, such an Oriental rug would probably come across the Pacific from China or the Philippines. The Rococo in Mexico, as in Europe, borrowed from the Far East; textile patterns, wallpapers, and household furnishings imitated the Chinese. The same influence is manifest also in the shapes of some Mexican pottery. The Chinese type of decorative screen—significantly called "Spanish wall" in some European languages—executed in leather and wood, with painted and lacquered scenes and metal trappings, was a favorite and useful object of the gentry household.

A highly effective Rococo atmosphere is evoked by one such screen, made in Mexico; it measures some 18 by 6½ feet, is divided into ten panels, and is painted in oil on canvas. Here an anonymous artist from the second half of the eighteenth century depicted scenes from a garden party, held perhaps near some seignioral mansion in New Spain. Music is being made in the two panels illustrated. The flutist (*fig. a*) is quite realistically portrayed; the young woman beside him may be holding the notes or the text of a song. In the other picture (*fig. c*) the bass viol is strung with only three strings, in the Italian manner of that age. Color adds considerably to the animation of the scenes; the flutist wears blue, with a scarlet vest, the cellist a scarlet coat over a sky-blue suit, and the woman a gown of a darker red. Jardinieres of majolica stand on the garden wall, and meticulously varied bouquets are set about. The other panels in the screen show servants bringing up refreshments and elegant men and women in costumes of the period engaged in conversation.

Thus the screen, a furniture piece of Oriental ancestry, is painted in the European Rococo manner; but its entire spirit, as well as the lushness of the vegetation and the volcanic peaks in the background, places the scene in colonial Spanish America.

In this chapter, over twenty Latin American organs have been presented—from the primitive to the most magnificent. Many more remain there, neglected, some mere shells, in no condition to be played. Their noble tone belongs to the past. Silenced, they stand in dignity through much turmoil, monuments to a splendid phase of colonial life, the beauty of which is known to all too few.

ROCOCO IN BRAZIL

Bᴙ the Treaty of Tordesillas (1494) the pope effected a division of the New World according to longitude between the two kingdoms of the Iberian Peninsula. In contrast to the Spanish possessions, which spread widely throughout Middle and South America, the Portuguese holdings consisted of one compact area, a single colony—Brazil. It covered an immense territory, however, larger than the United States and comprising almost half of South America. Tropical vegetation came down to the water's edge on the Atlantic shore, and the Amazon was a river of mystery and terror, whether the explorer set out from the delta or, more daringly, broached it at the headwaters in the Andes.

This land did not reveal immediate riches, as did the Spanish viceroyalties. The culture of the sparse aboriginal population was semi-savage, far below the level attained by the pre-Columbian peoples in either Middle America or the Andean areas, with their splendid cities and religious centers. Furthermore, as the Portuguese widened his grip along the coast and inland, many natives retired into the well-nigh limitless world of the interior jungle and distant high plateaus, greatly reducing the available native labor.

The word "brazil" was current before the discovery of the Americas, used to designate plants and woods that rendered a crimson dye. Portugal's colony in the New World was first called Santa Cruz, but because in the begin-

ning brazilwood was one of its chief economic assets—samples of the precious material were carried home by the first expedition—the whole region soon came to be known as Brazil.

The quantity and the quality of the other native woods simplified many problems of construction for the Brazilian builder. Unlike Europe, where wood was scarce and stone was the principal building material, here a virgin forest offered an unlimited supply of durable timber for structural beams and columns. Often they carried an incredible weight of masonry. In those days, too, every seafaring nation needed vast quantities of wood for its ships.

The harbor just below the bulge, where stands today the city of Salvador, offered an excellent anchorage for the first comers. The expedition of Pedro Alvares Cabral landed in the vicinity in 1500—almost twenty years before Cortés reached Mexico—and two years later the first settlement was founded. In 1530 the first royal agent was sent over, and in 1549 Tomé de Souza, supported by a large military force, established the Captaincy of Bahia and made the seaport its capital.

At first Brazil was divided into captaincies, which were later consolidated under the administration of a single viceroy. Colonization was a private enterprise, that is, undertaken through the award of feudal grants. The landholders received practically full authority over, as well as hereditary rights to, their lands, which they were supposed to develop at their own expense. In return they made regular payments to the king; the right of coinage, the death penalty, and certain other matters remained under the jurisdiction of the crown.

Before the end of the seventeenth century cities and towns had spread along the coast and up the fertile valleys and river beds. Sugar, cotton, rice, and tobacco were then the main products; in the eighteenth century gold, diamonds, and coffee became important. The centers of development and wealth shifted as new areas were opened to production. Growing numbers of Negro slaves were imported. The Negro took to this climate, which was well suited to his constitution, and today about a third of the population has Negro blood, either pure or mixed.

The lack of native craftsmen with a high indigenous artistic culture and the indifference of Portugal toward her colony in the sixteenth century are mainly responsible for the simple, unadorned buildings of the early epoch. Only a few of these remain, but a number are preserved in prints and paintings. The widespread activities of pirates along the coast accounts in part for the destruction of many early edifices. In the first century of Brazil's colonial life, little attempt was made to transplant here Portugal's ornate Manueline Gothic style, as the Spaniards had done with their contemporary architecture in Santo Domingo (see Pl. 1). In Brazil the typical early church façade shows a small entrance porch—usually with columns of the durable native wood, more rarely of stone—a single doorway, and a circular window placed between and above two rectangular ones. This type of structure was quite different from the barn-shaped church of the early Spanish American colonies. A predilection for windows is noticeable throughout colonial architecture in Brazil, while in the Spanish colonies it became markedly so only with the Rococo. On the other hand Brazil shows little preoccupation with domes and vaults. For Portugal had already experienced violent earthquakes and learned

that they toppled vaulted constructions first. Indeed, much of Portugal's early architecture had been destroyed by earthquakes, and thus, side by side with the old styles, the new came into its own there (see Appendix, Pl. 192, fig. a).

In coastal Brazil an ebullient Baroque arose. The coming of the Rococo coincides with the discovery and exploitation of the mines in the mountains. A clean and undiluted Rococo flourished especially in the Captaincy of Minas Gerais, and for this reason most of the Rococo examples presented here were selected from that region.

Because Salvador was the first capital of the colony and remained so until 1763, the general trends of colonial architecture and art can best be traced there. Colonial towns in Brazil were not laid out in a checkerboard pattern, like those in Spanish America; like Lisbon and Oporto, they spread according to the need of the times. Salvador (also called Bahia, because of its location on the Bahía de Todos os Santos—All Saints' Bay) was no exception and today it is virtually two cities —the lower, with its magnificent harbor, and the upper, where colonial churches, monasteries, and government buildings are still preserved. By the end of the eighteenth century the city had a population of some seventy thousand; it boasted six monasteries and six nunneries and buildings that were six or seven stories high.

One of the oldest structures illustrated here, the church of the Third Order of St. Francis, built in 1703 (Pl. 161, fig. a), stands in the picturesque section of the upper town. Although at first glance its richly decorative exterior of stone may bring to mind the Spanish colonial Baroque, a study will reveal differences. In this small building the three entrances leave little space for ornamentation on the ground floor. The four allegorical figures in the second story are the most striking elements of its façade. Noteworthy also are the wrought-iron balconies, typically Brazilian, and the repeated use of volutes and consoles. The pilasters between the doors show heads below the capitals—a Baroque arrangement frequent in Central European architecture and already familiar in this volume from Spanish American wood carving. The pediment is not drawn up to any special height but is dramatized with great scrolls and with tall finials which suggest Portuguese taste.

A detail of the second order of the façade (*fig. d*) shows a certain placidity in the various motifs when considered separately; each panel seemingly is a unit. In the pediment alone is a flowing and florid effect achieved. But even this mildly Baroque ornamentation was found too strong for a later generation who stuccoed it over; only recently was it restored to its original beauty.

Adjoining this edifice is the Franciscan monastery, with its colonnades (*fig. b*), and beyond that stands the church of São Francisco, finished in 1710. Its twin towers are covered with tiles; between them rises a freestanding pediment with a tall cross, seen here from the rear. (The interior of this church is shown on *Pls. 164, 165*). The walls of the monastery cloister are adorned with a scenic dado of Portuguese blue tiles presenting a series of allegorical pictures, each enclosed in Baroque scrollwork. Plain columns support both galleries, and the roof hangs low, producing welcome shade in this tropical climate.

Belém, the capital of the state of Pará, lies on the Amazon delta, the nearest large port to the motherland. Commerce in wood, oil, nuts, spices, fruits, honey, dyes, and skins brought great wealth to the region, and in addition the fertile soil produced cotton, cocoa, sugar, tobacco, and, later, coffee. The tremendous opportunities for making quick fortunes found expression here in an exaggerated scale of living.

Belém's church of Santo Alexandre (*fig. c*), however, displays a rather sober and controlled spirit. This structure, the third on the site, was built by the Jesuits in 1718. Windows break the second and third tiers in the façade as well as in the flanking towers—indeed, the Jesuits are said to have introduced glass window panes into Brazil.[229] The pilasters, barely suggested, are ornamented with strongly tempered floral and geometric motifs, and pediments are placed only over the entrances and the niche. That niche, with its twisted columns, and the bracket-like lines which define the major pediment are Baroque touches. Santo Alexandre exemplifies the dwelling-house type of façade that was common on the coast of Brazil but most unusual in the Spanish colonies.

The capital city of Pernambuco, Recife—so-called from its outlying reef—is situated on that great elbow of land which is nearest to the Old World. In colonial times ships arrived here weeks earlier than in Rio de Janeiro and the other more southern ports. Beginning with three small trading posts and a little fort, it functioned first as the harbor port for Olinda, an older town on the bluff beyond it which has now dwindled in importance to a suburb.

During the period when Portugal and Spain were under one sovereign (1580–1640), the colony of Brazil was somewhat neglected because it was thought to possess little mineral wealth. Consequently, in 1630, the Dutch West India Company was able to gain a foothold here and establish "Holland in Brazil" along the northeast coast. Realizing the strategic importance of Recife as a harbor and impressed by the commercial possibilities in the nearby waterways, the Dutch laid plans to develop this fishing village into a beautiful city. But in 1654 Portugal regained control once more, and the city continued to flourish and expand under Portuguese rule. A widespread republican uprising occurred in 1710, which expelled the governor and established its own government; not until aid arrived from the motherland was this rebellion suppressed. Built on strips of land between converging rivers, Recife has been compared to Venice, its buildings, bridges, and squares gaining an especially picturesque touch from the tropical setting.

The church of São Pedro dos Clérigos (*Pl. 162, fig. b*) in Recife dates from 1729; its architect was Ferreira Jacomé. In its façade, unusually tall and slender, many of the distinguishing characteristics of coastal Baroque can be observed. It has three entrances, the center one emphasized, and many windows; even in the gable, where in Spanish America one would normally find a niche, there is an attic window flanked by volutes, typically European. The excellence of the plastic ornament can be seen in the detail of the main portal (*fig. c*). In Baroque fashion it has twin columns; but they are classically fluted rather than twisted. The opulence of the Baroque is evident also in the bombastic heraldic shield that fills the central space, in the garlands of fruit at the sides, and in the mermaids ending in scrolls. The massive wooden door has the quality of bronze. In the general design of its façade, this church reminds one of that in Oporto, Portugal, dedicated to the same saint and built in 1732–1748 by the Italian Nicoló Nasoni. Further, Central European architecture may have furnished inspiration especially for the attenuated towers (*see Appendix, Pl. 192, fig. d*).

The entrance to the Saldanha palace at Salvador, Bahia (*fig. a*), today a trade school, is dated about 1720. When this portal, also with a coat of arms, is compared with that of the Recife church, contemporary in date, the variety found in coastal Baroque becomes evident. No attempt was made to have the figures against the pilasters appear functional, as caryatides. Somewhat like those on the façade of the Third Order in Salvador, they stand as statues, with massive volutes as pedestals and capitals. Note the spiraling grapevines with clusters of fruit on the engaged columns. In the second story the carving is less protruding. Again the general build-up is remarkably different from that presented by Spanish American portals, in spite of a number of similar decorative elements.

Recife has sixty-two churches, many of them built in the eighteenth century. The three grouped here (*Pl. 163*) have several features in common. All of them were planned with lofty twin towers. In each the central doorway is emphasized. Elaborate French windows open onto balconies on the second floors, and round or star-shaped windows are employed. The pediments are drawn high and kept somewhat separate from the towers; when provided with a window they recall steep-sided Flemish gables (*see Appendix, Pl. 190, fig. a*). The whitewashed wall surfaces provide a pleasing contrast to the light gray stone throughout.

The church of the Carmelite Third Order (*fig. c*) was started in 1687 on the site where formerly the palace of the Dutch governor had stood. In mid-eighteenth century it was provided with a new façade, the pediment of which has been described as one of the most "contorted" in all Brazil. Nevertheless, when it is compared with the two on this plate—as well as with others along the coast—it is unquestionably a version of the coastal type. The tendency to modulate a basically uniform design will become evident again when the architecture of the mining district is presented, although the type there is quite different from this. Carmo's ambitious façade reveals sculptural originality and verve, qualities which later were abandoned in the interest of speedy production.

Individuality also characterizes the church of Rosário (*fig. a*), dated 1725–1777, especially in its exquisite central window, the Rococo hexagonal grilled opening in its tower, and the floral richness and fine design of its pediment.

In the church of Santo Antônio (*fig. b*), dated 1750–1753, there are no statues and little individual warmth or vibrancy, except in the pediment. Though many of the decorative elements seen in the others are applied here, a certain formalism prevails. A somewhat uniform ornament is used above the doors in the first and second stories, and no attempt is made to break the monotonous regularity by varying the system of openings. In its total effect, the building has great elegance. Here the uneven cornice line employed in the other two façades is used most effectively; the pediment rises gracefully from three scallops, which accommodate the three round windows below.

This device of modifying the powerful horizontal of a cornice to free and lighten the ornate pediment can be observed very often in Brazil. The bulk of the towers seldom provides contrast, as is so frequently the case in Spanish America. The large crosses which top all the pediments are typical of this country; rarely in the Spanish colonies are they so dominant.

Sometimes plain colonial buildings that survived the vicissitudes of the sixteenth and seventeenth centuries were rewarded, so to speak, in the eighteenth with a magnificent interior. Such is São Bento (Pl. 164, fig. b), one of the earlier churches of Rio de Janeiro, dating, together with its Benedictine monastery, from 1623–1642. In the early eighteenth century it came under bombardment by the French, and cannon balls are still embedded in its walls. Inside, highly plastic and heavily gilded foliage carved of wood constitutes the prevailing motif for the decoration. It is modified and varied to spread over straight and arching surfaces and is ingeniously composed to cover the bulging sides of the boxlike pulpit. A number of cherubs can be discovered among the leaves. The saints between the arches are quiet in appearance and gesture. Organization in this luxuriant mass of compact ornament was achieved by dividing the surface into fields and by the rhythmic repetition of line.

The cathedral at Salvador, also rather austere in its outer aspect, has a superbly ornate interior; the edifice, as has been mentioned, belonged to the Jesuits (see Pl. 10). Shown here is the altar in the left transept dedicated to St. Ignatius (fig. d). He stands on a high pedestal, and below him is the Virgin, with angels at her feet—all carved in the best eight-

eenth-century tradition. The twin columns of gilded wood on either side spiral in opposite directions. Note the saints under baldachins placed against the plain concave surfaces of the pilasters and, on the inner frame of the niche, the caryatides, whose upraised arms may once have held lamps. This altar is a fine example of Brazilian Baroque—already moving, in its use of color, into the Rococo. (For interesting differences, compare this altar with those in certain Jesuit churches in Spanish America, some of them contemporary, illustrated on Pls. 43, 99, 109.)

The façade of the church of São Francisco in Salvador, Bahia, is quite plain, but the interior is one of the richest Baroque manifestations in all coastal Brazil, lined with wood carving and stucco ornaments, gilded and polychromed (fig. a). It was completed in general construction in 1723, but its decoration took more than a quarter of a century longer. Panels in plastic relief, with deeply undercut motifs, alternate with the flatter carving. Caryatides support the garlanded columns of the altar (lower right), and others, more decorative than functional, are represented as holding up the baldachin to the pulpit. A plain strip of wall above the frames of the panels (upper left) provides a welcome margin to set off the magnificent painted ceiling. Note also the great oval medallions, with their candelabra, flanking the window.

In the other detail (fig. c) a composition from the left transept can be studied. In the center stands the Virgin of the Immaculate Conception, her robes executed in good Baroque estofado; but the swirling scrolls and the various groupings of angels with their alive gestures distract the eye somewhat from the main figure. There are angels in figured gowns, putti ending in scrolls holding the conventional crown, and cherubs dangling in the leafy background of the pilasters. Again considerable organization is gained by the use of panels and a precise balancing of the ornament. Perched in the capital at the upper right is the carved figure of a symbolic bird.

Many of the churches in Brazil, modeled after Portuguese structures, had a gallery above the side aisles opening onto the nave through a series of loges or balconied windows. The effect inside was that of a clerestory (*figs. a, b*); outside, this arrangement is indicated in the rows of second-story windows.

Another interior view of São Francisco in Salvador shows its sumptuous main altar and apse (*Pl. 165, fig. b*). The deep and narrow sanctuary is characteristic of church architecture in Portugal and Brazil. Strips of white define the intricate pattern of the barrel-vaulted ceiling and serve to emphasize the burnished gold of the heavy coffered fields. In the altar the lines of the ornate engaged columns and their arches are all but lost in the plethora of ornament, centered on the touching statue of St. Francis, embracing and embraced by the Crucified. The catafalque-like build-up, here comparatively low, provides a most effective podium for the sculpture. On the wall beside the sacristy door the soft blue and white of tile pictures add to the exposition of color.

A full view of the sanctuary of São Pedro dos Clérigos (*fig. a*), in Recife, shows the narrow and lofty interior indicated by the exterior (*see Pl. 162*). The walls are plain, broken only by elegant balconies, but the ceiling of masonry vaulting is unusually elaborate. The columns are entwined with garlands spiraling in opposite directions. Behind the altar the usual catafalque-like construction rises tier on tier, reaching nearly to the ceiling—a Portuguese feature adopted in Brazilian churches.

Both structures on this plate date from the first half of the eighteenth century and both are on the coast, not far from each other. A comparison of their interiors reveals considerable diversity in the local taste. Differences can be noted also between the typical Brazilian sanctuary and the Spanish American. The latter usually extends the full width of the nave and is separated from it by a broad triumphal arch; furthermore, the retable usually

covers the entire end of the apse, and light from the outside is focused upon it. It should be mentioned here that Brazil is not an earthquake country.

Beginning with the middle of the eighteenth century a distinct daintiness is apparent in the coastal architecture. Light curves and cornices replaced the heavy striving ones, and more and more of the wall space was left empty or filled with larger windows and doors. The parish church of Pilar, in Salvador (*Pl. 166, fig. a*), from late eighteenth century, is a remarkable example of this type. It has but one tower, which like its pediment is kept low. Decoration is on an exquisite scale, every detail masterly in design and execution. The windows might be regarded as out of proportion with the rest of the building were they not treated with infinite grace; divided into small panes, they present a checkered pattern that fills in the dark openings. The surrounding decoration has the tenuousness of a picture frame, and the lines of the fancifully shaped gable window could have been inspired by a Rococo jewel box. Both the flaming urns and the cross are still present but scaled down to harmonize with the rest of the structure. Standing on a steep flight of steps and bathed in the strong white sunlight of the tropics, the building has the unreality of a Rococo stage backdrop.

Throughout the state of Paraíba, farther to the north, are scattered churches that exemplify an early and lavish Baroque; unfortunately many of them are now neglected and overgrown with tropical vegetation, their windows broken or gaping.

In the church of São Francisco at João Pessoa (*fig. b*), the capital, the captivating illusion of a stage setting is still more marked. This church, renovated to its present form in 1779, is approached through an atrium between tiled walls. A rhythmic series of scrolls decorates the coping of these walls, punctuated at intervals by the finials of the piers and the ornamental pediments that crown the Stations of the Cross. Three broad low steps augment the dramatic effect of the building. All five doorways still possess their original wooden grilles. In the second story, French windows open onto balconies. The pediment is low, but the scroll design carried down on either side gives it the appearance of a two-story structure. The tower, except for the framing piers of stone, is faced with pale blue tiles, even to the Oriental cupola. One cannot look at this building without visualizing the Rococo ceremony and splendor which enlivened the scene about it—the palanquins borne by barefoot Negro slaves in uniforms of velvet and gold, the carriages with grooms and postilions, the extravagant display of Oriental and European finery. It has much of the mood of contemporary country mansions in the motherland (*see Appendix, Pl. 192, fig. f*).

The pulsing enjoyment of the Brazilian carver in his craft is revealed in many details of interior decoration whether small or large. Though the elaborate cornice inside the choir loft of this church (*Pl. 167, fig. a*) may appear heavy to some, it is not at all awkward. The frame of the adjacent window overlooking the nave shows the same approach, demonstrating the excellence of the material and the expertness of the craftsmen; its heavy volutes are typical of Brazil. And all this for a room remote from the public eye, used only by members of the choir.

Like the two other examples on this plate, the pulpit from São Francisco Xavier in Belém (*fig. b*) dates from the first half of the eighteenth century. Beginning with the two cherubs who hold back the looped drapery above its baldachin, the canopy rises in a polychrome pyramid of angelic and allegorical figures. The supporting bracket carries angel busts—perhaps Hope and Charity beside the blindfolded Faith—and ends in a leafy bouquet, counterbalancing the crown and cross at the top.

In the sacristy of Carmo in Salvador (*fig. c*) both wall and ceiling are sheathed with panels

containing canvases, gilded stucco work, and wood carving. Fitted into a door frame (center) is a highboy of a beautiful local wood. (*See also Pl. 186.*) The stone pavement—in two tones and varied in pattern, following the tradition of wall tiles—produces a pleasant coolness in that tropical climate. Despite the altar with its crucifix at the far end of the hall and the large statues of saints between the doors, the impression is that of a mundane salon.

A luscious Rococo spirit, adjusted to tropical conditions, permeated the manner of life in the coastal cities, and by mid-eighteenth century this region had established a style in which the Rococo was grafted onto the Baroque. The use of statuary, never in very great favor here, gradually was discontinued; decoration was concentrated on the pediment and the door and window framing. Increasingly the ecclesiastical building took on the worldly elegance of a princely palace, both within and without.

When the towers and cross of the church of Conceição in Salvador are covered (*Pl. 168, fig. a*), few marks remain to identify the edifice as dedicated to the service of God. The ornamentation over the doorways is restrained in line and bulk, and the windows above them are framed simply. Delightful is the bracketing together of the window cornices, forming a single undulating line and ingenious shadow play. Through the subordination of other embellishment, the curves of the pediment are given dramatic emphasis, and the cross at the top a striking position. In the center is a shell, itself a holy emblem, containing a sickle moon; as there was scarcely room for a statue it would seem that the builders were content with this one symbol of the Virgin of the Immaculate Conception. The building may have been constructed by local artisans who were familiar with, and had even worked on, much more pretentious edifices. In this simply conceived and tastefully executed church, without any striving for pomposity, they achieved an expression of sincerity.

The town of Igarassú, near Recife, grew up on the site of early plantations. Its church (*fig. b*), dedicated to the sainted martyrs Cosmos and Damian, was founded in 1553 and is reported to be the oldest in the country. Although it was redone in the taste of the late seventeenth century, such structural features as the single doorway, the porch, and the triangular placement of the windows in the façade are preserved from the pioneering period. In the later decoration elements appear that have been seen elsewhere; noteworthy is the strong and rhythmic line of the cornice below the modest pediment.

This photograph is one of a number furnished for this chapter by Robert C. Smith, eminent authority on the art of Portugal and Brazil. He has pointed out that this little church in its tropical setting provided the Dutch artist Frans J. Post (1612?–1680) with a subject for a painting.[230] Post was the first painter of Brazil whose work can be identified. He lived in Recife during the Dutch occupation, and his paintings of the sugar plantations and opulent landscape, the buildings, and the flora and fauna of the region, done with the clarity of a Canaletto, help reconstruct the picture of seventeenth-century coastal Brazil.

The seminary church in Belém (*fig. c*) shows how the style on the coast was modified for the comfort of the congregation. Here, in the damp and heavy climate of the Amazon delta, an open gallery, its roof drawn low, runs the length of the edifice. The façade has the usual features: plain tall pilasters, a scrolled pediment rising slightly higher than the roof, and a squat tower. A simple and practical structure, it is well suited to the conditions of the land. Were not the date 1689 inscribed below the cross, it might be judged as somewhat later.

When the coastal churches of Brazil were being erected, Baroque was the prevalent style throughout Europe. To the casual observer this coastal Baroque may not seem to differ

much from the Baroque of other lands, but to the student it reveals a character of its own. Throughout Latin America the climate, soil, and vegetation, the materials at hand, and the presence or absence of aboriginal traditions in art and craftsmanship all helped to individualize the arts of a colony. In Brazilian as well as in Spanish American Baroque, the emphasis was not on varied ground plans and brilliant architectural solutions but on ornamentation. In Brazil most of the colonial churches along the coast adhered to a rectangular three-aisle plan, with both apse and sacristy enclosed within the regular frame; the decoration is characterized by a discriminating balance, often achieved by confining the ebullient elements within panels.

As has been indicated, for almost two centuries the major development of Brazil was along the coast. At the close of the seventeenth century, however, both gold and diamonds were discovered in the mountains of the south central regions of the colony. Gold had been the dream from the very beginning in all Latin America. Scheduled armadas laden with gold and silver from the expanding mines of the Spanish colonies moved regularly to Spain, and it was argued that, as Brazil was a part of the same continent, her mountains also should contain precious metals. Numerous expeditions were sent inland to seek deposits, but it was long before success came. Finally, in 1692, an iron-colored pellet scooped up from a shallow river bed in the pail of a thirsty mulatto proved to be gold, and the feverish search began. Soon other veins in other valleys were discovered. The district was miles inland, unexplored, and inhabited by hostile Indians. After the natives had been driven out and the customary fights among the white rivals had decided who of them had the right to exploit the mines, the region was declared a captaincy under a Portuguese officer and called Minas Gerais (general mines). It filled rapidly with settlers from other parts of Brazil, and a mass of immigrants poured in from

Portugal, resulting in one of the great migrations in history. Mining on a grand scale was commenced.

The mining district was under very strict surveillance to make sure that every grain of gold dust and every splinter of diamond reached the authorities. Five hundred Portuguese dragoons were stationed in scattered companies about the mines to forestall bootlegging. The roads over which the treasure passed were bordered with stone walls, sometimes skillfully disguised with moss to prevent any by-passing of toll stations and tax officials. For so long as it could, the Portuguese crown tried to keep this vast source of wealth secret from the rest of the world. No foreign travelers or visitors of any sort were permitted in Minas Gerais; enslavement was the penalty. Agriculture and industry were forbidden there; schools were not allowed; none of the religious orders was permitted to gain a foothold. Every effort of the population had to be directed toward the mines. And these were so productive [227] that the value of the annual mining output during the first fifty years is reported to have run as high as $8,500,000. The covetous motherland squeezed all possible wealth out of the province. Before the eighteenth century had drawn to a close, the mines were exhausted and a general decadence had set in, aggravated by rebellion and revolution. More than half a century passed before even a fraction of the former prosperity was recovered.

The architecture of Minas Gerais was a purely eighteenth-century development. The primitive clay and rubble chapels of the first decades, with their thatched roofs, were built on much the same plan as the very early coastal churches; the small porch was omitted and sometimes the bell tower stood free. By 1730 larger constructions of masonry were being raised and on a more pretentious plan. The eighteenth century had not passed its halfway mark before the mining cities could boast finely executed edifices. As both monasteries and nunneries were excluded, white and Negro lay societies competed with one another in erecting and adorning their churches. A local quartz made its structural as well as its aesthetic contribution. Because of an abundance of superlatively hard wood for beams, few of these churches were vaulted. Despite the great wealth that was extracted from the Minas district and the influx of new people, the architecture of the area possesses a rustic beauty all its own. The region was still too far from Rio de Janeiro—its nearest port and the seat of the new viceroyalty—to emulate the lavishness and elegance of the coast. Domestic architecture followed the pattern of northern Portugal, from where a large percentage of the miners came.

As for the church building itself, a rather small, low edifice was favored. It had an elaborately decorated single doorway and two towers, which usually were integrated into the façade. In the central section were windows of a Rococo design, irregular and scalloped in outline, while for the towers elongated ovals were preferred. To the pediment went the dramatic emphasis. Rounded and oval ground plans, such as are rarely seen in Spanish America, were common.

Those dark grains which proved to be gold gave to Ouro Preto (black gold) its name; in colonial times it was known too as Vila Rica (rich town). And the gold in the nearby hills also gave the place its rich art and architecture, making of it a unique site, a veritable open-air museum in which the artistic atmosphere of the golden era is today held fast. Its thirteen churches, its numerous government buildings (dating from the period when it was the seat of the captaincy-general), its ornate public fountains, the graceful stairways and ramps connecting the many levels of its hilly terrain, all are preserved. In 1933 a government decree declared the town a national monument.

A section of Ouro Preto (*Pl. 169, fig. a*) shows a winding street that probably has changed little in the last century and a half. Its houses are generally two-storied, sometimes with a dormer added, and the heavily tiled roofs project to shade the upper windows. The windows have the same kind of eighteenth-century framework as the churches. A goodly number of the balconies originally were constructed with wooden railings and shutters. Throughout Brazil, whether on the coast or in the mountains, windows and doors were protected from the sun and the eye of the curious by wooden shutters, sections of which often were ingeniously fitted together in geometric patterns, Mudéjar in manner. But the Mudéjar was not confined to the woodcarver's craft; glazed tiles, imported from Portugal and the Netherlands, were used for coolness and cleanliness, and they lent their brilliance and color to church and convent walls as well as to garden walls and the patios of mansions. In the Mudéjar tradition also, geometric patterns were pressed into stucco surfaces.[225]

Most of Ouro Preto's public buildings reflect its prosperity. The former penitentiary (fig. b), which combined the functions of town hall and prison, has a Rococo elegance in its lines; only a close view reveals that the small crisscross pattern at the windows is made up of iron bars. This prison building—the third of its kind to stand here—was designed by the governor Luiz da Cunha e Meneses, and seemingly it was his pet project; he impressed labor and forced contributions for the enterprise. Despite the resultant scandals, the major part of it went up between 1784 and 1788, with the aid of the architect Francisco Pinto de Abreu. Work stopped when the tyrannical official was recalled to Lisbon,[227] and certain minor sections, together with some of the interior, were not finished until 1869. This edifice is the only one in Minas Gerais constructed entirely of masonry and without a covering of plaster. A classically formal, closed pediment tops the central section, and the pilasters and columns harmonize with it. Grace is lent especially by the statues at the corners of the balustrade and by the double stairway that leads up to the entrance. Throughout, the carving and masonry are excellent. The fountain is a comparatively recent addition.

The church of Carmo (fig. d) was designed by Manoel Francisco Lisbôa in 1766. Francisco de Lima contracted to execute the soapstone carvings on its façade in 1771, and the building was completed about a decade later. The entrance and the "bull's eye" window—actually rather a carp's mouth in shape—are one composition, with fine detail in the petaled decoration. The molding about the central window is like a picture frame and the cartouche serves as a connecting ornament. Noteworthy is the rounding of the main cornice, above this window, a feature often seen on the coast. Carmo is the church that stands out on the hill in the photograph of the city.

The Negroes of the town and their various lay brotherhoods were zealous in their religious endeavors. The church of Rosário in Ouro Preto (fig. c) documents the high standard of their work. Completed in 1785 by José Pereira Arouca, the building, unique with its doubled-oval ground plan and rounded façade, is a brilliant example of the Rococo's imaginative use of the curving line. The problem of a pediment is beautifully solved; shaped like a coronet, it crowns the façade.[227]

Certain churches in Ouro Preto immortalize the name of the great architect and sculptor Antônio Francisco Lisbôa, through whom the Rococo of Brazil achieved its most striking expression. He was born in Ouro Preto in 1730, the natural son of a Negro slave, Izabel, and a Portuguese father, the *carpintero* Manoel Francisco de Costa Lisbôa just mentioned as the designer of Carmo.

The life of this famous artist is partly legend—a legend that is still gathering fantastic allegations—out of which emerges an arresting personality. He learned his craft from his father's contemporaries Antônio Francisco and João Bautista Gomes, when they were working in the booming mining towns. As a youth he drafted building plans, carved wood, and cut reliefs and figures out of the local soapstone; until then this material, which is soft when quarried but hardens with time, had been little used. He is described as small and sturdy of build, with a dark complexion, a low forehead, short curly hair, a sharp-cut chin, and clear burning eyes. A man of violent temperament, sensual and licentious, he seemingly enjoyed life to the full until in his late forties he contracted a severe illness—probably leprosy. From his disfigurement he acquired the nickname O Aleijadinho (the little cripple); under this sobriquet he enters the pages of art history. According to his biography, written by his daughter-in-law, he lost some of his fingers and toes and was so repulsive in aspect that he shunned contacts; he was carried through the streets in a curtained palanquin. Like Renoir of a later epoch, he continued to work, however, fixing his pen or carving tool to the stump of his hand. Some of his best and finest sculpture was produced during his last years. Up to the end of his life —he died in 1814 at the age of eighty-four— he signed his receipts himself, in a thin and even script. Aleijadinho lies buried in the parish church of Conceição in his native town, before the Altar of Hallowed Death.[231]

The church of São Francisco in Ouro Preto has much within and without that makes it an outstanding example of Minas Rococo (Pl. 170, fig. a). The plan is attributed to Aleijadinho, under whom work was proceeding in 1766, as is also the sculptural decoration on the façade. The building was finished about 1794. Its rather solid cylindrical towers are lightened by elongated oval windows and the crownlike cupolas which cap them. The rounded walls of the towers are ingeniously integrated into those of the building. In front of them the façade is set forward, its line defined by engaged columns and the broken pediment. Here the early arrangement of a single doorway and a triangular grouping of openings above it persists, though with Rococo modifications. The center window has become a medallion, a focal point for decoration; to accommodate it the cornice molding has been pushed far upward into the pediment. Above the doorway and flanked by the Franciscan coat of arms and that of Portugal's king, is placed a medallion with the Immaculate Conception; the larger relief shows St. Francis receiving the stigmata.

Inside, on the unplastered boards of the ceiling—flat at the top and following the angle of the rafters on the sides—Manoel da Costa Ataíde, in 1801–1810, painted a Glorification of the Virgin (fig. b). The favorite Rococo shell frame is skillfully filled in with an orchestra of angels, some playing quite modern instruments and others singing, holding their music. The single column, used architecturally on the façade, is carried up pictorially beyond the walls and across the slanting sides of the ceiling with an amazing feeling for perspective, exaggerating the height.

The painted illusionistic atmosphere is excellently supported by the plastic decorations of the interior. Aleijadinho's creations are the two delicately carved, small stone pulpits. On the one here Jonah and the whale appear beside a panel of John the Evangelist with his symbolic eagle (fig. d). The precision of the carving—especially clear in the Rococo angel heads amid flowery garlands on the base of the pulpit—gives to the stonework the quality of bronze.

This type of soapstone carving, using small motifs and exquisitely proportioned detail in the spirit of the best Rococo, characterizes many churches in Ouro Preto; outside, it was employed on the portals, and inside on pulpits, lavabos, and other ornamented surfaces. Tradition has it that Aleijadinho and his associates carved most of this work, though there is little documentation to prove it. However, the manner is singularly homogeneous and the attribution seems justified.

The subject of angel heads amid garlands is used with immediacy in polychrome and gilded wood on the high altar of the parish church at Caeté (fig. c); note the unusual manner of portraying the feathers in the wings. Caeté was one of the smaller mining settlements in the Minas district and was elevated to a town only in 1855. The church, the plan of which is said to have been sent from Portugal, was finished in the last third of the eighteenth century.[227] It follows the familiar Minas type. Comparable in the excellence of its interior and exterior decoration to churches in larger and better-known towns, it documents the general high standard of the artists and craftsmen in that epoch throughout the region.

Four churches from other towns in the Minas district, all started in the last third of the eighteenth century, show variations on the same theme. They are constructed on a noticeably uniform principle—a rectangular plan, two towers, a single doorway, a flaring pediment with a stone cross, and pilasters in the original color of the stone. All have another highly enjoyable characteristic in common: the separation of the upper towers and pediment from the lower section of the façade by means of a powerful cornice. However, as closely related as they are in general design, they differ in aspect because of the many varied details.

The church of São Francisco in the town of Mariana (Pl. 171, fig. b) was begun in 1763 and finished in 1794 by Pereira, mentioned in connection with Rosário in Ouro Preto. Its façade is sober and distinguished. Here there are no curvilinear walls. The central section, including the pediment, is stepped forward somewhat from the towers, and the belfries are set back even behind the plane of their bases. The placement of the rectangular windows brings out the horizontal. There are no story-telling reliefs; a composition of small Rococo motifs above the door provides the only sculptural ornament. Interest is directed toward the central window, which breaks into the pediment.

On the same square in Mariana stands the church of Carmo (fig. c). It was begun in 1784 by Domingos Moreira de Oliviera, who had worked under Aleijadinho on São Fran-

cisco in Ouro Preto; but it took three other architects and more than three decades to finish the building and its interior. Here the bases of the rounded towers are interestingly digested into the façade of the structure; only a suggestion of them remains in the small narrow windows and in the close triangular grouping of the larger ones above the door. Note the profile of the cornice and the roof tiles. The pediment seems to spring from the towers. Two carp's-mouth windows adorn this façade, the upper one an echo of the lower.

Sabará is one of the oldest of the gold-mining towns and in its heyday had a population of eighty thousand. The Carmo church there (fig. d) boasts a painted ceiling and is lavishly decorated throughout with gold leaf and Chinese red lacquer. A touch of chinoiserie is apparent also in the exterior, in the deep overhang of the cornice and the curving lines of the pediments. A riotous composition, with a "winged shell" as center, leans against each belfry wall, linking the towers with the ornamental gable. The bell of this church is dated 1772.

Another version of the Minas district type is seen in the church of São Francisco in São João d'El Rei (fig. a). This town was named in 1713 in honor of the Portuguese king John V, who reigned from 1707 to 1750. The church, dated 1774 on its façade, stands on a raised atrium approached by stairways leading up from either side of the gate. Its towers project boldly. The pilasters are decorated with delicate carving, and a framing of lacy detail sets off the large rectangular windows. Above the doors the scrolled segments of a sharply broken pediment make way for a heraldic composition, which is surmounted by a relief of the Immaculate Conception. In the somewhat massive gable pediment, a second relief shows St. Francis at the foot of the Cross, an unusual sculptural detail. The large round central window gains emphasis from its sheer simplicity and from the curving cornice and moldings which accentuate its line. The narrow windows in the tower bases are characteristic of this Rococo; where they are found in Spanish America they often have the shape of a star (*see Pls. 41, 42, 49*).

All four churches were the creation of lay brotherhoods, which, since religious orders were forbidden in Minas Gerais, attained more than customary prominence and power. The Negroes, brought in as slaves to work the mines, revered the Virgin of the Rosary especially and honored a number of Negro saints. In this hard-working region, where a religious celebration was a major event, the Negroes had their own festivals with colorful pageantry, dancing, and sometimes such barbaric touches as the crowning of a king of the Congo. The churches of Minas Gerais fall into several categories: the parish church, or *matriz;* those raised by the brotherhoods—white, mulatto, or Negro; and the pilgrimage church. Architecturally they all belong to one type; however, as has been seen, rivalry stimulated many original details.

There was another and grim side to the delightful picture of Rococo splendor. From the very beginning the Portuguese law had discriminated against the colonist in Brazil, ruling that the opulence and luxury produced by the thriving colony should be, in the main, for the sole enjoyment of the Portuguese. The colonists were not allowed to use gold, silver, or even imitations of these metals in their households or on their persons. In 1766, when goldsmithing was prohibited by virtue of a royal letter, 142 goldsmiths' workshops, with their forges, were demolished. (Less than a quarter of a century later, however, 375 masters and 1500 workmen were practicing their craft illegally in the viceroyalty.[222]) Negroes were supposed to wear only coarse sacking. The gifts of a bridegroom to his bride were limited, and any Portuguese who married a colonist was déclassé. No one could own oil paintings, and the importation of newspapers and printed books, except for a few religious volumes, was forbidden. No agricultural products could be raised which would compete with those of Portugal or of the Portuguese colonies in the Orient. Only Portuguese ships were permitted to enter Brazilian ports, and their wares brought extraordinarily high prices whereas native products were sold at the lowest.[224] In accordance with general colonial policy everywhere during this period, colonial industry was discouraged by the mother country. The great Portuguese minister of the crown, the Marquis of Pombal (1699–1782), instituted various reforms under his enlightened rule, but they were too few and too late to satisfy the colonists.

In 1789 the Viscount of Barbacena became the captain general of Minas Gerais. The royal fifth had been lazily collected and reluctantly paid, and much was in arrears. The newly arrived official showed an energetic hand. By this time signs of discontent were apparent in many parts of Brazil. Colonies in North America had already fought for and won their independence, and revolt was in the air. Creole officers, priests, and civilians gathered in the various villages and towns to air their grievances and indignation. Among those who laid plans for a republic was a young doctor—whose duties also included those of the dentist of that day. His name was Joaquim José de Silva Xavier, but he was better known by his nickname, Tiradentes (the tooth puller). Though a slight and unimpressive man, he was a burning protagonist of the independence movement, and upon the betrayal of the conspiracy and the defection of most of those involved in it, he took upon himself all responsibility. In 1792 he was hanged in Rio de Janeiro and his body quartered; to augment the effect of the medicine meted out to revolutionists, his head was sent to Ouro Preto to be raised aloft in the public square. Now he is spoken of with reverence and pride, and to honor him, an early martyr of Brazilian independence, the name of the place where he was born and lived has been changed from São José to Tiradentes.

This little town is one of the many mining settlements which sprang up in the first years of the eighteenth century. It has the typical winding streets of a mining village, with cobblestone pavements and low houses. Here a decorative fountain, there the Rococo contours of a church give atmosphere to the picture. But wherever the eye falls, the mineral-bearing hills, silhouetted against the horizon, close the perspective.

An interior detail from the parochial church at Tiradentes (*Pl. 172, fig. a*) shows its tray-shaped ceiling constructed of wide boards. The square coffered panels are painted with medallions and the frames gilded. A part of the organ loft that was shown earlier (*see Pl. 156*) can be seen in the foreground (upper left).

In the apse and on the archway (*fig. b*) angels and allegorical figures, small and large, nude and elaborately costumed, are joined in a polyphony of white and shining gold. Note the floating figure in the upper left on the curve of the cornice, visible also in the preceding photograph. The ornamentation on the soffit is developed—as it frequently is in Brazil—by the repetition of a volute. Typical Rococo arabesques, painted in tempera, cover the ceiling in an all-over pattern, and a lively sculptured frame compensates for the *rigueur* of the round window.

Atlantes, half life-size, and fantastically powerful scrolls support the piers at either side of the main altar (*fig. c*). Such statues occur also in other churches of Minas. The whole posture of the figure gives the impression of a man staggering under a crushing weight. It is far from classic or Renaissance models; there is much realism in the tired face and in the hand resting on the leg. As an independent piece of sculpture, it has merit and would make an even stronger appeal were it not almost suffocated under the giant scrolls. Note the human head in the panel at the left, completely subordinated into the composition.

The apse of the parish church in São João d'El Rei (*fig. d*) reveals a scheme of decoration quite different from the one just shown. Interest centers on the large paintings, which are framed in elaborate Rococo moldings and

mounted on the side walls. Gold is applied to walls and ceiling in plastic motifs as thick as jungle vines, kept separate by fields of white. On the main altar the lower section of the twisted columns is lightly grooved, while the upper part is garlanded. Angels sit in the arch and on segments of the broken pediment. Compare the Eternal Father here with similar compositions in Spanish America (*see Pls. 45, 52, 109*); instead of dominating the scene, the figure is framed in and held as one detail within the general rhythm and color scheme of the whole. The build-up of the catafalque-like structure behind this altar is especially clear, a feature seen earlier in coastal churches.

Our last illustrations of Rococo in Brazil show a famous pilgrim church from the Minas district. To make clear the many sources which contributed to the artistic outfitting of such an establishment, a slight digression is necessary. In eighteenth-century Europe the pilgrimage church was already an age-old institution. And the impetus at that time to restore and enlarge such shrines is easily understandable. In 1699 the Turks, who had occupied a goodly part of Europe and menaced the rest of it for nearly two centuries, were driven back to the Balkans, and almost immediately a religious revival began to sweep over the liberated countries. Moreover, in Western Europe the Counter Reformation was continuing its campaign against Freemasons, free-thinkers, and the like. To help erect new buildings for the faith, gold, silver, diamonds, pearls, and emeralds poured in from colonies in the New World and the Orient.

Pilgrim places, many of which had been founded in the Middle Ages, bloomed again, refurbished and enlarged if not completely re-edified. The eighteenth-century pilgrimage often had the character and fervor of a political demonstration, and its destination had to be large enough to accommodate huge crowds. Such sites still abound, not only in Portugal and Spain but also generally throughout Europe. Some of them have retained their landscaped parks, their mounting stairways with elaborate balustrades, their fountains, flower beds, and terraces with statues; for formal gardens, which, like Isola Bella on Lake Maggiore, integrated the ever-changing surface of water into a bizarre design with Baroque éclat, were not confined to the palaces of nobles. On the island in Lake Orta, also in northern Italy, an early-eighteenth-century garden provided a setting for a Via Crucis in which life-size statues of carved wood stand in pavilions at the Stations of the Cross; similar arrangements survive in Portugal and Brazil. Architecturally the pilgrimage church in the Valley of La Brianza (*Appendix, Pl. 192, fig. c*), again in northern Italy, reminds one of the Minas churches in Brazil.

Cultural ideals traveled easily to and fro throughout Europe, carrying with them the artistic modes and styles from one land to another. The vast extent of the Holy Roman Empire had much to do with this. Members of the Habsburg family, whose seat was in Vienna, held sovereign positions throughout Europe as emperors, kings, archdukes, and princes. From Flanders to Sicily, from Poland to Portugal, their influence was firmly embedded, cemented by marriage ties as well as by alliances and kept strong generation after generation by prolific families. A Bavarian princess was the second wife of the Portuguese king Pedro II, and his successor, John V (reigned 1707–1750), was married in 1708 to Maria Ana, a daughter of the Austrian king. (The Minas town of Mariana and the Mariana Islands were named for Austrian-born queens.) When John V's skillful ambassador, the Portuguese Marquis of Pombal, was sent in 1745 to Vienna to mediate between Maria Theresa and Pope Benedict XVI, he married the Austrian Princess Daun. Thus, as the century passed its halfway mark, not only was the Queen Mother and Regent of Portugal an Austrian, but the wife of Portugal's great reform minister, the antagonist of the Queen Mother, also was an Austrian.

With Portugal oriented politically toward the center of the Holy Roman Empire, it is small wonder that an influx of artistic modes and manners from Central Europe made itself felt there. To a greater degree than is generally recognized, the Baroque and Rococo were fertilized and cross-fertilized by the talent of artists and craftsmen of the lesser publicized nations. Holland, Denmark, Sweden, and Norway, as well as the eastern countries within the orbit of the Holy Roman Empire, developed their distinctive and delightful adaptations of these two styles. Any mention of Rococo examples from countries connected with Portugal through a royal marriage must give first place to the Bavarian churches of the Asam brothers, which have a grace of line and an atmosphere reminiscent of contemporary work in porcelain. Indeed, some of the statuary of the great sculptors Balthasar Permoser and Johan Joachim Kändler served as models for Europe's first manufactory of hard-paste porcelain, at Meissen in Saxony. In such art centers as princely courts and theaters, music salons and ateliers, a Rococo was formulated which soon became an export article.

Portugal has several famous Baroque or Rococo pilgrim churches which have strongly influenced those in her colony Brazil. Bom Jesus do Monte, near Braga, Portugal, goes back to the early sixteenth century, but the present establishment was not begun until the 1720's; contributions for the new building were collected even throughout the Portuguese colonies.[28] It is approached by a series of well-composed stairways and esplanades, with small chapels containing tableaus of the Passion carved of wood. The church is large and the entire layout grandiose, benefiting in its total effect from the cultivated landscape that surrounds it. Another such sanctuary in Portugal is at Lamego. In type this church, dated in mid-eighteenth century, is closer to some of those in Brazil, but in its milder sylvan atmosphere of rolling hills again the effect is different. A third Portuguese example, Bom Jesus do Matosinhos, is dedicated to the same patron as the famous shrine in Brazil. It is located north of Oporto and houses a miraculous crucifix, which at the beginning of the present century received the homage of some thirty thousand pilgrims yearly.

The Brazilian pilgrim church of Bom Jesus do Matosinhos (*Pl. 173, fig. a*) stands on a hilltop near Congonhas do Campo, where it commands a magnificent view of the subtropical countryside and dominates the small town below. It was founded (1757) in fulfillment of a vow by the Portuguese hermit Feliciano Mendes, who for the last eight years of his life collected alms for its construction. Work began in 1758 under Antônio Roiz Falcato as stonemason and Antônio Gonçalves Rosa as carpenter and joiner, both of Ouro Preto. Between 1765 and 1777 the nave was completed and the two towers were raised. The same Francisco de Lima who worked on Carmo in Ouro Preto contracted to finish the main chapel.

The approach to the sanctuary leads up a sloping hillside through a religious "garden." Small square pavilions roofed with cloister vaults are ranged on either side—pilgrimage chapels, for which Aleijadinho and his assistants carved (1780–1790) sixty-six large wooden figures representing scenes of the Passion. The painting of the statues was done by Francisco Xavier Carneiro, who had previously gilded the high altar of Carmo in Mariana,[227] and Manoel da Costa Ataíde (*see Pls. 170, 171*).

There is a rustic air about this church. In style it is related closely to the other late Rococo twin-towered churches in Minas. It has the single doorway with a large heraldic medallion flanked by rectangular windows. A straight, unbroken cornice extends across the entire front, and the traditional window is placed in the pediment, set off by a heavy, decorative molding. This pediment, in spite of the abrupt breaks in its outline, gives a stronger illusion of an arc than the others illustrated from this district. The towers are slender and their small narrow windows are without ornamentation. The ground plan is simple, and there is little sculptural decoration—as if the climax of the dramatic movement was deliberately left to the statues and the theatrical setting of the open terrace.

Amazing spirit and power emanate from the heroic figures of the twelve prophets at the corners of the barrier. They bring movement and dramatic intensity into the general picture. Late works of Aleijadinho, carved of native soapstone, they stand in close architectonic relationship with one another and with the building to which they serve as overture, each oriented to a different direction. Highly theatrical, the figures show individuality and an inner greatness, held fast by the massiveness of their material—stone. Through the rhythm of the various postures, the series builds up to a crescendo as the eye travels along from one to another.

Aleijadinho's remarkable talent manifests itself not only in the grouping but also in the varied and emotionally articulate gestures with which he enlivens the more or less conventional iconography of the prophets. Names carved on scrolls or on shields at their feet identify them all. On this plate are pictured Joel, who preached repentance to his people that their old men might dream dreams and their young men see visions, Isaiah, full of righteous wrath, and Hosea, the loving and forgiving (*figs. b, c, d*). An especial histrionic effect is achieved by the costumes and headgear of Oriental inspiration; note the carved detail in the drapery folds, the braiding, and even the buttons.

It has been remarked that these figures show technical deficiencies—the last of them were executed when the sculptor was in his eighties. It is possible that had he been commissioned for this work when he was a young man, they would have had more elaboration and ebullience. But here is evidence that the artist who carved graceful portals and pulpits in other Minas churches turned with the years from the fragile and charming to the virile and intense. These prophets of his are startlingly somber—sometimes even foreboding—both in feature and in pose; they exhibit an immediacy of experience and an economy of line which only a mature master could have achieved. We are reminded that during this period of his life he was carried concealed behind curtains to his workshop, and returned only after dark to avoid being seen by his fellowmen. These twelve statues, his final work, were carved when he had to have his chisel and mallet strapped to the stumps of his deformed hands.

With little learning and without ever leaving the remote hill towns of his native province, Aleijadinho carried Brazilian Rococo to its fullest flowering. It is highly probable that he saw Rococo objects, such as porcelains and terra-cotta *bozzetti* of European sculptors (*see Appendix, Pl. 192, fig. b*), as well as engravings and books. But though they give a clue as to how the style was communicated to him, they do not explain the high standard of his achievement. In spite of his handicap, he infused each of his prophets with a strange, Biblical grandeur and an eloquent spirituality which grew out of the soil of this Brazilian world. A rare human story lives in his masterpieces; his gift was genius.

15

THE WOODCARVER'S LANGUAGE

In Europe, even before the Renaissance, popular taste in interior decoration turned toward marble and other types of fine stone, bronze, wrought iron, stucco, and tiles; the less affluent districts painted wood to imitate these materials. In the New World, however, where virgin forests provided woods of undreamed strength and beauty in great abundance, wood again came into its own. For the Indian craftsmen it was a familiar medium. With the tools of iron and steel furnished by the conquerors they achieved amazing dexterity and showed a many-sided ingenuity in translating a two-dimensional design into three-dimensional reality. The colonial woodcarver may have been unlettered, but he was highly articulate in the florid and expressive language of his craft. Alfred Neumeyer considers such decorative detail of special importance in evaluating the Indian's contribution to Latin American colonial art.[67] While contemporary Europe was emphasizing grandeur and virtuosity in architectural construction, here the decorative was predominant—the embellishment of basically simple buildings to achieve a maximum of splendor.

Fire, earthquakes, and floods have destroyed many masterpieces of the woodcarver's art in Latin America. Perhaps fire has been the greatest hazard; for buildings were illuminated by tapers and candles, often incorporated into altar designs amid inflammable oil-painted canvases, cotton cloth, and objects of dry wood.

Nevertheless a vast artistic treasury survives to perpetuate the regional artist's lively and appealing talent.

The great economic upswing in the first half of the eighteenth century did away with many wood carvings from the earlier period. Fortunately in the church of La Asunción in Juli, Peru, a large relief of the Assumption (*Pl. 174, fig. a*) remains from an early era, though now discarded. Originally it was part of the main retable of that church; the irregular hole at the bottom could have been cut later to make a place for a sagrario. The life-size depiction of the Virgin, the arrangement of the angels with their medieval instruments, the delicate gilding, the fine soft colors—all are remarkable. This church building was finished by 1620, and from its general style the relief would date from about that time or at most only a few decades later.

Maní, a town in Yucatán, Mexico, which lies southwest of the great Maya religious center Chichen Itzá, was important in both pre-Columbian and Conquest history. The Franciscan order succeeded in obtaining from the Spanish crown exclusive rights for the indoctrination of the Indians in Yucatán; they divided the peninsula into districts, with an administrative center at Mérida and four branches, one of which was at Maní.[96] Two friars took up residence there in 1547. All the Indian chiefs and their people were baptized at the instigation of the Maya ruler, and he himself, Kukum Xiu, adopted the Christian name Francisco. He is reputed to have furnished six thousand Indians to build the Franciscan establishment at Maní on the ruins of a Maya settlement. It was here that Bishop Landa destroyed over five thousand clay idols, some forty stone statues, nearly two hundred ceremonial vessels, and twenty-seven codices.[97]

The date of the present Franciscan church, dedicated to the archangel Michael, is given as 1630. Reminiscent of the early fortress-like edifices, it is very spacious. The altar of St. Anthony (*fig. d*), standing on the right side of the nave, probably is more or less contemporary with the building. A statue of the patron carrying the Christ Child occupies the single large niche. On the retable the four caryatides holding swags of flowers in their hands and standing on bearded human heads recall the halbardiers on the Casa de Montejo in Mérida, which also was built by Indians from Maní (*see Pl. 32*). The reliefs depict episodes from the life of the saint.[95] This retable has been repainted but fortunately is not completely ruined. A fascinating barbarism pervades the work, from the scene in the lunette to the small decorative medallions in Plateresque tradition on the base. A companion piece, dedicated to the Virgin of Sorrows, was published by Elizabeth Wilder Weismann.

The panel of the Virgin Martyrs (*fig. b*), one of a pair now in the Museum of Colonial Art, Bogotá, Colombia, is believed to date from the seventeenth century and to have come from the nunnery of Santa Clara in Tunja. Each of the maidens carries the palm of martyrdom. The carving, in rather high relief, shows an estofado excellent in quality and unusual in its variety (*see also Pl. 84*).

In the other panel on this plate, today in the Colonial Museum of Antigua, Guatemala, a somewhat similar subject is presented—St. Clara and her nuns, who quelled the invading Saracens by going out to meet them with the uplifted pyx. This relief (*fig. c*) is considerably lower, and the coloristic effect has been impaired by the repainting. It probably dates from the early eighteenth century; license to build the Clarissa nunnery in Antigua was granted in 1698, but not until the following year did six nuns from Mexico arrive to found the institution. On the upper left the treated cloth has begun to peel away, revealing that at this late date an early technique was still practiced—a textile was glued over the carved wood and upon it gilding was applied which was later painted over.

When the two reliefs are compared, the Tunja piece exhibits more individuality and its grouping is more animated; a subdued rhythm can be sensed in the halos and drapery of the Guatemala carving.

In Europe the Counter Reformation inspired the refurbishment of old altars and the installation of new ones along the side walls of churches. This movement, carried into the New World, sometimes resulted in gilded paneling throughout the nave and a multiplicity of side altars (*see Pls. 34, 44*).

The side retable at the end of the right aisle in the cathedral of Comayagua, Honduras, dedicated to the Virgin of the Rosary, provides a rare example of relief technique (*Pl. 175, fig. a*). Here in the lower section are recorded the Joyful Mysteries of Mary—episodes of her youth and Jesus' childhood; above them are the Sorrowful Mysteries—scenes of the Passion. At the top are depicted the Glorious Mysteries: two small carvings in octagonal frames show the Pentecost and the Assumption, while the large central panel portrays the Coronation. A beguiling charm is evident in the story telling, the waxy smooth surfaces, and the mild quality of the pastel coloring. Over the retable proper the composition continues in a series of oil paintings, framed by wide decorative scrollwork, likewise exquisite.

The contract for this retable, drawn up in Comayagua, July 9, 1708, was discovered in Guatemala by Heinrich Berlin, that indefatigable delver into archives.[139] Its sculptor was Vicente de la Parra, *maestro de ensamblador*, a resident (not a citizen) of Comayagua. He was born in Guatemala about 1667 and at the age of thirteen seems to have been apprenticed to Agustín Nuñez, a distinguished master of the province. Apparently he worked independently from 1690, for contracts survive signed by him from that year on. Besides outlining the iconographical subject matter, the Comayagua document gives the measurements required and calls for ten salomonic columns to be disposed in two stories and a pediment, all to be finished within six months. The price agreed upon was 380 pesos. This date is the last for de la Parra in the Guatemala archives; Berlin suggests that he may have ended his years in Honduras. (For the main retable in this cathedral with statues set in niches see *Pl. 6.*)

A conservative compositional tradition is embodied in the work just discussed; the retable ends on a line with the altar table and the rest is treated as a decorative base. An eighteenth-century side altar in the nunnery church of Santa Catalina (*fig. b*), in Cuzco, displays a considerably freer movement of line. The two sham doors beyond the lilies —sometimes found beside the altar table in place of lower niches—call to mind the iconostas of the Greek Orthodox church. Unusually well preserved, this piece has retained its original sagrario with rounded sliding doors of wood, subtly carved; all too frequently, even in colonial times, a silver construction in a later style was fitted into this section. In the upper part of the retable, set off by a filigree crest, three reliefs illustrate the phrases of the Creed: "He descended into Hell . . ., He ascended into Heaven and sitteth on the right hand of God the Father. . . ." This altar, fortunately unharmed by the 1950 earthquake, is unsurpassed in the delicacy of its carving and the mildness of its opal tones and antique gold. A detail of the columns will be shown later in this chapter (*see Pl. 189*).

As has been mentioned, in 1671 the old capital of Panama was sacked by Henry Morgan, after which the city was removed to a new and better-fortified location. The priest of the church of San José in the old city saved his beautiful "golden altar" from the raiders by taking down the statues, the gilded columns, the pediments, and other removable ornamentation and whitewashing the body of the retable, thus concealing the goldleaf. According to legend this is the retable which now stands in the church of San José in Panama City (*fig. c*). However, such an early date for this carving is open to question. In spirit it is eighteenth century and in type strongly coastal Peru. It shows a close relationship to the main retable of Magdalena Vieja in Lima (*fig. d*)—which definitely dates from the first half of the eighteenth century—notably in the yawning segments of its broken pediments, in the rosette (not grape) decoration on its columns, and in the scalloping around the central shell and side niches. Such a close stylistic connection is easily understandable since the regular passage of the fleet linked Panama with Lima. Note the finely carved doors at the sides and the Byzantoid painting of God the Father.

In conventual churches, as noted earlier, often the choir was placed in a gallery included in the clausura. Frequently such choirs retain a strong ascetic character. From the back of the deep choir loft of the Franciscan church in Quito, Ecuador, little of the magnificent church interior can be seen, except for a section of the ceiling and the statues and paintings ranged just below it. As early as 1581 this church was mentioned as one of the finest in the province.[166] The two Peruvian Indians Jorge de la Cruz and his son Francisco Morocho reputedly participated in the decoration of the choir about 1610. The choir stalls (*Pl. 176, fig. a*), built of cedar, at present number sixty-two. Each panel, polychromed and gilded, contains a saint in high relief. There is severity in the poses as well as in the strongly classicizing columns. Even though this church has undergone considerable refurbishment, the choir seems to have suffered little change.

Eighteenth-century Baroque characteristics are evident in the choir stalls of La Merced in Cuzco, Peru (*fig. b*). The carving, dated around 1710, includes thirty-five saints and notable Mercedarians, all lively in gesture. The striking row of oval medallions above the stalls proper may have been inspired by the two-tier arrangement in the Cuzco cathedral (*see Pl. 155*). A plethora of rich carving fills the limited space. Over the two entrances are oblong reliefs of Mary Magdalene and Mary of Egypt, both as penitents—subjects which are found also over the doorways to the sacristy in San Francisco Bogotá. (The opposite side of this choir was shown on *Pl. 155*.)

The choir in a colonial cathedral, unlike that of a conventual church, often occupied, as in Spain, an enclosed section in the center of the nave, opposite the main altar. A throne for the bishop or archbishop stood in the center, and ornately carved choir stalls lined the walls. Here at special hours the many members of the cathedral clergy assembled daily. Dressed in their impressive robes, laces, and jewelry and resplendent in the slanting rays of the sun or the flickering candlelight, they made a dramatic spectacle as they chanted their service accompanied by the organ.

The feeling for pomp and the general high standard of workmanship which distinguish Mexico City's cathedral are evident also in its choir stalls of cedar (*Pl. 177, fig. a*). Juan de Rojas won the contract to carve them, in 1696, in competition with a number of famous sculptors; the execution of the work is said to have taken around thirteen years to complete.[128] Holy scenes and fifty-nine saints adorn the panels. These figures step interestingly out of their frames and are set in rhythmic succession, one augmenting the effect of another. They were gilded later, but the backgrounds and the rest of the woodwork retain the natural tone.

Generally accepted as one of the most notable and artistic monuments of wood carving in all Mexico, the choir stalls remaining from the former Augustinian monastery church of Mexico City are now preserved in an *aula* of the National Preparatory School, part of the university. They contain scenes from the Old and New Testaments, among them the loading of Noah's Ark (*fig. b*), the expulsion of Adam and Eve from the Garden of Paradise (*fig. c*), and the creation of birds and fishes (*fig. e*). A total of 253 panels was recorded in mid-nineteenth century, but a hundred of these have since been lost.[104] An immensely articulate technique transmits successfully the Biblical atmosphere, even beyond the mere telling of the stories. Bust caryatides ending in leaves—a Baroque feature favored throughout Spanish America—and swags of fruit are incorporated into the pilasters that separate the stalls. Rich carving covers the arm rests and the *misereres*, the small consoles on the under sides of the hinged seats against which the clerics might rest.

The contract for this great work, published by Berlin, proves that it was executed by Salvador de Ocampo, the son of one of the great Indian sculptors of the period, Tomás Xuárez.[89] Ocampo received his certificate as master of joinery in 1698, the year in which he finished the high altar in the Augustinian church at Metztitlán. The choir stalls were contracted for in 1701 and were to be delivered by May 1, 1702. The short time span implies a number of assistants, and Ocampo agreed to employ only the best craftsmen. According to the document the subject matter for the many "histories" was furnished by the superior of the order. It may have been selected from several different sources, probably all engravings, or perhaps from some large "anthology," like the later *Figures des histoires de la Sainte Bible* by Alexis de la Roche and Jean Lesclapart (published in 1724). In such albums many traditional ideas and designs were recut and assembled. However, a strong relationship of spirit can be discerned between the creation scene shown here and an engraving by Jan Sadeler after a much earlier painting by Martin de Vos, though the figures are by no means identical (*see Appendix, Pl. 192, fig. g*).

Cedar was specified for the framework, and mahogany, already in the possession of the order, for the stalls. Nails, braces, and other metal parts were to be supplied by the sculptor; he also agreed to work inside the monastery, to take nothing away, and to reimburse the monastery for any wood which might be spoiled in the carving. An irony of dependence on documentation appears in the fact that the choir stalls as they stand are made almost entirely of walnut. There is no mention of gilding and polychroming and the carving remains in the natural color of the wood. The juxtaposition of two unmatched pieces in the creation scene, however, suggests that a gold or polychrome finish was intended.

A few choir stalls surviving from the former Franciscan establishment of San Bernardino at Xochimilco, Mexico, show the variety of decorative detail then current (*fig. d*). Xochimilco, still famous for its "floating gardens," was a powerful community in pre-Columbian times, and in the sixteenth century it became an important ecclesiastical and military center. Numerous artists and craftsmen from among its Indian population were employed throughout the whole region. In contrast to the elegance of the carving from the metropolis, the Xochimilco example has a robust, somewhat rustic spirit. Eucharistic grapes entwine its columns, while flowers predominate on those of the cathedral. A feeling for wood as a medium and the enjoyment of the carver in working with it are equally sensed. Several dates [134] appear on the façade of the church—1590, 1682, and 1716; the choir stalls may well fall between the last two.

As if to compensate for the sobriety of the massive iron bars which closed off the upper and lower choirs of a nunnery church from the nave, the surrounding wall surface often was treated lavishly. The choirs of Santa Clara and Santa Rosa in Querétaro, Mexico, reveal all the Rococo finesse of the mid-eighteenth-century arts and crafts then flourishing in that city. An exquisite perforated wooden screen extends into the arch of each, and colorful decoration enriches the solid barrier of the gallery. In Santa Clara (*Pl. 178, fig. a*) a crucifix occupies the center of the subtly carved wooden grille. Textiles, starched and painted, are draped at the sides. Along the gallery railing are ranged medallions containing carved figures. In Santa Rosa (*fig. d*) this space is filled with canvas paintings variously framed, a veritable exhibit of gilded wood carving, and the screen has the appearance of a gigantic lace fan. Santa Rosa was dedicated in 1752; Santa Clara dates somewhat later.

In the nunnery church known as Las Nazarenas in Lima—also called Santo Cristo de los Milagros—wooden grilles stand on either side of the sanctuary (*fig. c*). Several intricate motifs commingle in this carving, some characteristic of ironwork, others of woodwork; one might even discover a suggestion of weaving or tile patterns—Rococo blended with Mudéjar through the wonderful quality of the material. A more lacy design fills the archway. This building, consecrated in 1730, was rebuilt between 1766 and 1771 under the patronage of the viceroy Amat.

A side retable in San Francisco in Antigua, Guatemala (*fig. b*), also displays masterly wood carving. Here the openwork in the upper section produces a marked contrast to the solid lower part where there are niches and statues. Each column is divided and decorated in two different patterns. Noteworthy are the large rosettes below the statues, a much-repeated motif in this captaincy-general. The flowery spirals, though differently applied, are similar in their pictorial effect to the carving in the upper choir of Santa Clara in Querétaro.

Many conventual churches had a small *tribuna* like a theater loge—or sometimes a pair—placed close to the main altar and overlooking the entire nave. The three illustrated here, though rather close in date, are unalike in their ornamentation. The first (*Pl. 179, fig. a*), in the nunnery church of Santa Catalina in Cuzco, Peru, gives the appearance of a balcony screened off by a wide-spaced wooden grille, painted red and gilded. The scrollwork and petaled rosettes make it highly Rococo. Much more massive is the bulging tribune in the San José chapel of El Tejar in Quito (*fig. b*). Solid panels form the railing, and the crossbars are very close, imitating a fine basket weave. It is painted a rich red, and each of the three parts is carved with a different pattern and gilded. Note the neo-Mudéjar pendants on the bottom of the balcony. An impressive wrought-iron grille distinguishes the tribune of Santa Clara, Querétaro, which is placed above the portal leading to the sacristy and the nunnery (*fig. c*). The vast corbel and the surrounding magnificence of plastic ornament in stucco and wood are worked into a spectacular composition.

The three following illustrations display wood carving in small patterns and delicately detailed. A section of the San Agustín sacristy in Lima (*fig. d*) presents figures of such lesser-known Augustinian saints as Veronica, Antonio Amandula, Brigida (holding the church), and Antonio del Aquila. These statues are probably some of those contracted for by Diego de Medina in 1643 (*see also Pl. 94*). But the niches with their flamelike tongues and lacy ornamentation appear to date from mid-eighteenth century. Busts with scrolls for torsos rise from vaselike pedestals to separate the niches. (Compare with the Mexican version on the San Agustín choir stalls seen earlier.)

Unknown even to many long-time residents of Quito is the interior of the church of San Juan de Dios, which adjoins the hospital. Illustrated here is the small double door that leads from behind the pulpit into the cloister (*fig. e*). When closed, its wings present in relief a drawn curtain with cords and pompons and, in the center on a slender Rococo stand, a flower arrangement which tastefully fills the space without crowding. It is an illusionistic performance of much charm.

Work on the façade of the church of San Francisco in Puebla, Mexico, continued from 1743 to 1767, and the choir stalls there (*fig. f*) may date from that period or even later. They show how the decorative language was increasingly simplified as the late Baroque turned into the Rococo style. Here nothing bulges, much of the surface is left undecorated, and few figural elements appear. Nevertheless, through the liveliness of its combined motifs, the composition is fully mature and satisfying to the eye. (For similar tray-shaped panels and play with wavy lines see *Pls. 94, 95*.)

It is significant that when this selection was made from hundreds of photographs to show exquisite examples of Rococo in Spanish America, two of the examples turned out to be from Mexico, two from Ecuador, and two from Peru.

In Romanesque and Gothic Europe, the ceiling was conditioned by the constructional limitations of the age. The Renaissance developed a rich coffered ceiling that could hold its own with the ornate furniture, the tapestries, and the canvas paintings of the lavishly decorated rooms of the period. Contemporary Moorish craftsmen on the Iberian Peninsula were perpetuating the methods by which they had constructed and ornamented ceilings for generations. As has already been noted in Chapters 5 and 6, Spanish carpenters had to pass an examination on the various types of ceiling before they could be admitted as masters into the guild. These styles were brought by craftsmen to America. The examples illustrated on *Plates 180* and *181* are lettered consecutively for the convenience of the reader.

A typical Mudéjar ceiling survives above the choir loft of San Francisco in Quito (*fig. a*), its rafters crossed and recrossed with narrow strips of wood in geometric patterns, inlaid, and set with gilded cones. It is worth noting that the Mudéjar method of constructing with small pieces of wood, which originated in North Africa or the Near East and continued in Spain, all lands poor in forests, should be carried over into the New World where timber colossal in size and unparalleled in strength abounded.

The ceiling of La Concepción in Bogotá (*fig. b*) presents a variation of the Mudéjar in which the structural members are hidden. It is executed on sheets of silver, enlivened by the delicate coloring of painted bouquets. Here the conservative Mudéjar rule of using only geometric or non-figural patterns is broken, for angel heads are painted all around the border. Tradition has it that this ceiling was brought from Spain. It was in the villa of Juan Díaz in Tocaima until a great flood destroyed that building in late sixteenth century, after which it was transferred to its present location.[169]

In the ceiling over the apse of the nunnery church of Santa Clara in Tunja, Colombia (*fig. h*), the rafters are exposed in their full length; a lively design is painted over the entire construction, giving a Mudéjar impression. The long cross beams with their interlaced pattern, like those in the nave of this church (*see Pl. 24*), are thoroughly orthodox; but the blazing sun applied in the center and the seraphim in their octagonal frames are highly original.

Another type, a Gothic survival into Renaissance times, was the straight horizontal ceiling with exposed beams.[34] These as well as the heavy supporting *zapatas*, or brackets (Mudéjar in origin), carried more and more ornament as time went on; often the spaces between the rafters also were inlaid or painted. This type, its rich carving brought out by the application of color, is illustrated in the ceiling detail from the former Palace of the Inquisition in Lima (*fig. c*).

The waiting room of the Dominican monastery in Lima has a low coffered ceiling (*fig. e*). It followed a design published in Villalpando's edition of Serlio[203] and was finished under the supervision of Salvador de Ribera between 1582 and 1586. Similar ceilings in the church and cloister were destroyed

in an earthquake. This type of construction, made up of coffers shaped like a kneading trough or *artesa*, is the *artesonado* in the strict sense of the word. The bulblike pendants are a conventionalization of the wooden pegs which were once necessary to hold the structure in place.

In the antesacristy of San Agustín in Lima (*fig. j*), rather shallow coffers are applied on a tray-shaped ceiling. Diego de Medina signed a contract for this work, as well as for the ceiling and statuary in the sacristy, in 1643 and promised completion within a year and eight months. Specifications required that the ceilings be of oak, except for the carving in the coffers, which should be of cedar.[198]

The sacristy of Santa Teresa in Cuzco shows a variant of the coffered ceiling, rather rustic but powerful (*fig. l*). The joists are worked into a checkerboard system and originally were painted, producing a lively effect. Renaissance disks alternate with Mudéjar panels within the coffers. The central pendant, purely ornamental, is a perfect example of pseudo Mudéjar. This Carmelite foundation, established in 1673, was ready for inauguration by 1676.

As far back as the Gothic period ceilings were decorated with painted designs on stuccoed wood. One of the richest examples of this type of work to survive in Latin America comes from the ambulatory in a sixteenth-century Dominican monastery at Coyoacán (*fig. d*), in Mexico. Each of the cloister corners boasts such a ceiling, painted on a checkerboard construction with nine fields to a side. A great variety of designs was used; signs of the zodiac, Christian symbols, and some emblems from martyrology, as well as various types of rosette, can be distinguished, evenly spaced and precisely composed, like the initial letters of an illuminated monastic book.

A less lively ceiling of the same type covers the reception hall of the Dominican monastery at Cuzco, Peru, which was badly damaged in the earthquake of 1950. Here in the square panels the shield of the order alternates with angel heads in octagonal medallions, all modeled in stucco and painted (*fig. f*). The painting of the small squares in both examples displays an amazingly fine brushwork, even though they were intended to be viewed from quite a distance.

A detail from the cloister walk of the Augustinian monastery in Quito (*fig. i*) shows a horizontal ceiling in which coffers are suggested by moldings and the staggered fields are painted with flowers and studded with gilded cones. The photograph also gives a glimpse of the gallery arches, fully paneled in the same elegant style. Large canvases line the inner walls, framed elaborately above and below and separated by pilasters carved with busts. This cloister was finished about 1657, and reportedly Miguel de Santiago painted a life of St. Augustine for its walls.[183] In the diapered sectors a certain relationship to ceilings in Colombia can be noted (*see Pl. 27*).

In the ambulatory at La Merced in Cuzco (*fig. k*) the arches formed by the heavy beams and their supporting brackets are emphasized by ornate carving. Here, also, paintings probably once lined the wall, but the unity of their arrangement has been disturbed by the vicissitudes of time.

Finally, a ceiling detail is presented from El Topo in the outskirts of Tunja, Colombia (*fig. g*). The simple roof construction is undisguised but most decoratively covered. The gilded motifs are repeated all over a white ground, like cutout stars for Christmas. This edifice was erected in 1729 as an Augustinian retreat. In 1870 it was taken over by the nuns of La Concepción, and the grille may have been put in place at that time in the changeover from men to women residents.

While many colonial ceilings may give the impression of grandeur, often their construction is primitive. A photograph taken during the renovation of the church of Santa Barbara in Tunja, Colombia (*Pl. 188, fig. e*), reveals the uneven poles, which served as rafters, and the outer covering of reed matting—such as that used on roofs and fences in tropical countries. It is very possible that the method of

binding this mat with vegetable fiber goes back to pre-Columbian times. The ceiling proper consists of whitewashed boards on which gilded decoration is applied. (*Compare Pl. 119.*)

Plates 182 and *183*, showing pulpits, also are treated as one. After the altar the pulpit was perhaps the most important part of a church. From it the Gospel was preached, and thus the attention of each member of the congregation was focused upon it. The number of truly magnificent pulpits in colonial Latin America is so great that the twelve examples gathered here from eight lands, as different as they are in detail, can give only a faint idea of the full glory expressed in such wood carving.

The simplest type, harking back to the seventeenth century and earlier, shows a many-sided box placed on a columnar support carved in a harmonious style. One such example stands in the modest church of San Francisco at Comayagua, Honduras (*fig. l*). The wood is gilded and a nonfigural pattern covers the entire piece; the fringed lambrequins indicate the mid-eighteenth century. Note the palm and pineapple motifs on the pedestal, the base of which is of stone. This pulpit is entered through a door in the wall.

Another example is found in the church of San Francisco in Veraguas, Panama (*fig. c*). The decoration here combines the Rococo and the neoclassic, in a curious blend of imported iconography carried through by rustic talent. The supporting column is carved into what has been interpreted as an Indian woman, wearing the long earrings and loose gown of the local native costume, her head wreathed with the red hibiscus. In the relief medallions around the box the Evangelists alternate with the three virtues, Faith, Hope, and Charity. Painted flowers make the transition from the balustrade of the stairway to the once-bright carvings. After the Conquest the province of Veraguas, Panama, was given by the Spanish king to Christopher Columbus and his family.

The region was agriculturally rich, exporting much of its produce to distant parts. In addition the Grand Admiral, who held the title of Duke of Veraguas, received a share from the production of the district's gold mines. The mountain village of San Francisco Veraguas lies twelve miles north of Santiago, the present-day capital of the department.

Another type of pulpit hangs like an oriel, suspended from the wall. The parish church of Checacupe, Peru, offers an outstanding example of this type (*fig. e*). It is entered from a passage through the wall by means of a small landing. Unusually rich and varied, its carving is comprised of elaborate niches and numerous columns in various sizes. Its base has the lines of a bowl, decorated with ornate grotesques. Stylistically this work is closely related to the better-known pulpit in the church of San Blas in Cuzco, which dates before 1696; several pulpits in and around Cuzco show kinship and all probably come from about the same period. It is worthy of note that the Indian Juan Tomás Tuyru Tupac, whose name is often linked with the pulpit of San Blas, was born in a small village in the vicinity of Checacupe and that a Quechua family of the same name is still living there. He is believed to have carved the pulpit and some of the other decoration in the Checacupe church; a number of wood carvings in Cuzco are known to be his work. Contemporary documents reveal that he was not only a sculptor and master carpenter but also an architect and a specialist in "hydraulic works," which probably included organs.[187]

La Merced in Sucre, Bolivia, also has an oriel pulpit (*fig. a*), dating from about 1710, when this section of the church was decorated.[221] Its curving base carries the figures of bird sirens, favorite symbols of the Augustinians in the Middle Ages but rare in Latin America. Just above them puma heads form corbels for the grape-wound columns. Amid all this exquisite carving the decisive line of the circular rim of the pulpit is especially noteworthy.

A chalice-shaped pulpit with a stairway stands in San Diego in Quito (*fig. j*). While in the Checacupe example the protruding grotesque heads of the separating members received the main emphasis, in Sucre the emphasis was shifted to the sirens in the center of the panels. In contrast to both of these, the individual motifs in the Quito example are submerged in a wealth of carving. There are few figures and the principal decoration of the base is a cluster of spirals and floriated elements. The balustrade, with its elegant newel post, is unusually well integrated into the design. This pulpit is said to date[176] from about 1738.

The stair railing at San Francisco in Popayán, Colombia, develops single motifs (*fig. d*), a contrast to the polyphony manifest in the preceding example. A large canephora bearing a basket of tropical fruits forms the newel post, and on the balustrade, amid intertwining grape-vines, leaf-sprites are worked into a clean-cut design that has the precision of metalwork. The pulpit itself is akin to that just shown from Quito (*see also Pl. 28*).

In the pulpit of San Agustín in Popayán (*fig. k*), again a chalice shape, the figures are small in relation to the body of the piece. The polychrome and gilding are even and unobtrusive. A canvas painting is placed in the back wall. With its simple graceful base and open crownlike canopy, this little-known piece has rarely harmonious proportions. Though it probably dates from the second half of the eighteenth century, it harks back to the early type, which had an appeal for certain sculptors throughout the colonial period. (Compare the medallion on the landing with that in the same position at Checacupe seen on the opposite plate.)

The drawn-out ramp to the pulpit in the church of Santo Domingo in Las Casas, Mexico (*fig. b*), carries an unusual pattern—a different interpretation of the basic elements of construction and decoration realized by a different Indian cultural circle. The pulpit box rests on a heavy globelike base and the ramp has a support at the turn. No figural decoration is used. As much as one can see of the woodwork underneath, it too is elaborately carved and is well integrated into the paneling of the wall.

In the pulpit of La Compañía at Córdoba, Argentina (fig. i), the ornamentation was kept quiet and organized into strictly demarcated, small panels; figural elements were avoided. At the back, scrolls lead up to and over the shell-shaped canopy in a burst of virtuoso decoration, heavily loaded on but not pompous. The interior of this church was finished in 1690. Across the Andes, in the Peruvian viceroyalty, the same type of pulpit survives in several other Jesuit churches. Arequipa's Compañía has a somewhat similar one, dated about 1675. The pulpit in the chapel of the Jesuit Rosario College (founded in 1653), in Bogotá, Colombia, likewise shows plain panels decorated with compact nonfigural carving.

The name of Jujuy, a village in the Argentine Andes, is a corruption of the Quechua name of a former Indian chief. Undoubtedly the fantasy of Indian carvers was responsible for the Jacob's ladder on the pulpit stairway in its Rosario chapel (fig. f), for the adjoining parish church served a large Indian population. The story here is told with the power of conviction and a rare feeling for material and form. Jacob lies at the foot of the stair and at the top the Saviour in a mandoral beckons with a welcoming gesture, while angels seem to move up the steps amid curling clouds. Figures of the Evangelists are carved on the box and again bird sirens adorn the pendent base. The two great panels on the wall record the "generations" from Adam to Solomon (left) and from Abraham to Jesus (right). In the center is carved a relief of Augustine clasping a flaming heart, and on the canopy an angel sounds a trumpet. This work dates from the eighteenth century.[211]

With the coming of the Rococo the attitude toward decoration changed and with it sometimes even basic shapes. The pulpit box of San Carlos in Lima, Peru (fig. g), is as neatly articulated as a piece of furniture. The lower section is playfully expanded, and ribbon-like volutes exaggerate the bulge. The canopy in itself presents a complicated piece of work, a monumental baldachin. This pulpit dates, with the interior of the church, between 1758 and 1766.

Later in date and still less typical is the San Agustín pulpit at Salamanca, Mexico (fig. h). Here swags studded with flowers and inlaid —dark wood alternating with ivory or bone— bedeck the box. Matching inlay decorates the canopy. (Compare Pl. 42.) The curving surface of the stair rail carries a continuous story, like a screen, a full scene painted in fresh colors seemingly depicting the ascent of laurel-crowned souls to a somewhat neoclassic Heaven. The supporting column of heavy stone is remarkable for its architectural character. (For other pulpits illustrated in this volume see Pls. 11, 24, 26, 108, 164, 167, and 170.)

The crown of Mary, Queen of Heaven, caught the fancy of the colonial artist, and on occasion he developed it into an amazing ornament. Sometimes a crown of stone was placed on the outside of a building (the papal tiara and bishop's miter also can be found as decorative motifs). In Chiapa de Corzo a public fountain from the sixteenth century was constructed of brick in the shape of a crown. At the sanctuary of Atotonilco, near San Miguel de Allende, Mexico, it lends its form to the lantern of a dome. Usually, however, it was an element in interior decoration. In the sixteenth-century church at Maní, Yucatán, it makes a graceful canopy over the pulpit, adjacent to a side altar shown earlier in this chapter (see Pl. 174).

In the St. Joseph retable of the Augustinian church in Salamanca, Mexico, probably dating from the 1760's, crowns are developed into massive structures of exquisitely carved and gilded wood. Used architecturally, they give dramatic focus to the tableaus placed under them, in this case the Annunciation to St.

Joseph (*Pl. 184, fig. a*). Note the fine scroll-work at the sides, reminiscent of drapery, the splendid angel canephorae, and the subtle interlacing pattern of the background. (*See also Pl. 45.*)

The crown in the Franciscan church at Trujillo, Peru (*fig. b*), dates from the late seventeenth century or the early eighteenth and is quite different in execution. On this masterly retable, with its polychromed story-telling reliefs of Mary's life, the crown is not strictly a part of the composition. Carved in relief and upheld by two angels at the top of the structure, it is thrust forward so far that it overhangs the altar table. Note the swag of fruit and the leaf-sprite among the scrolls (lower right). The Dominican church in Trujillo also uses a crown in the same way (*see Pl. 97*).

An impressive crown, projecting like a baldachin, decorates the altar to the right of the sanctuary in Santa Rosa in Querétaro, Mexico (*fig. c*). Here, as at Salamanca, it is an integral part of the design. The retable's cornice juts out to serve as a base for it. Its scrollwork curves up to a considerable height, and the light falling through the window illuminates the angel placed upon its crest. Below, the starched and painted curtains are held in place by two angels—as in many paintings—and carved drapery falls in folds beside them, framing the central figure. In spite of a wealth of detail, the composition has a floating quality, an amazingly light touch. (Compare with the crown in the Rosario chapel of Santo Domingo in Oaxaca, *Pl. 33.*)

The last crown shown here tops the main altar of the Jesuit church in Quito, Ecuador (*fig. d*). It is an airy construction, suspended like a chandelier. Upheld by four angels—whose gestures are remarkably alive—it is built up of only those parts needed to convey the form and seems almost weightless. The whole group fits beautifully between the segments of the broken pediment. A sumptuous main altar in this church is described shortly after mid-seventeenth century,[183] but considerable redec-

oration took place at the time of Legarda. (For others crowns on altars see *Pls. 97, 111, and 164.*)

Many confessionals, too, exemplify the exquisite woodwork that once decorated colonial churches. In its present-day form the confessional dates no farther back than the second half of the sixteenth century. The examples here discussed are mainly from the eighteenth. The piece now standing in the Museum of Religious Art, connected with the cathedral of Mexico City, may be of a somewhat earlier date (*Pl. 185, fig. a*). It represents a type which seemingly was later abandoned; the confessant knelt in front of the booth and a hinged panel concealed the face of the priest. Coffered paneling decorates the front section, and a convulsive all-over pattern the background; within the arch is carved a papal tiara.

Close to this in style and type is the confessional in the cathedral of Ayacucho, Peru (*fig. c*); its design also is strongly frontal. The saint and two angels are carved in the flat manner characteristic of the Andean region. Perforated scrolls lighten the whole piece. Four such confessionals stand in this cathedral; all come from La Compañía in the same town, where still others are extant.[204]

The confessional in the cathedral of Comayagua, Honduras, has something of a Chinese palanquin about it (*fig. b*). Its sides are drawn forward and the hoodlike baldachin consists only of a large graceful leaf. Here the confessor was approached from the side. The sinuous pattern decorating the side panels is well adapted to their peculiar shape, and the oval grille with its daintily gilded frame is another finely integrated element.

Both of the following confessionals come from Guanajuato, Mexico (*figs. e, f*), the first, from the parochial church there and the second, from La Valenciana, a suburb of the town. Basically they are much alike. In each case the door has a low bay shape, irregular panels break the rigidity of the side pieces, and the baldachin projects over the confessor's chair like a separate member. In their decoration, however, they differ considerably. The conelike scrolls on the canopy of the first are especially graceful. In its angular build-up and its massivity the second reminds one of a wardrobe detail. (Compare it with the Mexican armoire on the following plate.)

From the same region is the confessional in Santa Rosa, Querétaro (*fig. d*). Here ingeniously stylized motifs mount at the sides like fragile columns of flowers and a large gilded shell forms the canopy. A very lively zigzag pattern decorates the bay, and light-colored flowers were painted on the inside walls, as in a Rococo interior. (A fine confessional very close to this in style can be seen in the Augustinian church at Salamanca, *Pl. 45*.)

The colonial production of furniture, textiles, silverware, and pottery was so vast and so varied that each of these crafts deserves a separate volume. Some publications on the subject have already appeared, and it is to be hoped that the whole field will be covered before the best examples still extant have gone to pieces or been cast aside. Although only a few furniture pieces can be presented in this book, they belong here, for they add considerably to the picture of artistic life in the colonies.

A cabinet of unusual size and workmanship is in the Prado collection at Chorillos, near Lima, Peru (*Pl. 186, fig. b*). Its many drawers and cupboards, by offering an opportunity for variety in design, kept the large surface from appearing at all monotonous. Even the cockscomb ornaments on the top are preserved, reminding one, with their lacy floral and heraldic shapes, of the confessional from Ayacucho on the preceding plate. This cabinet is probably the earliest of the examples shown here; the table and chair standing before it might be called Spanish colonial Chippendale and are of a somewhat later date.

La Cata, near Guanajuato, Mexico, which is described by Humboldt as having one of the three richest silver mines in the province,

also boasted a magnificently outfitted church. Dilapidation set in after the mines were abandoned, and today the settlement is a sorry sight, the church a shadow of its former glory. In a dark and out-of-the-way corner of the sacristy stands a wardrobe which reveals the splendor that once characterized this interior (*fig. a*). The radiating rays of its paneling echo the Mudéjar. The ornamentation of its heavy top is developed as for a building—indeed it reflects the style of the stonework on the church's façade. Thick gold leaf against a background of bright blue brings out the design. Note the glazed tiles set into the floor.

As in the case of the two confessionals, two contemporary secretaries were selected from one city—Recife, Brazil—to show the individuality occurring within one period and place. The first piece (*fig. c*) stands in the sacristy of São Francisco, the second (*fig. d*) in that of Santo Antônio.[230] Both show an amazing *bonhomie* in their shape, and in both the craftsmanship is of the highest quality. Remarkably shallow in depth for their bulk, they are constructed like a console to lean against the wall. The faces of fauns are carved on their curving legs. Both carry cascades of volutes like side garlands. Cube-shaped drawers make up the entire front of the first secretary; the central section could be dropped to form a writing desk. The wood carving in the Franciscan establishment has been declared as some of the finest in the country. Nevertheless the secretary in the sacristy of Santo Antônio is equally impressive in conception and execution. It offers fewer small compartments, and an etching-like design, different on every tier, covers its surface. The open space above the writing section offsets the somewhat top-heavy effect.

Here mention should be made of the traveling desks or *vargueños*, so-called because they were first manufactured in Vargas near Toledo, Spain.[41] This type became popular in Spanish America in the seventeenth century[205] and was made in several centers there. To trace not only the sources of the designs, which were inlaid, but also the influence which they in turn may have exerted on other wood carving elsewhere would make an interesting study.

In colonial times the humble spent much time in waiting. And many of the benches which stood in the anterooms of palace, monastery, and parish house received truly artistic decoration. Here are shown examples from Peru, Mexico, and Honduras, all highly ornate (*Pl. 187*).

A bench in the Prado mansion at Lima (*fig. a*) may be the earliest in date. Birds amid flowers, such as were woven into tapestry in this viceroyalty, adorn the topmost panel. The rows of spindles on the back and at the bottom of this rare piece of furniture are turned in different patterns.

The bench in the Augustinian church at Salamanca, Mexico (*fig. b*), was designed to stand against the right wall near the entrance; the protruding section fitted around a pilaster. Note the asymmetry of the gilded Rococo motifs that cross the top and fringe the seat. Leather upholstery, still visible on the back, once covered the seat also.

Of the benches in the Popenoe collection at Zamorano, Honduras, the one at the left (*fig. c*) came from San Antonio del Oriente. It is constructed of honey-colored cedar and makes its appeal through a massive undercut pattern. Two birds hold the central medallion with its crown and monogram; the flower elements are airily distributed and fill with a warm plasticity the edges as well as the back. The piece has claw legs. The second (*fig. d*), somewhat longer yet less weighty, is gracious in a different way. Both the seat and the back were once upholstered, as the nail heads prove. Across the top a stylized floral cresting is brought out by delicate gilding on a painted gray background. This piece came from the town of Danlí and is dated 1789 on the back. The arm rests of both benches, turned in powerful scrolls, have a living, animal quality. The first piece is the embodiment of a robust Ba-

roque; the second shows the healthy daintiness of a rustic Rococo.

Many visitors are too overwhelmed by the general impression of colonial church interiors to perceive the immense variety and superlative craftsmanship revealed in the details. Nearly all of the examples of wood carving shown on the next two plates are taken from buildings that have already been illustrated in this volume. The reader is referred to the place names in the index for the related photographs.

The colonial craftsman applied human bodies and faces in many cases where his European contemporary would have thought them inappropriate. Highly unusual is the side garland on the main altar of Tegucigalpa's cathedral, dating from late eighteenth century (*Pl. 188, fig. a*). An angel—more of a winged siren—holding a bouquet and placed as if on a ship's prow emerges out of the rhythmic scrollwork. One of the altar columns, more like a lace valentine than woodwork, can be seen in the illustration; even candle holders are included in the vivacious composition.

Somewhat more functional is the figure from Quechólac, Mexico (*fig. c*); it rises out of a twisted column draped with flowers and leaves and ends in an elaborate capital that forms a multiple crown for it. This work, beautifully three-dimensional, probably dates from mid-eighteenth century.[134] Never having received the customary gold leaf and polychrome, it retains the blond color of the natural wood.

Angular figures are interwoven in a manner typical of Tunja's woodwork on a column in that town's cathedral (*fig. d*). Behind the relatively thin, screenlike façade, an undecorated upright carries the weight of the structure. (*Compare Pl. 23.*)

The church of the Franciscan Third Order at Cuernavaca, Mexico, as its name implies, belonged to a lay brotherhood, and the regional craftsman heaped the fruits of his fantasy upon its decoration. On the main altar (*fig. f*) alternating flat and rounded members serve as background for angel heads and *putti*. Note the little nun at the right and above her the carved drapery that encloses the central niche. This altar, dated 1735, shows the *estípite* used in a most original manner. As was discussed in Chapter 6, that ornamental shape appeared in Mexico in early eighteenth century and belongs to the polyphony of the Churrigueresque style. As early as the sixteenth century, however, it was applied in Florentine architecture (*see Appendix, Pl. 190, fig. f*). Topped by a bust, it appeared as a decorative initial in a book printed in Antwerp in 1571, and one of the Sadelers put it into an engraving printed by Plantin in 1577.

A strong folkloristic fantasy created the rampant lions which serve as candelabra in the parish church at Colohete, Honduras (*fig. b*). Again the carving is flat, but through the decorative sense of the craftsman a naïvely charming effect was produced. Few such candelabra have survived to recall the former method of illumination in churches. In Nindiri, Nicaragua, where oxcarts are still the main means of transportation and electricity is unknown, the author saw another set in use in 1947.

The salomonic or twisted column has its ancestry in classical Greece as well as in the Near East. The term derives from the sacred column in St. Peter's, Rome, which according to legend came from Solomon's temple but really is Roman. Further, a twisted column of gilded bronze was unearthed on the site of the hippodrome in Constantinople, within the complex of Hagia Sophia. Made up of the intertwining bodies of three serpents, it was identified as the base for a golden tripod (long vanished) dedicated to the "god of Delphi." [20]

The adoption of the twisted column in Venice and her domains is logical, for an intensive commerce was carried on between that port and the Byzantine capital. In Byzantine, Romanesque, and Gothic art this type of column usually was slender and comparatively short, its surface plain or spirally fluted. In the Renaissance, more ornately decorated, it was applied on jewel caskets, clocks, and other objects of the goldsmith's art. Raphael and Veronese used it, enlarged to an impressive size, especially in scenes of Old Testament pomp. The twisted columns in their paintings are close to the shape which the Baroque, with its sense of the monumental, translated into three dimensions. The most notable example is on the bronze baldachin designed by Bernini (c. 1627–1633) in St. Peter's. Here, as well as in many other seventeenth-century European versions, the ornamentation consists of a garland of acanthus or flowers. [19]

The salomonic column appeared in Latin America in mid-seventeenth century, first in wood but soon also in stone. One of the earliest examples on record appears on an engraving of the former main altar of the Puebla cathedral. [203] Often in the colonies the shaft was divided (as in the prototypes) and carried at least two kinds of ornament. Vines heavy with grapes became as frequent a decoration as garlands of flowers.

Seven details of columns from five countries—Bolivia, Peru, Ecuador, Brazil, and Honduras—are placed side by side for comparative study (*Pl. 189*). The Eucharistic grapes, changed by the fertile imagination of regional artists, sometimes resemble tropical fruit. The individual composition of the columns and the secondary designs surrounding them serve to augment the differences.

Two types of column can be seen in the detail from the main altar at Copacabana (*fig. e*). The larger still recalls the Plateresque, while the smaller is salomonic, divided into three sections and tapering toward the top. Exquisite openwork distinguishes the side garland on the right. The running atlantean figure, with one arm uplifted, is a motif encountered also on some façades, carved in stone. The gilding of this altar was finished in 1684.

The main altar of San Pedro Mártir in Juli (*fig. d*) dates from the same period, or perhaps earlier. Here grapes and highly stylized leaves alternate, carved in full three dimensions. The capital is a study in the folkloristic interpretation of European models, and the bull above it, symbol of Luke (the other three columns bear the winged symbols of the other Evangelists), brings home what liberties the regional artist took with Old World tradition—and with what stunning results. This altar is ungilded, very beautiful in the beige tone of the natural wood.

Birds are perched among the Eucharistic grapes on a side altar in Quito's Compañía (*fig. b*). It may be that they were intended to symbolize the human soul; in Coptic and Byzantine representations the dove and the peacock placed among grapes have that significance. It is interesting to note that this side chapel is dedicated to the Polish saint Stanislaus, whose statue appears on the retable as well as on the façade of the church.

Birds among grapes are found more frequently in Portuguese carving than in Spanish. The extremely long-stemmed stylized leaves that decorate columns in Recife's Capela Dourada (*fig. c*), in Brazil, may have had a bird as prototype. This chapel of the Franciscan Third Order, opening off the conventual church, was finished in the last years of the seventeenth century. Its carving is remarkable for the absence of all figural motifs. Excep-

tionally thick gilding throughout gave rise to the name Golden Chapel.[228] Another version of birds among grapes can be seen in the Tunja altar illustrated on the preceding plate.

In the detail from a side altar of Santa Catalina in Cuzco a number of decorative motifs are combined (*fig. g*). Besides being spirally ridged, the long twisted column is hung with grapes. Note the extension with cherubim above the capital. The smaller column is wound with flowers. On the panel at the left the regional artist made effective use of repetition, superimposing the popular vase motif with its spreading bouquet.

The third altar from Comayagua's cathedral to be illustrated in this volume (*fig. a*) stands in the sagrario chapel. It shows salomonic and candelabra columns side by side. Here the grapes and leaves are very flat. The divisions are interestingly proportioned, and each section carries different ornamentation.

A still more pungent folkloristic talent is revealed in the altar of San Pedro in Zepita (*fig. f*). Its twisted column is ornamented most heavily in the lower third and carries angel heads in its spiraling garland, while the little columns at the right are studded with dainty rosettes. Filigree volutes and stylized flowers as side garlands bear witness with their upsurging Rococo rhythm to the vigor and eloquence of the regional woodcarver.

POSTSCRIPT

THE extant remnants of Latin American colonial art are still numerous enough to form a representative corpus of the creative achievement of that age. But the forces of destruction, which set in early in the nineteenth century, are increasingly active. The animosity toward Spain and her traditions then went so far as to drag the bones of Cortés from their resting place in an attempt to scatter them. The anticlerical feeling that rose and waned at intervals also has contributed to the destruction. Today an important factor is the urge to modernize and renovate, coupled with a limited understanding of the value of this art. Poverty, too, plays its role. This author has seen a large and exceptionally fine colonial rug in a church in the Titicaca region folded into a small square to keep the feet of the priest warm as he stood before the altar; when attention was called to the fact that this extraordinary piece should be preserved, the priest replied that he had no money to buy himself a hassock.

But chiefly it is ignorance that is destroying the legacy from the colonial past. The formation of committees in various capitals for the preservation of colonial monuments is in vain so long as only a few miles away the local populace continues to follow a false ambition to be "modern." The people do not seem to realize that they can be modern and still preserve their splendid heritage. It is possible to strengthen an aging building with cement and iron girders without making it completely over. Old statues need not be "refreshed" with entire coats of new cheap paint, nor paintings touched up by those who lack a feeling of their basic style; no authorities should have the power to order nude angels of the colonial era painted over with garments. Also, it is doubtful whether neon lights around an altar or a bare electric bulb dangling in front of a main statue adds to the devotional atmosphere. And to condone the wrecking of an old church or palace by promising to deposit its best sections in some museum is indeed a weak apology for destruction; such a transfer cannot be carried out without the loss of much of the original spirit.

In the prologue to the *Guide to Bogotá* by the distinguished diplomat Guillermo Hernández de Alba, a former professor of the Jesuit college there, colonial monuments are referred to as among the greatest assets of Latin American culture, a never-failing attraction for the tourist and scholar. In the same book the proposal is made to create chairs in the seminaries for teaching the history of religious art in America; thus the oncoming priests could gain an appreciation of the treasures entrusted to their hands and assist in educating the general public.

In the archives of the various countries other constructive work is awaiting unselfish hands. Whether the volumes and fascicles that remain lie in moldy corners of convents or on cobwebby municipal shelves, they need to be studied thoroughly, especially while the monuments to which they relate can still be admired. Considerable specialized knowledge is necessary to decipher their contents. To date, zealous private persons can be thanked for most of the research that has been done.

The failure of neighboring countries or even towns to exchange material and information of mutual interest is regrettable. Too often a local savant has no knowledge of—and seemingly no interest in—what exists beyond his own mountain range, and the books which treat the regional art are not available a few hundred miles away from the towns where they were published. Thus it is impossible to construct a sweeping panorama of Latin American colonial art, and without it the various artistic manifestations do not fall into proper focus.

With conditions in the Old World as they are, Latin America offers to the younger generation of investigators a fertile and rewarding field. But just as in pre-Columbian archaeology, research had to work out, from the methods of the classical field, a modified discipline, so in the colonial art of Latin America it must evolve new techniques and methods, for the conditions under which this art was produced are utterly different from those encountered elsewhere. It is a matter of primary importance to record in word and picture and to preserve. Involved speculation as to artists and dates has its place in this research, to be sure. But it has to go much farther than the mere repetition of the names of officials and curates, except as such information offers dates. Few are interested in what captain commanded the garrison in Florence or what bishop presided in Venice when Donatello and Titian created their masterpieces.

Time for salvage is fast running out. Since the plan for this book was laid down, the volcano of Paricutín in Mexico has obliterated villages, and floods in Guatemala, seismic catastrophes in El Salvador and Ecuador, civil strife in Colombia, and an earthquake in Cuzco have all taken a tragic toll. But if the interest and appreciation of a greater public are awakened soon, the legacy remaining from a unique epoch can still be preserved for the enjoyment of posterity and a new and refreshing chapter added to the history of art.

BIBLIOGRAPHY

····•———◆———····

THE mere acknowledgment of the existence of arts from the colonial period of Latin America came belatedly. Not until the very end of the nineteenth century—if not the beginning of the twentieth—did there appear in a magazine article or a slim travel book an aesthetic appraisal of colonial art in one area or another. It is interesting to note that the pre-Conquest art of Middle America was appreciatively treated in the first half of the nineteenth century. A native of the United States, John Lloyd Stephens (1805–1852), wrote the first books to describe with sound judgment and a clear eye the pre-Columbian wonders of the Maya area; and similarly another citizen of the same country was responsible for one of the earliest comprehensive works on colonial art in Latin America. *Spanish Colonial Art in Mexico* by Sylvester Baxter (1850–1927), published in 1901, was so rich in descriptive information and illustrative material that in 1934 Manuel Toussaint found it worthy of translation and brought it out in Mexico, with amendments resulting from more recent research. Neither Stephens nor Baxter was what today would be called a "professional." The first was a lawyer and a railroad builder, and the second a foreign news correspondent and publicist.

This Bibliography includes the books consulted during the years that my work was in preparation. Further titles, which may be just as good, can be found in comprehensive bibliographies published both in this country and abroad by various institutions which devote themselves to the subject. Among these, an especial place must be given to *A Guide to the Art of Latin America*, edited by Robert C. Smith and Elizabeth Wilder (Washington, 1948), a work that contains a vast amount of information as well as clear-cut and attractive introductions to each country's literature. *The Handbook of Latin American Studies* (Cambridge, Mass.), an annual volume amazing in its scope started so ably under the guidance of Lewis Hanke, takes over with the year when that bibliography ends—1942.

Very great help was obtained from the data and the excellent essays on geography, history, and art in the three volumes of the *New World Guides to the Latin American Republics*, edited by Earl Parker Hanson (New York, 1945). Vázquez' *Compendium* furnished much of the atmosphere and description of early seventeenth-century colonial life. For general reference, use was made of the *Encyclopædia Britannica*, the *Catholic Encyclopedia*, *Enciclopedia Italiana*, and the Spanish *Enciclopedia universal ilustrada*.

The numbers indicate source references as well as works where fuller information on a particular subject can be found. Books with an extensive bibliography are marked here with an asterisk (*), and the dagger (†) denotes those with rich illustrative material.

EUROPE GENERAL

Alvin, Louis, *Catalogue raisonné de l'oeuvre de Wierix*. Brussels, 1866

—— *Catalogue raisonné des portraits gravés par les trois frères Wierix*. Brussels, 1867

Atkinson, Robert, and Hope Bagenal, *Theory and Elements of Architecture*. New York, 1929

Baum, Julius, *Martin Schongauer*. Vienna, 1948†

Bemden, J. J. P. van den, *De Familie Galle*. Antwerp, 1863

Berliner, Rudolf, "The Origins of the Crèche," *Gazette des Beaux-Arts*, Oct., Nov., Dec., 1946

Bode, Wilhelm von, *Die Kunst der Frührenaissance in Italien*. Berlin, 1926†

The Book of Saints. New York, 1950

Brieger, Peter, "The Baroque Equation, Illusion and Reality," *Gazette des Beaux-Arts*, March, 1945

[1] Briggs, Martin Shaw, *Baroque Architecture*. New York, 1914

[2] Brown, Lloyd A., *The Story of Maps*. Boston, 1950

Brugge die Schoone. Bruges, 1942

Cheney, Sheldon, *A World History of Art*. New York, 1937

Chledowski, Casimir von, *Neapolitanische Kulturbilder XIV.–XVII. Jahrhundert*. Berlin, 1918

Croce, Benedetto, *Der Begriff des Barock*. Berlin, 1925

[3] —— *Storia della Età Barocca in Italia*. Bari, 1929

Decker, Heinrich, *Barock-Plastik in den Alpenländern*. Vienna, 1943

[4] Delaumay, M. l'Abbé, *Les Évangiles de dimanche et fêtes de l'année*. Paris, 1864†

Delen, A. J. J., *Christophe Plantin*. Brussels, 1944

[5] —— *Histoire de la gravure dans les anciens Pays-Bas et les provinces belges*. Paris and Brussels, 1924

Denucé, J., *The Antwerp Art Galleries*. Antwerp, 1932

[6] —— *Kunstuitvoer in de 17e Eeuw te Antwerpen de Firma Forchoudt*. Antwerp, 1931

D'Ors, Eugenio, *Lo barroco*. Madrid, n.d.

Eich, Ernst, *Vom Werdegang des Madonnenbildes*. Zurich, 1947

Fletcher, Sir Banister F., *A History of Architecture on the Comparative Method*. New York, 1943†

[7] Floerke, Hanns, *Studien zur niederländischen Kunst und Kultur Geschichte*. Munich, 1905

Fokker, T. H., "The First Baroque Church in Rome," *Art Bulletin*, Sept., 1933

Ganz, Paul, *Hans Holbein d. J.* Stuttgart and Berlin, 1919

Gorissen, Friedrich, *Gent, de Fiere*. Bruges, 1941

Grimschitz, Bruno, *Wiener Barockpaläste*. Vienna, 1944†

Gurlitt, Cornelius, *Geschichte des Barockstiles*, 3 vols. Berlin, 1887–89

Hamlin, Talbot, *Architecture through the Ages*. New York, 1944

Hausenstein, Wilhelm, *Vom Geist des Barock*. Munich, 1921

Hauttmann, Max, *Die Kunst des frühen Mittelalters*. Berlin, 1929

Hind, Arthur M., *History of Engraving and Etching*. London, 1923 (Dover reprint, 1963)

Holbein, Hans, *Die Todesbilder und das Todesalphabet*. Berlin, 1922†

[8] Holt, Elizabeth Gilmore, ed., *Literary Sources of Art History*. Princeton, 1947

[9] Jameson, Mrs. Anna Brownell (Murphy), *Legends of the Madonna*. London, 1857

Kehrer, Hugo, *Alt-Antwerpen*. Munich, 1917

Kimball, Fiske, *The Creation of the Rococo*. Philadelphia, 1943

Knipping, B., *De Iconografie van de Contra-Reformatie in de Nederlanden*. Hilversum, 1939†

Kreisel, Heinrich, *Würzburg*. Berlin, 1930†

Kristeller, Paul, *Die Apokalypse*. Berlin, 1916

—— *Kupferstich und Holzschnitt in vier Jahrhunderten*. Munich, 1921†

[10] Künstle, Karl, *Ikonographie der Christlichen Kunst*, 2 vols. Freiburg, 1926–28

Lang, Ludwig, *Was ist Barock?* Zurich, 1924

[11] Legrand, F. C., Brussels. Correspondence

Liefmann, M., *Kunst und Heilige*. Jena, 1912

[12] Mâle, Émile, *L'Art religieux après de Concile de Trent*. Paris, 1932

[13] Maroger, Jacques, *The Secret Formulas and Techniques of the Masters*. New York, 1948

Mayor, A. Hyatt, *The Bibiena Family*. New York, 1945†

[14] Mccall, John E., "Early Jesuit Art in the Far East," *Artibus Asia*, 1947–48

McComb, Arthur, *The Baroque Painters of Italy*. Cambridge, Mass., 1934†

Michel, André, ed., *Histoire de l'art*, 18 vols. Paris, 1905–29†

Michel, Wilhelm, *Das Teuflische und Groteske in der Kunst*. Munich, 1911

Milliken, William M., "Two Sculptures of St. Margaret by Antonello Gagini," *Gazette des Beaux-Arts*, April, 1943

Morgan Library, *The Animal Kingdom*. New York, 1940

Muñoz, Antonio, *Iconografia della Madonna*. Florence, 1905

Müseler, Wilhelm, *Geist und Antlitz des Barock*. Berlin, 1943

Novák, Arne, *Baroque Prague*. Prague, 1947†

Ojetti, N., L. Dami, and N. Tarchiani, *La Pittura Italiana del Seicento e del Settecento alla Mostra di Palazzo Pitti*. Milan and Rome, 1924†

Osborn, Max, *Die Kunst des Rokoko*. Berlin, 1929†

[15] Penney, C. L., *Spanish Publications at Antwerp*. In press. Catalogue of books printed in the House of Martin Nucio

Peusner, Nikolaus, *An Outline of European Architecture*. New York, 1948

—— and Otto Grautoff, *Barockmalerei in den romanischen Ländern*. Wildpark and Potsdam, 1928†

[16] Pope, Arthur Upham, *Iranian and Armenian Contributions to the Beginnings of Gothic Architecture*. New York, 1946

Popp, Hermann, *Die Architektur der Barock und Rokokozeit in Deutschland und der Schweiz*. Stuttgart, 1913

Praz, Mario, *Studies in Seventeenth Century Imagery*, 2 vols. London, 1939, 1947

Raisz, Erwin, *General Cartography*. New York, 1948

Riegl, Alois, *Die Entstehung der Barockkunst in Rom*. Vienna, 1923

—— *Stilfragen. Grundlagen zu einer Geschichte der Ornamentik*. Berlin, 1932

Riehl, Hans, *Barocke Baukunst in Osterreich*. Munich, 1930†

[17] Robeck, Nesta de, *The Christmas Presepio in Italy*. Florence, 1934

Rooses, Max, *Les Bois gravés pour le bréviaire et planches*. Antwerp, 1910–11

[18] —— *Le Musée Plantin Moretus*. Paris, n.d.†

Scherer, Valentin, *Dürer*. Berlin, n.d.

Scholz, János, ed., *Baroque and Romantic Stage Design*. New York, 1950†

[19] Schubring, Paul, *Die Kunst der Hochrenaissance in Italien*. Berlin, 1926

Semrau, Max, *Die Kunst der Barockzeit und des Rokoko*. Esslingen, 1913

Sitwell, Sacheverell, *German Baroque Art*. London, 1927

Sturgis, Russell, *A Dictionary of Architecture and Building*, 3 vols. New York, 1902

[20] Swift, Emerson Howland, *Hagia Sophia*. New York, 1940

Thieme, U., and F. Becker, *Allgemeines Lexicon der bildenden Künstler*. Leipzig, 1907–50

Thompson, D. V., *The Materials of Medieval Painting*. London, 1936 (Dover reprint, 1956)

Tietze-Conrat, E., "Giovanni Bologna's Bronzes as Painter's Cribs," *Gazette des Beaux-Arts*, Jan., 1947

[21] Van der Elst, Joseph, *The Last Flowering of the Middle Ages*. New York, 1944

Van Marle, Raimond, *Italian Schools of Painting*, 19 vols. The Hague, 1923–38†

Van Puyvelde, Leo, *Les Primitifs flamands*. Brussels, 1947

Voss, Hermann, *Die Malerei des Barock in Rom*. Berlin, 1924

Weisbach, Werner, *Barock als Kunst der Gegenreformation*. Munich, 1921

—— *Die Kunst des Barock in Italien, Frankreich, Deutschland und Spanien*. Berlin, 1924†

Wijngaert, Frank van den, "Balthasar Moretus II, III en IV," *De Gulden Passer*, Antwerp, nos. 1, 2, 1948

[22] Willumsen, J.–F., *La Jeunesse du peintre El Greco*. Paris, 1927

Wölfflin, Heinrich, *Kunstgeschichtliche Grundbegriffe*. Munich, 1918

[23] —— *Renaissance und Barock*. Munich, 1907

Yamada, Chisaburo, *Die Chinamode des Spätbarock*. Berlin, 1935

SPAIN AND PORTUGAL

Angulo, Diego, "Martin Schongauer y algunas miniaturas castellanas," *Arte español*, no. 5, 1925

[24] Bevan, Bernard, *History of Spanish Architecture*. London, 1938*†

[25] Camón Aznar, José, *La arquitectura plateresca*, 2 vols. Madrid, 1945†

Camps Cazorla, Emilio, *Cerámica española*. Madrid, 1936

[26] Dieulafoy, Marcel, *La Statuaire polychrome en Espagne*. Paris, 1908

[27] *Documentos para la historia del arte en Andalucía*, 10 vols. Seville, 1927–46

Domínguez, Bordona Jesús, *Manuscritos con pinturas*, 2 vols. Madrid, 1933

Dos Santos, Reynaldo, *A arquitectura em Portugal*. Lisbon, 1929

[28] Feio, Alberto, *Bom Jesus do Monte*. Braga, 1930

Ferrandis, José, *Marfiles y azabaches españoles*. Barcelona, 1928

Filgueira, J. Valverde, *La iconografía de Santiago y el grabado compostelano*. Santiago de Compostela, 1944

[29] Florit, José M., *Aranjuez*. Barcelona, n.d.†

García, Simón, *Compendio di arquitectura y simetría de los templos*. Madrid, 1681

Gardner, Arthur, "Benedictine Cloisters of Spain," *Geographical Magazine*, Aug., 1942

Gómez-Moreno, María Elena, *Juan Martínez Montañés*. Barcelona, 1942†

Hagen, Oskar F. L., *Patterns and Principles of Spanish Art*. Madison, Wis., 1936

Hernández Díaz, José, *La ruta de Colón*. Madrid, 1946

—— *La universidad hispalense y sus obras de arte*. Seville, 1942

"Igreja de Cheleiros," *Boletim da Direcção Geral dos Edifícios e Monumentos Nacionais*, Porto, 1947

"Igreja de S. Quintino," *Boletim da Direcção Geral dos Edifícios e Monumentos Nacionais*, Porto, 1946

Keil, Luís, *Inventário artístico de Portugal: Distrito de Portalegre*. Lisbon, 1943†

King, Georgiana Goddard, *Mudéjar*. New York, 1927

[30] —— *The Way of St. James*. New York, 1920

Lampérez y Romea, Vicente, *Historia de la arquitectura cristiana española en la edad media*, 2 vols. Madrid, 1908–09†

Livermore, H. L., *A History of Portugal*. Cambridge, Eng., 1947

[31] Loga, Valerian von, *Spanische Plastik*. Munich, 1923†

López Martínez, Celestino, *Arquitectos, escultors, y pintores vecinos de Sevilla*. Seville, 1929

—— *Desde Jerónimo Hernández hasta Martínez Montañés*. Seville, 1929

—— *Desde Martínez Montañés hasta Pedro Roldán*. Seville, 1932

—— *Retablos y esculturas de traza sevillana*. Seville, 1928

Lowe, S. L., *Paleographic Guide for Spanish Manuscripts, Fifteenth–Seventeenth Centuries*. New Orleans, 1943

Lozoya, Marqués de (Juan de Contreras), *Historia del arte hispánico*, 4 vols. Barcelona, 1931–45†

Lucka, Emil, *Torquemada und die spanische Inquisition*. Vienna, 1926

Mayer, August L., *Alt–Spanien*. Munich, 1921

—— *Meisterwerke der Gemäldesammlung des Prado in Madrid*. Munich, 1922†

Museo de América, *Guía de su instalación provisional*. Madrid, 1944

Oliveira, Martins J. P., *Historia de la civilización ibérica*. Buenos Aires, 1944

Orduña Viguera, Emilio, *La talla ornamental en madera*. Barcelona, 1930†

Orozco Díaz, Emilio, *Temas del barroco*. Granada, 1947

[32] Pacheco, Francisco, *Arte de la pintura, su antigüedad y grandezas*. Madrid, 1866

Passos, Carlos de, "Architetti Toscani in Oporto," *Illustrazione*, April, 1934

[33] Peers, E. Allison, *Studies in the Spanish Mystics*, 2 vols. London, 1927

Pérez Embid, Florentino, *El mudejarismo en la arquitectura portuguesa de la época manuelina*. Seville, 1944†

Pinedo, Ramiro de, *Ensayo sobre el simbolismo religioso en las construcciones eclesiásticas de la edad media*. Burgos, 1924

Proske, B. G., *Castilian Sculpture: Gothic to Renaissance*. New York, 1951†

[34] Ráfols, J. F., *Techumbres y artesonados españoles*. Barcelona, 1926†

Real Academia de Bellas Artes de Santa Isabel de Hungría, *Homenaje a Martínez Montañés*. Seville, 1939

[35] Ruiz de Arcaute, Agustín, *Juan de Herrera, arquitecto de Felipe II*. Madrid, 1936†

Sánchez Moreno, José. *Vida y obra de Francisco Salzillo*. Murcia, 1945

Sancho Corbacho, Antonio, *Jerez y los puertos*. Madrid, 1947†

—— *La cerámica andaluza*. Seville, 1948

[36] Schubert, Otto, *Geschichte des Barock in Spanien*. Esslingen, 1908†

Sitwell, Sacheverell, *Southern Baroque Art*. London, 1924

—— *Spanish Baroque Art*. London, 1931

Smith, Robert C., "Alguns desenhos de arquitectura existentes no Arquivo Histórico Colonial Português," *Revista do Serviço do Patrimônio Histórico e Artístico Nacional*, Rio de Janeiro, no. 4, 1940

—— "A arte barroca de Portugal e do Brasil," *Panorama*, Lisbon, no. 38, 1949†

—— "Portuguese Baroque Woodcarving," *Magazine of Art*, Oct., 1950

—— "The Portuguese Woodcarved Retable 1600–1750)," *Belas artes*, Lisbon, no. 2, 1950 (2nd series)

—— "Recent Publications on the Fine Arts

of Portugal and Brazil," *Art Bulletin*, June, 1944*

Soria, Martin S., "Some Flemish Sources of Baroque Painting in Spain," *Art Bulletin*, Dec., 1948

Tamayo, Alberto, *Las iglesias barrocas madrileñas*. Madrid, 1946

[37] Taylor, R. C., "Francisco Hurtado and His School," *Art Bulletin*, March, 1950*†

Tormo y Monzó, Elias, *La Inmaculada y el arte español*. Madrid, 1915

[38] Trapier, Elizabeth du Gué, *Velázquez*. New York, 1948†

Trens, Manuel, *El arte en la Pasión de Nuestro Señor*. Barcelona, 1945†

[39] —— *María, iconografía de la Virgen en el arte español*. Barcelona, 1946†

[40] Virrié, F. P., Barcelona. Consultation

Weisbach, Werner, *El barroco arte de la Contrarreforma*. Madrid, 1942

—— *Spanish Baroque Art*. Cambridge, Eng., 1941

Weise, Georg, *Spanische Plastik*. Reutlingen, 1925–29

—— and G. Otto, *Die religiöse Ausdrucksgebärden des Barock und ihre Vorbereitung durch die italienische Kunst der Renaissance*. Stuttgart, 1928

LATIN AMERICA GENERAL

[41] Alcázar Molina, Cayetano, *Los virreinatos en el siglo XVIII*. Barcelona, 1945

[42] Alcedo y Herrera, Antonio de, *Aviso histórico, político, geográfico*. . . . Madrid, 1740

[43] Angulo Íñiguez, Diego, *Bautista Antonelli*. Madrid, 1942

[44] —— and Enrique Marco Dorta, *Historia del arte hispanoamericano*, vol. 1. Barcelona, 1945†

—— Enrique Marco Dorta, and Mario J. Buschiazzo, *Historia del arte hispanoamericano*, vol. 2. Barcelona, 1950*†

[45] —— *Planos de monumentos arquitectónicos de América y Filipinas*, 3 vols. Seville, 1933–39

[46] Arciniegas, Germán, *Germans in the Conquest of America*. New York, 1943

Arnaud, Leopold, "The South American Heritage," *Journal of the American Institute of Architects*, Dec., 1944

[47] Bancroft, Hubert Howe, *History of Central America*, 3 vols. San Francisco, 1882–87

[48] Berlin, Heinrich, "Los archivos notariales como fuentes para la historia del arte colonial en Latinamérica." Paper read at the 29th International Congress of Americanists, New York, 1949

Bermúdez Plata, Cristóbal, ed., *Catálogo de pasajeros a Indias*, 3 vols. Seville, 1940–46

Buenaventura, Manuel M., *El libro*. Cali, 1944

Buschiazzo, Mario J., *La arquitectura colonial en Hispano América; catálogo razonado*. Buenos Aires, 1940

[49] —— *Estudios de arquitectura colonial hispano americana*. Buenos Aires, 1944*†

—— "Exotic Influences in American Colonial Art," *Journal of the Society of Architectural Historians*, 1945–46

—— "Indigenous Influences on the Colonial Architecture of Latin America," *Bulletin of the Pan American Union*, May, 1941†

—— "Kolonialische Malerei," *Lasso*, Buenos Aires, Nov., 1935

Cobo, Bernabé, *Historia del Nuevo Mundo*, 4 vols. Seville, 1890–93. Written c.1653 in Peru

Crow, John A., *The Epic of Latin America*. New York, 1946

[50] Desdevises du Dézert, G., *L'Église espagnole des Indes à la fin du XVIIIᵉ siècle*. Paris, 1917

Díaz Ordóñez, Virgilio, "Columbus in Hispaniola," *Bulletin of the Pan American Union*, Oct., 1942

Diffie, Bailey W., *Latin-American Civilization, Colonial Period*. Philadelphia, 1946

Documentos de arte colonial sudamericano, 6 vols. Buenos Aires, 1943–50

[51] Douglas, Norman, *Siren Land*. New York, 1923

[52] Fisher, Lillian Estelle, *Viceregal Administration in the Spanish American Colonies*. Berkeley, 1926

[53] —— Correspondence (Berkeley, Calif.)

Flexner, James Thomas, *First Flowers of Our Wilderness*. Cambridge, Mass., 1947

Flores Aráoz, José, "La pintura colonial en América," *Cultura peruana*, Lima, Dec., 1942

[54] Frézier, Amédée François, *A Voyage to the South Sea and along the Coasts of Chile and Peru in the Years 1712, 1713, & 1714*. London, 1717

[55] Gage, Thomas, *The English-American. A New Survey of the West Indies, 1648*. London, 1928

García Gutiérrez, Jesús, *Santos y beatos de América*. Mexico, 1946

Gardner, Helen, *Art through the Ages*. New York, 1948*†

Gillin, John, "Mestizo America," in *Most of the World.* New York, 1949

Gómez Sicre, José, "Colonial Religious Painting," *Américas*, March, 1949

Guide to the Art of Latin America, edited by Robert C. Smith and Elizabeth Wilder. Washington, 1948*

Guido, Angel, *Redescubrimiento de América en el arte.* Buenos Aires, 1944†

Hamilton, Earl J., "Imports of American Gold and Silver into Spain, 1502–1660," *Quarterly Journal of Economics*, vol. 43

56 Hanke, Lewis, *Bartolomé de las Casas.* Havana, 1949*

—— *The Spanish Struggle for Justice in the Conquest of America.* Philadelphia, 1949*

Haring, C. H., "American Gold and Silver Production in the First Half of the Sixteenth Century," *Quarterly Journal of Economics*, vol. 29

57 —— *The Spanish Empire in America.* New York, 1947*

—— *Trade and Navigation between Spain and the Indies in the Time of the Habsburgs.* Cambridge, Mass., 1918

58 Humboldt, Alexander von, *Essai politique sur le royaume de la Nouvelle-Espagne.* Paris, 1811

59 —— *Travels to the Equinoctial Regions of America 1799–1804.* London, 1852

60 Juan y Santacilia, Jorge, and Antonio de Ulloa, *Noticias secretas de América.* London, 1826

61 —— *Relación histórica del viaje a la América meridional.* Madrid, 1748

Karraker, Cyrus H., *The Hispaniola Treasure.* Philadelphia, 1934

62 Kelemen, Pál, *Medieval American Art,* 2 vols. New York, 1943

Lanning, John Tate, *Academic Culture in the Spanish Colonies.* New York, 1940

Leonard, Irving A., *Books of the Brave.* Cambridge, Mass., 1949

—— *Romances of Chivalry in the Spanish Indies.* Berkeley, 1933

63 Lipman, Jean, *American Primitive Painting.* New York, 1942†

—— "The Composite Scene in Primitive Painting," *Gazette des Beaux-Arts*, Feb., 1946

Lozoya, Marqués de (Juan de Contreras), *Historia del arte hispánico,* 4 vols. Barcelona, 1931–45. Especially vols. 3 and 4†

MacLeish, Archibald, "The American Experience," *Bulletin of the Pan American Union*, Nov., 1939

64 Madariaga, Salvador de, *The Fall of the Spanish American Empire.* New York, 1948

—— *The Rise of the Spanish American Empire.* New York, 1947

Manzano Manzano, Juan, *La incorporación de las Indias a la corona de Castilla.* Madrid, 1948

Marco Dorta, Enrique, and Diego Angulo Íñiguez, *Historia del arte hispanoamericano,* 2 vols. Barcelona, 1945, 1950

Means, Philip Ainsworth, "Biblioteca andina," *Connecticut Academy of Arts and Sciences, Transactions*, 1928

65 Meléndez, Juan, *Tesoros verdaderos de las Indias,* 3 vols. Rome, 1681–82

Mendieta, Jerónimo de, *Historia eclesiástica indiana.* Mexico, 1870. 16th century

Métraux, Alfred, "General Statement" in *Handbook of Latin American Studies 1941.* Cambridge, Mass., 1942

66 Moses, Bernard, *The Establishment of Spanish Rule in America.* New York, 1898

67 Neumeyer, Alfred, "The Indian Contribution to Architectural Decoration in Spanish Colonial America," *Art Bulletin*, June, 1948*†

68 —— Correspondence (Oakland, Calif.)

Newcomb, Rexford, *Spanish-Colonial Architecture in the United States.* New York, 1937*†

—— "Studies in Regional Architecture," *College Art Journal*, Jan., 1946

69 Noel, Martín S., *Contribución a la historia de la arquitectura hispano-americana.* Buenos Aires, 1921

—— *Teoría histórica de la arquitectura virreinal.* Buenos Aires, 1932

Northrop, F. S. C., *The Meeting of East and West.* New York, 1947

Palm, Erwin Walter, "Estilo y época en el arte colonial," *Anales del Instituto de Arte Americano*, Buenos Aires, 1949

70 —— "Zur Situation der spanischen Baudenkmäler in der Neuen Welt," *Österreichische Zeitschrift für Denkmalpflege*, nos. 5–6, 1949†

71 *Pan American Yearbook, 1945.* New York, 1945

Picon-Salas, Mariano, *De la conquista a la independencia.* Mexico, 1944

72 Pinkerton, John, ed., *A General Collection of Voyages and Travels,* vol. 14 of "South America." London, 1813. Capt. Betagh's observations on Peru

73 Priestley, Herbert Ingram, *Coming of the White Man, 1492–1848.* New York, 1929*

[74] Rios, Fernando de los, "Action of Spain in America," in *Concerning Latin American Culture*. New York, 1940

Ryan, Edwin, "Central America," *The Americas*, Jan., 1948

—— "What Is 'Latin America'?" *The Americas*, April, 1947

Sánchez, Luis Alberto, *Existe América Latina?* Mexico, 1945

[75] Schurz, William Lytle, *The Manila Galleon*. New York, 1939*

Sierra, Vicente D., *Los Jesuitos alemaños en la conquista espiritual de Hispano-América*. Buenos Aires, 1944

Smith, Robert C., *The Colonial Art of Latin America*. Washington, 1945*

—— "The Evolution of Latin-American Art," *Inter American Intellectual Interchange*, Austin, Texas, 1943

—— "The Hispanic Foundation in the Library of Congress," *Bulletin of the Pan American Union*, Nov., 1939

Smith, Robert S., *The Spanish Guild Merchant. A History of the Consulado, 1250–1700*. Durham, N. C., 1940

[76] Solá, Miguel, *Historia del arte hispano-americano*. Barcelona, 1935†

Squier, E. G., *States of Central America*. New York, 1855

Stanislawski, Dan, "Early Spanish Town Planning in the New World," *Geographical Review*, Jan., 1947

—— "The Origin and Spread of the Grid-Pattern Town," *Geographical Review*, Jan., 1946

[77] Terry, Adrian R., *Travels in the Equatorial Regions of South America in 1832*. Hartford, Conn., 1834

Torre Revello, José, "Obras de arte enviadas al Nuevo Mundo en los siglos XVI y XVII," *Anales del Instituto de Arte Americano*, Buenos Aires, 1948

[78] Toussaint, Manuel, *Arte mudéjar en América*. Mexico, 1946*†

—— "A Defense of Baroque Art in America," *Inter American Intellectual Interchange*, Austin, Texas, 1943

[79] Trenti Rocamora, J. Luis, *El teatro en la América colonial*. Buenos Aires, 1947

Ulloa, Antonio de. See Juan y Santacilia, Jorge

[80] Valle, Rafael Heliodoro, *Santiago en América*. Mexico, 1946†

Vargas Ugarte, Rubén, *Historia del culto de María en Hispano América y de sus imágenes y santuarios más celebrados*. Lima, 1931

[81] Vázquez de Espinosa, Antonio, *Compendium and Description of the West Indies, 1612–1630*. Washington, 1942

Walker, Martha Ann, Marie Schmitt Ely, and E. Boyd Hall, *Sacred Paintings on Skin*. Santa Fe, 1944

[82] Weyl, Nathaniel, "Mexico, European and Native," in *Concerning Latin American Culture*. New York, 1940

Whitaker, Arthur P., ed., *Latin America and the Enlightenment*. New York, 1942

Wilder, Mitchell A., and Edgar Breitenbach, *Santos*. Colorado Springs, 1943†

Wilgus, A. Curtis, *The Development of Hispanic America*. New York, 1941

MEXICO

Anderson, Lawrence, *The Art of the Silversmith in Mexico, 1519–1936*, 2 vols. New York, 1941†

Angulo Íñiguez, Diego, "Las catedrales mejicanas del siglo XVI," *Boletín de la Real Academia de la Historia*, Madrid, 1943

—— *La cerámica de Puebla*. Madrid, 1946

—— "Eighteenth-Century Church Fronts in Mexico City," *Journal of the Society of Architectural Historians*, 1945–46

—— "The Mudéjar Style in Mexican Architecture," *Ars islamica*, no. 2, 1935

—— "Pereyns y Martin de Vos: el retablo de Huejotzingo," *Anales del Instituto de Arte Americano*, Buenos Aires, 1949

Bancroft, Hubert Howe, *History of Mexico*, 6 vols. San Francisco, 1883–88

[83] Barber, Edwin Atlee, *The Maiolica of Mexico*. Philadelphia, 1908†

[84] Baxter, Silvestre, *La arquitectura hispano colonial en México*, with introduction and notes by Manuel Toussaint. Mexico, 1934†

[85] Bello, José Luís, and Gustavo Ariza, *Pinturas poblanas*. Mexico, 1943†

[86] Benítez, José R., *Las catedrales de Oaxaca, Morelia y Zacatecas*. Mexico, 1934

[87] —— *Morelia*. Mexico, 1936

[88] Berlin, Heinrich, "Artífices de la catedral de México," *Anales del Instituto de Investigaciones Estéticas*, Mexico, no. 11, 1944

—— *Códice de Yanhuitlan*. Mexico, 1947

—— "El convento de Tecpatán," *Anales del Instituto de Investigaciones Estéticas*, Mexico, no. 9, 1942

[89] —— "Salvador de Ocampo, a Mexican Sculptor," *The Americas*, April, 1948

[90] —— "Three Master Architects in New Spain,"

Hispanic American Historical Review, May, 1947

[91] —— Consultation and correspondence (Mexico City)

[92] Bonavit, Julián, "Esculturas tarascas de caña de maiz y orquideas," *Anales del Museo Michoacano,* Sept., 1944

Brenner, Anita, *Idols behind Altars.* New York, 1929†

[93] —— *Your Mexican Holiday.* New York, 1941

Carrera Stampa, Manuel, *Zacatecas.* Mexico, 1948

Carrillo y Gariel, Abelardo, *El Cristo de Mexicaltzingo: técnica de las esculturas en caña.* Mexico, 1949

—— *Las galerías de pintura de la Academia de San Carlos.* Mexico, 1944

—— *Imagineria popular novoespañola.* Mexico, 1950†

[94] —— *Técnica de la pintura de Nueva España.* Mexico, 1946*

Catálogo de construcciones religiosas del estado de Hidalgo, edited by Justino Fernández. Mexico, 1940*†

[95] *Catálogo de construcciones religiosas del estado de Yucatán,* edited by Justino Fernández. Mexico, 1945*†

[96] Chamberlain, Robert S., *The Conquest and Colonization of Yucatán.* Washington, 1948

Chauvet, Fidel, *Tlatelolco.* Mexico, 1946

[97] Cogolludo, Diego López, *Historia de Yucatán.* Mérida, 1867–68

[98] Cornejo Franco, José, *Guadalajara.* Mexico, 1945

[99] Cortés, Antonio, *Valenciana.* Mexico, 1932†

Couto, José Bernardo, *Diálogo sobre la historia de la pintura en México.* Mexico, 1947

Danes, Gibson, "Baltasar de Echave Ibía," *Anales del Instituto de Investigaciones Estéticas,* Mexico, no. 9, 1942

[100] Díaz del Castillo, Bernal, *The Discovery and Conquest of Mexico.* London, 1933

Dirección de Monumentos Coloniales, *Edificios coloniales artísticos e históricos de la Republica Mexicana.* Mexico, 1939†

Enciso, Jorge, "El convento de Actopan," *Archivo español de arte y arqueología,* Madrid, Jan.–April, 1935

[101] Espinosa, Luís, ed., *Chiapas.* Mexico, 1925

El estado de Michoacán. Mexico, 1932

Estrada, Genaro, *El arte mexicano en España.* Mexico, 1937

Fernández, Justino, *Las ilustraciones en el libro mexicano durante cuatro siglos 1539–1939.* Milan, 1939

—— "Rubens y José Juárez," *Anales del Instituto de Investigaciones Estéticas,* Mexico, no. 10, 1943

—— "Tiepolo, Mengs and Don Rafael Ximeno y Planes," *Gazette des Beaux-Arts,* June, 1943

—— See also *Catálogo . . .*

Fernández Villa, Agustín, *Antigua escuela de pintura en México.* Mexico, 1919

Fisher, Lillian E., "Commercial Conditions in Mexico at the End of the Colonial Period," *New Mexico Historical Review,* 1932*

Gante, Pablo C. de, *La arquitectura de México en el siglo XVI.* Mexico, 1947†

—— *La ruta de Occidente.* Mexico, 1939

[102] García Granados, Rafael, "Capillas de indios en Nueva España, 1530–1605," *Archivo español de arte y arqueología,* Madrid, Jan.–April, 1935

[103] —— *La ciudad de Oaxaca.* Mexico, 1933

[104] —— *Sillería del coro de la antigua iglesia de San Agustín.* Mexico, 1941†

[105] García Preciat, José, "La catedral de Mérida," *Archivo español de arte y arqueología,* Madrid, Jan.–April, 1935

[106] Gómez de Orozco, Federico, *El convento franciscano de Cuernavaca.* Mexico, 1943

Gutiérrez de Medina, Cristóbal, *Viaje del virrey Marqués de Villena.* Mexico, 1947

Gruening, Ernest, *Mexico and Its Heritage.* New York, 1928

[107] Helm, MacKinley, *Journeying through Mexico.* Boston, 1948

[108] Instituto de Investigaciones Estéticas, *La primera universidad de América.* Mexico, 1940

Janvier, Thomas A., *The Mexican Guide.* New York, 1887

Jiménez Rueda, Julio, *Herejías y supersticiones en la Nueva España.* Mexico, 1946

Kelemen, Pál, *Battlefield of the Gods.* London, 1934, 1937†

[109] —— "Religious Sculpture of Colonial Mexico," *Art in America,* July, 1944

Kilham, Walter H., *Mexican Architecture of the Vice-regal Period.* New York, 1927†

[110] Kubler, George, *Mexican Architecture of the Sixteenth Century,* 2 vols. New Haven, 1948*†

Le Duc, Alberto, *Una casa habitación del siglo XVIII en la ciudad de México.* Mexico, 1939

Leicht, Hugo, *Las calles de Puebla.* Puebla, 1934

León, Francisco de P., *Los esmaltes de Uruapan.* Mexico, 1939

Leonard, Irving A., "The Mexican Book Trade in 1600," *Hispanic American Historical Review,* Jan., 1941*

Louchheim, Aline B., "The Church Façades of Lorenzo Rodríguez." Thesis manuscript in New York University Library, 1941

MacGregor, Luis, *Arte colonial mexicano.* Mexico, 1946

—— "Cien ejemplares de plateresco mexicano," *Archivo español de arte y arqueología,* Madrid, Jan.–April, 1935

Martínez Cosio, Leopoldo, *Los caballeros de las ordenes militares en México.* Mexico, 1946

[111] Maza, Francisco de la, "El arte en la Ciudad de Nuestra Señora de los Zacatecas," *México en el arte,* no. 7, 1949

—— "Fray Diego Valadés, escritor y grabador franciscano del siglo XVI," *Anales del Instituto de Investigaciones Estéticas,* Mexico, no. 13, 1945

—— "Mexican Colonial Retablos," *Gazette des Beaux-Arts,* March, 1944†

—— *Las piras funerarias.* Mexico, 1946

[112] —— *San Miguel de Allende.* Mexico, 1939†

[113] McAndrew, John, "The Relationship of Mexican Architecture to Europe: Problems in the Field of Colonial Studies," in *Studies in Latin American Art.* Washington, 1949

[114] —— Consultation (Wellesley, Mass.)

Meade, Joaquín, *San Luis Potosí.* Mexico, 1946

Medel, José V., *La capilla del Rosario.* Puebla, 1940

Medina, José Toribio, *Historia del tribunal del Santo Oficio de la Inquisición en México.* Santiago, 1905

Méndez Plancarte, Gabriel, ed., *Humanistas del siglo XVIII.* Mexico, 1941

México en el tiempo, 2 vols. Mexico, 1945–46†

Monroy, Salazar, *Santuario de Ocotlán.* Tlaxcala, 1938

Moreno Villa, José, *La escultura colonial mexicana.* Mexico, 1942†

—— *Lo mexicano en las artes plásticas.* Mexico, 1948

[115] Ortega y Pérez Gallardo, Ricardo, *Historia genealógica de las familias más antiguas de México.* Mexico, n.d.

Pach, Walter, "Unknown Aspects of Mexican Painting," *Gazette des Beaux-Arts,* Oct., 1943†

Palacios coloniales de México, D. F. Mexico, 1946†

Peñafiel, Antonio, *Ciudades coloniales de Puebla.* Mexico, 1914

Pineida, Vicente, *Historia de las sublevaciones indígenas en el estado de Chiapas.* Chiapas, 1888

[116] Pérez Salazar, Francisco, *El grabado en la Ciudad de Puebla de los Angeles.* Mexico, 1933†

Prescott, William H., *History of the Conquest of Mexico.* New York, 1936

[117] Ramirez A., J. Guadalupe, *Querétaro.* Querétaro, 1945

Revilla, Manuel G., *El arte en México.* Mexico, 1923

[118] Rhode, Francisco José, "Anagahuan," *Anales del Instituto de Investigaciones Estéticas,* Mexico, no. 14, 1946

[119] Ricard, Robert, *La conquista espiritual de México.* Mexico, 1947

Rojas Garcidueñas, José, "Acta de fundación y petición de Merced del convento agustino de Salamanca," *Anales del Instituto de Investigaciones Estéticas,* Mexico, no. 17, 1949

Romero de Terreros, Manuel, *Arte colonial,* 3 vols. Mexico, 1916–21

—— "Bodegones y floreros en la pintura mexicana. Siglos XVIII y XIX." *Anales del Instituto de Investigaciones Estéticas,* Mexico, no. 14, 1946

—— *Breves apuntes sobre la escultura colonial de los siglos XVII y XVIII en México.* Mexico, 1930

—— *Grabados y grabadores en la Nueva España.* Mexico, 1948†

—— *Los jardines de la Nueva España.* Mexico, 1945

[120] Rosell, Lauro E., *Iglesias y conventos coloniales de la ciudad de México.* Mexico, 1946†

Roys, Ralph L., *The Indian Background of Colonial Yucatán.* Washington, 1943*

[121] Rubio Mañé, J. Ignacio, *La Casa de Montejo en Mérida de Yucatán.* Mexico, 1941

[122] Simpson, Lesley Byrd, *The Encomienda in New Spain.* Berkeley, Calif., 1950

[123] —— *Many Mexicos.* New York, 1941*

[124] —— Correspondence (Berkeley, Calif.)

Smith, F. Hopkinson, *A White Umbrella in Mexico.* Boston, 1890

Taxco. Mexico, 1946

Templos coloniales de México, D. F. Mexico, 1946†

[125] Thompson, J. Eric S., *Tattooing and Scarification among the Maya.* Washington, 1946

Three Centuries of Mexican Colonial Architecture. New York, 1933†

Torres Quintero, Gregorio, *México hacia el fin del virreinato español.* Mexico, 1921

[126] Toscano, Salvador, "Chiapas: su arte y su his-

toria coloniales," *Anales del Instituto de Investigaciones Estéticas*, Mexico, no. 8, 1942†

[127] Toussaint, Manuel, *Arte colonial en México*. Mexico, 1948*†

—— *El arte flamenco en Nueva España*. Mexico, 1949

[128] —— *La catedral de México y el Sagrario Metropolitano*. Mexico, 1948†

—— "La escultura funeraria en la Nueva España," *Anales del Instituto de Investigaciones Estéticas*, Mexico, no. 11, 1944

—— "Fray Andrés de San Miguel, arquitecto de la Nueva España," *Anales del Instituto de Investigaciones Estéticas*, Mexico, no. 13, 1945†

—— *Guía ilustrada de Tasco*. Mexico, 1935

—— "Mexican Colonial Paintings in Davenport," *Gazette des Beaux-Arts*, Sept., 1943

[129] —— *Paseos coloniales*. Mexico, 1939†

[130] —— *Pátzcuaro*. Mexico, 1942*†

—— *La pintura en México durante el siglo XVI*. Mexico, 1936

20 Centuries of Mexican Art. Mexico, 1940†

[131] Vargas, Fulgencio, *Historia elemental del estado de Guanajuato*. Mexico, 1940

[132] Velázquez Chávez, Agustín, *Tres siglos de pintura colonial mexicana*. Mexico, 1939†

Vetancourt, Agustín de, *Teatro mexicano*. Mexico, 1870

[133] Ward, H. G., *Mexico in 1827*. London, 1828

[134] Weismann, Elizabeth Wilder, *Mexico in Sculpture*. Cambridge, Mass., 1950*†

[135] —— "Stone Sculpture of Colonial Mexico," *Magazine of Art*, March, 1950

Wethey, Harold E., "Mexican Fortress Churches in the 16th Century," *Art Bulletin*, Dec., 1942

Wroth, Lawrence, *The Book Arts of Early Mexico*. Cambridge, Mass., 1945

Wuthenau, Alexander von, "The Spanish Military Chapels in Santa Fe and the Reredos of Our Lady of Light," *New Mexico Historical Review*, July, 1935

—— *Tepotzotlán*. Mexico, 1941†

Zavala, Silvio, *Ordenanzas del trabajo, siglos XVI y XVII*. Mexico, 1947

CENTRAL AMERICA AND THE WEST INDIES

[136] Aguilar, Arturo, *Reseña histórica de la diócesis de Nicaragua*. León, 1927

Angulo Iñiguez, Diego, *El gótico y el renacimiento en las Antillas*. Seville, 1947

[137] Annis, Verle L., "El plano de una ciudad colonial," *Antropología e historia de Guatemala*, 1949

[138] —— Correspondence (Los Angeles, Calif.)

[139] Berlin, Heinrich, Guatemala City. Correspondence

[140] Borhegyi, Stephen F., "Reconocimiento arqueológico de los sitios indigenos sobre la falda norte del volcán de Agua," *Revista de antropología e historia de Guatemala*, no. 1, 1951

[141] —— Correspondence (Guatemala City)

[142] Brigham, William T., *Guatemala*. New York, 1887

[143] Cuadra Cea, Luis, Managua. Correspondence

[144] De Varona, Esteban A., *Orosi*. San José, 1949†

[145] Díaz, Victor Miguel, *Las bellas artes en Guatemala*. Guatemala, 1934

[146] Durán, Rómulo E., *Bosquejo histórico de Honduras*. San Pedro Sula, 1927

Garavito, Humberto, *Francisco Cabrera miniaturista guatemalteco (1781–1845)*. Guatemala, 1945

[147] García Peláez, Francisco de Paula, *Memorias para la historia del antiguo reino de Guatemala*. Guatemala, 1943

Guerra Trigueiros, Alberto, "The Colonial Churches of El Salvador," *Bulletin of the Pan American Union*, May, 1938

Instituto de Antropología e Historia, *Catálogo del Museo Colonial de Antigua*, Guatemala. Guatemala, 1950

—— *La ermita de Nuestra Señora del Carmen*. Guatemala, 1949

—— *La iglesia catedral metropolitana*. Guatemala, 1950

Juarros, Domingo, *Compendio de la historia de la ciudad de Guatemala*, 2 vols. Guatemala, 1936*

[148] Kelemen, Pál, "Colonial Architecture in Guatemala," *Bulletin of the Pan American Union*, Aug., 1941 ("Arquitectura colonial en Guatemala," *Boletín de la Unión Panamericana*, Nov., 1941)†

[149] —— "Guatemala Baroque," *Magazine of Art*, Jan., 1942†

—— "Observaciones sobre el arte colonial y precolombino en Honduras," *Honduras Maya*, Sept., 1947

[150] —— "Some Church Façades of Colonial Guatemala," *Gazette des Beaux-Arts*, Feb., 1944†

—— "A Tapestry in the Morley Collection," *El palacio*, Dec., 1945

[151] Kelsey, Vera, and Lilly de Jongh Osborne, *Four Keys to Guatemala*. New York, 1939

Lunardi, Federico, *La fundación de la Ciudad de Gracias a Dios*. Tegucigalpa, 1946

—— *Iglesia y convento de San Francisco*. Tegucigalpa, 1945

[152] —— *El Tenguax y la primera iglesia catedral de Comayagua.* Tegucigalpa, 1946

McBryde, Felix Webster, *Cultural and Historical Geography of Southwest Guatemala.* Washington, 1945

Minter, John Easter, *The Chagres: River of Westward Passage.* New York, 1948

[153] Osborne, Lilly de Jongh, "Pilgrims' Progress in Guatemala," *Bulletin of the Pan American Union,* March, 1948

—— See also Kelsey, Vera

Palm, Erwin Walter, *El estilo imperial de Felipe II y las edificaciones del siglo XVII en la Española.* Ciudad Trujillo, 1943*

—— "A Descendant of the Arfe Family in Spanish America," *Gazette des Beaux-Arts,* Aug., 1946

[154] —— *Documentos y testimonios relativos al arquitecto Rodrigo Gil de Rozillo, llamado Rodrigo de Liendo.* Ciudad Trujillo, 1947

[155] —— "Observaciones sobre la arquitectura colonial en Honduras," *Boletín de la Unión Panamericana,* March, 1947*†

—— "Plateresque and Renaissance Monuments of the Island of Hispaniola," *Journal of the Society of Architectural Historians,* 1945–46*†

—— *Rodrigo de Liendo, arquitecto en la Española.* Ciudad Trujillo, 1944

—— "The Treasure of the Cathedral of Santo Domingo," *Art Quarterly,* Spring, 1950

[156] —— Correspondence (Ciudad Trujillo)

[157] Popenoe, Dorothy H., *Santiago de los Caballeros de Guatemala.* Cambridge, Mass., 1940

Prat Puig, F., *El pre-barroco en Cuba.* Havana, 1947†

Recinos, Adrián, "La ciudad de Guatemala, 1524–1773," *Antropología e historia de Guatemala,* 1949

Rodas N., Flavio, and Ovidio Rodas Corzo, *Simbolismos de Guatemala.* Guatemala, 1938

Schultze Jena, Leonhard, *La vida y las creencias de los indigenas Quiches de Guatemala.* Guatemala, 1946

[158] Squier, E. G., *Nicaragua,* 2 vols. London, 1852

Trapnell, Agnes Wilcox, "See All of Panama," *Bulletin of the Pan American Union,* Oct., 1947

[159] Toscano, Salvador, "La escultura colonial en Guatemala," *Anales del Instituto de Investigaciones Estéticas,* Mexico, no. 5, 1940†

Valladares R., Juan B., *La Virgen de Suyapa.* Tegucigalpa, 1946

[160] Villacorta C., J. Antonio, *Historia de la capitanía general de Guatemala.* Guatemala, 1942*

[161] —— *Prehistoria e historia antigua de Guatemala.* Guatemala, 1938

Weiss y Sánchez, Joaquín E., *Arquitectura cubana colonial.* Havana, 1936†

[162] Wells, William V., *Explorations and Adventures in Honduras.* New York, 1857

[163] Ypsilantys de Moldavia, Jorge, *Parroquia del Señor San Miguel de Heredia de Tegucigalpa.* Tegucigalpa, 1944

Zimmer, Agnes Stephens, "Córdoba," *Bulletin of the Pan American Union,* Aug., 1939

COLOMBIA, ECUADOR, VENEZUELA

Acuña, Luis Alberto, *La escultura religiosa en Santa Fé de Bogotá.* Bogotá, 1932

Bernal, Cristóbal, "La capilla del Rosario de Tunja," *Santa Fé y Bogotá,* Aug., 1923

Caldas, Francisco J. de, *Viajes.* Bogotá, 1936

Centenario de la independencia de la provincia de Tunja. 1913

[164] Compte, Francisco María, *Varones ilustres de la Orden Serafica en el Ecuador desde la fundación de Quito hasta nuestros dias.* Quito, 1885

Correa, Ramon C., *Historia de Tunja.* Tunja, 1944

[165] Delft Museum, Het Prinsenhof, Delft, The Netherlands. Correspondence

García, Juan Crisóstomo, "Guía de las principales iglesias bogotañas," *Boletín de historia y antigüedades,* April–May, 1943

Gento Sanz, Benjamín, "Colonial Art of Quito," *The Americas,* April, 1946

[166] —— *Historia de la obra constructiva de San Francisco.* Quito, 1942*

[167] —— "The History and Art of the Church and Monastery of San Francisco de Quito, *The Americas,* Oct., 1947

Habig, Marion A., "The Franciscan Provinces of South America (Ecuador, Colombia, Venezuela, Guiana)," *The Americas,* Oct., 1945

[168] Hernández de Alba, Guillermo, "Arte en Colombia: el santuario de Monguí," *Arte en América,* Seville, 1949

—— *Estampas santafereñas.* Bogotá, 1938

[169] —— *Guía de Bogotá.* Bogotá, 1946

—— *La iglesia de San Ignacio de Bogotá.* Seville, 1948

—— *Panorama de la universidad en la colonia.* Bogotá, n.d.

[170] —— *Teatro del arte colonial.* Bogotá, 1938*†

[171] —— Correspondence (Bogotá)

Jaramillo, Gabriel Giraldo, *El arte en Colombia*. Bogotá, 1944

——— *La pintura en Colombia*. Mexico, 1948

Kelemen, Pál, "El retrato de Gaspar de Figueroa," *Revista del Colegio Mayor del Rosario*, Bogotá, 1945

Lehmann, Henri, "Colonial Art at Popayán," *Gazette des Beaux-Arts*, July, 1943

[172] Marco Dorta, Enrique, "La arquitectura del renacimiento en Tunja," *Revista de Indias*, Madrid, 1942

[173] ——— *Viaje a Colombia y Venezuela*. Madrid, 1948

[174] Marden, Luis, "Hail Colombia," *National Geographic Magazine*, Oct., 1940

Martí, Mariano, *Relación de la visita general en la diócesis de Caracas y Venezuela, 1771–1784*. Caracas, 1928–29

Möller, Carlos Manuel, "Caracas ciudad colonial," in *La Caracas de ayer y de hoy*. Caracas, 1950

——— "La catedral de Caracas," *Arte en América y Filipinas*, Seville, no. 3, 1949

[175] ——— Correspondence (Caracas)

Museo de Arte Colonial. Catalogue. Bogotá, 1943

[176] Navarro, José Gabriel, *Artes plásticas ecuatorianas*. Mexico, 1945†

——— "Ecuadorian Sculpture," *Metropolitan Museum of Art Bulletin*, New York, May, 1945

——— *La escultura en el Ecuador*. Madrid, 1929†

——— *La iglesia de la Compañía de Jesús en Quito*. Madrid, 1930†

[177] ——— *Religious Architecture in Quito*. New York, 1945

——— *Summary of Ten Lectures on Ecuadorian Art*. Panama, 1935

[178] Negret, R., *Guía histórico–artística de Popayán*. Popayán, n.d.

Nuñez, Enrique Bernardo, *La Ciudad de los Techos Rojos*, 2 vols. Caracas, 1947–48

Parker, Helen, "The Museum of Colonial Art in Quito, Ecuador," *Bulletin of the Pan American Union*, Nov., 1947

Pizano Restrepo, Roberto, *Gregorio Vásquez de Arce y Ceballoz*. Paris, 1926†

Planchard, Enrique, *Tres siglos de pintura venezolana*. Caracas, 1948†

Las procesiones en Popayán. 1937

[179] Rackham, Bernard, Guildford, Surrey, England. Correspondence

[180] Recio, Bernardo, *Compendiosa relación de la cristianidad de Quito*. Madrid, 1947

[181] Rojas, Ulises, *Escudos de armas e inscripciones antiguas de la ciudad de Tunja*. Bogotá, 1939

Salamanca, Aguilera Rafael, *Guía histórica ilustrada de Tunja*. Bogotá, n.d.

[182] Solano, Armando, and G. Troconis Porras, *Cartagena de Indias*. Bogotá, 1942†

Vaquero Dávila, Jesús, *Génesis de la nacionalidad ecuatoriana*. Quito, 1941

[183] Vargas, José, *Arte quiteño colonial*. Quito, 1944*†

——— *El arte quiteño en los siglos XVI, XVII y XVIII*. Quito, 1949

——— *La cultura de Quito colonial*. Quito, 1941

Velasco, Juan de, *Historia del reino de Quito*. Quito, 1844

Villanueva, Carlos Raul, *La Caracas de ayer y de hoy*. Caracas, 1950

[184] Wuth, Bodo, Quito. Correspondence

[185] Zawadzky, Alfonso, *Necrología de San Francisco de Cali*. Cali, 1933

PERU

Barriga, Victor M., *Documentos para la historia de Arequipa*, 2 vols. Arequipa, 1939–40

——— *Los Mercedarios en el Perú en el siglo XVI*, 3 vols. Arequipa, 1939–42

——— *El templo de la Merced de Lima*. Arequipa, 1944

[186] Basadre, Jorge, *El Conde de Lemos y su tiempo*. Lima, 1948*

Benavides Rodríguez, Alfredo, *La arquitectura en el virreinato del Perú y en la capitanía general de Chile*. Santiago, 1941†

Clark, Mary Doris, "Santiago de Pomata, a Colonial Church on Lake Titicaca," *Bulletin of the Pan American Union*, Nov., 1930

Cobo, Bernabé, "Historia de la fundación de Lima," *Monografías históricas sobre la ciudad de Lima*, 1935

Cossío del Pomar, Felipe, *Pintura colonial; escuela cuzqueña*. Cuzco, 1928†

Cuadros, Manuel E., *Historia y arquitectura de los templos del Cuzco*. Cuzco, 1946†

[187] ——— Correspondence (Cuzco)

[188] Cuentas, Alberto J., *Chucuito*. Lima, 1929

Davis, Harold E., "The Chinchereños," *Acta americana*, July–Sept., 1945

Di Doménico Suazo, M. Haydeé, *La fuente de la Plaza Mayor de Lima, 1651–1944*. Lima, 1945

Flores Aráoz, José, "Iconografía de Santa Rosa de Lima," *Cultura peruana*, Lima, Nov., 1944

[189] Freyer, Mrs. Frank B., Denver, Colo. Correspondence

—— See also McNeil, Paul A.

Gallagher de Parks, Mercedes, *La escultura popular y costumbrista en piedra de Huamanga*. Lima, 1942

García, José Uriel, "La arquitectura colonial del Cuzco," *Revista universitaria*, Cuzco, 1936

[190] —— *La Ciudad de los Incas*. Cuzco, 1922

—— *El nuevo Indio*. Cuzco, 1937

Gento Sanz, Benjamín, *San Francisco de Lima*. Lima, 1945

[191] Gerbi, Antonello, *Caminos del Perú*. Lima, n.d.

Habig, Marion A., "The Franciscan Provinces of South America (Perú and Tucumán)," *The Americas*, July, 1945

Harth-Terré, Emilio, *Artífices en el virreinato del Perú*. Lima, 1945

—— "La obra de la Compañía de Jesús en la arquitectura virreinal de Perú," *Mercurio peruano*, Lima, Feb., 1942

—— "Tesoros de la catedral de Lima," *Anales del Instituto de Investigaciones Estéticas*, Mexico, no. 11, 1944

—— "Las tres fundaciones de la catedral del Cuzco," *Anales del Instituto de Arte Americano*, Buenos Aires, 1949

Kelemen, Pál, "El sentido y la expresión del arte de las culturas americanas," *El comercio*, June, 1945

[192] *Lima, precolombina y virreinal*. Lima, 1938*†

[193] Lohmann Villena, Guillermo, *El Conde de Lemos Virrey del Perú*. Madrid, 1946*

—— *Historia del arte dramático en Lima durante el virreinato*. Lima, 1941

—— "Noticias inéditas para ilustrar la historia de las bellas artes en Lima durante los siglos XVI y XVII," *Revista histórica*, Lima, 1940–41

[194] Lozoya, Marqués de (Juan de Contreras), *El arte peruano y sus possibles relaciones con Canarias*. Tenerife, 1944

Marechal, Leopoldo, *Vida de Santa Rosa de Lima*. Buenos Aires, 1943

Mariategui Oliva, Ricardo, *Escultura colonial de Trujillo*. Lima, 1946

McNeil, Paul A., "A Peruvian Art Collection [Freyer] in Washington," *Bulletin of the Pan American Union*, Aug., 1936

[195] Means, Philip Ainsworth, *Fall of the Inca Empire and the Spanish Rule in Peru: 1530–1780*. New York, 1932

[196] Medina, Pio Max, *Monumentos coloniales de Huamanga (Ayacucho)*. Ayacucho, 1942

Morales, Macchiavello Carlos, *San Francisco de Lima su iglesia y convento*. Lima, 1941

[197] Prescott, William H., *History of the Conquest of Peru*. New York, 1936

Santibáñez Salcedo, Alberto, *El monasterio de Nuestra Señora del Prado*. Lima, 1943

[198] —— "La restauración de la sacristía del templo de San Agustín," *Cultura peruana*, Lima, 1945

[199] —— Correspondence (Lima)

Skinner, Joseph, ed., *Peru*. London, 1805

[200] Squier, E. George, *Peru*. New York, 1877

Toussaint, Manuel, "El arquitecto de la catedral del Cuzco," *Anales del Instituto de Investigaciones Estéticas*, Mexico, 1941

Tschopik, Harry, Jr., "An Andean Ceramic Tradition in Historical Perspective," *American Antiquity*, Jan., 1950

[201] —— *Highland Communities of Central Peru*. Washington, 1947

Ugarte Elespuru, Juan Manuel, *Exposición de la pintura peruana*. Lima, 1946

Vaillant, George C., "Peruvian Art, Past and Present," *Gazette des Beaux-Arts*, Apr., 1945

Vargas Ugarte, Rubén, *Los Jesuitas del Perú*. Lima, 1941

—— "Notas para un diccionario de artífices coloniales," *Instituto de Investigaciones Históricas, Cuadernos de Estudios*, Lima, 1942–43

[202] Verger, Pierre, *Fiestas y danzas en el Cuzco y en los Andes*. Buenos Aires, 1945†

—— *Indians of Peru*. New York, 1950†

[203] Wethey, Harold E., *Colonial Architecture and Sculpture in Peru*. Cambridge, Mass., 1949*†

—— "Iglesias de Cajamarca," *Cultura peruana*, Lima, 1945*†

—— "La Merced in Cuzco, Peru," *Journal of the Society of Architectural Historians*, 1945–46

—— "The Problem of Toribio de Alcaraz," *Gazette des Beaux-Arts*, May–June, 1947

—— "Saña, a Dead City of Peru," *Michigan Alumnus Quarterly Review*, 1946

[204] —— Correspondence (Ann Arbor, Mich.)

[205] Zimmern, Nathalie H., "A Peruvian Bargueño," *Gazette des Beaux-Arts*, Mar.–Apr., 1947

[206] —— "The Tapestries of Colonial Peru." *Brooklyn Museum Journal*, 1943–44

ARGENTINA, BOLIVIA, CHILE

[207] Benavides Rodríguez, Alfredo, *La arquitectura en el virreinato del Perú en la capitanía general de Chile*. Santiago, 1941†

"Bolivia," *Turismo*, Lima, June, 1943†

Buschiazzo, Mario J., *Bibliografía de arte colonial argentino*. Buenos Aires, 1947*

—— "Un interesante expediente arquitectónico del siglo XVIII," *Anales del Instituto de Arte Americano*, Buenos Aires, 1948

208 —— *El templo de San Francisco de La Paz.* Buenos Aires, 1949*†

209 —— Correspondence (Buenos Aires)

Caillet-Bois, Horacio, *Primer salón de arte sagrado y retrospectivo de Santa Fé.* Santa Fé, 1940

210 Cobb, Gwendolin B., "Supply and Transportation for the Potosí Mines, 1545–1640," *Hispanic-American Historical Review*, Feb., 1949*

Documentos de arte argentino. Buenos Aires, 1939–50†

Documentos de arte colonial sudamericano. Bolivia. Buenos Aires, 1943–50†

211 Giuria, Juan, *Apuntes de arquitectura colonial argentina.* Montevideo, 1941†

212 —— "Organización estructural de las iglesias coloniales de La Paz, Sucre y Potosí," *Anales del Instituto de Arte Americano*, Buenos Aires, 1949

Habig, Marion A., "The Franciscan Provinces of South America (Bolivia and Chile)," *The Americas*, Jan., 1946

"Historia de la Villa Imperial de Potosí." Manuscript no. 2065 in the Library of the Royal Palace, Madrid

Kirchhoff, Herbert, *Bolivia.* Buenos Aires, 1942†

La Barre, Weston, *The Aymara Indians of the Lake Titicaca Plateau, Bolivia.* New York, 1948

213 Lascano González, Antonio, *Monumentos religiosos de Córdoba colonial.* Buenos Aires, 1941*†

Marco Dorta, Enrique, "Andean Baroque Decoration," *Journal of the Society of Architectural Historians*, 1946–47*†

214 —— "El barroco en la Villa Imperial de Potosí," *Arte en América*, Seville, 1949*†

Nadal Mora, Vicente, *El azulejo en el Rio de la Plata.* Buenos Aires, 1949

215 Noel, Martín S., *Rutas históricas de la arquitectura virreinal altoperuana.* Buenos Aires, 1948†

216 *Nuestra Señora de Copacabana y su santuario.* Copacabana, 1943

Otero, Gustavo Adolfo, *La vida social de coloniaje.* La Paz, 1942

Ribera, Adolfo Luis, "Los pintores del Buenos Aires virreinal," *Anales del Instituto de Arte Americano*, Buenos Aires, 1948

—— and Héctor Schenone, *El arte de la imaginería en el Rio de la Plata.* Buenos Aires, 1948

217 Sanjinés, Fernando de M., *Historia del santuario e imagen de Copacabana.* La Paz, 1909

218 Schenone, Héctor, "Tasación e inventario de la iglesia de San Ignacio en Buenos Aires," *Anales del Instituto de Arte Americano*, Buenos Aires, 1949

Taullard, Alfredo, *Platería sudamericana.* Buenos Aires, 1941†

—— *El mueble colonial sudamericano.* Buenos Aires, 1944†

Torre Revello, José, *La orfebrería colonial en Hispano-América y particularmente en Buenos Aires.* Buenos Aires, 1945

Tschopik, Harry, Jr., "The Aymara," in *Handbook of South American Indians*, vol. 2. Washington, 1946

219 Vignale, Pedro Juan, "El maestro anónimo de la portada de San Lorenzo de Potosí," *El arquitecto peruano*, Lima, Jan., 1946

220 Wethey, Harold E., "Hispanic Colonial Architecture in Bolivia," *Gazette des Beaux-Arts*, Nov., 1949*†

221 —— Correspondence (Ann Arbor, Mich.)

BRAZIL

222 Azevedo, Fernando de, *Brazilian Culture.* New York, 1950*†

Calmon, Pedro, *Historia de fundação da Bahia.* Bahia, 1949

Cardozo, Manoel, "The Brazilian Gold Rush," *The Americas*, Oct., 1946

Carvalho Lisbôa, Elisio de, "Colonial Art in Bahia," *Bulletin of the Pan American Union*, Jan., 1946†

Corrêa da Costa, Sérgio, *Every Inch a King.* New York, 1950

Falcão, Edgard de Cerqueira, *Relíquias da Bahia.* São Paulo, 1941†

Goodwin, Philip L., *Brazil Builds.* New York, 1943. Photographs by G. E. Kidder Smith†

Guido, Ángel, "O Aleijadinho, the Little Cripple of Minas Geraes," *Bulletin of the Pan American Union*, Aug., 1931

223 Jardim, Luiz, "A pintura decorativa em algumas igrejas antigas de Minas," *Revista do Serviço do Patrimônio Histórico e Artístico Nacional*, Rio de Janeiro, 1939

224 Kelsey, Vera, *Seven Keys to Brazil.* New York, 1941

Kochnitzky, Leon, "Black Gold of Brazil's Baroque," *Art News*, Jan., 1942

Lima, Augusto de, Jr., "Evolução do barrôco

no Brasil," *Estudos brasileiros*, May–June, 1939

Lino, Raul, and Ribeiro Couto, *Ouro Preto*. Lisbon, 1943†

[225] Mariano, José (filho), *Influências muçulmanas na architectura tradicional brasileira*. Rio de Janeiro, n.d.†

Martins, Judite, "Subsídios para a biografia de Manuel Francisco Lisbôa," *Revista do Serviço do Patrimônio Histórico e Artístico Nacional*, Rio de Janeiro, 1940

[226] Mattos, Aníbal, *Monumentos históricos, artísticos e religiosos de Minas Geraes*. Belo Horizonte, 1935

Smith, G. E. Kidder, photographer, *Brazil Builds*. New York, 1943†

Smith, Robert C., "A arte barrôca de Portugal e do Brasil," *Panorama*, Lisbon, no. 38, 1949†

[227] —— "The Colonial Architecture of Minas Gerais in Brazil," *Art Bulletin*, June, 1939*†

—— "The Colonial Churches of Brazil," *Bulletin of the Pan American Union*, Jan., 1938*†

[228] —— "The Golden Chapel of Recife," *Brazil*, April, 1948

[229] —— "Jesuit Buildings in Brazil," *Art Bulletin*, Sept., 1948*†

—— "Recent Publications on the Fine Arts of Portugal and Brazil," *Art Bulletin*, June, 1944*

[230] —— Correspondence (Philadelphia, Pa.)

Sousa-Leão, Joaquim de, "Brazilian Colonial Architecture," *Studio*, London, Oct., 1943

Valladares, José, "Bahia and Its Museum," *Bulletin of the Pan American Union*, Aug., 1948

[231] Waagen, Ludwig, *Rio de Janeiro als Kunststadt*. São Paulo, 1940†

ORGANS

Anglés, Higinio, *La música de las cantigas del Rey Alfonso el Sabio*. Barcelona, 1943

[232] —— *La música en la corte de los reyes católicas*. Madrid, 1941

—— *Orgelmusik der Schola hispanica vom XV. bis XVII. Jahrhundert*. Leipzig, 1926

Araiz, Andrés, *Historia de la música religiosa en España*. Barcelona, 1942

Audsley, George A., *The Art of Organ Building*. New York, 1905 (Dover reprint)

[233] Ayestarán, Lauro, *Domenico Zipoli*. Montevideo, 1941

Azcárate, Andrés, "El uso de los instrumentos músicos," *Revista de estudios eclesiásticos*, Bogotá, July, 1938

Baldelló, Francisco, "Órganos y organeros en Barcelona," *Anuario musical*, Barcelona, 1946

[234] Barwick, Steven, "Sacred Vocal Polyphony in Early Colonial Mexico." Thesis manuscript in Harvard University Library, 1949

[235] Basile, Mrs. David G., Cuenca. Correspondence

[236] Bernal Jiménez, Miguel, *Morelia colonial; el archivo musical del Colegio de S. Rosa de S. María de Valladolid (sig. XVIII)*. Mexico, 1939

[237] —— Consultation (Morelia, Mexico)

Bishop, W. C., *The Mozarabic and Ambrosian Rites*. London, 1924

Esclava, F., *Música religiosa en España*. Madrid, 1860

Escobar, José Ignacio P., *Historia de la música en Colombia*. Bogotá, 1945

Furlong, Guillermo, *Los Jesuítas y la cultura rioplatense*. Buenos Aires, 1933

Hamilton, Mary N., *Music in 18th Century Spain*. Urbana, Ill., 1937

Hernández, F. J., "Órganos de la Nueva España," *Hoy*, Mexico, 1939

Hopkins, E. J., *The Organ, Its History and Construction*. London, 1855

[238] Kelemen, Pál, "Church Organs in Colonial Mexico," *Bulletin of the Pan American Union*, March, 1942 ("Órganos eclesiásticos de México en la época colonial," *Boletín de la Unión Panamericana*, April, 1942)†

[239] Klotz, Hans, *Über die Orgelkunst der Gotik, der Renaissance, und des Barock*. Kassel, 1934

[240] Mayer-Serra, Otto, *La música y músicos de Latino-América*, 2 vols. Mexico, 1947

[241] Mitjana, Rafael, "Histoire de la musique espagnole," in Lavignac's *Encyclopédie de la musique*. Paris, 1920

[242] Nagy, Lajos, *Az aquincumi orgona*. Budapest, 1934

Romero de Terreros, Manuel, *Las artes industriales en la Nueva España*. Mexico, 1923†

[243] Sachs, Curt, *The History of Musical Instruments*. New York, 1940*†

[244] Salazar, Adolfo, *La música en la sociedad europea*. Mexico, 1944

Saldívar, Gabriel, *Historia de la música en México*. Mexico, 1934

[245] Schneider, Marius, "A propósito del influjo árabe," *Anuario musical*, Barcelona, 1946

[246] Smith, Carleton Sprague, New York. Correspondence

[247] Spell, Lota M., "Music Teaching in New Mexico in the Seventeenth Century," *The New*

Mexico Historical Review, Santa Fe, Jan., 1927

[248] —— Correspondence (Austin, Texas)

[249] "Uruguay's Musical Prospector [Curt Lange]," *Américas*, April, 1949

Vente, M. A., *Bouwstoffen tot de Geschiedenis van het nederlandse Orgel in de 16ᵈᵉ Eeuw*. Amsterdam, 1942

[250] —— Correspondence (Zwolle, The Netherlands)

Winternitz, Emanuel, "Bagpipes and Hurdy-Gurdies in Their Social Setting," *Metropolitan Museum of Art Bulletin*, New York, Summer, 1943

—— "Music for the Eye," *Art News*, June, 1946

[251] —— Consultation (New York)

Wörsching, Joseph, "Der künstlerische Orgelprospekt," *Die Christliche Kunst*, Jan., 1937

INDEX

(Plate numbers are in italic)

INDEX

INDEX

[292]

INDEX